Celebration 2000

Catch the Millennium Bug with Eric and

Young Writers

Preston

Edited by Dave Thomas

First published in Great Britain in 2000 by
YOUNG WRITERS
Remus House,
Coltsfoot Drive,
Woodston,
Peterborough, PE2 9JX
Telephone (01733) 890066

HB ISBN 075431 700 5
SB ISBN 075431 701 3

Foreword

Young Writers have produced poetry books in conjunction with schools for over eight years; providing a platform for talented young people to shine. This year, the Celebration 2000 collection of regional anthologies were developed with the millennium in mind.

With the nation taking stock of how far we have come, and reflecting on what we want to achieve in the future, our anthologies give a vivid insight into the thoughts and experiences of the younger generation.

We were once again impressed with the quality and attention to detail of every entry received and hope you will enjoy the poems we have decided to feature in *Celebration 2000 Preston* for many years to come.

Contents

The Poems

The Countryside

Look at the trees that blow in the breeze
and the bees that live in the trees.
See all the birds
that sing all their words
down in the dancing countryside.

See all the leaves that blow in the breeze
and the birds that live in the trees.
See all the bees
that buzz in the trees
down in the pounding countryside.

See all the bees that blow in the breeze
and the trees that sway in the breeze.
Look at the bees that blow to the trees
and the ants that climb on the plants
down in the jumping countryside.

Sally Summersgill (8)
Alston Lane RC Primary School

Countryside

Deep in the countryside, bees fly around,
insects and bugs underground, people dig all around.
Insects and bugs go deeper down,
bees and bugs fighting for slugs.
The ducks are playing in the pool,
people get ice-creams that are really cool.
The countryside is full of life,
full of life, full of life.

Victoria Wright (8)
Alston Lane RC Primary School

Countryside

In the countryside near to me,
there lives an owl in a tree.
He is fluffy and white
and goes hunting in the night.

Near the tree near to me
lives a bumblebee.
He has some lovely wings
but he has also given me lots of stings.

Near the bee
that lives near the tree
there lives a little mouse
that has a little house.

Near the mouse
that lives near the bee
a little cuckoo
sings in a tree.

Hannah Cowell (10)
Alston Lane RC Primary School

Countryside

I like to pick the flowers
In the beautiful month of May,
I like to have picnics and play and stay all day.
The ducks are messing about in the pond,
That is why the countryside
Is full of life, full of life.

Andréa Egidi (8)
Alston Lane RC Primary School

Countryside Poem

The countryside has flowers all different colours,
yellow ones, red ones and blue ones.
There are trees all different shades of green.
There are lots of farms in the countryside
with lots of fields and hedges
and cows grazing on the grass.
With the sun shining in the sky,
the countryside is hot, lovely and sweet.

There are people everywhere
walking up and down the country lanes,
cats and dogs walking,
flowers and grass growing on the sides of the roads.

So do not forget
Countryside!

Christopher Eccles (9)
Alston Lane RC Primary School

Sheep

Walking round the field,
Eating all the grass,
Giving birth to baby lambs,
Getting milk from their mums.

Running round the field,
Devouring all the grass.
Giving birth to baby lambs,
Gulping milk from their mums.

Anthony Murphy (8)
Alston Lane RC Primary School

COUNTRYSIDE

The countryside is very green,
and there is lots to be seen.
Mice are playing in fields of wheat
as farmers grow the food we eat.

Funny days
Sunny days
Walking in the country.

Tractors in the fields are ploughing,
cows and sheep are happily grazing.
Peace and quiet all around
birds and bees are the only sounds.

Funny days
Sunny days
Walking in the country.

Daniel Livesey (9)
Alston Lane RC Primary School

THE COUNTRYSIDE

Deep in the country live the bees and trees
that blow in the breeze,
and among the bees and trees
live the plants.
What the plants do is a dance
where the toads come to prance.
Look at the magnificent ants
that climb the plants
and patrol the plants.

Victoria Goldsmith (8)
Alston Lane RC Primary School

Spring Is Coming

Spring is coming,
Here at last,
Flowers are growing,
Winter is past.

Flowers are growing,
Daffodils too,
Rivers are flowing,
Birds anew.

Rivers are flowing,
Animals out,
Sun is shining,
There's no doubt.

Spring's nearly over,
Time to pack up,
Come on summer,
Spring's finished, *good luck!*

Jacob Walker (9)
Alston Lane RC Primary School

Countryside

Down at the pond the ducks are swimming.
In the deep grass, the flowers are budding.
The birds in the trees sing all day
and the wonderful trees come in May.

The cows and the sheep are munching at grass.
The wonderful sun shines in the sky.
The little ants are working all day
and I like the countryside.

Karen Eastham (9)
Alston Lane RC Primary School

Countryside

The countryside is sunny,
It's really nice,
I've been there already,
I'd like to go twice.

Derbyshire I went to,
It's the best,
I'd go there again,
To get a rest.

I also live in the countryside,
But it's not the same,
But I still think it's great,
So I'm not ashamed.

Jake Jackson (9)
Alston Lane RC Primary School

Lambs

With a beautiful white wool coat
What little baby lambs like to wear
They cuddle their mums to keep safe.
When the lambs are playing
And eating the grass.

When day turns to night
And it's time for the lambs' bedtime,
The mothers come and tuck them in
And they all say goodnight.

Rebecca Coleman (9)
Alston Lane RC Primary School

The Countryside

I live in the countryside.
There are lots of children,
villages, houses and trees.
Oh, I do love the countryside.

There are birds nesting in trees,
Badgers making holes,
Horses eating ripe green grass,
Cows eating sharp thistles.

There are lots of things to do
In the countryside.
Oh, I do love the countryside.
Don't you?

Victoria Richardson (10)
Alston Lane RC Primary School

Countryside

Look at the woodpecker
pecking at the tree.
Look at the ants
climbing on the plants.
Look at the daisies
that blow in the wind.
Look at the people
sitting on the grass
drinking a bottle of wine.
Look at the river
running very fast
splashing on the side of the path.

Ben Shaw (9)
Alston Lane RC Primary School

Our Countryside

Flowers growing, birds twittering,
Cows munching at the juicy grass,
All these things are in our countryside,
Spring is here at last.

Chorus: Here it is, here it is,
Come and look, it's great,
The countryside is what we love,
It's something that you'll never hate.

The rivers are flowing,
The trees are tall,
You can hear,
The sparrows call.

Chorus: Here it is, here it is,
Come and look, it's great,
The countryside is what we love,
It's something that you'll never hate.

Anne Seed (9)
Alston Lane RC Primary School

Countryside

It's as big as two schools, it's as big as five hotels.
It's as colourful as a rainbow.
It is like a nature reserve because there are lots of animals small and big.
It is like a garden with all the flowers.
Yes, you've guessed it - it's the countryside.

It's like a farmer's delight.
It's as quiet as an old man's coffin.
It's like a wood factory with all the woods.
It's an animal's home.
Yes, you've guessed it - it's the countryside.

Oliver Pedley (10)
Alston Lane RC Primary School

COUNTRYSIDE

Look at the bees
Buzzing in the trees.
Look at the lambs
Playing with the rams.
Look at the nests
Where the birds rest.
Look at bugs
Playing with the slugs.
Look at the ants
Climbing down the plants.
Listen to the robin
Hopping and bobbing.
Look at the sun
When the taps run.
Now it's spring
Let the birds sing.
Look at the woodpecker
It's a little wrecker.

Aimèe Bolton (8)
Alston Lane RC Primary School

COUNTRYSIDE

In the countryside live the homeless animals
going all over the land,
collecting all the nuts and berries
all around the land.
Squirrels dancing here and there,
The wild birds flying and flitting through the trees
and passing by the quiet village roads.

Dancing and prancing through the land,
prancing and dancing all around.

The trees for the animals homes
and for fresh air for everything that lived and is living.
The farmers ploughing and planting throughout the land
where the cows graze.

Andrew Banks (8)
Alston Lane RC Primary School

THE SUNNY COUNTRYSIDE

Oh, sunny, sunny countryside, how beautiful you are.
Sunny, sunny countryside, you shine like a gleaming star.
Countryside, sunny countryside, come to me.
Sunny countryside, you're beautiful to see.

All the animals are munching at the grass, *munch munch.*
All the little ants are marching in and out.
All the birds sing a lovely song, *tweet tweet.*
Oh, sunny countryside, you're the best.

Catherine Holden (9)
Alston Lane RC Primary School

COUNTRYSIDE

Big growing flowers
No big towers
Woolly old sheep
And a roaring jeep.

A big old house
And a little mouse
One white duck
Paddling in the muck.

There's a duck having a fly
In the dark blue sky
Landing on a ledge
Near a green hedge.

Nicholas Grime (9)
Alston Lane RC Primary School

NEST

In a tree there was a nest
Where little chicks went to rest,
And then at last
The chicks flew past
And sat on the window ledge
Near the big green hard hedge.

The chicks sleep in their nest,
Keep warm and have a rest.
They sleep all day,
in and away.

Lucy Gallagher (8)
Alston Lane RC Primary School

IN THE COUNTRY

In the country there are cows, birds and plenty of fields.
There are trees and bees.
The farmers are going backwards and forwards cutting the grass in the fields.

There are sheep and hills.
It is sunshiny and windy and sometimes there is a lot of rain.
We live in the countryside.
I love the countryside, it is lovely.

The countryside has trees and flowers of all different colours.
The trees are big and the flowers are small.
The trees are thick, bushy and they're green and brown.

David Shannon (10)
Alston Lane RC Primary School

THE COUNTRY

Every day and every hour,
A little bud starts to flower.

In the country there is beautiful weather,
And up in the hills there are fields full of heather.

There are little woods full of trees and bushes,
And down by the river there are reeds and rushes.

Birds and animals in their habitat,
There is a woodpecker on that tree *rat-a-tat-tat.*

I love the country, I think it is great,
I think I'll go there, I just can't wait.

Daniel Cullen (8)
Alston Lane RC Primary School

My Garden

My garden has lots of flowers
You'll find lots of powers.

Gardens have plants
And lots of ants.
Red, green and brown leaves
Endless black soil
Never seems to spoil.

My garden has slugs
You'll also find some interesting bugs.

Gathering lots of roses
Aroma for your noses.
Reddy-pink, slimy worms
Deadly fire starts to burn
Every flower spreads its seeds
No more room left for weeds.

Sarah Worrall (9)
Bamber Bridge Methodist School

Windy Weather

W indy weather
E veryone is cold
A rctic winds
T hunder and lightning
H ot and sunny
E veryone is warm
R aindrops are falling.

Kelvin Marshal (9)
Bamber Bridge Methodist School

My Favourite Animal

I've patted the dog,
Stroked the cat,
Caught the frog -
I've done all that
But
My favourite animals are dolphins.

Not mice, not lice,
Not hares, nor bears,
Not cats, or rats,
But dolphins.

I could like pigs or cows,
I could like monkeys
Who shout out loud,
Or maybe horses
But
My favourite animals are dolphins.

Not bugs, not slugs,
Not snails, nor whales,
Not dogs, or frogs,
But dolphins.

Zoe Evans (8)
Bamber Bridge Methodist School

CHOCOLATE

C hocoholics love it
H ot
O r
C old
O range chocolate is the best
L o bars and all the rest
A nimals love it - even mice
T hat's why I think it's nice
E ventually it will banish so at the end
make that chocolate smudge vanish.

Jenny Worth (10)
Bamber Bridge Methodist School

THE FOOTBALL POEM

F owler is the best
O vermars can beat the rest
O wen can score a goal
T oo bad he is so small
B eckham can shoot from far
A nd hit a brand new car
L iverpool are the best
L iverpool can beat the rest.

Liam Warbrick (9)
Bamber Bridge Methodist School

Fast Food

Go to McDonald's,
Go to Burger King,
If you want something spicy,
Buy an onion ring.

Go to a restaurant,
Or Pizza Hut,
If you buy a Snickers,
Take out the nuts.

Go to Kentucky,
In the USA,
Go on Concorde,
Have an nice day.

Eat fast food at home,
Put the chips in the chip pan,
Pick up the bread,
Slap down some ham.

Michael Kellett (8)
Bamber Bridge Methodist School

Sam's Pear

Sam went up and up, and down and down,
And he found a pear and he put it on his hair,
And walked and walked,
And he said, 'There's my pear.'
He looked up and up, but it was not there.
He looked down and down, but it was not there
And he found it on his hair.

Pamela Kelly (9)
Bamber Bridge Methodist School

My Sister Called Sarah

My big sister gets on my nerves.
She hates me.
She likes having a look at the locks in Liverpool,
She's always eating.

She's very big,
She has a lot of friends,
Sarah talks too much,
She loves it when it's summer.

Her best friend is called Laura,
She never lets me play,
I always get left out.

Rachael Worsley (9)
Bamber Bridge Methodist School

Football

F ootball is the best,
O vermars can beat the rest,
O wen plays for Liverpool,
T oo bad because he's so cool,
B eckham shoots from afar,
A nd scores a goal or hits the bar,
L ots of people go wild, everyone shouts and screams,
L ike that's too cool.

Shaun Delaney (10)
Bamber Bridge Methodist School

A Lonely Mountain

Peak so high,
Above the sky,
Head so proud,
Above the clouds.
Lonely mountain way up there,
You have secrets we can't share.

Head so high,
Know it all,
You seem, oh so tall.

Your snow so white
Your rock black as night,
Skiers skiing,
Sledgers sledging,
Lonely mountain way up there,
You have secrets we can't share.

Head so high,
Know it all,
You seem, oh so tall.

Sarah Huntley & Jamie Creeley (9)
Holme Slack County Primary School

Similes

Imagine a fox as smelly as socks
Imagine a dog as dumb as a hog
Imagine a boy as small as a toy
Imagine a snail as hard as a nail
Imagine a school as wet as a pool
Imagine a cat as flat as a mat
Imagine a mole as thin as a pole.

Oliver Howard (10)
Holme Slack County Primary School

SIMILES

Imagine a whale as small as a nail,
Imagine a fox as stinky as socks,
Imagine a monk as smelly as a skunk,
Imagine a mouse as big as a house,
Imagine a rat as thin as a mat,
Imagine a bug as slimy as a slug,
Imagine a fish as round as a dish,
Imagine a moth as wet as a cloth,
Imagine a mutt as tiny as a butt,
Imagine a pig as hairy as a wig,
Imagine a hare as large as a bear,
Imagine a mole as deep as a hole.

James Goodbourn (11)
Holme Slack County Primary School

I AM A . . .

You can screw me up
I am used for many different things
I can't walk
I can't talk
I am used for display
Teachers have a lot of me
I was alive
I can be used for maths, English, geography, science
Get me in different sizes
Everyone has me.

Lauren Dineley (11)
Holme Slack County Primary School

What Am I?

I boil water
You turn me on

You put water in me
I have a plug

I turn cold water hot
You use me for a drink

I am sometimes small and sometimes tall
I have a scale up my side

I come in the colours of green, yellow, white and blue
I scold you sometimes when I'm hot.

Hayley Murphy (10)
Holme Slack County Primary School

I Am A . . .

I have blonde hair
I am married
I can walk
I can talk
I have a nice face
I can drive
I can shout loud
I can move
I wear glasses
I am a size 4 and 5.

Rachael Bennett (11)
Holme Slack County Primary School

I Am . . .

I can be crunched up really tight,
Spaced out but still in touch with others
And even spread out.
You can pour me,
You can move me and not change shape.
I can move on my own.

Dayna Murray (10)
Holme Slack County Primary School

Similes

Imagine a snake as tiny as a flake
Imagine a skunk as holy as a monk
Imagine a bee as big as a tree
Imagine a mole as round as a hole
Imagine a mouse as wide as a house
Imagine a moth as dirty as a cloth.

Faye Parkinson (11)
Holme Slack County Primary School

There Was A Man From France

There was a man from France
Who went to a ball for a dance
For he slipped on the floor
And banged his head on the door
That silly old man of France.

Luis Sumner (10)
Holme Slack County Primary School

My Mum

A money giver
A bed-maker

A child carer
A kind carer

A friendly mother
A cuddle-maker

A meal-maker
A family helper

A catalogue
to make my mum.

Scott Anderton (11)
Holme Slack County Primary School

What Am I?

I can be read
I was alive
I can be scribbled in
I could be fiction
I could be seen in a library
I can be thrown
I could be funny
I could be talked about
I can be boring.
What am I?

Richard Leniewski (10)
Holme Slack County Primary School

Mum

A family helper
A house ruler

A money giver
A food shopper

A child carer
A cuddle giver

A kind carer
A bill payer

A catalogue
  to make
    my mum!

Brett Thornton (10)
Holme Slack County Primary School

Christmas Metaphors

C hristmas is a shop
H olly is a hedgehog
R eindeers are teddy bears
I ce is a freezer
S now is icing on a cake
T insel is the stars
M istletoe is a lampshade
A ngels are the sparkling moon
S anta is a big fat cherry.

Samantha Dawson (10)
Holme Slack County Primary School

Christmas Metaphors

C hristmas is a chocolate bar,
H olly is a hedgehog,
R obin is the baubles on the Christmas tree,
I cing is the snow in the winter season,
S tockings are monkeys hanging on the branches,
T rees are happiness,
M istletoe is a porcupine,
A ngels are canaries,
S now is as white as a beard.

Hugh Sneddon (11)
Holme Slack County Primary School

Similes

Imagine a boy as small as a toy
Imagine a fish as wide as a dish
Imagine an ox as flat as a box
Imagine a mouse as big as a house
Imagine a lizard as fun as a wizard
Imagine a fox as smelly as a sock
Imagine a pig as thin as a twig
Imagine a dog as mouldy as a log
Imagine a flea as yellow as a bee.

Jason Stewart (10)
Holme Slack County Primary School

There Was An Old Lady . . .

There was an old lady of Lea,
Who loved to drink gallons of beer,
She said 'How do you do?
Can I come for a brew?'
That silly old lady of Lea.

Amey Astley (10)
Holme Slack County Primary School

There Was A . . .

There was an old lady of Lea,
And she loved to drink lots of beer,
She called out her name,
And said 'I am in pain,'
And that's the old lady of Lea.

Rebecca Whelan (11)
Holme Slack County Primary School

A Man In A Mood

There once was a man in a mood,
Who always ate rabbit food,
For he said 'It's so cool,'
And said 'Yo moo,'
That silly old man in a mood!

Zulakha Desai (11)
Holme Slack County Primary School

My Mum

A child carer
A money giver

A bargain buyer
A bill payer

A food shopper
A house cleaner

A cuddle giver
A clothes buyer

A catalogue
  to make
    my mum.

Samantha Brown (11)
Holme Slack County Primary School

The Witch

A grubby old witch
Lives in a ditch.
Horrible witch
In the ditch.
Smelly witch
Big eyes
Black hat.
Green old hands
Green old face.

Garrie Mirza (8)
Longridge GM Primary School

MICE

Chorus: They scrape the carpets,
And roam the house,
Looking for food!

They scratch the furniture,
They eat almost anything,
From scented candles to story books,
From sneaking to not be seen!

Chorus: They scrape the carpets,
And roam the house,
Looking for food!

They look like balls of fur,
Their long thin tails are strong,
They scamper about all over the place,
With long thin claws they run about!

Heather Bryan (8)
Longridge GM Primary School

ROBOTS

A robot is an electronic moveability machine.
If I had one
I would call it Judge.
It would trudge along.

A robot is a computerized machine
Made for bionic assembly lines.
It is wicked to have a robot
To do the work.

Christopher Melling (9)
Longridge GM Primary School

My Life

Sonia is my name.
I live on the plains of Africa.
At 3.00am I wake
To go to the sandy village of Bomtake.
We have no water for days.
Our crops are on the bay,
Where the sun is at its hottest.

After a day of back-breaking labour,
I return to my town to have a short nap.
I return to see my family again.
I pass most towns, including Twanbow,
Which is dangerous with dark alleys and traffic.

When I get home I pull open the door
To see one small cramped room.
My mother is feeding my sister,
My dad is making matchboxes.
Why does nobody help us?

Lucinda McDade (9)
Longridge GM Primary School

Bugs

Slimy bugs
Little bugs
Under the ground
Running round and round
Little eyes, little legs
Biting little pegs
But I like bugs best.

Kenny Chow (8)
Longridge GM Primary School

Aliens

Aliens are very unfamiliar,
They have got very big heads and very small bodies,
Their eyes are big and black,
Their eyes glow in the dark.

They fly high in the sky,
The UFOs look like pancakes,
They can fly very fast,
They make quick escapes.

They are unfamiliar,
They are strange,
They are foreign,
And most of all, they are weird.
What do you think aliens look like?

William Metcalf (9)
Longridge GM Primary School

Rally

Some people are lucky,
They get to see the cars as black as a cooked sausage,
Which makes my mouth water.

Screeching tyres as they rev their engines,
Smoke coming off their tyres when they turn,
Immobilized cars after they've crashed,
With Colin McRae ramming down the track at
The speed of 200mph.

Sean Winder (9)
Longridge GM Primary School

ANIMALS

Animals are lovely creatures,
They dance around the room.

They make funny noises.
Dogs bark,
Cats miaow,
Horses neigh,
Donkeys hee-haw.

Animals have lovely colours.
It is brilliant to watch them run wild.
They are lovely and furry and very very fast.
Animals are very sweet creatures.

Katie Arrowsmith (8)
Longridge GM Primary School

A DRAGON

I dream about a dragon,
I think about a dragon,
I even talk about a dragon.

Its scaly back,
Its fire glazing in the sun,
Its wings so big,
They block out the sun.

I like to think of a certain dragon,
Its scales are beautiful colours,
Red, yellow and orange,
They shine in the sun.

Nathan Bibby (9)
Longridge GM Primary School

Dogs

Dogs can be good,
Dogs can be bad,
Dogs can be happy,
Dogs can be sad.

Fat dogs,
Thin dogs,
Long dogs,
Short dogs,
Dogs can be different in many ways.

Dogs can be brown,
Dogs can be black,
Dogs can be many different colours.

Fat dogs,
Thin dogs,
Long dogs,
Short dogs,
Dogs can be different in many ways.

Amy May (9)
Longridge GM Primary School

Dog

A dog, spotty black
And white paws
Home is red and yellow
Big brown eyes and
Big wet nose
Eats his dog food
Drinks his water
Goes for a walk.

Jennifer Melling (9)
Longridge GM Primary School

PETS

Dogs bite,
Cats miaow,
Rabbits are lovely
And soft.
Pigs roll in mud
And go *oink oink.*

I love pets,
You get joy
Out of them.
Rabbits run
In their runs,
What would we do
Without them?

Chipmunks,
Chimpanzees,
Beautiful little hamsters
And lovely woolly sheep.

I love pets,
You get joy
Out of them.
Rabbits run
In their runs,
What would we do
Without them?

Beautiful cute kittens,
Six, seven or eight weeks,
Lambs are trying to walk,
They are all very precious.

Jazzie Knight (8)
Longridge GM Primary School

A Footballer

A footballer's
Big red shirt is like fire
Slicing like a knife for a tackle
Dirt on them looks like a brown racing horse
Their voices are like cackles
The girls admire them so much.

After it all
It's off to the pub
Meet some friends
And have some grub.

A tired footballer at home
and goes to bed.

Christopher McGuigan (9)
Longridge GM Primary School

A Sheep

A big woolly sheep
So fast and quick,
1 lamb, 2 lambs, 3 lambs or 4,
They still run fast and quick.

Like a lawnmower
Fast and quick,
Grass away
And off they go to a new patch.

Mark Ward (8)
Longridge GM Primary School

A WITCH

A witch is ugly and spooky
And green with red fiery eyes,
She has a black fierce cat
With red glowing eyes.

She lives in a spooky old cottage
With mice and rats in it,
Bats flying everywhere
I don't know how she can live there.

She makes horrid spells
And bubbly potions to make things die,
She loves to make scary spells
And poisons apples, she scares me.

Alice Newby (9)
Longridge GM Primary School

THUNDER

Flashing light from the night
Not knowing what's going to happen.
It's scary, thunder *crash bang*, UFO passing by.

It's a spaceship sweeping by,
Knocking trees all over the place,
Plants destroyed forever.

Emily Scott (8)
Longridge GM Primary School

Ponies

The bays, the blacks and chestnuts all mixed together,
Look like a mass of books cramped on one shelf.

All the bits, the snaffles, the pelhams and the kimblewick,
How do you know which is which?

The different sorts of breeds,
The lively Arab as quick as lightning,
The tiny Shetland, as big as a mouse
And the Welsh Mountain, as hard and sturdy as a rock.

Charlotte Nuttall (8)
Longridge GM Primary School

Rabbits

Black rabbits, white rabbits
And brown rabbits.
Sniff sniff
They like to run in the garden
And be tickled.
They live in a hutch
Sniff sniff sniff
They eat brown pellets and a mixture.

Clare Briggs (9)
Longridge GM Primary School

SCISSORS

The scissors in our classroom
Don't cut card or paper,
They don't cut card or paper.

We could swap our scissors
For the ones that cut better,
For the ones that cut better.

Scissors are not very expensive,
But if we use the money we can't
Spend it on books or computers,
Then we can't spend it on books or computers.

Jennifer Hartley (8)
Longridge GM Primary School

THE TRACTOR

A tractor is a big strong machine
With wheels big and small.
The best part is when it roars
Through the farm and down the road,
With a big trailer of hay, when
You go down the road dropping
Bits on the way.
On the cars behind the trailer
Onto a bike, a three-wheeler.

Christopher Procter (8)
Longridge GM Primary School

WHAT DOES A FRIEND NEED?

A lot of money?
A classy car?
To be funny?
Or good at art?

Or does she need a great big house?
Pierced ears?
Or a pet white mouse?

Does she have to wear short skirts?
Or platform shoes so high it hurts?

Does she need to have cool friends?
If she's not cool the friendship ends.

No, all she needs is a kind heart and mind,
And to be there for me to find.

Maria Nowell (10)
Our Lady & St Gerard's RC Primary School

THE BEAR

Cubbie the bear
Ate only bread and honey
What happened to him was very funny.
He got stung by fourteen bees,
Now all he eats is broccoli and cheese.

Now Cubbie the bear
Hasn't any hair,
He is completely bald
And has a severe cold.

James Gorman (10)
Our Lady & St Gerard's RC Primary School

ROLLER-COASTER

I've been on a galleon
And I threw up my dinner that day
And when they said 'Go on it again'
I said sharply 'No way.'
This year I promised I'd go on the big one
So a favour to me, may you do
Will you go on the roller-coaster as me
While I'll dress up as you?
You can hear all the screaming
The yells and the noise
The wails and cries
From all the girls and boys.
The man's measuring me
And I pray I'm too small
And when I step aside, he says
'You're nice and tall.'
The queue's getting smaller
The ride is really near
My heart thudding loudly
Is all I can hear.
I go on the roller-coaster
And bite hard on my lip
And get prepared
For my scary trip.
I grab on tight
Ready for my fright
Up bumps I fly
I'm vertical in the sky
My heart's beating very fast,
The ride has finished at last.

Suzanne McGarry (10)
Our Lady & St Gerard's RC Primary School

Bear Rap

Roar, roar,
Here comes a bear,
Yeh, yeh, yeh,

A fierce creature,
looking for a feature,
Toooo eat,
It might be,
A tasty treat,
Foooor a bear.

Roar, roar,
Here comes a bear,
Yeh, yeh, yeh.

Christopher Scott (8)
Out Rawcliffe School

Cakes

Cakes can be yummy,
Cakes can be scrummy,
I love them in my tummy.

Cakes can be big,
Cakes can be small,
I love the ones with silver balls.

Cakes can be round,
Cakes can be square,
I had one with a grizzly bear.

Rachel Collinson (11)
St Clare's RC Primary School, Fulwood

HEY CAT

Hey cat, get off my mat,
Hey cat, give me that,
Hey cat, give me my bat,
Hey cat, you're too fat.

Hey cat, eat your food,
Hey cat, don't be rude,
Hey cat, get off my bed,
Hey cat, I'm going red,
so you'd better get off my bed.

Hey cat, be good,
Hey cat, don't go in the mud,
Hey cat, just be good.

William Gregson (10)
St Clare's RC Primary School, Fulwood

IN THE FOREST . . .

In the forest you'll see bears,
They snore in their sleep
And cuddle little sheep.
In the forest you'll see wolves,
They live in dens
And take chickens from pens.
In the forest you'll see a stream,
Where people sit and have a dream.
You'll hear the rippling of the stream.

Gillian Newton (11)
St Clare's RC Primary School, Fulwood

SEASONS

Spring
The flowers are a-bloom, the lambs are a-leaping
The children are a-laughing, the willows are a-weeping
I stand here in the big, big world and shout out 'Spring.'

Summer
The sun it shines like bars of gold, it shines on the birds and the bees.
I take no breathe of wind just a gleam of sun for
I can see that summer has begun.

Autumn
Leaves are falling to the ground, the wind blows them up
And they twirl round and round.
Conkers crack upon the ground and very soon they will be found.

Winter
The frosty dew on a spider's web, the snow on the
roofs of the houses ahead.
The twinkling lights of the Christmas tree with a big
pile of presents just for me.

These are the things from the seasons I see, they bring
Lots of different feelings to me.

Kathryn O'Gara (11)
St Clare's RC Primary School, Fulwood

I AM

I am like a comfortable chair sitting all alone.
I am dark as dark as can be.
I am a cake with a chocolate flake.
I am a beer waiting to be drunk.
I am the planet Uranus.

Joseph Farrell (10)
St Clare's RC Primary School, Fulwood

I Wish I Wasn't A Mum!

I wash the dishes
Clean the clothes
Hoover the hallway
Wipe baby's nose
Dust the front room
Tidy the shed
Make a good job of the bed,
Mike comes in
And throws his lunch in the bin
I tell him to come down
But he just looks at me with a frown
He storms upstairs in a mood
And shouts out words which are mostly rude
When the clock strikes 9
I open the fridge and pull out some wine
I sit down with a bag of Maltesers
And pluck my eyebrows with some tweezers
If you've read my poem, all impressed
Just think of me when I'm depressed!

Jake Welsh (11)
St Clare's RC Primary School, Fulwood

Lazy Cat

Lazy cat get off that hat,
Stop chewing that rat,
Or you will end up fat,
Like your brother on that mat.

Martin Garsed (10)
St Clare's RC Primary School, Fulwood

CHRISTMAS

A Christmas tree in the corner of my big hall,
With its little angel lying on top,
Without that angel it would look so small,
Even when the champagne top comes off with a loud *pop, pop!*

Everyone rejoices,
They give a large shout,
Then the Christmas cake is quickly given out!

Everyone is happy,
Nobody is sad,
Not even my poor old grumpy dad!

Matthew Sutherst (10)
St Clare's RC Primary School, Fulwood

CHOCOLATE

Chocolate is brown,
Some people treat it as a crown.
It can come in different shapes and
You can find it on cakes, but
I love it on my plate.

Chocolate is yummy,
Especially in my tummy,
Chocolate can be big, it can be
Small, it also can be very tall.

Claire Young (10)
St Clare's RC Primary School, Fulwood

My Day

As the dog wagged its tail,
And the mouse gave a squeak,
I was hunting for chocolate, not making a peep.
As the sun was setting high up in the sky,
I was at the sink making apple pie.

As the clock was ticking up on the wall,
I was going shopping down at the mall.

As the babies were crying in their cradles,
I was at the supermarket buying a ladle.

After the supermarket I went back to
Bed, with thoughts of my day going round in
My head.
Goodnight!

Victoria Bamber (11)
St Clare's RC Primary School, Fulwood

Metaphor Poem

I am a soft, comfy settee,
I am rich and powerful. Gold, I am.
Red juicy beans. I am fizzy
Exploding Tizer. I am tall and strong as
The Statue of Liberty. I am a big hairy
Bear. I am the crashing of drums.
I am the big Pluto planet. I am
A red, raging fire. I am a wonderful
Speeding gift Z3. I am a fast
Football game.

Adam Norris (11)
St Clare's RC Primary School, Fulwood

Me And My Family

She does the work
She cleans the dishes
She mops the floor
She dusts the rooms
She hoovers the house
She's my mum.

He goes to work
He works all day
He has a motorbike
He comes home at 6.30
He likes Maltesers
He's my dad.

He's really annoying
He goes to High School
He messes up my room
He plays with my toys
He bosses me about
He's my brother.

He's a big fur ball
He's really big and cuddly
He's like a teddy bear
He stays out at night
He's my cat.

I like playing football
I play on my PlayStation
I like watching soaps
I like doing art
I'm me.

Philip Yates (10)
St Clare's RC Primary School, Fulwood

Sweets Can Be

Sweets can be hard,
Sweets can be soft,
Sweets can be different colours.

Sweets can be nice,
Sweets can be yummy,
Sweets can be gummy
To make you look funny.

Sweets can be as big as a hole
Or as small as a mole.

Clare Battersby (11)
St Clare's RC Primary School, Fulwood

Teatime

This evening at tea
as I cut my chip
something jumped out
it was a pip.
The pip which came from my chip
was small and brown
and it made me frown,
as it looked at me
it was slurping my tea.

Jenny Casey (10)
St Clare's RC Primary School, Fulwood

DINOSAURS

Clashing teeth and clashing jaws
Herbivores and Carnivores.
In the long grass velociraptors
Sneak and now and then they
Take a peek, the prey squeal and
Squeak as they are eaten alive by
A vicious T-rex.
A Triceratops comes running in and
Knocks people over like a rolling pin.

Nicholas Aikman (11)
St Clare's RC Primary School, Fulwood

THUNDERBOLTS

They are big, sharp and scary.
They come in all shapes and sizes
If it hits you it will kill you.
They are round, big and bulgy.
If they hit the ground they will make a big sound.
They come out of space and they look like a face
It is as big as the moon.
It can blow up the moon.
It is called a thunderbolt.

Jack Huggonson (11)
St Clare's RC Primary School, Fulwood

The Monster Under My Bed

The monster under my bed,
Is big, green and hairy,
He's got sharp gruesome teeth,
But he isn't at all scary.

The monster under my bed,
Came to school with me today,
He scared the wits out of the Head,
And the teacher made me pay.

The monster under my bed,
Is the latest attraction at the fair,
For two rides it's one pound,
And the rides are a real scare.

The monster under my bed,
Won't live in my room anymore,
Because my bed is too small,
And makes my feet sore.

The monster under my bed,
Has packed his bags to leave,
Because we're chucking my bed out,
And it's a very sad time indeed.

The monster under my new bed,
Isn't very friendly at all,
He snores really loudly,
And he's driving me up the wall.

One day there was a knock at the front door,
It was the monster from under my old bed!
He was looking very hurt and sore,
'I am very pleased and I welcome you back,' I said.

Tegan Miller (10)
St Clare's RC Primary School, Fulwood

Room 2

There is a ghost in room 2,
And nobody really cares,
I lie in bed frightened with fear
And I know it's really here.

Everybody thinks I'm stupid,
But I don't really care
When I go in that room
My knees start to shake,
And sometimes I feel like a piece of steak!

Every time I go in there,
I hear a scream or shout,
I always try to forget what I've heard,
And all of a sudden I hear a bird.

Nicola Lindsay (10)
St Clare's RC Primary School, Fulwood

Murder

I drive home in my car
I open the door and there they are
Ready to pounce, ready to kill
I am the next person on their bill.

They say to me
'Do you have any last words?'
And I say 'Yes,
Help!'

Thomas Flett (11)
St Clare's RC Primary School, Fulwood

I Want - I Don't Want

I want to be a bird in the fresh blue sky
I want to be a dolphin splashing in the deep blue sea
I won't want to be a bee hard at work
I want a tan from the sun so high
I want to cool off in the blue lagoon
I don't want to smell my dad's big shoes
I want
I don't want.

Rochelle Crichton (10)
St Clare's RC Primary School, Fulwood

The River Poem

Tumbling down the mountainside,
Little insects hitch a ride.
Foamy water swirling round and round
Sticking close towards the ground.

Tributaries come to join in with me
Following until I reach the sea.
Bubbling, babbling over the golden gravel
Letting all my darkest secrets unravel.

Meandering through the great big town
Passing all the factories make me frown.
Under the bridges, near the sea
I'm getting very close now
And I've started to smile with glee.

Dominic Baxter (9)
St Oswald's RC School, Longton

The River's Journey

I tumble down the mountain
And splash with white foamy water.
I gurgle and laugh.

I soon start to slow down and
I pass tiny houses.
I swish under small bridges,
I murmur through the countryside.
Herons glide past.

I met the sea at last, exhausted.
I stagger through the mighty sea
And I join the waves.
Then splash back down again.

The sun beams at me with its hot shine.
Fish swim around me.
The waves almost drown
The little seagulls.

Callum Roxburgh (9)
St Oswald's RC School, Longton

A River

I rush and push past the rocks.
Rocks banging and crashing, bashing
Along the crooked river flow.
Tired but then I go quieter.
But their dead old factories are
Polluting my skin.
Then I come to a rough sea
Wild as a horse.

Jonathan Waite (8)
St Oswald's RC School, Longton

WHERE I WAS ONCE

Where I was once
The mountains high,
The silver trickles sparkled.
Over the waterfalls I flowed.
I fell into the river,
With a bubble at the pebbles,
And a babble as I met the golden gravel.
The sunbeams danced on my sandy shallows.
The summer had gone,
The last sigh of summer on my back.
A single blossom sailing.
I started to meander,
Not knowing where I was.
I fell into the city's grasp.
It killed me.
The factories vomited their poisons into me.
I had flowed through history.
I used to be a mighty force.
Now I am a wet dirty puddle,
Waiting to die.

Elizabeth Boyce (9)
St Oswald's RC School, Longton

A RIVER POEM

Today is a lovely day.
Pebbles beneath me.
I am swishing away to sea.
I am at meanders now,
Fish are tickling my skin.
I tumble to the sandy shore,
Damselflies hover above me.

I am going through a town now and
I am getting dirty.
I am near to sea,
I am exhausted,
I get trapped by some rocks,
My friends help me to get out.
I am in the sea now waiting to die.

Heather Cookson (8)
St Oswald's RC School, Longton

THE RIVER JOURNEY

I start high up in the mountains
Gushing over rocks side to side.
Bashing into pebbles,
Falling down waterfalls.
I can't stop myself,
Fish as silver as torpedoes.

I am slowing down now,
People chucking waste into me.
I see rubbish drifting past.
I plod under a bridge.
I see people and cars above.

Tired, dozy, I slide over golden gravel.
Boats whizzing past me.
The sun shining on me.
Birds flying over me.
The wind pushing me this way and that way,
Then I take a trip to the Atlantic Ocean.

Rachel Quilliam (8)
St Oswald's RC School, Longton

RIVER POEM

My journey started at the top of a mountain.
I gushed and tumbled down.
Then I came to a waterfall.
I shut my eyes then . . .
Then I fell down.
I picked up a bit of gravel,
But I didn't mind.

The fish under me were going to the Crystal Ball
All in fancy dresses.
They looked really funny.
I carried on.
I stared down, down a bit.
It started to snow in flakes,
It was as beautiful as a bird on a warm day.

I knew I was getting near to the sea,
I felt tired, drowsy.
I'm snuggling for a cold winter's nap.

Nicola Bowker (9)
St Oswald's RC School, Longton

MY JOURNEY

I splish and splash over rocks
down a waterfall and over a stone.
I bubble and chatter as I go.
The fish are lazy as junk.

Then I go slowly.
Then I see I have made it to the sea.

Amy Ford (9)
St Oswald's RC School, Longton

The River's Life Story

I started as a little droplet in the clouds
Then the clouds burst!
I crashed down the mountain
And gushed at the grass.
I trampled over the fish below.

I bubble, babble over golden gravel.
I sally over stones.
I wind like a roller-coaster and a whirlwind put together.

Then I slow down as the days grow older and
The winds grow colder,
I am now exhausted,
As tired as can be.
I flutter, I flatter and I am now asleep at sea.

Philippa Mercer (9)
St Oswald's RC School, Longton

River Poem

I slip and slide and glance and glide.
Birds fly over me high in the sky.
I laugh and smile with reflections in me.
Other streams joining onto me.
I crash against rocks and form rapids like crashing waves.

Fish as scaly as a dragon swim under me.
Soon I go under bridges.
I pass hamlets, villages, towns and cities.
Soon I come to the sea and relax gently floating
Across the sea where boats float.
I am now the sea.

Ashley Yates (8)
St Oswald's RC School, Longton

River Poem

I crash through the mountains lancing at rocks
as I tear through the mountains
like a knight fighting in battle.
Then falling to the ground
as I thrash down the waterfalls.
Then all is silent.
All I can hear is the birds and the trees
as the wind flows through the leaves.
Then I can hear the roar of cars and motorbikes
and people as they talk and shop through the village.
I flow slowly like a knight who has lost a battle he's fought in.
Then I hear the birds again
but this time the birds are seagulls flapping and calling
like a dog that's lost his mother.
Then I fight my way through the sand
like a knight charging into battle with a broken leg.
I feel myself sinking all the time like a snowman melting in the sun
then I feel myself piecing back together like a jigsaw
And I realise I've made it to the sea.

Alex Seed (8)
St Oswald's RC School, Longton

My River Poem

I sally down the mountain gushing all the way.
I babble over golden gravel tumbling over rocks.
Foamy water swirling round and round.
I will go on forever.

I scatter down under bridges making ripples all the way.
You may come and you may go, but I will always stay.
I will go on forever.

Alice Stirzaker (9)
St Oswald's RC School, Longton

My Journey Through Life

I remember when I was small,
I was white and foamy.
As small as a trickle.
I slipped over waterfalls,
Guided by my friends.
They helped me, and I grew quickly.
Sparkling in the sunshine.

As I grew bigger
I taught the ducks to float.
I babbled over the rocks, bubbled on pebbles,
Gave frogs a lily ride,
Chattering to the streams.
The kingfishers took
The itchy fleas off me
Called fish.

I stretched under bridges.
The horrible giants polluted me.
Then I slowed down.
I was exhausted, limbering, plodding,
To the open world, the sea.

Becky Turner (8)
St Oswald's RC School, Longton

A River Poem

I shower down the mountain tops
Flowing very fast.
I start as a trickle but then start to tumble,
I linger over rocks causing a meander,
I swivel round the bluebells
Growing in the moss.

Kingfishers standing over me,
Perching on the rocks.
As night falls and the stars
Are starting to glow,
I make a little trickling noise,
So that all is not quiet.

As the sun is rising,
A start of a new day,
I start my busy work again.
Tumbling over rocks
On my way to the big wide sea.
Travelling under bridges
All wet and damp,
Sometimes I think
I will never reach the sea.

But what's that underneath me?
A pike swimming along,
I hear a seagull calling,
I must be near the sea.

A graceful breeze
Blowing me in all different directions.
At last I've met the sea.
So happy I shall be!

Alice Park (8)
St Oswald's RC School, Longton

A River Poem

The wrens fly over me as
I depart for my long journey.
Tumbling wildly as I travel along,
I swish and splash,
I gush and crash,
I feel so relaxed.

I flow merrily and happily
I bicker down into the middle.
I slow down,
The water seems so silvery.
I'd like to go to sleep.

I go under a tall, narrow bridge.
Then I go down to the sea.
When the sun comes out I begin my journey again.

Jenny Wileman (8)
St Oswald's RC School, Longton

A River Poem

I remember when I was tumbling and crashing
over and round the mossy rocks,
splashing in foamy waterfalls.

I was slowing down,
lots of turrets joined me.
I went through 1000 bridges.

I was dozy, tired, shattered
and I was paddling to the sea.

Carl Titherley (8)
St Oswald's RC School, Longton

The River's Journey

Tumbling, crash, crash, crash,
I gushed down as a waterfall,
I felt fierce trying to get to the end,
The trees around protected me as I went down.

As I went slowly down
I saw the towns and villages.
When I meandered around,
In and out.
I started to meet the dirty, scratty factories
After I passed under lots of bridges.
Then I started to go drowsy,
I was very tired, plodding along,
I was at the end at last!

Helen Wilson (8)
St Oswald's RC School, Longton

The River Flows

At the top of a mountain,
Washing down,
Rivers join me as I go.
Kingfishers fishing,
Coming to the middle.
I am spoilt.

Junk being thrown into me as I go,
Junk is slowing me down.
Getting lazier and lazier.
Then I come to the sea.

Boats drive all over me,
Twisting me up with their propellers,
Fish wiggling their way through.
Children paddling all over me
While I am pulling their sandcastles.

Benjamin Sinkinson (8)
St Oswald's RC School, Longton

A River Poem

I remember rushing and sliding
Down the mountains at a tremendous speed.
Crashing down the waterfalls
Trickling past the bridge.
Rushing to the river,
Not knowing where to go.

Then I just flowed and flowed,
Suddenly I fell down a waterfall into the plunge pool.
I had the kingfisher as my guard.
Still not knowing where to go,
I flowed into the meanders.
I stayed there a while.

Then the wind took up and I whizzed to the sea.
The men polluted me.
I went to the sewer, now I am dead.

Oliver Yates (8)
St Oswald's RC School, Longton

The Journey Of Me

I remember when I was small.
I slipped and splashed around the pebbles,
I was white and clear,
But now I am green and dirty.
I was as slippery as a big green frog
That jumped around in me.

I whooshed down the waterfall.
The fish swam inside me.
I floated around the town
While I got cans and old boots
Thrown at me.

The dirt gathered around me like big bullies
I ended up at the bottom of the sea.

Elizabeth Case (9)
St Oswald's RC School, Longton

River Poem

I remember when I used to be
Friends with the mountains.
I fell off and made new friends with the bluebells.
I soon lost them because of the horrible factories
And had to make friends with some fish.

Then I started to enjoy life.
When I got near the sea I started to get lazy
And managed to slow down.
I told my journey to everyone in the sea
And they all enjoyed it.
They especially enjoyed the part about
Passing loads and loads of bridges.

Christopher Morris (8)
St Oswald's RC School, Longton

THE RIVER

Crashing, sliding, tumbling,
I fall down the waterfall.
I meet another stream
I meander a tiny bit.
I pass under bridges.
I slowly go through the town while
People throw things in me.
I slow down as I reach the sea
I feel tired and exhausted.

Samuel Stefan (8)
St Oswald's RC School, Longton

WATCH OUT - THE YEAR 2000

The year 2000 is coming our way!
So all the kids come out to play.
The whole world's celebrating already,
Booking holidays so that they can enjoy the grand day.
After all, they can only live the moment once,
They can't go back, no matter what.
So listen up people,
Put down all your things,
Come out into the sun
Don't miss all the fun.
Whilst you're dancing, screaming enjoying
This fun,
Stop and listen for the clock to strike twelve
For that will remind you,
That the year 2000 has just begun!

Eman Hassan (8)
St Peter's CE School, Meadowfield

DOG

My next door neighbour's dog
Is very annoying,
Her name is
Super Sandra Saucy Sandy,
She licks and pricks and even nips
Until she hears a call,
Her owner will say,
'Super Sandra Saucy Sandy'
And then it is time,
She will leap and run and even jump,
Then . . . .
Munch, munch, munch very quietly, then after that?
Bang! Goes the door,
She's outside again.

Rebecca Stuart (10)
St Peter's CE School, Meadowfield

MY CAT

My cat has white and black fur.
My cat has white paws and sparkling eyes.
My cat that sleeps by the fire.
That's my cat that sleeps by the fire,white and black fur,
white paws and sparkling eyes that sparkle when she looks at the fire.
Who pulls up the carpet and rips the wallpaper and scratches the door and digs in her nails.

But after all she is my cat!

Joseph Marshall (10)
St Peter's CE School, Meadowfield

The Aliens

It was mid-December and snowing hard
When the aliens landed in my backyard.
The funny queer little alien was deep, deep blue
And it looked as sticky as snow-white glue.
We soon became friends, he showed us some photos
Like Venus and Mars, then he showed us the
Sun, moon and stars.
His wife was quite pretty and had a beautiful
Young cute kitty,
We still receive letters from the alien in Mars
And still get photos of the sun, moon and stars.

Naomi Rigby (10)
St Peter's CE School, Meadowfield

Getting Up

Rain splatters on the window
My mum shouts from downstairs
'Get up, your breakfast is ready'
The smell of bacon travels to me
I hear hissing from the kitchen
As I crawl out of bed, my brother
Walks downstairs.
I hear my parents muttering
And I find out we are having
Bacon and egg.

Sam Ashworth (11)
St Peter's CE School, Meadowfield

Whether Or Not It's Lancashire Weather

Oh I wish it were summer
I'm sick o' the cowd
It's mekin' mi shiver
And feel so owd.

Mi wellies are muddy
Mi scarfs full of 'oles
Mi gloves look like Schmeichel's
'Ad 'em in goals.

Oh I wish it were summer
I'm sick o' the cowd
It's mekin mi' shiver
And feels so owd.

I want to put away mi jumper
And mi long woolly vest
I want to walk to church
In sunshine wearing mi Sundi best.

Oh I wish it were summer
I'm sick o' the cowd
It's mekin mi shiver
And feel so owd.

I want to sit in mi deck chair
Wi' a couple o' beers
And mi knotted 'anky over mi ears.

Oh I wish it were summer
I'm sick o' the cowd
It's mekin mi shiver
And feel so owd.

Well I suppose it'll come
When it's good and ready
So for now I'm off to bed
To keep warm, wi mi teddy.

Oh I wish it were summer
I'm sick o' the cowd
It's mekin mi shiver
And feel so owd.

Nikolas Prescott (9)
St Peter's CE School, Meadowfield

My Hamster

My hamster is a great runner
He runs on his wheel all night.
He chews at his bars and then goes for a drink
That's my hamster, full of joy.

Then he becomes very hungry
So he goes for a munch
After that he goes for a run
That's my hamster, full of fun.

Time is passing
It's 7.30 and he's getting tired
He's off to Dreamland, to his bed
That's my hamster, very tired.

Laura Whitelaw (11)
St Peter's CE School, Meadowfield

Ten Slimy Snakes

Ten slimy snakes slithering in a line
One got eaten up, then there were nine.
Nine slimy snakes going to a fete
One got trodden on, then there were eight.
Eight slimy snakes on their way to heaven
One vanished in a puff of smoke, then there were seven.
Seven slimy snakes eating a Twix
One choked and then there were six.
Six slimy snakes happy to be alive
One dropped dead, then there were five.
Five slimy snakes broke the law
One went to jail, then there were four.
Four slimy snakes happy as can be
One broke wind, then there were three.
Three slimy snakes went to the loo
One got flushed away, then there were two.
Two slimy snakes squeezing a man called Don
One let go then there was one.
One slimy snake went on a plane
Flew off to America and was never seen again.

Samantha Jayne Bedford (9)
St Peter's CE School, Meadowfield

My Cat

My cat is called Spotty,
His fur is all knotty,
The reason for this I am told,
Is because he is now very old,
He lies on the bed all day,
But at night he comes out to play.

Rebecca Anne Denoual (9)
St Peter's CE School, Meadowfield

My Friendly Cat

Green shining eyes and silk soft ginger fur,
Pink padded paws which make little noise.
Curled up on my bed, sleeping peacefully,
I look at her with affection and love.
Then when she lifts her head and yawns a weary yawn.
I walk up to her and scratch behind her ear, I hear her purr
Which makes me very happy as I know she loves me.
Then when she is tired I stroke her very gently until she
Falls asleep.
I love and care for Molly and all my other pets a lot.
They are very important to me.

Emma Seed (11)
St Peter's CE School, Meadowfield

My Cat Zippy

I have a cat
Called Zippy,
She runs around the room
Like a hippy.
She always wants to play
With me when I don't want her to
But she always jumps on my knee
When I want her to.
She sleeps all day in the house
But she's out at night looking for a mouse.

Robert Fair (9)
St Peter's CE School, Meadowfield

Getting Up

I awoke on New Year's Day
To find the world had changed,
The world was flat not round,
And I was made from paper,
The paper I was made of
Was as smooth and thin as string.
The trees were made of cheese,
And so was the grass.
'What has happened?' I cried
And then I awoke,
To find the new year had begun.

Racheael McGregor (11)
St Peter's CE School, Meadowfield

Anita

Anita is brown,
She is a hot autumn morning,
In the car.
Anita is a spring lady,
She is a cool dresser,
She is a neat table
And Home and Away
She is spaghetti Bolognese.

Rosie Burman (10)
St Peter's CE School, Meadowfield

MOTHER'S DAY AT THE BEACH

As the tide comes in
It seems to wash away my sin,
As I lie on the sand,
It runs through my hand.
Then I build a sand chair,
And I say look over there
'Cause I see a dolphin
It's the colour of a pin,
Under the sea can there be,
Many fishes of the sea,
They're all different colours,
And have all got mothers,
They all come out from March to May
That makes it a good Mother's Day.

Leanne Gavaghan (9)
St Peter's CE School, Meadowfield

MY DOG

My dog is a naughty cheeky dog
He can run very fast.
He's black and white called Boris
Boris is soft and nice and cuddly.
He is small with a big head
He likes licking people's lips,
Boris is a small Jack Russell,
I love my dog Boris.

Simon Bleasdale (11)
St Peter's CE School, Meadowfield

10 Little Aliens

Ten little aliens praying in a shrine,
One fell through the floor, then there were nine.
Nine little aliens on a dinner plate,
One got chopped in half, then there were eight.
Eight little aliens, one began to yell,
He was going up to heaven but then he went to hell.
Seven little aliens all began to do tricks,
One went and got it wrong, then there were six.
Six little aliens doing a groovy jive,
One missed a vital step, then there were five.
Five little aliens (5-1 the score) one went and
Missed a shot, then there were four.
Four little aliens on a shopping spree, one went
And dropped his cash, then there were three.
Three little aliens going to the zoo, one fell
In the mud, then there were two.
Two little aliens, chewing on a scone, one nearly
Choked on it, then we had one.
One little alien played with Ben. He went to his
House and was never seen again.

Andrew Mortimer (11)
St Peter's CE School, Meadowfield

Hopper

I've got a black rabbit called Hopper,
Who hops around all day,
She nibbles at the grass
And then she runs away.

She zooms around the garden,
And stops to sniff a leaf
She's just like Linford Christie
With those gigantic feet!

Robert J Lowe (9)
St Peter's CE School, Meadowfield

CATS

(A tribute to Mitzy)

Cats sleep anywhere
Any table
Any chair
Top of the piano
Window ledge
Cats sleep anywhere.

Cats eat anything
Protein biscuits
Dog food
Or even
Weetabix
Cats eat anything.

Cats play anything
Any roof
Any tree
Any street
Cats play anywhere.

Kelly Cartmell (10)
St Peter's CE School, Meadowfield

Ten Little Aliens

Ten little aliens sitting on a vine,
One threw up, and then there were nine.
Nine little aliens, seeing a play called Kate
One ran away, then there were eight.
Eight little aliens seeing the views of Devon
One saw Madonna, then there were seven.
Seven little aliens, eating a king-size Twix
One saw Mel B, then there were six.
Six little aliens, daring to do a dive
One slipped up, then there were five.
Five little aliens, were walking through a door,
One alien fainted, then there were four.
Four little aliens, running after a bee,
One slipped in mud, then there were three.
Three little aliens, naming a baby called Noo
One disappeared, then there were two.
Two little aliens, preparing to do a con,
One chickened out, then there was one,
One little alien, eating an ice-cream cone,
He froze to death, then there was none.

Heather Robinson (10)
St Peter's CE School, Meadowfield

Aliens

Once I saw an alien, he was two-headed and green,
He looked nasty and filthy and big and ugly.
He climbed out of a spaceship, it was large and futuristic.
He had a whole army of small two-headed aliens.
He said, 'I will rule the Galaxy' and jumped back
Into his spaceship with the other aliens.

David Wall (11)
St Peter's CE School, Meadowfield

Getting Up

I just opened my eyes with a start
The gloomy day awaiting for me
Through my window
As I smelt the cooking
I jumped on the floor with
A thud.
When I walked to the bathroom
And poured water on my face.
I raced downstairs smelling the
Mouth-watering food.
Sitting at the table waiting
For my breakfast.

Francesca Summers (10)
St Peter's CE School, Meadowfield

My Cat

I used to have a cat and her name
Was Suzie
I loved her very much
And she had a gentle touch.
She used to doodle around
And pounce on my feet
She used to eat fried eggs
And chicken, sweetcorn and meat.

Christopher Blake (11)
St Peter's CE School, Meadowfield

GETTING UP

I awoke to feel my mum pushing and shoving me out of bed,
I slowly opened my eyes.
Kicked off my duvet, got changed and went straight into
The bathroom.
I washed myself and ran down the stairs as fast
As my legs could carry me,
I had my breakfast, got ready and to my surprise
It was 10 to 9.
I ran straight to school,
Lucky for me I was on time.

Richard Sharp (10)
St Peter's CE School, Meadowfield

ALIENS

There go some aliens round and blue
Up in a spaceship that looks brand new.
They're jumping out and coming down,
One's the king, he's wearing a crown.
They start walking up to me,
They're saying 'bluber, uber, te, te, te.'
'What does that mean?' I said,
The king's name's Fred and I'm Ted.
Oh come on as if,
They suddenly stopped frozen stiff.

Kimberley Straker (10)
St Peter's CE School, Meadowfield

My Hamster

I have a little hamster called Daisy,
Sometimes she sits around being lazy,
But I don't care because she's my little hamster called Daisy.
She sleeps in a large bed-box full of straw (which seems
To be her favourite place)
For a little bit of exercise she speeds around in her tubes
And plops down into a smaller cage.
All night all she does is run up and down in her noisy tubes
But her favourite thing of all is when I stroke her
Behind the ears.

Hannah Moore (10)
St Peter's CE School, Meadowfield

Cats

Cats are beautiful but very mysterious animals
Bright, shining eyes that glow and reflect in the moonlight.
Silky soft furry coats of 1, 2 or even 3 colours
Soft paws with a padded texture next to
Sharp claws about a centimetre long.

Cats look like shadows in the moonlight
Or a blur dashing across a road
Cats are wondrous creatures
Small, but wonderful.

Nicola Crane (11)
St Peter's CE School, Meadowfield

The Whale

When you're swimming do not fail
To keep a look out for that whale!
He's got the most annoying knack
Of taking people on his back.
When he's picked up two or three,
He whisks them off right out to sea.
When you ask him to land
He doesn't seem to understand.
For he lands you on a deserted island
Until some ship appears,
Often you have to stay for years.

Lisa Hall (8)
St Peter's CE School, Meadowfield

Alien

I was walking through the forest and I heard a rattle.
It was the birds singing nice and firmly.
Then I came to a beautiful pond full of fish
Like trouts and sticklebacks. Then all of a sudden
An eagle came shooting down at me.
And I fell down, smack on the grass.
And all of a sudden I heard a noise
'Hello, I'm sorry that I hurt you.'

Scott Iddon (11)
St Peter's CE School, Meadowfield

FISH

My fish lives in a tank,
He has 2 eyes and 2 gills,
But he never pays the bills,
He is quite round,
He once almost drowned,
He almost got killed by a cat,
Now he's really fat.
My fish called Little
He once had a brother called Large, he was always in charge.
Large died and everybody cried.
I love my fish called Little and Large.

David Callaghan (10)
St Peter's CE School, Meadowfield

SEASHORE

Sandy shore and seaweed
Rocks and cockle shells,
Pebbles round,
Fishy smells.

Sun on clear water,
Donkeys jingling bells,
Hoof prints in sand ripples,
Seagulls squealing yells.

Susan Rodger (10)
St Peter's CE School, Meadowfield

My Cat

I'd loved my cat as she loved me
She had a meal 2 times a day
And she loved to play.
She winked with her left eye
And never liked milk.
She saw me grow up 0 to 10
But then one day her life ended.

So now we've got a new cat
Who winks with her left eye
And does not like milk.

Yolanda Hopkins (10)
St Peter's CE School, Meadowfield

My Dog

I loved my dog with all my heart,
Even though I did not take him for a walk.
I knew he loved me a lot.
He was very helpful and very cute,
He never liked other dogs but he was good.
When he died we were very sad,
I still remember even now.
We bought a stone dog to remind us,
He sits in the corner of the living room.

Ben Slater (10)
St Peter's CE School, Meadowfield

Alien

If I met an alien,
I'd ask him where he's been
The kind of people he has met
The stars that he has seen.

If I met an alien
I'd ask him what he wears
I'd ask him what fruit he eats
Like apples, plums and pears.

If I met an alien
I would ask his name
Before he answered he would go
Never to be seen again.

Hannah Shelstone (10)
St Peter's CE School, Meadowfield

My Friend

My friend is great,
She sometimes meets me at the gate.
When we're at school
She looks so cool.
But when it's home time
She leaves me behind.
So I dawdle along,
Sing a song,
And then at the end of the street,
I look at my feet,
And say 'Is she still my friend?'

Lydia Speariett (9)
St Peter's CE School, Meadowfield

I SAW A PIG

I saw a pig with a furry white tail,
I saw a spider with a snorting nose,
I saw an owl spinning a web,
I saw an elephant in a pea-green boat,
I saw a caterpillar with a big grey trunk,
I saw Mum with tiny hairy legs,
I saw a serpent dancing to the Beatles,
I saw a butterfly with hard rough scales,
I saw a giraffe with colourful wings,
I saw a rabbit with a long neck.

Emily Barker (10)
St Peter's CE School, Meadowfield

ALIENS

Here comes a spacecraft enormously big
When it had landed big shiny and new
Something stepped out, bigger than me or you.
He adjusted his translator and said rather loud,
'Can I have some fish and chips mate, I'm starved.'
I thought, that's a bit queer what happened to the old
Traditional 'take me to your leader routine'?
He mind-read and said
'Oh come on it's the 20th century.'

Andrew Addison (11)
St Peter's CE School, Meadowfield

My Dog Charlie

C harlie is so cheeky, he is always chewing things,
H e can talk, howl and sing
A nd every time Coronation Street is on he waits for the cat
 and barks.
R abbits are probably bigger than him.
L ook he is giving us his cute begging eyes.
I t's cool having a dog like Charlie,
E very time you've got chocolate in my house, you've got a friend.

Verity Collins (10)
St Peter's CE School, Meadowfield

My Mum

I have a mum who's lots of fun,
She's always there to brush my hair,
She's always there when I am down,
She's the greatest mum in town.

Catherine Phillips (9)
St Peter's CE School, Meadowfield

Alien

I had a dream
About an alien, it was very weird
As they always are.
Funny colours and funny sounds
They speak in funny ways.

Rickesh Chauhan (11)
St Peter's CE School, Meadowfield

ALIEN

I went upstairs into my room,
To my telescope,
Thinking I would see an alien,
My heart was full of hope.
As I gazed up into space,
My heart was thumping and began to race.
There upon the black of night,
I saw a marvellous trembling sight.
It was plummeting down to Earth,
At the speed of sound.
When it came there was a bang,
As it crashed to the ground.
I pulled on my slippers and ran
Down the stairs,
Full of worries and full of cares.
I ran through the door to his mess
Where a green man was waving and
Shouting distress.
I tugged on his arm to get him out.
I saw his face and began to shout,
I stopped, I stared, he looked kind.
Down in my heart I did not mind,
I wondered if he had magic powers,
He bent over to sniff the flowers.
Then with a huff and a phew,
His spaceship was as good as new.
I walked in hoping I'd see him
Again some day.

Beau Mulley (10)
St Peter's CE School, Meadowfield

MUNCHING BUNCHING APES

The hungry apes go munch, munch, munch
They go around in a bunch
Pulling faces at the spectators
Acting like dictators
Thumping their hairy chests
With their mighty fists
At last they settle down to a feast.
Munch, munch, munch.

Minal Mistry (9)
St Peter's CE School, Meadowfield

MY FRIEND

My friend King Cole,
He looks like a mole.
And his belly's so round,
He can't sit down,
His bum's so big,
And he eats like a pig,
Actually King Cole isn't my friend at all.

Philip Donnelly (9)
St Peter's CE School, Meadowfield

MILLENNIUM BUG

Millennium Bug it's big,
It's hairy, it's not very scary.
It will eat you in one bite,
It does not like to fight.
It has fleas and it eats cheese.

Peter Downey (9)
Sacred Heart Primary School

CELEBRATION 2000

Man U, Man U are the best
and have passed every test,
With Beckham running down the wing and
crossing the ball with Yorke scoring a goal.

> Chorus
> Oh Man U we do, Oh Man U we do,
> Oh Man U we do, Oh Man U we love you.

Man U, Man U hear the fans cheers,
So sell your fear and buy a beer.

Man U, Man U have no bug
but Villa have the Millennium Bug.

Jordan Frye (10)
Sacred Heart Primary School

MILLENNIUM POEM

A Millennium Bug is coming to town
and I will not have a big frown.
The PC we got this year, I don't know
I think it has got a can of beep.
It's a slug, it's a slug, it's the Millennium Bug,
It's sliding quite fast and I want it to go back
to the past.
It's a Bug, it's a Bug, I can't believe it's
the *Millennium Bug!*

Christopher Addison (10)
Sacred Heart Primary School

Football In Year 2000

PNE, PNE they're the best,
They pass every test.
Going round everywhere,
Sean Gregan's got fuzzy hair.

PNE is going to be the best team in the millennium,
Cartwright playing down the wing,
Hear the North End fans sing,
Tepi is a brilliant keeper.

The millennium, the millennium,
In the year 2000 the Euro Championships are being held
in Holland and Belgium,
Brazil are the best,
But Bulgaria pass every test.

Matt Murphy (10)
Sacred Heart Primary School

Millennium Will Soon Be Here

Millennium will soon be here,
Millennium will be here next year.
Millennium will be a lot of fun because
We can have much more fun.
Millennium will soon be here,
So don't worry you can wait till next year.
Millennium is the time to play,
Millennium is the time to have fun,
Millennium will soon be here so
Wait till next year.

Abbie Ruks (10)
Sacred Heart Primary School

Celebration 2000

There'll be parties in the streets
And everybody that we meet
Will have something to say on this very big day,
You've guessed it, the millennium.
When the clock strikes 12 there'll be cheers and claps
In every house especially mine.
Then we'll be sing good Auld Lang Syne.
Everybody is going to have fun, even you and me,
You'll see.
Then I'll have to find the key to the
Next hundred years ahead of me!

Stephanie Lawson & Paula Riley (11)
Sacred Heart Primary School

Celebration 2000

I zoomed to the Millennium Dome,
it was shaped as a cone.
I thought this is not right, I thought it is
not a pretty sight.
So I clambered up it and cut off the top,
it still wasn't right.
So I curved it, then it looked right, then
I saw the real Millennium Dome, the one
that I did is the Triangle Dome.
I screamed with terror.

Ryan Helm (9)
Sacred Heart Primary School

It!

It's big, it's small,
No it's not, it's very tall.
It's fat, it's thin,
It's an alien.

It's microscopic, it's humongus,
It's a giant about to bong us.
It's a wish, it's a swish,
It's a nanny on a fish.

It's a table in a stable,
It's Blobby's Aunty Mable.
It's a slug, it's a plug,
It's the Millennium Bug!

Hannah Gallagher (10)
Sacred Heart Primary School

The Millennium

PNE, PNE are going up,
PNE are the team to stop.
With Nogan on fire and
they never tire,
North End are going up.
With Moyes there, there
will always be a care and
Nogan and Basham are a
great pair.

Kevin Duffy (10)
Sacred Heart Primary School

MILLENNIUM

Millennium, millennium
It's finally here,
People will celebrate with wine and beer.
Millennium Dome,
Millennium gnome.
Fireworks go bang,
Cymbals go clang,
Bang, bang,
Clang, clang,
It's the millennium.
The Millennium Bug,
The millennium thug!
Watch out at night
Or you might get a fright!

Darren Walls (10)
Sacred Heart Primary School

MILLENNIUM

Millennium are the best,
They are not a pest.
Millennium, millennium,
Millennium are the best.

Bugs, bugs are very slimy,
Trees, trees are very climby,
People, people are very friendly,
People, people are treated very badly,
So try hard for the Millennium Dome.

Belinda McCann (9)
Sacred Heart Primary School

MILLENNIUM BUG

Millennium is nearly here,
So raise your glass and let's all cheer.

A Millennium Bug is fat and strong,
It's always singing a millennium song.

It might be in your rooms tonight,
Beware because it might give you a fright.

Katy Nuttall (10)
Sacred Heart Primary School

THE MILLENNIUM BUG CHUMS

This is the Millennium Bug, you've
got to beware, it's down your plug.
It will eat a million pears,
it might be sitting on your chairs.
It might be fat like a slug,
beware it's the Millennium Bug!

Terri-Louise Cromie (10)
Sacred Heart Primary School

THE MILLENNIUM BUG

It's a Bug, it's a Bug, it's the Millennium Bug,
It's big, it's scary,
It's not hairy.
It's round, it's fat,
It's having a snack,
Beware it's the Millennium Bug.

Owen Henry (10)
Sacred Heart Primary School

MILLENNIUM BUG

Millennium Bug is very strange,
It won't even cure your dog's mange.
Little will it cure,
Little will it do,
Except make your cows go moo.
New diseases spread around,
New diseases may be found
In the Dome, it's very big,
Ultimate fun it will be.
Millennium Bug
Biting ugly goats.

Matthew Walmsley (10)
Sacred Heart Primary School

SPACE

Mercury is my favourite
But Venus is even better.
Earth is where I live
And Mars is completely red.
Jupiter is weird
And Saturn makes patterns.
Uranus I don't like,
Neptune I've never seen
And last of all
Is very small -

Pluto!

Caroline Hamer (10)
Sacred Heart Primary School

Let's Celebrate Millennium

M illennium is coming soon
I t's going to be a real boom.
L et's all party, let's all cheer,
L et's all celebrate, the millennium's here.
E njoy the millennium, it might be your first time,
N othing will be better, so drink some white wine.
N othing with be better, than millennium new year,
I t's going to be a blast, so let's all cheer.
U nbelievable it may be,
M illennium will be here for all to see.

So raise your glasses and give a cheer,
The millennium will soon be here.

Olivia Carroll (10)
Sacred Heart Primary School

What Is A Celebration?

A celebration is not education,
It is not a computer
Unless it's a tuber
Oh no it's not, it must be a top,
Switch it off and then it's a cop.
Oh no, oh no, he's gonna arrest me for sailing with Katie,
Oh no, I think I will faint, I've just had a race with the policeman.
Now you know a celebration is none of these
Unless it's some cheese with a cherry on top,
Hey look out there's the Millennium Bug.

Ainé Henry (9)
Sacred Heart Primary School

The Millennium Celebrations

T is for television
H is for helicopter
E is for E-mail

M is for millennium
I is for Internet
L is for light
L is for leaves
E is for electricity
N is for nuclear
N is for new year
I is for infantry
U is for universe
M is for me.

Francesca Waszczuk (10)
Sacred Heart Primary School

Celebration 2000

Marais Hall is on the ball,
Oh look he's scored a goal.
Now David May is on the ball,
Hey, look he's scored a great goal.
Man U have no bug
But Arsenal have a mug.
Newcastle are scary
But Liverpool are hairy.

Jonathan Curry (10)
Sacred Heart Primary School

Millennium

The millennium is coming,
Everyone is running
To get the latest toy
For all girls and boys.
There's Teletubbies, Furbys too
And everyone wants a Furby
Just like me and you.
Our PC now has E-mail
And bad people are in jail.
So get up, have some fun in the Millennium
Dome all day long.

Liam Magee (11)
Sacred Heart Primary School

Celebrate

21st Century
E-mail
MiLlennium
Electricity
Brilliant
Rollerblades
DigitAl
Two Thousand
Explosion

Nicola Sherrington (10)
Sacred Heart Primary School

CELEBRATION

C is for century
E is for enjoy
L is for light
E is for electricity
B is for brilliant
R is for roads
A is for alarm clock
T is for two thousand
E is for E-mail

T is for twenty-first century
H is for happy
E is for estate car

M is for me
I is for infant
L is for leaf
L is for lead
E is for equal
N is for numbers
N is for nuts
I is for impatience
U is for unhappy
M is for millennium

Rachael Hatton (10)
Sacred Heart Primary School

OXFORD HISTORICAL MONOGRAPHS

THE CAROLINE CAPTIVITY OF THE CHURCH

Charles I and the Remoulding of Anglicanism 1625–1641

JULIAN DAVIES

CLARENDON PRESS · OXFORD

This book has been printed digitally and produced in a standard specification in order to ensure its continuing availability

OXFORD
UNIVERSITY PRESS

Great Clarendon Street, Oxford OX2 6DP

Oxford University Press is a department of the University of Oxford.
It furthers the University's objective of excellence in research, scholarship,
and education by publishing worldwide in

Oxford New York

Auckland Cape Town Dar es Salaam Hong Kong Karachi
Kuala Lumpur Madrid Melbourne Mexico City Nairobi
New Delhi Shanghai Taipei Toronto

With offices in

Argentina Austria Brazil Chile Czech Republic France Greece
Guatemala Hungary Italy Japan South Korea Poland Portugal
Singapore Switzerland Thailand Turkey Ukraine Vietnam

Oxford is a registered trade mark of Oxford University Press
in the UK and in certain other countries

Published in the United States
by Oxford University Press Inc., New York

Reprinted 2011

ISBN 978-0-19-820311-7

Printed and bound in Great Britain by CPI Antony Rowe,
Chippenham and Eastbourne

Cover illustration: *The Last Supper*, by Bernard van Linge, 1631.
Photograph by Neil Percival. Reproduced with permission of the
Rector and Fellows of Lincoln College, Oxford.

To My Parents

ACKNOWLEDGEMENTS

It is particularly pleasant for me to acknowledge that in writing this book I have incurred the debts of many people. Dr Gerald Aylmer, Master of St Peter's College, Oxford, acted as sub-editor for the University Press and scrutinized innumerable drafts with painstaking effort. I should like to thank him also for examining my thesis and for offering such constructive recommendations for its improvement. Similarly, I should like to express my gratitude to Dr Felicity Heal for supervising the original thesis, broadening my historical horizons and encouraging my early research into the period. Dr John Morrill (my other examiner) and Dr Kevin Sharpe also read over earlier drafts of the work and gave generous advice about its improvement. Dr Mark Dever, Dr Steven Gunn, Dr Anthony Milton, and Dr Sears McGee kindly scrutinized individual chapters, while Ms Anne Gelling carefully steered the text towards publication.

In recent years the historical questions addressed by this work have become increasingly controverted. At times the debate has become so heated that I have felt it better to observe the confrontation from the sidelines, rather than from the midst of the fray. Yet I have profited enormously from the discussions which followed the innumerable papers which I read at seminars during the past six years. This work would have been inferior had it not been for the efforts of many other historians in the field before me. Although sometimes we might disagree over interpretation, I should like to thank Dr Nicholas Cranfield, Lord Dacre, Dr Kenneth Fincham, Dr Andrew Foster, Dr Christopher Haigh, Dr Peter Lake, Professor the Earl Russell, Dr Paul Seaver, Mr Peter White, and especially Professor Patrick Collinson, Dr Christopher Hill, Sir Keith Thomas, and Dr Nicholas Tyacke for helping me to formulate the ideas within this book. Its mistakes and central thesis, of course, remain my own.

The text was written for the most part between 1988 and 1990 in Oxford or at my parents' farm, high above the Honddu Valley, on Mynydd Epynt. Much of the research for the original thesis was conducted in over fifty record repositories. I can only express my deep gratitude to all those office staff who responded to my many queries and who hauled vast quantities of documents from the stacks for me to inspect. In particular, I should like to thank Mrs Alison Keneally of the Greater London Record Office for her exceptional kindness, and the staff of the Bodleian Library for their availability and patient assistance over many years.

As far as funding was concerned, the research for this work would not have been possible without the support of the postgraduate award which I received from the Department of Education and Science, under the auspices of the British Academy. I am deeply grateful also to the Principal and Fellows of Jesus College, my undergraduate college, for electing me to a scholarship, and later to a Lectureship and the post of Junior Dean. Similarly I should like to thank the Principal and Fellows of Brasenose College for electing me to a three-year Lectureship in Modern History. The final stages of this work would have been delayed had it not been for the facilities of the Refugee Studies Programme at Queen Elizabeth House, and I should like to acknowledge my gratitude to its Director, Dr Barbara Harrell-Bond, for permitting me to use its computing facilities while I was working there. Thanks are due also to Dr Peter Carey, Dr Cliff Davies, Dr Robert Evans, Revd Bruce Gillingham, Revd Julian Hubbard, Dr John Robertson, Dr Mark Smith, Dr Lawrence Snell, Mr David Thomas, Dr John Walsh, Revd John Wenham, and Dr Anne Whiteman, for their assistance over issues indirectly connected with this book, but of no less importance to me during its time of writing. The final version of the text was laser-printed at the Computing Centre of the University of Cambridge, shortly after I had embarked upon ordination training at Ridley Hall.

My interest in the subject of the work stems, to a large extent, from my early contact with Welsh Anglicanism in rural Breconshire. The text also bears the imprint of the effects of my coming to faith in 1979, and my subsequent charismatic awakening in 1986. To the ministry of St Aldate's Church, Oxford, and my fellowship group there, and to my friends at the Oxford Overseas Centre and elsewhere, I can only acknowledge my deep gratitude for their generous agape and fellowship. In particular I should like to thank the following for facilitating the writing and completion of this work, not least through their prayers, supplications, and hospitality: Hélène André, Sr. Leonard Azzopardi, Andrew Bailey, Ken and Phyllis Bennett, Simone Campling, Caroline Dobson, Marianne Dorman, Sarish Despande, Rosa Flores, Daniela Guiliani, Patricia Jimenez, Alison

Jones, Felix Leinemann, Ming Li, Jeo-Yang Noh, Jean and Cecile Menetrier, Lena Ng, Ananta Parajuli, Thuy Phung, Steven Tam, Deborah Thomas, Bill Wilson, Barnabas Wong, Zhi-chao Zhang, and Gianghuo Zhu. Finally, I should like to express my gratitude to my parents for uncountable years of sacrificial affection and support, and for giving me roots to cherish and wings to spread.

J. E. D.

Llanfihangel-fechan
December 1990

CONTENTS

ABBREVIATIONS

Unless otherwise stated, place of publication is London.

AO = archive office
RO = record office

Ball	Thomas Ball, *The Life of... Dr Preston*, ed. E. W. Harcourt (1885)
Barnard, *TH*	John Barnard, *Theologico Historicus or the True Life of Peter Heylyn* (1683)
BDRO	Bedfordshire RO (Bedford)
BERO	Berkshire RO (Reading)
BI	Borthwick Institute, York
Birch	*The Court and Times of Charles I*, ed. T. Birch, 2 vols. (1848)
BKRO	Buckinghamshire RO (Aylesbury)
BL	British Library, London
Bodl.	Bodleian Library, Oxford
BRO	Bristol RO
Calamy	E. Calamy, *The Nonconformist's Memorial*, ed. S. Palmer, 3 vols. (1802)
CARO	Cambridgeshire RO (Cambridge)
CBRO	Cumbria RO (Carlisle and Kendal)
CC	*The Correspondence of John Cosin*, ed. G. Ornsby (Surtees Soc., 53, 1869)
CCL	Canterbury Cathedral Library
CCO	Corpus Christi College, Oxford
CCRO	City of Chester RO
Ch. Ch.	Christ Church, Oxford
CJ	*Commons' Journal*
Clarendon	Edward Hyde, earl of Clarendon, *History of the Rebellion*, ed. W. Dunn Macray, 6 vols. (Oxford, 1888)
CLRO	Clwyd RO (Ruthin)
Collinson, *GP*	P. Collinson, *Godly People: Essays on English Protestantism and Puritanism* (1983)

Collinson, *RP*	P. Collinson, *The Religion of Protestants: The Church in English Society 1559–1625* (Oxford, 1982)
CRO	Cheshire RO (Chester)
CSPD	*Calendar of State Papers Domestic*
CSPV	*Calendar of State Papers Venetian*
CUL	Cambridge University Library
CVRO	Coventry RO
CWRO	Cornwall RO (Truro)
DBRO	Derbyshire RO (Matlock)
DCL	Durham Cathedral Library
D'Ewes, *Autobiography*	*The Autobiography and Correspondence of Sir Simon D'Ewes*, ed. J. O. Halliwell, 2 vols. (1845)
DFRO	Dyfed RO (Haverfordwest)
DNB	*Dictionary of National Biography*
Documentary Annals	*Documentary Annals*, ed. E. Cardwell, 2 vols. (Oxford, 1844)
DPD	Dept. of Paleography and Diplomatic, Durham University
DRO	Devon RO (Exeter)
DTRO	Dorset RO (Dorchester)
DURO	Durham RO (Durham)
DWL	Dr Williams's Library (London)
ERO	Essex RO (Chelmsford)
ESRO	East Sussex RO (Lewes)
ESFRO	East Suffolk RO (Ipswich)
Fuller, *AII*	Thomas Fuller, *The Appeal of Injured Innocence* (1659)
Fuller, *CH*	Thomas Fuller, *The Church History of Britain*, ed. J. Nichols, 3 vols. (1868)
GCC	Gonville and Caius College, Cambridge
GCL	Gloucester Cathedral Library
GERO	Greenwich RO
GL	Guildhall Library, London
GLRO	Greater London RO (Clerkenwell)
GRO	Gloucestershire RO (Gloucester)
Hacket, *SR*	John Hacket, *Scrinia Reserata* (1693)
HCL	Hereford Cathedral Library
Heylyn, *CA*	Peter Heylyn, *Cyprianus Anglicus* (1668)
Heylyn, *EH*	Peter Heylyn, *Examen Historicum* (1659)

HFRO	Herefordshire RO (Hereford)
Hill, *SP*	Christopher Hill, *Society and Puritanism in Pre-Revolutionary England* (1964)
HLRO	House of Lords RO
HMC	*Historical Manuscripts Commission*
HNRO	Huntingdonshire RO (Huntingdon)
HRO	Hampshire RO (Winchester)
HTRO	Hertfordshire RO (Hertford)
IWRO	Isle of Wight RO (Newport)
KAO	Kent AO (Maidstone)
Knowler	*The Letters and Dispatches of Thomas Wentworth, Earl of Strafford*, ed. W. Knowler, 2 vols. (Dublin, 1759)
KTRO	Kingston (Surrey) RO
Lake, *AP*	Peter Lake, *Anglicans and Puritans? Presbyterianism and English Conformist Thought from Whitgift to Hooker* (1988)
LAO	Lincolnshire AO (Lincoln)
LJ	*Lords' Journal*
LJRO	Lichfield Joint RO (Lichfield)
LJU	*A Collection of... Letters (of)... James Ussher*, ed. R. Parr (1686)
LLRO	Liverpool RO
LPL	Lambeth Palace Library
LRO	Leicestershire RO (Leicester)
Nalson	John Nalson, *An Impartial Collection... of the Great Affairs of State*, 2 vols. (1682–3)
NLW	National Library of Wales (Aberystwyth)
NNRO	Norwich and Norfolk RO (Norwich)
Northcote	*The Notebook of Sir John Northcote*, ed. A. H. A. Hamilton (1877)
NRO	Northamptonshire RO (Northampton)
NTRO	Nottinghamshire RO (Nottingham)
NYRO	North Yorkshire RO (Northallerton)
ORO	Oxfordshire RO (Oxford)
Parentalia	*Parentalia... or Memoirs of the family of the Wrens*, ed. S. Wren (1750)
Parker, *ES*	Kenneth Parker, *The English Sabbath: A Study of Doctrine and Discipline from the Reformation to the Civil War* (Cambridge, 1988)

PCR	*Proceedings ... in the County of Kent in connection with ... the Committee of Religion* (Camden Society, OS, 80, 1862)
PRO	Public RO (London)
Prynne, *CD*	William Prynne, *Canterburies Doome* (1646)
PTRO	Portsmouth RO
QCO	The Queen's College, Oxford
RCHM	*Royal Commission on Historical Monuments*
Rushworth	John Rushworth, *Historical Collections*, 7 vols. (1659–1710)
Seaver, *PL*	Paul Seaver, *The Puritan Lectureships: The Politics of Religious Dissent 1560–1662* (Stanford, CA, 1970)
SERO	Sheffield RO
SFRO	Staffordshire RO (Stafford)
SFRO (WSL)	Staffordshire RO (William Salt Library, Stafford)
SHRO	Shropshire RO (Shrewsbury)
SJC	St John's College, Cambridge
SPRO	Southampton RO
SRO	Somerset RO (Taunton)
SSC	Sidney Sussex College, Cambridge
Synodalia	*Synodalia*, ed. E. Cardwell, 2 vols. (Oxford, 1842)
SYRO	Surrey RO (Guildford)
TRHS	*Transactions of the Royal Historical Society*
Tyacke, *AC*	Nicholas Tyacke, *Anti-Calvinists: The Rise of English Arminianism c.1590–1640* (Oxford, 1987)
UCS	University College AO (Swansea)
WARO	Warwickshire RO (Warwick)
WCL	Winchester Cathedral Library
WCO	Worcester College, Oxford
WDRO	West Devon RO (Plymouth)
WERO	Westminster RO (Westminster)
WJC	*The Works of John Cosin*, ed. J. Samson, 5 vols. (Oxford 1843–55)
WJH	*The Works of Joseph Hall*, ed. P. Wynter, 10 vols. (Oxford, 1863)
WKC	*The Works of King Charles I* (1662)
WLA	*The Works of Lancelot Andrewes*, ed. J. Bliss, 11 vols. (Oxford, 1841–54)

WORO	Worcestershire RO (Worcester)
WRS	*The Works of Robert Sanderson*, ed. W. Jacobson, 6 vols. (Oxford, 1954)
WSFRO	West Suffolk RO (Bury St Edmunds)
WSRO	West Sussex RO (Chichester)
WTRO	Wiltshire RO (Trowbridge)
WWL	*The Works of William Laud*, ed. J. Bliss and W. Scott, 7 vols. (Oxford, 1847–60)
WYAS	West Yorkshire Archives Service (Leeds and Calderdale)

Manuscript Sources: Glossary and List of Abbreviations

acta	acts of court
Ad.	archdeacon
AO	Archives Office
APec	archiepiscopal peculiar
Ay	archdeaconry
Bp.	bishop
ca	churchwardens' accounts (mostly under parish)
Ch.	chapter
Chan.	chancellor
coll.	collection
comperta	visitation findings
Comm.	commissary
Con.	consistory
Corr.	correction
corr.	correspondence
DCh.	dean and chapter
Dn.	dean
detecta	digest of presentments drawn up before visitation
Dy	deanery
ecc.	ecclesiastical
ep. reg.	episcopal register
instance	cases between parties
met.	metropolitical
office	cases of criminal prosecutions, usually summary
pb	parish book
Pby	prebendary
Pec.	peculiar

Prec.	precentor
pres.	churchwardens' list (presentment) of defects
reg.	register
RO	record office
RPec.	royal peculiar
speculae	special survey
subs.	clerical subscription to articles, and recognizing the Royal Supremacy and Book of Common Prayer
tr.	transcript
Treas.	treasurer
Vch.	vicars' choral
vm	vestry minutes

Its better that men be disorderly saved, than orderly damned: and that the Church be disorderly preserved, than orderly destroyed

(Richard Baxter, *Five Disputations* (1659), 165)

INTRODUCTION

This work, based upon my Oxford doctoral thesis of 1987, addresses revisionism in the neglected area of ecclesiastical policy between the accession of Charles I in 1625 and the calling of the Long Parliament in 1641. Within this field, it is offered both as an in-depth historical analysis of major themes of controversy and as a reference work for the local historian. To claim that it is a revisionist work would not be particularly controversial, if it were not for the fact that the word 'revisionist' has particular connotations for the study of early seventeenth-century history.

During the last twenty years so-called 'revisionists' have challenged two of the main, if not the main, shibboleths of traditional historiography, advanced to explain the collapse of the Stuart regime in 1640 and the eventual slide into Civil War. These were that the political crisis represented first, *a constitutional struggle over issues of principle and the structures of authority*, and second, the surfacing of the revolutionary potential of *Puritanism*. Instead, 'revisionists' suggest that the political crisis stemmed from first, *a functional crisis in the apparatus of government*, and second, from the revolutionary effects of *Arminianism*.[1] While it is important not to over-rationalize the revisionist platform (many revisionists differ over analysis within these categories) such a synopsis probably fairly depicts the broad agreement among individual revisionists, and their differences with traditional historiography.

Such revisionist historiography stems, it would appear, from two main presuppositions: first, that principled ideological considerations are of little importance in explaining historical motivation and change,[2] and second, that religion is easily separable from

[1] For an overview and critique of revisionism see Richard Cust and Ann Hughes, 'After Revisionism', and some of the other essays in their (eds.) *Conflict in Early Stuart England: Studies in Religion and Politics 1603–1642* (1989); Derek Hirst, 'Local Affairs in Seventeenth Century England', *Historical Journal*, 32 (1989), 440–8. See other works critical of aspects of revisionism, Epilogue, n. 100.

[2] Derek Hirst, 'Local Affairs', 440–8. Lawrence Stone, *The Past and The Present* (1981), 93.

politics.[3] Underlying this book are different presuppositions. They rest on the belief that the opposition which the Stuart regime faced in the 1640s is inexplicable other than in an ideological framework of reference, and that at the heart of the debate and struggle were fundamental constitutional considerations. Secondly, given the existence of an established, state Church (regardless of the fact that the language of religion is often political or that Charles I was using the Supremacy to promote his idiosyncratic style of sacramental kingship), to differentiate, as revisionism does, between religious and political factors is unwarranted. A religious–political dichotomy cannot be equated with a spiritual–secular one.

Within revisionist historiography it is impossible to overestimate the significance of *Arminianism*, both as a cause of Charles I's troubles but also as the pivot upon which a not inconsiderable part of the revisionist case rests.[4] This work is critical of Dr Tyacke's thesis, while acknowledging that it offered the wrong answer to a correctly diagnosed problem, that problem being that the innovations which occurred during the reign of Charles I explain the radicalization of Puritanism and a considerable part of the opposition faced by the government in 1640–1. In place of Arminianism, it offers an alternative thesis, that of Carolinism (and its subsidiary and less important handmaid, reinterpreted Laudianism). These, it suggests, better explain the reasons for attack on the Church in 1640–1. The term 'Carolinism' does not represent the redundancy of analysis or the violation of the historical context under the umbrella of yet another vaguely defined '-ism'. Its utility rests in its descriptive content as the lowest common denominator of ecclesiastical policy after 1625 and the suggestion, borne out in this study, that a greater coherence exists behind the royal policy than previously uncovered. Its use in preference to 'Laudianism' emanates also from its pronounced politico-ecclesiastical connotations, since the usage of Laudianism to describe the innovations of the reign has always given the impression that their source was inherently ecclesiastical, that they were political only in consequence, and that they emanated invariably from Laud. Laudianism still has a prominent place in explaining the events of

[3] This revisionist presupposition is implicit in the 'Arminian' thesis but brought to its logical conclusions in John Morrill, 'The Religious Context of the English Civil War', *TRHS*, 5th ser., 34 (1984), 165–75.

[4] Tyacke, *AC*, and his 'Puritanism, Arminianism and Counter-revolution', in C. S. R. Russell (ed.), *The Origins of the English Civil War* (1973), 119–43.

1640, as this work shows, but it is a Laudianism reorientated and more contextualized than before.

Carolinism never constituted a coherent philosophy of absolutist kingship (although it had absolutist tendencies); rather it represented the policy of Charles I to realize his highly personal notion of sacramental kingship by exploiting his prerogative as Supreme Governor of the Church. Thus the established Church under Charles I (as a vital arm of the political apparatus of the state and the vehicle for Caroline ideology) became more highly politicized than it had under any of his predecessors. Consequently this work does not subscribe to the revisionist view that the major constitutional problem in the 1630s was *functional*. Rather it elevates *the importance of ideological debate and conflict over constitutional issues fomented by the pursuit of Carolinism*. Although the Supremacy went unquestioned, the ecclesiastical innovations of the reign could not fail to provoke principled and constitutional evaluation, when the demands of royal authority within Church and Commonwealth appeared to conflict with the authority of God, the conscience, or the congregation.

'The cause of the Church' was rejected less because of its attempt to reinvest the catholicity of Anglicanism than because, for Charles I, this policy was indistinguishable from his obsessive drive to eradicate 'profanity', 'popularity', and disorder. Given its politicization of religious belief and practice, combined with its attempted reversal of basic reformation principles, the Caroline Church represented not the apogee of Anglicanism, but a very weird aberration from the first hundred years of the early reformed Church of England. Certainly the Supremacy had entailed that the monarch would mark the state Church with his or her personal stamp, but no monarch had questioned the populist and parliamentary basis of the Reformation Church as much as Charles I, nor unsettled to such an extent the consensual accommodation of Anglicanism.[5]

Since this work concentrates on the ecclesiastical context, to resolve whether a distinctive Anglican spirituality existed in the early seventeenth century has not been its concern. In this respect, however, it is worth pointing out that the term 'Caroline' to embrace the likes of Donne, Herbert, Ussher, Hall, Taylor, or Ken gives

[5] G. Bernard, 'The Church of England c.1529–c.1642', *History* (1990), 183–206, underestimates the novelty of Caroline policies (both in terms of content and impact), as well as ignoring the populist and parliamentary origins of the Anglican Church.

erroneous impressions about their views and associations within any seventeenth-century contextualization.[6] If the Caroline Church left its mark it was in the realm of political ideology and practice rather than spirituality. Its legacy was to be seen in the survival of opposition to Anglican moderation manifested in events, such as the expulsion of nonconformists after 1660;[7] the reintroduction of the communion rail after 1673, when conservative interests sought to consolidate an Anglicanism purged of nonconformity,[8] and the attempted restraint of preaching by James II.[9] By the end of the seventeenth century, with the concept of the divine right of the monarchy finally discredited by the Glorious Revolution of 1689, Carolinism was dying a strange death.[10] It was singularly unfortunate for those former loyal Anglicans, whose exclusion from the Church it had sought, justified, or brought about, that it had not passed away earlier.

[6] e.g. G. H. Tavard, *The Quest for Catholicity: A Study in Anglicanism* (1963), 44.

[7] A. Whiteman, 'The Re-establishment of the Church of England, 1660–1663', *TRHS*, 5th ser., 5 (1955); I. Green, *The Re-Establishment of the Church of England 1660–1663* (Oxf., 1978); R. Beddard, 'The Restoration Church', in J. R. Jones, (ed.), *The Restored Monarchy 1660–1668* (1979); R. S. Bosher, *The Making of the Restoration Settlement* (1951); N. Sykes, *From Sheldon to Secker: Aspects of English Church History 1660–1765* (Camb., 1959); T. Harris, P. Seaward, and M. Goldie (eds.), *The Politics of Religion in Restoration England* (Oxford, 1990); P. Seaward, *The Cavalier Parliament and the Reconstruction of the Old Regime, 1661–1667* (Cambridge, 1988).

[8] C. Firth and R. S. Rait (eds.), *Acts and Ordinances* (1911), i. 265; W. Scudamore, *Notitia Eucharistica* (1876), 166. Many rails reappeared after 1685.

[9] Bodl. Tanner MS 31/268–70. In 1686 James II attempted to revive Charles I's instructions of 1629, which Compton among others, stalwartly opposed.

[10] G. V. Bennett, 'Conflict in the Church', in G. Holmes (ed.), *Britain After The Glorious Revolution 1689–1714* (1982).

I

CAROLINISM

A prince 'who knew not how to be, or be made great.'

(Laud on Charles I, *WWL* iii. 443)

I. 'ANGLIANISME'

'I call the religion of England Anglianisme, because it among the rest hath no one especial author, but is set forth by the Prince and Parliament.' So wrote Thomas Harrab in his *Tessaradelphus* of 1616, a comparative study of the branches of European Protestantism.[1] Although this appears to be the first instance of 'Anglianisme' in print, the word 'Anglicanism' had no popular currency in the seventeenth and eighteenth centuries, and it did not enter the first English dictionaries.[2] Only during the second half of the last century did it find an established niche within the English vocabulary when the Tractarians popularized the word, and bestowed upon it a meaning somewhat distinct from that known to Harrab.[3] 'Anglianisme' for Harrab was a useful term because it served to denote that the Anglican Church, unlike its Lutheran or Calvinist relatives, acknowledged no great reformer as its founder, and that in contrast to most other reformed Churches its basis was national rather than territorial. It might suggest also that the Church of England, in the best tradition of Jewel, was not newly established at the Reformation, but reformed in such a way that it preserved the universal and catholic apostolic faith proclaimed in England from the earliest times. But here the

[1] T. Harrab, *Tessaradelphus or the Four Brothers* (1616), 'to the reader'.

[2] According to Professor Russell (*The Causes of the English Civil War* (Oxford, 1990), 104–5), 'Anglican' was not in usage before 1635. This overlooks the frequent use of 'ecclesia anglicana': see *The Oxford English Dictionary*, 2nd edn., ed. J. A. Simpson and E. S. C. Weiner, 20 vols. (1989), i. 464; see also PRO SP 16/203/30.

[3] 'Anglicanism', *The Oxford English Dictionary*, i. 464, which gives the earliest examples of the word in print as 1838 and 1846. *The Study of Anglicanism* (1988) ed. S. Sykes and J. Booty; P. Avis, *Anglicanism and the Christian Church* (Edinb. 1989).

common ground ends. For the Tractarians, Anglicanism was pre-eminently a system, a *via media* in doctrinal, ecclesiological, and evangelical matters, founded upon a delicate equipoise between Scripture, tradition, and reason and not upon the infallibility of any of these elements, in particular the first two, as represented in 'Puritanism' or Rome.[4] This interpretation of Anglicanism, alien to Harrab's, rested in part upon the work of a minority of commentators who had depicted Anglican history in terms of a dialectic struggle between the opposing forces of Anglicanism and Puritanism on the one hand, and Anglicanism and Rome on the other.[5] Harrab's definition, in contrast, lacked any such notion of Anglicanism as a *via media* in doctrinal or evangelical matters, and as far as ecclesiology was concerned, he noted that the ceremonies of the Jacobean Church were 'daily decreasing'. Like most of his contemporaries he would have had no conception of Puritanism as a system alien to Anglicanism; rather it was a manifestation of evangelical zeal and nonconformist inclination accommodated within the flexible structures of the English Church.[6]

A rational conclusion to be drawn from a study of the etymology of Anglicanism is that it has become more exclusive over time. The Anglicanism of the first-century reformed Church of England was far more inclusive than the Church which grew out of the exclusion of puritan and evangelical identities, which resulted from the onslaught of Carolinism, the persecutions of the Cavalier Parliament, and the rigid and stultifying strait-jacket which eventually orphaned its Methodist offspring.[7] But it is not just the word Anglicanism which

[4] Harrab, *Tessaradelphus*, 'to the reader'; J. F. New, *Anglican and Puritan: The Basis of their Opposition 1558–1640* (1964); F. A. Clarke, *Life of Thomas Ken* (1896), 234; E. C. E. Bourne, *The Anglicanism of William Laud* (1947); 'Anglicanism' in *Oxford Dictionary of the Christian Church* (1974), ed. F. L. Cross and E. Livingstone, 57. P. E. More and F. L. Cross (eds.), *Anglicanism* (1935), pp. xxiv, xxvii, xlvii, lii; *The Via Media of the Anglican Church by John Henry Newman* (Oxf., 1990), ed. H. D. Weidner, pp. xxx–xl, ch. 2.

[5] In particular Heylyn, *CA*; R. K. Faulker, *Richard Hooker and the Politics of a Christian England* (1981), 33, 39–58; Lake, *AP, passim*; and G. Veith, *Reformation Spirituality: The Religion of George Herbert* (1985), 12, 16.

[6] Harrab, *Tessaradelphus*, 'to the reader'; P. Lake, 'Puritan Identities', *Journal of Ecclesiastical History*, 35/1 (1984), 112–23; 'A Comment: Concerning the Name Puritan', *Journal of Ecclesiastical History*, 21/4 (1980).

[7] Anglican writers appear increasingly to divest Anglicanism of its Hookerian spectacles: 'The popular account of Anglican moderation, that it consisted in steering a steady middle path between the exaggerated positions of Rome on the one hand and Geneva on the other, simply will not bear examination,' O. O'Donovan, *On The Thirty-Nine Articles: A Conversation with Tudor Christianity* (1986), 13–14.

has altered over time. Its liturgical and architectural setting has also changed. Although the Prayer Book was widely used, it was rarely seen as self-sufficient. As for the archaeological evidence of the early reformed Church, much of this was swept away during the reign of Charles I, or later under the Victorian 'restorations'. What now appears as a liturgical setting sanctioned by time immemorial might appear as innovatory in the early seventeenth or later nineteenth centuries. Well into the last century, many churches were more like barns than the emphatically 'ecclesiastical' structures of today.[8]

In addition to the contribution of Tractarian and late Anglican writings, the perceived polarity of Anglicanism and Puritanism owed much to the Marxist undercurrent of seventeenth-century historiography. This saw Puritanism as the creed of the rising middle classes, destined to criticize and then subjugate the outmoded structures and ways of a Church that hindered the rise of capitalist enterprise. Whig historiography reinforced this interpretation by characterizing the period before 1640 as a pre-revolutionary age and Puritanism as the progressive advocate of change and revolution. These views were seemingly confirmed by and partly based upon the very biased accounts of some Caroline apologists, in particular Heylyn, who wished to marginalize Puritanism from the mainstream of English church life.[9] Within the last twenty years this antithetic edifice of Anglican against Puritan has come tumbling down. Puritans, as now understood by historians, were essentially the more enthusiastic, evangelical type of Protestants, not necessarily nor particularly nonconformist in their attitudes to the Church. They were more concerned with social redemption than with social revolution; with godliness in the Commonwealth rather than with political upheaval or Presbyterian programmes.[10] Indeed, if puritans posed a

[8] J. Stow, *Annales*, ed. E. Howes (1615), 892; G. Parry, *The Golden Age Restored: The Culture of the Stuart Court 1603–42* (Manchester, 1985), 262; Bodl. MS Rawl. D353/82; T. Jones, *The History of Breknockshire*, 4 vols. (Brecknock, 1911), for the state of churches in one county before extensive Victorian reconstructions; J. Barlow, *An Exposition of the Second Epistle to Timothy* (1625), 248. For occasional conformity see Ch. 2 section ii and K. Fincham, *Prelate as Pastor: The Episcopate of James I* (Oxford, 1990) *passim*; Bodl. MS J. Walker c. 9/31–57^{v}.

[9] C. Hill, *Society and Puritanism in Pre-Revolutionary England* (1964); W. Haller, *The Rise of Puritanism* (New York, 1938); Heylyn, *CA*, and his other works.

[10] N. R. N. Tyacke, 'Puritanism, Arminianism and Counter-Revolution', in C. S. R. Russell (ed.), *The Origins of the English Civil War* (1973), 119–43, and intro. to the same by Russell; Tyacke, *AC*; Collinson, *RP*; Collinson, *GP*; Lake, *AP*; P. Lake, *Moderate Puritans and the Elizabethan Church* (Cambridge, 1982); P. Lake, 'Puritan Identities', 112–23; Parker, *ES*; C. S. R. Russell, *Parliaments and English Politics*

threat to the state and unsettled the peace of the Church it was less because of themselves than because the authorities attempted to restrict the free expression of their evangelical and reformed interests. In this respect, Elizabeth I might appear as one of the elements making for instability in the Elizabethan Church: a cause of much controversy over rites and ecclesiastical discipline, and of the increased appeal of Presbyterianism in the 1580s and 1590s.[11] Fortunately for evangelical Protestants neither the Elizabethan Settlement nor the Canons of 1604 were wholly enforced in the localities, permitting James I for much of his reign to accommodate Puritan interests within the Church by condoning occasional conformity, at least until 1622.[12]

Professor Collinson has depicted the Jacobean age as the time when the reformed Church of England finally came of age. Within the Jacobean Church, as in its Elizabethan predecessor, many clergy and laity supplemented its rather limited evangelistic and congregational tools by establishing and supporting voluntary forms of religion, such as prophesyings, fasts, repetitions, prayer-meetings, and lectures. The evangelistic thrust of Puritanism—the most vital force for reform and renewal within the Church—entailed a considerable cross-section of English society placing a high premium on personal faith, vocational election, and godliness in Church and Commonwealth, values which might diverge from the demands of a state Church and the possible moral relativism of some of its leaders.[13] But as long as the bishops were reformed, enthusiastic supporters of

1621–1629 (Oxf., 1979), 28; K. Fincham and P. Lake, 'The Ecclesiastical Policy of James I', *Journal of British Studies*, 24 (1985), 169–201; Fincham, *Prelate as Pastor*. For the contribution of literary historians, see: Veith, *Reformation Spirituality* 12–23, 31–41, 246–50; B. Lewalski, *Protestant Poetics and the Seventeenth Century Lyric* (1979); L. Sasek, *The Literary Temper of English Puritanism* (Baton Rouge, LA, 1961); H. Fisch, *Jerusalem and Albion: The Hebraic Factor in Seventeenth Century Literature* (New York, 1964).

[11] P. Collinson, *The Elizabethan Puritan Movement* (1967); C. Haigh (ed.), *The Reign of Elizabeth I* (1985), essays by Collinson and Haigh in particular.

[12] Fincham, *Prelate as Pastor, passim*; Fincham and Lake, 'The Ecclesiastical Policy of James I', 169–207; K. Fincham, 'Archbishop Abbot and the Defence of Protestant Orthodoxy', *Historical Research*, 61 (1988); id., 'Ramifications of the Hampton Court Conference in the Dioceses 1603–1609', *Journal of Ecclesiastical History*, 36/2 (Apr. 1985), 208–227; P. Collinson, 'The Jacobean Religious Settlement: The Hampton Court Conference', in H. Tomlinson (ed.), *Before the English Civil War* (1983); Lake, *AP* 145–6; Bodl. MS J. Walker c. 9/31–57^{v}.

[13] Collinson, *RP*, *passim*; Collinson, *GP*, (esp.) 468–99; Lake, *AP*, 240ff.; Lake, 'Puritan Identities', 112–23.

the Gospel, and reluctant to press conformity, little unsettled the shared interests of the hierarchy and the godly. Bishop Williams of Lincoln believed that the best way to win Puritans to conformity was to outpreach them, while in the neighbouring diocese of York, Archbishop Matthew almost paralleled apostolic efforts by preaching thousands of sermons throughout his parishes.[14] In addition to such shared evangelistic concerns, a common doctrinal platform served to accommodate Puritan and bishop within the Jacobean Church; a 'doctrinal consensus' more reformed than Calvinist, since not all the shared doctrinal issues were specifically Calvinist.[15]

Although the Jacobean Church was praised for its scholarship and eirenicism, it was not without its critics. Drs Lake and Fincham have highlighted the tensions which sometimes threatened its peace. Underlying much of the later Caroline critique of the Jacobean establishment was the judgement that it had occasioned the decay of worship by attaching too much importance to preaching.[16] Yet within the Jacobean Church such differentiation between sermonic and sacramental piety was not only theologically impossible but institutionally unlikely, given reformed eucharistic views and the Anglican retention of infant baptism.[17] During the reign of James I, a steadily increasing outlay on church fabrics and furnishings, a perceived (if difficult to prove) increase in the number of communicants, the greater professionalization of the clergy, and the growth of *iure divino* ideas of episcopacy all suggest that Jacobean piety was not simply

[14] Hacket, *SR*, i. 27, 34; Collinson, *RP*, 46–50; John Fisbroke, *Six Sermons delivered in a Lecture at Kettering* (Camb., 1633); Seaver, *PL* 23; P. Lake, 'Matthew Hutton: A Puritan Bishop?', *History*, 64 (1974); Fincham, *Prelate as Pastor*, 253–76; P. Collinson, 'Popular Prelates: Elizabethan and Jacobean Roots of the Low Church Tradition', *Lambeth Palace Lib. Ann. Report* (1982).

[15] Tyacke, *AC*, 1–105; Parker, *ES*, 178; R. T. Kendall, *Calvin and English Calvinism to 1649* (Oxf., 1979); Collinson, *RP*, *passim*; P. Lake, 'Protestants, Puritans and Laudians', *Journal of Ecclesiastical History*, 42/4 (1991), 618–28.

[16] R. Shelford, *Five Pious and Learned Discourses* (1635), 12.

[17] Lake, *AP* 176, 229; Veith, *Reformation Spirituality, passim*; P. Lake, 'Calvinism and the English Church, 1570–1635', *Past and Present*, 114 (1987), 74; *WLA* v. 296; Bodl. MS Tanner 71/30, 39^{v}, 57, 62, 148; J. Tombes, *Felo de Se, or Mr Richard Baxter's Self-Destroying* (1659); for frequent communions in Calvin's Geneva see H. Höpfl, *The Christian Polity of John Calvin* (Camb., 1982), 61–2. It was Bishop Lewis Bayley's discussion of the sacraments in his Jacobean classic, *The Practice of Piety*, which helped to convert the eighteenth-century evangelist, Howell Harris: Richard Bennett, *Howell Harris and the Dawn of Revival* (Bridgend, 1962), 240. For the centrality of Christology in Puritan works see Lake, 'Protestants, Puritans and Laudians', 624; id., *Moderate Puritans*.

pedagogical and that 'parish Anglicanism' was not the preserve of rustic Pelagians.[18] It was in fact a reformed Church of England in which George Herbert felt more at home than the less reformed Laud.[19]

The religious peace of Jacobean England rested upon the promotion of a popular Anglican conformity, as Puritans were won over to the established Church by James I's conscious policy not to force conformity or conscientious issues. The policy of Charles I and most of his episcopal bench to reverse this practice, and to marginalize and anathematize the most vital force within the Church as sectarian and subversive, was disastrous for themselves and for the country. The king marked out evangelical Puritanism as a popularist threat to hierarchy and authority, which elevated individualism over deferential principles, and questioned his own inflexible views. Yet as Professor Collinson has shown, the voluntarism of Jacobean Puritanism existed within a contractual framework which limited its subversive potential. Thus historians who try to ascertain why religion was a factor in the causes of the British Civil War and the English revolution ought to start with Charles I's tragic and remarkable statement to Neile in 1634: 'the neglect of punishing puritans breeds papists.'[20]

It is not surprising that among the three works which Charles I recommended to his children, shortly before his execution in 1649, was Hooker's *Laws of Ecclesiastical Polity*, the first major critique of evangelical Puritanism within the later reformed Church of England.[21] Hooker, as Peter Lake has shown, arrived at a very different notion of the relationship between Scripture and reason from that which had passed as orthodox in Elizabethan Protestantism. He played down the internal testimony of the Spirit and denied that Scripture was either self-authenticating or self-interpreting. What

[18] C. Haigh, 'The Church of England, the Catholics and the People', in Haigh (ed.), *The Reign of Elizabeth I*, 169–220; J. Boulton, *Neighbourhood and Society: A London Suburb in the Seventeenth Century* (Camb., 1987), 282 ff.; J. Stow, *Annales*, ed. Howes, 892; R. O'Day, *The English Clergy: The Emergence and Consolidation of a Profession 1558–1642* (Leicester, 1979); P. Lake, 'Presbyterianism, the Idea of a National Church and the Argument from Divine Right', in P. Lake and M. Dowling (eds.), *Protestantism and the National Church in Sixteenth Century* (1987), 193–213; Birch, i. 81; W. Lamont, *Godly Rule: Politics and Religion 1603–1660* (1969), 36–45; Fincham, *Prelate as Pastor, passim*.

[19] Veith, *Reformation Spirituality*, 12–23, 31–41, 246–50.

[20] PRO SP 16/259/78; Tyacke, *AC*, 223–4; Fincham, *Prelate as Pastor, passim*; Collinson, *RP*, *passim*.

[21] *WKC*, ii. 448–9; i. 115; Faulker, *Richard Hooker*, 49, 51, 38–58.

was novel in this synthesis was less the interplay of Scripture, reason, and tradition (which all Protestant theologians emphasized to a greater or lesser extent) than Hooker's depiction of the Spirit as past or as the mere exercise of reason. Thus he did not see the Reformation as a progressive revelation of the Word through the Spirit. This led him to attack the importance laid on pulpit preaching by the later reformed Church.[22] Dr Lake shows how Hooker then proceeded to shift the contemporary emphasis on instruction and doctrine towards worship and in the process helped to reclaim the symbolism and ritualism of the visible Church from the status of popish superstition to that of a very necessary and essential mode of communication and edification.[23] Although the Jacobean Church might thank him for this (his 'sacramental virtualism' was shared by Ussher and others), the notion that the efficacy of the sacrament was no longer dependent upon the preaching of the Word was both novel and disturbing.[24]

Although there is every reason to assume that these Hookerian views informed the later, Caroline attempt to marginalize Puritanism, Charles I could not accept them without qualification. Hooker certainly did not provide the king with a policy, for he was no consistent advocate of theories of divine right, which he had somewhat discredited when attacking *iure divino* Presbyterianism.[25] Moreover Carolinism united a Hookerian view of the Church with an intolerant and exclusive concept of divine-right episcopacy, which few episcopalians before or after were prepared to defend.[26] In this respect, Hooker was certainly one of the foundation stones of the Caroline Church, a necessary but not a sufficient explanation for Charles I's stigmatization of nonconformity and evangelical enthusiasm.[27]

Recent revisionist historians suggest that Charles I anathematized Puritanism because he had imbibed Arminian doctrine. This, it is held, led him to proscribe its doctrinal opposite, Calvinism, the perceived doctrinal base of Puritanism.[28] Such an argument is based upon two related and unproven assumptions: first, that the doc-

[22] Lake, *AP* 158. [23] Ibid. 158–78. [24] Ibid. 176. [25] Ibid. 220–5.

[26] H. R. McAdoo, *The Spirit of Anglicanism: A Survey of Anglican Theological Method in the Seventeenth Century* (1965), chs. 3–5; G. V. Bennett, 'Archbishop Laud and Episcopacy', in Geoffrey Rowell (ed.), *To The Church of England* (1988), 34–47; A. McGrath, 'Reformation to Enlightenment', in P. Avis (eds.), *The Science of Theology* (1986), 107–205.

[27] Lake, *AP* (1986), 179–87; *The New Criterion: A Quarterly Review*, 4/2 (Apr. 1926), 222; More and Cross (eds.), *Anglicanism*, 342.

[28] Tyacke, *AC* 246–7.

trine of the Jacobean Church was specifically Calvinist (rather than reformed) and second, its corollary, that it could therefore be criticized only from an Arminian platform. The first of these assumptions is briefly addressed in the third chapter. As to the second, Peter Lake has shown that it was possible to criticize the reformed piety of the Jacobean Church from a *Calvinist* platform within the Church.[29] Moreover Charles I was no Arminian revolutionary. As far as can be ascertained, the king was doctrinally dyslexic rather than doctrinally illiterate. He did not articulate his beliefs in the systematic way that his father did, and apart from his espousal of the doctrine of the divine right of kings his ideological baggage was light.[30] Although intelligent, he lacked his father's erudition and wisdom.[31] Certainly he was no Calvinist: according to Clarendon, the king was 'sufficiently indisposed towards the person or the principle of Mr. Calvin's disciples'.[32] That he disliked those parts of Calvin's *Institutes* which appeared to condone resistance to authority is not in question: when Morton suggested that the *Institutes* provided no support for the Scottish rebellion, the king ordered the bishop to drop his thesis before he passed his sermon for publication.[33] Clearly, Charles I did not need to understand the religious significance of election in order to recognize in it a dangerous threat to his notion of social uniformity and civility. But if Charles was not Calvinist, neither was he Arminian: he was quintessentially and self-consciously Caroline. The policy of neutralizing doctrinal controversy during the 1630s was a reflection of his lack of interest in academic theology and his determination to impose silence on the predestinarian debate, regardless of the effect this might have upon current reformed orthodoxy.[34] In the last resort, doctrine for him was less important than morality. As he told Davenant in 1630, points concerning 'reformation and newness of life were more needful and profitable' than controversy over predestination, which was 'too high for the people's understanding'.[35]

[29] Lake, *AP* 228–9; id., *Moderate Puritans*, *passim*; id., 'Protestants, Puritans and Laudians', 618 ff.

[30] Tyacke, *AC* 7–8.

[31] *Parentalia*, 45–7; Bodl. Tanner 70/103; PRO SP 16/437/56; J. N. Figgis, *The Divine Right of Kings* (1896); R. Cust, *The Forced Loan and English Politics 1626–28* (Oxf., 1987), 325; J. P. Sommerville, *Politics and Ideology in England 1603–1640* (1986), 9–46. According to his one-time tutor Bishop Carleton, Charles was more intelligent than his brother Prince Henry: PRO SP 14/80/27. *WKC* i. 115; *Brief Memoirs of Nicholas Ferrar*, ed. T. MacDonough (1987), 151–3, 199–202.

[32] Clarendon, i. 121.

[33] PRO SP 16/437/56.

[34] See Ch. 3 section iii in particular.

[35] Bodl. Tanner MS 290/86v.

If Charles's doctrinal beliefs allow of some categorization, then they are probably best likened to an anti-dogmatic, anti-fideistic Erasmianism.[36] Certainly some of those whom Charles promoted in the 1630s were, in varying degrees, either cool towards Calvinism or anti-Calvinist in their orientation, and many of them made some association of it with Puritanism in order to unsettle the likes of Abbot. Such association helped to raise the king's already entrenched views against the Jacobean polity, but it did not predispose him to see Puritanism in any worse light than before, for running deeper than the king's distrust of Calvinism, and anterior to it, was a pronounced subjective hatred of Puritan voluntarism. Puritanism for Charles I was the disease, and if it was more pervasive than he had previously thought, or if it had a doctrinal complexion, as Buckingham was wont to tell him, then it merely confirmed his worst suspicions.[37]

The royal fear of Puritanism was at its heart a dread of disorder, disunity, and the contamination of 'popularity'. In fact the attempt to eradicate these cancers constituted the salient marks of much royal policy throughout the reign.[38] The king's insecurity, isolation, intransigence, and inability to understand others meant that he easily succumbed to theories of Puritan-inspired conspiracies. Prerogative rule and the reconstruction of the Church after 1629 constituted the royal response to a sincerely held conviction that there existed a deeply entrenched plot, orchestrated by popular Puritan elements in the House of Commons and within the judiciary, to undermine monarchy.[39] Although, as Professor Russell has shown, no identifiable 'Puritan' opposition existed, Charles I believed that it did. Notestein's notion of a parliamentary opposition attempting to unsettle authority may well have been the king's perception. At the same

[36] I cannot accept Lord Dacre's opinion that Arminianism has its origins in Erasmianism, since Erasmianism is opposed to the scholasticism and fideism of Arminianism: H. R. Trevor-Roper, 'The Religious Origins of the Enlightenment', in his *The European Witch-Craze of the Sixteenth and Seventeenth Centuries and Other Essays* (New York, 1967), 204–36, and *Catholics, Anglicans and Puritans* (1987), 41–2.

[37] R. Cust and A. Hughes (eds.), *Conflict in Early Stuart England: Studies in Religion and Politics 1603–1642* (1989), 18–19, 21.

[38] K. Sharpe, 'The Personal Rule of Charles I', in Tomlinson (ed.), *Before the English Civil War*, 58–63, and his *Criticism and Compliment: The Politics of Literature in the England of Charles I* (Cambridge, 1987); R. Smuts, *Court Culture and the Origins of a Royalist Tradition in Early Stuart England* (Philadelphia, 1987), 258–62; Cust and Hughes (eds.), *Conflict in Early Stuart England*, 84; Cust, *Forced Loan*, 328–9, 332, 336.

[39] L. J. Reeve, *Charles I and the Road to Personal Rule* (1989), ch. 6, 172–80, 295–300; Cust, *Forced Loan*, 13–90, 324–32; Cust and Hughes (eds.), *Conflict in Early Stuart England*, 18–21, 84–6.

time, Charles's failure to distinguish between his person and his office, or between public loyalties and personal beliefs, made him suspect Puritan leanings in those in whom he detected the slightest disaffection to his will. As John Reeve has suggested, there was no limit to his authoritarianism and paranoia about loyalty. When he challenged the earl of Leicester to answer the accusation that he was one of these ubiquitous Puritans, the earl acknowledged the king's twisted comprehension of Puritanism, by replying that he could not absolutely deny that he was a Puritan because he did not 'perfectly know what it is to be one'.[40] So pervasive was the royal conviction that an undercover Puritan conspiracy aimed to unsettle authority that he suspected it was the major cause of opposition to his policies during the later 1620s and 1630s. Hall could only clear himself from the accusation of supporting (what he called) 'modern Puritanism' by showing that he had not only curtailed the growth of nonconformity but that Devon and Cornwall had responded well to the king's financial demands.[41] Laud and Wren knew the king's mind well. As early as 1626 both had made a clear connection between Puritanism and political subversion, by which they meant the recent parliamentary opposition to Charles I. This was music to the king's ears. Those who sought his patronage in the 1630s played on the royal dread of disorder and disaffection to close the curtains on the Jacobean Church. In seeing Puritanism too ubiquitously and in subscribing to its redefinition, Charles I and his bishops laid themselves open to the charge that if they were not revolutionaries, they were certainly political reactionaries. 'They have brought it to pass', exclaimed Rudyerd in 1640, 'that under the name of puritan all our religion is branded.'[42]

In a sermon preached before the king during April 1628, Phineas Hodson rooted the strength of the court and Commonwealth 'principally . . . in order and beauty'. As Charles I's aestheticism was deeply appreciative of both, during his reign court ritual and art became active instruments in the banishment of Puritan disorder from the theatre of kingship. Caroline court culture attained a quasi-religious character as the king bestowed upon it the liturgical sanctions of the Church. Contrary to what is thought, Charles I, more

[40] *HMC De Lisle and Dudley vi*, 356. For the best character sketches we have of Charles I see Reeve, *Charles I*, ch. 6, *et passim* and Russell, *The Causes of the English Civil War*, ch. 8.

[41] SRO DD/PH 221/40.

[42] *WWL* i. 121–47; Bodl. Tanner MS 361/68–9^{v}; *CJ* i. 1355.

effectively than his predecessors, employed ceremony as a conscious act of propaganda by harnessing to his services the liturgy and rites of the *ecclesia anglicana*.[43] By impressing upon the nation the culture of the Chapel Royal, he effectively diffused throughout the parishes of his realm his own cult and apotheosis—an *imago dei*, which found its most disturbing icon in the face of Christ, commissioned by John Williams in 1631 for the east window of his new chapel at Lincoln College, Oxford.[44] Through the manipulation of divine worship and its setting, Charles I's pretensions to sacramental kingship received not only visual expression but the cloak of divine respectability. As God's lieutenant on earth, whose power reaches 'but to an ordinary man', he saw it as his duty to inculcate in others his vision of religion.[45] As the editor of *The King's Works* put it,

> he was not satisfied in being religious as a particular christian but would be so as a king and endeavour that piety might be as universal as his empire. This he envisaged by giving ornaments and assistances to the external exercise . . . that so, carnal minds, if they were not brought to an obedience, might yet to a reverence and if men would not honour, yet they should not despise religion.

In fact the cult of the Caroline Church had become the masque of Charles I, his most effective and very unplatonic re-creation.[46]

But the visual apotheosis of divine kingship under the second Stuart had its historical antecedents. Although a cult of Elizabeth I had developed in Tudor England, a Virgin Queen was no match for an *Eikon Basilike*. The native notion of the Supreme Governor as the godly Constantine, which James I had done so much to inculcate, served to elevate respect for the office of kingship in early Stuart England, as did the mutual support of divine-right episcopacy. As Charles gave his support to Laudianism, high clericalists intent on tracing their professional identity from heaven sought to extricate *iure divino* kingship from its Foxeian conditions. Rooted more securely in natural law and freed from its constitutional inhibitions, the divine right of kings advanced towards absolutist heights. At the same time

[43] P. Hodson, *The King's Request or David's Desire* (1628); Parry, *Golden Age Restored*, 193, 242; and Smuts, *Court Culture*, 217–41.

[44] *RCHM City of Oxford*, plate 124.

[45] Smuts, *Court Culture*, 234–8; *WKC* i. 98; PRO SP 16/182/31.

[46] *WKC* i. 98; Sharpe, 'The Personal Rule of Charles I', 60; Smuts, *Court Culture*, 253–7. R. E. Clements, *God and Temple* (Oxf. 1965), 68. Charles' notions of kingship were probably influenced by the books of Kings and Chronicles, see *Brief Memoirs of Nicholas Ferrar . . . by Dr Turner* (Bristol, 1829), 137–9.

such principles would receive greater prominence under Charles I because of the king's conscious desire to put into practice what for his father had been more of an ideal. One ironic effect of Charles I's interference in church affairs was to blur the lines of demarcation that Laud, Cosin, and others envisaged in their idea of the Supremacy, between the authority of God, who allowed them their spiritual rights, and the divine authority of the king who permitted their exercise and jurisdiction.[47] In fact the role of Charles I was at times more redolent of the Lutheran *summus episcopus* than of Supreme Governor. This was graphically expressed in the coronation of 1626, when the king, instead of receiving the fealty of his bishops on oath, embraced them from the throne.[48] It may have been a source of serious concern both that the role of the Governor within the Church had not been defined, and that Charles I had not systematically declared the extent of his ecclesiastical prerogative. The scope for royal interference was in fact limitless, and thus Laud's attempts to define the boundaries of ecclesiastical prerogative were of no small professional interest to the clergy. Laud acknowledged the possibility that a king might attempt to undermine the true faith. Consequently only when the bishops suffered 'an unjust violence' from the Crown did Laud see it as incumbent upon them to defend themselves, although even under these conditions they were not to break their oaths of allegiance.[49] But although the theories of the divine right of kings and bishops might not in the last resort be mutually compatible, there was little prospect of a serious fissure between the pillars of the State and the Temple. After all Charles and Laud had similar visions for the Church, if somewhat different ways of realizing them. Moreover, in order to secure its ascendant pretensions, Laudianism was obliged to dance to the call of the Caroline concept of divine right.

Charles's obsession with order and deference go far to explain why he should restrict Puritan and noncomformist persuasions. But the roots of his dislike of evangelical freedom extend further. It seems that true religion for Charles I consisted of following an exemplary,

[47] P. Lake, 'Presbyterianism', id., *AP passim*; Parry, *Golden Age Restored*, 202, 192, 242; Smuts, *Court Culture*, 230–4; *WWL* iii. 406–7, vi. 43, 114–15; PRO SP 16/121/33 (1, 11); Collinson, *RP* 18; *CC* i. 147–51; *Northcote*, 62.

[48] Fuller, *CH* 385; Lamont, *Godly Rule*, 57; *Reliquiae Sacrae Carolinae* (1650), 143.

[49] *WWL* vi. 142–3; i. 5–6, 64 As such Laud laid down the premiss upon which both the Seven Bishops and the Nonjurors subsequently acted.

moral code of conduct, along a path illuminated less by the Word than by capturing a sense of the numinous. Gifts such as personal faith in Christ or the working of the Holy Spirit may well have escaped him. Although he recognized a 'true light', he nevertheless proceeded to restrict its illumination to an ordained ministry rather than corporately to the ministry and the congregation, or individually to the believer.[50] If someone other than a beneficed minister assumed a preaching role, this could be only 'false' or 'uncertain'.[51] Thus it seems that the king had little interior understanding of the basic doctrinal platform of the English Reformation: justification by faith and the priesthood of believers. Consequently one must seriously question Sir Philip Warwick's assertion that no contemporary 'better understood the foundation of the Church and the grounds of the Reformation' than Charles I.[52] In fact, not unlike the drift of some recent historiography, he conceived of the Reformation as little more than a state act, inaugurated by authority, without any impulse from below. The 'Reformation of my mother', the Church of England, 'was done ... neither with multitude nor with tumult', he informed Henderson, 'but legally and duly and by those whom I conceive to have the reforming power.'[53] Yet once the Reformation involved the people it had assumed the aspect of subversion; in the words of Charles I, 'popular reformation' was 'little better than rebellion'.[54] There is little surprise therefore that he came to anathematize the reformed polity of Jacobean England, and in particular the voluntarism of the Jacobean Church. His narrow vision of the ecclesiastical past ensured more than anything else that he would visualize the most vital force of the Reformation as the enemy within. Religion became the major cause of the British Civil War not because of the bugbear of Arminianism but because Charles I was in conscious rebellion against lay and popular Protestantism—the very Reformation itself. There is little wonder therefore that he helped to create much of the opposition which faced him in 1640 and singularly failed to distinguish between Puritanism and disloyalty to the Crown, between those whom he had alienated and those who were his

[50] *WWL* v. 320; Smuts, *Court Culture*, ch. 8.
[51] *WWL* v. 320.
[52] *Characters of the Seventeenth Century*, ed. D. N. A. Smith (1918), 56.
[53] *WKC* ii. 156; I refer in particular to G. W. Bernard, 'The Church of England c.1529–c.1642', *History* (1990), 184.
[54] *WKC* ii. 176.

opponents in war.[55] Well might Fuller write that 'King James spoke not so confusedly as if Puritanism were a Religion and all that disliked bishops and ceremonies were of that Religion: and all of that Religion were enemies of kings.'[56]

II. CAESARO-SACRAMENTALISM

In 1625 a Florentine diplomat wrote of the changed atmosphere at court two months after the death of James I. The new king removed himself into the inner recesses of the household, bringing to an end the royal accessibility to courtiers. Strict Elizabethan codes of conduct for observation in the antechambers were introduced, and distance, reverence, and deference conditioned all movements within the court. One commentator wrote that Charles I showed 'himself so strict that a great change is observable. Dignity, respectful demeanour and regularity are insisted upon; from which everyone readily conjectures how much weight his Majesty will attach to deference and obedience in matters of serious importance.'[57] Thus the marks so characteristic of Caroline religion in the 1630s—distance, deportment, and reverence—had already made their début in 1625. Such notions became established themes in the sermons of the court, or in those which propagated the language of the Chapel Royal in the localities. 'Good carriage', preached Richard Steward, Charles's fifth clerk of the Closet, 'is as well a part of religion as of civility' and was to be observed no less 'in the Temple than in the court'.[58] Foulke Robartes, prebendary of Norwich, and Wren, his

[55] Tyacke, 'Puritanism, Arminianism and Counter-Revolution', 119–43, *passim*; see also Ch. 3 section i.

[56] Fuller, *AII* iii. 46; see also H. Parker, *A Discourse Concerning Puritans* (1641).

[57] *HMC Skrine*, 6. For an introduction to the Caroline court, see Smuts, *Court Culture*, 183–212; Parry, *Golden Age Restored*, ch. 9; O. Millar, *The Age of Charles I* (1972), and his *Vandyke in England* (1982); D. Lindley (ed.), *The Court Masque*, (Manchester, 1984); M. Butler, *Theatre and Crisis 1632–42* (Cambridge, 1984); J. Harris, S. Orgel, and R. Strong (eds.), *The King's Arcadia: Inigo Jones and the Stuart Court* (1973); C. J. Summers and T. L. Pebworth (eds.), *Poetry and Politics in the Seventeenth Century* (Columbia, MO, 1988); Sharpe, *Criticism and Compliment*; E. Veevers, *Images of Love and Religion: Queen Henrietta Maria and Court Entertainments* (Camb., 1989); *Ceremonies of Charles I: The Notebooks of Sir John Finet, Master of Ceremonies, 1628–1641*, ed. A. J. Loomie (New York, 1987); Reeve, *Charles I and the Road to Personal Rule*, ch. 6.

[58] R. Steward, *Three Sermons Preached by ... Dr. Richard Stuart to which is added a fourth ... by Archbishop Harsnett* (1658), 1.

bishop, likened bowing towards the altar to bowing towards the royal chair of state.[59] Both Thomas Lawrence, chaplain to the earl of Pembroke, and Peter Hausted visualized the ascent to the altar as the approach to the king through a series of presence chambers, passing through stages of holiness and demanding different degrees of adoration, depending on 'the degree of consecration in all things'. Walter Balcanquall, chaplain in ordinary and Calvinist delegate at Dort, stressed the exemplar of Charles's approach to the table, 'be sure you make a curtsie low enough with David, I am a worm and no man, or if you will, a little lower with Abraham since dust and ashes begin to speak with you.' A prebendary of Wells, Edward Kellet, was even convinced that the manner in which Charles received the communion could convert recusants from popery.[60] Through sermons such as these, printed often by the king's special command for diffusion across the country, Charles was consciously moulding his own image of religious observance and grafting upon the nation liturgical practices (kneeling, bowing, genuflecting, and standing) often unaccommodating to pre-existing gestures. Such worship was an expression less of 'Arminian' sacramentalism than of Caesaro-sacramentalism, since Calvinists as well as those whom Dr Tyacke designates as 'Arminians' were prepared to practise and vindicate the novel modes of worship.[61] 'The spiritual worship of God', wrote John Preston, 'is never well performed but when it's signified by the comely gesture of the body as far as we may . . . they must concur, the body must go with the spirit.' Daniel Featley bowed at the name of Jesus and wrote a vindication of it. Although he did not bow towards the table, he did not object to it in principle.[62] Whereas Dean Young

[59] F. Robartes, *God's Holy House and Service, according to the primitive and most Christian Form thereof* (1639), 91; *Parentalia*, 82.

[60] T. Lawrence, *The Duty of the Laity and the Privileges of the Priest* (Oxford, 1635) 13, and id., *A Sermon Preached before the King's Majesty at Whitehall* (1637), 1–10; P. Hausted, *Ten Sermons* (1636), 121; W. Balcanquall, *The Honour of the Christian Churches* (1633), 12; Edward Kellet, *Tricoenium Christi, in Nocte Proditionis Suae* (1641), 645, 634. See also H. Valentine, *Sermon Preached March 27 1639* (1639), 5; *Parentalia*, 81–2; H. King, *Two Sermons Preached at Whitehall in Lent* (1627), 25.

[61] Tyacke, 'Puritanism, Arminianism and Counter-Revolution', 119–43; Tyacke, *AC*, esp. ch. 8; Parry, *Golden Age Restored*, 268. H. Burton likened bowing in the Chapel Royal to bowing to Nebuchadnezzar's golden image: C. Dow, *Innovations unjustly charged* (1637), 190; *HMC De Lisle and Dudley vi*, 99.

[62] J. Preston, *Life Eternal or a Treatise of the Knowledge of the Divine Essence and Attributes* (1629), 11, 38; Daniel Featley, *The Gentle Lash or the Vindication of Dr. Featley* (1644), 9.

of Winchester bowed towards the east only during the eucharist at his cathedral, he always did so both at Wells and in the Chapel Royal, and did not 'disallow those that did it'.[63]

Apologists for the Caroline liturgical innovations such as Peter Heylyn, chaplain in ordinary to the king, appealed to the tradition and practice of the Chapel Royal, as the prototype for change.[64] In his preamble to the Canons of 1640, Charles I himself referred to those rites and ceremonies which had fallen into disuse since Elizabethan times but which had survived intact in some churches and within the Chapels Royal. In this appeal to the past, to an illusory 'former splendour of uniformity, devotion and holy order', there was a good deal of unconscious and probably conscious myth-making. In fact there is no evidence to substantiate the royal claim that such practices were ever used by the Edwardian reformers or 'taken up by the whole Church' for most of Elizabeth's reign.[65] The liturgy and ecclesiology of the Caroline Chapels Royal was of comparatively recent development and originated almost certainly during the time that Andrewes was dean of the Chapel between 1618 and 1626. James I, like several of his bishops, such as Neile, Buckeridge, and Laud, came to visualize in Andrewes's private form of worship the essence of primitive, liturgical practice.[66] Moreover Andrewes almost certainly advised James I about the furnishing of the chapel which was to accompany Charles to Spain in 1623 and which was intended to exhibit to the Spanish Church that England was visibly part of the catholic, apostolic fold, but purified of the corruptions of Rome.[67] At what juncture Charles became attached to these liturgical arrangements remains unclear, but it is apparent that at the time of James I's funeral in 1625, the rail, that peculiar mark of Andrewes's influence, was visibly present within the Chapels Royal.[68]

[63] WCL MS xxii/88.

[64] P. Heylyn, *Antidotum Lincolniense* (1636), epistle dedicators; Dow, *Innovations unjustly charged*, 190.

[65] *WWL* v. 610–12. For Charles's orders 'under his own hand' for the Scottish Chapels Royal see *HMC Appendix to the 9th Report*, 245. See also ibid., 248, 258; PRO SP 16/582/31; P. Heylyn, *Observations on the History of the Reign of King Charles* (1650), 143; *Parentalia*, 98, 79.

[66] HLRO Braye MS 8/38; PRO C115/N4/8049; Bodl. Rawl. MS 674/66.

[67] PRO SP 14/142/38; Bodl. Rawl. MS 674/66.

[68] *The Old Cheque Book of the Chapel Royal*, ed. E. F. Rimbault (1872), 155. Other notable innovations occurred during the time that Wren was dean of the Chapel, after 1636, such as receiving at the rail (*WWL* v. 360) and the large east-end crucifix, erected in April 1637 towards which Davenant refused to bow (*HMC De Lisle and Dudley vi*, 99).

The rail stood at the heart of Charles's programme of 'restoring' uniformity and order within Church and Commonwealth. Like the rails surrounding the royal beds, it inculcated respect for the consecrated place and person.[69] Chapter 6 suggests that the king rather than Laud was more effectively the author of the metropolitical order, designed to create a uniformity across the whole country in the placing of the table and the reception of the communion: a uniformity destructive not only of the Canons of 1604 but of St Gregory's declaration of 1633 which had safeguarded the rights of the ordinary.[70] Charles's personal involvement in the evolution and enforcement of the altar policy emanates from several sources. 'The king's injunctions concerning divine service' (possibly a draft for the metropolitical order, if not the original order itself) specified that tables should be railed in, that communicants should receive there, and that the priest should not leave them at the time of the administration.[71] Other evidence includes Charles's pledge in 1629 to revive the Elizabethan Injunctions of 1559, which had positioned the table where the altar stood outside communion; his prosecution of Williams for writing the *Holy Table, Name and Thing* against the metropolitical order;[72] and finally the instructions which he gave to individual parishes (such as those of Coventry, while on progress through Tutbury in 1635, or those of Newcastle, during the Scottish campaign of 1639). These orders involved the wholesale reconstruction of the east end, the erection of steps for the table, and the destruction of galleries, all redolent of Wren's practices in Norwich.[73] By 1640 through ritualistic innovations and the reorientation of the table, Charles I had effectively enrolled the parish church as the main vehicle for the propagation of his sacramental kingship. Within this new perspective theatre (in some ways similar to the stage sets of Inigo Jones), the royal and divine attributes merged in a synaesthesia of awe and spectacle. The parish church had veritably become 'thy glorious Temple, thy Whitehall'.[74]

[69] PRO SP LC/9/99/51. [70] See Ch. 6 section i. [71] PRO SP 16/474/60.

[72] PRO SP 16/153/44, 51; LPL MSS 1030/68(b).

[73] PRO SP 16/351/18; Heylyn, *CA* 288; Prynne, *CD* 91; *The Memoirs of Ambrose Barnes*, ed. W. H. D. Longstaffe (Surtees Soc., 1, 1866), 327; DURO Ep/Ch/le Street/CWA/136^{v}, DURO Ep/NI/1639. Bodl. MS Tanner 314/160: Wren justified the costly removal of seats to the corporations of Norwich and Ipswich as obedience to the king's command. The rails erected by Charles I in the Chapel Royal at Hampton Court survive in a cellar of the palace, see *RCHM Middlesex* (1937), 42 and plate 106. See also WTRO P 562/2/118, and *Parentalia*, 98.

[74] J. W. Legg, *English Orders for Consecrating Churches in the Seventeenth Century* (Henry Bradshaw Soc., 41, 1911), 202.

In a sermon preached before the king, Archdeacon Brownrigg of Coventry likened Charles I to Zerrubabel, the restorer of the worship of God within the *Books of Haggai* and *Ezra*.[75] Yet in spite of his religious externalism and possibly in deference to his father's greater wisdom, Charles I was never associated with Solomon.[76] For the king, as for Laud, there could be no inner piety without its visible manifestation. It is no coincidence therefore that the author of *De Templis* dated from his reign the restoration of English churches after years of neglect during the Reformation.[77] Many Puritans, however, suspected that this external worship of the heart, rather than developing into a charitable construction of the religious intentions of others, resolved itself into a concern for passing, cosmetic appearances. Certainly behind these initiatives lay a deep craving to instil deference. The efficacy of exemplar meant that Charles I saw the cathedrals not just as the mother-churches of their dioceses but as pace-makers for royal policy.[78] The restoration of St Paul's, sponsored by Laud, which Charles encouraged, was part of a wider restoration programme envisaged and scrutinized. From Newmarket in September 1636 Wren wrote to inform Bishop White that within a few days the king intended to visit Ely to examine the state of the cathedral.[79] Not long before he had visited Winchester, where he had summarily ordered the destruction of the chapter house in order to open up a prospect of the east end.[80] Like Laud he paid close attention to the ordering and removing of pews within churches and cathedrals in an endeavour to manufacture order out of confusion and to instil deference in the minds of those who had abnegated their social reserve.[81] Similar interests revealed themselves in the royal determination to make his servants and the nobility marry according to their status, and his isolation of the royal children from all but

[75] R. Brownrigg, *Sixty-five Sermons* (1674), i. 21. It was an epithet also applied to Wentworth by Archbishop Ussher, *LJU* 460.

[76] David was a more usual ascription: BL Portland Loan MS 29/173/243; Brownrigg, *Sixty-five Sermons*, i. 1; Robert Skinner, *A Sermon Preached before the king at Whitehall, December 3 1634* (1634); H. Burton, *An Apology of An Appeal* (1636), epistle dedicatory; Parry, *Golden Age Restored*, 26, 31, 242.

[77] R. T., *De Templis: A Treatise of Temples* (1638), section xxi, p. 183.

[78] *WWL* v. 319. On the cathedral as exemplar see Dow, *Innovations unjustly charged*, 188–9; H. Burton, *For God and the King* (1636), 159–61.

[79] Bodl. MS Tanner 70/103–4.

[80] Ibid.

[81] PRO SP 16/312/84, SP/16/239/56, SP/16/241/28; *WWL*, v. 324, vii. 556; Bodl. Ashmole MS 1131/3/53.

noble offspring.[82] If the king's mentality was stiflingly aristocratic perhaps it owes much to the concept of divine-right episcopacy that such prejudice did not clash with the more plebcian inclinations of the bench of bishops, who were content with banishing obtrusive funerary monuments to the more obscure corners of their churches.[83]

The bishops and those whom they ordained were subjected to the same royal scrutiny as other marks of the visible church. When Heylyn became a royal chaplain in 1631, Laud informed him that the king did not love silk or satin chaplains; Heylyn thereafter respected the king's wishes by wearing a 'plain and decent habit'.[84] Although Charles did not have such a high view of episcopacy as Laud,[85] he was reportedly 'much troubled' on hearing that Scottish deacons were in effect only lay officers (in the Scottish act of admission the essential words of conferring orders were omitted) and told the Scottish bishops either to admit the English book of ordination or to amend their manual.[86] Motivating much of this concern with the external visibility of the Anglican Church was a sincere desire to carve out a more distinct Anglo-Catholic identity and to show Catholic Europe that the English Church was not just a rival to Rome, but a better advertisement than it of the catholic, apostolic Church. In this respect, Charles's personal contacts with the Spanish Church in 1623 (and the French Church through Henrietta Maria) almost certainly deepened his catholic awareness.[87] Thus he took offence at the reluctance of the Irish bishops to wear episcopal habit claiming that what was at issue was less their dependence on the Anglican Church (over which they scrupled) than their identification with Catholicity.[88] The royal promotion of Anglo-Catholicism sur-

[82] BL Add. MS 37/11–12^{v}, 343; PRO LC5/134/87.

[83] Sharpe, 'The Personal Rule of Charles I', 61; *WWL* v. 358; vii. 116, 157, 174; PRO SP 16, 351, 100; *LJU* 460; PRO SP 16/260/60, SP/16/244/48; J. Hacket, *A Century of Sermons* (1675), p. xiv; Prynne, *CD* 381; *Parentalia*, 74.

[84] Barnard, *TH* 121.

[85] *WKC* i. 86–7; *WWL* iii. 194–200; HLRO 28 Nov. 1640 (petition of Thomas Brewer).

[86] *WWL* vi. 456.

[87] Reeve, *Charles I*, 177, 181–4, *et passim* for Charles's Hispanophilia; T. Cogswell, *The Blessed Revolution: English Politics and the Coming of War: 1621–1624* (Camb., 1989), *passim*. Edmund Atwood saw the ecclesiastical changes of the reign not as an attempt to create an Anglo-Catholicism but what he called an Anglo-Protestantism (Bodl. MS Clar. (SP) 18/1381). Did Charles learn anything from his Danish relatives? See Steffan Heiberg (ed.), *Christian IV and Europe* (Copenhagen, 1988), 475–82.

[88] *WWL* vii. 293.

faced also in his advocacy of priestly confession,[89] his affection for the lay monasticism at Little Gidding,[90] the encouragement of holy days, and his commission from Cosin of a substitute primer for that used by Henrietta Maria's ladies in waiting, the *Collection of Private Devotions*,[91] which Cosin may have compiled originally for the countess of Denbigh.[92] In the long term the Caroline attempt to reinvest the catholic apparel of the Anglican Church was bound to blur the visible boundaries between orthodoxy and popery, and this, in spite of the king's resolution 'to deal with . . . the Pope, as wrestlers do with one another, take him up to fling him down'.[93]

III. CAESARO-SACERDOTALISM

That Charles I had no desire to change the Jacobean Church before Laud's ascendancy was not a view widely held by contemporaries. In 1641 the parliamentary opponents of Carolinism traced its descent not from 1629 or 1633, but from 1625. In fact as early as April 1626 it seems likely that Charles had selected Bishops Harsnett of Norwich, Laud of St David's, and Morton of Coventry and Lichfield to advise him on church affairs.[94] On this particular occasion the king may have delegated responsibility for tendering advice on certain issues. To Laud, he may have assigned economic problems, for on the night of 9 April 1626, a few days after receiving the royal request, Laud gave to Charles I 'an account of what I had received in command on April 5th and of other things relating thereto. Among the rest

89 *CSPV 1636–9*, 217; *HMC Appendix to the 9th Report*, 496 (21 Oct. 1638).

90 But Charles's association or interest in Little Gidding should not be exaggerated (that of Laud and Williams was greater): see the essays by Pamela Tudor-Craig and Roger Van der Weyer in R. Ollard and P. Tudor-Craig (eds.), *For Veronica Wedgwood These: Studies in Seventeenth Century* (1986), 152–88; *Brief Memoirs of Nicholas Ferrar*, ed. Macdonough, 139–40; Parry, *Golden Age Restored*, 247.

91 *WWL* vii. 299.

92 *The Diary of John Evelyn*, ed. E. S. de Beer (Oxford, 1955), iii. 45–6; J. Collier, *An Ecclesiastical History of Great Britain* (1708), 742; W. Prynne, *A brief survay and censure of Mr Cozens his couzening devotions* (1628); Bodl. MS Smith 23/31. For Charles's counter-reformation tastes in art see among others, Smuts, *Court Culture* chs. 5–7; and for a contemporary's response: *HMC Appendix to 9th Report*, 496 (21 Oct. 1638).

93 *Characters of the Seventeenth Century*, ed. Smith, 56. For Charles I and the Vatican see G. Albion, *Charles I and the Court of Rome* (1935) and the forthcoming work of Anthony Milton; *CSPV 1636–9*, 217.

94 *Lords Journal*, iv. 392; *WWL* iii. 186–7.

concerning ... impropriations.'[95] Morton's inclusion within this group of close consultants suggests that the king was not restricting his ear to anti-Calvinists, as Morton was a strong Calvinist determinist.[96] Although it is important not to overestimate the significance of these early consultations in 1626 (the king sought wider episcopal advice about what he termed the 'cause of the Church' during the same year) they nevertheless helped to secure Harsnett and Laud among the closest advisers of the king and led to the formulation of several important policies.[97]

The picture of the king which emerges out of these early consultations is of a monarch more receptive to the advice of others than original in his views. This, however, does not mean that Charles I had no distinct vision of what his Supremacy entailed. He consciously visualized himself in the role of his Tudor predecessors, paternalistically moulding the Church and restoring what he saw as its 'true former splendour of uniformity, devotion and holy order'.[98] The preamble of the Canons of 1640 professed his 'princely inclinations ... to uniformity and peace', a desire to redirect the Church along the lines of its first Reformation (conducted under Edward VI and during the early years of Elizabeth I) and to redress those later developments which had threatened its foundation. These were listed as 'the want of an express rule therein', 'subtle practices', 'the devices of some ill-affected to sacred order', and 'inadvertancy of some in authority'.[99] Basically, this meant that the king had taken upon himself to root out of the Church those very voluntarist tendencies which had made later Elizabethan and Jacobean Anglicanism the catholic and eirenic accommodation that it was.

As early as December 1629 Charles I informed Laud of his intention to revive one of the first Elizabethan codes for the Church: the Injunctions of 1559. This caused the bishop no little consternation. Laud questioned their legal force and consulted with several of his colleagues whether or not they were still binding. It appeared that James I had ratified only a few of the injunctions, and that these had reappeared in the Canons of 1604. When legal opinion was sought, the Caroline judges differed, like their Jacobean predecessors, over

95 *WWL* iii. 187–8. See also Bodl. MS Smith 23/11–23.
96 Parker, *ES* 149–52.
97 *WWL* iii. 189; Prynne, *CD* 368; LPL MS 943/347; Bodl. MS Smith 23/11–23.
98 *WWL* v. 609–13; Bodl. Tanner MS 70/103.
99 *WWL* v. 609–13.

whether the remaining injunctions were binding.[100] Nevertheless, in response to the royal request, Laud proceeded to ask some of the bishops to find out which injunctions had been left out and whether any of them were worth revamping. He himself suggested that they should also be compared to other Elizabethan canons and constitutions, possibly to dampen the king's enthusiasm for their revival, for as late as 1635 Laud was still opposed to their re-enactment and denied that they had any binding legal force.[101] In December 1629 Laud informed Dorchester, the Secretary of State, that 'some things will fall out so cross that the business will hardly be mastered which . . . the bishops will submit to his Majesty's wisdom.'[102] Not until Heylyn drew up the canonical book of visitation articles in 1640 did some of these earlier Elizabethan orders see the light of day, although throughout the 1630s they had received some sanction in various visitation articles.[103]

This incident in 1629 has wider implications for a study of Charles's policy as it reveals his ready propensity to elevate orders of questionable legality over those of canonical authority, which Laud's legalism did not easily admit. Laud gave his full support to measures only so long as they were canonically binding.[104] Consequently during the 1630s he was placed in some difficulty when measures were prosecuted forcefully which had no canonical sanction. This explains his relatively lethargic prosecution of ministers for failing to read the book of sports and of lecturers for not complying with the letter of the Instructions, as well as his failure to implement the full metropolitical altar policy. On the other hand it explains his thorough enforcement of the Canons of 1604 and his unrelenting defence of the Book of Common Prayer. It probably also confirms those rumours which said that Laud wanted a Parliament, and thus Convocation in the 1630s so that canons could be made more in tune with Caroline policy.[105] Finally it explains his unconditional support for the Canons of 1640.

During the 1630s, if there was one policy which Laud was solidly associated with then that policy was the enforcement of the legal sanctions of the Church, the Canons of 1604. Laud's archiepiscopate

[100] PRO SP 16/153/44, SP/16/158/18; Bodl. Rawl. MS A 127/59, 75.
[101] LPL MS 1030/57, 137; PRO SP 16/158/18.
[102] PRO SP 16/158/18; *WWL* vii. 33.
[103] See Ch. 7 section ii. [104] See Ch. 2 section ii.
[105] *CSPV 1632–36*, 225; Ch. 2 section ii.

witnessed the first serious attempt not just to introduce the canons but to enforce them over most of the Southern Province.[106] This was controversial enough within a Church where occasional conformity had long conditioned many to accommodate their ecclesiological differences. But it was aggravated by the king's drive not only to prosecute non-canonical measures, but to undercut the canons by appealing to the authorities upon which they rested. The appeal to precedent and primitivism which characterized much intellectual debate was made by Charles I also, for as his attempt to revive the Injunctions of 1559 reveals, he was determined to revamp the earliest codes of the institutional Church.[107] A story related by Matthew Wren sufficiently betrays the king's cavalier attitude to canonical authority. In September 1633 Charles commanded Wren to inform Laud that 'his Majesty held it fitting' to reduce the prayers before the sermon in the Chapel Royal and elsewhere to the form in canon 55 of 1604.[108] As soon as he received this message, Laud told Juxon, recently made dean of the Chapel, of the royal wish.[109] Yet before long the king had chided Juxon for failing to inform him that the canon had derived from earlier forms evolved under the Tudors, which he appears to have thought more worthy of reviving because of their greater age.[110]

The publication of the Royal Instructions of 1629 suggest that the king saw his Supremacy in both an explanatory and a declaratory role.[111] These Instructions constituted a radical, if somewhat disorganized programme to subordinate the pulpit to the liturgy, and to uproot nonconformity within the Jacobean Church. They can also be seen as Charles's decision to resort to more authoritarian modes of control after the dissolution of Parliament and his determination to go it alone. The most controversial stipulations concerned its restrictions on lectures, which had grown up within the later reformed Church of England to supplement its insufficient number of sermons and to provide some vocational training for the clergy. Instruction 5 asked lecturers to read the liturgy before they preached and to turn

106 See Ch. 2 section ii.

107 As recognized by Fuller, *AII* iii. 92: 'the controversy in hand is about additional ceremonies enjoined by no Canons' ('save some men's over imperious commanding, and other over-officious complying'). See also Bodl. Tanner MS 70/103.

108 *Parentalia*, 89; Bodl. Tanner MS 314/152^v.

109 Bodl. Tanner MS 314/152^v.

110 *Parentalia*, 89; Bodl. Tanner MS 314/152^v.

111 *WWL* v. 307–9.

all their afternoon sermons into catechizing by question and answer. All lecturers maintained by corporations had either to accept a cure within the town or undergo suspension, while all market-town lectures had to be converted into combinations of ministers beneficed within the same vicinity.[112] Other Instructions reinforced these, by permitting only those allowed in statute to employ household chaplains (7), and by inviting clergy to attend lectures and to inform against any 'misdemeanours' (6). Instruction 3 reinforced the observation of the declaration of 1628 circumscribing doctrinal discussion. Others (1, 2, 4, and 9) asked the bishops to return to their sees, to practise good estate management, and to tighten ordination procedures. In short the Instructions provided the king with a solution to the Jacobean Church, an establishment which in his eyes had betrayed the principles of the early Reformation and infected consecrated heights with popular and Puritan contamination.[113]

Considering the attention which the Instructions have received, it is rather surprising that little is known of their formulation. It is widely assumed that Laud was solely or primarily responsible for the document, an interpretation which has its roots in *Canterburies Doome*.[114] That Laud was involved with the king in their formulation is not in doubt as both their hands appear upon some of the final drafts of the code.[115] But according to Heylyn, Laud's involvement in the whole affair equalled that of Harsnett, archbishop of York. This is confirmed, if not based upon, a letter addressed to both of them by Bishop Wright of Bristol, asking for a clarification of certain Instructions.[116] Yet Laud's involvement in the formulation of the Instructions was one thing. His involvement in the formulation of the Considerations, a document which formed their basis, was another. At his trial, Laud said that Harsnett had played a far more significant role than himself in the stages leading to the appearance of the Instructions.[117] Harsnett had drawn up a document, the 'Considerations for the Better Settling of Church Government' in which he

112 *WWL* v. 307–8.

113 *WWL* v. 307–9; PRO SP 16/205/4; 16/148/41. Charles's personal orders to Field of St David's and Potter of Carlisle turning down their requests to leave their sees reveals how seriously and personally he regarded the instructions: PRO SP 16/159/50; *The Diary of Thomas Crosfield*, ed. F. Boas (1935), 93.

114 PRO SP 16/153/100; LPL MS 943/103; Prynne, *CD* 368; BL Add. MS 29 975/119.

115 PRO SP 16/153/41.

116 HLRO MS Braye 8/52; Prynne, *CD* 368; PRO SP 16/160/68.

117 HLRO MS Braye 8/52; *WWL* iv. 273; Prynne, *CD* 287.

addressed solutions to ecclesiastical problems.[118] The first seven Considerations eventually appeared as the first seven Instructions of 1629. According to Laud, his own involvement at this stage was only to tender the Considerations on Harsnett's behalf to the king. In Laud's trial, Prynne produced a copy of these Considerations, which he had discovered in the archbishop's study and which Laud claimed as his own copy of Harsnett's text.[119] The question to ask therefore is not whether Harsnett formulated the Considerations, but whether he did so with Laud's assistance. Two facts reinforce Laud's claim that he was not their author. In the first place, it became apparent at Laud's trial that he disliked consideration 9, which he termed a 'sour expression'.[120] This had designated Sidney Sussex and Emmanuel Colleges as 'nurseries of puritanism' and had petitioned the king to appoint only 'grave and orthodox' clerics as their heads.[121] In the second place, Laud appears to have tendered his own proposals to the king at the same time as or after he presented Harsnett's Considerations. Of the ten Instructions which appeared in December 1629, instructions 8 and 9 were not included among Harsnett's proposals. On one of the final drafts for the Instructions, a proposal was inserted which eventually appeared as instruction 9: that leases for lives be turned into leases for years.[122] Dr Heal has shown Laud's singular attachment to this initiative during the 1630s and it seems reasonable to suggest that Laud petitioned for its acceptance in December 1629.[123] There is also the possibility that he was behind the inclusion of instruction 8, which asked that the liturgy and catechizing were as well attended as sermons. While dean of the Chapel, in November 1626, he had relayed these concerns to the king and had asked him personally to set the example of attending public prayers as well as the sermon.[124] As neither instructions 8 or 9 were included with the Considerations and as both have some association with Laud, it seems unlikely that he formulated the Considerations with Harsnett, but rather tendered his own proposals to the king while Charles was drafting the Instructions from the Considerations in December 1629.

118 Prynne, *CD* 287; *WWL* iv. 273–4.
119 *WWL* iv. 274; HLRO MS Braye 8/52; Bodl. MS B8/52.
120 *WWL* iv. 273.
121 Prynne, *CD* 287.
122 PRO SP 16/153/41.
123 F. M. Heal, 'Archbishop Laud Revisited', in F. M. Heal and R. O'Day (eds.), *Princes and Paupers in the English Church* (Leicester, 1981), 129–42.
124 *WWL* iii. 197; PRO SP 16/153/41.

Charles converted Harsnett's first seven proposals into the first seven Instructions, but dropped considerations 8–11, probably because they were more in the nature of advice and less easily translated into specific orders. However there was a further reason why he left out consideration 9, which asked for the internal overhaul of the two Cambridge colleges. According to Laud the king 'thought fit to leave [it] out'.[125] The inclusion of an Instruction which would cast aspersions upon Calvinist divines in high places might have wrecked the royal plans for the 'peace of the Church' and for the cessation of the predestinarian controversy.[126] That Laud as well as Charles should have found this Consideration distasteful suggests that Harsnett was far more anti-Calvinist than either of them. It was Harsnett after all who led the prosecution against Davenant at court in 1630; 'Laud walking by, all the while in silence, spoke not one word.'[127] Harsnett's last consideration (12) became the last instruction (10) and as such formed the basis of the Accounts of the Provinces, the annual accounts tendered to the king by the two archbishops, informing him of the promotion of the Instructions throughout the 1630s. Harsnett had suggested that the Accounts be returned twice a year, but Charles thought best to receive only one, each January.[128] During his trial, Laud denied responsibility for the idea of the Accounts, while praising their intent to prevent the king from falling out of touch with ecclesiastical affairs.[129]

'To be a great stranger to all church proceedings' was clearly not Charles I's desire in the last days of 1629, when the advent of a new decade and the dissolution of a Parliament which appeared bent on his humiliation jolted the king into a fresh assertion of his Supremacy over the Church. On 8 December he discussed ecclesiastical issues with Laud; perhaps the date when he drafted the final version of the Instructions.[130] Harsnett's Considerations were by this time within the king's hands, as they must have been presented sometime between May 1629 (the publication date of the letters reissued as instructions 1 and 2) and 9 December, the first date for which there is conclusive evidence of the existence of the Instructions.[131] Once the king had approved the final draft, copies were dispatched to

[125] Prynne, *CD* 287; *WWL* iv. 274. [126] See Ch. 3 section iii.
[127] Bodl. Tanner MS 290/86; Fuller, *CH* 410.
[128] PRO SP 16/153/41; LPL MS 943/247–291; *WWL* iv. 66.
[129] *WWL* iv. 274. [130] PRO SP 16/153/44; *WWL* iv. 274.
[131] PRO SP 16/153/44, 40, SP/16/142/75.

Archbishops Abbot and Harsnett for their final approval. Abbot returned his on the 9th and suggested a slight alteration (in instruction 9 dealing with estate management) which was included. Harsnett returned his copy three days later and urged the king to pass them 'in due and speedy operation'.[132] Thus the Instructions were born, and copies, written by Baker, Abbot's secretary, and signed by Charles I and Dorchester, Secretary of State, were sent to the archbishops for distribution throughout their respective provinces.[133] Not until January 1634 was any alteration made to the Instructions, when as a result of Laud's accession to Canterbury, a new edition was issued with four additional items all concerning economic matters.[134]

The king's marginalia to the Accounts suggest that he visualized these annual reports not as general surveys of ecclesiastical problems but as updates on the progress of the enforcement of the Instructions in the dioceses.[135] However as they constituted one of the direct channels of communication between centre and locality, the archbishops could use them to alert the king to certain problems. As Laud and Neile edited the episcopal reports in their hands, the Accounts reveal something about their own perceptions as well as those of their episcopal colleagues. For his own part Laud took the opportunity to convey to the king his own unease at the practice of receiving at the rail, the spread of popery, and the lay stranglehold over the Church, issues outside the immediate perimeter of the Instructions.[136] Laud also used the Accounts to convey to Charles the impression that there existed very little nonconformity across the country. Alternatively, we have exaggerated the degree of opposition to the Canons and the extent of nonconformity during the 1630s, which seems unlikely. In the account for 1634 Laud informed the king that there had been 'a great clearing' of nonconformists within the diocese of Gloucester, 'of late . . . so much suspected'.[137] During the following year he told him that there was only *one* nonconformist cleric within the entire diocese of Lincoln and that he was now in the hands of the High Commission.[138] He reassured Charles that no one

[132] PRO SP 16/153/40, 42, 50.
[133] *WWL* v. 309; iv. 274. [134] *WWL* v. 311–4.
[135] *WWL* v. 317–70. Over-concentration on Laud has obscured the fact that Charles I took as much interest in Neile's accounts from the Northern Province as in Laud's from the Southern Province. PRO SP 16/312/84, SP/16/259/78.
[136] *WWL* v. 317–70. [137] *WWL* v. 330. [138] *WWL* v. 334.

had been presented to Piers during 1635 for breaking the canons or the Instructions of 1629, which, given the bishop's rigorous detection of nonconformity in Bath and Wells, was wishful thinking.[139] Again, in the account of 1638 he noted that only one 'refractory person... stands out' in London diocese, and he was 'now under suspension'.[140] In these accounts Laud was conveying to the king reports which had been forwarded by individual bishops, who themselves may have wished to reassure Charles that everything was under control and that little nonconformity existed. Laud's assumption that the king would accept the picture that he was conveying was clearly not as naïve as Charles's belief that it gave a true impression of the extent of nonconformity, and of episcopal success in containing it. Only a king severely isolated from the state of the country could write in the margin of the last account, in 1640, 'I hope it is to be understood, that which is not certified here to be amiss, is right touching the observation of my instructions, which granted this is no ill certificate.'[141] In lulling the king into a false sense of security to allay his paranoia about nonconformity, Laud was guilty of misleading him. Yet it was not only the king's security that he guaranteed in so doing but his own as well. Laud was morbidly conscious of his own standing in the king's eyes and consistently exercised the greatest discretion and circumspection. But it was true to his character that just as he did not wish Charles to think that he was lax, at the same time he did not wish to appear 'ruthless' in the eyes of nonconformists. He informed Quartermayne in 1640 not 'to represent that we are cruel, merciless, oppressors of men's conscience. You have found no hard measure at our hands, we have not dealt unkindly with you.' However, as he had recently accused Quartermayne of sheltering seditious conventicles when he had only held religious meetings with his

139 Ibid.

140 *WWL* v. 356. Contrary to what may be thought, Laud was very protective towards his fellow bishops when discussing their activities with the king. He certainly did not use the accounts to blacken the reputation of those with whom he may have differed over doctrine or discipline; take for example his recounting of the troubles at Hereford in 1638 to the king (*WWL* v. 357) and his previous forthright confrontation with Coke over these very issues (*HMC Cowper ii*, 199–200, 208). For the king's prosecution of Bridgeman see B. W. Quintrell, 'Lancashire Ills, the King's Will and the Troubling of Bishop Bridgeman', in J. I. Kermode and C. B. Phillips (eds.), *Seventeenth Century Lancashire* (Liverpool, 1983), 95, 67–95; see also Ch. 6 nn. 142, 165–66, 220, 223.

141 *WWL* v. 370.

neighbours, Laud's perception of nonconformity, if not as distorted as the king's, was certainly more pliable.[142]

That Charles I could not face the true extent of nonconformity might suggest that his interest in ecclesiastical affairs was at best superficial. Yet the king's participation in the formulation of policy was in contrast to his relative isolation and disengagement from direct involvement in the localities. This emanates from the crucial role he played in the genesis and formulation of those policies, which are considered in the remaining chapters of this work, and his very personal influence in four further areas: the publication of controversial books; the suspension of his two main clerical opponents, Abbot and Williams; the bringing of Scotland and Ireland into conformity with the English Church; and the issue of preferment.

As bishops of London, Laud and then Juxon (and their chaplains, or Archbishop Abbot when he was amenable) controlled the licensing of books throughout the 1630s.[143] During his trial Laud admitted that he had altered some works on his own initiative or on that of other bishops, although not without first consulting the king. But he confessed also that certain works were passed to him with alterations already annotated by the king for the press.[144] Charles I personally expunged out of the collect for the royal family the words 'father of thine elect and of their seed', while in October 1633 he further altered it by dropping all references to Elizabeth of Bohemia and her family, and then told a disillusioned Juxon to inform the archbishop of what he had done.[145] The republication of the book of sports was largely the decision of the king, as was the commissioning of its theological and historical apologies from Heylyn and White.[146] According to his biographer, Heylyn became something of a royal press secretary on a whole variety of issues. It was the king not Laud who asked him to write the *History of St George*, in vindication of the Garter and as a reply to Hakewill's work; the official replies to Prynne's *Histriomastix* and Williams's *Holy Table, Name and Thing*;

142 R. Quartermayne, *Quartermayne's Conquest over Canterburies Court* (1642), 20.

143 For aspects of censorship see F. B. Williams, 'The Laudian Imprimatur', *Library*, 29 (5th ser., 1966), 96–104; S. Lambert, 'Richard Montagu, Arminianism and Censorship', *Past and Present*, 124 (Aug. 1989); P. M. Olander, 'Censorship of the Press during the Personal Rule of Charles I' (Oxford B.Litt. thesis, 1976).

144 HLRO MS Braye 8/53; *WWL* vi. 49–50.

145 LPL MS 943/229, 231; *WWL* vi. 49–50.

146 See Ch. 5 section i.

and the articles against Williams.[147] Again Charles appears as personally responsible for the publication of what were arguably the two most controversial works to appear during the reign: Mainwaring's *Religion and Allegiance* and Sibthorpe's *Apostolike Obedience*, both of which justified the king's arbitrary financial expedients on near absolutist grounds.[148]

In 1628 Williams investigated claims, aired in the Lords, that Laud had licensed some objectionable works, including Mainwaring's sermon.[149] Laud admitted that he had conveyed the royal command to Montaigne of London for publication, but declared that he personally thought the book should not have been published. In the Lords, the earl of Montgomery, a man in no way sympathetic to Laud, corroborated his testimony by revealing that he had been present at Woodstock when Charles ordered the publication and that Laud advised the king against it on the grounds that 'there were many things therein which (would) be very distasteful to the people'.[150] After Buckingham and other lords, who had also been present at the same meeting, supported Montgomery's testimony, Williams dropped the accusation. Not until the Long Parliament was the archbishop questioned again about this particular issue.[151] Charles's very personal support for Mainwaring surfaced in July 1628 when he sent an order 'three times in one day' (the last at twelve o'clock at night) to Montaigne in the Lords commanding the bishop to restore to Mainwaring his full preaching licence.[152] Although Montaigne finally gave in to this blatant pressure, his prolonged resistance must bring into question Abbot's characterization of him as a rubber stamp for anything that came from Whitehall for his imprimatur.[153]

In 1627 Abbot himself refused to license Sibthorpe's controversial

[147] Barnard, *TH* 124, 141–2, 156, 158, 165, 169, 198; Heylyn, *CA* 332. Charles I also ordered the publication of Laud's speech at the censure of Prynne, Bastwick, and Burton: 'I had no purpose to come in print, but your Majesty commands it, and I obey,' *WWL* vi. 37.

[148] R. Mainwaring, *Religion and Allegiance* (1627); R. Sibthorpe, *Apostolike Obedience* (1627). See also Cust, *Forced Loan*; Sommerville, *Politics and Ideology*; *WWL* iii. 207.

[149] *LJ* iii. 856; *WWL* iv. 83–4.

[150] *LJ* iii. 856.

[151] Ibid.; *WWL* vii. 14; iii. 207.

[152] Birch, i. 371–2. The king elevated Mainwaring to St David's in 1636. His consecration was the only one attended by members of the royal family during the reign: (28 Feb. 1636) LPL Reg. Laud i/12–73^{v}, ii/25–102.

[153] Rushworth, i. 444; Birch, i. 291.

sermon, which, like Mainwaring's, had attempted to justify arbitrary taxation.[154] Charles probably guessed that Abbot would object to it and that he should have sought his imprimatur rather than Montaigne's suggests that he was looking for an opportunity to test his archbishop's obedience. Abbot sent a list of principled objections against its publication and asked that he might discuss further reservations with Laud.[155] Charles refused this request and so ignored Abbot's objections that the archbishop was convinced that the king had resolved that the book should 'go forth to his good or harm'.[156] When Abbot subsequently lodged a further set of objections, the king asked Neile and Laud to reply, but at the same time, to spite Abbot, elevated them to the Privy Council.[157] Finally in July 1627, at the request of Buckingham, Charles ordered Abbot into confinement in Kent and henceforth to desist from meddling any further in the High Commission. Before the duke left for France, he informed Charles that it would not be safe for him to leave the country if Abbot were still at Whitehall, who would 'there ... cross all things that I intend'.[158]

Charles I's role in the confinement of Abbot is better known than his involvement in the prosecution of that other noted episcopal opponent, Williams. The bishop of Lincoln's favour with Buckingham declined in proportion to Laud's rise. The countess of Buckingham assured Williams that Laud had undermined him in her son's eyes and that he had such an aspiring nature 'that he will undercut any man in the world, so that he may gain by it'.[159] Laud appears to have distanced himself from Williams, one of his original patrons, once it became clear that the Lord Keeper had lost the duke's confidence

154 Rushworth, i. 436–40, 445–6, 456. Selden informed Abbot's chaplain, Worrall, that if the book appeared it would abolish all notion of '*meum et tuum* and leave no man in England possessed of property': Rushworth, i. 439; Heylyn, *CA* 108; Cust, *Forced Loan, passim*.

155 Rushworth, i. 437; *WWL* vii. 7. Abbot disliked Sibthorpe's support for the poll-tax, and warned that 'although it was by a law, [it] produced a terrible effect in King Richard the Second's time ... [and that] it was a marvellous fault, the blame was not laid upon the rebels of that age': Rushworth, i. 442, 437 ff.

156 Rushworth, i. 438. For some of the king's personal objections see Bodl. MS Sancroft 18/21–22.

157 Rushworth, i. 437–8, 440; HLRO MS Braye 8/53.

158 Rushworth, i. 445. Charles also published Dean Bargrave's sermon which 'imputed rebellion to those who refuse the loan and much urged obedience' (Birch, i. 214). For the novelty of its argument see Smuts, *Court Culture*, 235, 238.

159 Rushworth, i. 440. For Buckingham, see R. Lockyer, *Buckingham: The Life and Political Career of George Villiers, First Duke of Buckingham 1592–1628* (1981).

after Williams's opposition in 1624. The rift between Laud and Williams was acute. According to Hacket, Laud's dissociation from his former patron, and his subsequent participation in Williams's humiliation, was the archbishop's 'great fault'.[160] Yet deep as was the rift between the two bishops, it went deeper between Williams and the king. In 1634 Williams used Laud as a go-between in an attempt to restore his favour with the king, which only exasperated Charles further. He told Laud that he had 'forewarned him enough of this error' and that he could not distinguish sufficiently between 'a churchman and a churchcause'.[161] Charles maintained that Williams's offences in 1634 were temporal and therefore could be tried in the lay courts. Subsequently Williams stayed in Star Chamber since Charles refused to release him because he had published objections to the metropolitical order.[162] According to Barnard, no sooner had Charles heard of Williams's book than he ordered Heylyn to reply to it. On 30 July 1637 Charles, in his own hand, sent five propositions to Laud to tender to Williams as the condition for his release. These included relinquishing all his commendams, exchanging Lincoln for an Irish or Welsh see, and acknowledging his offence in writing the book.[163] By 9 June 1638 Williams had craved the king's pardon 'having justly procured your Majesty's displeasure'.[164] However this recantation remained unpublished and Williams remained in confinement for failing to clear himself on the other grounds. In March 1640, at the request of Henrietta Maria, Charles sent Laud further propositions to tender to Williams for subscription.[165] According to Charles, only the mediation of the queen could induce him to this act of clemency 'none else having power to move his Majesty . . . to free him from suits now depending in the Star Chamber and the High Commission'.[166]

Given the king's religious preconceptions, not the least of his problems stemmed from the fact that in his three kingdoms there

[160] Hacket, *SR* ii. 65, 63.

[161] LPL MS 1030/83.

[162] Bodl. MS Carte 103/71; *WWL* vii. 337.

[163] Barnard, *TH* 169–70; G. Vernon, *The Life of Heylyn* (1682), 90; LPL MS 1030/68(b); Bodl. MS Cherry 2/143–144ᵛ.

[164] LPL MS 1030/91, 110. There appears to have been a measured recantation sometime before, Bodl. MS Cherry 2/169–173.

[165] LPL MS 1030/97, 91; Bodl. MS Cherry 2/169–207. Bodl. MS Cherry 2 contains some very interesting and little-known information about Williams.

[166] LPL MS 1030/97.

existed three different Churches, each with their different theories of authority. In the process of bringing Scotland and Ireland into greater ecclesiastical conformity with England, the significance of Laud and Wentworth was considerable.[167] As early as the 1610s, when James I wished to streamline the Scottish Church along English lines, Laud had suggested proposals for its realization. These James had rejected, on the grounds that his own more moderate scheme of conformity would win greater acceptance.[168] In 1629, however, some Scottish bishops revived the idea of bringing Scotland into a greater conformity by asking Charles I to sponsor a new Scottish Prayer Book.[169] While encouraging greater conformity, Laud opposed the idea for an alternative Prayer Book. He told Charles I that he was 'clear of opinion that if his Majesty would have a liturgy fitted there different from what they had already, it were better to take the English liturgy without any alteration' so that 'the same ... book might be established in all his Majesty's dominions'.[170] Charles, after initially agreeing with this suggestion, eventually decided to back the bishops' request, a mistake, as it turned out retrospectively, since it led to the formulation of a liturgy far nearer to 1549 than 1552.[171] The ill-fated book was drawn up by the Scottish bishops with the assistance of Wren, Laud, and Juxon, whom Charles delegated to co-operate. All the major alterations in the book passed with the royal consent: 'whenever I had any doubt,' Laud wrote, 'I did not only aquaint his Majesty with it, but writ down most of the amendments or alterations in his Majesty's presence.'[172] Some of the earlier drafts contain Charles's personal alterations, which, according to Professor Donaldson, 'reflect the views of a somewhat small-minded sacerdotally-inclined layman, rather than a churchman interested in doctrine and other larger issues'.[173] When the book was finally introduced, Laud was held responsible for it. In fact there were so many

[167] G. Donaldson, *The Making of the Scottish Prayer Book of 1637* (Edinburgh, 1954); F. R. Bolton, *The Caroline Tradition of the Church of Ireland* (1958); H. F. Kearney, *Strafford in Ireland 1633–41* (Manchester, 1959); C. V. Wedgwood, *Strafford 1593–1641* (1935); T. Ranger, 'Strafford in Ireland: A Revaluation', *Crisis in Europe 1560–1660*, ed. T. Aston (1975); C. S. R. Russell, 'The British Problem and the English Civil War', *History*, 72/236 (Oct. 1987), 395–415.

[168] Hacket, *SR* i. 64; Fuller, *CH* 444.

[169] *WWL* iii. 278–9, 335–47, 336, 350–61, 427–32; vi. 456.

[170] *WWL* iii. 427, 342–3.

[171] *WWL* iii. 428, 342–3; Fuller, *CH* 444.

[172] *WWL* iii. 428; vi. 456.

[173] Donaldson, *Making of the Scottish Prayer Book*, 39.

accusations against him that in 1637 the king felt obliged to announce in the Privy Council that the 'archbishop of Canterbury was scandalously and without reason blamed as the man who upholds him in this resolution in these affairs' (of Scotland) and 'that he (the king) had never taken the advice of anyone soever but everything happened from his motion alone, and those who thought differently deceived themselves'.[174] The method of introducing the book advocated by Laud was not followed and when the book was finally condemned he prided himself on having predicted all the troubles that had come to pass. In fact Laud had made it clear to the king that he wanted nothing to do with the introduction of the book, because he was ignorant of Scottish law and custom.[175] Clearly he had learned the lesson of his earlier intervention in Scottish affairs under James I.

Charles I was as deeply concerned to bring the Irish Church into similar conformity with the English Church. 'It is certainly deeply seated in his Majesty's thoughts,' Laud informed Wentworth in 1635.[176] But the archbishop believed that the royal intentions would come to nothing unless the economic base of the Church was first restored: 'the material Church must be built and an abler clergy in some measure provided or else it will be vain to attempt it.'[177] In fact it was Charles I rather than Laud or Wentworth who advocated an intransigent, impulsive policy of British conformity. 'It will be ever forforth of my heart to conceive that a Conformity in Religion is not above all other things principally to be intended,' Wentworth informed the Secretary of State, Coke, in November 1636, 'but yet the time and circumstances may very well be discussed and I do not hold this a fit season to disquiet or sting them in this kind, and my reasons are divers.'[178] Subsequently, in April 1637, Wentworth

[174] *CSPV 1636–9*, 394. Laud asked Heylyn to write an apology exonerating him from formulating the Scottish Prayer Book: Barnard, *TH* 177.

[175] *WWL* vii. 461: concerning these issues, Laud informed Wentworth that 'the king is more willing not to hear than to hear'; *WWL* iii. 278–9, 336. During his confinement in 1647 Charles promised to reintroduce episcopacy in Scotland 'when all was quiet': Bodl. MS Sancroft 78/23.

[176] *WWL* vi. 354; Knowler, i. 187; Fuller, *CH* 426; Bolton, *The Caroline Tradition of the Church of Ireland.*

[177] *WWL* vi. 354; not dissimilar to Laud's comments (*WWL* vii. 78): 'I am heartedily set for uniform Church service . . . if God's service stay a little for the king's that the king may be better able to set forward and to maintain God's'; see also Knowler, i. 187.

[178] Knowler, ii. 39. Professor Russell has also noted Laud and Wentworth's reservations about Charles I's methods of achieving conformity: 'The British Problem

advised the king (without effect) to defer the task of bringing Ireland into greater conformity with England, an initiative which paralleled Laud's attempts to cushion the impact of the implementation of extra-canonical Caroline conformity within the Church of England.[179] If 'thorough' had any application in ecclesiastical affairs for Laud and Wentworth then its usage was clearly conditioned by their practical appreciation of what was equitable and pragmatic.

The issue of preferment provides further evidence that Laud's influence has been exaggerated and that of the king underestimated. For nomination to bishoprics and deaneries, the archbishop could certainly submit several names to the king from among current holders or from among chaplains in ordinary, although other interested parties might attempt to attract the royal attention through key figures (such as one of the Secretaries of State, the Lord Chamberlain, or the queen of Bohemia) in favour of another chaplain in ordinary, one of the chaplains in extraordinary, or a total outsider, these last two options invariably failing.[180] The fundamental reason for this was that Charles chose to prefer none but his chaplains in ordinary to higher ecclesiastical preferment. In January 1635 Laud informed Wentworth that it was impossible for him to help any man 'forward in the Church, unless he can ... come into the court service and be the king's (chaplain) in ordinary. For that rule the king hath set ... himself.'[181] In January 1636 he further expressed doubts about his ability to procure a placement because the 'king will be for his chaplains'.[182] The reason why Bramhall, alone of Wentworth's chaplains, received royal preferment, was that he had temporarily served the king as chaplain before going to Ireland.[183] All those nominated to bishoprics during the reign had at one time or other been chaplains in ordinary to Charles as king, or as prince of Wales. In 1637 he gave the bishopric of Limerick to George Webb, who had

and the English Civil War', 400. His analysis of the British context of the collapse of Charles's regime has superseded all others; *The Fall of the British Monarchies 1637–1642* (Oxford, 1991).

179 Knowler, ii. 63.

180 *WWL* vii. 79, 102, 167–8, 238, 431, 440; PRO SP 16/88/18, SP 16/49/40, SP/16/65/78, SP/16/107/31, SP/16/183/42; PRO LC5/134/5 gives a list of all chaplains in ordinary for 1635–7 and LC3/1/4 for 1641.

181 *WWL* vii. 102: and reiterated to Elizabeth of Bohemia (11 Sept. 1635), 'the king will make none bishops but such as he hath some knowledge of himself, as having been his own chaplains in ordinary or otherwise' (*WWL* vii. 167).

182 *WWL* v. 238.

183 *WWL* vii. 79; Barnard, *TH* 121.

served him in this capacity before his accession. Very shortly afterwards, Laud received a letter from the dean of Limerick asking him to support his candidature. Yet Laud believed that even if the letter had arrived earlier 'it would not have varied his Majesty's resolution for Dr Webb'.[184] Charles I kept a tighter control over episcopal and decanal appointments than James I, who, according to Laud, had been more easily swayed by noble representation. Even as prince of Wales, Charles had asserted the right to nominate to all major ecclesiastical posts within the Principality, which possibly helps to explain why Laud received St David's in 1621.[185] Certainly the candidates of 1640–2 for the vacant bishoprics and deaneries were personally chosen by the king, after some consultation with Juxon. In September 1641 when the Secretary of State, Nicholas, suggested that Charles might fill the vacancies in order to reinforce the royal cause in the Lords, the king informed him that he and Juxon had already drawn up a provisional list of candidates. However, with the widening parliamentary division over religion between moderates and radicals in 1641, he later decided to make some alterations to this former selection in order to win over more moderate Anglicans to his cause.[186]

The chaplains in ordinary, and to a lesser extent the chaplains in extraordinary, received not only the larger but the smaller livings in the royal gift. In 1638 Laud again failed to prevail with the king for one of Wentworth's candidates because of 'the suits of his own chaplains in ordinary coming so thick upon him for all those few preferments which are now left in the crown'.[187] Of course, from Laud's point of view, the king's election and preferment of his own chaplains was not necessarily a bad thing. Yet on occasions, it meant that his influence was so circumscribed that his own candidates suffered the same fate as those of Wentworth. In September 1630 Laud attempted to secure the wardenship of Winchester for his

[184] *WWL* vi. 400–1. The king also refused to elevate to bishoprics those under forty years, *WWL* vii. 102. He preferred those who received his clerical patronage to be unmarried: Bodl. MS Jones 17/304.

[185] *WWL* vii. 102; Hacket, *SR* i. 207; PRO C115 M 24/7770; *The Memoirs of John Evelyn*, ed. W. Bray, 2 vols. (1819), ii. 21–2, 28, 31–2, concerning Charles's personal involvement in the election to the vacant bishoprics and deaneries in 1641–2. The king also exerted a tight control over the selection of the Prince's chaplains, *WWL* vii. 123.

[186] *The Memoirs of John Evelyn*, ii. 21–2, 28, 31–2, 46–7, 63; see Ch. 3 nn. 65–70.

[187] *WWL* vi. 557. For lists of chaplains extraordinary in 1641 see PRO LC3/1/36.

chaplain, Stanley, only to find that the king's letters overruled his own, 'and in some ways that I had no great cause to like'.[188] The tight control over the election to the highest echelons meant that the scramble for places occurred lower down the ladder. Here Laud confronted considerable noble competition. In 1638 he obtained Halifax for Marsh, but only just in time, as on the following day the earl of Elgin nominated someone to the king and 'had carried it, if the diligence I used had not prevented it'.[189] But during the same year, he failed to promote another of Wentworth's candidates because of Lennox's favour with Charles. 'At my entreaty be not too sudden,' he informed the Lord Deputy, 'I see plainly the king is made in the business, and out of all doubt he will not like it well if you do not gratify my Lord Duke in this particular.'[190]

In order to become a chaplain in ordinary the first qualification of a minister was to preach before the king and to his liking.[191] Richard Marsh received such preferment only because Charles was so impressed when he heard him preach at Worksop on his progress to Scotland in 1633. In spite of having at various times the backing of both Laud and Williams, the talented Theodore Price failed to achieve a chaplaincy simply because he had never preached before the king. When Laud subsequently supported his candidature for the bishopric of St Asaph (which was contested also by a protégé of the

[188] *WWL* vi. 288. Among Laud's close acquaintances who did not receive high ecclesiastical preferment in his lifetime were Richard Bailey, William Bray, William Chillingworth, William Heywood, Joseph Mede, John Oliver, Christopher Potter, Jeremy Taylor, Thomas Turner, Thomas Weeks.

[189] *WWL* vii. 440. Marsh had been chaplain to Archbishop Matthew of York; see his *Sermon Preached at the consecration of (Richard) Senhouse, Sept. 1624* (1625).

[190] *WWL* vii. 431. Lists in the extant docquet books can be categorized according to the name of those who 'procured' the preferment and the officer who gave the 'order' for it. Between 1627 and 1635 Laud is mentioned as having 'procured' the preferment of at least five bishops: Buckeridge to Ely, Curle to Rochester, Mawe to Bath and Wells (all 1628), Lindsell to Hereford, and Dee to Peterborough (1634). Among those 'procured' by others were Montagu to Chichester (by Porter, 1628), Owen to St Asaph (by Secretary Dorchester, 1629), Corbet to Oxford (by Secretary Conway), Hall to Exeter and Wren to Hereford (by Secretary Coke, 1627 and 1634): PRO SP 38/14, 15. The Secretarial procurement can be taken as evidence of direct royal involvement in the preferment procedure, while Endymion Porter's procurement of Montagu's preferment is conclusive evidence of Buckingham's key role in his elevation. PRO SP 38/14, 182–182^{v} shows that the names of the person who had 'procured' Mainwaring's appointment to Stanford Rivers and that of the person who had given the 'order' for Montagu's elevation to Chichester were later respectively erased, but not vice versa.

[191] *WWL* vii. 79, 102.

earl of Montgomery) Charles bestowed the see on John Owen, one of his former chaplains.[192] In October 1640 Laud wrote to Pembroke, recommending his own chaplain, John Oliver, as chaplain in ordinary, yet only on the criterion that he had 'preached twice to the king with great' approval,[193] a letter incidentally which also casts doubt on the accusation that Laud had usurped the normal process of electing chaplains which traditionally belonged to Pembroke, as Lord Chamberlain.[194] Clearly therefore the most important step was to secure a preaching slot before the king. So valuable were these that some chaplains might voluntarily relinquish one for a friend, as Accepted Frewen did for Henry Hammond.[195] The Lord Chamberlain, the Secretaries, Laud, and others tried to obtain a pulpit for their protégés, or if they supported the candidature of a particular chaplain, tried to influence the compilation of preaching lists for the court calendar. This is graphically illustrated by an event during 1631 when Pembroke altered the list drawn up by the Secretary, Dorchester, for the Lenten preachers. The earl informed him that he had dropped the name of Richard Steward because he had preached so often that he had deprived others such as Hacket and Towers of their preaching slots.[196] Pembroke was taking a bold stand because Steward was not only one of the king's favourite preachers but appears to have been a protégé of both Dorchester and Harsnett.[197] Arising out of comparative obscurity he eventually succeeded Wren in the two offices which gave him the closest accessibility to the king, clerk of the Closet and dean of the Chapel. Apart from his catechetical style of preaching he was known for his exceptionally good looks.[198] Another of Charles's favourite preachers

[192] PRO LC5/134/87; Birch, ii. 21–2; *WWL* vii. 79, 102; Hacket, *SR* i. 207. In May 1634 before the royal progress to the Midlands, Pembroke wrote to Bishops Williams, Dee, and Wright asking them to supply a rota of preachers at places where the king stopped. He suggested also that they might consult with the earls of Rutland and Stamford about suitable candidates: PRO LC5/134/9.

[193] LPL MS 943/603.

[194] *WWL* iv. 87, 294–5; vi. 583; Bodl. MS Rawl. D 353/Jan. 30.

[195] J. Fell, *The Life of Dr Henry Hammond* (1661), 8.

[196] PRO SP 16/183/13; PRO LC5/132/1^{v}–4^{v} for list of Lenten preachers 1627–34. Steward's name appears on all save that for 1631.

[197] PRO SP 16/184/57; R. Steward, *Three Sermons Preached by . . . Dr Richard Stuart to which is added a fourth . . . by Archbishop Harsnett* (1658).

[198] Knowler, i. 524. The king offered him the bishopric of Chichester in 1641 (which he rejected) and then the deanery of Westminster: *Memoirs of John Evelyn*, ii. 31–2.

was Robert Sanderson, who first came to court in November 1631 and whom Laud introduced to the king as someone who could brilliantly resolve scruples of conscience, which appear to have troubled the royal pillow on more than one occasion (the king had one 'great case of conscience' which he informed Laud about but which Laud never committed to paper).[199] Charles frequently attended Sanderson's sermons at court and was heard to say that 'I carry my ears to hear other preachers, but I carry my conscience to hear Mr. Sanderson and to act accordingly.'[200]

With regard to the issue of preferment, as in other areas, Laud only too readily realized that he was the king's man in the first place and that Charles had set limits to his influence. Laud was poised to assume a high position in the Church after 1625 because of his close association with Buckingham and because he was everything which Abbot was not. As early as 1626 Charles had possibly promised Laud the deanery of the Chapel, the clerkship of the Closet, and even the see of Canterbury.[201] The king may even have contemplated moving Abbot from Canterbury in September 1626 and making Laud archbishop instead. Buckingham asked Rives, the king's advocate, to inform him whether the pope had ever possessed the power of removing bishops from one see to another at his own will, and, more importantly, whether such power passed to the king at the Reformation. Not surprisingly, Rives thought that to remove bishops from their sees or clergy from their livings at discretion 'would fill the whole Church with outcries'.[202]

The king permitted Laud to consult him on any ecclesiastical matter but not to meddle in other issues, unless specifically ordered, which may well have restricted Laud's influence at the council board.[203] If the archbishop prosecuted any personal measures, such as restricting the liberties of the Stranger Churches, suppressing the Feoffees for Impropriations, or rebuilding St Paul's, he was careful to present these as the personal objectives of the king, for as Laud informed Wentworth the king loved to appear as the author of policy.[204] If Charles gave his full backing to Laud, as he did in those three cases

199 *WRS* vi. 296; *WWL* iii. 213.

200 Izaak Walton, *The Life of... Sanderson* (1678; 1907 edn.), 445–6.

201 *WWL* iii. 161, 196. Laud was seen as a future bishop of London as early as June 1623: PRO SP 14/137/5.

202 PRO SP 16/306/107.

203 *WWL* vii. 175, 288, 359.

204 *WWL* v. 323–4; Heylyn, *CA* 445.

above, then the alliance of king and archbishop was unshakeable. John Bulteel wrote that no one 'durst . . . oppose the archbishop in that business (of the Stranger Churches) lest they should incur the king's indignation for his sake, who was so potent and gracious with the king'.[205] Yet on occasions Charles gave only lukewarm endorsement to Laud's policies. In one notable area, that of improving the economic state of the clergy (and for Laud the fundamental problem), the archbishop's concerns fell on deaf ears, while the proposals recommended in the Considerations of 1626 came to little.[206] Charles promised to restore impropriations to the Irish Church (which he eventually did) but Laud continually feared that he would go back on his promise. In October 1635 he asked Wentworth to 'settle (them) with all the speed you can, for if they die in your hand, I will never hope to see them live again; nor the Church by them'.[207] Throughout the 1630s Laud continually conveyed to Charles I the need to augment livings and stipends, and in January 1636 reminded Charles that he had 'often told [him] upon [his] own experience [that it was a work] very necessary and fit to be done, and . . . worthy of your Majesty's royal care and consideration'. Yet the archbishop's frustration at the royal inactivity was made evident in the Account for 1638, when he confessed that he had expected 'your Majesty's reign [to] be so blessed as [the clergy] might in time find some relief. But this is quite beyond episcopal power.'[208]

Although courtiers might attempt to unseat the archbishop, his position of trust was never seriously in doubt until the last months of 1640. Laud remained aloof from the court, despising as he did its flattery and corruption. He was, as Clarendon pointed out, 'of too warm blood and too positive a nature towards asserting what he believed truth, to be a good courtier . . . let the case be what it will, he did court persons too little'. After Laud's death, Richard Steward gave a similar testimony, 'that he had but little love in the Court . . . chiefly [because] he there found so little honesty'.[209] In fact Laud

[205] J. B(ulteel), *A Relation of the Troubles of the Three Foreign Churches in Kent* (1645), 134, 139.

[206] LPL MS 943/347. However Laud was posthumously vindicated: on April 1646 Charles I made a vow to return all impropriated property held by the Crown to the Church and to pay rent instead: Bodl. MS Carte 103/396.

[207] *WWL* vii. 175.

[208] *WWL* v. 333–4, 356.

[209] Clarendon, i. 125; *CC* i. 228. Confirmed also by Herbert Croft's view that Laud chose 'not friends to himself but to the Church and Commonwealth, for he considereth not himself as a total, but as a part': Bodl. MS Tanner 102/164.

appears to have feared his unseating less at the hands of courtiers than of clergymen. The reason why he secured the clerkship of the Closet for the unambitious Juxon in 1633 was in order to have someone near to the king whom he might 'trust'.[210] He would remember that Abbot's fall from grace began when he failed to appear at court through increasing ill health. There was never a lack of clergy to advise the king on doctrinal and disciplinary matters.[211] If there was one cleric whom Laud feared might eclipse him in the king's favour, that cleric was probably Matthew Wren. He had been chaplain to Charles in Spain and two years later, in 1626, became dean of Windsor.[212] As the following chapters reveal, while Wren and Laud shared basic assumptions about the Church, their attitudes to the object and mode of enforcing Carolinism were fundamentally different. Such a divergence did not merely reflect the distrust between Wren, the doctrinaire reactionary, and Laud, the conservative legalist; its roots lay in a personality clash which was clearly discernible to, and readily exploited by, their contemporaries. In November 1633 (shortly after Juxon's accession to London, and doubtless partly because of it), Hacket (and Williams?) attempted to 'kindle coals' between the archbishop and Wren.[213] Within the year, the dean had ousted Juxon from the clerkship of the Closet and two years later, in 1636, he succeeded him as dean of the Chapel.[214] Secure as he was, the archbishop could never take the king's confidence for granted. It was a relationship best summed up in Laud's words to Wentworth: 'since you desire not only my counsel but his Majesty's resolution, you shall here have it, as far as he is pleased to give it.'[215]

[210] *WWL* iii. 221.

[211] *WWL* iii. 215–16. According to Crosfield (*Diary*, ed. Boas, 88) the king made Juxon Lord Treasurer in 1636 because he was above corruption and without family.

[212] Bodl. Rawl. MS D. 392/356; (PRO SP 16/117/56 for Wren's early proposals to the king for altering the liturgy at Windsor, Sept. 1628).

[213] *Parentalia*, 45–50. Contrast Clarendon's warm study of Laud (Clarendon, i. 120) with that of Wren whom he dismissed as 'of a severe, sour nature': Clarendon, i. 137. Grimstone described Wren as 'the least of all these birds but one of the most unclean': Bodl. Tanner MS 65/236.

[214] Knowler, i. 524.

[215] *WWL* vi. 354.

2

LAUDIANISM

> I will touch that fault . . . with a gentle hand, because of the good which was in him; because in other things, I believe, for my part, he was better than he was commonly thought; because his death did extinguish a great deal of envy.
>
> (Hacket on Laud, *SR* ii. 65).

I. INFLUENCES AND INFERENCES: PATRISTIC, SCHOLASTIC, AND PROTESTANT

'The archbishop is a stranger to me,' remarked a barrister during Laud's trial in 1644, 'but Mr Prynne's tampering about the witnesses is so palpable and foul that I cannot but pity him and cry shame it.'[1] Prynne's perversion of evidence was manifest in Laud's trial, but it was even more marked in his *Breviate of the Life of Laud* and *Canterburies Doome*, published respectively in 1644 and 1646. The *Breviate* was ostensibly a copy of Laud's diary but proved in fact to be a grossly perverted edition. Laud, in his *History of the Trial*, showed how Prynne had dropped out key passages and materially altered others.[2] But the archbishop was unable to reply to the various misrepresentations made in Prynne's other work, *Canterburies Doome*, an account of the trial and of Laud's policies.[3]

That Prynne's analysis was readily received in the 1640s reveals Laud's widespread unpopularity and the extent to which he had become the scapegoat for the problems of the Personal Rule. But Prynne's account was influential not just because of Laud's unpopularity but because of certain historiographical accidents. In *Cyprianus Anglicus*, his biography of Laud, published posthumously in

[1] *WWL* iv. 51.
[2] *WWL* iii. 111–27, 261–72, 275–462; iv. 1–419; HLRO MS Braye 8; WCO MS Clarke 5/11.
[3] Prynne, *CD*.

1668, Peter Heylyn used Prynne's work extensively as a source, while offering an alternative interpretation. Where Prynne had condemned Laud, Heylyn merely eulogized him.[4] This helps to explain the expression of fundamentally divergent opinions about Laud, based on essentially the same evidence. Towards the end of the seventeenth century Archbishop Sancroft, aware of the serious inaccuracies in Heylyn's account, commissioned Henry Wharton to write a new history of Laud's archiepiscopate, based on manuscript sources.[5] Fuller, another seventeenth-century historian, was also influenced by Prynne, although to a lesser extent than Heylyn, as exemplified in their conflicting interpretations of the 1630s in works such as *The Appeal of Injured Innocence* and *Examen Historicum*.[6]

Later historiography followed similar lines, devolving into either adulation or condemnation. Victorian historiography was heavily biased from entrenched positions of Anglo-Catholicism or English liberalism.[7] Within the liberal tradition, however, there was a breadth of perceptions. Macaulay's 'ridiculous old bigot' needs to qualify Gladstone's characterization of Laud as the most tolerant statesman of the seventeenth century, as well as C. H. Simkinson's panegyric epitaph to the 'reformer par excellence of his own day, the chief advocate of the working classes, the defender of the poor, the leader of the educational movement, an administrator who endeavoured to exterminate the corruptions of the civil service and an ecclesiastic who proposed to widen the boundaries of the English Church'.[8] Only in the work of S. R. Gardiner in the 1880s did there surface a more serious attempt to study Laud with significantly more detachment.[9] Gardiner's work, however, appears to have had considerably less influence on more modern interpretations of the Caroline Church than that of his seventeenth-century predecessors. In fact underlying much current historiography is a notion of Laudianism which is little

[4] Heylyn, *CA* 55–525, where he uses Prynne's 'evidence' more than thirty times. See A. Wood, *Athenae Oxonienses* (1817 edn.), iii. 557, for a low estimation of Heylyn as a historian.

[5] *WWL* iii. 93, 111–27, 251, 259–72. It is apparent that Heylyn did not know Laud very well, as evidenced by the special emphasis which he attached to those rare occasions when they met, Heylyn, *CA* 47–8 and *EH* 260.

[6] H. Wharton, *The History of the Troubles and Trial of William Laud* (1695); Fuller, *CH* iii; Heylyn, *EH*; Fuller, *AII*; *WWL* iii. 113–14.

[7] W. Collins (ed.), *Archbishop Laud Commemoration* (1895), has a good sample of the range; H. R. Trevor-Roper, *Archbishop Laud* (1940), 430–3.

[8] Collins (ed.), *Archbishop Laud Commemoration*, 124, 142, 158.

[9] S. R. Gardiner, *The History of England*, 10 vols. (1884), x. 315–16.

different from that of Prynne's. Revisionist works which attached considerable significance to the phenomenon of Arminianism also belong to this tradition, because Prynne more than anyone else popularized the notion of an Arminian conspiracy.[10]

Since Gardiner's day extensive research has uncovered much of the ecclesiastical history and religious mentality of the early seventeenth century, but large lacunae remain.[11] The only substantial biography of Laud to appear since *Cyprianus Anglicus* was Lord Dacre's *Archbishop Laud*, which was as spirited an attempt to understand its subject as Heylyn's, but not based upon an extensive reading of primary sources.[12] Ironically, the explosion of local studies has not greatly aided our understanding of religious developments in the reign of Charles I, because these studies, for the most part, concern the socio-political scene rather than the ecclesiastical, and more the period after 1640 than before.[13] Moreover in historiography too often a stereotypical notion of Laudianism has been visualized in a particular diocese (especially Norwich) and its marks looked for elsewhere.[14] Laud's role as ordinary within the diocese of Canterbury or as metropolitan within the Southern Province has been largely ignored.

[10] N. R. N. Tyacke, 'Puritanism, Arminianism and Counter-Revolution', in C. S. R. Russell (ed.), *The Origins of the English Civil War* (1973), 119–43; Tyacke, *AC*, *passim*; A. J. Fletcher, *A County Community in Peace and War: Sussex 1600–1660* (1975), 76–94; A. G. R. Smith, *The Emergence of a Nation State* (1984), 287, 284; C. S. R. Russell, *The Crisis of Parliaments* (Oxford, 1971), 216–17; W. Prynne, *Anti-Arminianisme or the Church of England's Old Antithesis to New Arminianisme* (1630). See also Heylyn's dispute with Baxter over these issues in *Certamen Epistolare* (1659) and his *Historia Quinqu-Articularis* (1660).

[11] Two of the more important are: C. Hill, *The Economic Problems of the Church from Archbishop Whitgift to the Long Parliament* (Oxford, 1956); K. V. Thomas, *Religion and the Decline of Magic* (1971). For a selection of relevant works see bibliography; my dissertation, 'The Growth and Implementation of "Laudianism", with special reference to the Southern Province' (Oxford D.Phil. thesis, 1987) investigates one neglected theme.

[12] Trevor-Roper, *Archbishop Laud*, 3rd edn. (1989). Some of its themes are pursued in his more recent, *Catholics, Anglicans and Puritans* (1987), 40–119. For other biographical attempts see C. Carlton, *Archbishop William Laud* (1987); and K. Sharpe, 'Archbishop Laud', *History Today*, 33 (1983), 26–30.

[13] See the bibliography for local studies. The local approach to seventeenth-century history was disabled in the study of ecclesiastical aspects because it focused too much on the county community: diocesan boundaries cut clean across county borders, while ecclesiastical courts provided entirely different systems and agencies of local government from those of shire administration.

[14] W. Lamont correctly gauged the state of affairs: 'when we begin with Archbishop Laud we begin with a type and usually end with nothing except clichés', *Godly Rule: Politics and Religion 1603–1660* (1969), 56.

Invariably, he is depicted as the *dominus factotum*, the moving force behind all the ecclesiastical developments of the reign, which are then given an uneasy coherence under the term 'Laudianism'. Laud's enforcement of these measures is invariably depicted as hurried, oppressive, and implemented under pain of the heaviest court censure, with no condescension to conscience.[15] Within individual historical works, however, there often exist unreconciled interpretations of laudianism, which beg but never receive the requisite explanation. At times Lord Dacre characterized Laud in much the same way as Prynne, but noticed uncomfortably that he could not be duly charged with having enforced innovations during the metropolitical visitation.[16] Dr Seaver thought the Instructions of 1629 were Laud's 'brutal and drastic proposals' for the restraint of lecturers, but failed to explain why he did not rigorously enforce them in London.[17] Both were confronted with the same problem of attempting to accommodate evidence into a conventional picture of Laudianism, with which it sits all too uneasily. Within Laudian studies generally there has always existed a tension between portrayals of a man who was tolerant doctrinally (as exemplified in his friendship with Andrewes, Ussher, Selden, Grotius, Chillingworth, and Hales) and of one who could be so intolerant over matters of secondary importance, rites and discipline.[18] The result of recent 'revisionist' studies of the early seventeenth century has been to widen further the chasm that exists between laudianism as perceived (whether by historians or contemporaries) and laudianism as it existed in the mentality and actions of Laud and his disciples. With the challenge to traditional Whig historiography, Laud, an already maligned figure in seventeenth-century studies, was cast in the role of villain of the piece. It is axiomatic to the revisionist history of the early seventeenth century, from which constitutional conflict has temporarily absconded, that ecclesiastical issues should be the chief catalyst of the British Civil War, and Laud, in the traditions of historiography, its chief incendiary. However, it was not simply the collapse of the Whig interpretation of the early

[15] Although see G. Cragg, *Freedom and Authority* (Philadelphia, 1975), 113: 'Laud wanted to change the pattern, not to punish the individual, and if there were signs of amendment he was prepared to suspend proceedings.'

[16] Trevor-Roper, *Archbishop Laud*, 192–4.

[17] Seaver, *PL* 255.

[18] See *DNB* entries; *WWL* iv. 3; *Briefwisseling van Hugo Grotius*, ed. P. C. Molhuysen and B. L. Meulenbroek (The Hague, 1936), ii. 241. Lord Dacre has emphasized Laud's intellectual latitude in his *Catholics, Anglicans and Puritans*, 41.

seventeenth century which led to the characterization of Laud as the greatest calamity ever visited upon the Church, but a new view of Laudianism itself.[19]

A significant lacuna in past historical works was the absence of any recognition of the role played by doctrinal issues in the formulation of ecclesiastical policy during the reign of Charles I. In recent years 'revisionist' historians, led by Dr Nicholas Tyacke, have stressed the importance of the rise of free-will doctrines over the prevailing predestinarianism of Jacobean England. This thesis depicts Charles I and Laud as Arminians, spearheading an Arminian faction within the Church and outlawing the Calvinism of the majority. This, it is held, effectively brought to an end the Elizabethan and Jacobean 'calvinist consensus' which held together in one Church those of widely divergent ecclesiological opinions. Then, during the 1630s, Laud embarked upon a programme of 'arminianization' in the Church, with Arminian doctrine finding visible expression in the sacramental and ecclesiological changes of the 1630s.[20] Thus for revisionist historiography religion was a factor in the causes of the Civil War, not because of the rise of Puritanism but because of the rise of Arminianism. Laud, always the religious reactionary, was now the religious revolutionary. While Dr Tyacke's work has helped to alter our perspective of early seventeenth-century history, its simple Weberian polarization of grace and predestination hinders rather than aids our understanding of the early seventeenth-century Church.[21] Moreover by equating Laudianism with Arminianism, Laudianism has become identified as a narrow doctrinal influence, imposed from above, devoid of popular support and much historical context. It seems that one doctrinal theme (predestination) has been emphasized out of proportion to a wider doctrinal context and then conflated with ecclesiology. This is not to gainsay that Arminian doctrine existed, that Laud was anti-Calvinist in some respects, or that, to a certain extent, he redefined Puritanism.[22] But we do not need the rise of Arminianism (even if

[19] Russell, *The Crisis of Parliaments*, 216–17; Smith, *The Emergence of a Nation State*, 282, 284; Collinson, *RP* 90. 'If there is one person to whose actions and policies the fall of the Stuart monarchy may be attributed, that person is William Laud': R. Ashton, *The English Civil War: Conservatism and Revolution 1603–1649* (1978), 110.

[20] Tyacke, 'Puritanism, Arminianism and Counter-Revolution', 119–43; Tyacke, *AC*, ch. 8 in particular; Collinson, *RP* 85, 112; 118.

[21] Tyacke *AC* and his, 'Puritanism, Arminianism and Counter-Revolution', 119–43.

[22] See Ch. 3 sections i, iii; Tyacke, *AC* 10, *et passim*.

Arminianism needed to rise) to explain Laudianism (which may be accounted for in other ways) or the Carolinism with which it overlapped and to which it eventually succumbed.

In 1601, when Bishop Young of Rochester ordained Laud as deacon, his ordinand's patristic knowledge so impressed him that he predicted that he would be an instrument of restoring the Church from its narrow reformed basis to the wider catholic sentiments of apostolic times.[23] For the Laudian mind the traditions of the early Church constituted the context in which both the Church and the Bible had origin and meaning. Patristics were the means of discovering these traditions unadulterated by Roman glosses.[24] In 1616 Laud was probably the prime mover in procuring from James I an order encouraging the greater study of the Fathers within the universities. It is difficult to substantiate this conclusively, but during the 1631 visitation of Dunmow, when Thomas Shephard informed him that he studied the Fathers, Laud replied that he 'might thank him for that'.[25] To a considerable extent, Laud's mentor in this patristic renaissance was Lancelot Andrewes, arguably the greatest patristic scholar of the seventeenth century. Throughout his life, Andrewes's singular purpose had been to employ ancient sources in the enrichment of the spiritual and devotional life of the Church. His liturgies, consecration forms, and sermons were imbued with patristic imagery and ideals, which prepared the way for placing the English Prayer Book in a wider liturgical setting, and the Reformation in a richer catholic context than had hitherto been feasible.[26]

However the appeal to the Fathers was not the preserve of the Laudians, it was increasingly the mark of reformed scholarship.[27]

[23] W. Hutton, *St John's College* (1898), 97.

[24] Cragg, *Freedom and Authority*, 126–97; Hacket, *SR* i. 9; *WWL* ii. 361.

[25] Bodl. MS Jones 56/3; LPL MS 595/117; H. Smith, *The Ecclesiastical History of Essex* (n.d., Colchester), 46–7.

[26] *WWL* vi. 342; H. Davies, *Worship and Theology in England*, 5 vols. (Princeton, NJ, 1975), ii. 292–343; G. J. Cuming, 'Eastern Liturgies and Divines', *Studies in Church History*, 13 (1976), 231; F. E. Bright, *Liturgies Eastern and Western* (1986); *The Greek Devotions of Lancelot Andrewes*, ed. P. G. Medd (1892); *WLA*; *CC* i. 74, 92; H. McAdoo, *The Spirit of Anglicanism: A Survey of Anglican Theological Method in the Seventeenth Century* (1965), 331, 24–81; PRO SP 16/168/7; PRO SP 16/1865/108; *WWL* iii. 196.

[27] A. McGrath, 'Reformation to Enlightenment', in P. Avis (ed.), *The Science of Theology* (1986), 137–41; Lake, *AP* 226; W. Perkins, *A Reformed Catholic* (Cambridge, 1598); *LJU* 12, *et passim*; Fuller, *CH* 379; *The Works of... Robert Bolton*, ed. E. Bagshawe (1641), 22.

What distinguished the Laudian from the more overtly reformed appeal was that the Laudian sought in patristics the arbitration of Scripture and tradition, while the reformed sought through them their confirmation. The ultimate distinction between these approaches rested in a different view of Scripture: the reformed notion, on the one hand, of Scripture as self-authenticating and self-interpreting, and the Laudian, on the other, which saw its interpretation as fundamentally subordinate to tradition. The Fathers provided a platform for most interested parties. It was not so much the appeal to the Fathers that was important as the Fathers to whom the appeal was made. Certainly individual authors could be cited against those who claimed an exclusive monopoly of interpreting doctrinal or disciplinary matters. As far as Laud was concerned patristic scholarship had to inform and uphold ecclesiastical sanctions. Thus in 1624 he probably helped to secure the resignation of the cathedral lecturer at Hereford by 'imputation of learned puritanism' in spite of his 'expertise in fathers and councils'.[28] Like Andrewes, Laud did much to popularize the study of the Greek Fathers over the Latin Fathers. In 1631 he established a press in London for the printing of Greek works, and projected another for Oxford, which failed to materialize. Andrewes's popularization of Greek patristics helped to shift attention away from the Latin tradition towards St Basil, St John Chrysostom, and St Gregory Nazianzenus.[29] In its turn, this patristic reorientation might at the same time facilitate and reflect a shift away from works of reformed divinity to those which stressed the importance of the sacramental life and the historical Church. Thus Laud believed that Calvin's *Institutes*, 'may profitably be read . . . as one of the first books for divinity', but if students read it before the Fathers, this would 'hinder them from all grounds of judicious learning [and] too much possess their judgements before they are able to judge'.[30]

During the 1630s conflicts arose less between Calvinists and Arminians than between those who remained staunch disciples of

[28] BL Portland Loan 29/120 (Mar. 1624); *WWL* iii. 155; Cragg, *Freedom and Authority*, 249.

[29] *WWL* iv. 202–3; *WWL* iii. 253 (12); vi. 342–3; McGrath, 'Reformation to Enlightenment', 185–6; Cuming, 'Eastern Liturgies and Divines', 231; N. Lossky, *Lancelot Andrews, the Preacher (1555–1626): The Origins of the Mystical Theology of the Church of England* (Oxford, 1991). For popular recognition of this shift, see R. T., *De Templis: A Treatise of Temples* (1638), 200.

[30] *WWL* v. 117.

reformed literature, and those who saw these works as increasingly threadbare and limited. In 1638 Laud intervened in the affairs of Shrewsbury to support the nomination of Lawson as the curate of St Chad's, instead of Poole, the nominee of the trustees and a cleric of 'the school of Perkins and Dr. Downham'. Poole's Greek had been so deficient that it had prevented him from becoming master of Shrewsbury School. Lawson, on the other hand, was an able scholar, well read 'in the Fathers, schoolmen, councils and history of all sorts (and) a great honourer of Archbishop Laud'.[31] When describing Heylyn's education, his biographer wrote that he did not receive it in 'compendiums and little systems of divinity ... but the main body of Divinity, by studying the Fathers, Councils, ecclesiastical Histories and schoolmen, the way which King James commended to all younger students for confirming them in the doctrine and discipline of the Church of England, that is most agreeable to the doctrine of the Primitive Church'.[32]

With this greater patristic saturation within the universities came a more pronounced emphasis upon the visibility and catholicity of the historical Church, upon the liturgy, and a deeper sacramental theology, all salient features of the Laudian renaissance. For Laud, as for Hooker, the church building was 'the house of prayer ... a court beautified, with the presence of the celestial powers ... here we stand, we pray, we sound forth hymns to God, having his Angels intermixed as our associates'.[33] In that patristics often stressed the inherent holiness of the consecrated place and object, they might run counter to aspects of reformed theology. In 1625 John Prideaux argued against the inherent sanctity of the church building, as churches were 'holy' not in an objective sense but through 'Christ's promises, sacred meetings, united devotion ... [and] participating [in] ... the Word and Sacraments'.[34] For Laud, however, the Church could not have just a subjective, monitory, or didactic purpose. It was '*extra usum*' and 'the greatest residence of God upon earth', which was evident above all in the body and blood of Christ in the eucharist,

[31] PRO SP 16/375/55; Clarendon, i. 123.

[32] Barnard, *TH* 93–4; *Brief Memoirs of Nicholas Ferrar*, ed. T. Macdonough (1837), 170; C. Dow, *Innovations unjustly charged* (1637), 32–4.

[33] H. Davies, *Worship and Theology*, ii. 16; R. Hooker, *Of the Laws of Ecclesiastical Polity: The Fifth Book of Richard Hooker*, ed. R. Bayne (1902), 125. See also W. Hardwick, *Conformity with Piety* (1638), 13.

[34] Davies, *Worship and Theology*, ii. 16.

centred on the table during the communion.[35] Thus the Laudian emphasis on the sacraments and the institutional Church stemmed not from the rise of Arminianism but from the patristic reorientation and historical reinvestment of Anglicanism.

A deeper sacramental awareness carried with it a higher evaluation of the two indelible marks of the visible church, the bishops and those whom they ordained. This helped to reinforce the Anglican assertion of *iure divino* episcopacy (particularly after 1590 when countering Presbyterianism) and served to legitimate the increasing sense of corporate and professional feelings among the ministry.[36] As a result of the increased importance attached to the succession of grace, benediction (the channel through which grace became immanent) attained greater significance through an increased emphasis on a number of related functions: the consecration of the elements,[37] the sign of the cross at baptism,[38] the consecration of church structures and objects,[39] the blessing after marriage[40] and at the end of the service,[41] the confirmation of the young,[42] churching after childbirth, and hearing confession,[43] and of course the ordination of priests and deacons.[44] But along with the increased aura of benediction went its corollary, 'the doome of benediction'—excommunication.[45] To a certain extent Laud regarded excom-

[35] *WWL* vi. 51–7; Knowler, ii. 263. For the particular eucharistic theology of Laud and others see Davies, *Worship and Theology*, ii. 292–342. This shows that Laud's eucharistic beliefs were not Lutheran (contrary to D. Hirst's argument, *Authority and Conflict: England 1603–1658* (1986), 165).

[36] R. O'Day, *The English Clergy: The Emergence and Consolidation of a Profession 1558–1642* (Leicester, 1979).

[37] Davies, *Worship and Theology*, ii. 292–342: Bodl. MS Add. a. 55/27.

[38] Bodl. MS Add. a. 55/29; Thomas Morton, *A Defence of the innocency of the three ceremonies of the Church of England* (1618); *Synodalia*, i. 245–330; P. E. More and F. L. Cross (eds.), *Anglicanism* (1935), 430–8.

[39] J. W. Legg (ed.), *English Orders for Consecrating Churches in the Seventeenth Century* (Henry Bradshaw Soc., 12, 1911); Prynne, *CD* 120–1; HLRO MS Braye 8/38; Bodl. MS Add. a. 85/30; PRO SP 16/204/92; BRO P/Xch/Chw/16/1636; GRO R 14a/32; HFRO AL19/18; LRO DE 1784/17/32^{v}.

[40] Bodl. MS Add. a. 55/29; PRO SP 16/456/44.

[41] PRO SP 16/293/128.

[42] PRO SP 16/201/42, SP 16/456/44—made canonical in 1640 but 'somewhat out of practice of late years'; Collinson, *RP* 52; PRO SP 16/260/90; G. Nuttall, *Richard Baxter* (1965), 11.

[43] ERO D/ACA 51/196; Bodl. Tanner MS 68/210/3; Mr Sp. (Anthony Sparrow) *A Sermon Concerning Confession of Sins and the Power of Absolution* (1637).

[44] *WWL* vi. 327; Bodl. MS Add. a. 55/29, 30; PRO SP 16/108/75.

[45] Bodl. MS Add. a. 55/31.

munication as a greater episcopal power than benediction, as it was on the jurisdiction 'intrinsic and original' in the episcopal act of excommunication rather than on the audience of ecclesiastical cases (which as *iure positivo* marked a difference only by degree) that he rested his fundamental distinction between bishop and priest. Such a distinction could not be defined simply by a superiority and imparity of jurisdiction, since all archpresbyters and archdeacons might claim the same. It had to be defined clearly by a separation of order, for, as he informed Hall, this is how the Fathers had described it, '*ordinatio episcopi*'.[46]

Laud's view of episcopacy was necessarily high, but it could never be for him simply *iure apostolico*; it was of divine right as well. 'Episcopacy is not so to be asserted to apostolical institution, as to bar it from looking higher, and from fetching it materially and originally, in the ground and intention of it, from Christ himself, though perhaps the apostles formalised it.'[47] Ultimately, however, the question was less whether episcopacy was *iure divino* than what kind of divine right. As Laud noted, Theodore Beza believed that episcopacy was of divine right but argued that it was never intended to be universally prescriptive, a recognition which, according to Laud, constituted 'the great rock in the lake of Geneva'.[48] If, as in Geneva, episcopacy had been abolished, this could only be temporarily, otherwise its absence was an abdication of responsibility and it ought to be restored. These high and exclusive views on episcopacy meant that Laud could give only the coolest response to Dury's attempts to create a pan-Protestant union in the 1630s and that he would seek in the first place the friendship of the Danish and Swedish Churches before those of the Swiss and Huguenots.[49]

As Laud believed that the bishops were the essential link with the primitive church, to abolish them would sever the connection with the source of all reliable tradition, and leave the door open to 'parity . . . the mother of confusion'.[50] Laud's strongly held opinions (which few before or after shared) brought him into early conflict in

[46] *WWL* vi. 573–7.
[47] *WWL* vi. 573–4, 577. For the different views of Laud and Williams over divine-right episcopacy see *WWL* iii. 199–200; Hacket played down the difference: *SR* ii. 87.
[48] *WWL* vi. 574.
[49] W. Tighe, 'William Laud and the Reunion of the Churches', *Historical Journal*, 30/3 (1987), 717–27.
[50] *WWL* vi. 173.

Oxford with reformed theology: in 1602 when he asserted that the Church of Rome provided the visibility of the Church of England until the Reformation, and in 1604 for claiming that there could be no true Church without diocesan bishops.[51] Many years later, Archbishop Abbot (who had criticized Laud in Oxford) published what was clearly meant as a reply: *A Treatise of the Perpetual Visibility and Succession of the True Church in all Ages*, which traced the visible Church not through Rome or bishops but through those 'noble worthies of the Christian world' who had found themselves in conflict with Rome. Included among these were Wycliffe, the Albigenses, and the Pauperes of Lyons. While Abbot's opinions would find favour with many nonconformists within the Church, there were probably few if any of his fellow bishops who could subscribe to this almost sectarian notion of visibility. In fact seeing these views as a fundamental threat to the catholicity of the established Church, Laud informed James I about them. Apparently the king was suitably shocked that his archbishop could ever have countenanced such opinions.[52] Although both Laud and Abbot's doctrinal views on this issue of visibility were unrepresentative, the clash was not without its parallels after 1625. For in England the major doctrinal debates were less over predestination than over the external visibility and historicity of the Church. They were not, however, disconnected, for what was really at issue in the Caroline Church was not one but two mutually exclusive doctrines of predestination and visibility: the elect believer against the elect bishop. Conceivably what might have kept them together was an elect king, but this was one role that Charles I did not condescend to play.

Thus, the reign of Charles I witnessed both an increase in episcopal court activity and in the number and quality of censures meted out to offenders, as the concept of divine-right episcopacy in its more aggressive Laudian mould fought its way to recognition. Laud's exalted views on episcopacy explain his attachment to the rights of the ordinary within ecclesiastical jurisdiction, as in the St Gregory's case and in the Canons of 1640.[53] On the other hand such high episcopal views meant also that he did not invest the metropolitical office with as much authority as is sometimes thought. For Laud the difference between archiepiscopal and episcopal authority was not

[51] *WWL* iii. 132–3. [52] *WWL* iii. 145.
[53] See Ch. 6 section i; Ch. 7 section ii; *WWL* vi. 429.

one of order but of degree, as archbishops, unlike bishops, were not consecrated. He did not resurrect any long-dead metropolitical or (as has been asserted) 'pre-Tridentine' powers, nor were his metropolitical articles materially different from those of Abbot in any significant respect.[54] The visitorial powers of the High Commission were invoked to reinforce the proceedings of the metropolitical courts but this was not arbitrary as the practice rested firmly on Elizabethan letters patent.[55] In fact those instances where Laud championed metropolitical authority are less evidence of any desire to establish an overriding authority over the episcopate than of a desire to protect either ecclesiastical privilege, as in the controversy over his right to visit the universities, or his personal interest in the dispute with Williams over the visitation of Lincoln.[56]

In 1626 Laud suggested to Charles I a plan for the dismemberment of Lincoln and other large sees into smaller administrative units, by making all sees in England and Wales coterminous with shire boundaries. Although this would have diminished the prestige of certain bishops, such proposals if put into practice would have vastly increased episcopal authority. In the Lords the clerical vote might have risen to something near to its pre-Reformation levels, while within the shires the episcopal presence would have been enhanced, as each diocesan would reside within the county town and all peculiar jurisdiction would have disappeared.[57] Not surprisingly, given the nature of this remarkable overhaul of diocesan jurisdiction, the plan was shelved, although it may have partially surfaced in the 1630s in Charles I's plans to create a new diocese at Bury St Edmund's, by dividing the see of Norwich along the border of Suffolk and Norfolk.[58] As with other things, the Church of England had to wait until industrialization and the growth of population before anything similar to it was realized.

With respect to other major influences, scholastic ideas were as prominent within Laudianism as within other contemporary systems of divinity, such as seventeenth-century Bezan Calvinism or Orthorox Lutheranism.[59] The problem, however, is less one of ascertaining

[54] A. Wright, *The Counter-Reformation* (1982), 190; *WWL* v. 419–35; vi. 577.

[55] R. G. Usher, *The Rise and Fall of the High Commission* (1910), 241–54; *WWL* iv. 178; PRO SP 16/499/29. From Abbot, not Laud, Hacket traced the sentences of 'great correction or rather destruction', *SR* i. 97.

[56] PRO C115/N4/8610; *WWL* v. 553–82.

[57] LPL MS 943/347. [58] BL MS Harl. 7032/160.

[59] McGrath, 'Reformation to Enlightenment', 154–65; Lake, *AP* 226.

scholastic undercurrents than of isolating particular influences and explaining the uses to which they might be put. With respect to methodology, Laud's *Conference with Fisher the Jesuit* constitutes one of the last great scholastic works of divinity.[60] Laud was certainly more influenced by Thomist Aristotelianism than the Neoplatonic influences which moulded the mind of Thomas Jackson. Whether or not this helped to moderate Laud's antipathy to Calvinism is open to question, although a causal connection has been made between Neoplatonic ideas and Arminianism.[61] In at least four areas, an incipient Aristotelianism underwrote Laudianism.

The reassertion of the Aristotelian connection between nature and grace, and the natural theology which the reformers had discarded served to provide Laud with a particular integrated ethical and social view. It was no coincidence therefore that the Church was accused of meddling too much in political affairs and moral issues. His assertion that it was as important to preach within the council chamber as within the pulpit was also a reflection of this perception and not just a cover for his indifferent sermon oratory.[62] Again a Thomist association of nature and grace meant that Laud could in no way subscribe to the identification of the spiritual with the non-material, the material dimension of the Church being no less important than its spiritual: 'For my part I take myself bound to worship with body as ... in soul.'[63] Although he recognized that reverence was essentially an expression of the inward heart, he believed that this had to be externally manifested in worship. Thus he aimed to inculcate reverence within the service through ceremonies and gestures, for 'it is superstition nowadays for any man to come with more reverence into a church than a tinker and his bitch come into an alehouse'.[64] His integrated view of Church and Commonwealth doubtless stemmed from the same philosophy ('(Jerusalem) stands not ... for the City and ... State only ... nor for the Temple and Church

[60] Cragg, *Freedom and Authority*, 112; *WWL* ii for the *Conference*. Hacket, *SR* i. 172 called it a 'masterpiece of divinity'.

[61] McAdoo, *Spirit of Anglicanism*, 338; S. Hutton, 'Thomas Jackson, Oxford Platonist and William Twiss, Aristotelian', *Journal of the History of Ideas*, 39 (1978). For Hooker's Aristotelianism: Gunner Hillerdal, *Reason and Revelation in Richard Hooker* (Lund, 1962), 63; R. K. Faulker, *Richard Hooker and the Politics of a Christian England* (1981), 7–9.

[62] *WWL* vi. 150–8, 187, 191, 199, 213–14.

[63] *WWL* vi. 56–7; *WWL* vi. 143; i. 5–6, 64.

[64] *WWL* vi. 57.

only . . . (for) both are but one Jerusalem'), although here he was possibly more directly influenced by Hooker.[65] Thus, at least in theory, Laudianism dissociated itself from the Erastianism or theocraticism which marked contemporary reformed disciplines and which were soon to assert themselves in the various ecclesiastical settlements introduced in England.[66]

In the emphasis which Laud attached to communication and association may rest a second Aristotelian influence: 'In all ages of the Church the touchstone of religion was not to hear the Word preached but to communicate.'[67] Within the Church, its members were not just communicative with each other but with the priest as well. As one minister said in 1631, 'there can be no expectation of a communion of saints *in spiritualibus*, unless the laity doth communicate to the clergy *in temporalibus*.'[68] At the heart of this vision was communion, which made the association more than the sum of its parts and, most importantly, communicative with God. A third Aristotelian influence can be found within the emphasis which Laud placed upon habituation. He envisaged both Church and Commonwealth as inculcating certain habits that would lead to an ultimate realization of essential objectives. Policy was not an end in itself but a means to an end and, in Laud's eyes, primarily educative. Contrary to what Trevor-Roper has written, Laudian policy marked less of a preference for repression over education than a preference for education over revelation. Thus Laud placed greater emphasis on codes of conduct and ethical enlightenment than on spiritual nourishment.[69]

A fourth Aristotelian influence existed in Laud's understanding of the mean—his vision of the Anglican Church as a *via media* between Rome and Puritanism, and beyond the constraints of canonical law, a persuasive policy of implementing change—'*moderata semper suasi*' as he informed Vossius.[70] Fatally, it found expression also in an attempt

[65] *WWL* i. 5–6.
[66] C. Cross, 'The Church in England 1646–1660', in G. E. Aylmer (ed.), *The Interregnum: The Quest for a Settlement* (1972) 99–120.
[67] *WWL* iv. 284.
[68] Bodl. MS Add. a. 55/6–7. For Laud's eucharistic views see Davies, *Worship and Theology*, ii. 292–342.
[69] E. Baker, *Plato and Aristotle* (1906) 247; Trevor-Roper, *Archbishop Laud*. For Laud and the University of Oxford see K. Sharpe, 'Archbishop Laud and the University of Oxford', *History and Imagination: Essays presented to Lord Dacre*, ed. H. Lloyd-Jones, V. Pearl, and B. Worden (1981), 1.
[70] *WWL* vi. 265; iii. 412.

to establish the mean in evangelical matters, a novel departure, for in the English Protestant tradition it has no parallel outside Hooker.[71] Parker might talk of a golden mediocrity but what balance existed when Whitgift located a mean between the poles of popery and Anabaptism, Bancroft, one between popery and Presbyterianism and Laud, another, between popery and Puritanism?[72] As Professor O'Donovan has written, there was nothing particularly middle about most of English Protestantism.[73] With respect to the role of reason, this was far more circumscribed for Laud than commentaries on Anglicanism allow, as he believed that 'reason by her light can discover how firmly the principles of religion are true; but all the light she hath will never be able to find them false.'[74] In spite of his patronage of the likes of Hales, Mede, and Chillingworth, his contribution to the ideas of the Cambridge Platonists and the Latitudinarians was minimal. Moreover even if laudianism had assigned a special role to reason this would not have been particularly distinctive within Protestant thought, as all contemporary Protestant systems stressed the interrelationship of reason with Scripture and tradition.[75]

Of the native influences within Laudianism, apart from Carolinism, that of Andrewes was undoubtedly the greatest. For Laud he was none other than 'the greatest light of the Christian World'; for Montagu and Cosin he was simply 'our Gamaliel'.[76] In fact Andrewes could be seen as a mentor behind much of the shift represented by the Caroline Church, although as Fuller hinted he would never have forced upon the nation his own religious prejudices. Certainly Charles I's attachment to Laud and especially to Wren suggests a posthumous affection for Andrewes, whose sense of the numinous and of an indigenous Anglican and Catholic past probably made a profound impact upon the king's aesthetic appreciation.[77] Like Andrewes, Laud and others who rose to prominence under Charles I harkened back to the Edwardian Reformation and in particular to the

[71] Lake, *AP, passim*; O. O'Donovan, *On the Thirty-Nine Articles: A Conversation with Tudor Christianity* (1986), 13–14.
[72] Lake, *AP* 159; *WWL* ii, p. xiii.
[73] O'Donovan, *Thirty-Nine Articles*, 14.
[74] Cragg, *Freedom and Authority*, 120–2.
[75] A. McGrath, 'Reformation to Enlightenment', 154–68, 187–90; McAdoo, *Spirit of Anglicanism*, 337, 341–2, chs. 3–5.
[76] *CC* i. 74, 92; *WWL* iii. 196, 199–200.
[77] Fuller, *CH*; *WLA* i (pp. xiii, xv) and ix.

first Edwardian Prayer Book, which expresses eucharistic views similar to their own and was untainted with the Zwinglianism that influenced the later editions of 1552 and 1559.[78] Weighing heavily also upon Laud's mentality was the native, medieval past. He was steeped in history and saw the pre-Dissolution days as a time when the Church was socially and politically respected—a time, as Curle wrote, when 'religion was in life'.[79] With respect to more continental Protestant influences, that of Lutheranism was less direct than derivative, as the Laudians saw the polemical advantages of appealing to a Protestant tradition which was not Reformed.[80] The influence of Bucer and Calvin, however, was probably considerable, and not just in a reactionary sense. For both can be said to have provided Laud with discipline as the third mark of the Church, along with the preaching of the Word and the administration of the sacraments, a recognition which he used to devastating and ironic purpose.[81]

II. LAW AND GOSPEL

Like Chillingworth, Laud probably believed that only two possible ways existed to induce Christians to a 'unity of communion': either to remove the diversity of their opinions or to reveal that their different opinions were no hindrance to their unity.[82] Yet the emphasis which Laud placed on the visibility of the Church meant in effect that he could conceive of such a 'unity of communion' only through the uniformity of outward expression. 'Unity', he claimed, 'cannot long continue in the Church where uniformity is shut out at the church door.'[83] Thus he signally failed to appreciate that the result of a

[78] H. Davies, *Worship and Theology*, 13; PRO SP 16/168/7; O'Donovan, *Thirty-Nine Articles*, 92.

[79] HRO Reg. Curle: A/1/1/31/13; *WWL* ii, *passim* (Conference with Fisher the Jesuit) *CSPV 1636–9*, 156.

[80] D. D. Wallace, 'The Anglican Appeal to Lutheran Sources: Melancthon's Reputation in Seventeenth Century England', *Historical Magazine of the Protestant Episcopal Church*, 52/4 (Dec. 1983), 355–60. I owe this reference to the kindness of Dr Judith Maltby; *WWL* i. 64; iv. 268; vi. 16; B. Hall, 'The Early Rise and Gradual Decline of Lutheranism in England 1520–1660', in D. Baker (ed.), *Reform and Reformation in England and the Continent c. 1500–1700* (Oxford, 1979).

[81] B. M. G. Reardon, *Religious Thought in the Reformation* (1981), 153–5, 163–72, 197–8.

[82] Collins (ed.), *Archbishop Laud Commemoration*, 143.

[83] *WWL* iv. 60.

policy of enforcing uniformity of rites would be to create the very divisions which he aimed to remove. Nevertheless the enforcement of an authentic Laudian policy was not as rigorous as is usually thought, since Laud contemplated uniformity only through canons, not non-canonical stipulations. He wished the representatives of the Stranger Churches, for example, 'good but in a canonical way'. Later he would inform them that his intention 'was to govern the Church of England according to the Canons except the king would restrain him'.[84]

It seems to have gone unnoticed that the archiepiscopates of Laud and Neile (1632–40) witnessed the first serious attempt to enforce the Canons of 1604 throughout the two Provinces of the Church. As early as 1622 Laud appears to have extracted a greater canonical observance in St David's, in the wake of James I's volte-face during that year.[85] In London diocese his episcopate was controversial because of its concern with basic canonical nonconformity. There were probably many parishes within the diocese where the Canons of 1604 had made very little impression, even though there were others which were islands of canonical conformity.[86] Shortly after his accession in 1628, about fifty conformable clergy petitioned Laud to take the diocese into his 'fatherly consideration' and 'not to be lax unto us' but to force all nonconformist clergy into conformity.[87] During Laud's episcopate all clergy were called upon canonically to wear the surplice, to use the sign of the cross at baptism, to bow at the name of Jesus, to be properly licensed (if preachers), and to subscribe fully to the articles. Canonical stipulations affecting the congregation, such as that they should kneel at communion and stand at the creed, were also introduced although rarely enforced.[88]

[84] J. B(ulteel), *A Relation of the Troubles of the Three Foreign Churches in Kent* (1645), 135. Before the reality of the Anglican Communion, Laud recognized the autonomous interdependence of the other provinces. While favouring a canonical uniformity of Ireland and Scotland with England, he informed Archbishop Ussher, 'yet since you, and that Church have thought otherwise; I do very easily submit to it,' *WJU* 476; *WWL* iv. 60.

[85] PRO SP 16/455/59; *WWL* vi. 368; UCS D2/89; A. Foster, 'Church Policies of the 1630s', in R. Cust and A. Hughes (eds.), *Conflict in Early Stuart England: Studies in Religion and Politics 1603–1642* (1989), 85.

[86] PRO SP 16/455/59; PRO SP 16/152/4; ERO D/ABA 5 Commissary/25^{v}–173, D/ALV 1/72^{v}.

[87] PRO SP 16/152/4.

[88] GLRO DL/C/343/79–80^{v}; PRO SP 16/161/43, SP 16/218/43; ERO D/ABA 5/25^{v}, 71^{v}, 94^{v}, 104^{v}, 107, 114^{v}, 118, 125, 125^{v}, 139, 142, 156–7^{v}, 160, 168–9, D/ABA 4/105^{v}, D/ALV1/72^{v}, 74; GL 9531/15/21–6^{v}, 38–9; PRO SP 16/474/67; PRO SP 16/210/41–2; PRO SP 16/261/54^{v}.

As archbishop of Canterbury (whether in his capacity as ordinary within the see or metropolitan within the province) Laud pursued the same policy of enforcing only canonical orders.[89] This policy needs to be distinguished from that in certain dioceses, where the bishops prosecuted parishioners for not observing some non-canonical rites.[90] The instructions which Laud gave to Brent at the beginning of the metropolitical visitation and the reports which he returned to the archbishop reveal that the visitation occasioned the first serious attempts to enforce the Canons of 1604 across the Southern Province. In this respect the proceedings of the metropolitical courts in some sees marked a watershed in court activity. Virtually all the metropolitical censures were for canonical offences, and as a rule it was a few clergy rather than their congregations who were censured.[91] Often Brent merely attempted to inculcate canonical practices among congregations where they were lacking. At Northampton, for example, he showed parishioners how to bow at the name of Jesus: 'the greatest matter they stick upon' and during morning service took off his hat to impress upon the males that they should remain uncovered in church.[92]

If contemporary complaints against Laud were correct, then throughout the Southern Province after 1633 there was a greater observance of the canons than before.[93] Only during the last stages of his reign had James I tightened his policy from one of tolerating occasional conformity towards a general enforcement of the canons.[94] Occasionally, however, he appears to have asked certain congregations to observe individual canons, such as in 1611, when he refused to grant a charter to Coventry unless all its parishioners, in their several churches, knelt at communion.[95] Nevertheless it is important

[89] LPL VG 4/22/97, VG 4/13/148; CCL PRC 18/23/Dec. 1636, V/P/636/15, J/J/57/32; *WWL* vi. 368.

[90] ORO ODP c. 27/14^v, c. 13/288^v, CUL B/2/53/24, NRO PDR Corr. Bk. 66/99, 123^v, ; SRO D/D/Ca 313/178^v, D/D/Ca 297/Mells (unfol.).

[91] *WWL* vi. 368; SP 16/474/67, SP 16/260/90, SP 16/293/128, SP 16/274/12, SP 16/455/59. For Laud's visitation of the cathedrals see *HMC Appendix to the 4th report*, 124–59.

[92] PRO SP 16/293/128.

[93] The works of Prynne and Burton listed in the bibliography, for example.

[94] K. Fincham and P. Lake, 'The Ecclesiastical Policy of James I', *Journal of British Studies*, 24 (1985), 169–207; Bodl. MS Walker c. 9/31–57; P. Collinson, 'The Jacobean Religious Settlement: The Hampton Court Conference', in H. Tomlinson (ed.), *Before the English Civil War* (1983).

[95] CVRO CAR AC A79/35.

not to overestimate the greater degree of canonical conformity even under Charles I. An unpopular policy of enforcement generated disaffection, while in some parishes there might be considerable ignorance of as well as opposition to the most basic canons. When in April 1637 the dean of Bristol donned the surplice and hood at Wherwell in Winchester diocese some parishioners believed that they had just witnessed 'the marks of the beast' and subsequently left the church.[96] Even in London diocese during Laud's episcopate it proved possible for a particular minister not to wear his surplice and to go undetected for several years, although Laud eventually tracked him down.[97]

As the Canons of 1604 had never been systematically introduced, their introduction during the 1630s often proved as controversial as the introduction of non-canonical orders. Not surprisingly, many people were unable to discriminate between canonical and non-canonical innovations. Clergy might be petitioned against in 1640 for canonically bowing at the name of Jesus and using the cross at baptism, as well as for non-canonically bowing towards the altar and making their congregations receive at the rails.[98] Although there was a concerted episcopal attempt at least to introduce the Canons of 1604, what was enforced within a particular diocese depended upon the predilection of the individual bishop.[99] Coke of Hereford, for example, pressed the wearing of the surplice and the cross in baptism, but probably not bowing at the name of Jesus.[100] In his inaugural speech, preached to the first Convocation of 1640, Thomas Turner, Laud's chaplain, painted a varied picture of the enforcement

[96] PRO SP 16/352/29; PRO SP 16/474/67.

[97] GL 9531/15/38; see also the extensive canonical non-observance in the Arches peculiar during the 1630s: PRO SP 16/474/67. For the difficulties in bringing one parish into conformity ('that hath been disorderly fifty years'), as well as the reluctance of its rector (Samuel Collins, Provost of King's) to press things too quickly, see PRO SP 16/210/41.

[98] *PCR* 190; *The Suffolk Committee for Scandalous Ministers 1644–6*, ed. C. Holmes (Suffolk Record Soc., 13, 1970); John White, *The First Century of Scandalous Priests* (1643); John Walker, *The Sufferings of the Clergy* (1714); BL Add. MS 15672/1–55, 441; MS Egerton 2651/97, 150.

[99] BL Portland Loan MS 173/99. The case for the greater episcopal enforcement of canonical conformity in the reign of Charles I than before is made in my thesis 'The Growth and Implementation of "Laudianism" with special reference to the Southern Province', and in that of K. Fincham, 'Pastoral Roles of the English Episcopate in Canterbury Province, 1603–1625' (London Ph.D. thesis, 1985).

[100] *HMC Portland iii*, 76; Davenant called for a canonical confirmation of the innovations in the 1630s: Bodl. MS Tanner 67/147.

and observance of the canons across the Southern Province, and criticized those bishops who in their desire for 'popular praise' were less enthusiastic in enforcing uniformity and in consequence had brought down upon their colleagues 'the unjust imputation of rigour and tyranny'.[101] But most bishops appear to have preferred persuasive means to censure. As a result of such a policy, Hall wrote that he had won over many nonconformists to conformity.[102] During the metropolitical visitation Brent described Laud's policy as one of 'strong persuasion and vigour mixed with mildness'. Clearly even Laud's efforts ought to be contrasted with the policy of Wren, Piers, and others. The enforcement of the canons and the means by which they should be enforced were two entirely different objectives.[103]

As ordinary in Canterbury and metropolitan within the Southern Province Laud did not use his authority to enforce non-canonical stipulations, such as standing at the gospel, the gloria, and the psalms, bowing towards the table, or, as the later chapters relate, the full metropolitical order.[104] At the same time he fundamentally altered the letter of, or cushioned the impact of, other non-canonical initiatives, such as the reading of the book of sports or the enforcement of the Instructions of 1629. Nor did Laud exploit the oath of canonical obedience to extract acquiescence to these policies, which conceivably he might have done had he so wished.[105] With some justification, therefore, he could tell Saye and Sele in 1641 that he could legally prove that he had not 'commanded or enjoined any (ceremony) or other, upon any . . . congregation in England, much less upon all, to be either practised or suffered, but that which is directly commanded by law'.[106] In Laudianism there was a strong legalistic strain, which Laud himself traced from the teaching of his self-styled '*master in humanis*', Aristotle.[107] 'How dangerous it was', Laud quoted on

101 Fuller, *CH* 456; LPL Conv. 1/1/1/50.

102 SRO DD/PH 221/40.

103 PRO SP 16/351/100.

104 CCL V/P/636/15, 23, 31, PRC 18/23 See Ch. 6 sections ii and iii.

105 Wren on the other hand widened the oath of canonical obedience to encompass not just obedience to the canons but to his personal orders; Bodl. MS Tanner 315/135.

106 *WWL* vi. 126.

107 *WWL* iv. 59. In the Smart controversy at Durham, Howson exploited Laud's legalistic attachment to the letter of the Prayer Book, by pointing out to him that it contained no sanction for Cosin's liturgical innovations (PRO SP 16/174/64; *CC* i. 16 ff.). Thomas Wilson refused to read the prayer against the Scots in 1640, for similar reasons! (G. Swincock, *The Life of Thomas Wilson*, 12–15).

one occasion, 'to trust... the will of the judge rather than the written law.' When accused of enforcing non-canonical stipulations or advancing arbitrary forms of government, Laud implied that it might be a good idea for Parliament to draw up a written code of common law to prevent arbitrary judgements against himself.[108] There was more than a grain of truth in the contemporary perception that Laud's policy approximated to an almost judaical legalism, or, as Tombes termed it, 'the leaven of pharisaical wil-worship'.[109]

The furthest that Laud might go to press a non-canonical practice was to advertise it as a sound custom, creative of order and decency within the Church or as promoted by the king. People might become habituated to it over time, but it was never his intention nor inclination to enforce that which was not required by law. Such a policy was cogently expressed in a letter to the vice-chancellor of Oxford over the novel and contentious practice of bowing towards the table.[110] During the 1630s many clergy adopted this gesture, especially in court circles, after the example that had been set by Andrewes. Charles I also practised it whenever entering or leaving church, and during the parliamentary service at Westminster Abbey in November 1640 he created a spectacle by bowing to the altar in full sight of the congregation. The title of Bishop Skinner's sermon, 'Judge not by appearances', preached on this occasion may not have been coincidental.[111] The controversy at Oxford in 1638 arose when the vice-chancellor asked Corbet, one of the fellows of Merton, to bow towards the altar at the University Church. Corbet refused, made a public show of his refusal, and petitioned Laud, as chancellor, to issue an express command ordering him to comply or permitting him to do as he wished. Laud informed the vice-chancellor that he had no intention at all of making Corbet submit: 'I will not give him a command, either to do, or to desist, [nor] to appoint any substitute, but leave him, and let him do as it shall please God and himself.' He also made it categorically clear that it was not his intention that this ceremony should be enforced unless warranted by 'public authority'; without this 'they shall never have' a command. However Laud did

108 *WWL* iii. 59; Cragg, *Freedom and Authority*, 122.

109 J. Tombes, *Fermentum Pharisaeorum, or, the Leaven of Pharisaical Wil-Worship* (1643).

110 *WWL* v. 204–6; HLRO MS Braye 8/41; *The Diary of Ralph Josselin*, ed. E. Hockliffe (Camden, 3rd ser., 15, 1908), 8.

111 *HMC Buccleuch iii*, 387; P. Heylyn, *Observations on the History of the Reign of King Charles* (1650) 85; BL Sloane MS 827/81; Dow, *Innovations unjustly charged*, 190.

inform Corbet that he considered the practice to be indifferent and that for decency's sake it could be adopted, for if all such practices were 'kicked out, you may bid farewell to all decency and order'.[112]

As the canons authorized the established liturgy, a central theme within Laudian policy was the enforcement and popularization of the Book of Common Prayer. Shortly after coming to London, he asked churches to observe prayers on Wednesdays, Fridays, and holy days.[113] Laud disliked any deviation from the main text and consequently scorned the intrusion of extemporary prayer in services, although not in private.[114] Extemporary prayer in public worship he considered as 'public abortion': it being 'an over hasty mother that brings forth so soon as she has conceived'. But there existed another reason why he disliked the intrusion of extemporary prayer in worship. He appears to have believed that the Holy Spirit could only be accessible in limited ways to those who came after the apostles, which thereafter had necessitated the use of set forms.[115] Although this was a contemporary and widely believed conception, it appears to have received one of its most negative expressions in Laud's characterization of those 'bold, ignorant . . . men . . . "foaming out their own shame" to the great disorder and scandal of . . . Christ'.[116]

Laud's vision of the limited accessibility of the Holy Spirit to the individual went a long way towards determining his views on preaching. He disliked lay preachers not simply because they were unbeneficed but because he failed signally to appreciate their vocation to preach. He told Saye and Sele that he knew no 'gifts and graces set aside, much less thrust out but such as are neither gifts and graces of Christ but the bold . . . impudent attempts of weavers, cobblers and felt-makers . . . to preach without . . . knowledge, warrant or calling'.[117] His views on preaching were conditioned also by his sacramental theology, which meant that for him preaching could only be a means rather than the means to salvation. Sermons, he considered, were not properly worship but were designed to teach 'faith and obedience, and how we are to pray and give worship to

[112] *WWL* v. 206.

[113] ERO D/ALV 1/Feb. 1628–Nov. 1629; GL 9064/20/78^{v}; Hacket, *SR* i. 122: one of Williams's abortive recommendations to James I in October 1623 was for increased attendance at Wednesday and Friday services.

[114] *WWL* vi. 98.

[115] *WWL* vi. 108, 113.

[116] *WWL* vi. 100–1. Laud seems not to have given the Holy Spirit its due recognition elsewhere, *WWL* ii. 103.

[117] *WWL* vi. 102–3.

Him'.[118] Whereas for Herbert preaching and prayer were equal in importance (evidenced in his placing the reading-desk and pulpit opposite to each other in Leighton Bromswold), for Laud prayer had the upper hand. While preaching was 'a speech to man for his edification and instruction in faith and good life', prayer was 'a speech to God, to honour and worship Him'.[119] All these factors conditioned Laud's attempt during the 1630s to redress the balance in favour of the liturgy over preaching. Many of those who rose to prominence in the Church during the last years of James I and under his successor characterized the Jacobean Church as an institution where the worship of God had been edged out by the prostitution of the pulpit to the populace. 'The beauty of preaching', wrote Shelford, had 'preached away' the 'beauty of holiness'.[120] Such views did not emanate from the rise of Arminianism, although they provided evidence of growing disenchantment with reformed divinity. Rather they were corollaries to the patristic and catholic reinvestment of the Anglican Church. There is, after all, no necessary connection between Arminianism and an attack on preaching. In fact some of Dr Tyacke's 'arminians' were among the most enthusiastic preachers in the Caroline Church, the most notable being Samuel Harsnett, archbishop of York. During the debate in February 1629 on the restoration of churches, which led to the proclamation of 1629, while Harsnett agreed that 'it were necessary . . . material churches were looked to', he drew attention to the fact that there 'is an inward and spiritual church more to be cared for with the preaching of the Word to the salvation of . . . souls'.[121] In May 1624, when accused by the city of Norwich of suppressing lectures, he revealed that he had preached thousands of sermons and was reckoned 'more than half a puritan for so doing'. In 1627 he even went so far as to suggest that the most important clerical function was 'preaching in season and out of season' to which the administration of the sacraments necessarily took second place.[122] Most bishops, however, in the Caroline Church were far less assiduous in fulfilling their pedagogical duties. Prynne and others pilloried many of them in the 1640s for their

[118] *WWL* vi. 114–15.
[119] *WWL* vi. 119; *Brief Memoirs of Nicholas Ferrar*, ed. Macdonough, 104.
[120] R. Shelford, *Five Pious and Learned Discourses* (1635), 12.
[121] *HMC Buccleuch iii*, 342.
[122] Bodl. Tanner MS 114/204; LPL MS 943/127 (incorrectly indexed in Todd as Corbet).

infrequent or unedifying preaching, an incompetence which contrasted them unfavourably with the thousands of sermons preached by the evangelically inclined Jacobean bench.[123]

Yet the decline of preaching during the 1630s, as perceived by contemporaries, was relative to the increased importance attached to the liturgy and the sacraments, rather than absolute. Not without reason, this appeared to many as a frontal attack on the preaching of the gospel. Had Charles I and his bishops gone out of their way to encourage preaching, while at the same time reinvesting the catholic life of the Church, they might have been more cushioned against the crisis of 1640 and preserved the unity of Anglicanism. Instead the 1630s witnessed attempts to restrict the freedom of religious expression of the itinerant or conventicle preachers, and unparalleled interference in the parishes to control the authorized preaching of the clergy. Laud had no more sympathy for those who separated from the Church than Abbot, who had informed Charles I in 1632 that 'separatists (were) contemptible (and) fit to be punished'.[124] However Laud's notion of separatism was wider, serving to comprehend not just conventicles proper but a considerable amount of extra-parochial activity as well, which had been tacitly accepted and condoned in the Jacobean Church. At the same time, consistorial pressure to conform, as well as the perception that Charles I and his bishops were either hostile or lukewarm to the gospel, forced many into separatist activities or to leave the kingdom. The only religious meetings which Laud appears to have condoned outside public worship were those within the nexus of the family or household. Conventicles, on the other hand, for Laud consisted of ten or more meeting together 'to read, preach and expound'.[125] On this criterion even the twelve disciples would have been branded as conventiclers!

It was the unlicensed preachers, the conventiclers, and a cross-section of the laity, rather than the beneficed clergy, who suffered at the hands of the Star Chamber and the High Commission under

[123] Prynne, *CD*; *The Answers of John Bastwick . . . to . . . Sir John Bank(e)s* (1641), 4; Collinson, *RP*, ch. 2; K. Fincham, *Prelate as Pastor: The Episcopate of James I* (Oxford, 1990), 253–76.

[124] *WWL* v. 309 (but notice also Abbot's qualification).

[125] R. Quartermayne, *Quartermayne's Conquest over Canterburies Court.* (1642), 28–9. One of the results of the wider definition of separatism was emigration to New England. For this see the (1951) London Ph.D. thesis of N. C. P. Tyack: 'Migration from East Anglia to New England before 1660.'

Laud.[126] The shortage of clergy, Laud's high notions of priesthood, and his belief that the clergy had been downtrodden all help to explain his reluctance to impose heavy clerical censures. In his trial, he countered the suggestion that he had censured clergy heavily by showing that during the seven years of his archiepiscopate as few ministers were prosecuted in High Commission as during any of the three periods of seven years under Abbot's twenty-one years.[127] Few of the records which Laud produced in his trial to substantiate this have survived, but S. R. Gardiner examined the almost complete series of records for the two-year, three-month period after February 1634 and concluded that there were during this period remarkably few clerical censures.[128] Of the fourteen cases of clerical condemnation, at least five or six were for criminal offences. In five of the remaining cases (for nonconformity), the penalty was remitted either wholly or in part.[129]

The notion that Laud heavily censured ministers for canonical nonconformity during the metropolitical visitation also needs to be seriously questioned especially in light of the reports which Brent sent to Laud, in which he recorded his proceedings during the visitations of 1635.[130] In the royal peculiar of Stratford, Brent suspended Wilson, its vicar, for 'grossly particularising in his sermons, for suffering his poultry to roost and his hogs to lodge in the chancel', but shortly afterwards released him because he was the son of a conformable minister. At Warwick (Worcester) he questioned Roe, one of its ministers, who was 'suspected' of nonconformity, yet failed to 'foster anything upon him'.[131] Hall, one of his fellow ministers, informed Brent about the nonconformity of Clarke of Alcester, but this was countered by a timely letter from Sir Richard Knightley,

[126] For the Star Chamber see H. Phillips, 'The Last Years of the Court of the Star Chamber 1630–41', *TRHS*, 4th ser., 21 (1939); Rushworth, iii, appendix, 1–109; PRO Sta. Cha. 9 1625–40; and entries in *CSPD*. For the High Commission, see Usher, *Rise and Fall of the High Commission*; and entries in *CSPD*. For individual cases in both courts see *Cases in the Courts of Star Chamber and the High Commission*, ed. S. R. Gardiner (Camden., 39, 1886). Stray papers in Laud's hand such as Bodl. MS Add. c. 303 (82) (dealing with the dispute between Lord Powis and Sir Edward Vaughan), reveal the extent to which he involved himself with civil cases in these courts.

[127] *WWL* iii. 420–1; vi. 92.

[128] Gardiner, *History of England*, x. 224–5.

[129] Ibid.

[130] PRO SP 16/293/128, SP 16/351/100, SP 16/274/12, SP/16/474/67.

[131] PRO SP 16/293/128.

testifying to Clarke's good behaviour.[132] Within the diocese of Chichester, Brent carefully examined the ministers of Warningcamp, Felpham, and Clapham with a view to suspending them, but nothing could be found against them and he merely inhibited them from preaching. He did the same to Peartree, in the diocese of Norwich, who could not inform him what *ecclesia* meant.[133] At Shrewsbury (Coventry and Lichfield), because he could prove nothing against Burton of St Chad's, (although he questioned him publicly), he only temporarily suspended him. He released another minister, Bedford, from suspension with an admonition because no witnesses appeared against him.[134] In Derby archdeaconry he suspended two ministers for performing clandestine marriages but only *parte poena* because of their poverty, which made him doubt whether anyone would prosecute them in the High Commission.[135] Others were suspended but released on the following day upon their submission, or the intercession of those who testified in their favour, or who hoped to win them over to conformity. Even when there was clear evidence of nonconformity, calling them into the High Commission did not always entail prosecution if no witnesses appeared. In 1636 Brent informed Laud of two nonconformist curates at Chelmsford (London): no 'good course ... can be taken against them but in the High Commission ... there is no other way to punish them sufficiently ... but I fear it will be hard to find the parties'.[136] These reports cannot be dismissed as Brent's reluctance to employ heavy court censure, because he produced them expressly for Laud's examination and made no attempt to cover his proceedings. Moreover during the time that they were compiled, Brent was in the archbishop's total confidence: in 1636 Laud described his vicar-general as an 'honest' man. Moreover he could have dismissed him had he so wished.[137] It was only after the archbishop accused Brent of corruption in the management of Merton College that any notable rift occurred between them.[138]

In his capacity as ordinary within London and Canterbury Laud also censured very few clergy. In his account for 1632 Abbot re-

[132] S. Clarke, *The Lives of Sundry Eminent Persons* (1683), i. 7.
[133] PRO SP 16/293/128.
[134] Ibid. [135] Ibid.
[136] PRO SP 16/351/100.
[137] PRO SP 16/330/17; *WWL* vii. 268.
[138] Heylyn, *CA* 463–4; *WWL* vii. 268; HLRO MS Braye 8/29.

ferred to only one or two deprivations inflicted by Laud in London diocese.[139] In his own account of the diocese for 1633 Laud informed Charles I that during that year he had deprived only Nathaniel Ward, who had refused to conform to the articles after 'long patience and often conference'. The entries relating to this particular case in Laud's register confirm this testimony, save for one significant fact. Laud deprived Ward in December 1632, a year after he first appeared in court. Laud wrote his account of 1633 in December 1633, to give to the king by 2 January 1634. This might suggest not only that Laud had inflicted no deprivations after December 1632 (an opinion confirmed by the register) but also that in order to impress the king he felt the need to refer to a deprivation which, without informing Charles, he had inflicted long before.[140] He called another minister, John Beadle of Barnston, into court during the same year for omitting parts of the liturgy, but then merely dismissed him with a canonical admonition 'upon his submission and promise of reformation'.[141] As far as Canterbury diocese was concerned, Laud asserted that 'I think it will appear, that as few . . . have been suspended or deprived . . . as in any diocese in England. Nor have I by these suspensions hindered the preaching of God's word, but of schism and sedition.'[142] The extant records of Canterbury diocese confirm this picture. The difference between Abbot and Laud's policies as ordinaries within Canterbury was probably less in the number or quality of the clerical censures than in the greater pressure under Laud to conform to the canons and in the heavier interference in the parishes. Laud might hold out the threat of clerical censure but invariably used persuasive tactics rather than penalties to obtain conformity. The same goes also for his policy as metropolitan, when he would often interview conscientious objectors himself or refer them to popular conformists, such as Featley, Brownrigg, or Holdsworth (Harsnett's 'conformable puritans').[143] On his own testimony Neile pursued a similarly persuasive policy, confessing that after twenty-eight years as bishop he had 'never deprived any man but . . . endeavoured their reformation'.[144]

139 *WWL* v. 310.
140 GL 9531/15/23^{v}, 38–9; *WWL* v. 318.
141 *WWL* v. 318.
142 *WWL* iii. 420.
143 PRO SP 16/351/100; Quartermayne, *Quartermayne's Conquest*, 17.
144 PRO SP 16/345/85/5^{v}; although this somewhat underestimates the pressure he could apply, see Ch. 4 n. 123; Foster, 'Church Policies of the 1630s', *passim*.

Although the Caroline Church brought unprecedented pressure upon clergy to conform (which might weigh as heavily upon the conscience as censures) the number of clerical deprivations between 1625 and 1640 was possibly less than twenty, a figure much smaller than the eighty deprivations inflicted by James I during the first years of his reign or during the purges of the 1640s.[145] The greatest number of deprivations occurred almost certainly in Norwich between 1636 and 1638. In December 1637 seven ministers were deprived by Wren for the offence of non-residence, but only after he had first consulted the king, whose reply was 'proceed to deprivation'.[146] Even if the number of Caroline resignations were greater than Jacobean resignations (given the end of the policy of occasional conformity and more subtle modes of extracting conformity) the resignations listed in Laud's register for metropolitical and *sede vacante* jurisdiction are relatively small.[147] Thus in spite of all their difficulties under Charles I's rule, the clergy had found professional favour within the Caroline Church. It was a very different story for those laity, summoned to Star Chamber and High Commission, for whom Laud reserved his heaviest censures.[148]

III. LAUDIAN PROJECTS

The patristic emphasis on the visibility of the Church and the inherent holiness of the church fabric necessarily led to a concern for the restoration of churches in the seventeenth century. Donne's words, 'he that cares not though the material church fall . . . is falling from the spiritual,' attained a striking relevance as contemporaries contemplated the sorry state of their churches.[149] According to Stow's editor, when London parishes started repairing their churches

[145] B. W. Quintrell, 'The Royal Hunt and the Puritans 1604–5', *Journal of Ecclesiastical History*, 31 (1980), 53; Bodl. MS J. Walker c. 9/31–57v, 31; Fincham and Lake 'The Ecclesiastical Policy of James I', *passim*; Bodl. MS J. Walker c. 9/31; suspensions however were higher under Charles I than James: see, as a sample, the long list of Norwich suspensions in Bodl. Tanner 314/120–122v, 181–95, Tanner 89/182. See also Fincham, *Prelate as Pastor*, appendix vi.

[146] *WWL* v. 350; *Parentalia*, 95; Bodl. Tanner 314/120–122v, 181–94, Tanner 89/175–6.

[147] LPL Reg. Laud i/175–306v, ii/1–27v (*sede vacante*); i/72–185 (metropolitical institutions), i/308–323v (ordinary institutions).

[148] Fuller, *CH* iii. 535.

[149] *The Works of John Donne*, ed. H. Alford, 6 vols. (1839), ii. 330.

after 1615, this was 'not without good cause for there was not any church work done in fifty years until then'. For Fuller, Laud was preeminently the 'grand causer of the repairing of churches' and dated from his archiepiscopate 'the general mending, beautifying and adorning of all English churches'. His desire to externalize religious expression meant that much court activity under Laud was spent in reinforcing church walls. As bishop of London he issued many commissions for rates and impressed upon parishes the need to restore their fabrics in visitation addresses. Perhaps his greatest contribution to the ecclesiastical rebuilding of England was the proclamation of 11 October 1629.[150]

The origins of the committee which led to the formulation of this document can be traced to debates in the Lords in February 1629, during the second session of Charles's third Parliament.[151] Certain peers expressed concern that too many petitions for briefs for the repair of churches were entering the House and slowing down business. On the introduction of yet another brief from the earl of Clare, Lord Keeper Coventry took the opportunity to suggest that it was time to limit the number of petitions either to churches whose restoration was beyond parochial means or whose decay was caused by factors other than parish negligence. Coventry told the House how he had often raised the problem with the bishops, with the implication that they should be doing more to solve it. Laud, who was present at the debate, cleared the bishops of any negligence and stressed that on several occasions their good intentions had come to nothing because of the refusal of churchwardens to present decays and because of the reluctance of many lay impropriators to repair their chancels. Often those cited into court would seek a prohibition, as had recently occurred in cases in the High Commission.[152] With his retort, Laud had effectively raised the debate to a discussion of what he considered to be two of the greatest banes of the contemporary Church—prohibitions and impropriations.[153] He had also established the basic premisses of the proclamation. In its final form,

[150] J. Stow, *Annales*, ed. E. Howes (1615), 892; Fuller, *CH* 536–7; QCO MS 390/174ᵛ; GLRO DLC/343/65–159ᵛ; Hacket, *SR* i. 122 (Williams had called for the restoration of churches in October 1623); *Stuart Royal Proclamations*, ii, ed. J. F. Larkin (Oxford, 1983).

[151] *LJ* iv. 31; *HMC Buccleuch iii*, 342.

[152] *HMC Buccleuch iii*, 342.

[153] *WWL* ii. 120. Bancroft and Abbot had been concerned with the problem, Bodl. Tanner MS 280/119.

this asked judges not to send many prohibitions. Yet not until 1637, when Laud secured from the king an order preventing prohibitions from drawing cases away from the High Commission, did they decrease in any meaningful sense.[154] For much of the 1630s Laud's words to Wentworth rang true, that the Church was so enmeshed in the common law that it was impossible 'for any man to do that good which he would or is bound to do'.[155]

In spite of the continued resort to prohibitions the proclamation facilitated the restoration of churches across the country. For the first time it established diocesan commissions to survey churches and to order repairs to be carried out within a specified time, thus supplementing the decanal and archidiaconal commissions instituted under the Canons of 1604.[156] Such commissions were established in the sees of Exeter, Oxford, Peterborough, Bath and Wells, Gloucester, Norwich, Worcester, Coventry and Lichfield, York, and probably in most other sees during the 1630s.[157] Certainly in all dioceses there was greatly increased activity in calling parishioners and impropriators into court to make them restore their churches and chancels.[158] Some courts appealed directly to the proclamation rather than canonical precept as the justification for their actions.[159] The resulting episcopal commissions effectively bypassed the churchwardens' presentment as the main instrument of detection. In fact in some parishes the proclamation occasioned so much restoration work that the parish might exceed their original estimates, leading to the procuring of letters patent for briefs.[160] The problem of assess-

[154] Usher, *Rise and Fall of the High Commission*, 319; PRO SP 16/383/44.

[155] *WWL* vi. 310.

[156] *Synodalia*, i. 295.

[157] DRO Ch. 854d. 179, Ch. 866/1638 Jan. chw. of Buckfastleigh con. Frowde, 2914A/PW1/1636; Dartington PW2/1633; SRO D/P/Ilm/52^{v}, D/P/Ax 4/1/1/1633/4; ORO MS archd. papers C. 2/120^{v}, 178; St Martin's a. 1/179; NRO PDR x2159/5/11; GRO P329/CW 2/1/283; Bodl. Tanner MS 68/240; WARO DR 87/2/137; SFRO D9/A/PC/1/55, D113/A/Pc/1/30; LJRO B/V/1/53, B/C/3/15; Foster, 'Church Policies of the 1630s', 203, 215–16.

[158] This could be substantiated by enumerable references, for a selection: Birch, i. 81; LJRO B/V/1/52–5, 60 (unfol.); DPD Corr. Bk. 1635–6/14, 19, Corr. Bk. 1637–8/12^{v}; WSRO Ep. 11/15/1; PRO SP 16/259/78, 16/351/38, 16/304/15, 16/312/84, 16/398/99, 16/499/50; NRO X2159/5/11, X622/4/6, Corr. Bks. 66/1^{v}–154^{v}, 68/4^{v}–136^{v}; R. A. Marchant, 'The Restoration of Nottinghamshire Churches 1635–1640', *Thoroton Society Transactions*, 5 (1961); E. R. C. Brinkworth, 'The Laudian Church in Buckinghamshire', *University of Birmingham Historical Journal*, 5 (1955–6), 31–59. For many other references see my thesis.

[159] DTRO E /PUD: CW8; GLRO DL/C/343/207^{v}.

[160] GLRO DL/C/343/95, 73^{v}, 207^{v}.

ment and collection was fraught with difficulties, which, together with disputes over tithes and pews, went far to monopolize court activity.[161] Often those who held land in a particular parish, yet lived in another, would refuse to contribute to the costs of restoration, which might lead all concerned into long, drawn-out legal disputes. The churchwardens of Churchill (Oxford) were sued by two such landowners. Eventually the parish appealed to Arches with the result that Laud required Lambe to support the churchwardens, 'for if this cause be held there will be but few churches repaired'.[162] There were disputes also over different methods of assessment, which often ended up in the secular courts. Not only parishes but a good many clergy (two notable examples were Heylyn and Pocklington) might find themselves heavily involved in lengthy dilapidation suits.[163]

The extent to which detection or parochial presentment restored the fabric of churches in the 1630s differed from parish to parish, and from diocese to diocese, it being contingent upon a whole variety of circumstances. Although much of the increased parish expenditure was remedial and preventive, it might cost as much and very often more than the ostensible Caroline innovations.[164] However, in some city parishes congregations vied with each other to see who could outlay the most on their parish churches. The army officers who visited Bristol in 1634 were amazed at how the citizens had 'spared no cost nor forwardness to beautify and adorn (their churches) for they daily strive in every parish, who shall exceed the other in . . . generous and religious bounty, most to deck and enrich those sanctified and heavenly mansions'.[165]

The restoration of St Paul's Cathedral was, according to Fuller, 'the masterpiece of (Laud's) performance'. It was also his most fitting, if short-lived, memorial.[166] When bishop of London, he

[161] This is my own impression after sifting innumerable court records. For the importance of the proprietorial pew see R. Gough, *The History of Myddle*, ed. D. Hey (1981), 77, 96, 117, and the doctoral work in progress of Kenneth Dillow; for tithes see W. Kennet, *The Case of Impropriations* (1704).

[162] PRO SP 16/316/71 ii.

[163] Barnard, *TH*, 142–4; BDRO J. 1224–30; PRO SP 16/437/27; WTRO D1/42/57/131, 150–1; ORO c. 2/301^{v}, c. 26/218, c. 27/21–22^{v}; SFRO D260/M/PV/1; WSRO Dep. Bk. Ep. 1/11/16/1–135, Ep. 11/9/18/71–104; PRO DEL 3/2 Stackpoole; BERO D/A2 c. 79/184; NRO Corr. Bk. 68/4–136^{v}; ERO D/ALV 2/162.

[164] Clarendon i. 199–202; for verification see a sample of churchwarden accounts listed under parish records in the bibliography.

[165] L. G. Wickham Legg (ed.), *A Relation of a Short Survey of 26 Counties* (1904), 92.

[166] Fuller, *CH*, 537.

assumed a special responsibility for the restoration of its structure, and during the 1630s he provided much of the drive behind the programme of assessment and collection of funds. In official dispatches and personal correspondence he continually impressed upon clerics and lay bodies across the country the necessity of the work and the need to speed up their contributions.[167] In 1637 he finally managed to secure from the king permission to channel all the profits and fines of the High Commission into the rebuilding of the cathedral.[168] Under the original commission of 1631 justices of the peace were responsible for the clerical as well as the lay assessment and collection. But in 1633 Montagu of Chichester asked Laud to change this practice so that the bishops could take over responsibility for the clerical contributions. This resulted in the new commission of January 1634.[169] In circulars sent to every diocese Laud invited the bishops to contribute personally to the restoration. Many did so handsomely, although Wren does not appear to have contributed at all.[170] A significant number of clergy also gave personal donations, among them several of Laud's former Welsh clerical colleagues, including Morgan Owen (later bishop of Llandaff), Thomas Howell (later bishop of Bristol), and Archdeacon Brand of Cardigan. The largest clerical donation came from Robert Skinner, which almost certainly helps to explain his otherwise meteoric elevation to Bristol in 1637.[171] Throughout the Southern Province the restoration of St Paul's became a standard theme of visitation addresses and even sermons.[172] Some bishops, including Goodman and Williams, attached special enquiries to their visitation articles, others such as Corbet, Curle, Davenant, and Montagu issued episcopal letters to their clergy.[173] Only one bishop, Piers of Bath and Wells, appears to

[167] PRO SP 16/175/45, SP 16/213/6a, SP 16/216/70, SP 16/259/22, SP 16/266/21, 50 SP/16/276/42; *WWL* vi. 546, 561; vii, 189, 440, 465; *HMC Various Collections viii*, 50; Bodl. Rawl. MS B. 372(11); BL Stowe MS 743/103–4, BL Sloane MS 34/3ᵛ–4, KAO U350, C/249; SRO DD/PH 222/33; CCL Z. 3. 14/35; *WWL* iv. 92.

[168] *WWL* iii. 255; LPL MS 943/559.

[169] PRO SP 16/357/110; *WWL* vii. 400; CCL Z. 3. 14/35.

[170] PRO SP 16/257/114, SP 16/259/69; GL 25,474/1–6; SFRO D13 23/E/1/208ᵛ; BL Harl. MS 984/164ᵛ; WORO 2648/716. 093/83; BRO Ep/A/30/1.

[171] GL 25,474/1–6.

[172] Giles Fleming, *Magnificance Exemplified, the Repair of St. Paul's Exhorted Unto* (1634); LPL MS 1030/67; *Articles to be enquired in the visitation of... Godfrey (Goodman) Lord bishop of Gloucester* (1637) see *prefix*; *Articles to be enquired in the visitation of... John (Williams) Lord Bishop of Lincoln* (1635), see last clause.

[173] PRO SP 16/574/58; HRO Reg. Curle A/1/1/31/13; PRP SP 16/257/114; Bodl. Rawl. MS C. 579/47ᵛ.

have called ministers systematically into court to receive their contributions and to censure them for non-payment, which was not officially required as Laud had invited only a 'voluntary' clerical contribution in his letter of 1634.[174]

Although after 1634 the lay and clerical assessment and collection were separate, to a certain extent there was still some interaction as the parish minister often recorded the lay contributions. These were then collected by churchwardens and constables and taken to a suitable place where they could be given to the justices.[175] Those who had promised to contribute yet failed to pay might be summoned to appear before the justices, as happened in Herefordshire.[176] However those invited to pay were numerically relatively few in each parish, as they comprised only subsidy men and those of 'ability', although this might make any refusal particularly sensitive.[177] The motives for refusal were varied. For some it was ostensibly a shortage of cash. In Wentlog in Monmouthshire they needed the money to repair the sea walls. In Roydon in Essex they had spent so much on the restoration of their parish church that they could afford little for St Paul's.[178] But the refusal of others might rest on more ideological foundations. For Thomas Wilson the restoration was conclusive evidence that 'Israel hath forgotten his maker and buildeth... temples'.[179] Others voiced a more overtly political objection. In Herefordshire, James Clarke thought the collection contrary to the Petition of Right, as 'an extorting and exacting of all the subjects and that the projectors of such business in other countries had their skin flayed off their heads'.[180] Perhaps such a response was not surprising considering that some clergy advertised the collection not as a benevolence but as a 'prerogative royal'.[181] Although Laud did not go

[174] SRO D/D/Ca 302/18; PRO SP 16/259/69. The clergy paid less than the laity, which was not well received in some quarters: SRO DD/PH 221/33.

[175] BL Add. MS 11051/197, 199; CWRO DDP 162/5/1; WARO DR 50/9/192.

[176] BL Add. MS 11051/197.

[177] BL Add. MS 11051/191; BRO Ashton Court MS 36214.

[178] PRO SP 16/291/105; ERO D/D Ba 0/1; the vicar of Little Canfield was summoned into court for saying that the City was 'as able to maintain [St. Paul's] as his parish': GLRO DL/C/322/158v. See also PRO SP 16/378/73 (evidence of reluctance to contribute because of demands of ship-money and plague relief) and PRO SP 16/371/14.

[179] Swincock, *The Life and Death of Thomas Wilson* 81; Heylyn, *Observations on the History of the reign of King Charles I*, 104.

[180] BL Add. MS 11051/224.

[181] BL Add. MS 11051/224. In a similar way some clergy justified ship-money: CCO MS 206/6v; Bodl. Tanner MS 299/171.

this far, he himself advertised the collection as a royal rather than an ecclesiastical initiative, in order to encourage contributions.[182]

The restoration of St Paul's appeared as one of the objectives which Laud listed within his diary as 'things which I have projected to do if God bless me in them'.[183] This list has been ignored presumably because other measures seemingly more indicative of Laudianism—the republication of the book of sports, the restraint of lecturers, the Instructions of 1629, and the metropolitical altar policy—have received undue attention in comparison. This is not to say that Laud was unconcerned with these policies during the 1630s; far from it; but what this work shows is that they were not as identifiably or authentically Laudian as these 'projects'. This is gleaned not just from Laud's testimony but from the evidence of other records which reveal his personal prosecution of these particular measures.[184] Apart from the restoration of St Paul's, these authentically Laudian projects were the overthrow of the Feoffees for Impropriations (a syndicate of Puritan laymen who tried to buy up livings so that they could appoint to them); the augmentation of livings (crucial to his programme of restoring the economic power of the Church); the revision of the statutes of Oxford and the cathedrals of the new foundation; attaching commendams to the smaller bishoprics; settling the tithe dispute in London; buying impropriations through the fines of the High Commission; establishing a Greek press at London and Oxford; and the return of crown impropriations to the Church. Two of the entries were erased and it is impossible to say exactly what these were although one of them appears to concern Oxford.[185] The remaining entries all concern Laud's charitable bequests or the universities. Many of these 'projects' have received individual attention from historians and there is no need to repeat what they have said elsewhere.[186] There were, however, two other

182 CCL Z. 3. 14/35.

183 *WWL* iii. 253–5.

184 HLRO MS Braye 8/12, 36–7, 59; *WWL* vi. 307–8, 342, 484; *WWL* iv. 176, 303; LPL MS 943/299, 301, 303; *WWL* iii. 253–5; *WWL* v. 332, 353; LPL MS 728; PRO SP 16/376/7, SP 16/376/7, SP 16/345/88; *Parentalia*, 50–1; Bodl. MS873; BL Harl. 832/48ᵛ–64ᵛ; PRO/E/112/211/533.

185 *WWL* iii. 253–5.

186 Among the more important are: Hill, *Economic Problems of the Church*; E. W. Kirby, 'The Lay Feoffees: A Study in Militant Protestantism', *Journal of Modern History*, 14 (1942), 1–25; I. M. Calder (ed.), *Activities of the Puritan Faction of the Church of England 1625–1633* (1957); A. Hamilton Thompson, 'The Statutes of Gloucester, Canterbury and Winchester Cathedrals', *The Antiquary's Journal*, 7 (1927),

policy initiatives which Laud more than any other person sponsored in the 1630s, which were not included in the list: his measures to curtail the activities of the Stranger Churches and the nonconformity of the English merchants and regiments abroad.[187] In 1634, when representatives of the Stranger Churches in Norwich approached Laud to seek his support for a petition against the recently introduced restrictions, he informed them that he could not intercede for them as he 'was the man that had set this business on foot'.[188] As early as March 1632 Laud had presented proposals to both the king and the council asking that all those 'strangers' born in England should resort to their local parish church, while all native refugees might retain their own churches only so long as they used the Book of Common Prayer translated into their own tongue.[189] These measures were first introduced during the metropolitical visitation but not enforced until July 1635 and certainly not observed in any meaningful way until a year later.[190]

As early as 1628, Carleton had alerted Laud to the nonconformist activities of English merchants in the Low Countries, information which he then presented to the council.[191] As a result, by 1634 the Prayer Book was being read in Lord Vere of Tilbury's regiment in the Netherlands and among the Merchant Adventurers.[192] The Dutch Reformed Church took particular offence at these developments as they maintained that they should determine the form of

85; *The Statutes governing the Cathedral Church of Winchester given by King Charles I*, ed. A. W. Goodman and W. Hilton (1925); *Statuta Ecclesiae Cathedralis Herefordensis 1636*, ed. J. Jebb and H. W. Phillot (1882); H. R. Trevor-Roper, 'The Church of England and the Greek Church', *Studies in Church History*, 14 (1978), 213; Fuller, *CH* 407–18; Fuller, *AII* iii. 13.

[187] Plans for the reduction of churches in the Channel Islands to conformity with the Church of England were shelved at the representation of the earl of Danby: PRO SP 16/537/13; for the wider Caroline policy to establish British conformity with the Church of England, see Ch. i section iii and C. S. R. Russell, 'The British Problem and the English Civil War', *History*, 72 (1987).

[188] J. B(ulteel), *A Relation of the Troubles*, 140. The Stranger Churches of England were the Dutch (London, Colchester, Norwich, Maidstone, Yarmouth, Sandwich); the Walloon (Southampton, Norwich, Canterbury), and the French and Walloon (London), see *ibid.* For the sixteenth century background see Andrew Pettegree, *Foreign Protestant Communities in Sixteenth-Century London* (Oxford, 1986).

[189] *WWL* v. 323–4, vi. 22–8; J. B(ulteel), *A Relation of the Troubles*, 45–8; *WWL* vii. 134; iv. 314.

[190] B(ulteel), *A Relation of the Troubles*, 142–3.

[191] *WWL* vii. 12.

[192] *WWL* vi. 380, vii. 12, 14; PRO SP 16/274/2; *WWL* iii. 375; Gardiner, *History of England*, viii. 314–5; PRO SP 16/437/59.

worship used by foreigners within their own country. Laud had in fact denied them the very principle which he had broached to determine the liturgy of the Stranger Churches in England.[193] Laud's rationale for these restrictions was his paranoid fear of any nonconformity to the discipline, canons, and liturgy of the Church of England. He told representatives of the Norwich Stranger Churches that he knew 'their doctrine, parity of ministers' which was not apostolic.[194] If they continued as 'Israel in Egypt' as he called them, they would endanger not only the Church but the Commonwealth as well.[195] Yet as with the Feoffees, there is no evidence that the Stranger Churches constituted the slightest danger to the Anglican Church. Perhaps none of Laud's policies went so far as these to create the impression that he intended to undermine Protestantism. Richelieu was reported to have asked that if a king who is a Protestant would not permit two disciplines in his kingdom, why should a king of France?[196] Laud's cool reception of John Dury's attempt to create a pan-Protestant union during the 1630s is further confirmation of how far removed the archbishop was from the Protestant sympathies of his predecessor and the prevailing preconceptions within the country. When Laud extended overtures to the Protestant churches, it was less towards the Huguenots, the Dutch, and the Bohemians than to the Swedish and Danish Lutherans, who had retained the office if not the full prescriptive power of episcopacy.[197] When Laud was accused in 1641 of aspiring to divide the English Church from the Reformed Churches abroad, he stood defenceless.[198]

Laud's integrated social perspective, as well as his desire to make the laity feel the heavy hand of the Church helps to explain why the Star Chamber and the High Commission were abolished in 1641. His activities here need far closer investigation than has been conducted in the past or than is possible in this work. It was in these

193 B(ulteel), *A Relation of the Troubles*, 132–43, *passim*.
194 Ibid. 134.
195 Ibid. 139; *WWL* iii. 422.
196 B(ulteel), *A Relation of the Troubles*, 134, 139.
197 W. Tighe, 'William Laud and the Reunion of the Churches', 717–27; BL Add. MS 11044/92–3v; PRO C115 Bundle M 12/7223. Dury himself was somewhat disabled in the task of reconciliation, as he believed in conscience that the ordination he had received from the reformed Churches was insufficient, and so he sought episcopal orders from Hall and Laud: *The Time-serving Proteus, and Ambidexter Divine, Uncased to the World* (1650), letters, 1–5.
198 *WWL* iii. 421; HLRO MS Braye 8/61; PRO SP 16/499/63v.

courts that Laud, according to Fuller, was seen to concur with the side advocating the heaviest censures. Moreover, as Clarendon noted, the High Commission meddled in matters which were outside its jurisdiction. The archbishop's attempts to restrict prohibitions doubtless helped to foster this image but so also did the increased court activity during the 1630s over tithes, administrations, marriages, adulteries, rape, theft, felony, and other issues, which according to some voices in 1641, ecclesiastical jurisdiction had no inherent right to try.[199] Possibly to an unprecedented extent the church courts under Charles I were concerned with the morality of contemporary society. At times the king may not have appeared very righteous, yet he was certainly very moralistic: 'so severe an exactor of gravity and reverence in all mention of religion . . . that he could never endure any light or profane word'.[200] According to Clarendon, he not only permitted but directed Laud and the bishops to prosecute the gentry and his own personal servants for their moral offences. During most sessions of the High Commission 'persons of honour and great quality' were summoned 'upon report of their incontinence . . . or conduct in their lives'.[201] The heavy fines which Laud imposed upon these offenders in Star Chamber were then channelled into the rebuilding of St Paul's. This, according to Clarendon, 'sharpened men's minds against the bishops before they had any ill intention towards the Church'.[202] Richard Steward gave a similar impression. He believed that Laud had few friends at court because there were 'few of the greater quality whom he had not some time or other much contestation with, either in defending his master from abuse or the Church from injury'.[203] Such interference in the lives of the well-to-do was deeply resented and surfaced explicitly in Laud's trial, when he was accused of humiliating Sir Robert Howard and Viscountess Purbeck. It was in fact the king who was more behind this particular prosecution; one day at court he took Laud aside and asked him to bring the viscountess 'to penance' as her offence was a 'great

[199] Fuller, *CH* iii, 535; Clarendon, i. 372–3; see Bodl. Tanner 65/272 for the Commons' case against the High Commission. Hacket, *SR* i. 97 compares the mild use of the High Commission under Bancroft with that under Abbot and Laud. For another appreciation of Bancroft's moderation see Bodl. MS J. Walker c. 9/31–57^{v}.

[200] Clarendon, iv. 489.

[201] Clarendon, iv. 489; i. 125, 372, Usher, *Rise and Fall of the High Commission* 201 ff.

[202] Clarendon, i. 125.

[203] *CC* i. 228.

reproach' to the nation.[204] There can be little doubt that Laud's greatest mistake was to get involved with the prosecution of Prynne, Bastwick, and Burton. Prynne returned with vengeance in 1641 to bring his former enemy to justice. Yet as intense as was Laud's contempt for Prynne he informed Wentworth in 1637 that for his 'own part (I thank God) I desire no blood'.[205] The infamous censure when carried out was a secular not an ecclesiastical censure, and neither Juxon nor Laud voted in the case. Nevertheless Laud failed signally to absolve himself from involvement in the humiliation of Prynne, and just as he became the scapegoat for much that occurred in the 1630s, Prynne became the popular hero of its opposition.[206]

The High Commission and the Star Chamber may well have been more unpopular with the higher than the lower echelons of society. R. G. Usher pointed out that half of the cases *ex officio* were presented by the court on the petition of some poor or uninfluential person.[207] The one aspect of its proceedings which served to diminish its popularity as a court of appeal was probably the *ex officio* oath. The accused might be privately examined not only without knowing what charge he had to answer but without legal advice. Consequently he might be trapped into making an admission. If he then denied the oath tendered to him he might be compelled to answer a number of interrogations framed for the express purpose of making him incriminate himself.[208] According to Richard Steward, Laud wished 'to prevent the too frequent use of the *ex officio*, in the High Commission' and intended, had he lived, to propose to Parliament ways of overhauling its procedures. In 1640, however, members would hardly have been receptive to proposals which appeared to prolong the life of an institution which in their eyes had already relinquished its right to exist.[209]

Apart from his attack on prohibitions, a powerful factor in fusing together lay interests against Laud was his attempt to restore impropriations and other proprietorial rights to the Church, or as an intermediary step, to the Crown before their resumption by the Church. An important development in this procedure was his attempted restoration of the right of presentation to livings, alienated

204 *WWL* iii. 394; D'Ewes, *Autobiography*, i. 251–2; Bodl. MS Clar. 20/1510.
205 *WWL* vi. 36–70; vii. 329.
206 *WWL* vi. 36–70; HLRO MS Braye 8/13.
207 Usher, *Rise and Fall of the High Commission*, 323 ff.
208 Ibid. 247 ff. 209 *CC* i. 229.

from the Crown.[210] The campaign to restore tithes to the Church was also part of the same strategy. As all tithes were due to the priest alone by divine concession, according to Laud, those who retained them were sinning 'the sin of sacrilege'. Even if these impropriations had been bought from the Crown this did not absolve guilt as Henry VIII and his successors had had no right to sell them in the first place. The annual rent which the Tudors had reserved for themselves was merely to sell one part of the sin and retain the other. That such property had also passed through parliamentary hands did not give grounds for complacency either since statute could not absolve 'a sin against the moral law of God'.[211] It was through arguments such as these that Laud persuaded Viscount Scudamore to return his property to the Church, an example followed by Viscount Camden and Duchess Dudley, which contributed to the most significant reclamation of ecclesiastical property in England since the Reformation.[212]

As early as April 1626 Laud had drawn up for Charles I proposals which addressed the economic problems of the Church.[213] A document in Laud's hand entitled 'Certain considerations of church government and discipline to be offered to his Majesty' is almost certainly a copy of these very proposals. They highlight not only the radical nature of Laud's suggestions for solving the economic problems of the Church but also the central importance of the economic status of the clergy in his wider ecclesiastical programme.[214] After all it was not the extent of nonconformity which Laud impressed upon the king in his first provincial account, but the poverty of the clergy:

[210] J. P. Sommerville, *Politics and Ideology in England 1603–1640* (1986), 221; PRO SP 16/231/18 shows that at least 12 Peterborough livings had been alienated from the Crown since 1600; they included two of the most nonconformist parishes in the country: All Saints', Northampton and Patteshull. HLRO 1641 Jan 15/198; PRO SP 16/232/56. J. S. Hart *Justice upon Petition* (1991), 84–6.

[211] PRO C115 M 24/7772. Dean Potter was as critical of Elizabeth I's sacrilege, 'a national sin because confirmed by act of Parliament', *The Diary of Thomas Crosfield*, ed. F. S. Boas (1935), 74. For Laud's attempts to augment livings in impropriated hands see PRO SP 16/499/16ᵛ, 106–106ᵛ; *WWL* iii. 255.

[212] *WWL* vii. 376–7; *A Mirror of Christianity... the life and death of Alice Duchess Dudley* (1669); *Brief Memoirs of Nicholas Ferrar*, ed. Macdonough 144–5; G. W., *A Sermon at... All Saints, Worcester, June 3 1635* (1635), *epistle dedicatory*.

[213] LPL MS 943/347; Bodl. MS Smith 23/11–23; see Ch. 1. n. 95.

[214] Hill, *Economic Problems of the Church*; F. M. Heal, 'Economic Problems of the Clergy', in F. M. Heal and R. O'Day (eds.), *Church and Society in England, Henry VIII to James I* (1977), 99–119; F. M. Heal, 'Archbishop Laud Revisited', in F. M. Heal and R. O'Day (eds.), *Princes and Paupers in the English Church* (Leicester 1981), 129–42; *WWL* vi. 307–8.

'I find one great complaint, and very fit to be redressed. It is the great grievance of the poor vicars, that their stipends are scarce able to feed and clothe them.' Only when the Church had recovered its material strength did Laud believe that the problem of nonconformity would decrease.[215] It is no surprise therefore to find that the 'Considerations' called for the return to the Church of all former church lands and impropriations. Those who had purchased property in the past were to be content with leases only and to pay to the Church an annual rent. If this was unrealistic, Laud suggested that Charles should confirm the lay inheritance but that the Church rather than the Crown should receive rent, a rent based upon a new evaluation of wealth instead of the dated *Valor Ecclesiasticus*. The Crown should relinquish all clerical tenths to the bishops and receive instead the episcopal tenths. Ecclesiastical bodies which leased their own property to the nobility and gentry were not to renew any leases once they lapsed. Provision should be made through statute so that the minister within the impropriated living should receive at least half of the tithes and profits of the place, while the other half should go to the ecclesiastical body to which the living was appropriated, with a view to improving low clerical stipends. Laud also invited the king to barter with the nobility when granting them favours or pardons, in order to achieve a suitable maintenance for clergy on livings within their hands. Such far-reaching proposals naturally had implications for impropriations in royal hands also and Laud invited the king not to grant or alienate any further livings within his gift.[216] The clear invitation was for the king as well as the laity to return impropriations to the Church, a scheme partially successful in that during 1635 Laud, supported by Wentworth and Ussher, secured from Charles the return of the Crown's impropriations in Ireland.[217] However, the practical obstacles to the realization of many of these far-reaching proposals were enormous and the 'Considerations' remained an aspect of Laudianism which never was. Had they been realized, if only partially, then Charles I would have occasioned the greatest threat to secularized property since Mary I, and caused as much controversy as did his contemporary Ferdinand II in the ill-fated Edict of Restitution.[218]

[215] LPL MS 943/347. [216] LPL MS 943/347.
[217] *WWL* v. 327; *LJU* 459; Fuller, *CH* 426; *WWL* iv. 176; LPL MS 943/529.
[218] For the context of the Edict see G. Parker (ed.), *The Thirty Years War* (1984), 97–9, 111–18.

As it was, Laud's attempt to resolve the economic problems of the Church and to restrict prohibitions brought him into head-on collision with the apparatus and principles of common law. At the same time the archbishop's belief that the judiciary conspired to encroach upon the Church did not foster good relations. Laud clashed also with the common law because his legalism was more than a match for its own. But in this respect it is important to view the 1630s within their historical context. Abbot and Bancroft were as concerned as Laud to protect the Church's rights from legal encroachment, although the extraordinary consistorial activity of the 1630s considerably aggravated mutual animosity.[219]

By late 1640, then, Laud had ranged against him a powerful opposition of common lawyers, civil lawyers (whose rights, as Chapter 7 shows, were eroded in the Canons of 1640),[220] and many of the gentry and nobility, who had been humiliated by clergy bent on advertising their new professional confidence, reasserting their prescriptive rights, and impressing carolinism. Perhaps it goes almost without saying, therefore, that contemporaries were struck not by the discovery of a new-found freedom of the will, but by a general fear that they were returning to the bondage of an ecclesiastical tyranny. Thus the most disturbing doctrinal influence for the Protestants of early seventeenth-century England was not the rise of Arminian ideas of free will but the revival of patristic and scholastic doctrines of the Church. Well might Heylyn call Laud the English Cyprian, after the Father who had suffered for striving to attain the unity of the Church under the aegis of episcopacy.[221]

219 Hill, *Economic Problems of the Church*, 280–8, 124, 131; PRO SP 16/474/68 for Sir John Lambe's analysis of how the common law had encroached upon the Church; *WWL* vi. 310: 'as for the Church it is so bound up in the forms of the common law that it is not possible for me, or for any man, to do that good which he would, or is bound to do' (Laud); Sommerville, *Politics and Ideology*, 221.

220 See Ch. 7 section iii.

221 Johannes Quasten, *Patrology*, 4 vols. (Utrecht, 1986), ii. 340–3, 374–5.

3

ARMINIANISM

> For that Christ died for all men is the universal and constant doctrine of the Catholic Church in all ages, and no 'error' of Arminius: and are the express words of Scripture itself, in more places than one. And the Synod of Dort, called principally about the errors of Arminius, allows this for orthodox; '*Christum mortuum esse pro omnibus*'.
>
> (Laud, *WWL* iii. 304–5.)

I. DOCTRINAL ARMINIANISM OR DOCTRINAL PURITANISM?

In his preface to the *Treatise of Liberty and Necessity*, Thomas Hobbes remonstrated with those of his contemporaries who sought the origins of the English Revolution in doctrinal issues. As 'good lawful diversions for the duller sort of citizens who contract disease for want of motion', they inhibited the study of what he considered to be the true causes of the crisis.[1] Today if Hobbes were to return, he would still find doctrinal debate bedevilling historians of the early seventeenth century.[2] Although English Arminianism has a respectable pedigree in Stuart historiography, only in recent years has it come to the front stage.[3] Dr Tyacke took up the threads of a well-worn theme and

[1] *The English Works of Thomas Hobbes*, ed. Sir William Molesworth, 11 vols. (1840), iv. 233.

[2] See for example the exchanges in *Past and Present*: P. White, 'The Rise of Arminianism Reconsidered', 101 (1983), 34–54; W. Lamont, 'The Rise of Arminianism Reconsidered', 107 (1988), 227–32; P. Lake, 'Calvinism and the English Church, 1570–1635', 114 (1987), 32–77; N. Tyacke, 'The Rise of Arminianism Reconsidered' and P. White, 'A Rejoinder', 115 (1987), 201–29. The best review of Tyacke's work is Anthony Milton's in the *Journal of Ecclesiastical History*, 39/4 (1988), 613–16. For the five Articles: P. Schaff, *The Creeds of the Evangelical Protestant Churches* (1877), 549.

[3] C. V. Wedgwood, *The King's Peace* (1955), 90; Clarendon, i. 123–4; G. Davies, 'Arminian versus Puritan in England, c. 1620–1640', *Huntington Library Bulletin*, 5 (1934); J. W. Allen, *English Political Thought 1603–1644* (1938), 159–60; H. C. Porter, *Reform and Reaction in Tudor Cambridge* (Camb., 1958), 281, 330; G. Cragg,

worked them into a new synthesis which went further than describing the rise of Arminianism. He suggested that under the patronage of Charles I, Laud and his Arminian disciples were able to secure power at the centre and outlaw the Calvinism of the majority, thus effectively bringing to an end the Jacobean consensus which had bound together in one Church those of widely divergent views. Then during the 1630s the king and Laud embarked upon a programme of 'Arminianization' in the Church as Arminian doctrine expressed itself in the ecclesiological and sacramental innovations of the 1630s.[4] Thus for revisionist historiography, religion was a factor in the Civil War not because of the rise of Puritanism but because of the rise of Arminianism.[5] With the revision of traditional Whig historiography, this thesis offered itself as a convenient explanation of the crisis of the 1640s. In consequence few words have been bandied about with such indiscriminate and frequent application as 'Arminian' or 'Arminianism'. In fact the situation envisaged by Francis Rous of Arminians multiplying spawn upon spawn has veritably come to pass.[6]

This revisionism is a salutary corrective to traditional historiography in that it has helped to restore religious values to our perception of the past, has served to reinterpret Puritanism, and has aided the unmasking of the remarkable institution that was the Jacobean Church.[7] Nevertheless the thesis of a rise of Arminianism is to be criticized not least because, as an explanation for the problems of the Stuart monarchy, it is as reductionist as the thesis of the rise of Puritanism which it has attempted to displace. The first and obvious question one needs to ask is whether Arminianism had to rise within

Freedom and Authority (Philadelphia, 1975), ch. 4; T. M. Parker, 'Arminianism and Laudianism in Seventeenth Century England', in C. Dugmore and C. Duggan (eds.), *Studies in Church History* (1964).

[4] Tyacke, *AC*; and his, 'Puritanism, Arminianism and Counter-Revolution', in C. S. R. Russell (ed.), *The Origins of the English Civil War* (1973), 119–43.

[5] Tyacke, 'Puritanism, Arminianism and Counter-Revolution', 132.

[6] *Commons Debates for 1629*, ed. W. Notestein (Minneapolis, 1921), 12–15; Tyacke, *AC*, *passim* which employs the word very loosely throughout; C. S. R. Russell, *The Crisis of Parliaments* (Oxford, 1971), 216–17; A. Fletcher, *A County Community in Peace and War: Sussex 1600–1660* (1975), 74–94; A. G. R. Smith, *The Emergence of a Nation State* (1984), 282, 289; A. Foster, 'Church Policies of the 1630s', in R. Cust and A. Hughes (eds.), *Conflict in Early Stuart England: Studies in Religion and Politics 1603–1642* (1989), 193–224; D. MacCulloch, 'Arminius and the Arminians', *History Today*, 39 (Oct. 1989), 33; S. Doran and C. Durston (eds.), *Princes, Pastors and People: The Church and Religion in England 1529–1689* (1991), 196.

[7] The works of Patrick Collinson; Kenneth Fincham; Peter Lake; John Morrill; and Kenneth Parker (all listed in the bibliography) in particular. For the contribution of literary historians see Ch. 1 n. 10.

what is seen as an unquestionably Calvinist Church? The reformed Church of England, like its Calvinist and Lutheran neighbours on the continent, was not a gathered Church of the elect but a community with multifarious doctrinal views. The work of Kenneth Parker has seriously questioned Tyacke's notion that a specifically Calvinist doctrinal consensus existed in Jacobean England, by showing that Calvinist doctrine did not underwrite the sabbatarian doctrines shared by hierarchy and Puritan alike. Moreover, the practice of divinity was often far removed from its doctrine. Sir Robert Harley once said of Lord Herbert of Cherbury that 'my lordship loves a puritan but hates a predestinator'. It was quite possible to believe in one's eternal election without translating that belief into a concrete, systematic doctrine of predestination. In other words it was possible to be reformed in Jacobean England without being Calvinist.[8] Certain ideas, which in retrospect can be seen as formative in the later development of a fully ingrained Arminian theology within the eighteenth century, were implicit if not explicit in both the Elizabethan and Jacobean Church, and their successor. They should not be traced to Erasmianism (where Trevor-Roper has located them) since Erasmian ideas are incompatible with a strongly scholastic and fideistic Arminian theology. Rather their origin can be found in the pastoral problem implicit in the reconciliation of free evangelical grace with a rigidly predestinarian theology, a problem which increased across Europe as Calvinist theology was placed on the defensive and required to rationalize its doctrine in the last quarter of the sixteenth century. This was a problem in England during the 1620s and 1630s, but as the thrust of this work suggests, a far greater problem was that of reconciling Anglican free grace with the restrictions of an increasingly authoritarian doctrine of the Church, which placed the evangelical promise under constraint. This is why English Arminianism did not come into its own until after the overthrow of Caroline censorship and why it never developed into the coherent theology which appeared in the Netherlands. It comes as little surprise, therefore, that in contemporary English works Arminianism attained far less importance than in the works of present-day historians.[9]

[8] Parker, *ES* 178; *HMC Portland iii*, 30; Lake, 'Protestants, Puritans and Laudians', 618 ff.

[9] Porter, *Reform and Reaction* chs. 15–17; O. O'Donovan, *On The Thirty-Nine Articles: A Conversation with Tudor Christianity* (1986); CCO 288/364–5. H. R. Trevor-Roper, *Catholics, Anglicans and Puritans* (1987); R. T. Kendall, *Calvin and English Calvinism to 1649* (Oxford, 1979).

In the list of doctrinal innovations drawn up by Williams and Ussher for the committee of religion in 1641, out of eighteen points, only the thirteenth explicitly mentioned Arminianism, and only one other, the fourteenth, can be construed as referring to any of the five Arminian heads. The other doctrinal innovations concerned popery, Socinianism, and other heterodox ideas. The committee carefully discriminated between what they considered to be points of popish doctrine and points of Arminianism. None of these popish doctrines are necessarily consequential to an 'Arminianization' of the Church but to its catholicization in its widest, patristic sense. Clearly those who sat on the committee for religion believed that there existed a doctrinal and ecclesiological explanation for what had occurred during the previous twenty years which was more embracing than doctrines of free will. Unlike some of their contemporaries, they certainly did not conflate Arminianism with ecclesiological issues, as they singled out separate innovations in discipline.[10] In fact when the Short Parliament met in 1640 there was little talk of 'Arminian' policies or of 'Arminian' doctrine. The perception of Arminianism in the 1620s had succumbed to the perception of popery, and a whole variety of heterodox ideas. The accusations of 'Arminianism' continued in occasional petitions and in some of the sessions of the 1640s, but they were insignificant when compared to the anxieties about popery and other doctrinal innovations.[11] In fact it is not going too far to suggest that 'Arminianism' as perceived by Parliament in the 1620s was to all intents and purposes a dead letter by 1640. It had certainly played a part in 1629, the first occasion when, according to Professor Russell, more than just a minority of members perceived it. The reason why 'Arminianism' attained significance in 1629 lies less in the doctrinal issue *per se* than in its perceived connections with the subversion of the Church, Commonwealth, and property rights.[12] 'Arminianism' was looked upon as a bridge to popery of which Neile and Weston were the architects. A connection was made with facility between an attack on Calvinist predestination and the growth of ritualism on the one hand, and the undermining of property rights on the other, a conflation occasioned by the concurrency of the liturgical

[10] Bodl. Eng. misc. c. 92/39.

[11] *The Short Parliament Diary of Sir Thomas Aston*, ed. J. D. Maltby (Camden, 4th ser., 1988).

[12] C. S. R. Russell, *Parliaments and English Politics 1621–1629* (Oxf., 1979), 31, 207, 233, 298, 345, 396–404, 415–16.

practices of the Durham House circle with the king's sponsorship of arbitrary views of kingship. Laud was accused of 'arminianism' in the Remonstrance not because of any overt doctrinal statement on his part but because he was believed (incorrectly) to have licensed the sermons of Sibthorpe and Mainwaring, which justified arbitrary taxation.[13] Members conveniently chose not to accuse Harsnett of Arminianism, doubtless because he had supported the Petition of Right and had risen to power outside the entourage of Buckingham or Neile.[14] Nevertheless, to recognize that the parliamentary perception of Arminianism fluctuated a good deal according to the political index is not to deny the sincerity with which a few members, including Pym and Harley, appreciated the doctrinal credentials of Arminianism.[15]

The Lords may have been more doctrinally illiterate than their neighbours in the Commons if the York House debates which several of them attended are taken as representative.[16] Certainly most did not participate in the theological gymnastics and the game of doctrinal divide and rule, cherished by the likes of Warwick and Saye, who had sponsored the meetings under Buckingham's auspices. Their failure to condemn Montagu as an Arminian stemmed directly from the fact that other peers present did not perceive the issue in such clearly defined terms. When, during the first conference, Saye, supported by Coke, Secretary of State, suggested that the conclusions of the Synod of Dort should be introduced to prevent future Montagus from misinterpreting the articles of religion, Carlisle and Pembroke quickly retorted that the Synod's doctrine was binding only to those who had 'submitted themselves' to it.[17] Pembroke thought that Morton had gone too far in his objections to Montagu, exclaiming that it was a 'marvellous thing to me to hear Mr. Montagu accused for popery in saying that a man made just by the grace of God, through faith is also declared to be just by his holy life and conversation'.[18] With a measure of self-interested social reserve the

13 Ibid. 396, 404, 415–16; Bodl. Tanner MS 72/329, Bodl. MS Eng. hist. d. 222/20 Jan. 1629; Ch. 1 section iii.

14 Russell, *Parliaments and English Politics*, 31; Bodl. MS Rawl. A 441/28.

15 Russell, *Parliaments and English Politics*, 29–32, 404; Tyacke, *AC* 125–63.

16 T. Ball, *The Life of... Dr Preston*, ed. E. W. Harcourt (Oxf., 1885), 126–30; *WJC* ii. 17–71. For a recent treatment see B. Donagan, 'The York House Conference Revisited: Laymen, Calvinism and Arminianism', *Bulletin of (Institute of) Historical Research*, 64/155 (Oct. 1991), 312–31.

17 *WJC* ii. 65, 63–4.

18 *WJC* ii. 49.

earls identified the Calvinist opinion that the elect remained justified even in sin as 'most pernicious' and 'unfit for any people to hear'.[19] According to Cosin, those peers who attended the second conference a few weeks later were also unconvinced (with the exception of Warwick and Saye) by the bishop's criticism of Montagu's ideas.[20] Even if we accept that Cosin's account is the most biased narrative of the York House meetings, it reveals conclusively enough that the peers differed in their opinions about Montagu, and sometimes appeared vague and confused about the subtleties of the doctrinal points in contention. Perhaps this explains why two years later in 1628 Jackson dedicated his near-arminian treatise to Pembroke.[21] Doubtless, for many across the social spectrum the doctrinal debate lacked any relevance at all, as Dean Potter believed.[22] Certainly the application of Arminianism could be as loose and as indiscriminate as other terms of denomination or abuse. An alteration might be perceived and then without much comprehension identified with a current label, which according to the parishioners of Holdcastle (Lincoln) in 1640 was 'Ormianism'.[23]

During the 1630s some ministers took the opportunity to preach fully-fledged Arminianism, and the advocates of true doctrinal Arminianism were possibly greater than the small figures collected by Dr Tyacke on the basis of surviving depositions.[24] Yet for many clergy the perception of an Arminian–Calvinist division was not the perception of a simple Weberian polarity between grace and predestination. All divines ostensibly accepted predestination as biblical teaching and as rooted in the articles. As Sir Dudley Digges said, 'it seems that the arminians do all agree on the article but the difference is on the sense of it.'[25] The question was not whether there was predestination, but 'when' decreed and in what way, not whether there was a decree, but whether it was absolute or conditional, dependent on the foresight of faith or not. It was less predestination

19 *WJC* ii. 58–9. 20 *WJC* ii. 74.

21 T. Jackson, *A Treatise of Divine Essence and Attributes* (1628), epistle dedicatory.

22 *Dr Potter's Vindication of Himself... 1629* (1651). Nor should we forget that even noted reformed ministers such as Robert Jennison and Paul Micklewaite sought clarification on the doctrinal subtleties in question: Bodl. Tanner MS 72/294. Micklewaite consulted Ward, Brownrigg, Sanderson, Laney, and Cotton of Boston: Bodl. Tanner MS 71/53.

23 J. Walker, *The Sufferings of the Clergy* (1714), i. 93.

24 Tyacke, *AC* 188–99; Bodl. MS Carte 103/62–5; SRO D/D/Ca 282/236.

25 *Commons Debates for 1629*, ed. Notestein, 122.

per se which was attacked than predestination to reprobation (which was not necessarily synonymous with Calvinist doctrine and certainly alien to Augustinian doctrine).[26] As the articles of religion espoused single predestinarianism rather than rigid or double predestinarianism, and as there existed no systematic plan of predestination laid out for human eyes, it was possible to reach a position extraneous to the main Calvinist or Arminian systems, while agreeing in part with them both.[27] In this way Sanderson in *Pax Ecclesiae* and Playfer in *Appello Evangelium* bypassed the alternative schemata, evolving their own doctrines of predestination and advertising them as consistent with the confession of the Church of England.[28]

The difficulty in perceiving a clear Arminian–Calvinist division among the clergy was furthered by the existence of certain Calvinist sublapsarians who subscribed to hypothetical universalism: that Christ had died for the sins of the whole world, even if the divine decree of predestination was efficacious for the elect alone.[29] Within this category fell those Calvinists who were influenced most probably by Overall's teaching: Lake of Bath and Wells, Davenant of Salisbury, Hall of Exeter, Ussher of Armagh, and Samuel Ward.[30] To some of their contemporaries their position looked analogous to the Arminian view of grace. As early as 1617, Ussher, a Calvinist of impeccable hue, was slandered with the charge of Arminianism.[31] That Calvinists might hold neither an exclusive nor a monolithic position on the wider doctrines of authority, the Church, and the sacraments (in particular baptism) meant that some of them might be accused of Arminian heterodoxy, as was Joseph Hall, formerly one of the delegates at Dort. In his *Old Religion* of 1627, he asserted

26 A. McGrath, 'Reformation to Enlightenment' in P. Avis (ed.), *The Science of Theology*, (1986), 157–8; Kendall, *Calvin and English Calvinism to 1649*, 13–42; and for a reply, P. Helm, *Calvin and the Calvinists* (Edinburgh, 1982). Calvin, *Institutes* 3, i. 1.

27 O'Donovan, *On The Thirty-Nine Articles*, 85.

28 J. Playfer, *Appello Evangelium* (1652); CCO MS D288/358; BL Add. MS 5783; Bodl. Rawl. MS A 419, C 167.

29 J. E. Platt, 'Eirenical Anglicans at the Synod of Dort', *Reform and the Reformation: England and the Continent c. 1500–1750*, ed. D. Baker (Oxford, 1979); see also Richard Sibbes' introduction to Paul Baynes's *Commentary on the First Chapter of Ephesians* (1618).

30 Playfer, *Appello Evangelium* (1652) 'third opinion'; *LJU* 49–51; *WRS* v. 308; M. Fuller, *The Life, Letters and Writings of John Davenant* (1897), 221; Bodl. MS Tanner 71/148, Tanner 80/137. For their differences with others, in particular Twiss over predestinarian issues see Bodl. Tanner MS 71/146–8.

31 *LJU* 49.

that Rome was a true Church, without sufficiently explaining his definition of truth.[32] Consequently, in answer to the accusations of Burton and others, he had to write both the *Apologetical Advertisement* and the *Reconciler* in order to vindicate himself from the charge of Arminianism.[33]

Perhaps because they were more doctrinally sensitive than their lay contemporaries, the clergy appear to have been reluctant to accuse fellow clerics of Arminianism. They realized that however near a doctrinal opinion was to Arminianism it had an indigenous growth in England and stemmed from a possible construction or misconstruction of the articles. John Goodwin, certainly among the most doctrinally literate of clerics, doubted whether those called Arminians by their contemporaries were such, and suggested that if any adopted Arminian tenets, it was less for doctrinal reasons than because they wished to unseat the likes of Abbot and alter the course of the Jacobean Church.[34] Thus Goodwin would agree with Collinson but not with Tyacke. Another seventeenth-century commentator, John Walker, believed that 'few or none' of the so-called English Arminians 'held in all the points of it'.[35]

Neile's defence, drawn up in 1629, reveals that although he might patronize anti-Calvinists, personally he had good grounds for rejecting the accusation of Arminianism.[36] Reprobation he believed was merely *non eligere*, while faith, repentance, and obedience were the effects of election, not its cause, views which were decidedly not Arminian. As Burghley's chaplain thirty-five years earlier, he had written against Baro's contention that God elected on account of foreseen faith. As for the issue of falling from grace, this he had never determined, but believed, that in the end the elect could never fall; if they sinned God would restore them by faith and repentance.[37] Thus Neile was not an Arminian, but at most an anti-Calvinist. Others such as Christopher Potter, dean of Worcester, resolved 'never to be an Arminian and ever to be moderate . . . to stand fast in that liberty . . . I love Calvin very well and I must tell you I cannot hate Arminius'.[38]

32 *WJH* viii. 631–718; Fuller, *John Davenant*, 243–6.

33 *WJH* viii. 719–57; vol. i, p. xlv.

34 J. Goodwin, *Redemption Redeemed* (1651), 170–1. I owe this reference to the kindness of Miss Elaine Walker.

35 Walker, *Sufferings of the Clergy*, i. 42.

36 DCL MS Hunter 67/14.

37 DCL Hunter 67/14.

38 C. Potter, *Vindication of Himself . . . 1629* (1651), 2.

Some who received preferment from Neile might edge in some respects towards Arminianism, as Dr Tyacke shows, yet to call even these Arminians does not do justice to the eclecticism of their views.[39] In spite of Montagu's near-arminian views on foreseen faith and falling from grace, Hall (one of the English delegates at Dort) confessed that he personally did not think that Montagu was Arminian, finding that 'mistaking was more guilty of this dissension than misbelieving... it plainly appeared to me, that Montagu meant to express not Arminius but Bishop Overall, a more moderate and safe author.'[40] Overall had in fact been the former patron of both Montagu and Cosin. To prove his thesis, Hall wrote the *Via Media*, for 'I desired to rectify the judgement of men concerning this misapprehended controversy showing them the true party in this unseasonable plea.' Since Overall went 'a midway between these two opinions which he held extreme, and must needs therefore somewhat differ from the continually received tenet, in that point', Hall gathered from Overall and the English delegates at Dort 'such common propositions concerning these five busy articles as wherein both of them are fully agreed'.[41] Given that a distinguished Calvinist did not perceive the controversy in terms of a simplistic polarity between Arminian and Calvinist it seems incongruous for historians to visualize doctrinal positions in terms of opposed camps. It is even more incongruous for them to do so when examining the very eclectic doctrinal position of Laud.

'I have nothing to do to defend Arminianism, no man having yet charged me with the abetting any point of it,' Laud testified during his trial.[42] Laud was clearly not referring to the charge made against him in the Commons Remonstrance of 1629, which resulted in both Neile and Laud protesting their innocence before the Privy Council and the king, and declaring 'that they hated such opinions'.[43] Although some contemporaries were sceptical of this renunciation, there appear to have been sound grounds for Laud's rejection of the charge. The evidence adduced for Laud's doctrine is certainly insufficient to indict him of Arminianism. Rather it places his position on the five points somewhere between the poles of Arminianism and Calvinism. That Laud should urge Vossius to publish a revised

[39] Tyacke, *AC* 106–24.

[40] *WJH* i, pp. xliii–xliv, which implicitly questions Professor Collinson's assertion that Hall saw an Arminian threat to the Church of England in 1626; *TLS* 489 (13 May 1983) and *RP* 90.

[41] *WJH* ix. 488–519; i, pp. xliii–xliv.

[42] *WWL* iv. 267. [43] Birch, i. 439.

edition of his *History of Pelagianism* clearly indicates a dislike of rigid predestinarianism, as the purpose of the work was to show 'that there was a great difference between a reasonable view of the free-will of man, which the Church had never condemned, and extreme views of human independence which set at nought the grace of God'.[44] On the same account it clears him of Arminianism. Vossius, according to Montagu's opponent, Carleton, was wrongly traduced for Arminianism, he being 'no arminian but a very honest man'. In fact the Dutch allowed him a professorship at Leyden, a bastion of Calvinist orthodoxy, while in his last work, *De Scriptoribus Latinis*, he reiterated an Augustinian position on predestination.[45]

Among other evidence cited for Laud's Arminianism is the letter concerning Montagu's opinions, the Lambeth Articles, and the Synod of Dort, which he sent to Buckingham in August 1625. Yet the fact is invariably ignored that in this letter, Laud distinguished between predestination to election and predestination to reprobation: those doctrines of Dort and Lambeth which were 'fatal' (i.e., reprobation) and contrary to Montagu's opinions, and those which were not (i.e., election).[46] In his *History* Laud likened his doctrinal position on two of the five points, to that held by James I at the Hampton Court Conference. On the issue of perseverance, the king had determined that 'we may often depart from grace' without determining 'totally' or 'finally', but 'wished that... doctrine... handled... with great discretion lest on the one side God's omnipotency be called in question by impeaching the doctrine of His eternal predestination; or on the other... a desperate presumption... by inferring the necessary certainty of standing and persisting in grace'.[47] But elsewhere Laud was more explicit, asserting that while the elect might fall they would not do so finally. Thus he could personally affirm Calvin's tenet '*renatos... non posse per finalem impoenitentiam cadere... et hoc verum est*'. This was a far more moderate and orthodox position than Montagu's.[48]

[44] G. Vossius, *Historiae de controversiis quas Pelagius ejusque reliquiae moverunt* (1618); Bodl. Tanner MS 314/55.
[45] *Dr Potter His Vindication of Himself... 1629.*
[46] *WWL* vi. 244–6. For the controversy surrounding the Lambeth Articles see Porter, *Reform and Reaction*, 314–40; P. Lake, *Moderate Puritans and the Elizabethan Church* (Camb., 1982), 209–26.
[47] *WWL* iv. 267, 453, 267–8; R. G. Usher, *The Reconstruction of the English Church*, 2 vols. (New York, 1910), ii. 344–5.
[48] *WWL* vi. 704.

As for the question of the irresistibility of grace, Laud believed that although man had the will to resist grace, yet if God so wished he could bestow a grace so powerful that man would not resist. In reply to Bellarmine's assertion that '*potest ille libere gratiam repudiare, sed certum est non repudiaturum*', Laud wrote, '*possum libere si volo; et tamen certum est me non velle; simul stare possunt*'.[49] The same notes reveal that Laud had believed in predestination to election, which he later described in a sermon of 1626 as one of the fundamental points of divinity.[50] But such a predestination was not inconsistent with human responsibility under God: 'let every man that calls on the name of Christ, depart from iniquity. If he do not that, he is not Christ's; let him talk of predestination while he will.'[51] Such evidence is enough to place Laud within a broad Augustinian tradition, a moderate position that adhered to single predestination to election but one which regarded as anathema the notion that God actively predestines some to reprobation. For Laud this was nothing better than a philosophical intrusion upon orthodox divinity, for the 'question is not here what God may do by an absolute act of power would he so use it upon the creature which he made of nothing but what he hath done, and what stands with his wisdom, justice and goodness to do'.[52] In the last resort an over-scrupulous inquest into the divine decrees was inadvisable, for, as he told Wentworth in 1636, the 'truth whatsoever it be [with relation to predestination] is not determinable by any human reason in this life. And therefore [it] were far better . . . to be referred up to the next general known truth in which men might rest, than to distract their conscience and the peace of the Church, by descending into interminable particulars.'[53] Thus Laud had no 'arminian' confidence in man's nature or in his innate ability.

It has been suggested that when Laud used the terms 'orthodox' and 'puritan' he meant respectively 'Arminian' and 'Calvinist', enabling him to overturn the Calvinist orthodoxy of the Church, and smearing Calvinist conformists with the taint of Puritanism.[54] In 1625 Buckingham asked Laud to draw up a list of clergy denoted by 'o' and 'p', representing, it is assumed orthodox and Puritan, so that Charles I could promote only Arminians.[55] Yet if orthodox means Arminian here then it makes the preferment of Calvinists after 1625

[49] *WWL* vi. 699; PRO SP 16/4/20. [50] *WWL* i. 130; vi. 607–708.
[51] *WWL* i. 131. [52] *WWL* vi. 133. [53] *WWL* vii. 275.
[54] Tyacke, *AC* 167 ff. [55] *WWL* iii. 159.

inexplicable. Whatever the term 'orthodox' meant, it clearly comprehended some Calvinists as well, as the criterion for preferment after 1625 lay not so much in a particular doctrinal position, as in an ideal of churchmanship. After all, no Calvinist was promoted during the 1630s solely for his doctrine. In 1641 when Saye and Sele accused Laud of promoting only those who held the same doctrinal opinions as himself, Laud showed how he had helped the preferment of 'many . . . who yet went not with them which my Lord will needs miscall my party'.[56]

Only at the cost of the greatest distortion can divines be placed within closed categories of Arminian and Calvinist. Moreover patronage connexions would have transcended such clear lines of demarcation had they in fact existed. Heylyn, an Arminian, for example, was originally affiliated to the Winchester–Wells axis outlined by Professor Collinson. He regarded Arthur Lake as a father of the Church and travelled all the way from Burford to Wells to receive from him 'fatherly benediction, devout prayers' and confirmation.[57] Dean Young, another member of this connexion, was Heylyn's 'dear friend' and one of the first men at court to introduce him to Charles, then prince of Wales.[58] On the other side of the spectrum, Bishop Morton, the most prominent Calvinist determinist on the episcopal bench and Montagu's main opponent at York House, was Cosin's foremost patron during the 1630s. In July 1639 he wrote to Laud asking that Cosin, then Master of Peterhouse, be preferred to higher office. Over a year later, Charles I, who had 'a very good opinion of him', elevated him to the deanery of Peterborough.[59] It is not a little incongruous, therefore, to see both Cosin and Heylyn as among the most important scions of the same 'arminian faction'. At the same time serious rifts might exist between 'arminians' not least within the Durnam House circle itself, most notably between Neile, Howson, and Cosin.[60]

In the light of much recent historiography it would be naïve to suggest that many Calvinists were promoted during the 1630s. Yet the conclusion is as inescapable as it is unconventional: James I possibly

[56] *WWL* vi. 92. [57] Collinson, *RP* 85; Heylyn, *CA* 159.

[58] Barnard, *TH* 94; Heylyn's main patrons were the earls of Danby and Ancram: G. Vernon, *The Life of Heylyn* (1682), 35–6.

[59] DPD Mickleton and Spearman MS 20/11; also DPD Cosin Letter Book 1A/27. Cosin became a chaplain in ordinary only in April 1636 (PRO LC5/134/168). See also Bodl. Tanner MS 70/105; PRO SP 16/382/31.

[60] *CC* i. 200–10.

elevated more so-called 'Arminians' to the higher echelons of the Church than his successor. On the Caroline bench Skinner and Curle were orthodox in a very reformed sense as they were among the clergy who collected over fifty doctrinal errors within contemporary works for the committee of religion.[61] Others such as Piers, Howson, Duppa, Warner, and Williams had good Calvinist credentials although they belonged to a more liberal reformed tradition than Hall, Davenant, and Morton,[62] who, according to Montagu, were the only bishops 'violently bent against' Rome.[63] Even Mainwaring spent time delineating and recording the ways of providence in the world.[64]

Given the salient criteria conditioning preferment to the higher echelons during the reign, the episcopal appointments of 1640–1 appear less surprising, although they are usually depicted in terms of a Calvinist reaction.[65] The king would not overtly offend parliamentary susceptibilities by choosing bishops who did not appear to be doctrinally orthodox, but at the same time he would not elect nonconformists or those who were not royal chaplains. Perhaps what is most remarkable about these elections (in the light of historiography) is that overtly Calvinist chaplains were overlooked, such as Featley, Bargrave, Young, and Balcanquall. That Hacket was not selected suggests that Williams played little or no part in the elections. In fact the king consulted Juxon and drew up a provisional list of candidates before Nicholas, Secretary of State, advised him to fill the vacancies to strengthen the royal and episcopal voice in the Lords.[66] Nor can any of those selected be described fairly as 'anti-Laudian', since

[61] BL Harl. MS 6424/84.

[62] Tyacke, *AC*, 60; Bodl. MS Eng. Misc. MS fos. 49/24–24ᵛ; F. L. Huntley, *Jeremy Taylor and the Great Rebellion* (Michigan, 1970), 64, 76, 89, 91; NNRO Lee Warner MS 1/6; Bodl. MS Cherry 2/5; *WWL* iv. 297.

[63] J. Berington (ed.), *The Memoires of Gregorio Panzani* (Birmingham, 1793), 246. Montagu assured Panzani that all the other bishops were 'very moderate' in their attitude to Rome; two were 'almost catholic'—Goodman and Wright; G. Albion, *Charles I and the Court of Rome* (1935), 412–14.

[64] E. Yardley, *Menevia Sacra*, ed. F. Green (1927), 111; Walker, *Sufferings of the Clergy*, i. 42.

[65] C. S. R. Russell, *The Fall of the British Monarchies 1637–1642* (Oxford, 1991), 411–12, *et passim*.

[66] *The Memoirs of John Evelyn*, 2 vols., ed. W. Bray (1819), 21–2, 28, 31–2. These elections were made personally by Charles I who had already consulted with Juxon about the most suitable candidates before the Secretary of State, Nicholas, approached the king on September 1641 to fill the vacant sees. Hacket appears to have crossed the king on a number of occasions: BL Sloane MS 4177; *LPL* MS 1030/65–7; *Parentalia*, 45–7, 49–50.

all were implicated to some degree in the changes of the 1630s. Brownrigg had offered constructive bridge-building in the Convocation of 1640.[67] Winniffe, dean of St Paul's, and King, archdeacon of Colchester, were the authors of the original capitular order altering the position of the table at St Gregory's, while Westfield was Laud's appointee as archdeacon of St Alban's.[68] Prideaux was perhaps most out of tune with the developments of the Personal Rule, but he had lost some of his popularity during the 1630s over the sabbatarian question (with the help of Heylyn). Perhaps more important was his long-standing acquaintance with Laud, who had saved him from disgrace in 1631 through a timely intercession with the king.[69] Another of those selected, Richard Steward (who rejected Chichester, probably on the promise of the deanery of Westminster), was heavily implicated in the changes of the 1630s and had been slandered for 'Arminianism'.[70]

If 'orthodox' did not mean 'Arminian' in the 1630s, then what of its corollary. Was Calvinism a Puritan doctrine? In 1611 Archbishop Abbot wrote that 'such as you call puritans did never differ from the rest in any part of substance but about circumstances and ceremonies, and about the manner of ecclesiastical regiment'.[71] As mentioned earlier, historians in recent years have helped to uncover the reformed doctrinal consensus which bound together in one Church those of differing ecclesiological views,[72] and which meant that before the 1620s Puritanism rarely, if ever, had a doctrinal identification separate from the doctrine of the established Church.[73] According to Fuller, the identification of a Puritan doctrine was in the first place a Catholic ploy first popularized by Spalato and then adopted by Harsnett and others, not only to bring to an end the policy of occasional conformity tolerated within the Jacobean Church but also to de-Calvinize it.[74] As early as the Convocation of 1621 the term of abuse was circulating, when Robert Sanderson noticed the opposition to those who fetched 'within the company of this title of puritan all

[67] See p. 264.
[68] *DNB*; *WWL* iv. 297; Bodl. MS Walker c. 3/341.
[69] Vernon, *Life of Heylyn*, 63; Parker, *ES* 314–26; Bodl. MS Jones 17/309^{v}; *WWL* v. 165.
[70] *Memoirs of John Evelyn*, ii. 31–2; *CC* i. 228; Tyacke, *AC* 241.
[71] P. A. Welsby, *Archbishop Abbot: The Unwanted Archbishop* (1962), 25.
[72] Collinson, *RP*; Lake, *AP*; Tyacke, *AC*; Parker, *ES*.
[73] Lake, 'Puritan Identities', *Journal of Ecclesiastical History* 35/1 (1984), 112–23.
[74] Fuller, *CH* 418.

orthodox divines that oppose against their semi-pelagian ideas, of purpose to make sound truths odious and their own corrupt novelties more . . . plausible'.[75] Certainly the term puritan was sufficiently elastic for its user to bestow upon it whatever meaning he wished. But the extent to which anti-Calvinists invested it with a Calvinist connotation differed considerably in relation to their divergence from Calvinism. Moreover, as was pointed out earlier, the doctrinal consensus of the Jacobean Church was only in some respects Calvinist.[76]

Whereas Montagu and others may have included under Puritanism much of Calvinism, Laud invested it with far fewer Calvinist connotations. Among Laud's personal reasons for identifying doctrinal Puritanism lay a desire to return a compliment. In his Oxford days some Calvinists had called him a papist; he now retorted by smearing them with the name of puritan. According to Clarendon, 'as they accused him of popery because he held some doctrinal opinions, which they liked not, though they were nothing allied to popery, so he entertained too much prejudice to some persons, as if they were enemies to the discipline of the Church, because they concurred with Calvin in *some* doctrinal points.'[77] In December 1624 he drew up for the duke of Buckingham a scheme of 'doctrinal Puritanism' in ten heads. This has not survived, but a list of Brownism in ten heads, which Laud drew up when replying to Saye and Sele's allegations in 1640, has.[78] Although these doctrinal heads were probably not the same substantive points as those presented to Buckingham in 1624, they enable us to ascertain the extent to which Laud would have comprehended the doctrine of predestination within 'Brownism' and 'Puritanism'.

Among those Brownist beliefs which Laud isolated for condemnation were denial of Christ's descent into hell, denial of the universal catholic Church (belief in particular churches only); belief that the Church of England was antichristian; that Christ will live on earth and not depart again; and that it was sinful to use the Lord's Prayer as a prayer. Those doctrinal points within 'Brownism' which expressly concerned the doctrine of predestination were that God decrees some to reprobation (double predestination) and its corollary, that God is the author of sin and that he works everything in us,

[75] *WRS* ii. 32.

[76] Even Heylyn did not think Calvinism and Puritanism were equatable: Tyacke, *AC* 8.

[77] My italics. Clarendon, i. 121.

[78] *WWL* iii. 155–6; vi. 130–3.

including evil. The last point concerned an antinomianism attendant on an over-rigid notion of election; that it was unlawful to pray for forgiveness of sins after conversion and that the elect were saved without repentance.[79] These points constitute sufficient evidence that Laud comprehended within Brownism only double or rigid predestinarianism—predestination to reprobation—and its corollaries. Therefore for Laud single predestination to election, interpreted in a Calvinist sense (conditional upon it not being antinomian) could not be a 'Puritan' doctrine, as it was not even a Brownist doctrine, Brownism being a more radical position than Puritanism in the eyes of contemporaries. Even so Laud's designation of predestination to reprobation as a Brownist doctrine was extreme by any standards, and smeared a lot of conformist Anglicans, not least a few bishops, with the charge of heterodoxy. Predestination to election, however, was an orthodox tenet, affirmed in the articles and not something which Laud need associate with Calvin in particular, although among reformation theologians Calvin had highlighted it. Thus, as far as Laud is concerned, historians have smothered important doctrinal subtleties in interpreting his understanding of 'orthodox' as Arminian and 'Puritan' as Calvinist. Moreover Laud's notion of both doctrinal Puritanism and Brownism, as the above shows, accommodated doctrinal views not necessarily associated with predestinarianism.[80]

Clearly when attempting to define 'doctrinal Puritanism' as understood by Laud and others, the elasticity of the designation is all important. It might cover a whole range of reformed doctrinal issues, rather than specifically Calvinist doctrines which might be related or not, depending upon the perception of the beholder—doctrinal issues not just of predestination and grace, but of the Church, authority, and the sabbath. Laud's notion of doctrinal Puritanism, it should be remembered, covered *ten* doctrinal heads. Giles Widdowes gave a wide range of definitions for the 'schismaticall puritan'.[81] Even the central ideas of the Reformation might be called 'puritanical doctrine', as William Gyles called them, regarding all those who 'taught men to apply Christ to themselves' as heretics and schismatics.[82] Clearly, then, in the designation of 'Puritan doctrine' not

[79] *WWL* vi. 130–3. [80] Tyacke, *AC* 186.

[81] G. Widdowes, *The Schismaticall Puritan* (Oxford, 1631), 'the preface'.

[82] HLRO Pet./Dec. 1640/Scotherne *v.* Gyles of Elm and Emneth; Hacket, *SR* ii. 39: the 'good office of preaching, performed often by a bishop was called Puritanism

only Calvinist election might be smeared but even the evangelical doctrine of salvation. Although the definition of an identifiably Puritan doctrine is not a sufficient explanation for the reaction against Jacobean Puritanism it was bound to intensify it. In an apology written to a friend at court clearing himself from the aspersions of Puritanism, Hall of Exeter distinguished between 'traditional' and 'modern' Puritanism. Before, Puritanism was understood only as a refractory opposition to the government, rites and customs of the Church but now some were identifying a 'modern puritanism... more subtle than in former times, and that under the colour of a full outward conformity, there may be nourished some unquiet and pestillent humours which may closely work danger to the churches peace'.[83] While Dr Tyacke may have overestimated the importance both of Arminian doctrine and anti-Calvinism in the 1630s, he is certainly correct to underline the significance of marking out a separate doctrinal Puritanism (if incorrect to equate this with Calvinism).[84] It implicated those who were tolerant of nonconformity within the Church with the stigma of disaffection and widened the climate of treason.[85] This in its own turn served to heighten anti-Puritan invective, and to reinforce Charles I's armoury against Jacobean Anglicanism.

II. THE MONTAGU CASE

The importance of the Montagu case was that for the first time, the Crown was seen to redefine Puritanism as a doctrinal system.[86] For much of his reign James I had contained a good many of the tensions implicit within Protestantism by defining Puritanism only in terms of nonconformity to matters of discipline and ceremonies.[87] At the same

by some in those times... that made the name of Puritan the very inquisition of England'; H. Parker, *A Discourse Concerning Puritans* (1641): 'If any preach constantly twice a Sabbath, this is enough to make him accounted a puritan,' J. Geree, *The Downfall of Antichrist and the Power of Preaching to pull down popery* (1641).

[83] SRO DD/PH 221/40.

[84] Tyacke, *AC* 7–8, 184–5, *et passim*.

[85] PRO SP 16/177/8; Jackson, *A Treatise of Divine Essence*, epistle dedicatory; Birch, i. 408.

[86] K. Fincham and P. Lake, 'The Ecclesiastical Policy of James I', *Journal of British Studies*, 24 (1985), 202–7.

[87] Ibid. 169–207.

time he promoted to the higher echelons of the Church many reformed Protestants who shared a common doctrinal base with Puritan nonconformists and who were not keen to unbalance the Jacobean religious settlement by forcing contentious ecclesiological issues.[88] This religious peace was placed in question by the European conflagration of the Thirty Years War. The wave of controversial, largely anti-Catholic preaching attendant on the announcement of the Spanish marriage plans and James's increasing overtures to Roman Catholicism (policies designed to achieve a cessation of hostilities and to prevent England's entry to war) resurrected the king's latent fear of Puritanism and its subversive potential, which all too clearly revealed the weaknesses in his eirenic policies.[89] Thus after 1618 James may well have been more open to a redefinition of Puritanism which was more attuned to his present predicament. Concurrent with these developments, his doctrinal position may have become less overtly reformed as a result of the death of his confessor, James Montagu, and because of the emergence of a more extreme predestinarian position after the Synod of Dort.[90]

In two books, the *New Gagg* and *Appello Caesarem*, Richard Montagu, a royal chaplain, proceeded to exploit his master's predicament and to redefine Puritanism in terms of doctrine as well as nonconformity. In *New Gagg*, he reduced the doctrinal points separating the Church of England from Rome to eight, implying that certain reformed doctrines were beyond the pale of orthodoxy. As Drs Fincham and Lake have shown, the prescription was clear: if the Anglican Church was to retain any credible claim to apostolic catholicity and if James was to retain his position as a peacemaker in confessional struggles, then the king had to dissociate himself from a good deal of current reformed doctrine. He implied also that James could not hope to defuse the Puritan threat through the usual policy of incorporation, while at the same time maintaining a moderate and eirenic stand towards Rome. By the time of his death in March 1625, James was converted to Montagu's position, having read over *Appello Caesarem* and approved it for publication.[91]

The opposition of prominent clergy, in particular Archbishop

[88] Ibid.; Collinson, *RP* 1–2.
[89] Ibid. 198–207.
[90] Ibid. 207.
[91] Ibid.; *CC* i. 37, 24, 21. The king asked White to scrutinize the work: Bodl. MS Rawl. c. 573.

Abbot, to the king's policies led James increasingly to turn towards the advice and support of those who were committed to the restoration of catholic order with the Church, and who disliked the churchmanship typified by Abbot, regarding it as narrowly Protestant. Historians have identified among these an Arminian party whose existence enabled Montagu to find supporters at court in 1624 and helped to pave the way for the capture of the Church after 1625.[92] The problem is that the word 'Arminian' confuses more than it clarifies. As suggested above, the doctrinal position of the so-called, 'Arminians' is to be found within a spectrum ranging from moderate Calvinism to anti-Calvinism, rather than Arminian. To designate them as Arminians gives their doctrinal opinions a coherence lacking in the extant records, while to visualize a party overlooks those who stood outside Neile's Durham House circle but who possibly welcomed Abbot's predicament, such as Williams of Lincoln, Harsnett of Norwich, and Howson of Oxford.[93] Nor did they hold a monolithic position on governmental policy: while Neile was a vigorous proponent of the Spanish war, Andrewes was not.[94] Again, the ascendancy of these clergy was relative to the decline in importance of Abbot and the more overtly Protestant presence at court. In fact their patronage by James I did not lead to any significant preferment as he had already promoted them to major appointments within the Church before 1618. The only significant exception to this was Laud, who was elevated to St David's in 1621 at the promptings of Williams, Buckingham, and probably Charles.[95] James had finally forgiven Laud for his involvement in the Devon divorce case of 1605, which had so alienated the king that at the time he pledged never to advance Laud. According to Williams, the king 'was constrained often time to say that he (Laud) would never desire to serve that master, which could not remit one fault unto his servant'.[96]

The extent to which these clergy supported Montagu has certainly been exaggerated. Montagu's main protagonist was Richard Neile,

[92] Tyacke, *AC* 106–24, 8.

[93] Hacket, *SR* i. 63; C. Dent, *Protestant Reformers in Elizabethan Oxford* (1983), 209–10; 'John Howson's Answers', in *Camden Miscellany*, ed. N. R. N. Cranfield and K. Fincham (Camden, 4th ser., 29, 1987), 319–43; Fuller, *CH* 418; Bodl. MS Rawl. D. 1349/156; Bodl. MS Rawl. C 573); K. Fincham, *Prelate as Pastor: The Episcopate of James I* (Oxford, 1990), 278.

[94] Russell, *Parliaments and English Politics*, 163.

[95] Hacket, *SR* i. 63; see Ch. 1 section iii for preferment policy.

[96] Hacket, *SR* i. 64; Rushworth, i. 440.

clerk of the Closet and bishop of Durham, who carefully examined Montagu's works and smoothed their passage to James I for publication.[97] The others were far more cautious. Buckeridge of Rochester was 'ever . . . to hold the reins hard that I went not too quick', while White, later bishop of Carlisle, to whom James I officially delegated the task of examining *Appello Caesarem*, was 'timorous . . . by his crossing out and putting in somewhat'.[98] As for Laud, he consistently remained aloof from Montagu throughout James's reign. After all, he was Buckingham's not the king's protégé and on this account alone would be more inclined to stay alongside Charles in the last stages of the reign when 'reversionary interests' came into play and Charles fell out with his father.[99] Once Charles succeeded, his position would be assured, as was evidenced during 1626 when he succeeded Andrewes as dean of the Chapel, and was probably promised the clerkship of the Closet after Neile and the see of Canterbury after Abbot.[100] Initially Montagu received little support from Buckingham. In fact in October 1624 he asked Cosin to approach Laud (then in Buckingham's household) in order to attract the duke's attention: 'the bishop of St. David's must now and in such cases put for the Church with the duke and use his great credit that we be not swallowed up with a puritan episcopate.'[101] Cosin approached Laud, but within six days he had received the reply that Laud was not prepared to help Montagu, causing the disheartened cleric to write 'for the bishop of St. David's . . . I smell a rat . . . I hope to see him one day where he will both do and say for the Church. Interim if he concede, I blame him not.'[102] Throughout this time Neile remained 'the only man that standeth up to purpose in the gapp'. 'I doubt not of his constancy and continuance,' wrote Montagu. In December 1624 Neile was still 'that worthy bishop, still like himself in his thorough courses for right, though alone and left alone'.[103]

Laud's movements in the last years of the reign reveal that characteristic discretion which accompanied him throughout his life. In August 1628 Edward Kellet, a prebendary of Wells, wrote that 'Bishop Laud's discreet proceedings, are too wise for me, and did somewhat deject me.'[104] Doubtless Montagu felt the same in 1624. Yet there

[97] *CC* i. 66, 49. [98] *CC* i. 49; Bodl. MS Rawl. C. 573.
[99] Russell, *Parliaments and English Politics*, 144–203.
[100] *WWL* iii. 161, 196.
[101] *CC* i. 24. [102] Ibid. [103] *CC* i. 34, 21, 65.
[104] Bodl. Tanner MS 72/292.

can be little doubt that they shared a similar vision of the Church. In 1638 Montagu would inform the archbishop that they both strove towards 'the same end, though not the same way'.[105] Both visualized the Church of England as buffeted on both sides by Puritanism and Rome, and both invested Puritanism with doctrinal connotations, although Laud with fewer Calvinist connotations than Montagu.[106] What enabled Laud and other cautious members of the Durham House circle to support Montagu was the projected marriage between Charles and Henrietta Maria, when the reversionary interest itself became reversed and when Charles began to face the opposition which he had previously used against his father. As mentioned earlier, by December 1624 Buckingham was sufficiently interested in the Montagu affair to ask his chaplain, Preston, to examine *Appello Caesarem* and to ask Laud to draw up in ten heads the content of doctrinal Puritanism for his own use.[107] After December 1624 Laud was clearly trying to educate Buckingham in the doctrinal controversy and its implications for the Church. Laud and Buckingham's dislike of Abbot was reciprocal. In the early years of Charles's reign, after the French marriage, Buckingham came to see in Montagu a political tool to beat the opposition posed by Abbot and others to his foreign policy.[108] For his own part Laud thought that Abbot's churchmanship was destructive of apostolic catholicity and a sell-out to Puritanism. It is unlikely that he would have been too distressed to see Abbot lose favour, the man whom he recognized from his Oxford days as the 'original cause of all my troubles', and who had accused him of being popish.[109] Later in 1627 Abbot depicted Laud as the person who had poisoned the duke's mind against him. Buckingham's consistent opposition to Abbot explains why the archbishop failed to solve the Montagu problem after Parliament delegated its resolution to him: 'three times I complained of it,' Abbot wrote in his apology of 1627, 'but he [Montagu] was held up against me, and by the duke, magnified as a clergyman.'[110]

Although Charles disliked Abbot's politics and his churchmanship,

105 PRO SP 16/383/63.

106 See Ch. iii nn. 47–50, 159–60; PRO SP 16/4/20 are possibly some of Laud's exceptions.

107 *WWL* ii. 155–6; Ball, *Life of... Dr Preston*, 114 (Preston also consulted Davenant).

108 Russell, *Parliaments and English Politics*, 13 *et passim*; see Ch. 1 n. 159.

109 *WWL* iii. 135.

110 Rushworth, i. 449–57, in particular 439, 453.

he was sufficiently shrewd to leave Buckingham to prosecute the Montagu affair alone. As he told Laud in 1634 he could discriminate between a church cause and a churchman.[111] In fact to speak of the king's commitment to Arminianism in 1625 forces upon the king's doctrinal position a strait-jacket which extant evidence will not allow.[112] Doctrinally Charles was neither Calvinist nor Arminian. That he disliked the confrontationist dogmatism of Montagu's personal religious opinions goes without question. In fact if support for Arminianism is measured by royal support for Montagu, then there is little evidence of it in the early stages of the reign. Montagu was sufficiently alarmed by the death of James I to anticipate a powerful reaction against himself.[113] Yet his perception of the king's motives in the early years of the reign needs to be read with caution. Deprived of preferment and accused of heterodoxy, he exemplified the traits of a marked, paranoid man. Charles's support appears to have waxed and waned in relation to his political requirements. The question in 1625 was not whether Charles would support doctrinal Arminianism (it never arose) but how far he could move against doctrinal Puritanism. As seen above, to this purpose, as early as April 1625, a few days after the accession, Buckingham asked Laud to draw up for the king a list of clergy with their names annotated by 'o' and 'p' to denote which were 'orthodox' and which were 'Puritan'.[114]

Montagu harboured fears, shared by Laud and others, that as a result of his appeal, Parliament might attempt to introduce the rulings of the Synod of Dort as a rule for the Church of England. Perhaps Charles decided to issue some statement specifying that Dort had no place in the Anglican confession, or he may have wished to have silenced Montagu altogether, recognizing in him an irritant to peaceful parliamentary proceedings, while at the same time wishing to prefer those opposed to 'doctrinal Puritanism'. It was clearly to seek advice on these matters that Charles sent Laud in the first few days of the reign to Lancelot Andrewes to ascertain what 'he would have done in the cause of the Church and bring back his answer especially in the matter of the five articles' (i.e., the five Arminian heads condemned at Dort). That Charles should refer this problem to Andrewes suggests not only his great respect for the bishop's opinion, but that he was keeping an open mind on the Montagu affair

[111] *WWL* vi. 338. [112] See Chapter 1 nn. 34–7.
[113] *CC* i. 67–8. [114] *WWL* iii. 159.

and almost certainly distancing himself from the more adversarial line advocated by Neile. Laud, true to character, played the discreet and cautious go-between.[115]

The first Parliament of Charles I met in June 1625 only to find that Abbot through 'remissness by command' had yet again failed to solve the Montagu controversy.[116] In order to prevent Montagu's impeachment Charles intervened in July 1625 and claimed that as a royal chaplain, it was for the Crown, not Parliament, to prosecute him.[117] Charles then decided to refer the problem to the Church, which was probably the line advocated by Andrewes, who had suggested the same in 1624. As Laud noted, this was for Montagu the first indication of the 'king's favour [towards] him'.[118] Yet this was no guarantee that Charles would continue to shield Montagu from Parliament once it returned after the recess. In August 1625, two days after the conclusion of the first session of the first Parliament, three of Montagu's more reserved supporters, Laud, Howson, and Buckeridge, were sufficiently concerned about this possibility to recommend his cause personally to the king in a letter which they addressed to Buckingham.[119] In this private missive they expressed gratitude to Charles for referring the problem to the Church as the correct arena for its resolution, but also stressed the danger of allowing any other judge in doctrinal matters. Their letter had the desired effect in the short run.[120] In December 1625 Charles sent Montagu's apology to Neile and White, and at about the same time he invited Andrewes and others to consult again about what should be done about Montagu in the forthcoming second Parliament, due to meet in February.[121] On 16 January this group asked Charles not only to prefer Montagu but to prohibit all parties from preaching or writing about the predestinarian controversy (which provided the basis for the June proclamation). However Charles had different ideas, and, as the three bishops had originally feared, he made a conscious decision to distance himself from Montagu and to leave him to his parliamentary accusers.

According to Fuller, early in 1626 the king informed Buckingham

[115] *WWL* iii. 160; *CC* i. 42.

[116] Russell, *Parliaments and English Politics*, 232; Tyacke, *AC* 116.

[117] Tyacke, *AC* 117; Russell, *Parliaments and English Politics*, 234; PRO SP 16/4/29; the king consulted the Solicitor-General before taking this action.

[118] *WWL* iii. 167–8. [119] *WWL* vi. 244–6.

[120] *WWL* vi. 245. [121] *WWL* iii. 178.

that because there was a great deal of ill feeling against Montagu he intended to leave him to Parliament 'to stand or fall according to the justice of his cause'.[122] This decision helps to explain Laud's mood of disillusionment on 29 January 1626 when he recorded in his diary that on the basis of the evidence collected by Buckingham concerning 'the cause, book and opinions of Richard Montagu . . . King Charles had determined himself therein. I see a cloud arising and threatening the Church of England. God of His Mercy dissipate it.'[123] But there were possibly other reasons for this mood of dejection. It seems likely that Charles had recently read Hall's work, *Via Media*, which attempted to show that the teachings of Dort, like Montagu's doctrinal position, were not irreconcilable with the articles of religion.[124] There can be little doubt that this would have appealed to the king's Erasmian temperament and his intense dislike of religious dogmatism. Laud, on the other hand, may have feared a subtle intrusion of Dort's teachings through this channel. Certainly before June 1626 Hall had presented to Montagu and his opponents copies of the work in an attempt to reconcile their differences.[125] Hall himself acknowledged that the treatise was presented to the king by Dean Young of Winchester together with a motion to enjoin a general moratorium on all the related points of controversy. Ironically it was the appearance of the proclamation of June 1626 which buried the treatise 'in a secure silence'.[126] In the end the disappearance of the work may have been part of a compromise package: in November 1626 Hall was nominated at the council board for either Ely or Bath and Wells.[127] When in 1627 he received Exeter it was with Laud's support and not Buckingham's. He himself wrote years afterwards that had the duke's letters arrived a few hours later from France he would have almost certainly lost the bishopric (possibly to Montagu).[128] Charles continued to keep Montagu from high office

[122] *WWL* vi. 249; BL Harl. MS 7000/193; Fuller, *CH* iii. 380.

[123] *WWL* iii. 179–80. Laud's words probably allude to Hall's introduction in *Via Media*: 'there need no prophetical spirit to discern by a small cloud that there is a storm coming towards our Church' (*WJH* ix. 489).

[124] *WJH* ix. 488–519.

[125] *WJH* i, p. xliv; PRO SP 16/20/23: in February 1626 Rudyerd informed Nethersole that 'My lord hath read the discourse concerning the Arminians, likes it very well and thinks it fit to be taken into particular consideration.' He was possibly referring to Pembroke and the *Via Media*.

[126] *WJH* i, p. xliv. [127] PRO SP 16/525/21, 23.

[128] *CC* i. 103; *WJH* i, p. xlv; *WWL* iv. 297.

and when he eventually elevated him to Chichester it was a concession to Buckingham, Montagu's main patron after 1626.[129] In fact it was the duke rather than the king who surfaced as the main advocate of so-called 'Arminianism'.

The York House Conferences can be seen as an attempt by the duke to keep the issues open after Charles had decided not to distance himself from Montagu.[130] Whatever their main purpose, they did little for Montagu's cause. Although he might take comfort in the fact that some Calvinists present felt that he was more ambiguous than heterodox in his opinions, he was forced to admit that in two crucial areas, the foresight of faith and falling from grace, his views were not orthodox. Nor did the conferences lead to any parliamentary support.[131] When Pym announced the decision of the parliamentary committee which had been set up to examine the issue, no one spoke in Montagu's favour.[132] Two months after the second Parliament Montagu wrote that the 'king and God favours us never so little', while in August 1626 he was led to believe that the king was not yet resolved 'against the side' (i.e., doctrinal Puritanism).[133] Moreover between 1624 and 1626 eight books appeared against Montagu. He replied to none of these, nor did anyone else on his behalf.[134]

The intensification of debate outside Parliament, in press and pulpit, provided sufficient justification for the publication of the proclamation of 14 June , silencing the controversy.[135] Several drafts for this survive, one with the king's corrections.[136] The preamble was drawn up by Laud, but the remainder by one of the Secretaries.[137] The entire corrected draft was then referred to Abbot and nine bishops, among them Laud and the Calvinists Felton and Davenant.[138] The personal corrections by Charles reveal his interest in the controversy and his desire to neutralize it to his own advantage. He toned down the accusation of 'Arminianism' by inserting 'schism'

[129] The royal assent for Montagu to receive Chichester was procured by Endymion Porter, Buckingham's associate: PRO SP 16/38/14/182v.

[130] *WJC* ii. 1–81, esp. 56–9, 64, 71; Ball, *Life of... Dr. Preston*, 126–30; Bodl. Tanner MS 303/32v; Fuller, *CH* 387.

[131] Ball, *Life of... Dr. Preston*, 126–34.

[132] Fuller, *CH* 380; Birch, i. 96.

[133] *CC* i. 90, 103. [134] Fuller, *CH* 380.

[135] *Stuart Royal Proclamations*, ii, ed. J. F. Larkin (Oxf., 1984), 90–3.

[136] PRO SP 16/29/78–9. [137] PRO SP 16/540/404.

[138] PRO SP 16/29/78–9.

instead, and altered the phrase 'opinions have been broached by Richard Montagu' to 'opinions seem to have been broached'.[139] Charles had little sympathy for Montagu's dogmatism, yet he probably thought that he was not an Arminian. He also altered the phrase stating that he was acting on the advice of his Privy Council to one claiming that it was on the advice of his bishops, since he did not wish to condescend to any recognition that laymen had the right to determine doctrinal issues.[140] In fact the proclamation can also be seen as an attempt to undercut the parliamentary bill for 'peace and unity of Church and Commonwealth', presented by four members who wished to give the Calvinist Irish Articles of 1615 statutory equality with the Articles of England.[141] The proclamation, however, shelved this issue altogether not so much by asserting the articles as the only rule of doctrine as by ordering no one further to controvert the predestinarian question in book, pulpit, or press, and by leaving the interpretation of doctrine in the hands of bishops.[142]

It is debatable, however, to what extent the proclamation enabled the king to appear as mediator. On 25 June 1625 Ussher suggested in the king's audience that it might lead to a decline in predestinarian orthodoxy.[143] Davenant feared that Durham House would exploit the ruling for their own interests, a fear which, as events turned out, was well founded, although Neile and his circle used the proclamation not (as has been asserted) to outlaw Calvinism on a national basis but to subtly prevent the publication of double predestinarian (reprobation) doctrine.[144] Shortly after its appearance Neile sent a copy to Cambridge almost certainly to thwart the attempt of some dons to proscribe the opinions of those opposed to double predestinarian beliefs.[145] Within a fortnight of the publication's appearance, the High Commission at Lambeth called the stationers and printers before them and charged them not to print or sell any of the books which had appeared against Montagu during the Parliament.[146] In the course of 1627 Neile and Laud strengthened their position at court, and thereafter exploited their position to further undermine

139 PRO SP 16/29/79. The personal reference to Montagu was eventually dropped, see *Stuart Royal Proclamations*, ii. 90–3.

140 PRO SP 16/29/79. 141 Tyacke, *AC* 154–5, 228–9, 23.

142 *Stuart Royal Proclamations*, ii. 90–3.

143 *The Whole Works of James Ussher*, ed. C. R. Elrington (Dublin, 1847–64), xiii. 351; *LJU* 368.

144 Fuller, *John Davenant*, 167.

145 Tyacke, *AC* 48–9. 146 Birch, i. 116.

the doctrine of the reformed Jacobean Church.[147] As clerk of the Closet Neile secured a pulpit for anti-Puritan invective. In November 1627 he effectively prevented Preston from preaching a sermon which depicted the rout at the Île de Rhé as providential judgement against a corrupt nation.[148] Some of the sermons preached before the king were abusive and sour, such as that given in 1628 by Matthew Wren, dean of Windsor, who compared Puritans to the assassin of Buckingham.[149] Neile also persuaded Montaigne of London to publish a book which was almost as provocative, if not as politically important, as *Appello Caesarem*: Jackson's *Treatise of Divine Essence and Attributes*.[150] Later, Laud, as bishop of London, used his own position as licenser to censor statements favourable to Dort and rigid predestinarianism.[151]

III. THE PEACE OF THE CHURCH

The idea of a pardon for Montagu was first aired by Laud and other bishops as early as January 1626, but not until June 1628 after his third Parliament did Charles ask Attorney Heath to draw one up, and not until December 1628 did he issue a warrant for it.[152] Laud

[147] Rushworth, i. 436, 445–56.

[148] Ball, *Life of... Dr. Preston*, 154–7, 158–61. Bodl. Tanner MS 72/269: on 21 Apr. 1628 the king ordered the ministers of London not to take note of the duke's defeat in France in their sermons.

[149] Birch, i. 408: 'a most pernicious sect, and dangerous to a monarch: as bad as Jesuits in their opinions. That they held the same tenet that their head fellow Felton doth... that it is lawful to kill any man that is opposite to their party and that all their whole doctrine and practice tendeth to anarchy.' (This could also have been a slur on Bishop Felton of Ely, a Calvinist). See also *The Confessions of John Bastwick* (1641): 'I have heard many sermons at the court yet never did I hear any, wherein I saw not the Puritans brought up with... some notorious lies told of them.'

[150] Jackson, *A Treatise of Divine Essence and Attributes* (1628), which caused a considerable parliamentary stir (Bodl. MS Tanner 72/150; MS Rawl. D 1347/114). It was published against the wishes of both Davenant and Morton, who examined it (Bodl. Tanner MS 290/84; *The Life of... James Ussher* (1686), 394; Bodl. Tanner MS 72/150.

[151] PRO SP 16/499/51; Bodl. Tanner MS 71/7; Tyacke, *AC* 151; Stationers' Hall: Company Records: Ct. Bk. 'C' 1602–54/7 Dec. 1628. The relationship between censorship and 'Arminianism' is examined by S. Lambert, 'Richard Montagu, Arminianism and Censorship', *Past and Present*, 124 (Aug. 1989).

[152] PRO SP 16/118/33; BL MS Harl. 7000/193; DCL Hunter MS 67/14/16—in June 1628 the king contemplated issuing pardons to Cosin, Sibthorpe, Mainwaring, and Montagu. Mainwaring received his in July 1628 (Birch, i. 379).

himself continued to distance himself from Montagu, and when the Commons investigated the granting of the pardon, it was Neile, not Laud, whom they implicated in its procurement.[153] The question remains why the king chose not to grant a pardon earlier than the last month of 1628. As late as October 1628 Heath, the Attorney-General, informed Montagu that, although the king had asked him to draw up a pardon, he had not given the warrant for its publication. However Heath promised Montagu that he would ask the king for a warrant on condition that he would 'review his book and take away things doubtful'.[154] Although Heath declined to advise Montagu in 'knotty points of controverted questions', he suggested that 'a sober ignorance may be safer and more valuable than a curious knowledge'. Heath wished Montagu to realize that if he refused to comply he would almost certainly not receive a pardon and would remain in the clutches of Parliament.[155] There can be little doubt that Heath spoke on behalf of the king and Privy Council, who were trying to secure more peaceful proceedings in the second session of the third Parliament, for at a meeting on 28 November 1628 the king informed the council that he wished the bishops in London to examine Montagu's book for any 'Arminianism'.[156] At the same time the assassination of Buckingham in the previous August meant that Montagu had lost his main supporter. Laud and Neile may also have been hoping for a more peaceful session as only five months before the Commons had voted them Arminians in the Remonstrance.[157] In November 1628 Montagu was informed that 'his great friends at court would take no blows for him', which is clear evidence that the court bishops wished him to relinquish his high parliamentary and public profile.[158] Moreover, given the fact that Laud's doctrinal position was more orthodox than Montagu's, it seems almost certain that he wished Montagu finally to come clean on his ambiguous statements by clarifying his doctrinal position precisely on those two crucial areas where he had failed to give satisfaction: the foresight of faith and falling from grace.[159] This interpretation receives support from a conversation

[153] DCL Hunter 67/14/16–17. The king asked the Attorney-General to consult Neile about the form of the pardon.

[154] PRO SP 16/118/33; DCL Hunter 67/14/16.

[155] PRO SP 16/118/33; Russell, *Parliaments and English Politics*, 404.

[156] Birch, i. 436–8. A few days after this council meeting the king asked Neile to procure the pardon from the Attorney-General.

[157] *WWL* vii. 632. [158] *CC* i. 152.

[159] Ball, *Life of... Dr. Preston*, 126–34; see p. 111; PRO SP 16/4/18–20.

between Samuel Ward and White of Carlisle in which the bishop made it clear that those who had originally countenanced Montagu's book had 'scrutinised it further' and 'had found in it some parts flat opposed to the received doctrine of our Church [and] are desirous to have those parts buried hereafter in silence'. White, in fact, had been one of the debaters at York House where he had revealed his doctrinal difference with Montagu precisely on these two issues.[160]

Thus in the last days of 1628, as the king looked for a more peaceful Parliament, pressure was brought to bear upon Montagu to alter his opinions.[161] With his position looking increasingly untenable, shortly before 12 December Montagu sent a letter to Abbot renouncing some of his opinions and clarifying his doctrinal position. It was even reported that Montagu had assented to Dort, but it is more probable that propositions, similar to Hall's *Via Media*, which interpreted Dort in the sense of Overall, were offered to Montagu for assent. The importance of Montagu's capitulation should not be underestimated. It took even the king by surprise, who as soon as he heard of the letter, summoned Secretary Coke to procure it from Abbot so that he could examine its authenticity.[162] Within ten days Abbot had convened the bishops at Lambeth to draw up the declaration for the peace of the Church.[163] In response to these developments, on 28 December Charles dispatched to Dorchester, Secretary of State, the royal warrant for the pardon which was then forwarded to Heath.[164] Finally on 17 January 1629 Charles published a proclamation authorizing the withdrawal of *Appello Caesarem* from the press.[165] Thus the events of December 1628 and January 1629 appear to have behind them an overall

[160] Bodl. MS Tanner 72/298; Ball, *Life of... Dr. Preston*, 126–8.

[161] *Barrington Family Letters 1628–1632*, ed. A. Searle (Camden, 4th ser., 28, 1983), 40. On 4 Dec. 1628 Sir Thomas Barrington heard a rumour that Montagu had converted from his former opinions, although he doubted its veracity.

[162] Birch, i. 449, 451; ii. 3–5; *HMC Cowper i*, 273 (in the same letter Coke referred to Montagu's retraction as a 'recantation or desertion of those opinions wherewith he hath been charged').

[163] Birch, ii. 3–5.

[164] DCL Hunter 67/14/17. After the warrants for the pardons were ingrossed, the Attorney-General sent those for Cosin and Sibthorpe to Neile in order to obtain the final signature from the signet office, but the two other pardons (Mainwaring and Montagu) were, according to Neile, 'never sent to me neither doth I know who got his Majesty's hand to them'.

[165] *Stuart Royal Proclamations*, ii. 218.

strategy not only to secure a peaceful Parliament but to stifle further doctrinal controversy.[166]

Possibly very few Calvinists saw the royal policy as an attempt to introduce Arminianism under the guise of pacifying predestinarian disputes. When Potter, provost of The Queen's College, praised the declaration in a sermon of March 1629, among those who congratulated his efforts were the Calvinists Morton, Winniffe, Young, and Goad (one of the delegates at Dort).[167] The events of winter 1628/9 appear to have convinced many that the king was not Arminian. The author of the 'reasons for the suppression of arminianism' was comforted by the proclamation for the withdrawal of *Appello Caesarem*, 'from whence we cannot but in reason presume that his highness utterly dislikes the doctrine therein contained, as being scandalous and repugnant to the most usually received and current doctrine of our divines'.[168]

The part played by Laud in the formulation of the declaration is not clear, but he was probably responsible for prefixing it to the articles, as Robert Baron of Aberdeen congratulated him for so doing.[169] To Laud was also delegated the task of answering the Commons vote (in reply to the declaration) that only Parliament could determine the doctrine of the Church, and that Arminianism was entirely incompatible with the articles.[170] Perhaps no document better reveals the principles which underlay Laud's attitudes and actions in the Arminian controversy. If the Articles admitted more than a single interpretation, then it was perfectly lawful for anyone to choose the sense he so wished, so long as it was consistent with 'the analogy of faith'. This opinion he might peaceably hold until the Church made an official interpretation of the same, for the 'wisdom of the Church hath been in all ages, or the most to require consent to articles in general, as much as maybe, because that is the way of unity'.[171] At the same time this policy necessitated the toning down

[166] *Articles agreed upon and reprinted by His Majesty's Command* (1628). See *WWL* i. 154 for an attempt to date the declaration. It appeared sometime between 24 Dec. 1628 and 7 Jan. 1629 (Birch, i. 449, 457; ii. 3–5); *Documentary Annals*, i. 43.

[167] Potter, *Vindication of Himself.*

[168] Bodl. MS Rawl. D. 1247/114.

[169] PRO SP 16/266/3.

[170] *WWL* vi. 11–12; PRO SP 16/499/45 (SP 16/108/66–7) reveals that this was never presented, causing Laud to write 'who altered the king's mind in this God knoweth').

[171] *WWL* vi. 11–12.

of some excesses, namely rigid predestinarianism. Consequently, for Laud, an Arminianization of the Church was an evil equal only to its Calvinization. Laud was not an Arminian, but his liberal interpretation of the Articles was bound to admit the airing of some arminian ideas. He attacked also the Commons' claim that the only interpretation of the Articles permissible was according to recent works of divinity. For Laud, on the other hand, commentaries could offer at the most only a 'probable' interpretation. Moreover, like Davenant, he believed that Parliament had no right to make an official interpretation of doctrine, 'for this belongs to them only that have power to make it'. In fact the Commons had contravened the recent declaration which had asked them to accept the Articles in their 'plain and literal sense'.[172]

The declaration asked no one to print or preach on the controversy, nor were the universities to dispute the issues in ways other than already approved by Convocation.[173] It did not proscribe single predestinarian Calvinism as it was still possible to receive article 17 in a single predestinarian sense.[174] In fact as the article endorsed predestination, the declaration called for a literal acceptance of predestination to election:

> Predestination to life is the everlasting purpose of God, whereby . . . he hath constantly decreed by his counsel secret to us, to deliver from curse and damnation those whom he hath chosen in Christ out of mankind . . . As the godly consideration of predestination, and our election in Christ is full of sweet, pleasant and unspeakable comfort to godly persons and . . . as feel in themselves the working of Christ . . . for curious and carnal persons, lacking the spirit of Christ, to have continually before their eyes the sentence of God's predestination, is a most dangerous downfall.[175]

That the declaration should actually reinforce predestination to election suggests that behind its publication lay an attempt to undermine predestination to reprobation (otherwise known as rigid or double predestination): the opinion that God had irrevocably condemned some men to eternal damnation, and its corollaries, that Christ had not died for all men but only for the elect, that God wills all sin and that man cannot attain to grace if once he falls. At the same time the declaration would undermine the opinions of those

[172] Ibid.; Bodl. Tanner MS 290/84.
[173] For a discussion of the doctrine of the Thirty-nine Articles see O'Donovan, *On the Thirty-Nine Articles* (for the single predestinarianism of article 17, ibid. 85).
[174] Contrary to Tyacke, *AC* 157, 49, 181.
[175] *Synodalia*, i. 43.

denied that the Arminian points could be, if only in some respects, compatible with the articles. Of course some Calvinists might object to such intentions. They might interpret an attack on predestination to reprobation as an attack on predestination *per se*, while an attempt to neutralize anti-arminian opinions would be construed as a subtle way of introducing Arminianism *en tout*. Even if Prynne and Burton misrepresented Laud's theological position and the rationale behind the declaration, their fears can be understood. They would meet any claims that the declaration was being pressed impartially with the objection that it should be used rather to protect rigid predestinarian teaching and to proscribe Arminianism.[176]

Apart from the fact that the declaration endorsed predestination to election, its limited circulation casts doubt on Dr Tyacke's assertion that it led to the proscription of predestinarian teaching in the 1630s. Whether it was known in the parishes depended on whether the clergy had bought an edition of the Articles after 1628 (to which it was prefixed) or successive editions of the Prayer Book which contained the Articles. Many parishes became aware of the declaration only through the Instructions of 1629 which reinforced it. When in 1636 the churchwardens of Walton, in the peculiar of the Sokens in Essex, were asked to certify whether or not their parish observed instruction 3 relating to the declaration, they confessed that they were unable to answer because 'we have not his Majesty's Declaration'.[177]

To what extent was the contemporary perception true that the declaration was not pressed impartially? Certainly on the basis of surviving evidence, very few preachers fell foul of Laud during the 1630s for breach of the declaration.[178] This does not mean that Laud was lax in its enforcement but that we have misinterpreted his intentions in applying it. Laud reproached only preachers who stressed predestination to reprobation, and who applied it to particular persons or to the nation. In 1629 Laud cited Daniel Votier of St Peter Cheapside for preaching that as some were condemned to reprobation, Christ had not died for the sins of the world.[179] On 20 December 1630 he called into court John Archer for depicting God as the author of sin. The views of John Vicars of St Mary, Stamford,

[176] Burton, *For God and the King* (1636), 114.

[177] Tyacke, *AC* 181; ERO D/APs VI/E6 1636; according to Heylyn, *CA* 120, the proclamation of 1626 had a similarly low circulation.

[178] Fuller, *CH* 415; Burton, *For God and the King*, 114, 116–22; Bodl. Tanner MS 71/66, 109.

[179] PRO SP 16/499/35.

whom he interrogated in October 1628, clearly fell within the exclusion zone laid down within the declaration, for he had to submit that he held 'no man by relapses to be made incapable of grace and repentance, whilst his soul is in his body, and so detest from my heart the heresy of the novations in this point'.[180] William Mady similarly fell into trouble with Laud in March 1631 for preaching on the decree of reprobation. Possibly many of those who preached predestination to reprobation remained undetected by informers or the London courts. The likelihood of detection increased when the preacher applied his teaching to the congregation by 'particularizing' in the pulpit.[181] When Votier was called into court a second time in 1637 it was because he had identified the elect and the reprobate among the pews, hardly a sop for the troubled conscience or for the parishioner who demanded respect from his social inferiors. One of the offended congregation reported Votier's sermon to Laud, who then summoned him to the High Commission.[182] Several others, such as Stephen Dennison of St Katherine, Cree, were similarly cited for particularizing in the pulpit.[183]

Apart from the fact that the number of ministers who fell foul was relatively small and that he attempted to curb rigid predestinarianism and its antinomian implications, Laud's application of the declaration has been misinterpreted in another way. It would appear that if Laud censured ministers who preached predestination to reprobation, then he did so because they were, in the first case, nonconformist to the Book of Common Prayer or canons, or particularized to such an extent that they questioned authority. Such a minister was Henry Burton of St Matthew, Friday Street, who marked out the bishops as reprobates, portrayed the country as on the road to apostasy, and vilified the Book of Common Prayer.[184] The reason for Archer's suspension was his failure to catechize properly, a suspension which lasted for only three months until April 1631.[185] Mady's predestinarian views fell into insignificance when compared to his anti-Trinitarian beliefs, for which he lost his licence to preach.[186] Votier's singular censure was to suffer Laud to dispute with him for one hour to try to make him see the error of his ways; then Laud, 'fearing

[180] Bodl. MS Tanner 71/66; GL 9531/15/22–3; PRO SP 16/176/63, SP/16/187/17, SP/16/186/75–6; BL Add. MS 34217/53.
[181] PRO SP 16/186/41, 75–6. [182] PRO SP 16/499/35.
[183] *CSPD 1634–1635*, 144, 318. [184] GL 9531/15/21.
[185] PRO SP 16/176/63, SP/16/187/17. [186] PRO SP 16/186/75–6.

the clamours of the world', merely dismissed him, and without censure.[187]

It was perhaps less in his capacity as bishop of London than as chancellor of Oxford that Laud had occasion to press the declaration.[188] Shortly after his election, information reached him that John Tooker of Oriel had preached Arminianism in its five points, and had publicly cast aspersions upon the Synod of Dort. Laud was swift to inform the provost of Oriel that Tooker should have been reprimanded for his impertinence, because 'I would not have sermons of such ill example lead the way into my government there,' and suggested that any who disobeyed the king's moratorium in future should be more severely reprimanded.[189]

Apart from Laud's personal intentions in pressing the declaration, his policy was conditioned also by the king's views. Charles I required him to keep the doctrinal peace and strictly laid down that he wished neither 'side' in the controversy to feel that they were prejudiced or favoured. The king informed Davenant in 1630 that his intention was not to have 'this high point meddled withall or debated, either one way or the other'.[190] As early as December 1630, when asked to publish what appears to have been a reasonably inoffensive tract on predestination, Laud replied that he much doubted whether the king would 'take any man's judgement so far, as to have (these) controversies any further stirred which God be thanked begin to be at more peace'.[191] Laud's communications to Oxford dons in the 1630s reveal an almost paranoid fear that this policy of impartiality would be unsettled by some hot-head and that the king would get to know about it. In 1630 he told Dr Tolson that 'the blame will fall on me more than upon another man, if such things as these pass without censure . . . be careful to maintain my honour in upholding the peace and government of the university.' In the summer of 1631 that very event occurred, when students at Magdalen Hall and Exeter broke the declaration and accused Laud and other bishops of bias towards

[187] PRO SP 16/499/35.

[188] For Oxford University see K. Sharpe, 'Archbishop Laud and the University of Oxford', in H. Lloyd-Jones, V. Pearl, and B. Worden (eds.), *History and Imagination: Essays presented to Lord Dacre* (1981).

[189] *WWL* v. 15–16; v. 48, 56, 78, 287–8.

[190] Bodl. Tanner MS 290/86ᵛ.

[191] *WWL* v. 15–16; PRO SP 16/176/46 (for context see SP 16/175/69 and SP 16/177/8). PRO SP 16/175/69 shows the king's displeasure over Brooke's previous discussion of the predestinarian question.

Arminianism. So bitter did the controversy become that the king personally heard their case at Woodstock on 23 August and then adjudicated between the various parties.[192] This Woodstock meeting has been ignored, yet its significance was greater than the York House Conferences because it was chaired by the king and established on even clearer principles than the declaration of 1628 the king's policy towards Arminianism. Charles reiterated his desire that the declaration be pressed impartially without favouring either interpretation.[193] This in itself is hardly sufficient to substantiate the king's doctrinal neutrality but the matter did not rest there. Charles personally and publicly embarrassed Laud by suggesting that his policy was not as impartial as he claimed. The king announced that he had been informed that Potter, provost of The Queen's College, had preached in favour of some Arminian heads without reprimand while the mouths of others had been stopped. As it turned out, the fellows of Potter's college were able to clear him from the charge, but henceforth Laud can have harboured no false illusions about the king's categorical requirements.[194] In the future he would have to exercise even greater discretion in pursuing his delicate policy of discriminating between single and double predestination, and in safeguarding a liberal interpretation of the Articles. Laud regarded the incident as so important that he inserted 23 August, 'the great hearing of the disorders at Woodstock', in the front of his diary among the very select dates which he observed as special days of remembrance. These included the dates of his parents' death, the Devon divorce case, the assassination of Buckingham, and of the audience which determined his election to the presidency of St John's, Oxford.[195]

In the immediate term the Woodstock meeting occasioned Laud's letter to the vice-chancellor in September 1631, beseeching him 'to proceed impartially against delinquents ... that neither one nor the other may have cause to say that you favour a party'.[196] As a result of the royal statement, the bishops were far more careful about what came under their censure. In the longer term the Woodstock meeting

[192] Bodl. MS Jones 17/300–310; *WWL* v. 50–71.

[193] Bodl. MS Jones 17/303.

[194] Ibid. 17/303–4; *WWL* v. 48–9. This possibly explains why Potter did not receive higher preferment.

[195] *WWL* iii. 130.

[196] *WWL* v. 48: followed by the king's personal letters to Laud and the university to put their affairs in order, *WWL* v. 72–8.

occasioned not just a greater scrupulosity but caused a distinct moderation of the programme of anti-Calvinism. On Christmas Day 1632 both Laud and White of Ely preached at court 'in favour of Calvin',[197] and directly against Arminianism which confuted 'the opinions of the vulgar'.[198] To suggest that a volte-face occurred in 1631–2 in Laud's doctrinal position does not do justice to the eclecticism of his opinions before, or to the fact that (as he informed Vossius) in these matters he had always counselled moderation.[199] But it does reveal how misleading is the current depiction of the 'rise of Arminianism' during the 1630s.

In terms of policy the Woodstock meeting certainly occasioned a distinct alteration. Henceforth there were no more Montagus or Jacksons, and a concurrent decline in predestinarian controversy occurred. As early as January 1633 Archbishop Abbot could inform the king that 'of the arminian points there is no dispute'.[200] Such an impartial testimony questions the notion that doctrinal controversy over the predestinarian question was endemic in the 1630s and that we should see the decade through spectacles of Arminian versus Calvinist, or a simple Weberian polarity of predestination versus grace. Nor, as the rest of this work reveals, were there clear 'Calvinist versus Arminian' divisions over the ecclesiological and sabbatarian issues of the Personal Rule. While some Arminian doctrine spread during the 1630s, the Arminianization of the decade is a myth. Moreover, as the first two chapters suggest, the reasons for the ecclesiological shift of the period are very different from those given in textbooks.[201] Another contributory factor to the peace of the Church was the parliamentary situation, or the lack of it, as doctrine ceased to have the same relevance as in the politically volatile situation of 1628–9. The Accounts of the Province reveal that there was no ostensible intensification of the predestinarian controversy during the 1630s.[202] Only once in the Accounts did Laud inform the king of any significant controversy, in 1638, when some clergy in the diocese of St David's breached the declaration, 'meddling in those points which your Majesty hath forbidden'. Other doctrinal controversies arose which Laud reported to the king, but their inclusion is not to be attributed to Laud's application of the declaration to cover all

[197] Birch, ii. 213–14; i. 439.
[198] QCO MS 390/63.
[199] *WWL* vi. 265–6.
[200] *WWL* v. 309.
[201] See esp. Ch. 2 section i.
[202] *WWL* v. 309–70.

doctrinal controversies but to his response to the additional instruction of 1634 which asked the bishops to report any major doctrinal disorders within their sees.[203]

During the metropolitical visitation, the declaration was republished and Brent asked to ascertain whether some ministers (whose names had been supplied by informers) at Gloucester and other places had preached against it.[204] Information collected by Lambe for the visitation of Peterborough also noted the same offence, such as that of Price of Brigstock, who preached for four hours on the theme that God 'created the greater part of the world of purpose to damn them'.[205] Perhaps the last occasion when Laud pressed the observance of the declaration in Oxford was after John Johnson of Magdalen preached universal grace in September 1640 and (on Laud's personal testimony) in contravention of the declaration.[206] Thus although Laud shared with Johnson a belief in universal grace (which many Calvinists also shared), he was prepared to suppress his own opinions under obedience to the king's moratorium. To this purpose, only four months earlier, he had prevented the publication of the works of Thomas Jackson, president of Corpus Christi. 'Both in regard of the duty which we owe his Majesty, and the peace of the Church,' Laud informed the vice-chancellor, 'no man should presume to print any [matter] which might break the rule given in his Majesty's declaration one way or the other.'[207] The situation was markedly different from that in 1628 and 1629, when Neile had published the very controversial and near-Arminian works of Jackson.[208]

As a result of instruction 3 of 1629, bishops and archdeacons encouraged the observation of the declaration through their visitations, and some expressly enquired into the declaration in their articles. Yet the attempt to pacify the predestinarian controversy of the 1630s should be seen in context. For both canonical and pastoral reasons clergy were obliged to curtail doctrinal controversy. Moreover James I's directions of 1622 foreshadowed the proclamation of 1626 and the declaration of 1628. Long before the reign of Charles I courts were engaged in the pacification of the predestinarian con-

[203] *WWL* v. 358, 311–14. [204] PRO SP 16/260/471.

[205] PRO SP 16/308/52.

[206] *WWL* v. 287–8.

[207] *WWL* v. 268. But of course neither Laud nor Calvinist 'hypothetical universalists' believed in a universal *saving* grace.

[208] See Ch. 3 n. 150.

troversy and were attempting to neutralize the more unfortunate pastoral consequences resulting from the preaching and application of double predestinarian opinions.[209] In 1623 Professor Collinson's archetypal evangelical Calvinist, Arthur Lake, bishop of Bath and Wells, preached that 'the world is much troubled now about universal grace, the resolution in short may be this, that (forbearing to be over busy with God's predestination, who is not pleased to acquaint us with his counsell in distinguishing persons), in a minister's commission grace is universal: we should labour the conversion of all and every one: neither should any man except himself, but to be in the number of that to whom God sendeth.' 'How absurd then are they that make this prophane collection,' he declared later in a sermon at St Paul's Cross, 'I am elected, therefore it skilleth not whether I serve God.'[210]

Court records are not the best means of measuring the extent of the episcopal promotion and the clerical observance of the declaration. Levels of detection probably varied from diocese to diocese, depending on the significance of the controversy and the interests of the diocesan. Some bishops, faced by a dispute, might attempt to defuse it and stress its anti-pastoral effects, others might stay clear altogether for fear that involvement would be construed as an attack on 'orthodox' doctrine and preaching. Ultimately the offence was in the hearer's ear. Goodman of Gloucester was offended by the claim of the rector of Little Dean that 'if we are saved, then all papists are damned,' and eventually suspended him.[211] In 1638 Juxon cited the near-Arminian, John Goodwin, of St Stephen, Coleman Street, for preaching universal redemption and breaking the declaration. In both accounts for 1638 and 1639, Juxon and Laud informed the king of his misdemeanours, which again reveals their impartial application of the declaration.[212] Like Goodman of Gloucester, Piers of Bath and Wells personally interviewed those whom he suspected of breaking the declaration, in order to convince them of the error of their ways. In October 1634 Richard Barnard of Batcombe appeared before him for preaching on 'apostasy and falling from grace', and received a reprimand for exercising (what he considered to be) his ministerial

[209] *Documentary Annals*, ii. 203; Hacket, *SR* i. 89.

[210] *Sermons with some religious and divine meditations by Arthur Lake, Bishop of Bath and Wells* (1629), 228, 259.

[211] GRO GDR 195/209.

[212] *WWL* v. 356, 362; *WWL* iii. 304–5.

duty 'to reprove general nations, cities, towns (and) particular persons, as by the example of Nathan to David'.[213] In neighbouring Exeter, Hall also interviewed suspects in audience and actually prosecuted (through personal suit) in consistory more cases over these issues than did his chancellor through parish presentments.[214]

Yet throughout the 1630s probably many engaged in doctrinal controversy and remained undetected. As the petitions of 1640s, sermons and reports of scandalous ministers reveal, clergy could advocate extremely controversial doctrines.[215] Some clergy, and even some surrogates, might interpret the declaration as an invitation to curtail Calvinist preaching altogether.[216] Some ministers took the opportunity to preach fully-fledged Arminianism, although on the basis of surviving depositions their numbers are small.[217] Significance, however, is not proportionate to quantity and such examples served to provide extra fuel against the Caroline Church in the 1640s. Certainly, reformed preachers were more wary of how they handled the question of predestination. Some of them even found it difficult to get their works published, as the king watered down the reformed orthodoxy of the Jacobean Church.[218] Thus it was singularly ironic that as Charles I strictly forced others to press the declaration impartially, he unwittingly bottled up Calvinist resentment, fermenting for change in 1640, while unconsciously fanning the flame of emergent free-will doctrine. In this respect, English Arminianism was less a cause of the anti-Calvinism of the Caroline Church than one of its consequences.

213 SRO D/D/Ca 319/87^{v}, D/D/Ca 299/56^{v}, 61.
214 SRO DD/PH 221/40, *WJH* i, p. xlvi; PRO SP 16/531/135.
215 HLRO 1641 Feb. 23/20; Bodl. MS Eng. th./20; Bodl. MS Carte 103/64–5; SRO D/D/Ca 282/236.
216 PRO SP 16/408/170.
217 Tyacke, *AC* 185–99; SRO D/D/Ca 282/236.
218 Tyacke, *AC* 248–65.

4
THE RESTRAINT OF PREACHING

> I cannot tell . . . what you call puritanical sermons; they come nearest to my conscience, and do me the most good.
>
> (*Mr. Bolton's Last and Learned Work of the Four Last Things* (1635), 168)

I. THE CONSIDERATIONS AND INSTRUCTIONS

Professor Collinson has written of the Jacobean Church that nowhere else in early modern Europe 'within a legally established Church was so much collective consciousness and behaviour conditioned not by regulations but by a more or less spontaneous consensus of private men, the religious public themselves'.[1] Jacobean England was a country on the move as the godly gadded between churches and households to hear sermons, to hold repetitions and fasts, and to participate in fellowship. The early seventeenth century witnessed perhaps the greatest evangelistic drive before the advent of the Evangelical Revival of the eighteenth century.[2] The thirst for preaching was deep and manifested itself in such phenomena as the development of the tester-pulpit with sounding-board, and a flood of parliamentary bills petitioning for more sermons and fewer restrictions on preaching.[3] Yet this comparative religious freedom was not without its critics. After the reaction of 1622, those who believed the 'beauty of preaching had preached away the beauty of holiness', looked forward to the day when they could overturn the primacy

[1] Collinson, *GP* 467–99.

[2] Collinson, *RP* 134–40, 242–83; Collinson, *GP* 467–99.

[3] H. Davies, *Worship and Theology in England* (Princeton, NJ, 1975–), ii, *passim*; *CJ* ii, *passim*; Bodl. MS Tanner 129/3; Collinson, *RP* 242–83, 134; N. Pevsner *et al.* (eds.), *The Buildings of England and Wales*, for the profusion of Jacobean pulpits; G. Nuttall, *Richard Baxter* (1965), 18; R. F. Young (ed.), *Commenius in England* (1932), 65.

of the pulpit, and quash the ascendant evangelical complexion of Anglicanism.[4]

Within the established structures of the Elizabethan and Jacobean Church, the lay-funded sermons supplemented the threadbare official provision of preaching.[5] Recent work has emphasized the extent to which the lectureship was a feature of the established Church rather than alien to it.[6] Traditional historiography, which visualized the lecture as radical and destructive of all order and uniformity in the Church, was based in part upon an uncritical adoption of the opinions of those contemporaries who wished to depict it in precisely this unfavourable light.[7] At the same time the characterization of the period before 1640 as a pre-revolutionary age led historians to emphasize only elements of opposition or revolution in the lectureship. Other, sometimes Marxist, historiography distorted the issue further by depicting lecturers as necessarily 'alienated' from the Church, or as a 'free-lance' clergy maintained and financed by the rising bourgeoisie who could only react to outdated ecclesiastical structures.[8] In place of these notions, Professor Collinson has stressed the 'accommodation' that existed between the established Church and lecturers during the late Elizabethan and Jacobean periods, an accommodation revealed most clearly in the number of lectures preached by combinations of beneficed ministers, designed to meet contemporary preaching needs, by working through existing parochial structures rather than outside them.[9] Far from being a threat to the very basis of the Church, such lectures were an element in cohesion and comprehension. In fact Professor Collinson has gone so far as to describe them as 'the most characteristic institution of the Jacobean Church'.[10]

The social acceptance of the lecture helps to explain James I's decision not to hinder its existence for much of his reign. It was also a reflection of the reformed consensus within the Church, in which a shared doctrinal platform, but, more importantly, a decision to tolerate ecclesiological differences served to diminish the inherent

[4] R. Shelford, *Five Pious and Learned Discourses* (1635), 12.
[5] Collinson, *RP*; *GP* 467–97.
[6] Collinson, *RP* 138–40; *GP* 497, 467–98.
[7] Collinson, *RP* 138–9; Bodl. Tanner MS 68/92; PRO SP 16/493/28.
[8] Hill, *SP* 79–80; M. Curtis, 'The Alienated Intellectuals of Early Stuart England', in T. Aston (ed.), *Crisis in Europe 1560–1660* (1965), 295–316.
[9] Collinson, *GP* 467–98; Collinson, *RP* 138–40.
[10] Collinson, *RP* 136.

difference between the hierarchy, lecturers, and Puritans.[11] Under new doctrinal and ecclesiological tensions such a consensus might face considerable strain. Fragmentation of groups and measured polarization might occur, as revealed by Drs Fincham and Lake. The early seventeenth century witnessed considerable doctrinal shift and debate across Europe but in England it was less liberal doctrines of grace which threatened the peace than more pronounced doctrines of the Church and authority. After the passing of the first and second generation of reformers, clergy looked more to the patristic Church upon which to model their own. They began to emphasize more the visibility and catholicity of the Anglican Church to defend it from, on the one hand, the taunts of Rome which denied it either and, on the other, from the over-rationalization of reformed doctrine, which threatened the doctrinal ambiguities of the Anglican Church. With the rise of an elevated view of episcopacy came a more assertive emphasis on the exclusivity of the ministry, and consequently on their sacramental office and functions. Combined with their increasing professionalization was a greater social confidence and corporate identity. An inevitable manifestation of these changes was less an Arminianization than a counter-reformation of the Church.[12]

It is impossible to understand the Caroline restrictions placed on the freedom of preaching other than in a context which examines the interplay of these doctrinal, ecclesiological, and (as shall be shortly discussed) political considerations. For those who questioned the nonconformist and evangelical inclinations of the Jacobean Church the unordained, non-beneficed lecturer might appear as a threat to established order within the Church, to its catholicity and visibility. At the same time the beneficed lecturer might come under greater scrutiny for his over-rationalization in the pulpit. The most popular type of preaching in the Lincoln combinations in 1614 was by 'doctrine and uses', preaching that was reformed in its concern with continual biblical exposition and experimental predestination.[13] Neile was informed that the lecturers would first read a passage and then

[11] Collinson, *RP*; Tyacke, *AC*; Parker, *ES*; Lake, *AP*.

[12] K. Fincham and P. G. Lake, 'The Ecclesiastical Policy of James I', *Journal of British Studies*, 24 (1985), 169–207; P. Lake and M. Dowling (eds.), *Protestantism and the National Church in Sixteenth Century* (1987); R. O'Day, *The English Clergy: The Emergence and Consolidation of a Profession 1558–1642* (Leicester, 1979); G. Cragg, *Freedom and Authority* (Philadelphia, 1975), 97–127.

[13] CUL Baumgartner MS 8/200–2. *Mr Bolton's Last and Learned Work of the Four Last Things* (1635), ed. E. Bagshawe, 183.

raise out of it a doctrine 'as far removed from their exposition as their exposition was short of the true meaning of the letter expounded'. From this doctrine they would then raise 'a use which stands in equal distance from their doctrine as their doctrine from their exposition'. But what was preaching by 'doctrine and uses'? There was certainly nothing particularly Calvinist about it. In one of his lectures Robert Bolton defended it as 'all edifying plainnesse and foolishnesse of preaching' which taught but not 'tickled' the conscience. Such preaching, as Neile's surrogates realized, was hardly censurable, for it was none other than evangelical teaching, which emphasized personal salvation and vocation.[14] As Professor Collinson has written, 'combination lecturers might preach little that was sensational or political [as] the themes of moral and practical divinity predominated.'[15] It was preaching that might draw crowds, was relevant to its audience, and food for hungry souls. But clearly some did not like it, and for these it might be 'puritanical'. Yet Sir Augustine Nicholls, judge of the Common Pleas, confessed that he did not know what such 'puritanical sermons' were, as 'they come nearest to my conscience, and do me the most good'. However this might not satisfy the criticism of those who complained that some lecturers in 'doctrine and uses' did not always keep within their analogy (resulting in some unfortunate pastoral effects) and dismissed all other kinds of preaching as 'carnal or at best academical'. According to Neile's surrogates, the minister outside the combination was all too often branded as a 'good moral man; for his learning . . . a dumb-dog, though he preach or catechise constantly in his own parish every Sunday'.[16] What irritated the surrogates more was that the popularity of this style of 'lecturing hath brought' the discipline and liturgy of the Church 'into contempt'.[17] As disturbing was the perception held by some that such evangelical preaching had fomented popular disaffection. For those Caroline clergy who wished to assert clerical rights, to externalize worship, and to turn the clock back to 1560 or 1540, such complaints received immediate audition. Edward Symonds believed that lecturers had stolen the 'affections of the people'. Clement Corbet, Wren's chancellor, believed that they had 'intoxicated' with their 'virulency' vast numbers of the nation. Wren himself claimed that 'the breach of

[14] CUL Baumgartner MS 8/201. [15] Collinson, *GP* 495.

[16] CUL Baumgartner MS 8/200–2; *Mr Bolton's Last and Learned Work of the Four Last Things* ('funeral notes upon my patron, Sir Augustine Nicholls'), 168.

[17] CUL Baumgartner MS 8/200–2.

that unity and uniformity in the Church hath principally been caused or occasioned by lecturers and lectures'.[18] Bishop Warner identified lecturers as little better than 'ballad singers and happy-horse sellers, for . . . they in the fair or market-town have the most crowd, while mercers and goldsmiths who sell rich commodities have nothing to do'. For clerics such as these the prescription was clear. The liturgy had to be elevated on a par with evangelical preaching and lecturing, in comparison with which it had declined in importance, while the lecturer had to show his conformity to the discipline of the Church.[19]

By the 1620s it was clear that James I had reservations about the liberty which he had previously allowed preachers. The reason for the royal reaction of 1622 was the threat posed to the king's authority by the wave of controversial preaching which swept the country following the announcement of the Spanish marriage plans and his overtures to Roman Catholics.[20] Some bishops, disillusioned by the toleration of nonconformity under Archbishop Abbot, used this as a pretext to discredit 'Puritanism' and popular preaching in the eyes of the king. Under the terms of the Directions of 1622 lecturers were required to avoid controversial doctrinal and political topics, to turn afternoon sermons into catechizing by question and answer (resurrected by Charles I in the Instructions of 1629), and to license themselves in the court of Faculties (on the recommendation of the diocesan, a fiat from Canterbury and authorization under the great seal).[21] These orders were distributed to all diocesan courts, and by some officials put into operation. From the circular which accompanied the orders, James I appeared to be acting in part on the advice of certain bishops. Hacket suggested that Williams was responsible for the measure, Heylyn suggested Laud. Laud can probably be discounted because he was in Wales on his primary

[18] Bodl. Tanner MS 68/92, Tanner 68/2/3 June 1636; Edward Symonds, *Four Sermons Wherein is Made a Fourfold Discovery* (1642), 28; Symonds himself often preached at the Stortford 'public lecture'.

[19] PRO SP 16/493/28; D'Ewes, *Autobiography*, i. 143. Richard Montagu claimed that lecturers 'brawl at the shadow of their own fancies': PRO SP 16/25/10.

[20] Fincham and Lake, 'The Ecclesiastical Policy of James I', 169–207; BL Harl. MS 159/136v; T. Cogswell, *The Blessed Revolution: English Politics and the Coming of War, 1621–1624* (Camb., 1989), 29–35.

[21] *Documentary Annals*, ii. 203; in the light of this surely G. Bernard, 'The Church of England c.1529–c.1642', *History* (1990), 195, underestimates the 'practical relevance' of predestinarianism for those who governed.

visitation of St David's between 5 July and 15 August.[22] Apart from Williams the most likely sponsor for this code was Harsnett of Norwich, the bishop who drew up the Considerations of 1629, which designated lecturers as 'the peoples creatures ... by reason of their pay' who 'blow the bellows their way, sedition'. Moreover the publication of the Directions coincided with Harsnett's measures to suppress 'sole lecturers' in his diocese, and to convert these into combinations, a practice which won the approval of James I, who during the prorogation of 1624 commended 'my lord of Norwich for suppressing ... popular lectures within his diocese'.[23]

The succession in 1625 of a king who perceived preaching as potentially subversive meant that the reaction of 1622 continued. It was not that Charles I was hostile to all preaching; he chose and preferred his chaplains on their ability to preach to his own liking.[24] Even attendance at a St Paul's Cross sermon was not beneath him, where he went in private in 1630 shortly after the birth of his son.[25] But Charles I had little sympathy for the relative freedom of religious expression found within the Jacobean Church, and anathematized evangelical Puritanism as a movement which subverted all forms of authority and hierarchy. Tragically he also made the association, like Laud and Wren, between Puritanism and the recent parliamentary opposition to his policies.[26] Consequently, if lectures were to survive at all under Charles I it was only under the most circumscribed conditions. When Goodman established several new lectures in Gloucester diocese in 1634, the king informed Laud that 'I must be satisfied that the occasions were very necessary otherwise he shall answer it'.[27] He certainly disliked those lectures established and financed by lay support outside clerical control, asserting that he would 'have no priest have any necessity of a lay dependency'.[28] With contempt he dismissed 'running lectures' with the words; 'if there be

[22] *Records of the old Archdeaconry of St Alban's*, ed. W. Hall (1908), 147–51; Bodl. MS Carte 77/93–94v; CVRO CA Records Art. Collect. A. 79/134; NNRO ANW/21/1/5; ESFRO FC 99/E1/1/1623; Bodl. Tanner MS 82/259–267v, MS Carte 77/93–4; Hacket, *SR* i. 89; Heylyn, *CA* 97; *WWL* iii. 139–40; Fuller, *CH* 355–9.

[23] PRO SP 14/165/2; Prynne, *CD* 368; Bodl. Tanner MS 114/204, 314/155v; BL Harl. MS 159/118, 136–136v. One of Williams's abortive recommendations to James I in October 1623 was the establishment of combination lectures in market-towns (Hacket, *SR* i. 122).

[24] See Ch. 1 nn. 191–3. [25] Bodl. MS Eng. letters b. 1/57.

[26] PRO SP 16/259/78. [27] *WWL* v. 330. [28] *WWL* v. 321.

dark corners . . . it were fit a true light should illuminate [them] and . . . not [one] that is false and uncertain,' evidence also of his conviction that only the ordained could preach.[29] So prejudicial were such royal views against independent religious expression that they go far to explain the reaction against lecturing which is a characteristic feature of his reign. Yet this does not mean that the king had evolved policy in his own mind and merely asked others to put it into practice. In 1634, when Laud informed him that the Mercers' Company intended to establish a lecture at Huntingdon without consulting Williams (and usurping his power of nomination and dismissal), Charles's reply was, 'show me the way to overthrow this, and to hinder the performance in time to all such intentions.'[30] Thus it is in the light of the king's receptivity to advice as well as of his own prejudices that the attempt to restrain preaching during his reign ought to be seen. In fact as early as 1626 Charles had sought the advice of his bishops in what he called 'the cause of the Church'.[31] One result of such consultations was Harsnett's 'Considerations for the better settling of church government' which Charles adopted with several alterations as the Instructions of 1629.[32] As seen above, Harsnett laid down four main recommendations concerning preaching: that all afternoon sermons should be turned into catechizing by question and answer; that all lecturers should read divine service before their lectures in surplice and hood; that only combination lectures, 'a company of grave and orthodox divines near adjoining' should preach in market-towns, and finally that all lectures maintained by corporations should take upon themselves a cure within the town and, until one became available, undergo suspension. Other proposals also restricted preaching, by inviting clergy to spy on lectures, that only those 'qualified by law' should employ domestic chaplains (which would prevent most gentry households from harbouring unlicensed preachers) and that the bishops should tighten up their ordination practices.

The Considerations constituted a radical programme to bind preaching to the liturgy and discipline of the Church. Once reformulated by the king they were distributed in January 1630 throughout the dioceses of the two Provinces. As early as 4 January

29 *WWL* v. 320.
30 *WWL* v. 321; LPL MS 1030/19.
31 *WWL* iii. 186–7.
32 Prynne, *CD* 368; *WWL* v. 307–9.

Laud had dispatched copies to his five archdeacons, suggesting that they pass on to the clergy only copies of those orders which directly concerned them.[33] On 27 January Hall of Exeter dispatched the Instructions to his four archdeacons for distribution, while in Lincoln Williams went so far as to sell copies to every minister, but not until after the second archidiaconal visitation, 'to avoid all occasion of putting the poorer sort of my brethren the clergy to . . . unnecessary trouble and expense'.[34] Although the bishops expected the clergy to make copies for their parishes, most of them neither expected the churchwardens to buy copies nor to possess them as a matter of necessity. Two exceptions to this rule were Curle in Winchester and Juxon in London, whose policy, although more expensive for the parishes to bear, effectively bypassed the clergy in the publication and the implementation of the Instructions.[35] This seems to have been paralleled by the general episcopal practice of appealing directly to the parishes by asking their archdeacons to publish the Instructions at their quarterly visitations, which countered possible claims by the churchwardens, who held annual office that they had not seen the orders.[36] They were republished also during episcopal visitations and some diocesans, such as Wren, Towers, Lindsell, and Montagu included them within their visitation articles.[37] Laud himself did not refer to the Instructions in his metropolitical or ordinary articles, although he asked Brent to see that they were respected throughout the Southern Province during the metropolitical visitation.[38] Heylyn saw the enforcement of the Instructions as one of the major tasks of the visitation but Laud's instructions to Brent and the vicar-general's returns suggest that they were not given preferential consideration.[39]

33 Prynne, *CD* 368, 371; Bodl. Tanner 82/262; *WWL* vi. 268.

34 DRO Chanter 57/7ᵛ; J. F. Chanter, *The Life of Martin Blake* (1910), 49–50; PRO SP 16/162/51.

35 *WWL* v. 324; STRO PR4/2/1/118; HRO 49M67/PRI/1625, 113M82/P22/21, 75M72/PW1/93; SYRO PSH/HORS/7/1/13, PSH/CHOB/7/1/3, PSH/MCH/1/2/8; GLRO 4825/1/36ᵛ, 4071/2/109, 1002/1/1634, 5714/1/116–126ᵛ.

36 PRO SP 16/162/51; Prynne, *CD* 371; Bodl. MS Tanner 82/262; *WWL* vi. 268; DRO Chanter 57/7ᵛ.

37 *Articles* for Norwich (Wren 1636, Montagu 1638), Peterborough (Lindsell 1633, Towers 1638), Hereford (Wren 1635), and Ely (Wren 1638).

38 PRO SP 16/260/471; WSRO Ep. 11/11/3/73; LAO Red Bk. Add. H. Reg. 3/197; *WWL* v. 399–452.

39 Heylyn, *CA* 288; PRO SP 16/474/67, 16/260/90, 16/293/128, 16/274/12, 16/455/59.

In fact the metropolitical courts did not occasion any marked intensification in their enforcement over the diocesan courts.[40]

Under the terms of the ninth clause of the Instructions of 1629, the two archbishops were required to send to the king by 2 January each year provincial reports on the progress of their enforcement within their respective dioceses.[41] This requirement entailed a close supervision of lectures at all levels through which the reports passed on their way to the king: from churchwarden to rural dean, from rural dean to archdeacon, from archdeacon to bishop; and bishop to archbishop. As early as the first quarter of 1630 most bishops appear to have carried out initial surveys of the lectures within their sees if the activities of Williams in Lincoln, Laud in London, Hall in Exeter, and Curle in Bath and Wells are representative.[42] The formulation of these early reports encountered a variety of problems, such as bad communications, dislike of surveillance or interference, a desire to protect parochial interests, bureaucratic delays, or sheer apathy among officials. The arrival of Archdeacon Rivet of Bath's survey was temporarily delayed because the lecturers within his archdeaconry lived 'far remote from one another'.[43] In February 1630 Laud had asked for the return of all the lecturers' names within London diocese, together with the places where they preached and the extent of their conformity in the light of the Instructions.[44] By September 1630, however, the officials of one of his five archdeaconries, St Alban's, had still not returned to the diocesan registrar the required information. Archdeacon Rayment realized the negligence of his officials only when Laud drew his attention to it.[45] Perhaps these initial surveys revealed most of all how little surveillance there had been in previous years and the extent of official ignorance that existed in the courts about lectureships. There were still delays in returning reports in London in 1635, when Juxon had to make an account to Laud, based upon the returns of only two of his five

[40] This is my impression gleaned from a reading of many of the extant court records.

[41] *WWL* v. 309; PRO SP/16/153/100.

[42] PRO SP 16/162/51; *WWL* vi. 268; Prynne, *CD* 371; Bodl. Tanner MS 114/115; SRO D/D/C/1878 bundle 3/14 Feb. 1630; DRO Ch. 57/7^{v}; Chanter, *Life of Martin Blake*, 48–51; *Records of the old Archdeaconry of St Alban's*, ed. W. Hall (1908), 155; Bodl. Rawl. MS D924/98.

[43] SRO D/D/C/1878 bundle 3/14 Feb. 1630.

[44] Prynne, *CD*, 371; Bodl. Tanner MS 114/115.

[45] *Records of the old Archdeaconry of St Alban's*, 155.

archdeacons.[46] The two bishops who continually failed to return Accounts in the 1630s were not, however, apathetic to the Instructions: Goodman consistently enforced them in Gloucester, while Wright of Coventry and Lichfield personally advocated them on visitation, such as in Salop archdeaconry during September 1633.[47]

In the diocese of Canterbury, Abbot established a commission to oversee the introduction of the Instructions, but it soon became apparent that he could not carry out all the orders with equanimity. When the commissioners suspended Udney and Palmer, lecturers respectively at Ashford and St Alphege's, Canterbury, Abbot merely relicensed them by exploiting the powers granted him under the terms of the Directions of 1622.[48] The commissioners, 'slighted and ridiculed', informed Laud that 'all conforming orthodox ministers were discomforted, His Majesty's Instructions annihilated and the archdeacon's jurisdiction inhibited'. Archdeacon Kingsley and Dean Bargrave petitioned the king against Abbot's actions, asserting that he was fomenting Puritan disaffection within Canterbury.[49] Abbot's conviction that conformist clergy, in particular the vicar of Ashford, were exaggerating the extent of nonconformity, fell on deaf ears. Consequently Charles I forced Abbot to suppress the Ashford lectureship, which he himself had previously sanctioned under the terms of the Directions of 1622.[50]

It would, however, be incorrect to see the enforcement of the Instructions through the spectacles of king versus archbishop, or Puritan versus Anglican. Paul Seaver's characterization of the code as 'brutal and drastic' is rather exaggerated.[51] When translated into practice the Instructions might be less offensive and might assume a different complexion within the parish than at the centre, whether that centre were focused in London or devolved upon the diocese. In fact the Instructions were in some respects sufficiently ambiguous to permit different interpretations. Wright of Bristol thought that they were 'a service due to his Majesty and most acceptable to God, the God of order', but he informed Harsnett and Laud that unless the

46 *WWL* v. 332.

47 GRO GDR 181, 185–200; P. Studley, *The Looking Glasse of Schisme* (1635), 284, 289, 299.

48 Bodl. Rawl. MS D. 924/98; *Documentary Annals*, ii. 203.

49 Bodl. Rawl. MS D. 924/98.

50 PRO SP 16/164/14: in 1629 the king conferred the lectureship upon Udney (a royal chaplain in extraordinary) at the request of Dorchester, Secretary of State.

51 Seaver, *PL* 243.

king explained certain words in the document and armed him with more than the general instructions, he could achieve little.[52] Consequently some bishops might exceed their letter, others might undercut and moderate them. The formulation and publication of the Instructions were one thing, their implementation another. Chapter 1 has already shown that Laud was less associated with the genesis of the document than we once thought. Developing this theme, the following analysis highlights, among other things, how historians have smothered over important subtleties in his attitude to the Instructions and ignored the extent to which he tempered or changed their letter. As early as February 1630, the Puritan Thomas Gataker had distinguished between a Laudian approach in London diocese and the more forceful line adopted by others: 'His Majesty's Instructions are in the City observed with some favourable constructions which it pleased that bishop (Laud) to give them, but our bishop (Neile) will not admit.'[53]

II. PREACHING AND CATECHIZING

Instruction 5 of 1629, which dealt specifically with lectures, consisted of four clauses. The first clause called for the conversion of all afternoon sermons into catechizing by question and answer, but whether this applied to all preachers or just lecturers was not immediately apparent. In November 1633 Lindsell of Peterborough informed Lambe of 'a puritan excuse' trumped up by several clergy within his diocese who were 'strong conceited that it belongs not to them, because the direction is for lecturers only'. But Lindsell himself was brought to question the real meaning and he felt obliged to consult the king.[54] From Laud's account in 1634 it is clear that he and Charles understood the clause to refer not only to lecturers but to preachers generally.[55]

Failure to distinguish between catechism and catechizing (the word used) on the one hand, and the sermon before, during, and after evening prayer (all of which might occur on the afternoon) on the other has led historians into assuming that the Instructions necessarily entailed the proscription of all sermons in the afternoon and

[52] PRO SP 16/160/68. [53] Bodl. Tanner MS 71/35.
[54] PRO SP 16/251/25. [55] *WWL* v. 320.

their substitution by the plain reading of the catechism in question and answer.[56] In order to understand the subtlety, the very flexibility of Laud's policy, it is necessary to keep in mind certain semantic difficulties which it left unresolved. Catechizing was considered a vitally important medium for the spiritual edification and education of the 'ignorant' in Reformation England. According to the Canons of 1604 ministers should catechize youths and apprentices for at least half an hour before evening prayer.[57] Among the Laudian bishops there was a clear conviction that catechizing was in decline, because preaching had encroached upon the sacramental and catechetical functions of the clergy.[58] Yet although instruction 5 addressed itself to these issues, it left unresolved something which contemporaries themselves could not easily resolve: what constituted an afternoon sermon? The Canons of 1604 suggested that two sermons should be preached every Sunday, in the morning and evening, but they laid down no time for evening prayer and it was left to the discretion of the ordinary or the clergy to establish one. Medieval canons, it would seem, regarded the time of services as flexible and dependent upon the seasons and the fall of dusk. The important fact is that during the early modern period evening prayer invariably took place in the afternoon.[59] Thus the sermon, before, during, or after evening prayer, was effectively an afternoon sermon and had canonical backing. The breadth of this loophole for those who wished to avoid a more radical interpretation of the instruction was considerable. In May 1637 Laud himself approved of the Worcester corporation's lectures on 'Sundays in the afternoon to be given (at) four o'clock after evening prayer'.[60] Earlier, when bishop of London, in January 1632 he had permitted William Jemmet 'to lecture . . . every afternoon'.[61] Again, during his trial Laud explicitly recognized the existence of the afternoon sermon when denying the assertion that the book of sports prevented preaching. The book of sports had, after all, approved of lawful recreations only after the end of the 'afternoon sermon', an inconsistency with

[56] Hill, *SP* 115.

[57] *Synodalia*, i. 280; Collinson, *RP* 232; I. Green, '"For Children in Yeeres and Children in Understanding": The Emergence of the English Catechism under Elizabeth and the Early Stuarts', *Journal of Ecclesiastical History*, 37 (1986).

[58] PRO SP 16/456/44.

[59] LPL 943/215; *WWL* iv. 252. I should like to thank Revd. Dr Nicholas Cranfield for discussions on this point.

[60] WORO 13945/712–17147(6).

[61] GL 9531/15/25–6; PRO SP 16/123/32.

the Instructions which Charles I had overlooked.[62] Moreover, as the second instruction required that lecturers should read prayers before their lectures, the Instructions unwittingly endorsed one type of afternoon preaching.[63] Others interpreted the instruction in a liberal way similar to Laud, who, like Juxon, approved of lectures on Sunday afternoon 'to begin after evening prayer and catechising'.[64] It seems that many court references to gadding to afternoon sermons refer as much to the sermon within evening prayer as to that after it. In the archdeaconry court of Essex, John Alex of Novendon was actually prosecuted for being absent from church and missing the afternoon sermon.[65] London churchwarden accounts reveal the existence of such sermons in the City.[66] When Nicholas Ferrar went up to London in the 1630s he attended afternoon sermons, while Christopher Dow depicted the scene of gadding from one city church to another on Sunday afternoon to hear different preachers.[67] In 1637 even a diocesan official recognized that baptism in several city churches was not performed until after the afternoon sermon.[68] Although Juxon prevented some preachers from preaching in the afternoon during his primary visitation of 1634, this was untypical as the preachers in question were prominent nonconformists.[69]

The archdeaconry court of Berkshire objected not to the existence of afternoon preaching at Sulhampstead Abbots but to the fact that people gadded to hear the preacher. The same courts prosecuted a parishioner of St Mary, Reading, for leaving his parish church and going to Caversham notwithstanding the fact that his own minister provided sermons in the afternoon.[70] In the neighbouring see of Oxford, Sunday afternoon sermons were preached in both the city church of St Martin, Carfax, and at the University Church throughout Laud's chancellorship. Throckmorton of West Malling fell foul of the archdeaconry courts of Rochester, not because he preached in the afternoon, but because he had disobeyed the chancellor's

[62] *WWL* iv. 251–2; Laud's *Articles* for the visitation of the Arches in 1639 have an insertion expressly recognizing the afternoon sermon (see Bodl. copy).

[63] *WWL* v. 308.

[64] GLRO DL/C/344/74.

[65] GL 2968/3/493^v.

[66] GL 9537/1541^v–2.

[67] *Brief Memoirs of Nicholas Ferrar*, ed. T. M. Macdonough (1637), 210; C. Dow, *Innovations unjustly charged unto the present Church and State* (1637), 208; J. Gore, *A Winter Sermon preached Shrove Sunday in the afternoon . . . 1634* (1638).

[68] PRO SP 16/371/39.

[69] ERO D/ABA 9/Commissary/251; HTRO AHH 5/13.

[70] BERO D/A2/c. 79/219^v, 253, D/A2/c. 77/89.

command 'to end his sermon in the afternoon upon Sunday in a seasonable time'.[71] The courts of Worcester, Peterborough, Exeter, Bristol, Norwich (under White) and Ely (under White) also permitted the afternoon sermons, as almost certainly did most other jurisdictions.[72] Thus historians incorrectly assume that the Instructions entailed the proscription of the afternoon sermon or lecture, as the evening sermon was widely recognized as taking place in the afternoon. Possibly only Wren showed any signs of wishing to exploit the Instructions to bring within their orbit the afternoon sermon in this widest sense.[73]

Yet the Instructions primarily addressed those afternoon sermons which occurred *before* evening prayer during the official time of catechizing. Instruction 5 specified that all such sermons should be turned into catechizing by question and answer.[74] But did 'turned' necessarily mean the proscription of this type of sermon? It is a measure of the historiographical distortion of Laudianism that we have failed to realize that Laud did not suppress this kind of afternoon sermon but allowed the preacher to preach on the catechism. Laud understood the instruction in terms not of the suppression of sermons but of the conversion of the pedagogical content, a policy totally distinct from the policy pursued by Wren.

Laud insisted that catechizing should first take place (with the measure of exposition that it allowed) but that then the minister, if he so wished, might preach on the catechetical heads. Contrary to what Dr Seaver suggests, it was not the king but Laud who petitioned in 1639 for the recognition of the catechetical afternoon sermon: 'I think your Majesty may be pleased to have the ministers preach if they will, so that they do first catechise orderly by question and answer, and afterwards preach upon the same heads to the people, for the better understanding of those questions.'[75] Unknown to the king, Laud was asking him to confirm a practice which he had permitted in London and Canterbury dioceses throughout the 1630s. His diocesan courts in these sees cited ministers for not catechizing but they did not attempt to prevent preachers from preaching in the

[71] C. Fletcher, *A History of St Martin's Carfax* (1890); *WWL* v. 287; KAO DRB/PA 33(1635).

[72] WORO 795. 02/2302/3/544; PRO SP 16/371/39; SRO DD/PH 222/40; BERO D/A2/c. 79/211v; see n. 92.

[73] W. Prynne, *A Looking Glasse for all Lordly Prelates* (1630), 71–3.

[74] *WWL* v. 307. [75] Seaver, *PL* 263; *WWL* v. 368.

afternoon before evening prayer, although they were expected to convert their preaching from an overtly rhetorical medium to a more catechetical one.[76] Within the diocese of Canterbury such afternoon sermons existed at Mersham and St Mary, Dover.[77] In November 1638 the churchwardens of St Mary, Canterbury, returned the presentment (without prosecution) that the 'sermon on the afternoon ... is by way of catechism according to the king's Majesty Instructions'.[78] Although clergy were encouraged to preach catechetically, at the end of the 1630s parishes could still present to the Canterbury courts again without prosecution that their sermons had not been converted.[79] This was a continuation of Laud's practice in London. In 1631 he suspended Archer for not catechizing properly but not because he had done so on Sundays 'in the afternoon',[80] while in September 1630 he licensed the Ealing lecture 'by way of catechising on Sundays in the afternoon'.[81] Only where ministers were particularly nonconformist to the catechism might Laud take measures to prevent the minister from preaching in the afternoon, as with Valentine of Chalfont St Giles, but of this there are very few examples.[82]

The episcopal response to the order to turn afternoon sermons into catechizing falls into two categories, those who adopted a similar approach to Laud's (first ordering ministers to catechize by question and answer and then allowing them to preach) and those who attempted to suppress afternoon sermons and confine the minister to the plain words of the catechism, notably Wren and Piers. Many bishops did not attempt to suppress the afternoon sermons and followed Laud's more accommodating line. Even Neile's visitation articles for 1635 allowed afternoon preaching 'in that kind of catechising, if he so preach'.[83] In Lincoln, John Williams ordered ministers to catechize first by question and answer and then to preach on the catechetical heads, which, as he told Lambe, would prevent the misconstruction of the order as an 'intent to take away preaching

[76] ERO D/ACv5; GL 2968/3/493v; ERO D/ABA 5 Commissary/152; CCL X. 6. 10./190v, Z. 3. 16/186, X. 6. 6./198v; CCL U3/30/8/1/22–8: the courts prosecuted people for gadding but not the ministers for preaching in the afternoon.

[77] CCL U3/30/8/1/22–8; *PCR*, 157; GL 2968/3/493v.

[78] CCL X. 6. 10/190v. [79] CCL Z. 3. 16/186; CCL X. 6. 6./198v.

[80] GL 9531/15/22–3. [81] GLRO DL/C/343/97. [82] PRO SP 16/326/18; Thomas Shepard, *God's Plot* ed. M. McGiffert (Amherst. Ma. 1972), 49.

[83] *Articles* (Neile) 1635; PRO SP 16/312/84 shows how he had brought many to perform 'both catechising and preaching'.

or to tire out preachers'.[84] Thus there can be little doubt that the catechetical sermon was recognized in most dioceses. The churchwardens of St Saviour, Southwark (Winchester), continually returned the answer during Surrey archidiaconal visitations that their minister had turned his sermons on Sundays and holy days into 'a catechising manner of preaching'.[85] During Wright's visitation of the archdeaconry of Salop in 1633, Peter Studley, one of the fiercest advocates of the Instructions, preached catechetical sermons at St Chad, Shrewsbury.[86] It might be objected that some bishops made no attempt to encourage the catechetical sermon and left preachers to preach very much as they had done before. If this was the case, then, as the courts could neither make the preacher preach catechetically nor preach upon the catechism, such practices marked a difference not of policy but of attitude. Only in the dioceses of Norwich and Ely (under Wren) and Bath and Wells (under Piers) was there a continuous, systematic attempt to prevent the preaching of sermons in the afternoon, by making the minister catechize only, and according to the plain letter of the catechism, a policy which was the exact antithesis of Laud's in this respect. Wren felt that 'catechising and preaching' could not sit well together, and claimed that if the minister was allowed to preach catechetically, he would ask only a few questions and then fall into a long sermon about the particulars in question, 'which', said Wren, '*could be no catechism*'.[87] It was a strict and possibly correct interpretation of the instruction, but one which Laud and other bishops chose to ignore. The difference between Wren and other clergy over this particular issue is humorously revealed in an entry in Dean Young of Winchester's diary for 25 November 1630, referring to a chapter meeting convened to elect a new cathedral lecturer to preach on Sunday afternoon: 'Dr Wren advised the lecture might be read once a weekday, because (the) reading on the Sundays crossed the king's order for catechising in parish churches. It was answered that they might catechise if they would, till three o'clock: *our lecture was after*.'[88] In Norwich and Ely,

[84] PRO SP 16/162/51. Among the charges brought by Allen against Williams in 1632 was that he had 'crossed the king's Instructions by allowing catechising and preaching' (PRO SP 16/211/47).

[85] GLRO P/292/SAV/533–4, 513, 516–17; Bodl. MS Rawl. E. 29.

[86] Studley, *Looking Glasse of Schisme*, 190.

[87] Bodl. Tanner MS 220/2, 8, 68/153, 137/7.

[88] WCL MS xxii/66; Young may have defended preaching at three on the basis of Acts 3:1 (see n. 99).

Wren suppressed afternoon sermons because he said, 'there was no mention in the rubric of divine service or canon for sermons in the afternoon but plenty of words in favour of catechising.'[89] In fact once bishop, he suppressed all afternoon sermons, whether before, during, or after evening prayer, catechetical or not. As early as March 1636 he had prohibited all preaching on Sunday afternoons within the city of Norwich. His visitation articles asked whether clergy had turned their sermons into catechizing 'and is this truly and sincerely performed, without mockery and show only'.[90] There was little room for Laudian flexibility in Wren's policy and the rigid application of his own interpretation brought him into conflict with those who, not without cause, disagreed with it. In short it helped to discredit the more moderate approach of Laud and the rest of the bench and in the long term helped to misrepresent their policies.

The tension aroused by Wren's inflexible policy is focused in an incident which took place at Dallam in Suffolk during one afternoon in 1636.[91] Lord Brooke had gathered together at his house several friends, including the earl of Bedford and Viscount Doncaster, to celebrate the christening of his child. Bedford asked his host for a sermon, which Ashe, Brooke's chaplain, then preached. The whole incident may have been carefully stage-managed to test their diocesan's nerve. Two days later, one of Wren's apparitors appeared with a citation calling Ashe into court on pain of excommunication and demanding to know why Brooke had permitted his chaplain to preach in the afternoon against Wren's express orders prohibiting such sermons within the diocese of Norwich. The apparitor informed them that the bishop intended to make an example of Ashe by calling him into the High Commission. This high-handed and provocative act brought Brooke to his feet. He instructed the apparitor to inform Wren that there was 'no law of God, or the realm, no canon of the Church, that inhibits ministers to preach on the Lord's day in the afternoon'. Brooke brought to his defence not only the book of sports, which Wren was forcing ministers to read and which expressly recognized the afternoon sermon; he also threw at the apparitor the words of a neighbouring bishop, White of Ely and Wren's predecessor at Norwich: 'therefore ... the bishops and the minister

[89] Bodl. Tanner MS 314/153^{v}; Tanner MS 220/8.

[90] Bodl. Tanner MS 137/7, 68/153, 333. At Hereford he had also suppressed all afternoon sermons: CCO MS 206/21.

[91] Prynne, *A Looking Glasse for all Lordly Prelates*, 71–3.

should preach on the Lords' Day afternoon, as well as in the forenoon and not be questioned, but commended for doing it.'[92]

Wren's strict interpretation of this instruction was equalled by that of Piers in Bath and Wells. Piers appears to have based his dislike of lectures on the reprobate belief that preaching had run its course: 'though there was need of preaching in the infancy of the Church as in the Apostles' time,' he informed the vicar of Limington in 1633 (who had just petitioned him for a lecture), 'yet now there was no such necessity, and thereupon he required the said minister upon his canonical obedience not to preach.'[93] He refused to allow ministers to give even the briefest exposition upon the catechism. The articles of impeachment preferred against him in 1641 said that he had prosecuted ministers whose only offence had been to pray before and after the catechism and threatened 'to punish ministers if they persisted in that way which he said was a catechism sermon-wise, and as if they preached', and he charged them '[to] ask no questions nor require any other answer from the people, but such as were contained in the catechism'.[94] The surviving court records of Bath and Wells fully confirm the justice of the charges.[95] In 1636, for example, Piers cited the churchwardens of Bridgewater for failing to present Devenish, their minister, for expounding upon the catechism in the afternoon. Bartholomew of Enmore was called into court for preaching on the catechism for half an hour, and for using what Piers considered to be an over-long prayer, and again in 1636 for preaching in the afternoon for several hours. In Bath and Wells if any afternoon sermons arose they were quickly put down, which Piers so successfully achieved that by 1637 he prided himself on having suppressed all afternoon sermons and lectures within the see.[96] Apart from Norwich, Ely, and Bath and Wells, preachers were restricted to the plain catechism and asked not to preach in Gloucester diocese and the archdeaconries of Northampton (Peterborough) and Derby (Coventry and Lichfield), where Samuel Clarke was respectively surrogate and archdeacon.[97]

92 Ibid. 71–3.

93 *Articles of Accusation and Impeachment... against William Piers* (1642), 2.

94 Ibid. 2.

95 SRO D/D/Ca 287/141ᵛ, 313/49, 309/74, 206, 319/33ᵛ, 326/239, 308/74ᵛ, 299/11.

96 SRO D/D/Ca/309/205, D/D/Ca/313/33v, 41ᵛ–42; *WWL* v. 334; PRO SP 16/499/59ᵛ.

97 GRO GDR 191/Nov.–Dec. 1636, GDR 195 Jan.–Mar. 1637, GDR 190/199; *HMC Appendix to the 9th Report*, 496 (4 Mar.); Bodl. MS Tanner 65/209–290ᵛ.

The few remaining instances of the suppression of afternoon sermons or lectures during the 1630s may be explained as infrequent expedients on the part of the courts, incited either by the preachers' refusal to catechize, or his general nonconformity.[98] In Norwich and Bath and Wells, on the other hand, the courts recognized afternoon sermons only to suppress them. Thus this particular instruction was sufficiently elastic to permit Laud and other bishops to moderate its force, but not to prevent the admission of extremist policies. It was also an invitation to individual ministers to prevent sermons within their parishes, and to reject requests from their congregations that they preach. Thomas Vaughan of Chatham in the diocese of Rochester informed his congregation that St Paul had taught him to be 'constant in season and out of season'. Since, according to the Instructions (he claimed), 'in season' meant 'to preach upon Sundays in the forenoon' and 'out of season' meant 'in the afternoon', he had made the conscious decision not to preach.[99] Clearly Vaughan was in clear contravention of the Canons of 1604 and the views of many of the clergy in the 1630s. Viscount Falkland was responsible for not a little historical misrepresentation when he accused the bishops as a whole of bringing in 'catechising to thrust out preaching'.[100]

Under the terms of instruction 8 of 1629, the bishops were to see that the catechism as well as the liturgy were as well attended as sermons. Surviving court records paint a varied picture of the extent of catechizing across the two Provinces, both in respect of the level of popular attendance and of clerical responsibility.[101] In several sees, including St David's and Bangor, it had fallen into disuse.[102] A similarly dark picture came in 1636 from Wren, who noted that there was a 'general defect of catechising' throughout the diocese of Norwich.[103] In all sees there were cases of clerical negligence and occasionally of some ministers not catechizing at all, but their number varied from diocese to diocese. In Winchester, according to Curle, only a handful of the clergy in any one year did not catechize. In 1638 Goodman reported that some clergy were opposed to catechiz-

[98] PRO SP 16/326/18; HFRO Box 27/vol. 97 Eardisley 27 Oct. 1636, 9 Dec. 1636; LJRO B/V/1/55.

[99] *PCR* 226; Bodl. Rawl. MS E 21/120 where Pocklington with difficulty tries to explain away the fact that St Peter preached at three in the afternoon (Acts 3:1–15).

[100] J. A. R. Marriot, *The Life and Times of... Viscount Falkland* (1907), 182–3.

[101] *WWL* v. 327, 339.

[103] Bodl. Tanner MS 68/26.

ing but because they were afraid of losing their livings they did not take their opposition too far.[104]

To make the clergy catechize was one thing, to make them catechize according to the catechism of the Book of Common Prayer was another. In 1635 children in many parishes within the archdeaconry of Buckingham were being instructed in Perkin's Six Principles. Laud insisted that catechizing must have its base in the official Prayer Book catechism, and during the metropolitical visitation, Brent issued orders to the clergy that they use no other.[105] Several preachers appeared before Laud for not obeying this requirement but they were relatively few. In December 1630, for example, Archer of All Hallows, Lombard Street, was suspended, but Laud absolved him three months later.[106] The Laudian attachment to the official catechism cannot be considered as an anti-Calvinist initiative, as predestinarian ideas underlay its doctrine.[107] Possibly, however, Laud wished to impress it upon the parishes because it was less overtly Calvinist than other versions. In fact there was wide consensus on the bench that it was the best catechism for clerical use. In 1635 Williams enquired in his articles whether ministers catechized according to the Prayer Book catechism, and he did not see fit to alter this article in 1641.[108] According to Morton's biographer, 'for the fuller instruction of children in the grounds of religion' the bishop printed many copies of the official catechism, at his own cost, for use in Coventry and Lichfield, and Durham, and gave strict orders to the clergy 'to be . . . careful in the catechising of their youth'.[109] Other bishops stressed the same through visitation addresses and sermons, such as Skinner of Bristol in 1637, who informed the clergy of the archdeaconry of Dorset 'to preach faith and good works . . . what to believe and how to live . . . [which] is briefly summed up in the Church's catechism . . . I will confidently say it, you cannot serve God nor the king nor the Church better than

[104] *WWL* v. 327, 339, 348, 359; William Jones, *The True Inquisition or the Sad Soules Search* (1633), 23.

[105] PRO SP 16/286/86; WSRO EP 11/11/3/73; LAO Red Bk. Add. H. Reg. 3/197.

[106] GL 9531/15/22–3.

[107] Ian Green has emphasized the mixed doctrinal complexion of cathechisms in this period: '"For Children in Yeeres and Children in Understanding"'.

[108] *Articles* (Lincoln) 1635; CCO D288/363^{v} (3).

[109] *The Life and Times of Thomas Morton* (York, 1669), 83; see also *The Vindication of the Bishop of Durham* (1641), 8.

by well catechising your cures.'[110] In the neighbouring see of Exeter, Hall also placed catechizing on a par with preaching.[111]

Although the attempt to increase catechizing met with difficulties when the minister wished to catechize according to other versions, extant records suggest that by the end of the 1630s the episcopal efforts were making some headway. Ultimately the campaign to increase catechizing would be weakened less by the clerical failure to catechize properly than by the apathy of many masters and parents to send their apprentices and children to be catechized. In 1634 the churchwardens of Wantage declared that 'the minister hath not of late catechised every Sabbath but the failure is rather in the parishioners not sending, than his (not) endeavouring.'[112] The vicar of St James, Dover despaired of catechizing during the harvest time when only a quarter of his congregation appeared in church.[113] It is impossible to say to what extent catechizing was better attended at the end of the 1630s than before. One can only refer to the concerted attempts made throughout the two Provinces to ameliorate the problem by prosecuting offenders for not appearing so that a fall in the numbers of prosecutions in any given area during the 1630s is unlikely to reflect decreased detection by the courts.

III. PREACHING AND THE LITURGY

The second instruction was potentially the most radical of all the stipulations concerning lecturers. It asked them to read prayers before each lecture, in an attempt to tie lecturing to the liturgy. This marked a considerable departure from the policy implicit in the Canons of 1604 where the lecturer was required to read prayers and to administer the sacraments only twice a year.[114] If rigidly enforced, this requirement would have helped to separate the conformist from the nonconformist beneficed lecturer, as obedience to this instruction meant in effect unequivocable acceptance of the Prayer Book. As such it served to bring down Ward at Ipswich and Workman at

110 Robert Skinner, *His Speech at the Visitation at Dorchester September 18 1637* (1744).

111 SRO DD/PH 222/46; J. Hall, *The Old Religion* (1627), 10. Some clergy, such as Crakenthorpe, welcomed the instruction: Bodl. Tanner MS 314/153^{v}.

112 WTRO D5/28/15.

113 CCL X. 6. 6./234; see also CCL VG/4/13.

114 *WWL* v. 307–9; *Synodalia*, i. 278.

Gloucester, and provided a measure of control over the ordinary parish lecture which was otherwise not provided for in the Instructions, such as the lecturer at Ringstead, in the see of Peterborough.[115] But this particular instruction was not rigorously enforced consistently or generally throughout all dioceses, and to a certain extent the recognition of the catechetical lecture before evening prayer diminished its impact.[116] As regards its enforcement by Laud in London, he asked at least one lecturer to read prayers 'wholly' before he preached,[117] but on other occasions, he merely asked lecturers to be assistants in the reading of divine service, as at St Mary at Hill in November 1632.[118] Churchwarden accounts reveal that at All Hallows the Great, St Botolph, Aldgate, St Michael, Battishaw, and elsewhere, members of the congregation were paid to read prayers for their lecturers.[119] This suggests that Laud permitted a general conformity to the liturgy rather than a full adherence to the instruction, enabling many London lecturers to ignore the full terms of the instruction without prosecution. The important principle for him was less that lecturers read prayers than that prayers were read.

Williams pursued a similar course in Lincoln. He informed Lambe that 'if the lecturer . . . in his surplice and hood read the confession and absolution, with the creeds and collects before his going up to the pulpit, he may be assisted by the parson or curate of the place in reading for him the other parts of the divine service.'[120] Yet Williams required that on at least some occasions throughout the year the lecturer should read the whole service (one of the stipulations of 1604). Under Juxon, in London, much the same policy of accommodation was pursued as under Laud. In 1637 the lecturers of Manningtree and Wetherfield did not read prayers before the lecture and the practice which had formerly existed in some London churches of allowing others to read them for the lecturer continued.[121] The flexibility of Juxon's policy is revealed in his personal orders of May 1640 for the Sunday and Wednesday afternoon lectures at Colchester.[122] On the Wednesday when few people would be present, the lecturer was to read the liturgy in surplice and hood, but on Sunday the parson of the parish was to catechize and read prayers

115 PRO SP 16/261/206–9; PRO SP 16/308/52.
116 See Ch. 4 Section ii. 117 GL 9531/15/26.
118 GLRO DL/C/343/144^{v}, 156^{v}. 119 GL 9235/2/1631; GL 818/1.
120 PRO SP 16/162/51. 121 ERO D/ABA 8/130^{v}, 243; GL 818/1.
122 GLRO DL/C/344/74.

for the lecturer before he preached. Unlike Laud and Juxon, Neile in Winchester did not show the same degree of accommodation over this particular instruction. When in February 1630 the preacher of St Mary, Ovary, invited Cornelius Burgess from the neighbouring diocese of London to preach in his stead, Neile insisted that Burgess would have to read prayers before his sermon, or not preach at all. Burgess gave the rather feeble excuse that he was too infirm to do both, and asked Neile to show the 'favour that his diocesan (Laud) did . . . that the curate of the place in case of infirmity might read in the lecturer's stead'. Neile retorted that since the king's Instructions were 'otherwise . . . he could not give way for doing the one without the other'. With Burgess's refusal to comply, Neile refused to permit him to preach, expelled him from Southwark, and ordered the churchwardens to read both the liturgy and the Instructions to the congregation. Furthermore, on that very afternoon he complained of Burgess in the High Commission and procured letters missive from Abbot summoning him to court.[123]

With respect to this second instruction, some lecturers were more amenable to control than others, such as those of the combinations, who as beneficed ministers were accustomed to reading the liturgy. Both Dove of Peterborough and Williams of Lincoln required their respective combinations at Kettering and Bedford to read prayers in surplice and hood, before their lectures, and in Williams's case before the appearance of the Instructions.[124] Within a few dioceses, Norwich under Wren, Peterborough under Towers (and Bath and Wells if Piers had not suppressed all lectures) the survival of the lecture was conditional not only on the lecturers' performance of divine service before the lecture, but on the congregational observance of orders regulating the conduct of worship.[125] In 1639 Towers so hedged the Brackley combination (which he had restored on the petition of the borough) with stipulations that Prynne cited it as evidence that Laud had irrevocably destroyed the authentic combination. Yet Towers's policy should not be taken as normative, especially since he appears to have modelled his policy upon Wren's in Norwich.[126] Nevertheless the requirement to read the liturgy before each lecture marked a significant departure from previous

123 Bodl. Tanner MS 71/35.
124 PRO SP 16/531/135; PRO SP 16/537/32.
125 Bodl. Tanner MS 68/36^{v}, 92, 332^{v}; LPL MS 943/637.
126 Prynne, *CD* 378–80; LPL MS 943/637.

procedures across the Southern Province. It placed increased burdens not only on the nonconformist lecturer but also upon the congregation and parson. Wright of Bristol complained that since many market-town lectures in Dorset started at seven, prayers would have to commence at six, which interfered with the working day. In other Dorset parishes incumbents who received an augmented salary for reading morning prayers would suffer financially if the lecturers assumed these duties for themselves.[127] This particular instruction caused more problems than it solved, and that it won only lukewarm support from Laud may help to explain why it alone of the Instructions of 1629 concerning lecturers failed to enter the canonical visitation articles, drawn up in 1640.[128]

Instruction 8 called for greater attendance at the liturgy. Failure to appear in church emanated from a variety of causes, not necessarily from a reluctance to attend services. Gadding, especially in the afternoon, was a national pastime—'the ordinary practice of this formal age', according to Peter Studley, vicar of St Chad, Shrewsbury.[129] In some areas it was more problematic than in others. Both Brent and Williams complained to Laud of the frequency of gadding, especially in the southern archdeaconries of Lincoln diocese.[130] The increase in the number of those presented for gadding has possibly less to do with its increase in real terms than in its increased detection. The existence of afternoon sermons engendered its survival, but it also thrived on institutional inconsistencies. Evening prayer began at different times in different parishes. Some attended evening prayer in their own parishes and then gadded to the evening prayer in another. Alternatively some went to a different parish to hear the sermon, but then returned to their own in time for evening prayer. At St Julian, Shrewsbury, divine service clashed with sermons in other churches, which resulted in a sizeable depletion in the congregation. At Lynn in Norfolk over ninety parishioners gadded from St Nicholas to St Margaret and many others in return, from St Margaret to St Nicholas.[131] Geographical mobility in early modern England occurred most frequently between the parish churches. Of course

127 PRO SP 16/160/68.

128 *Articles to be enquired at the... visitation of William (Juxon)... bishop of London* (1640).

129 *WWL* v. 308; Studley, *Looking Glasse of Schisme*, 25.

130 *WWL* v. 326; PRO SP 16/274/12.

131 LJRO B/V/1/48; NNRO ANW/3/35 (June 1640).

those who gadded did not always gad to the sermon. In Kent some gadded to the cathedral service at Canterbury.[132] Occasionally the ordinary might grant licences to parishioners to attend a different church other than their own, although with conditions attached. The archdeaconry court of Buckingham allowed some infirm parishioners of Waddesdon to attend a nearer church, so long as they resorted to their own parish church at least three times in the year, received holy communion there, and paid all 'dues, tithes and other rights' to their minister.[133] In the archdeaconry of Ludlow, David Lewis of Llanfairwaterdine absented himself because he went to hold 'wakes and pastimes' in neighbouring parishes. The number of those presented for playing recreations and for working on the sabbath were legion, but many offenders almost certainly went undetected. In several parishes people simply did not go to church, especially in the afternoon (for catechizing or evening prayer) or on holy days, as was the case in the populous parish of St Mary Somerset in London.[134]

During the 1630s the courts detected several clergy for failing to read evening prayer, but a more novel feature was the extent to which they pressed the reading of, and attendance at, prayers on holy days, in particular Wednesdays and Fridays, and summoned people for failing to attend on these days. There are signs of a tightening up of attitudes to this problem in the early 1620s. In October 1623 Williams suggested that two members of each family should always attend services on Wednesdays and Fridays. A strict policy in this respect existed in Hereford, where Coke's courts enjoined ministers to read prayers throughout the week.[135] Similarly, individual clergy sometimes initiated attempts to increase attendance at these less conventional times for public prayer. The vicar of St Mary Somerset (London) recommended that at least one member of each household should appear in church on Fridays and Wednesdays. However, his well-meaning efforts fell on deaf ears and 'accordingly few came'.[136]

132 CCL X. 7. 2./61 (see also PRO SP 16/105/26).

133 BKRO MS Archd. papers c. 289.

134 HFRO Box 39/vol. 146 Ap. 1636: GL 9057/1/c. 102; according to Rees Prichard, chancellor of St David's, Sunday for most people was 'a day for drunkenness, a day for sport, a day for dance . . . and excess too short': *The Morning Star or the Divine Poems of Mr Rees Prichard* (Merthyr Tydfil, 1815), 416); Stephen Geree, minister of Wonersh referred to 'empty churches': *The Ornament of Women* (1639), *epistle dedicatory*.

135 CCO MS 206/9v; ERO D/ALV 1/Feb. 1628–29 Nov.; Hacket, *SR* i. 122.

136 GL 9057/1/102.

In other parishes minister and congregation worked together to reach a mutually agreed time for morning and evening prayer. At St Martin, Carfax, in Oxford, in order to allow most parishioners to attend, they agreed to hold morning prayer at eight and evening prayer at six. The attempt caused a minor incident in the Oxford consistory during 1634, when only one parishioner out of several hundred refused to contribute towards the minister's new salary, established within the agreement: one parochial initiative for which Laud was uncharacteristically full of praise.[137] Whether St Martin's had many parallels or whether divine service elsewhere was more frequently attended at the end of the 1630s than before is difficult to ascertain. A decline or increase in the number of presentments may be interpreted in a variety of ways. What is apparent is that in some quarters a marked improvement was perceived, notably and unexpectedly from Wren, who informed Laud in 1637 that 'prayers, catechism, sermons' were better attended in the diocese of Norwich than before. Perhaps the situation across the country after 1637 was not dissimilar.[138]

IV. COMBINATION LECTURES

In an important article on the structures and features of church life in the early seventeenth century, Professor Collinson described the combination lecture as the 'most characteristic institution of the Jacobean Church'.[139] Neile's survey of 1614 is often cited as evidence of its popularity, yet in this survey there existed only eight combinations throughout the entire diocese of Lincoln, a relatively small number considering that the see covered six counties.[140] Moreover a survey which lists only combinations must necessarily give a partial impression of the state of lectureships. In a survey of all lectures in the diocese of Gloucester (the only complete diocesan survey of lectureships in the 1630s to survive) of twenty-four lectures only three (Chipping Sodbury, Thornbury, and Wotton-under-Edge) were combinations.[141] The rest were all single lectures, at least sixteen of which were preached by beneficed ministers. This amply confirms Dr Seaver's recognition of the parish lecture as the most common variety of lectureship, an opinion which Collinson doubted,

137 ORO ODP c. 27/266–8. 138 *WWL* v. 350.
139 Collinson, *RP* 136. 140 CUL Baumgartner MS 8/200–2.
141 GRO GDR/185 July 1634 (unfol.).

since Seaver had generalized from the evidence of London corporation, where virtually all lectures were of the single parish type.[142]

Harsnett's third consideration of 1629 had required that all market-town lectures be converted into combinations of neighbouring ministers. This appeared in the Instructions with only one alteration, that the ministers should be beneficed within the diocese where the lecture was held, which would effectively prevent any refractory lecture from claiming extra-diocesan immunity.[143] It seems that again Laud was prepared to forgo a rigid application of this instruction in order to obtain a general conformity. When in May 1630 the surrogates of the archdeacon of St Alban's suppressed the combination lecture at Winslow, which lay in the diocese of London[144] (but preached by lecturers beneficed within Lincoln diocese), the lecturers petitioned Laud to lift the order. The surrogates opposed the motion and informed Laud that if he gave in to the request they would 'not be able to do his Majesty's service, nor . . . make due certificate to the bishop of their conformity if that opposition to his Majesty's Instruction be amongst them'.[145] Nevertheless, shortly afterwards, Laud granted the lecturers' request and allowed the combination to continue. In return he merely asked them to subscribe a letter that they 'had continued (the) lecture in conformity with the Church of England and would continue it'.[146] On the related issue of single lectures supplied by a minister outside the see in which it lay, Laud appeared to adopt a firmer line at least on paper. In 1634, when Thornborough of Worcester suppressed the Stratford lecture, preached by Wheatley of Banbury (both places being peculiars outside the diocese), the archbishop commended his action 'for such a lecturer that is beneficed in another diocese shall preach anything to embroil the Church, or that which shall be otherwise false or untrue in itself he may slip always to his own home and there keep himself out of the reach of that bishop in whose diocese he hath been the hurt'.[147] However Laud may have encouraged other bishops to pursue a policy which he himself was not prepared to rigidly press: during the second metropolitical visitation of Lincoln in 1638, his surrogates allowed Whitfield to lecture at Stamford (which lay outside Peterborough diocese where he was beneficed) on the

142 Seaver, *PL* 88; Collinson, *GP* 212. 143 Prynne, *CD* 368; *WWL* v. 308.
144 PRO SP 16/168/6. 145 PRO SP 16/167/34, 168/6.
146 PRO SP 16/169/23. 147 WORO 2648/716. 093/83.

sole condition that Lady Armyne, the foundress of the lecture, repaired the church where it was preached.[148]

With respect to the more general requirement of the instruction, two lines of action might suggest themselves: the conversion of single market-town lectures into combinations (the policy suggested), or their suppression, which was not explicitly condoned. As bishop of London, Laud converted some single lectures into combinations, such as Thomas Hooker's lecture at Chelmsford in February 1630, which was not well liked by the townspeople or some of the local clergy, who were reluctant to offend local sensibilities by joining the combination.[149] Yet Laud evidently did not pursue a rigorous policy of conversion, as by 1632 there was still a considerable number of single lectures within market towns in Essex.[150] These he appears to have tolerated so long as lecturers were beneficed and not overtly nonconformist. Juxon pursued basically the same line and in 1637 there still existed several single lectures in market towns, such as at Manningtree Chapel in Essex, where the curate of Little Wigborrow preached.[151] In fact there is reason to assume that most bishops converted only a handful of single lectures into combinations as stipulated by the Instructions. In 1640 Bishop Coke's chaplain, who was beneficed elsewhere, still preached the lecture at Ross-on-Wye. In neighbouring Gloucester single lectures survived in market towns, among them Tetbury, Minchinhampton, Stroud, and Stow.[152] Piers in Bath and Wells pursued the most radical policy, aiming to suppress all market-town or week-day lectures, combination or not, which he appears to have achieved by 1637, when the Taunton lecture succumbed.[153] Among the casualties of his policy was the famous combination of Bath which Piers's predecessors, including Laud and Curle, had continued. The bishop objected to working-day lectures because (he claimed) they sheltered conventicles, 'for they may cloak their secret meetings in this kind under pretence of market-business'.[154] In Norwich Wren similarly disliked market-day lectures. He informed the bailiffs of Haverhill that Tuesday rather than

148 LAO Vj. 30/230; S. Clarke, *Lives of Sundry Eminent Persons* (1683), ii. 192; see Ch. 6 n. 169. The lecture had been set up in June 1632: LAO Corr. B/3/28.

149 PRO SP 16/161/54, 16/160/66.

150 PRO SP 16/218/43; ERO D/ABA 5/178.

151 ERO D/ABA 5/178; ERO D/ABA 8/130^v.

152 CCO MS 206/1^v; GRO GDR/185 July 1634; Bodl. Tanner 314/155^v.

153 LPL MS 943/563; Bodl. Tanner MS 314/153.

154 *Articles . . . against William Piers*, 1; Bodl. Tanner MS 68/92^v, 14–14^v.

market Wednesday was a more suitable day, since Tuesday was the day of deliverance from the Gunpowder Plot. But Wren did not need such a feeble excuse to suppress many of the combinations in Norwich; by 1638 there were only six left in the entire diocese.[155] Apart from these two dioceses, the only others which witnessed the suppressions of combinations were Peterborough and Oxford, where at least two lectures disappeared, those respectively at Kettering and Deddington.[156]

As Bishop Wright recognized, the third instruction overlooked the fact that several corporate towns were also market towns, which confused the lines of demarcation within the Instructions. Throughout the 1630s these might retain their combinations, although they were subjected to closer surveillance.[157] The bishop might assume to himself the nomination of all vacancies as Lindsell of Hereford did, in the case of Bishop's Castle, or he might ask the lecturers to renew their licence, as Juxon required of the Maldon combination during his triennial visitation in 1637.[158] Several courts tightened up their policies towards combinations even before the appearance of the Instructions. As early as 1627, Buckeridge permitted the Rochester lecture to continue only so long as he approved of the lecture list, on which the dean and prebends had to appear *ex officio*. All lecturers were to be beneficed within the immediate vicinity of the town, so that 'they might come in the morning and go home at night'.[159] But the combination was to continue only so long as there was no deputation without the bishop's approval, no doctrinal controversies, and a competent allowance from the corporation. In 1627, when Williams received complaints against the lecturers of the Ampthill combination for speaking irreverently about the Virgin Mary and for being in some points nonconformist, he revoked their licence, reissued a new one on his own terms, and replaced some of the clergy. Two years later

155 Bodl. Tanner MS 68/14–14ᵛ.

156 *HMC Buccleuch (Whitehall)* i. 275; *WWL* v. 330.

157 PRO SP 16/160/68. These included Guildford (PRO SP 16/293/128), Kingston (R. Mayo, *The Life and Death of Edmund Staunton* (1673), 14), Warwick (BL Add. MS 23146), Colchester (GLRO DL/C/344/14), Maldon (GL 9537/15 Dengie D/19ᵛ), Wainfleet (*WWL* v. 369), Kirton (*WWL* v. 369), Grantham (PRO SP 16/470/83), Bury St Edmunds (Bodl. Tanner MS 137/1; Bodl. MS Add. D. 78), Marlborough (PRO SP 16/260/90); Dudley (Nuttall, *Richard Baxter*, 18); Andover (HRO 35M48/16/8).

158 R. More, *The True Relation of Enoch ap Evans* (1641), 59–60; GL 9537/15/Dengie D./19ᵛ.

159 KAO DRC/R8/5/205ᵛ.

(and still before the appearance of the Instructions) Williams streamlined the Bedford combination along similar lines.[160] Prynne accused the Caroline bishops (and Laud in particular) of destroying the authentic combination lecture by binding it to the liturgy.[161] Yet the combination had always been more orderly and amenable to control than other lectures, as it was invariably preached by beneficed clergy. Laud's vision was of 'more ease to the people . . . by a combination of conformable . . . ministers . . . and not by some . . . humorous man who too often misleads the people'. Ironically it was under Charles I rather than his father that the combination became the most characteristic lectureship, if not the most characteristic institution of the Church.[162]

V. CORPORATION LECTURES

The fourth instruction, that all lectures maintained by a corporation should show a willingness to accept a cure within the town, modified Harsnett's corresponding consideration, which called for ministers to undergo suspension until such cures fell vacant.[163] Thus although the instruction left the door open to an extreme interpretation, it did not entail the immediate proscription of the single unbeneficed corporation lecturer. In some dioceses, as a result of this instruction, lectures might be suppressed, such as that at Woodstock in October 1633. When the corporation petitioned the king for its re-erection in 1637, Charles refused their request.[164] In Bath and Wells Piers suppressed all corporation lectures whether in accordance with instruction 4 or not, which exceeded even Wren's policy in Norwich, who stretched the instruction so as to allow no lectures unless the lecturer held the cure of the place where he preached.[165] There is little evidence that Laud suppressed any corporation lectures while bishop of London. He did however ask lecturers to assume a living

160 PRO SP 16/534/32, SP 16/537/32–3.

161 Prynne, *CD* 378–80. 162 *WWL* iv. 274.

163 *WWL* v. 308; Prynne, *CD* 368.

164 *WWL* v. 330, 356; Bodl. Film MS dep. 953 (Woodstock bor. MSS B. 78/3/4). Thus the corporation of Melcombe Regis appointed to a lectureship in December 1637 with no cure attached to it: *Weymouth and Melcombe Regis Documents*, ed. H. J. Moule (1883), 195–6. Similarly, the lecturer at Southampton ministered elsewhere; Roger Turner, *The Userers' Plea Answered* (1636).

165 *Articles . . . against William Piers*, 1; Bodl. Tanner MS 68/92, 160, 173.

once one became available. In May 1630 the bailiff of Colchester informed him that their lecturer, Richard Madden, had accepted the vicarage of St Peter's and that they wanted permission to remove the lecture to that parish from the one in which it had previously been held.[166]

On receiving the fourth instruction the reaction of some bishops was to ask for more specific information than that supplied in the official communication. Wright of Bristol was brought eventually to question what the king understood by 'corporation' and 'maintenance'.[167] His queries hinged on the essential question of whether lectures maintained by the corporations should be defined in terms of their location or status, as corporate towns might have lectures without actually maintaining them. Within the city of Bristol there existed both single and combination lectures. The single lectures, although supervised by the Chamber, were financed not by the city but by an impropriation in the country, which over the years had impoverished both the vicar and the parish, so that Wright feared that 'maintenance we have not but sacrilege'. As for the combination lectures, these were not maintained by the corporation but provided through the interest on the stocks and rents of several city churches. Thus if by 'maintenance' the king meant a sum financed by people and collected by the Chamber or paid by the Chamber out of the city rents, then the corporation of Bristol could justly claim that it maintained no lecture, and consequently stood outside the reference of the Instructions. The Bristol lectures, according to Wright, made 'a godly show yet they cost not the city one penny'.[168] The response to Wright's perceptive analysis has not survived, but single and combination lectures in Bristol appear to have survived the Instructions.[169]

In respects other than those highlighted by Wright, the fourth instruction belied a rather simplistic interpretation of the corporation lectureship. In some towns, lectures were supplied by the parish clergy, who received no financial support for their efforts, such as

166 PRO SP 16/166/72.

167 PRO SP 16/160/68. For a discussion of different types of towns in early modern England and Wales, see M. Weinbaum, *The Incorporation of Boroughs* (Manchester, 1937); id., *British Borough Charters 1307–1660* (Cambridge, 1943), pp. xxx–lxi. I should like to thank Dr Paul Slack for answering my queries about the different types of towns in early modern England.

168 PRO SP 16/160/68.

169 *HMC Appendix 4th Report*, 143; BRO churchwarden accounts listed p. 330; BRO Mayors' Audits 116, 270; *Merchants and Merchandise in Seventeenth Century Bristol* (Bristol Record Soc.), ed. P. McGrath, xix. 55–6 for a wider context.

John Tombes at Leominster (Hereford).[170] In Brecon (St David's) the local school provided the lecture, while in Stafford (Coventry and Lichfield) and Liskeard (Exeter) the corporation invited preachers to preach an occasional sermon, which was in all but name a lecture. These preachers might either be 'strangers' or neighbouring beneficed clergy, and, as licensed preachers, outside the reference of the Instruction.[171] At Northampton (Peterborough), Derby (Coventry and Lichfield), and Lincoln the lecturer or corporation preacher customarily held livings within the town before 1629, while at Derby the lectureship was already regarded as a stepping-stone to a living and a ready source of financial remuneration.[172] Other lectures in corporate towns were subsidized largely by London businessmen, such as those at Towcester (Peterborough) and Chumleigh (Exeter), the type of lectureship which Laud found the most objectionable. As with the Feoffees, he believed that it was the intention of those who supported them to advance clergy who were disaffected with the Church.[173] In such cases the bishops might try to assume for themselves the right of nomination and dismissal. Wright was exceptionally fortunate in the case of Ashbourne (Coventry and Lichfield). When five local townsmen failed to agree on a nomination with the six city representatives, they turned to the bishop, asking him to make the decision instead.[174] Williams confronted more difficulty at Huntingdon. Under the terms of Fishborne's will, the Mercers' Company established a lecture there and refused to allow the bishop any control over the post.[175] This incident (related by Williams to Laud, and by Laud to the king) occasioned the archbishop's petition to Charles that 'no lay man whatsoever and least of all companies or corporations may, under any pretence . . . have power to put in or put out any lecturer or other minister'. It was an opinion with which the king wholly concurred but the problem could only be solved by undermining the principle of lay patronage within the Church.[176]

There were many corporate towns with more than one lectureship

[170] BL Portland Loan MS 29/72.

[171] NLW SD/BC/3a/4; SFRO D/3 23/E/1/206ᵛ, 209, 240–1; CWRO DDP 126/4/1/158.

[172] *WWL* v. 349; LJRO Morton Reg. B/A/1/17; J. W. F. Hill, *Tudor and Stuart Lincoln* (Camb., 1956), 116.

[173] PRO SP 16/393/75; BL Add. MS 4460/4; *WWL* iii. 253.

[174] R. Porter, *The Life of Mr John Hieron* (1691), 8.

[175] LPL MS 1030/19.

[176] *WWL* v. 321; PRO SP 16/259/78 (where Neile highlights the same problem for the Northern Province).

throughout the 1630s. Other endowed sermons and lectures appear to have joined the Bristol lectures discussed by Wright.[177] Even after Workman lost his lectureship at Gloucester in 1634 (which had been endowed by the corporation) two town lectures continued weekly at St Michael's and St Marygate. In 1639 the common council established another on Thursday mornings.[178] They attempted also to revive Workman's lectureship on condition that the bishop approved of the nominee. Clearly Goodman did not, for within a month of the appointment of Robert Rogers to lecture, the city had to repeal his stipend.[179] From the 1630s onwards the common council also subsidized lectures expressly 'for the poor of this city and others that will resort to' them, while citizens continued to leave money for the preaching of sermons throughout the year, such as Redverne's bequests in 1639 and 1640 for St Michael's.[180] Thus in spite of unparalleled interference, some cities such as Gloucester may well have escaped the worst effects of the Instructions.

The lectures within the corporation of London presented a problem in their own right, as they were largely outside the reference of the Instructions. As early as 1628 Laud had conducted a survey of all the city lecturers.[181] Dr Seaver's thorough and systematic research uncovered at least 121 lectures within London in 1628, three times as many as had existed under Bancroft and Aylmer. Although he subjected lecturers to a closer scrutiny than his immediate predecessors, Laud did not attempt to put into practice before 1630 policies similar to those outlined in Harsnett's Considerations.[182] During four sessions of the consistory court in December and January 1628/9 seventeen lecturers were cited as curates into court, but in virtually all these cases Laud merely asked them to reveal their preaching licences. Of those cited, eight were unlicensed, and as far as can be ascertained, their future careers suggest that Laud gave them his licence and they retained their curacies. Two of the lecturers disappeared from the records, but there is no evidence that they were

[177] BRO P/Temple Ch./Ca 14(2)1, 14(13)1, 14(4)1, 13(4), P/St JB/CW/3(b)1635, 1639, P/St W/CW/36/66, 39, 101, P/St T./69, P/St J/CW/1(b)/29, P/Xch/CW/16/ 1636–7, 1639, 1633, P/St JB/CW/3(a) 1629–30, P/AllS/CW/1634–5, 1638–9.

[178] GRO B3/1/560–1, B3/2/63, 149.

[179] GRO B3/2/45, 50; F4/5/12.

[180] GRO B3/1/560, 51; B3/2/110, 133, 136, 164, 172, GRO/185 (July 1634) unfol.

[181] LPL MS 942/14 (1628), 942/16 (1629).

[182] Seaver, *PL* 244; PRO SP 16/579/36, 16/529/36, 16/123/32.

dismissed.[183] In 1632 Laud appointed Andrew Blackwell, one of the eight, to a new lectureship at St Mary at Hill. Among the remaining nine lecturers called into court who already had licences, Dr Seaver identified 'five' Puritans, yet only one of these was cited in 1631 (for seditious preaching). In fact, all retained their curacies and lectures except John Poynter, who left for Northamptonshire voluntarily and without prosecution.[184]

In his inability to explain Laud's comparatively mild treatment of London lecturers in consistory, Dr Seaver turned to the records of the High Commission and the court of Audience. However, these also failed to provide evidence for a Laudian policy of 'suppression'. In 1630 the High Commission referred to Laud the case of the four lecturers who had signed a petition urging relief for the Palatinate ministers. Laud merely required them not to intervene in matters of high policy again.[185] It seems that those lecturers who fell foul of Laud also did so because of 'seditious' statements. One such lecturer was Nathaniel Bernard of St Sepulchre, who was brought into the High Commission in May 1629 after praying for the queen's conversion. In cases of sedition, Laud soon released the offenders on submission, and only later, for continuous contempt of authority, was Bernard's lectureship terminated by the High Commission.[186] A characteristic feature of Laud's policy towards the London lecturers was the facility with which he granted pardons and preferred counsel to heavy court censure. In 1629 Laud suspended two celebrated lecturers, Henry Burton of St Matthew Friday Street, and James Walton of St Mary Colechurch, but shortly afterwards relaxed their suspensions and allowed them to return to their curacies.[187] In June 1629 he inhibited Thomas Edwardes, lecturer at St Botolph Aldgate, but by July 1629 Edwardes had shown his conformity by preaching a sermon on obedience to his superiors, and in 1631 was lecturing again.[188] Similar leniency was shown to Thomas Foxley, who was questioned but released on the promise of conformity, and to John Archer, whom Laud suspended for not catechizing according to the

183 GLRO DL/C/317/13^v–63^v; Seaver, *PL* 245, 240–66.
184 GLRO DL/C/343/156^v; Seaver, *PL* 246–7.
185 Seaver, *PL* 248; PRO SP 16/56/15.
186 GLRO DL/C/319/154^v, 162^v; PRO SP 16/261/1; Birch, ii. 255; Seaver, *PL* 249.
187 GL 9531/15/21^v; LPL MS 942/16; GL 9539/A/2, 1016/1; Seaver, *PL* 249.
188 PRO SP 16/142/51, SP 16/146/3, SP 16/152/32; GL 9235/2.

Prayer Book, but absolved three months later.[189] Other lecturers who were questioned or suspended by Laud (Ward, Jones, Martyn, and Gardiner), were never deprived and they retained their lectureships and curacies into the later 1630s.[190] It was indeed highly ironic that even when Laud suspended Stephen Dennison from his ministry at St Katherine, Cree, he allowed him to continue lecturing at Great Allhallows. After 1633, Laud's moderate measures in London were continued by Juxon. Those lecturers whom Laud had reprimanded remained unmolested throughout the 1630s.[191] In 1635 Juxon counselled five lecturers 'for breach of the canons ... in sermon ... practice or both', yet he did not prosecute them because, in Laud's words, 'all (five) promised amendment for the future and submission to the Church in all things, (and) my lord (Juxon) very moderately forbore further proceedings against them'.[192] Juxon suspended two lecturers in the same year, but in the case of John Wood, relaxation soon followed. Sparrowhawk, the other, withdrew voluntarily to another part of the diocese. Clearly 'all the disciplinary activity of 1635' identified by Dr Seaver does not amount to very much.[193]

In *Canterburies Doome* Prynne accused Laud of suppressing many lectures in London. In fact there is no evidence that Laud suppressed any, although some lecturers left and some benefactors were disinclined to establish new lectures.[194] Professor Trevor-Roper noticed that the measures which Laud undertook in London to restrain lecturers were not very stringent. Dr Seaver, on the other hand, saw the policies through very Puritan spectacles and concluded that Laud's measures were 'thorough with a vengeance'.[195] Yet he estimated ironically that of seventy 'Puritan' lecturers in London, during the six years of Laud's episcopate, only eighteen were questioned for nonconformity. Of these, only one, Meredith Mayday, was prohibited from preaching in the diocese; another, Nathaniel Bernard, died in prison, while a third, John Davenport, left for overseas.[196] Thus it seems that Laud became the general scapegoat for Puritan propaganda, and especially for those radical policies

[189] GL 1046/1/143^v; GL 9537/15/61–2.
[190] Seaver, *PL* 252; PRO SP 16/202/3.
[191] *CSPD 1634–35*, 613; PRO SP 16/261/187; Seaver, *PL* 245.
[192] *WWL* v. 333.
[193] *WWL* v. 333; Seaver, *PL* 258.
[194] Prynne, *CD* 373; *WWL* v. 310.
[195] Trevor-Roper, *Archbishop Laud*, 119; Seaver, *PL* 255.
[196] Seaver, *PL* 243, 254–5; HLRO Pet. 11 Dec. 1640 Meredith Mayday.

pursued by Wren and Piers, which either far exceeded the Instructions or represented its strictest possible interpretation and application. Laud's policy towards the lectures was less one of repression than of accommodation and streamlining, if motivated by his dislike of the Jacobean Church. Like Juxon, he was preferred to contemplate a promise of general conformity to the liturgy and canonical discipline, rather than a strict enforcement of the Instructions. As Dr Seaver noted, there existed no legal grounds for refusing to admit a lecturer, so long as he was properly ordained and willing to subscribe. When faced by a lecturer who, in submission, acknowledged his error and consented to reform, Laud had little option but to release him with an admonition to conform in the future.[197] No contemporary caught the essence of this 'Laudian' restraint of lecturers more poignantly than William Gouge, lecturer at St Anne, Blackfriars. He confessed that Laud's policy was misconstrued within the City; that he had never deprived any but those who refused absolutely to conform; and that he never proceeded against any on hearsay or before giving them lengthy counsel. If he inflicted suspension he invariably relaxed it after a short period, and required the offender to exhibit his conformity, usually by preaching a sermon.[198] In these cases Laud, like Juxon, preferred counsel and persuasion to retribution through the weight of court censure. Unlike Piers or Wren he did not cripple lecturers through excessive stipulations and unlike Charles I he did not contemplate their liquidation.

VI. OTHER REGULATIONS

The seventh instruction laid down that the bishop was to suffer none under 'noblemen or men qualified by law to have any private chaplain in his house', in accordance with the rules established in Henrician statutes.[199] Doubtless Heylyn was correct to see the instruction as an attempt to curb preaching by unbeneficed preachers who often sought the patronage of the gentry.[200] However, the degree to which the bishops prevented those 'not qualified' from harbouring preachers

[197] Seaver, *PL* 254. [198] PRO SP 16/202/3.

[199] *WWL* v. 308; *Statutes of the Realm*, iii. 295, 457 (Statutes 21 Henry VIII c.13, 25 Henry VIII c. 16); WSFRO E14/11/7; Bodl. MS Lister, ii, ch. 20.

[200] Heylyn, *CA* 253–4. Chancery Dispensation Rolls: PRO C58/40–3, for officially licensed chaplains; see also DRO CH 43 (Hall's licences).

is very difficult to ascertain. The accounts of the provinces reveal that although there was an attempt to impress the terms of the instruction, such were the practical difficulties encountered in its application that efforts were frequently stifled.[201] During the 1630s in the dioceses of Peterborough and Norwich and elsewhere, many gentry 'not qualified by law' illegally harboured chaplains by pretending that they were tutors for their children. Such 'chaplains' might read services according to their own fancy or hold lectures in contravention of the Instructions, such as Elm's outside Peterborough and Herrick's at Frowlesworth (Lincoln), both of which were subsequently suppressed.[202] In Ely diocese Wren highlighted a further, related problem. In 1639 at Childerley, Sir John Cutts, one 'not qualified', harboured a man whom he denied was his chaplain but was curate at the local church. In the rest of the diocese other clergy lived not on their cures but with the local gentry.[203] While Laud believed that they should live on their cures, he nevertheless recognized that the hospitality bestowed by the gentry was a valuable financial additive to an impoverished clergy. At least, in January 1630 Laud was aware of the financial hardships which might result if instruction 7 were strictly applied, as it 'would displace many young men particularly in London'.[204] In the Northern Province, Neile also saw difficulties in forcing the plain letter of the instruction. He informed Charles I that in the four northern dioceses there was a considerable number of gentry, who, although not qualified to have chaplains, nevertheless kept 'curates' for their impropriations which had no endowed vicarages. The cost of the curates' upkeep constituted part of their stipend and without this valuable remuneration, as Neile pointed out to the king, several poorly endowed parishes would have no ministers at all.[205]

Other than tightening up the licensing of chaplains, the bishops might further this instruction by restricting the consecration of domestic chapels. Some gentry would not seek a licence for consecration because they would not value the rite, but others, such as Sir Henry Slingsby, did. However, when he sought Neile's approval, the archbishop informed him that he 'had express command not to

[201] PRO SP 16/153/100. PRO SP 16/448/79 reveals that among the silenced clergy in Gloucester diocese, Marshall and Stubbes were 'chaplains' respectively to Sir William Guise and Sir Robert Coke.
[202] *WWL* v. 320, 364–5, 368; PRO SP 16/535/26.
[203] *WWL* v. 364–5. [204] Prynne, *CD* 368. [205] PRO SP 16/312/84.

consecrate any chapel less it may be the occasion of conventicles'.[206] Like Slingsby, others sought consecration unaware of potential impediments. In 1636 Sir Rice Rudd of Aberglasney, in the archdeaconry of Carmarthen, constructed a private chapel and asked Mainwaring, his diocesan, to consecrate it. The bishop, recognizing that Rudd was not qualified by law, presented the problem to Laud. The archbishop consulted with the king, and suggested that Mainwaring should consecrate the chapel but that he should license as chaplain the local minister on condition that Rudd also attended his parish church.[207] On other occasions, however, Laud may have gone further, by allowing private chaplains so long as they temporarily underwent suspension and resought episcopal licence.[208]

Ultimately, however, the attempt to control private chaplains would fail less through practical difficulties or court oversight than because those qualified, such as Lord Brooke, the earl of Warwick, or the countess of Chesterfield, would still offer asylum to itinerant or silenced preachers before attempting to intrude them into livings.[209] In October 1633 there was a rumour that Laud had attempted to restrict the activities of such noble chaplains and that he 'had forborne all preaching in private houses, among which is included her grace of Richmond'.[210] No documentary evidence exists to confirm this rumour, but it was certainly not out of character with the drift of Charles I's policy, who in 1636 impressed upon Laud the need to secure the conformity of chaplains even in the houses of those qualified in law: a task beyond the letter of the Instructions, well-nigh impossible to achieve, and, as John Davenport pointed out, one which contravened Magna Carta.[211]

In 1633, on the representation of some prominent lords, the king republished canon 33 of 1604 as a royal letter prohibiting the ordination of any minister without a proper title. This reinforced the terms of instruction 4 of 1629, which reminded the bishops that they

[206] *The Diary of Sir Henry Slingsby*, ed. D. Parsons (1836), 20. For allowing over 30 people to attend his private chapel Sir Henry Rosewell of Abbotsford (Dorset) was called into the High Commission during January 1640 (PRO SP 16/443/36).

[207] *WWL* v. 344. [208] LPL MS Reg. Laud i/189ᵛ, 281.

[209] Porter, *Life of John Hieron*, 4, 6; Clarendon, ii. 544; Prynne, *A Looking Glasse for all Lordly Prelates* 71–5; Clarke, *Lives of Sundry Eminent Persons*, i. 6; Bodl. MS Tanner 314/180.

[210] Knowler, i. 141.

[211] *WWL* v. 341; *The Letters of John Davenport*, ed. I. M. Calder (New Haven, Conn., 1937), and cited, J. P. Sommerville, *Politics and Ideology in England 1603–1640* (1986), 220.

should not hold 'frequent and unworthy' ordinations.[212] It constituted, as Heylyn saw, an attempt to curtail the activities of preachers and nonconformists. However, instruction 4 was less stringent than at first might appear, for what constituted an 'unworthy ordination'? Certainly the 1630s appear to have witnessed a tightening up of ordination procedures by paying greater respect to the canons, and at no time was Laud forced to invoke any of the penalties laid down in canons 31–9.[213] The situation was considerably different from pre-1622 years, yet the ambiguity of the word 'unworthy' meant that the instruction might condone activities which occasionally fell short of canonical requirement. Possibly only Wren interpreted the instruction in terms of a rigid adherence to the canons.[214] Laud broke canon 31, which laid down dates for ordination, and Harsnett disregarded canon 32, which specified that none should be made a priest and deacon on the same day.[215] Piers of Bath and Wells, Montagu of Norwich, Mainwaring of St David's, Morton of Coventry and Lichfield, Howson of Durham, Davenant of Salisbury, Hall of Exeter, Potter of Carlisle, and Neile at York all ordained 'literati', those whose only ostensible qualification was an ability to read, and in so doing broke not only canon 33 but the royal letter of 24 October 1633.[216] Several bishops also broke canon 39, which laid down that ordinands were to seek letters dismissory when seeking ordination outside the diocese. In 1639 twenty men whom Bancroft of Oxford had refused to ordain went to other bishops without his permission for ordination. Possibly these bishops acted in full knowledge of Bancroft's controversial ordination practices, which they might have regarded as exceeding canonical requirements.[217] The questions which his examining chaplain, Fulham, asked ordinands were considered by the Long Parliament an affront to individual conscience and were subsequently used by Prynne as 'evidence' that Laud had attempted to establish a tyranny over the soul as well as the Church.

[212] PRO SO3/10/Sept. 1633; *WWL* vi. 327; PRO SP 16/108/39.

[213] Heylyn, *CA* 255.

[214] K. Fincham, 'Ramifications of the Hampton Court Conference in the Dioceses, 1603–1609', *Journal of Ecclesiastical History*, 36/2 (Apr. 1985), 208–27; id., *Prelate as Pastor: The Episcopate of James I* (Oxf., 1990).

[215] LPL MS Reg. Laud/192v–193v; *WWL* iii. 142; NNRO Reg. 15/21 (24/7, 13, 21, 26v, 31v, 33).

[216] LJRO B/A/1/16/12–13, 15; DPD Bp. Reg. 1.4/110, 1.4/3, 19, 40, 50, 89; DRO Chanter 50; NLW SD/BR/3/13, 17; CBRO DRC 1/3; SRO D/D/B Reg. 20; NNRO Regs. 18/24/1–23, 16/23/152–185.

[217] *WWL* v. 363.

Ironically Bancroft himself was in breach of canon 34, which specified that the bishop should examine ordinands personally.[218]

Perhaps the question to ask is not whether the bishops broke the canons relating to ordination, but whether they did so with justification? The ordination of the clergy was linked most intimately to two fundamental problems of the Church: its education and material base. Laud believed that irregularities over ordination would disappear only when there were greater financial and pastoral incentives; in effect only with the return of impropriations to the Church.[219] In 1638 Bishop Roberts of Bangor lamented to Laud how impoverished the livings were in his diocese, which had forced him to ordain weak scholars. Laud took this opportunity to represent to the king that such problems were endemic in the Church. Goodman painted a not dissimilar picture in 1634, informing the archbishop that he had to ordain 'very mean ministers to supply very mean cures'.[220] When tightening up their ordination procedures the bishops often pitted themselves remorselessly against the structural deficiencies of the Church, and occasionally could make headway only by ordaining those whom they preferred not to ordain. If it were only for this reason, the attempt to restrict nonconformity in the Church would fail.

The restraint of preaching, in particular lecturing, may have been abetted more successfully by instruction 6, which invited clergy to attend local lectures and report any misdemeanours.[221] As a system of delation this was open to the usual abuses, and on occasions, Laud himself was the recipient and purveyor of false information. In 1635 he informed the king that the two lecturers of Worcester were 'very conformable'; a year later he had dismissed one of them because he was 'no graduate, an ignorant ass . . . talking false latin'.[222] Some parties might inform the courts of irregularities but decline to present any articles against lecturers, such as Morton did on one occasion.[223] However prosecution did not necessarily follow even when lecturers appeared in the Arches or in the High Commission. In December 1637 John Hieron, lecturer at Ashbourne (Coventry and Lichfield),

[218] Bodl. Rawl. D. MS 353 (16).

[219] Christopher Hill, *Society and Puritanism in Pre-Revolutionary England* (1964), and his *Economic Problems of the Church from Archbishop Whitgift to the Long Parliament* (1956).

[220] *WWL* v. 359, 330. [221] *WWL* vi. 308.

[222] *WWL* v. 343; WORO 13945/712. 17147.

[223] Clarke, *Lives of Sundry Eminent Persons*, i. 5.

was summoned to Lambeth for 'impertinent preaching'. Yet when he arrived no prosecutor appeared, and Hieron and his colleagues asked the court to appoint one so that he could be dismissed. Without relief they asked Dr Baker, Juxon's chaplain, to take up the case, but he refused.[224] Eventually, as a last resort they went to Dr Bray, Laud's chaplain, who 'courteously received them' and sent them to Sir John Lambe, who discharged them. Sometimes information did have an effect, although this might depend on the importance of the informer or the gravity of the offence.[225] Christopher Wren, dean of Windsor, asked Laud to prosecute Lee, a preacher within the royal peculiar of Wolverhampton. Consequently Laud informed Brent not to grant Lee any licence to lecture during the metropolitical visitation and, if sufficient charges could be brought against him, to summon him to court. As a result Lee underwent suspension in 1635, a case which was laid heavily against Laud at his trial.[226]

The depiction of Laud as continually prying into the affairs of lecturers and hauling them before the High Commission has little truth in it. Apart from Ward of Ipswich and Workman of Gloucester very few lecturers were prosecuted by this court.[227] The case of Angel, lecturer at Leicester, in 1634 provides a remarkable insight into the archbishop's treatment of lecturers as metropolitan. In June 1634 Sir John Lambe, the commissary of Leicester, prohibited Angel from preaching because he held no licence and would not conform to the liturgy. Lambe suspended him *ex tunc prout ex nunc* and told him to seek a licence from the archbishop.[228] When Angel appeared at Lambeth, Laud reprimanded him as a 'grevious transgressor' yet did not prosecute him. Instead, being 'sensible of his sad condition', he asked Lambe to be truly informed about 'his character and behaviour'.[229] Consequently Lambe allowed him to return to Leicester and gave him a 'toleration' until Easter to prove his conformity. Although subsequently questioned again, Angel continued to preach his lecture and was eventually cleared of the taint of nonconformity.[230] Passionate and threatening language followed by

[224] Porter, *Life of John Hieron*, 21.
[225] Ibid. 21.
[226] *WWL* iv. 301; Bodl. Tanner MS 140/169; Prynne, *CD* 380–1; A. G. Matthews, *The Congregational Churches of Staffordshire* (1925), 8.
[227] PRO SP 16/261/206–7, 304; Seaver, *PL* 96.
[228] LRO 1D41/13/61/83; PRO SP 16/540/18.
[229] PRO SP 16/535/27, 16/540/18, 19, 23.
[230] LRO 1D41/13/61/83, 1D41/13/63/128; PRO SP 16/540/23.

compassion and a failure to carry out censure were characteristic of Laud's attempt to reclaim nonconformists in other areas. As Sir Edward Dering noted, Laud's 'uncourtly nature sent most men discontented from him, yet would he often... sweeten many of them again, when they least looked for it'. As Clarendon and others intimated, Laud's 'immoderate heat', his very bad temper, was his worst failing.[231]

Another effective mode of regulation was the tightening up of licensing procedures. If the policy of Juxon and Goodman is taken as normative then most bishops granted licences sparingly.[232] Shortly after his elevation to Exeter in 1627, Hall asked the lecturer of Penzance to renew his licence, and subsequently issued several new ones.[233] When in 1635 the parishioners of Lanchester (Durham) rejected Morton's nominee as their lecturer, the bishop in turn refused to accept their candidate as a man 'altogether unknown unto me and one who aspires without my licence in the office of preaching', and prohibited him from preaching.[234] Episcopal licensing of lecturers, however, proved far more effective under Laud than under Abbot. In 1632, when Morton refused to grant Clarke a licence in Coventry, Abbot overruled the episcopal prohibition by invoking the powers laid down in the Directions of 1622. There is no evidence that Laud invoked the same power, nor did he require lecturers to seek confirmation in the court of faculties or under the great seal, also required in 1622.[235] Yet in default of a strict metropolitical surveillance, there existed a general tightening up of the episcopal licensing procedures. Such a policy probably did not result in an overall decline in the number of *licensed* sermons, as the bishops could grant as many preaching licences as they wished.[236] In fact

[231] BL 37/343 (11–12ᵛ); Clarendon, i. 49, 132; BL Harl. MS 6424/45; Dering cited by S. P. Salt, 'The Origins of Sir Edward Dering's Attack on the Ecclesiastical Hierarchy c.1625–1640', *Historical Journal*, 30 (1987), 20; R. Spalding, *The Improbable Puritan: A Life of Bulstrode Whitelocke 1605–1675* (1975), 16.

[232] GRO GDR/185 (July 1634); ERO D/ABA 7 Commissary/184ᵛ; *The Diary of Ralph Josselin*, ed. E. Hockliffe (Camden, 3rd ser. 15, 1908); John Geree, *The Downfall of Antichrist or the Power of Preaching to pull down Popery* (1641).

[233] DRO Moger Basket C/45; Thomas Bedford, *A Treatise of Sacraments* (1638), 'to the reader'.

[234] DPD Mickleton and Spearman MS 26/11; see also PRO SP 16/540/4.

[235] Clarke, *Lives of Sundry Eminent Persons* i. 5.

[236] *The Subscription Book of Bishop Tounson and Davenant 1620–40*, ed. B. Williams (Devizes, 1977), 5; DRO Chanter 43/533, 541, 547, 556, 558, 470, 479, 489; GRO GDR/185 July 1634; ERO D/ABA 7/184ᵛ.

both Laud and Brent gave a considerable number of such licences throughout the 1630s.[237]

The bishops might exert greater control over lecturers by suspending them temporarily during the outbreak of the plague as Thornborough did at Worcester in 1637, or as Dee's surrogates attempted to do at Northampton, only to find that the townspeople accused them of starving their souls.[238] Similarly Prynne accused Laud of suppressing Wednesday fast lectures within London, although Laud subsequently defended himself on the grounds that this had been a conciliar decision and never enforced.[239] Censorship also played its part in creating a climate unfavourable to lecturing, such as in 1636, when Juxon's chaplain published Peter Studley's *Looking Glasse for Schisme*, which attempted to show that Enoch ap Evans, the deranged murderer of Clun, was addicted to lecture gadding. Ultimately the intervention of king or council could be brought to bear upon the regulation of lectures, as it was during the Scottish rebellion, when several disappeared in the see of Durham.[240] In 1631 the king intervened on Laud's behalf to prevent the election of Thomas Ford as lecturer of Plymouth. Ford had slighted Laud in an Oxford sermon. Charles recommended instead Thomas Bedford, a judicious move as Bedford had preached within Plymouth for four years.[241] Yet the vetting procedures of the king and council were far from foolproof. In 1633 they nominated George Burdett as lecturer of Yarmouth, a decision with which Laud concurred; two years later Burdett was suspended and deprived for gross nonconformity.[242]

Noble interests sometimes proved an effective obstacle to the implementation of the Instructions: John Shawe escaped prosecution because he was chaplain to the earl of Pembroke. Corporations sometimes sought the help of noble patrons to further their own nominees as lecturers or to curb interference. Thus in April 1631 the bailiffs of Yarmouth looked for Dorset's support for Brinsley, their

[237] SRO D/D/C/1878 bundle 3/June 22 1634; WTRO D5/6; LPL reg. Laud 1/192^{v}, 195.

[238] PRO SP 16/393/15; *WWL* v. 354; Bodl. Tanner 68/3^{v} (Wren also).

[239] *WWL* vi. 46–7.

[240] Studley, *Looking Glasse of Schisme*, see imprimatur after epistle dedicatory; *The Memoirs of Ambrose Barnes*, ed. W. H. D. Longstaffe (Surtees Soc., 1, 1866), 328–9; PRO SP 16/444/34.

[241] GRO B3/2/134; WDRO W48/98; *WWL* v. 70; PRO SP 16/535/25; PRO SP 16/261/4.

[242] H. Swinden, *The History and Antiquities of Great Yarmouth* (1772), 851; BL Add. MS 4460/4.

own candidate.[243] On the other hand, corporations might take a lower profile for fear of attracting too much noble interest. When Alvey left his Newcastle lectureship in 1632, the aldermen cut the lecturer's stipend from £100 to £40 in order to make the post less financially attractive for the chaplains of court nobles.[244] The laity might also try to influence the course or timing of regulation, which some bishops might regard as an unnecessary provocation. When in June 1631 Sir Robert Phelips was slighted by one of the lecturers at the Ilchester combination (in which 'he had an interest'), he asked Curle to suspend the offender 'until he hath acknowledged his miscarriage to me and made his peace for the same'. Although Phelips was reluctant to presume to Curle ('I am to obey not to direct'), he suggested that the bishop might like to express his dislike 'of such malapertness in ministers towards their betters', especially with 'the aptness of this kind of people to grow impudent upon any sufferance'.[245]

Although lectures were often popular social gatherings in their own right, the laity were not universally enthusiastic about their establishment. Davenant's overtures to the Reading corporation to set up a single or combination lecture in 1626 continually fell upon deaf ears. When eventually they agreed, they refused to give the lecturer satisfactory financial backing, and for a long time his position remained tenuous. Similarly, in 1634 some parishioners of Sawbridgeworth appeared in court during Juxon's primary visitation for failing to pay their lecturer. While lectures might reinforce communal hospitality among some of the local clerics, this was not necessarily the case among the higher echelons of society. Robert Bolton advertised the fact that 'nobles, knights and gentlemen' rarely attended his lectures for fear of meeting their sins. He criticized them for preferring to play bowls, to hunt, or to go horse-racing. On the other hand 'many of the meaner sort' attended his preaching 'for spiritual food, as to the market for corporeal'. It was a picture reminiscent of that which Baxter depicted on entering upon his Dudley lecture: 'the poor nailers and labourers would not only crowd the church as full as ever I saw in London, but also hang upon the windows, and the leads without.'[246]

243 BL Add. MS 19398/62; Bodl. Tanner MS 68/127.

244 PRO SP 16/540/4.

245 SRO DD/PH 221/38; Bodl. Tanner MS 68/98.

246 *Mr Bolton's Last and Learned Work of the Four Last Things*, ed. Bagshawe, 176; Nuttall, *Richard Baxter* 18; *Reading Records*, ed. J. M. Guilding, 3 vols. (1895), ii. 250;

Some lectures disappeared in the 1630s for sheer lack of funding. In 1635, when London merchants drained off their support for the lectureship at St Ives (Lincoln), Oliver Cromwell implored them to continue their subscriptions, it being 'a piteous thing to see a lecture fall in the times when we see they are suppressed with too much haste and violence by the enemies of God's truth'.[247] Yet the regulation of lectureships doubtless created an unfavourable climate for the establishment of new ones. In 1640, when Rudge of Evesham (Worcester) left money for the provision of a lecture, he stipulated that if the lecture were discontinued its funding should be reallocated to poor relief.[248] But it was among the parish clergy themselves that the most unfavourable climate for the establishment of new lectures existed. As the scandalous minister reports and petitions of 1640 relate, some of them distanced themselves as much as possible from the interests of their sermon and lecture-gadding parishioners.[249] Reeve of Ampthill (Lincoln) read prayers for the combination in the later 1630s but rarely stayed behind to hear them lecture. Andrewes, vicar of Godalming (Winchester), designated lectures as 'good for nothing but for women to make gossiping matches', while the rector of Chalfont St Peter (Lincoln) wished all lecturers hanged. Others, such as the rector of Great Waldingfield (Norwich), were criticized by their parishioners for not maintaining or preaching at long-established lectures.[250] Elsewhere, clergy such as Buggs in Coventry and Hall in Warwick (Worcester), challenged the local attempt to erect lectures.[251] For other ministers the instructions were an invitation either to curb preaching, or not to preach at all.[252] As 'all edifying plainnesse and foolishnesse of preaching' fell out of favour, an increasing number of sermons appeared in print asserting

ERO D/ALV 2/80ᵛ. Collinson, *RP* 136, and *GP* 466–98 for the lecture as a social event for the clergy. In the Forest of Arden, however, lectures seem to have been better attended by the gentry than in Northamptonshire; S. Clarke, *The Lives of Thirty-Two English Divines* (1677), 320.

247 Hill, *SP* 93.

248 I. G. Smith and G. Onslow, *Worcester* (1883), 234–6.

249 *The Suffolk Committies for Scandalous Ministers 1644–6*, ed. C. Holmes, Suffolk Record Soc. 13 (1970), 37.

250 HLRO 1641 Feb. 23/20; *Surrey Archaeological Collections*, ii. (1864), 214; Bodl. Tanner MS 62/67; HLRO 1641/Feb. 9/127; PRO SP 16/219/20, 16/218/77.

251 Clarke, *Lives of Sundry Eminent Persons* i. 6–7; Bodl. MS Eng. misc. b. 193.

252 John Swan, *A Sermon Pointing Out the Chief Causes and Cure of Such Unruly Stirs as are not seldom found in the Church of God* (1639), 14–15; Bodl. MS Tanner 62/67.

Caroline conformity and legalistic issues.[253] Other sermons attacked some of the ideas at the heart of the Reformation, and were abusive of those who wanted to preach the gospel. In the wake of the Caroline dismantling of the Jacobean Church there surfaced a malignant swelling of anti-evangelical humours.[254]

According to Heylyn, by 1638 little trouble was 'expected from lectureships as they had been regulated'.[255] Certainly the surviving lectures were more conformable and tied to the discipline and liturgy of the Church than before. A policy of regulation had swept the country, save in Norwich and Bath and Wells, where suppression was the order of the day. Wren and Piers had not only interpreted the Instructions in their strictest application but had also exceeded their letter. Elsewhere the bishops, led by Laud, either moderated or undercut the code, which enabled lectures to survive in an attenuated or similar form as before, although these were concessions granted with increased conformity and unprecedented interference. Not surprisingly, many contemporaries failed to discriminate between these two policies and believed that they witnessed a frontal attack on the preaching of the gospel. Moreover a policy of restraint served to perpetuate a vicious circle. Disenchanted preachers simply joined the ranks of Hill's free-lance clergy, while attempts to prevent the laity from preaching made good apostles.[256] Consequently the problem of stemming 'disaffection' in the Caroline Church remained as illusory in 1640 as in 1625.

253 *Mr Bolton's Last and Learned Work of the Four Last Things*, ed. Bagshawe, 183; William Hardwick, *Conformity with Piety, requisite in God's Service* (1638), 155 ff.; Peter Hausted, *Ten Sermons* (1636), 219–30; John Featley, *Obedience and Submission* (1636), 4–9, 22; William Quelch, *Church Customs Vindicated* (1636), 12; J. Dyke, *Worthy Communicant or a Treatise Showing the Due Order of Receiving the Sacrament of the Lord's Supper* (1636); see *Short-Title Catalogue* for other examples.

254 John Gore, *The Way to Well-Doing: A Sermon of Faith and Good Works* (1638), 15; William Jones, *The True Inquisition or The Sad Soules Search* (1633); Thomas Drant, *The Royal Guest* (1637), 30; *The Confessions of John Bastwick* (1641), 1; Swan, *A Sermon, Pointing out the Chief Causes and Cure of Such Unruly Stirs as are not seldom found in the Church of God*; G. W., *A Sermon . . . at All Saints in Worcester . . . June 3 1635* (1635), 5–7; E. Kellet, *Miscellanies of Divinity* (1633), i. 182–3; HLRO Pet./13 May 1641; HLRO Pet./Dec. 1640/Scotherne *v.* Gyles. See *Short-Title Catalogue* for further examples.

255 Heylyn, *CA* 364.

256 Hill, *SP* 79–80; J. Taylor, *John Taylor's Last Voyage and Adventure Performed* (1641), last page.

5
THE BOOK OF SPORTS

> Many moderate men are of opinion, that this abuse of the Lord's Day was a principal procurer of God's anger, since poured out on this land, in a long and bloody civil war.
>
> (Fuller, *CH* iii. 425)

I. THE DECLARATION FOR LAWFUL SPORTS

To suggest that a 'moral majority' opinion existed in Jacobean England may not be as anachronistic as at first it may seem. In the seventeenth century moral issues were not as privatized as they are today. Moreover it was in the interest of all law-enforcing and law-abiding authorities to diminish disorder and not just the preserve of Puritans. Although many officials may have lacked the sense of urgency of the Puritan justice or constable, and although Puritans themselves might differ over the object and mode of moral restraint, as far as one particular area was concerned, Sunday observance, there appears to have been a near unanimity. Certainly the preservation of the religious sanctions and moral inhibitions of the Lord's Day (sabbatarianism) could never be solely the responsibility of the established Church; nor on the same account could it receive a monopoly of attention from the puritanically inclined. In historiography however, the doctrine and practice of sabbatarianism is seen largely as a 'Puritan' innovation, adopted by disaffected nonconformists in their attempts to reform the Church (from the outside), after their failure to introduce Presbyterianism during the last quarter of the sixteenth century. This perceived 'Puritan' doctrine of the sabbath depicted the fourth commandment as a perpetual and moral law, binding on Christians like the other commandments. The shift of the sabbath from Saturday to Sunday could not diminish its observance, as it now commemorated Christ's resurrection and was not simply a ceremony established by the Church. Sunday, the new sabbath day was to be kept holy, a day of rest and worship, especially consecrated to God.[1] In contrast to this 'Puritan' doctrine of the sabbath, historians opposed the 'Anglican' or 'catholic' doctrine. This visualized the fourth commandment as a ceremonial law, abrogated by Christ with the other laws of the Old Testament, and allegorized and treated as an injunction to rest from sin continually. Its observance was neither divinely instituted nor grounded in Scripture, but instead authorized by the Church and regulated by canon laws.

For the most part interpretations of the English Revolution assumed and reinforced this polarity of sabbatarian doctrinal platforms. More recently it has won advocates among those historians who have singled out the importance of sabbatarianism in the 'Puritan' reformation of manners, and in the (perceived) polarization of society in the later seventeenth century.[2] However this well-entrenched distinction of the Puritan sabbath from the Anglican Sunday, has been questioned fundamentally by Dr Kenneth Parker. He has shown convincingly that English sabbatarianism, far from being the preserve of 'Puritans', was an orthodox tenet held by many higher and lower *conformist* clergy, as well as many laity within the Church. Moreover as its origins were firmly rooted in the patristic and medieval past it could justly claim a greater degree of catholicity than the so-called 'Anglican' opinion.[3] Thus rather than being an innovation, sabbatarianism appears as another of those consensual doctrinal opinions which cemented the ecclesiological peace of the Jacobean Church, a peace which Charles I all too quickly destroyed. In fact, according to Parker, in carving out a separate 'Puritan' doctrine of the sabbath, Charles I and his apologists resorted to 'fraudulent means, distorting the doctrinal tradition of the English Church'.[4] The following pages deal with the central initiative behind this event: the republication and reception after October 1633 of James I's Declaration of Sports

[1] Parker, *ES* 1–7, 198–204; David Underdown, *Revel, Riot and Rebellion: Popular Politics and Culture in England, 1603–1660* (Oxf., 1985), 176–7.

[2] Parker, *ES* 2–7, Hill, *SP* 146; K. Wrightson, 'Alehouses, Order and Reformation in Rural England 1590–1660', in E. and S. Yeo (eds.), *Popular Culture and Class Conflict 1590–1914* (Brighton, 1981), 1–27; Underdown, *Revel, Riot and Rebellion*, 40–3; K. Wrightson, *English Society 1580–1680* (1982); for a critique see Margaret Spufford, 'Puritanism and Social Control', in A. Fletcher and J. Stevenson (eds.), *Order and Disorder in Early Modern England* (Cambridge, 1985); and Collinson, *RP*, chs. 4–6.

[3] Parker, *ES* 2–7, *et passim*.

[4] Parker, *ES* 7; PRO SP 16/248/13.

of 1618, which permitted certain recreations and pastimes on the sabbath.[5]

The book of sports was properly known as the king's declaration for lawful sports, and as such, contemporaries in the 1630s may be excused for associating Charles I with its reappearance rather than the bishops. 'Certainly,' said John Mundey in 'Sabbatum Redivivum', 'it was far enough from his Majesty's princely mind, that any of his liege people (should) take offence at the royal manifest.'[6] Those who spoke out against the declaration almost without exception held the king responsible for his own acts. John Metcalf thought 'that the king had done more than he could answer in publishing' it. 'Whatsoever the king is pleased to have done,' preached the vicar of Enmore in Somerset, 'the king of heaven commands us to keep the Sabbath.'[7] In neighbouring Combe Florey, William Treble refused to participate in Sunday sports because 'the king did allow of that which God did forbid', while in the Oxford parish of St Peter le Bailey, John Wildgoose declared that the sabbath day should be kept holy and that 'the king had made laws against it'.[8] Contemporary statements, such as these, which on the basis of surviving depositions represent a common perception, raise a fundamental question for the historian, for where does the opinion that Laud was responsible for the re-publication of the book emanate? It was after all Prynne and Burton who pointed the finger of accusation at the archbishop. To blame Laud in his trial, as in 1636 or in 1641, was the most effective way of implicating royal responsibility without accusing the king personally and without depriving him of room to manœuvre to alter his policy. Thus Burton blamed Laud but at the same time expressed disbelief that 'God's anointed' could ever have contemplated such a retrograde act as the publication of the declaration.[9] The question of the relative

[5] J. Tait, 'The Declaration of Sports for Lancashire', *English Historical Review*, 32 (1917), 561–8; L. A. Govett, *The King's Book of Sports* (1890); T. G. Barnes, 'County Politics and a Puritan Cause Célèbre: Somerset Church Ales, 1633', *TRHS*, 5th ser., 9 (1959), 103–22; PRO SP 16/248/13.

[6] SJC MS 1/25; Thomas Coleman likened Charles I to Jeroboam, who made a feast to ingratiate the people, *A Sermon Preached before the House of Commons August 30 1643* (1643), 40.

[7] Bodl. Tanner MS 68/338; SRO D/D/Ca 313/47.

[8] SRO D/D/Ca 301/56; ORO MS ODP c. 27/depos. 43^{v}–44.

[9] H. Burton, *For God and the King* (1636), 40, 60; Prynne, *CD* 149. See also Bodl. Rawl. MS A 409, where Humfrey Chambers renounces 'so presumptious an attempt as curiously to pry after, much more to question the . . . end of his Majesty's act'.

roles played by Laud and the king in the republication of the book, as in other policies of the 1630s, is not at all irrelevant, since its over-identification with Laud has shielded the king's role from greater investigation and led to the distortion of the constitutional implications of the policy by its dismissal as an 'ecclesiastical' issue.

That Charles I was not sabbatarian is evident from the masques and council meetings which he held on Sundays. Yet his dislike of strict sabbath observance alone is not a sufficient explanation for his republication of his father's declaration. Leah Marcus has suggested that behind the king's encouragement of rural pastimes lay a subtle attempt to bolster the social base of his sacramental kingship. She has suggested that the king saw holy day sports and customs as extensions of natural grace with the capacity of stemming disorder through their own sacred order. With the sanction of the Church, former rural customs might also help to diminish the social alienation generated by increased reverence for the church as a consecrated place. In that wakes and ales celebrated the origins and prescriptive rights of the parish, these customs also helped to give significance to a unit integral to Charles's notion of magisterial responsibility. At the same time, through the popularization of these practices, the king may have hoped to stem the decline of hospitality in the countryside, which he and others perceived to be taking place.[10]

While the resurrection of the moribund customs of the countryside might help to reassert the king's sacramental authority, an equally important if not more important consideration for him was that the book of sports provided fuel against Puritanism. Through its reappearance Charles would further isolate and stigmatize Puritanism as a disease within the body politic. In the preamble which James I had added to Morton's text, the definition of Puritanism had been considerably widened to include within it strict sabbath observance.[11] It had labelled as 'Puritans' those magistrates whose activity had

[10] PRO SP 16/470/107; Heylyn, *CA* 256–8; R. Cox, *The Literature of the Sabbath Question*, 2 vols. (1865), i. 480. For attempts by the Privy Council to suppress the sabbatarian controversy before 1632 see PRO SP 16/211/81; Leah S. Marcus, *The Politics of Mirth: Johnson, Herrick, Milton, Marvell and the Defense of old Holiday Pastimes* (Chicago, 1986), 17–19; Underdown, *Revel, Riot and Rebellion*, 40–1 ff., 176–7 ff.; Felicity Heal, *Hospitality in Early Modern England* (Oxford, 1990), 365, 352–403; id. 'The Crown, the Gentry and London: The Enforcement of Proclamation, 1596–1640', in C. Cross, D. Loades, and J. Scarisbrick (eds.), *Law and Government under the Tudors* (Cambridge, 1988), 211–12, 221.

[11] Parker, *ES* 150–4.

sparked off the original Lancashire dispute in 1617, and required ministers to conform to the Prayer Book or face deprivation. As such it smeared the attempt to restrict recreations with 'Puritan' nonconformity. Furthermore the requirement that 'judaising sabbatarians' should be reported to the authorities tainted the doctrinally orthodox with recusancy, which can only have pleased a king for whom 'the neglect of punishing puritans' bred popery.[12]

'The book was printed by the king it was not of my procuring.'[13] With such words Laud denied any responsibility for the republication of the book of sports. His explicit disavowal of culpability commands respect, if only because he was prepared to acknowledge his involvement in other more controversial policy initiatives of the 1630s. In fact during his trial he produced the document, signed by Charles I, authorizing its republication: 'Canterbury see that our declaration concerning lawful sports on the Lord's Day after evening prayer be printed.'[14] Heylyn, later Laud's biographer (but on his own testimony the king's apologist in the republication of the book), absolved Laud of any responsibility in the affair, there being 'no reason to charge that on my Lord Archbishop as if it were a matter of his procuring'.[15] Moreover in 1637, Dow, Juxon's chaplain, published his *Innovations unjustly charged* (written in answer to Burton's accusations), which attempted to exculpate the archbishop from any role in the republication and shift the focus of attention elsewhere: 'men may, at their liberty, father the king's acts upon the prelates or any other person whom they favour not, and then cavil at them at their pleasure and reject them as none of his.'[16]

According to Heylyn, two main events determined the timing of the republication: the appearance of Theophilus Braborne's *A Defence of the Sabbath Day* and the ales controversy in Somerset.[17] Braborne, whose work suggested that Saturday ought to be kept as the true sabbath, might well have escaped the king's wrath had he not dedicated the work to him. Heylyn's belief that Charles I was personally affronted by the epistle dedicatory receives confirmation from the fact

[12] Ibid.

[13] *WWL* iv. 251; HLRO MS Braye 8/47; WCO MS Clarke 5/11.

[14] *WWL* iv. 251; PRO SP 16/248/12.

[15] P. Heylyn, *A Brief and Moderate Answer* (1636), 80–1.

[16] C. Dow, *Innovations unjustly charged unto the present Church and State* (1637), 39.

[17] Heylyn, *CA* 256–8; his *Observations on the History of the Reign of King Charles* (1650), 113–14; and *The History of the Sabbath Day* (1636), 268.

that at Braborne's trial in the High Commission, the king's advocate led the prosecution.[18] However the offence attendant on the appearance of this treatise was soon overshadowed by the Somerset ales dispute. In 1633 several Somerset justices petitioned the Lord Chief Justice, Richardson, to issue a general order suppressing ales and wakes, the festivals which commemorated the dedication of churches.[19] If the resulting controversy had not become enmeshed in county factional disputes which subsequently involved the king, the Somerset order would have been unexceptional. The previous fifty years had witnessed the issue of many such orders; Richardson's itself was based on a precedent signed by Popham, Lord Chief Justice in Elizabeth's reign.[20] During his trial, Laud admitted that he had played a prominent part in rescinding Richardson's order, there 'being sufficient cause to regulate wakes but not to take them away'. Richardson himself revealed that Laud had savaged him at the council table, by informing the earl of Dorset after he had left the council chamber that he had almost been 'choked by a pair of lawn-sleeves'.[21] Laud, like the king, was undoubtedly taken aback by Richardson's provocative decision to publish the order in the churches without first consulting the ordinary.[22] Professor Barnes, and more recently Dr Parker, have closely studied the ales controversy and both have concluded that Laud's involvement emanated not from any identifiable anti-sabbatarian inclinations, but rather from a desire to protect ecclesiastical rights from judicial encroachment. In fact, when diocesan at Bath and Wells in 1628, Laud made no attempt to revoke a similar order issued by the Somerset justices.[23] Although the incident caused a rift between Laud and Richardson, which was not improved by Richardson's independent stand in the Sherfield case, their mutual antipathy should not be exaggerated.[24] Not long after the ales controversy he sent to Laud the names of noncon-

[18] Parker, *ES* 198–9; Cox, *The Literature of the Sabbath Question*, i. 480.
[19] Parker, *ES* 183.
[20] Parker, *ES* 182–91; *WWL* iv. 252.
[21] Parker, *ES* 182–8; *WWL* iv. 133, 252.
[22] The significance of these feasts has recently received fresh and perceptive treatment in Marcus, *Politics of Mirth*; Margo Todd, *Christian Humanism and the Puritan Social Order* (1987); and Underdown, *Revel, Riot and Rebellion*.
[23] Parker, *ES* 191; Barnes, 'County Politics', 103–22.
[24] Parker, *ES* 183–4; P. A. Slack, 'Religious Protest and Urban Authority: The Case of Henry Sherfield, Iconoclast, 1633', in *Schism, Heresy and Religious Protest: Studies in Church History*, ix. ed. D. Baker (Cambridge, 1972), 295–302; *WWL* iv. 252.

formists, while Laud and the other councillors helped to reconcile Richardson with Phelips, his local opponent, a reconciliation which appears to have lasted for the decade.[25]

It is generally assumed without question that as a result of the wakes and ales controversy, Laud asked the king to republish the declaration of 1618 and that so reluctant was the king that on 4 October, he requested Piers of Bath and Wells to inquire into the state of wakes within his diocese.[26] Yet this interpretation sits uneasily with the extant evidence. Charles was hardly reluctant to republish the declaration, which is precisely what he did on 18 October, before either Laud or Piers could report to him, which they eventually did in November.[27] Moreover in May, long before the republication or the council meeting that rescinded Richardson's order, Charles sent letters to the Somerset justices requesting that they issue no further orders against wakes and that they refrain from preventing people from playing lawful games after evening prayer.[28] Thus the king was using the rhetoric of his father's declaration and sponsoring its proposals before the official republication in October 1633.

Shortly after he republished the book, Charles I commissioned his almoner, Bishop White of Ely, and his chaplain, Peter Heylyn, to write respectively the theological and historical apologies for the work.[29] 'It was the king, our gracious master, his will and pleasure', declared White, in the epistle dedicatory to the *Treatise of the Sabbath Day*, written in 1635, 'that such a treatise should be set forth, to prevent further mischief and to settle his good subjects, who have long been distracted about the sabbath question.'[30] During the later 1630s other works appeared justifying the royal line on sports and sabbatarianism, such as Pocklington's *Sunday No Sabbath*, Primrose's *A Treatise of the Sabbath and Lord's Day*, Dow's *A Discourse of the Sabbath and Lord's Day*, and Sanderson's *A Sovereign Antidote Against*

[25] Knowler, i. 167; PRO SP 16/260/90.
[26] PRO SP 16/247/24; 16/248/24; Parker, *ES* 189–90. A conciliar committee to examine the issue was established, see PRO SP 16/534/54.
[27] PRO SP 16/250/20.
[28] SRO DD/PH 222/67.
[29] Heylyn, *History of the Sabbath Day*; F. White, *A Treatise of the Sabbath Day* (1635). The king also ordered the publication of sermons which promoted the book, see Thomas Turner, *A Sermon preached before the King at Whitehall . . . 1635* (1635).
[30] White, *Treatise of the Sabbath Day*, epistle dedicatory.

Sabbatarian Errors.[31] As Dr Parker has shown, these works advanced contradictory arguments about the morality of the fourth commandment. Heylyn and Pocklington both denied its morality, asserting that the commandment had no consequence for the observance of Sunday, which was established by the Church and not of divine but human institution. Consequently they elaborated the notion of sabbatarianism as a 'Puritan' doctrine, opposed to 'catholic' teaching, which the original book of sports had intimated, and in so doing helped to depict those who questioned the republication as opponents of royal and ecclesiastical authority.[32] The other writers tended to subscribe to a more patristic interpretation which rooted the morality of the fourth commandment and Sunday in divinity. John Cosin fundamentally disagreed with Heylyn and Pocklington.[33] Denying the perpetual morality of the sabbath, he asserted instead the perpetual morality of Sunday. While repudiating the novel views of these 'new writers' (as he called them), Cosin nevertheless saw their opinions as a resurgence of scholastic over patristic ideas, somewhat qualifying Dr Parker's belief that they lacked medieval antecedents.[34]

The royal sponsorship of the argument that Sunday was not the sabbath or more controversially that it was not immutable or of divine institution, meant that those (like Cosin) who disagreed with these opinions were very reluctant to air their objections.[35] Others were confused by the doctrinal differences in question, among them Collins, provost of King's, who sought clarification from Cosin.[36] In the last resort the clear divergence of doctrinal views which arose among the Caroline divines stemmed less from any ostensible dichotomy in an authentic 'Laudian' position (Dr Parker's explanation) than from the fact that as the king commissioned his own apologies for his own actions, there was little attempt to syncretize ideas.[37]

[31] The imprimatur lay with Laud, Juxon, and their chaplains. Laud's chaplain, Bray, gave the imprimatur for Pocklington's *Sunday No Sabbath*, for which he had to recant in 1641 (Bodl. Tanner 240/56). Others might advise on the publication of works, such as Bishop Lindsell of Hereford (HLRO 23 Jan. 1641/188–9). Bodl. Tanner MS 65/83 shows that Twiss and Archbishop Ussher were preparing evidence to use against the Caroline anti-sabbatarian authors in 1640.

[32] Parker, *ES* 196–204, 1–7.

[33] Bodl. MS Smith 40/123–6.

[34] Bodl. MS Smith 40/123–6.

[35] Bodl. MS Smith 40/123–6; HLRO 23 Jan. 1641/188–9; Bodl. Tanner MS 65/83.

[36] Bodl. MS Smith 40/123–6.

[37] Parker, *ES* 206, 200–6.

As far as can be ascertained, Laud's strict observance of Sunday suggests that he inclined towards a more moralistic interpretation of the Lord's Day,[38] even if he would find it difficult to dissociate himself from a polemic which placed as much emphasis upon tradition as revelation.[39] As for the king, however, no such case may be made. Charles I fully adhered to Heylyn's interpretation of Sunday as a human not a divine institution, thus downgrading the moral observance of the fourth precept and the Lord's Day. In answer to the question whether the same authority which changed the Jewish sabbath into Sunday had also instituted Easter, the king declared that 'it will not be found in Scripture where Saturday is discharged to be kept or turned into ... Sunday ... whereof it must be the Church's authority that changed the one (and) instituted the other.'[40] Such views thinly veil the royal sponsorship of the book of sports and consequent distortion of an authentic Laudian policy in relation to it.

II. DIOCESAN PUBLICATION AND CENSURES

The circular letter which Laud sent to every bishop in the Southern Province on 28 December 1633, announcing the republication of the declaration of 1618, specified that the bishops should see that the work was published in the parishes. It did not specify that only the incumbent should read it in his parish. There is no reason to doubt that Laud connived at the curate, a neighbouring minister, a court official (and possibly the churchwardens, although this must remain a matter of conjecture) reading the book on the minister's default. Diocesan officials were to consult with the bishops to ascertain the best way to distribute and publish the books in the parishes. The publication, its timing and method, was dependent on the will of each individual ordinary rather than on that of the archbishop.[41]

The survival of some diocesan correspondence for Bath and Wells permits a close reconstruction of the stages leading to the republication of the work within a particular diocese. On 2 November 1633

[38] Fuller, *CH* 424; *WWL* iii. 150. In March 1637 Laud asked the Council to prohibit plays in Lent, to the chagrin of Pembroke; Knowler, ii. 56; see also n. 196.

[39] Parker, *ES* 191. [40] *WKC* ii. 188.

[41] LPL Reg. Laud i/192: 'I am commanded to give you notice hereof, because his Majesty expects no little favour from you and your officers are to send for the books immediately;' SRO D/D/C/1878 bundle 3/30 Nov., 23 Nov.

Arthur Duck, the chancellor of Wells, informed Alexander Huish, the bishop's secretary, that the archbishop had dispatched to every bishop the circular letter of 28 October 1633. From this Duck knew that there was a declaration and that each parish would probably receive a copy, 'which . . . if I find it to be . . . I will send them down'.[42] Several days later, his opinions confirmed, Duck informed the secretary that he would receive the copies within the following week.[43] However not until 30 November did the 500 books arrive at Wells, by courtesy of the king's carrier.[44] Duck recommended that the declaration should sell for not under five pence: two pence for the printer 'and the hazard of some that may miscarry' and three pence for the apparitor, which was the same price he received for dispensing briefs. Eventually, as in most other dioceses, the books sold for six pence a copy.[45] Most significantly, Duck told Huish to consult with the bishop over the best way to distribute and publish the work in the parishes, revealing that the archbishop had given no specific instructions about the distribution or publication of the book of sports but left it to the discretion of the ordinary.[46] In Bath and Wells such liberty caused the diocesan secretary no little consternation, for Piers expected him to write within two days a note of fourteen lines to each minister explaining 'in what manner they shall publish the book in the church'.[47] As Piers proved to be one of the most enthusiastic protagonists of the book, it is unlikely that many other bishops gave such detailed specifications for its publication, although there is sufficient evidence to show that the bishops in every diocese distributed the book for publication within their parishes.[48]

The question arises, however, not so much whether the bishops ordered each incumbent to publish the book, as whether they asked him to read it in person. As stated, Laud's letter of 28 October suggests that he did not envisage the incumbent as the sole means of its publication.[49] During the metropolitical visitation Brent certainly encouraged incumbents to read the work in their parish church. Yet

42 SRO D/D/C 1878 bundle 3/9 Nov.
43 SRO D/D/C 1878 bundle 3/23 Nov.
44 SRO D/D/C 1878 bundle 3/30 Nov.
45 SRO D/D/C 1878 bundle 3/23 Nov.
46 Ibid.
47 SRO D/D/C/1878 bundle 3/30 Nov.
48 See my thesis, 'The Growth and Implementation of 'Laudianism', with special reference to the Southern Province' (Oxford D.Phil. thesis, 1987), p. 302, appendix ii.
49 LPL Reg. Laud 1/192.

in the particular instructions which Laud drew up for the vicar-general at the start of the visitation, the reading of the book is not listed, nor did the requirement enter the metropolitical visitation articles.[50] It seems very likely that the king required that each incumbent should read the work and that the names of those who refused should be returned to London. This seems to be the implication behind Laud's statement in his trial, 'His Majesty having commanded this, I could do little if I had not so much inquired what was done.'[51] It was this requirement, that names should be returned of those who refused to read the book, which Davenant declined to obey.[52] Archbishop Neile's letter to the king in January 1636 suggests that Charles I required Neile also to inform him of the clerical refusal to read the book in the Northern Province.[53] This pressure served to undermine some of that freedom which the diocesan as ordinary had in order to determine the best mode of publication in the parishes, a freedom allowed them not only by the declaration itself but by Laud's letter of 28 October.[54] On the other hand, it may have intensified episcopal efforts to have the book read. Even before the metropolitical visitation of their sees, Coke of Bristol, Davenant of Salisbury, and Bowle of Rochester had dispatched books to the parishes for the incumbents to read, and those bishops whose dioceses were visited metropolitically in 1635 had done the same in 1634.[55]

Charles I had not seen fit to alter the clause in James I's declaration which specified 'that the publication of this command be made by order of the bishops throughout all the parish churches of their several dioceses respectively'.[56] Thus although there was nothing novel in the requirement that the book be published within the churches, its appearance in 1633 could only seem a vindictive response to the Somerset order for the suppression of wakes, which

50 PRO SP 16/312/84; *WWL* v. 399–452.

51 *WWL* iv. 253; WCO MS Clarke 5/11.

52 Fuller, *CH* 425.

53 PRO SP 16/312/84; see R. A. Marchant, *The Church under the Law: Law, Justice, Administration and Discipline in the Diocese of York, 1560–1640* (Cambridge, 1969), 220 ff. for aspects of Neile's prosecution of the book of sports.

54 LPL Reg. Laud 1/192.

55 BRO P/St T./6 6/9; BL Egerton MS 784; WTRO D1/39/1/53, D5/28/34; BERO D/P 144/5/2/1633; PCR, 91–2; Prynne, *CD* 150–2.

56 *Documentary Annals*, i. 240–5.

the justices had asked the constable to read in the churches.[57] Moreover it was not now the justices who required compliance but 'supreme authority' itself. Fuller was not alone in questioning the tact of reading a declaration in church and thought that it would have been better if the tithing man or constable had read it at the market-cross, in the same manner as publishing proclamations.[58] Those who refused to read the book often did so in the knowledge that it contained no command whatsoever that the clergy should read it, nor did it lay down any penalties for such a default. Again, as the book was not a proclamation, it appeared in the parishes without the royal seal. Thomas Wilson of Otham (Canterbury) said that he refused 'to read the book not out of contempt for authority but as commanded by no law, for the king doth not in the book command or appoint the minister to read it, nor it to be read but published; neither came it with, nor know I of any seal; and his Majesty's writs, proclamations and mandates, use to come with a seal; and his Majesty intended (as I conceive) not to trouble any that refuse to read it, seeing there is no penalty threatened, nor authority given (that I know of) to any to question them that refuse to read it.'[59]

Wilson was certainly mistaken in his belief that the king never intended to trouble any who refused to read the book. Like the forced loan, the reading of the book was to become a test of loyalty to the Crown. That Charles ordered the prosecution of those who refused is not in doubt, as when informed of the refusal of William Twiss, chaplain to his sister, the queen of Bohemia, he told the bishops not to prosecute him. Moreover there is evidence that the Privy Council issued threats of deprivation to some clergy who refused.[60] But when did the practice of ecclesiastical censuring start and along what lines did it proceed in the dioceses? Rushworth believed that during the metropolitical visitation Laud censured

[57] Parker, *ES* 188–9.

[58] Fuller, *CH* 424; G. Swincock, *The Life and Death of Thomas Wilson* (1672), 12; R. Cust, *The Forced Loan and English Politics 1626–1628* (Oxf., 1987), 329.

[59] Swincock, *Life and Death of Thomas Wilson*, 67. Thus the book of sports should not be included in *Stuart Royal Proclamations*, ii. ed. J. F. Larkin, (Oxford, 1984). See also Bodl. Rawl. MS A 346/165ᵛ where Chambers makes comments similar to Wilson's.

[60] G. Kendall, *Tuissii Vita et Victoria* (1657), 80; Margaret Spufford, *Contrasting Communities: English Villagers in the Sixteenth and Seventeenth Centuries* (Cambridge, 1974), 231–2; Rushworth, iii. 1168, 1196.

recalcitrants and that only in response to this policy did other bishops initiate proceedings in their courts.[61] In his trial Laud asserted that he had given no instruction to Brent ordering the wholesale censure of those who refused. In fact remarkably few ministers underwent censure during Brent's visitations; only one in 1635: Pegges of Weeford (Coventry and Lichfield), whom he suspended *ex nunc prout ex tunc*, in case he did not read the king's declaration.[62] To others Brent appears to have offered time; he informed Laud that he had not suspended Fairfax of Rumburgh (Norwich) because he promised to read it in the future.[63] It is apparent then that Rushworth was mistaken about the importance of the metropolitical courts in the censure of recalcitrants. Again most bishops who inflicted censure did so not after but before the metropolitical visitation of their sees.[64] According to Heylyn it was the publication of his and White's apologies which encouraged the bishops to pursue a policy of censure rather than one of persuasion.[65] Yet, if there was a distinct alteration in policy after 1636, it was marked by the decrease not the intensification of censure in all dioceses where censures were inflicted, with the singular exception of Norwich under Wren. Most of those censured underwent censure before the appearance of the two apologies. Moreover to depict policy as Heylyn does in terms of a progression towards more stringent expedients ignores the fact that the courts preferred persuasive to penal methods of extracting compliance. Censure was infrequent (outside Norwich and Bath and Wells) and invariably an exemplary measure.[66] But if diocesan policies do not conform to the distinct division depicted by Heylyn, such a division may well reflect the perception of the king. With the publication of the apologies, justifying his republication of the book of sports, Charles possibly thought that there was less occasion for accommodation and more reason to invoke censure. This interpretation receives support from Neile's statement to the king in January 1636: 'touching your Majesty's declaration ... I have found some reluctancy in a few of the ministers but yet with this

[61] Rushworth, ii. 459.

[62] PRO SP 16/293/128. Thus during Laud's metropolitical visitation of Huntingdon archdeaconry, conducted by Lambe, Herbert Palmer, vicar of Ashwell, was surprised to find that he was not forced to read the book, discovering 'beyond expectation, rather a connivance at him, than an enforcement thereof': S. Clarke, *The Lives of Thirty-Two English Divines* (1677), 199.

[63] Ibid. [64] Rushworth, ii. 459; see section ii.

[65] Heylyn, *CA* 296. [66] See section ii.

petition of some time to consider better of the business, and liberty to read my lord of Ely's book lately written . . . upon reading whereof many promise either to conform or submit to ecclesiastical censure.'[67]

According to Prynne, as a result of his endeavours, Laud managed 'to suspend, sequester, excommunicate, censure, persecute, deprive . . . hundreds of godly ministers as capital offenders . . . for refusing' to publish the book.[68] Apart from Prynne's comments, the opinion that Laud was the main protagonist in the prosecution of clergy rests on the belief that he requested each minister to read it and that he censured all those who refused. Doubtless the incumbent suggested himself as the obvious candidate, but as Laud required the churchwardens or incumbent to certify that it was published (rather than read by the incumbent), he connived at neighbouring ministers or surrogates reading the book instead. Moreover Laud could not have censured all those who refused to read the book, as in the diocese of Canterbury he censured only four, the clerical refusal (to read the book) being far in excess of that number.[69]

The survival of court evidence and other material permits a careful reconstruction of the archbishop's policy as diocesan in Canterbury. Early in 1634 Brent, Laud's commissary, called several ministers before him to impress upon them that they should read the book. Of these, some proceeded to carry out his requirement, others did not.[70] Brent allowed time to those who refused and asked 'no more of it', which suggests that Laud did not press him to carry out a more stringent policy, at least at this stage. In May 1634, however, Laud became more personally involved in its publication, and at the request, according to Brent, of certain informers within the see.[71] Four clergy were singled out for not reading the book: Culmer of Goodnestone next Wingham, Player of Kennington, Hieron of Hernhill, and Gardiner of St. Mary, Sandwich. At this stage it was known that others had refused; this being so, why were only four ministers singled out?[72] It appears that these were singularly nonconformist clergy. Heylyn described them as 'the leading men, and the chief sticklers of the faction in all his diocese', a view with which

67 PRO SP 16/312/84. 68 Prynne, *CD* 153.

69 *WWL* iv. 253–4; Prynne, *CD* 128, 131–55, 505–6; Heylyn, *CA* 308; *PCR* 19; WCO MS Clarke 5/11.

70 *WWL* iv. 253–4; WCO MS Clarke 5/11.

71 HLRO MS Braye 8/47; WCO MS Clarke 5/11.

72 HLRO MS Braye 8/47; WCO MS Clarke 5/11.

Fuller concurred, if in far less heightened language.[73] Laud himself spoke of Culmer in his trial as the minister most deserving of suspension within his diocese, a suspension which proved ironic, in that Culmer had recently informed the council of a 'gentleman of quality' who had complained that the books were published in churches.[74] When Laud examined the four ministers, he did not suspend them peremptorily but gave them time to reform. During this period, one of the accused, Gardiner, promised conformity and was not prosecuted further, and on conditions which possibly entailed him not having to read the book.[75] Brent moved for a further reprieve for the three remaining clergy, which Laud refused on the basis that they had had long enough to conform, asserting that if they did not know 'how to obey' he did not know 'how to grant'.[76] However, when Laud censured them he suspended them only *ab officio* not *a beneficio* as well and did not carry out further prosecutions or implicate other clergy who had refused.[77] Thereafter he suspended only one minister, Thomas Wilson of Otham, in 1635, who testified to the fact that his censure, like those inflicted previously, was exceptional: 'I was singled out among the rest.'[78] Again, Wilson's suspension was only *ab officio*, and that only from the office of preaching, rather than the office of curate. Swincock, Wilson's biographer, claimed correctly that Wilson was suspended *a beneficio*, but this was later when he appeared in the High Commission for dilapidation suits and further nonconformity.[79] Culmer claimed that he also had been deprived of the profits of his place, but this occurred only after his patron had usurped the living during his suspension.[80]

After 1635 Laud called no other ministers to account for their failure to read the book, which confirms his testimony in the trial that

[73] Heylyn, *CA* 308; Fuller, *CH* 425.

[74] *WWL* iv. 254; PRO SP 16/301/68: the gentleman concerned was Edward Boys of Goodnestone, see *Antidotum Culmerianum* (1644), 35; R. Culmer, *A Parish Looking Glasse for Persecutors of Ministers* (1657), 3–4.

[75] LPL VG/4/22/103–4; *WWL* iv. 254; WCO MS Clarke 5/11; HLRO MS Braye 8/47; PRO SP 16/499/67.

[76] *WWL* iv. 254; HLRO MS Braye 8/47; WCO MS Clarke 5/11; PRO SP 16/499/67.

[77] *WWL* iv. 253; WCO MS Clarke 5/11.

[78] Swincock, *Life and Death of Thomas Wilson*, 12; *WWL* iv. 25; WCO MS Clarke 5/11.

[79] Swincock, *Life and Death of Thomas Wilson*, 67; WCO MS Clarke 5/11. Dering took up Wilson's case in 1640: Bodl. MS Add. c. 132/80/24.

[80] Culmer, *A Parish Looking Glasse for Persecutors of Ministers*, 3–4; *Antidotum Culmerianum* (1644), 35; WCO MS Clarke 5/11.

his policy with respect to the reading of the book of sports was 'far from rigour', there being 'in other dioceses far more than three . . . punished and their punishment greater'.[81] Laud's testimony received some unexpected confirmation from Fuller: 'as for the archbishop of Canterbury, much was his moderation in his own diocese silencing but three through the whole extent thereof.'[82] By 1639 Laud had absolved all the suspended clergy. Although Prynne saw this as a tactful response to the troubles in the North, Laud appears to have lifted the suspensions in response to personal requests from the individual clergy.[83] During November 1638, for example, Player of Kennington asked the archbishop that 'he be pleased to release him from . . . suspension according to your Grace's clemency towards others'. Laud informed Brent to absolve him if not 'wilfully refractory', and on conditions which did not entail his reading the book.[84] In 1638 Laud also received petitions from clergy in other dioceses for absolution from the censure inflicted by their ordinaries, and consequently absolved them, such as Thomas of Ubleigh (Bath and Wells), who had failed to obtain relief from Piers and Seaton of Apsley (Lincoln) whom Lambe had suspended only a few months before during the second metropolitical visitation of Lincoln.[85] In the words 'wilfully refractory' rested Laud's justification for prosecuting some ministers for failing to read the book, as refusal to read it did not constitute sufficient grounds for censure in the first place. Laud's clerical censures were infrequent, exemplary, and moderate with the aim of achieving a wider canonical obedience and stemming nonconformist inclinations. In 1640, during his visitation of Gloucester occasioned by Goodman's suspension, the archbishop inquired into and republished all of Goodman's articles for 1637 with one exception, that the minister should read the book of sports.[86] For Laud the reading of the book was less an aim in itself than a valuable test for conformity in particular cases.

With respect to episcopal efforts to enjoin the reading of the book, three categories suggest themselves: first, those who exceeded Laud's rather lethargic policy; second, those who adopted a similarly moderate course; and third, those who did not censure at all or for

81 *WWL* iv. 253. 82 Fuller, *CH* 424.
83 Prynne, *CD* 128; WCO MS Clarke 5/11; LPL VG/4/22/103–4.
84 LPL VG 4/22/103–4.
85 PRO SP/395/37, 49, SP 16/388/27; Calamy, iii. 213.
86 LPL VG 4/22/103–4; G. Soden, *Godfrey Goodman* (1953), 314.

whose policy there remains insufficient evidence. In historiography Wren's policy has invariably passed for Laudianism in this as in so many other respects.[87] Yet Wren's and Laud's attitudes and approach were quite distinct from each other. During his visitation of Norwich in 1636 Wren inquired into the reading of the book not only in his visitation articles but also through his visitation courts.[88] Returns revealed that a considerable number of clergy in Norfolk and Suffolk had not read the work. As a result of his findings Wren decided to choose sixty ministers, those whom he 'had most doubt of', to read it.[89] According to his own testimony, most of these ministers refused and were summarily suspended, although some were absolved at a later date on promise of conformity.[90] In his answer to the articles of impeachment preferred against him in 1641, he revealed that those whom he had suspended numbered thirty, sixteen of which were subsequently excommunicated.[91] Wren was the only bishop in the 1630s to mete out such extensive censures, and the only one who suspended clergy for not reading the book during 1636–7. Yet strict as his policy was, its severity has been exaggerated. As he discriminated between those whom 'he had most doubt of' and other clergy he must have asked only those clergy to read the book whom he suspected of canonical disobedience in the first place.[92] When Wren went to Ely in 1638, he appears to have carried out a similar policy during his first visitation there.[93]

Apart from Wren, three other bishops excommunicated or suspended *ab officio et a beneficio* over this particular issue: Piers of Bath and Wells, and, to a lesser extent, Curle of Winchester and Bowle of Rochester. A conservative estimate of the number of ministers Piers suspended is two, but this rests possibly on a misinterpretation of the articles of impeachment presented against him in 1641, where two ministers were named as having been suspended: Chambers of Claverton and Thomas of Ubleigh, who were singled out probably

[87] Although see Fuller, *AII* iii. 8.

[88] Bodl. MS Tanner 68/6^{v}, 30–3, 204, 332^{v} and refs. 89–91; *Parentalia*, 64; Heylyn, *A Brief and Moderate Answer*, 110–14.

[89] Bodl. MS Tanner 68/209; *Parentalia*, 64; Bodl. MS Tanner 314/155, 122^{v}, 180, 183^{v}–192, 132–6, 143^{v}–145.

[90] *Parentalia*, 64; Rushworth, ii. 461.

[91] *Parentalia*, 64; Heylyn, *A Brief and Moderate Answer*, 110–14. Bodl. Tanner MS 314/122^{v}.

[92] Bodl. MS Tanner 314/183^{v}–192.

[93] Bodl. MS Gough Eccles. Top 3 (SL 17679) 7/83, MS Tanner 65/4/5.

because they underwent suspension for a longer period than the other ministers and were eventually excommunicated.[94] Extant court records, however, suggest a much higher figure of suspensions, not less than twenty-five. The belief that Piers started suspending ministers in October 1634, when William Thomas was suspended, is also to be questioned not least because it is based only on the surviving court records.[95] William Whiteway of Dorchester noted in his diary that in July 1634 clergy suspended for not reading the book had appealed from the Wells courts to the court of Delegates.[96] Thus Piers not only suspended clergy before October 1634, but more than twenty-five ministers.[97] Between April 1634 and May 1635 the courts asked the incumbent to certify whether or not the book had been published.[98] Many of those who refused to certify were subsequently suspended, although this was generally for not more than six months, and it must remain conjectural whether a condition of their absolution was that they must read the book.[99] As the courts asked for a certificate that the minister had published rather than read, there were probably a considerable number of ministers in the diocese who did not read it. Certain clergy are known to have refused to read the book, but they remained unsuspended.[100] In some instances, however, Piers asked the minister to read the book in person, even when the book had been published in their parish. These ministers were probably singled out because Piers wished to suspend them on grounds of their nonconformity or because they had spoken out against the book. Like Wren's select recalcitrants in Norwich, they constituted the clergy whom Piers had 'most doubt of'.[101] Even so, both bishops pressed the reading of the book more vigorously than others elsewhere. According to Hill, the dioceses of

[94] *Articles of Accusation and Impeachment of the House of Commons against William Piers* (1642), 5.

[95] See T. M. Peake's fine study, 'Somerset Clergy and the Church Courts' (Bristol, M. Litt. thesis, 1978), 458–63.

[96] BL MS Egerton 784. On the relationship of the Delegates to other courts see PRO SP 16/350/82; R. G. Usher, *The Rise and Fall of the High Commission* (1910), 311; Duncon, *The High Court of Delegates* (Camb., 1971).

[97] *Articles ... against William Piers* (1642), 5; Peake, 'Somerset Clergy', 458–63.

[98] SRO D/D/Ca 294/60–5; Bodl. MS Rawl. A 409/72; D/D/Ca 302/17ᵛ–18, 301/13–18ᵛ, 309/327, 314a/327, 313/41.

[99] SRO D/D/Ca 301/13–18ᵛ.

[100] SRO D/D/Ca 302/17ᵛ–18; Bodl. MS Rawl. A 409/72–72ᵛ shows that Piers sent surrogates to read the book in parishes where it had not been read.

[101] Bodl. MS Rawl. A 409/72.

Bath and Wells and Norwich witnessed greater opposition because they were the major clothing districts of England; a safer explanation is the fact that greater activity by the courts resulted in a greater detection of opposition than elsewhere.[102]

Although Bishops Curle and Bowle censured few ministers in comparison to Wren and Piers, they censured more heavily than those in the second category, because they resorted to double suspension, from the office and its benefits.[103] Like Wren and unlike Laud, Curle inquired into the reading of the book in his visitation articles. During the early months of 1634, he asked for certificates of compliance from the clergy, and in June 1634 issued a letter ordering the suspension of certain ministers within the diocese of Winchester ostensibly for a failure to read the book, although it was not until January 1635 that suspensions were inflicted on, among others, Glover of Sutton and Bright of Ebbesham.[104] After these suspensions, Curle censured no others, as when Brent visited the diocese in mid-1635, he found that several ministers of the combinations at Dorking and Guildford refused to read the book, 'besides those that stood suspended for that fault'.[105] In neighbouring Rochester, Bowle, like Curle, suspended a few ministers *ab officio et a beneficio*. Ministers were asked to read the book within three weeks of the distribution.[106] However, not until one year later, in December 1634, did he issue an order to Wood, his chancellor, to suspend some of those who refused; one of these was Snelling of St Paul Cray, who eventually underwent excommunication in April 1635.[107] As the courts continued to question ministers for refusing to read the book during 1635 but refrained from censure, the likelihood is that those previously censured were prosecuted for their general nonconformity rather than for that particular offence.[108]

The second category is best defined as a policy of moderate censure, not dissimilar to that of Laud, suspension *ab officio* or suspension for a relatively short time. Perhaps the most pragmatic policy in this respect was conducted by Goodman in Gloucester.

102 Hill, *SP* 201.

103 For the relative difference between the various censures see E. Gibson, *Codex Juris Ecclesiastici Anglicani* (1713), index.

104 R. Mayo, *The Life and Death of Edmund Staunton* (1673), 14; *PCR*, 90; PRO SP 16/278/45.

105 PRO SP 16/293/128.

106 *PCR* 91–2.

107 Ibid.; Prynne, *CD* 150–2.

108 KAO DRB/PA33/113.

During 1634 the courts called for certificates from the parishes, but only where they suspected nonconformity in a particular minister did the courts ask the churchwardens not just whether the book had been read, but by whom it had been read.[109] On the basis of these certificates, Goodman cited to appear before himself those clergy who continually refused to read it, such as Prior of Sandhurst and Williams of Downhatherly, in an attempt to resolve their scruples of conscience.[110] Goodman suspended those who still refused, but only for a week so that during this time a neighbouring minister, recommended by the court, could read the book.[111] Caple of Eastington is usually cited as a minister suspended by Goodman for his refusal to read the book, but this censure was rather for his considerable nonconformity.[112] In the neighbouring see of Bristol, Coke asked for certificates early in 1634 and personally pressed some ministers, such as White of Dorchester. He, like others, refused but remained unsuspended.[113] Only one minister appears to have undergone suspension for any considerable length of time, the very nonconformist Williams of Shaftesbury, who preached 'terrification' against the book.[114] In the diocese of Oxford, Bancroft distributed the book as early as the winter of 1633. Thereafter the courts appear to have kept a close supervision over its reading, and detected some clergy, such as Wells of Bodicott, for preaching against it.[115] Only in 1638, however, did Bancroft inquire into its reading in his visitation articles, although his examining chaplain went so far as to question ordinands about the legality of reading it within the churches. Thus although there appear to have been no suspensions over failure to read the book (with the possible exception of Rogers of St Peter le Bailey) considerable pressure might be brought to bear upon individual conscience.[116]

Shortly before the metropolitical visitation of Peterborough in 1635, Brent received from Lambe a list of nonconformist ministers, some of whom were noted as not having read the book. As none of these were consequently suspended it is unlikely that either Dee or

109 GRO GDR 136 (Oct. 1637), 174 (Sept. 1634), 175 (Oct.–Nov. 1634), 186 (July 1634), 187 (Sept. 1634–Jan. 1635), all unfol.; GRO P230 CW2/1/1635.

110 GRO GDR 174/Sept. 1634, 187/Sept. 1634–Jan. 1635.

111 GRO GDR 187/Oct. 1634.

112 GRO GDR 186/Nov. 1634.

113 BL MS Egerton 784.

114 PRO SP 16/267/6.

115 ORO ODR c. 27/depos. 14ᵛ/43ᵛ–44.

116 ORO ODP MS Archd. c. 12/c. 279, ODP c. 27/14ᵛ.

Brent took any action against those who refused, as the bishop had enjoined the clergy to read it before 1634.[117] As early as January 1634 it was reported that at least sixty ministers within the diocese had refused to comply with the order. Although it was feared these would be deprived, they remained uncensured.[118] In neighbouring Ely diocese, White, who was a moderate voice in the High Commission, censured only very temperately. The case of Gibbs, curate of St Michael, Cambridge, exemplifies the limits of ecclesiastical policy before the advent of Wren's more rigorous activity.[119] Gibbs was clearly marked out for other reasons, as in other Cambridge churches the clergy did not have to read the book in person.[120] Gibbs received the book early in 1634 for publication in his church. On 9 August he appeared before Chancellor Eden and admitted his refusal to publish it, with the result that he was suspended from his curacy. Within five days, however, he was again in court and had received absolution, but with an admonition that he read the book and certify within a few weeks' time. Yet he still resisted and failed to appear in court and certify at the appointed time.[121] Not until 20 December did he finally appear, when he was again requested to comply. However by this time he could inform the court that he was no longer curate of St Michael's and that Lendall of Trinity College had published it for him. Gibbs was cited on further occasions for some reason, but it appears that he had in the meanwhile accepted a benefice in Lincoln diocese, where he read the book at Lambe's promptings.[122]

In neighbouring London, Juxon distributed copies of the book during November 1633 and then asked churchwardens in all rural deaneries to send in their certificates. Those churchwardens who failed to return certificates that the book had been published or certified that their minister had not published the book were cited in Juxon's visitation courts after December 1634.[123] On the return of a further negative answer the courts cited clergy for examination. But Juxon never pressed them to read the book under pain of censure

[117] PRO SP 16/308/52; NRO Corr. Bk. 63/160, 175, 177, 181, 197, 202, Corr. Bk. 65/51^{v}.

[118] Bodl. Tanner MS 71/186. [119] *PRC* 91; CUL F/5/4/206^{v}.

[120] CARO P22/5/2. [121] CUL F/5/41/206^{v}.

[122] CUL F/5/41/206^{v}.

[123] GL 2596/2/66, 823/1/1633; ERO D/ALV 2/18–157^{v}. Juxon drew up five articles concerning the book which were also distributed to the parishes: GL 3556/2.

and by allowing them to certify that the book was published rather than read by themselves he allowed them considerable freedom of manœuvre.[124] Peck of Prittlewell, who refused to read the book, was suspended by Juxon's visitation court but his presentment articles suggest that he was marked out for his considerable nonconformity rather than for this particular offence.[125] Among the many incumbents who refused to read the book were Burgess of Watford, Holdsworth of St Peter le Poor (also archdeacon of Huntingdon), the Gouges, and the Shutes.[126] There were four other dioceses where the courts prosecuted the reading of the book in a similar way. In Llandaff Murray took the opportunity to suspend probably his two most nonconformist clergy, Erbury of Cardiff and Wroth of Llanfaches, who then went to set up the first Welsh independent church. In neighbouring St David's at least one minister was suspended for various offences, which included his failure to read the work.[127] Within Coventry and Lichfield, two ministers, Bennet of Uffington and Simon Ashe, underwent deprivation, but this was only after they had left the diocese, Bennet to Lancashire and Ashe to the peculiar of Wroxhall and ultimately to the household of Lord Brooke in Suffolk.[128]

To this second category belongs also Williams's policy in Lincoln, who permitted Lambe to censure in particular cases of recalcitrance so long as it was inflicted 'duly and legally'.[129] Consequently at least three ministers suffered in the archdeaconry of Buckingham, where he was commissary: Valentine of Chalfont St Giles, Gladman of Chesham, and Woster of Olney. Since many clergy within the same archdeaconry refused to read the book, these three were singled out for their general nonconformity.[130] The suspension of Gladman and Valentine caused much ill feeling as in April 1635 it was reported that 'the women of Beaconsfield barred and cursed Sir John Lambe to the pit of hell' for his action.[131] Although he absolved both by June 1636, in December of the same year Valentine found himself suspended a second time. As in several other cases it was only when

[124] ERO D/ALV 2/18–157^{v}.

[125] ERO D/ALV 2/96. [126] Knowler, i. 166.

[127] LPL MS 943/261, 267; Calamy, iii. 506; G. Williams, *Recovery, Reorientation and Reformation: Wales c. 1415–1642* (Oxford., 1987), 484.

[128] Calamy, iii. 150; i. 94. [129] PRO SP 16/335/19, 30.

[130] PRO SP 16/286/40, 16/335/19, 30, 16/296/17, 16/300/2, 16/326/18, 49, 16/395/37, 49.

[131] PRO SP 16/287/31.

Valentine petitioned Laud in July 1638 that he was released from Lambe's censure.[132] Laud answered his petition by informing Lambe to absolve him for a year so that he could prove his conformity and on terms which meant that he did not have to read the book, which supports the argument of this chapter that the courts inflicted censure to obtain a wider conformity rather than to punish a refusal to read the book.[133]

The third category, which in some respects overlaps the second, comprises those who neither censured nor pressed its reading much beyond distributing the books to the clergy to read. According to Wren, there were many parishes in the diocese of Norwich where the book had not been published. The possibility exists, however, that he wished to paint a pessimistic picture to justify his own rigorous actions. In fact churchwarden accounts for Corbet's episcopate suggest that many parishes acquired the book even if the minister did not read it in person.[134] Certainly the archdeaconry courts cited clergy for refusing to read it, although when Fairclough failed to appear before the court of Sudbury, its surrogates merely adjourned to the parsonage house without prosecuting him, there being 'little more done than taking notice of his bodily weakness'.[135] Thornborough's courts in Worcester pursued a similarly moderate line. Clarke of Alcester wrote that he was 'often enjoined the reading of it, and much threatened for the refusal', yet the only retribution he suffered was to be 'envied and maligned' because all neighbouring clergy had obeyed the order.[136] In the dioceses of Exeter and Salisbury, Hall and Davenant ordered ministers to read the book in their churches (and in the case of Davenant, and possibly Hall) even before the metropolitical visitation.[137] Neither, however, liked the book and neither suspended any for their failure to read it. When Hall asked Bartlett of St Thomas, Exeter, to publish it from the pulpit, he read instead the fourth commandment, and without any episcopal prosecution.[138] In 1640 Davenant's chaplain, Pierce,

132 PRO SP 16/395/37.

133 PRO SP 16/395/37.

134 *Parentalia*, 64; ESFRO FC 147/E1/1/249, FC 67/E1/1/8^v, FC 101/E2/22, FB 123/E1/1 + 2 1634; NNRO PD 136/57.

135 Clarke, *Lives of Sundry Eminent Persons*, i. 170.

136 Ibid. i. 6–7.

137 DRO Dartington PW2/448; WTRO D1/39/1/531.

138 Calamy, i. 121; Knowler, i. 166.

preached both against the book and the abuse of the sabbath,[139] while during the 1630s the bishop had declined to return the names of those who had refused to read it, with the words (according to Fuller his nephew), 'I will never turn an accuser of my brethren; there be enough in the world to take that office.'[140] Apart from Worcester, Salisbury, and Exeter there are no known suspensions over the book for Chichester (Montagu and Duppa), Rochester (Warner), Bristol (Skinner), Durham (Morton), Chester (Bridgeman), St Asaph (Owen), Hereford (Lindsell and Field), or Bangor (Griffiths and Roberts), which suggests that the courts did not take a particularly firm line on the issue, although in these sees it was clearly distributed to the parishes for publication. Perhaps only in Carlisle did the courts actively discourage clergy from reading the book. According to one source Bishop Potter informed a minister that 'if it were sent to his diocese, he would slight it and urge none of his Jurisdiction to read it'.[141]

III. AUTHORITY AND CONSCIENCE

That the bishops and their chancellors were working together to further the publication of the book within the sees of Bristol, Rochester, and Winchester throws doubt on Heylyn's opinion that the bishops delegated responsibility on to the shoulders of their chancellors to shield themselves from reproach.[142] There may have been diversity in the intensity and frequency of censure yet there was an almost universal episcopal attempt to introduce the book. Only two chancellors, Mason of Winchester and Wood of Rochester, appeared before the committee of religion, charged with suspending ministers for refusing to read the book, but both cases revealed that they had acted only with the approval of their diocesans, Curle and Bowle.[143] Heylyn contended also that some bishops passed offenders on to the High Commission in order to avoid prosecuting them themselves.[144] This, however, ignores the fact that in their earlier stages, cases had been promoted within their diocese of origin, while

[139] PRO SP 16/470/107. (He called also for the restoration of those who had lost their livings in connection with the book.)

[140] Fuller, *CH* 425. [141] See n. 48. Clarke, *Lives of Thirty-Two English Divines*, 156. [142] Heylyn, *CA* 313.

[143] *PCR* 91–2. [144] Heylyn, *CA* 313.

they often returned to the diocesan for his audience (as was the case of Page of Ledbury in 1638) or for further examination by the consistory.[145] Moreover the High Commission was not the most suitable arena for such prosecutions, there being at all times a surplus of moral and defamatory cases for the court to deal with.[146] When ministers who had not read the book appeared in the High Commission that offence appeared only among others. General nonconformity marked out the ministers for prosecution rather than the particular offence of refusing to read the book. There exists no example of a minister prosecuted in the High Commission or in the ecclesiastical courts solely for his failure to read it. The notion that Laud used the High Commission to browbeat opponents of the book falls down on the fact that in the extant records of the court (even if they are not extensive they are intensive for particular periods) remarkably few ministers appeared for failure to read the book. Two ministers were almost certainly dismissed reasonably quickly on the promise of conformity: Sanger of Sutton Mandeville (Salisbury) questioned in April 1634 but not suspended, as he was still in office during the last years of the 1630s, and Page of Ledbury (Hereford), whose case was returned to the diocese in 1638.[147] Spencer of Scaldwell (Peterborough), Erbury of Cardiff, and Wroth of Llanvaches (Llandaff), Ward of Ipswich (Norwich), Workman of Gloucester (Gloucester), and Wilson of Otham (Canterbury) not only spoke out against the book but on all accounts in the 1630s were prominent nonconformists.[148] Worthen of Heydon (Lincoln) preached against 'theft in kings' and the judiciary.[149] In 1644 the singular case of Snelling of St Paul Cray (Rochester), was used against Laud as evidence that he suspended ministers in the High Commission for failure to read the book.[150] Yet it was the king's advocate who prosecuted Snelling. Laud said that he kept him from suspension 'as long as he could' and when the sentence was passed in court he was absent.[151]

145 PRO SP 16/375/78.

146 Usher, *The Rise and Fall of the High Commission* (1910), 256.

147 WTRO D5/28/34, D2/4 15 Office/181; PRO SP 16/375/78, SP 16/397/90.

148 PRO SP 16/308/52, SP 16/302/89; *WWL* v. 345, 340; LPL MS 943/261, 267; Clarke, *Lives of Sundry Eminent Persons*, i. 18; Swincock, *Life and Death of Thomas Wilson*, 74.

149 PRO SP 16/410/9; 16/261/72^{v}.

150 Prynne, *CD* 152; *PCR* 91–2, 93, 96–8; WCO Clarke 5/11.

151 *WWL* iv. 255; *PCR* 91–2; WCO MS Clarke 5/11.

It is difficult to estimate the total number of suspensions in the country as a whole, but on the basis of surviving depositions those suspended in Norwich and Bath and Wells almost certainly outnumbered those suspended in other sees. It is impossible to estimate the total number of clergy who read or refused to read the book, or the number of those parishes where the book was never published. In all dioceses, Norwich not excepted, there were possibly some parishes where the book was never bought.[152] On the calculation of Estwick of Warkton in January 1634, at least sixty ministers within his own diocese of Peterborough refused to read it.[153] In some jurisdictions there was considerable diversity in the clerical response: by April 1635, most clergy within the rural deaneries of Wendover, Wycombe, and Burnham (in contrast to other deaneries of the archdeaconry of Buckingham) had not read the book.[154] The records of only two dioceses, Gloucester and London, permit a quantitative analysis of the certificates returned by the churchwardens. Within London diocese (excluding those parishes under the commissary of London and within the archdeaconry of Middlesex, save for its Essex jurisdiction) at least sixty parishes had not certified that the book had been published by December 1634.[155] In Gloucester many parishes within the three rural deaneries of Winchcombe, Gloucester, and Fairford/Cirencester had not certified by September 1634 but most appear to have responded shortly afterwards as a result of court citations.[156] The return of certificates, however, tells us nothing more than that they were returned; it does not reveal the number of clergy who refused to read the book, nor in fact whether the book was published.

It is possible to underestimate the profound scruples of conscience occasioned by the book of sports. According to Estwick, many clergy who read it were seriously troubled by it. Others, such as Richard Condor and Vavasour Powell, it brought to the point of conversion.[157] For those who disliked the book but at the same time did not wish to

[152] The absence of references for disbursements in accounts does not necessarily mean that the book was not purchased. Most parishes surveyed in the Peterborough *speculae* of Aug.–Nov. 1637 (NRO PDR X2159/5/11) possessed a copy of the book; two which did not were Marston St Lawrence and All Saints Northampton, both centres of dissent to the Caroline innovations.

[153] Bodl. Tanner MS 71/186–7. [154] PRO SP 16/286/86.

[155] ERO D/ALV 2/18–157v. [156] GRO GDR 174, 175, 187 (unfol.).

[157] Anon., *The Life and Death of Mr Vavasour Powell* (1671), 2; Spufford, *Contrasting Communities*, 231–2.

disobey the royal request that it be read, one or two loopholes were available. In the first place, the courts invariably asked the churchwardens or clergy to certify whether the book was published, but not whether it was published to a full congregation. When some clergy returned the answer that they had read the book, it is conceivable that they had done so to themselves in their parsonage house. Others might read it in the church when there were few present. Williams of Shaftesbury read it before morning prayer when most of his congregation were absent and subsequently claimed that if they had not heard it published, it was their own fault for not coming to church.[158] At Holy Trinity, Dorchester (also within Bristol), a neighbouring minister read it against the wishes of the incumbent, John White, when only the churchwardens and the sexton were present.[159] For those who showed reluctance, Wednesdays, Fridays, and holy days proved to be ideal days for publication when few would come to church. Ferrar of Langham (London) read it at morning prayer on Wednesday in the presence of only six people. Occasionally the courts detected a minister for reading the book to only a handful of people (such as Juxon's courts in 1634), and they might ask him to read it again, but the general absence of such cases in extant records suggests that most clergy who read the book to a small congregation might have escaped.[160] There existed a further loophole in that the courts asked the clergy or churchwardens to certify whether the book had been published; they rarely asked by whom it had been published. Thus the clerical objectors could ask their curates, a neighbouring minister, or a surrogate to read it for them. Occasionally the courts (as in Bath and Wells) might ask a particular minister to read the book even when he had procured another to publish it.[161] But that this happened infrequently suggests reasons for the prosecution other than mere refusal to read it, in virtually all cases canonical nonconformity.

Some ministers might salve their conscience after reading the book by preaching on the fourth commandment, like the rector of St Giles in the Fields, or by reading out the ten, such as Dennison of St Katherine Cree, who then told his congregation 'dearly beloved you have heard now the commandment of God and man, obey which

[158] PRO SP 16/267/6. [159] BL MS Egerton 784. [160] ERO D/ALV 2/39v.
[161] SRO D/D/Ca 294/61v–65; Bodl. Rawl. MS A 346/165v.

you please'.[162] Others proceeded to undercut the book by pointing out that there was no command to play sports. 'These laws are left to everyone's choice,' said Spratt of Beaminster, although he subsequently advised his congregation 'to obey God's laws rather than the king's'.[163] Among both higher and lower echelons of the clergy there evolved an apology for those who, although not wishing to read the book, felt they had to because they had greater scruples about disobeying royal authority. The line advanced by Samuel Ward was that to read the book was not necessarily to approve of its contents: 'a minister . . . with a safety of conscience may publish it in his church being commanded by sovereign authority . . . the contents whereof he doth not approve in his own conscience.'[164] In November 1636 John Williams provided a similarly casuistical argument when attempting to encourage those who refused to read the book to comply, for 'the bishop measures obedience of his clergy by acting rather than allowing what is commanded in this kind'.[165] Later in 1641 he would make a similar distinction between private and public conscience for the king when Charles doubted whether or not he could with a safe conscience execute Strafford.[166]

But the conscience of some clergy was not as accommodating as Williams might have thought and they not only refused to read the book, but preached against it. Stranger preachers could more openly attack it but whether they secured a pulpit depended upon the co-operation of sympathizers within the parish. At Beaminster, a Sarum peculiar in Dorset, the minister, Spratt, accompanied by one of the churchwardens, allowed a preacher to speak against the book during the absence of the other churchwarden who was a keen supporter of the royal policy.[167] The motives of those who became informers were as diverse as human nature itself. Often they originated in social divisions within the congregation. When Page of Ledbury preached on the theme that it was as lawful for a 'weaver to shoot his shuttle on

162 Knowler, i. 166. 163 WTRO D5/28/34.

164 Bodl. MS Tanner 71/186, 279/352. See Bodl. MS Carte 197 for a comparison of the declaration with James II's declaration of liberty of conscience.

165 PRO SP 16/335/30.

166 *The Fairfax Correspondence*, 2 vols., ed. G. W. Johnson (1848), II, 127–8; Nalson, ii. 192. In his *Two Looks over Lincoln* (1641), 16, Richard Dey examined Williams's inconsistency in pressing the book of sports but not the full metropolitical order.

167 WTRO D5/28/34.

the Sabbath Day, as for a man to take his bow to shoot', a member of the congregation, whom Page had recently presented at Hereford for adultery, informed the consistory of the sermon.[168] In December 1633, shortly after the curate of Witney read the book, a parishioner absented himself from church. The curate threatened to present him for not attending but the parishioner replied that if the Oxford court summoned him he would take the liberty of informing it that the curate permitted unlicensed preachers.[169]

The role played by the justices of the peace in the introduction of the book was often ambivalent, given their position as upholders of royal authority and disarmers of popular licence. In 1637 Cole, a Suffolk justice, threatened to indict any minister who encouraged Sunday recreations.[170] Others were more obliging. In Somerset, Sir Robert Phelips drew up an apology for the local justices to show that the contents of the declaration in no way contravened the 'sabbatarian' statutes passed at the beginning of Charles's reign.[171] In certain cases the patron of the living might help to publish the book, such as Darcey of Sutton, who asked a neighbouring minister instead of the incumbent, although this action does not constitute evidence of a patron helping his minister escape censure as he wished to appoint a different incumbent. At Leominster, Wallop Brabazon went as far as to construct a bowling alley, with the express intention of irritating the Puritan Tombes.[172]

The book allowed only lawful sports after evening prayer. Like its predecessor of 1618, it explicitly prohibited bear-baiting, interludes, and bowls (for the 'meaner sort of people') at all times on Sundays and holy days, while allowing (only after evening prayer) archery, leaping, dancing, may-games, whitsun ales, and decorating the interior of churches with rushes.[173] Thus, contrary to what Prynne and others argued, it did not contravene but reinforced the two statutes passed in 1625 and 1628.[174] But the republication was for many an invitation to break all sabbatarian inhibitions. There were probably many like William Walker of Preston in Gloucestershire,

[168] PRO SP 16/375/78. [169] ORO Archd. c. 12/80.
[170] Birch, ii. 227. [171] SRO DD/PH 221/15, 28.
[172] PRO SP 16/278/45; BL Portland Loan MS 29/172.
[173] Tait, 'The Declaration of Sports', 561–8; PRO SP 16/248/13.
[174] *Statutes of the Realm*, v, pp. i, 25.

who felt that he could now play illegal sports 'because the king allowed him'.[175] The contemporary tract *A Divine Tragedy Lately Enacted* (written possibly by Burton) enumerates several examples of parishioners profaning the sabbath immediately after hearing their minister publish the book.[176] However it seems to have gone unnoticed that the ecclesiastical courts endeavoured to stem the profanation of Sunday.

Those prosecuted for sabbatarian offences were legion. In fact the courts used the book to enforce sabbath observance throughout the 1630s. It provided them with a code of proscribed recreations to which they might appeal without invoking statute law. Edward Hathaway of Chipping Sodbury appeared before the Gloucester court for 'abusing the king's majesty's liberty given in his late declaration by using unlawful games on the Sabbath'.[177] In 1636 the archdeaconry court of Ludlow detected William Aspenall of Long Stanton 'for playing his pipe and tuber on the Lord's Day between morning and evening prayer, contrary to the king's majesty's prohibition'.[178] The courts of Durham enquired whether the 'offence of unlawful gaming' was committed after or before evening prayer, to see if they had infringed the terms of the declaration.[179] In 1636 a Shropshire man appeared in the Hereford court for affirming that 'if the minister . . . would not give way to his dancing . . . contrary to the king's prohibition . . . he should catechise and preach to the walls'.[180] Those who played sports, prohibited under all circumstances on the sabbath, appeared frequently in the courts, such as the parishioners of Tawton, an episcopal peculiar in Cornwall, detected for playing bowls on Midsummer Day and the scores prosecuted for the same offence in Bath and Wells.[181] During 1636 Wren's courts prosecuted the curate of Wereham for playing unlawful games, which suggests

[175] GRO CDR 175; BL Portland Loan MS 29/172. The book of sports might affect one's employment: Thomas Hellyar, minstrel of Aldermaston, praised it for improving his material position: PRO SP 16/260/48.

[176] H. Burton, *A Divine Tragedy Lately Enacted* (1636); Birch, ii. 260.

[177] GRO GDR 138. For cases in the Northern Province see Marchant, *Church Under The Law*, 220.

[178] HFRO Box 39/A Bk. 146.

[179] DPD Corr. Bk. 1637–8 Dec. 1637/25^{v}.

[180] HFRO Box 39/A. Bk. 146.

[181] DRO C905a V. Bk. Bp. Pec./1637; SRO D/D/Ca 295/73, 293/13, 294/175^{v}, 308, 316/134^{v}; SRO D/D/Cd 76/Gatcombe Jan. 1634.

that they would not have looked very favourably on those 'scandalous ministers' accused in 1640 of sabbatarian offences.[182]

The metropolitical courts of the Southern Province also prosecuted those who took more liberty than allowed by the book. During 1634 they fined a parishioner of Bucklebury, in the archdeaconry of Berkshire, over three shillings for his 'offence in dancing before evening prayer on Sunday . . . contrary to the king's declaration'.[183] In the same year, during the visitation of Wells, they cited parishioners of St Cuthbert's for erecting a maypole before evening prayer.[184] Whilst visiting the archdeaconry of Totnes, Brent heard from the mayor and justices of Dartmouth about 'a company of yonkers' who had celebrated the erection of a maypole by drinking to its health and by playing drums so loudly that 'the inhabitants were affrighted . . . supposing some enemies had landed to sack them'.[185] In fact the metropolitical courts may well have associated the abuse of the declaration with its invitation to disorder and licence. In May 1635, during the visitation of Coventry and Lichfield, Laud's commissioners cited parishioners of Alveley, who had picked a fight with their neighbours from the parish of Enville after hearing the publication of the book.[186] Laud was sensitive to findings that the book was the cause of social disorder and asked Brent to investigate disturbances such as those at Clamford Bridge where he suspected that recusants (who were debarred from playing recreations) had stirred up trouble.[187]

In their efforts to impress sabbath observance on the parishioners the courts reflected the sabbatarian inclinations of the higher clergy. It is impossible to categorize the sabbatarian opinions of the higher clerical echelons into watertight camps of Puritan/Anglican and Calvinist/Arminian. Dr Tyacke's 'Arminian Sunday' is as misleading

[182] J. White, *The First Century of Scandalous Priests* (1643); NNRO ANF 9/3.

[183] BERO D/A2 c. 75/120^{v}; D/A2 c. 74/114.

[184] SRO D/D/Ca 297; D/D/Cd 78/1, 2.

[185] H. Burton, *For God and the King*, 16.

[186] Ibid. 47. The conflict may have been fuelled by the fact that the border between Staffordshire and Shropshire ran between the two villages.

[187] PRO SP 16/260/90. Laud's visitation for the episcopal peculiars also enquired into the abuse of the Lord's Day, 'since his Majesty's general pardon . . . and contrary to the order of the Church of England' (*WWL* v. 437–52). Throughout the 1630s there were serious disorders on May Day, which made the Council particularly fearful during April 1640, at the time of the apprentice disturbances in London: Rushworth, iii. 1169. It is interesting to conjecture whether the book of sports fomented some of this trouble.

as Heylyn's 'puritan Sabbath'.[188] Lancelot Andrewes and John Cosin, for example, were sabbatarians of an unequivocally strict complexion, while Prideaux, an impeachable Calvinist, came near to denying the morality of the fourth commandment, as Heylyn was so keen to publicize.[189] Another Calvinist, Joseph Hall, looked upon the pharisaical mentality of some sabbatarians with characteristic satire, being quick to detect 'a nice humorist that will not dress a dish, nor lay a cloth, nor walk abroad on a Sunday, and yet made no conscience of coercing his neighbour on the workday'.[190] As Dr Parker has convincingly shown, the sabbatarian consensus of the later Elizabethan and Jacobean Church did not rest on a specifically Calvinist interpretation of the fourth commandment.[191]

Among the bishops, possibly Wren, Curle, and Wright were the least sabbatarian inclined. Wren, as the petitioners of Cambridgeshire did not forget, played bowls on Sunday, while Curle, when bishop at Bath and Wells, acquired a reputation as an idolater for erecting maypoles.[192] Wright of Coventry and Lichfield allowed bear-baiting at Eccleshall and permitted, in certain circumstances, the sale of meat on Sunday, both of which were offences under the sabbatarian statutes. 'Suppose a labouring man', he informed the parishioners of Ashbourne, 'receives his wages so late on the Sunday night that before he can get home, the shops are shut ... and no meat then to be bought; shall not the poor man therefore have a chop of meat to his dinner the next day?'[193] Laud himself did not disallow lawful sports for those who wished to use them. In his trial he warned against falling into an almost Judaical superstition when seeking to extirpate profanity, bringing to his support Calvin's words in the *Institutes*, 'those men who stand so strictly upon the morality of the Sabbath, do by gross and carnal sabbatization, three times outgo the superstition of the Jew.'[194] As for his own observance of the sabbath, he kept it possibly more strictly than any of his episcopal

[188] Tyacke, *AC* 223; A. Foster: 'Church Policies of the 1630s', in R. Cust and A. Hughes (eds.), *Conflict in Early Stuart England: Studies in Religion and Politics 1603–1642* (1989), 216.
[189] Cox, *Literature of the Sabbath Question*, i. 153, 166; Bodl. MS Smith 40/123–6; Parker, *ES* 198.
[190] G. Lewis, *A Life of Joseph Hall* (1886), 301.
[191] Parker, *ES* 178.
[192] BL Egerton MS 1048/24; SRO D/D/Ca 299.
[193] R. Porter, *The Life of Mr John Hieron* (1691), 133.
[194] *WWL* iv. 255; iii. 209; WCO MS Clarke 5/11.

colleagues. He played no recreations himself, his only exercise being to swing a large book in his study, of which he was untimely deprived through a rupture.[195] According to Fuller, the archbishop strictly observed that day: 'a self-praise, or rather self-purging, because spoken on his life which seemed uttered without pride and with truth, and was not clearly confuted'.[196] It is not a little ironic therefore that Laud should have gone down unconditionally in history as the person who procured the republication of the book of sports.

But if the king's declaration for lawful sports opened the door to a greater profanation of the sabbath, then it went far to nullify any utility which Laud and his fellow bishops came to recognize in it as a means of achieving a wider canonical obedience and conformity. For, as this chapter shows, the censure of clergy often proceeded on principles other than a royal desire to have the book read. The few who were censured underwent censure for their nonconformity to the liturgy or church discipline, or for preaching so vehemently against the book that they negated their canonical obedience and questioned their allegiance to the Crown. No minister in the 1630s was censured solely for his failure to read the book. As a result of this policy of discrimination, together with the existence of various loopholes connived at by the courts, many ministers who refused to read the book were able to avoid censure, but not a profound dilemma of conscience. Such a policy found its most representative statement, not in the strictures of Prynne or Burton, but in Laud's answer to those who informed him that the noted Puritan, Arthur Jackson, beneficed within his own peculiar of the Arches, refused to read the declaration: Jackson 'is a quiet and peaceable man . . . therefore . . . I will not have him meddled with'.[197]

[195] *WWL* iii. 209. [196] Fuller, *CH* 424. [197] Calamy, i. 121.

6

THE TABLE OF SEPARATION

a table of separation . . . fortifi'd with bulwark and barricado, to keep off the profane touch of the laicks.

(John Milton, *The Complete Prose Works*, ed. D. M. Wolfe (Yale, 1953), i. 547)

In 1640 it was widely perceived that the Church of England had lost its Protestant bearings, and that its liberties were being usurped. The perception that the 'popish plot' was not spontaneous but hatched over time was seemingly confirmed by the sacramental innovations introduced during the Personal Rule of Charles I.[1] The most important of these was the removal of tables to the east end, their conversion from an east–west (tablewise) to a north–south (altarwise) axis, and the erection of rails to separate them from the church, at which communicants were ordered to receive the sacraments. The table, once the symbol of the Edwardian and Elizabethan Reformation, had become the lynchpin of the Caroline Counter-Reformation. As the Long Parliament dismantled the apparatus of Charles I's government, Laud suffered widespread reproach as the altar-monger who had conspired to reintroduce the trappings of Rome and to deprive congregations of their prescriptive rights.[2] Prynne marked out the lines of the conspiracy.[3] Laud arranged a test-case at St Gregory's in the City of London to create a precedent for the metropolitical changes. Then through an enforcement which was both hurried and oppressive, he quashed opposition into submission with full rigours of ecclesiastical justice, or, in the words of the seventh article of impeachment, 'he urged and enjoined divers popish and superstitious ceremonies without any warrant of law, and cruelly persecuted those who have opposed the same, by corporal

[1] C. Hibbard, *Charles I and the Popish Plot* (Chapel Hill, NC, 1983); Bodl. MS Clar. SP 19/1448.

[2] *WWL* iii and iv; *A Second Message to Mr. William Laud* (1641).

[3] Prynne, *CD*.

punishment and imprisonment, and most unjustly vexed others who refused to conform thereto by ecclesiastical censures of excommunication, suspension, deprivation and degradation, contrary to the laws of the kingdom.'[4] The following pages, however, offer an alternative interpretation, by attempting to answer that question which Heylyn asked Fuller: 'what (were) those private practices and opinions... which... Archbishop (Laud) with such a want of moderation, did enjoin on others?'[5]

The Caroline notion of religion as a matter less of revelation than of capturing and regulating a sense of the numinous helped to focus Charles I's attention upon the externals of worship within his kingdom. The communion table might be for him the metaphor of his authority within the Church as its divinely appointed governor and within the parish as its divinely appointed magistrate. Apart from any religious or aesthetic significance which the table may have had for him, he regarded it as a throne of presence to which as much respect was due as to his own chair of state. To elevate its significance was a visual and mnemonic means of impressing a greater respect for his pretensions to divine right among the people.[6] For Laud and other high sacramentarians the table had a more overtly religious significance: it was simply the 'greatest residence of God upon earth'.[7] It was a visual expression of their belief in a eucharistic sacrifice and a standard of their attempt to convert what they saw as the sermonic piety of Jacobean England into something far more overtly sacramental. The corollary of their high sacramentarian views was less a more liberal access of grace than a higher evaluation of the priesthood. This meant that in the first instance the sacramentalism of the 1630s was an expression not of Arminianism but of sacerdotalism. Thus the table was withdrawn from the 'midst of the people' into the relative seclusion of the presbytery, where only the priest held sway. The table of communion had become not a table of free access, but, as John Milton perceived, 'a table of separation'. In fact through its removal the clergy had reclaimed the impropriator's chancel, the ground lost to the laity at the time of the Reformation.[8]

[4] *WWL* iii. 407.

[5] Fuller, *AII* iii. 8.

[6] See Ch. 1 section ii; also K. Sharpe, 'The Personal Rule of Charles I', in H. Tomlinson (ed.), *Before the English Civil War* (1983), 62.

[7] *WWL* vi. 57, 51–6; H. Davies, *Worship and Theology in England*. (Princeton, NJ, 1975–), ii. 292–342; Bodl. MS Rawl. D. 353/104–5, 122ᵛ–124.

[8] *The Complete Prose Works of John Milton*, ed. D. M. Wolfe, (Yale, 1953), i. 547.

The insignificance which many attached to the communion table in early modern England was in part a consequence of the reformed mind, which attempted to wipe away any notion of sanctity in church objects. It was a result also of the lack of legislation establishing a uniformity of where and by whom the table should be placed within the church. In 1552 the rubric laid down where it should stand during communion, but not at any other time.[9] An attempt to remedy this was made in the Injunctions of 1559, which directed that the table be positioned where the altar stood, except at the communion, when it was to be placed within the chancel, where the minister could be conveniently heard. According to Grindal, these requirements were imperfectly obeyed and in their subsequent 'Interpretations' the bishops altered the force of the Injunctions by allowing the table to be removed into the body of the church, wherever the chancel was too small to contain the number of communicants.[10] It was this interpretation which prepared the way for canon 82 of 1604, which ordered that the table be placed in the position most convenient for the minister and the parishioners during communion. Consequently the Interpretations and the Canons of 1604 helped to undermine the basis for uniformity in the Injunctions.[11] Parishioners, left to interpret the most convenient position, placed and used their tables as they wished. For those who saw the table as the focus of order or greatest residence of God on earth this was an intolerable state of disorientation.

In order to restore the table to the east end, the ordinary had to assert his right of deciding where it should be placed, and the Injunctions (which had left the table at all times within the chancel) had to be preferred over other constitutions. It was precisely this line of argument which members of the Durham House circle, patronized by Richard Neile, advanced to justify the removal of the table within cathedrals. At Gloucester in 1617 Laud, as dean and ordinary, created a sensation by removing the table from the lower part of the choir to the very east end.[12] During the same year Francis Burgoyne,

[9] W. Scudamore, *Notitia Eucharistica* (1876), 157.

[10] *Documentary Annals*, i. 234, 238. At Herbert's Leighton Bromswold and Ferrar's Little Gidding it was customary to move the table from the east end into the chancel at the time of communion: R. Van de Weyer, *Little Gidding* (1989), 70, 74.

[11] *Synodalia*, ii. 211.

[12] GCL Chapter Act Bk. 1/4. *WWL* vi. 241 for Laud's words to Neile: 'a strange monster (is) lately born in that city of Gloucester. I pray God the Puritans which swarm in these parts do not say it is one of God's judgments for turning the communion-table into an altar.'

another of Neile's protégés, carried out the same procedure at Durham with the approval of his ordinary, Dean Hunt.[13] Traditionally the removal of these cathedral tables has been seen as a precedent for the later alterations. The principle that the ordinary should decide the position of the table had effectively been broached within the cathedral but it remained a matter of personal preference whether such a principle should be applied to the parishes. As for himself, Laud was far too conscious of convention not to realize that what was permissible within the cathedral (collegiate church or chapel) was not necessarily permissible within the parish. Consequently, as ordinary at St David's, Bath and Wells, and London, he did not attempt to put into practice the alteration which he had introduced in Gloucester.[14]

As ordinary in London the furthest that Laud was prepared to go in this respect was to order less than a handful of parishes to take away seats above the table.[15] This moderate application of ordinary power was in sharp contrast to the activities of Neile and Buckeridge, who encouraged the removal of tables to the east end in certain parishes under their personal jurisdiction within their sees of York and Rochester. Yet this did not constitute a general policy or a systematic enforcement; rather it was an identification with and an approval of a practice which they as ordinaries thought decent. As such, Neile and Buckeridge applied the principle that the ordinary might decide the position of the table within the parish long before it was given royal sanction in the St Gregory case of 1633.[16]

If it was the Durham House group who popularized both the east

[13] DCL Hunter MS 67/14: ii; Bodl. Rawl. MS A 441/128, Rawl. MS 821.

[14] This would explain Laud's rather ambivalent attitude to Cosin's innovations in Durham Cathedral, innovations which Howson thought 'indiscreet and unauthorised': PRO SP 16/203/90. In 1632 Laud suspended one of the surrogates of the archdeacon of Middlesex for removing the table out of its accustomed place at Great Dunmow: GL 9531/15/25 (this was also a convenient excuse to get rid of him—see PRO 16/223/4). For parish initiative not court's see *CSPD 1635–1636*, 123.

[15] *Cases in the Courts of Star Chamber and the High Commission*, ed. S. R. Gardiner (Camden, NS, 39,1866); GLRO 9531/15: 26.

[16] PRO SP 16/499/42; BI Chancery A.B. 25/28, 125, 130^{v}. For Neile's policy over the metropolitical order (he did not introduce the north–south position until after 1633, whereas the east-end position was introduced the year before) see BI Chancery A.B. 25/28-330^{v}; Chancery A.B. 26/26-203; PRO SP 16/259/78; R. A. Marchant, *The Puritans and the Church Courts in the Diocese of York, 1560-1642* (1960). For archdiaconal prosecution see: Nottingham archdeaconry (R. A. Marchant, 'The Restoration of Nottinghamshire Churches 1635–1640', *Thoroton Society Transactions*, 5 (1961), NTRO A42-7, PR 22765, 2794, 1517, 547); Cleveland archdeaconry (NYRO Thirsk ca); York archdeaconry (SERO PR 54/86; WYAS 40, Misc.: 8/125/1); Archiepiscopal peculiar of Ripon (NYRO Little Ouseburn ca, Kirby Malzeard ca).

end and altarwise positions, the rail came from an altogether different pedigree. In the extensive literature on the Durham and Grantham controversies (both associated with Neile) there is no mention at all of the rail.[17] The first bishop associated with the rail was not Laud but Andrewes, whose chapel possessed a rail running from north to south. In 1623 Andrewes's domestic chaplain, Christopher Wren, passed on a plan of this chapel to Laud and several other bishops, who then modelled their own chapels upon it. It seems likely that James I asked Andrewes (when dean of the Chapel) to introduce into the Chapels Royal the rites and ceremonies of his own chapel, which were generally considered to capture the essence of primitive worship.[18] By 1625 the rail was certainly present within the royal palaces. However, the rail had existed long before Andrewes. It seems likely that he based his own upon that at his London cure, St Giles Cripplegate, where one had existed since the earlier part of Elizabeth's reign. Rails existed in some parts of the country before 1634.[19] In an oblique way, the Advertisements of 1566 had encouraged their erection. This code ordered that tables should stand on a frame at the east end outside communion. Rails erected to surround the base might become a constituent feature of the frame and eventually the frame itself. Around this forms could be placed to facilitate the reception of the communion so that by the 1630s the rail and frame had become synonymous. In 1635 the rector of

[17] Bodl. Rawl. MS A 441/ 128, *CC* i. 155-99 (Durham); P. Heylyn, *A Coale from the Altar* (1637); J. Williams, *The Holy Table, Name and Thing* (1637) (Grantham); GCL Chapter Act Bk. 1/4; a rail was introduced at Kelvedon in 1633, but this was at the request of the commissary Aylett, who was rector there: ERO D/ACV 5/37^{v}, PRO SP 16/351/100).

[18] PRO C115/N4/8049; PRO SP 16/499/13; *WWL* iv. 251; HLRO MS Braye 8/40.

[19] *The Old Cheque Book of the Chapel Royal*, ed. E. F. Rimbault (1872), 155; PRO LC5/38/65; Bodl. Rawl. MS 674/66; BL Add. MS 12/222/73^{v}; LPL MS 943/283. For a sample of early rails: J. Walker, *The Sufferings of the Clergy* (1714), i, 76; *Historical Memoranda of Breconshire*, ii, ed. J. Lloyd (1904), 96; SHRO 4462/1/10; H. Owen and J. B. Blakeway, *A History of Shrewsbury* (1825), ii. 367; *Trans. of the Shropshire Archaeological and Natural History Society*, 1, (1878), 70; DRO DD 70963, P 51/1/5; CWRO DDP 162/5/1; SFRO D3710/1/1; BERO DP 97/5/3/112, D/P 114/5/2/ 162; *The Churchwardens' Accounts of St Mary Reading*, ed. F. N. A. Gary (1893), 153; DFRO HPR/68/33; LAO D+Ch. Fabric Rolls Bj/7 1629; *HMC X3 Wells Cathedral* (1885), 246; Bodl. Rawl. MS D/818/16; *The Churchwardens Accounts of St. Edmund and St. Thomas, Salisbury* (Salisbury, 1896), xxv. 200, 322; UCS D2/80^{v}; DTRO PE/SH/ cw/108; DBRO D638A/ PW1/307; SPRO PR4/2/1 (St Law), 118; *Precedents in Causes of Office*, ed. W. Hale (1841) 51; HLRO 1641: June 15/105, June 10/160; BL Add. MS 12,222/73^{v}, 81^{v}; Bodl. MS Tanner 314/110.

St Vedast's Foster Lane complained to Laud of the disorders in his parish 'for want of a frame of wood commonly called a rail'. Thus the rail had a long if not a widely established pedigree. According to Udall in 1640, 'they have been the custom, in many churches, town and country, beyond the memory of many people of sixty or eighty years old, who tell of rails in churches whereof there is sufficient record in the books of some churches in London, which mention the setting of them up in the beginning of . . . Elizabeth's reign.'[20]

I. ST GREGORY CASE

The practices of the Durham House group, the existence of the rail, and its popularization by Andrewes suggest that Charles I was not the sole promoter of these alterations, which predated his reign and arose in part from the preference of individual bishops within the Church. The year 1625 witnessed the accession of a king who, unlike James I, hankered after uniformity and order.[21] Charles I professed a concern for 'the cause of the Church' and invited his bishops to suggest policies which could promote his intentions. It is in this context of the king's receptivity to advice, as well as his concern for the externals of worship, that the evolution of the altar policy must be seen. As early as December 1629, when the bishops were engaged upon the comparison of the injunctions with the canons (occasioned by the king's desire to reissue the injunctions), Neile suggested that Charles I might 'by some declaration take away the scruple which some nowadays make of the placing of the communion-table'.[22] The placing mentioned here can only be the east end (often altarwise) which at this time was sanctioned in the Chapels Royal and among the disciples of Andrewes and Neile. Three years later, in 1633, the opportune occurrence of a controversy at St Gregory's, a church within the peculiar of St Paul's, provided Neile with the declaration for which he was looking.

The trouble at St Gregory arose when the dean and chapter as

[20] *Visitation Articles and Injunctions*, iii, ed. W.H. Frere (Alcuin Club Collections, 16, 1910), 381; PRO SP 16/168/24; Edmund Udall, *Communion Comeliness* (1641), 153.

[21] K. Sharpe, 'The Personal Rule of Charles I', 62; id., 'Archbishop Laud and the University of Oxford', in H. Lloyd Jones, V. Pearl, and B. Worden (eds.), *History and Imagination: Essays presented to Lord Dacre* (1981), 161.

[22] Bodl. Rawl. MS A127/73, 75 anonymous but in the hand of Neile and his secretary—compare PRO SP 16/167/25.

ordinaries moved the table from a tablewise to an altarwise position and railed it in at the east end of the chancel.[23] The architects of the alteration were two Calvinist royal chaplains, Dean Winniffe and Archdeacon King of Colchester.[24] Laud probably had nothing to do with the innovation: he had no jurisdiction within the decanal peculiar. Moreover it seems most likely that the royal chaplains were replicating the arrangements within the Chapel Royal, as had been adopted elsewhere in the City.[25]

In 1633 five parishioners appealed to the court of Arches in an attempt to revoke the dean's ruling on the basis that it was illegal and deprived them of the right of deciding where the table should stand, a right which they based on the Prayer Book, the Canons of 1604, and the Injunctions of 1559.[26] When Sir Henry Martin, dean of Arches, visited the church he sided with the parishioners, called the table 'a good court cupboard', and ordered its removal. Neile and Laud recognized that here was the opportunity for the king to make a declaration not only recommending the alteration but also asserting the ordinary's authority to determine the issue of conveniency and reinforcing episcopal authority within the parish. Thus in order to avoid an unfavourable verdict in the Arches, against the ordinary's power to decide where the table should be best placed, the case was transferred to the council in November 1633.[27] On 3 November 1633, in a plenary session of the council, Charles adjudicated in favour of the dean and chapter. Not without irony, he declared his dislike of 'all innovations receding from constitutions granted upon first and warrantable reasons . . . knowing how easily men are drawn to affect novelties'. Charles then placed the determination of what was 'convenient' into the hands not of the congregation but of the 'ordinary to whose place and function it doth properly belong'.[28]

23 PRO SP 16/499/42. The rail, like those favoured by Williams in Lincoln, was four-sided, *Surrey Archaeological Collections*, vi (1874), p. xiv.

24 Ibid.

25 GL 5090/2/192, 1188/1/139, 4215/1/13; GLRO P95/MRY 1/413/77; Vernon, *The Life of Heylyn* (1682), 52; *An Answer to a Lawless Pamphlet* (1641), 215; Sir Henry Martin's reference to the 'court cupboard' is also revealing (*WWL* iv. 225); PRO SP 16/96/63.

26 LPL MS 943/479.

27 PRO SP 16/499/42, SP 16/543/54; *WWL* iv. 225.

28 PRO PC2/43/404; PRO SP 16/499/42. For assertions of the ordinary's right to settle other rites, see *Parentalia*, 78–80. Howson asserted his discretionary, ordinary rights over 'things doubtful' when opposing the Durham innovations of Cosin: PRO SP 16/186/108.

Thus the king determined what the Injunctions of 1559 and the Canons of 1604 had not sufficiently determined: the power of the ordinary to alter, if he so wished, the internal arrangement of the parish church and contrary to the prescriptive rights of the congregation.

Charles's decision was as valid as Elizabeth I's in the 1559 Injunctions; neither had the force of law, but both rested on the ability of the governor of the Church to interpret and clarify its codes. Yet if the declaration established the ordinary's right to position the table, St Gregory's falls short of the test-case which it is invariably called. The king did not order the position of the table during or outside communion, but merely recommended it. Again he was seen to recommend an arrangement but only in a particular church. As Hacket said when he defended himself against Heylyn, 'the contention remains, whether that order of his Majesty with the Council hath influence upon other places, besides the particular of St Gregory which occasioned it.'[29] Moreover it was hardly the means of achieving uniformity: by asserting the ordinary's right the ruling provided the basis for unilateral episcopal action, out of step with a policy pursued by the Supreme Governor of the Church, and left the door open for lesser ordinaries to advance their own independent interpretations. It seems that Heylyn, more than any other person, propagated the notion that St Gregory's was a test-case for the metropolitical changes because he wished to give them a retrospective legitimation making St Gregory's the rule 'by which all ordinaries did proceed'.[30] He ignored both the fact that virtually all ordinaries enforced the alteration only after the start of Laud's metropolitical visitation, and that although the ruling reached the precedent books, there was little appeal to it as a precedent; appeals were made rather to Brent's order and its rationale.[31] Nor did St Gregory provide much support in those apologetics written to justify the alterations of the 1630s. Among the most important of these was the idea that the parish church should reflect the Chapel Royal. Yet the declaration itself recommended that St Gregory's should follow the arrangement of St Paul's, an opinion endorsed by some of the councillors present, notably Weston and Arundel.[32] In fact not until Heylyn's *Antidotum*

[29] Hacket, *SR* ii. 108. [30] Heylyn, *CA* 259.
[31] *Surrey Archaeological Collections*, vi (1874), p. xiv.
[32] *WWL* iv. 227.

Lincolniense of 1636 did the Chapel Royal publicly join the cathedral as the prototype for the parish church, at a time when the king was looking for a more effective legitimation for the metropolitical changes than that provided by the declaration.[33] Thus it was not coincidental in 1637 that the Privy Council ordered the demolition of St Gregory's church, which had occasioned the now redundant declaration. But the most substantial evidence to show that St Gregory's was not the test-case for the metropolitical order emerges from comparing it with the declaration. The one ordered what the other did not even recommend: the reception of communion at the rail.[34] Clearly, the origins of the metropolitical order lie elsewhere. As such, St Gregory's appears not as its test-case, but as a retrospective confirmation for the action of some ordinaries (such as Neile and Buckeridge) in placing their communion tables at the east end, an invitation to others to follow their practice, and a defence of ordinary authority.

The declaration had not resolved where the table should be placed during the communion, and as such it did not officially contradict the Canons of 1604. Yet before he issued it, Charles himself read aloud a passage from the Injunctions which implied that at all times the table should stay within the chancel.[35] Sometime after November 1633, however, he made a further recommendation to the bishops that they place their tables in the chancels and leave them there even during communion. Now the true limitation of St Gregory's was revealed: to order a fixed position for the table withdrew from the ordinary the right which the king had placed in his hands. It was in opposition to this that John Williams asserted his right as ordinary to decide the most convenient place for the table's position during communion in his own see long before he made the celebrated stand during the metropolitical visitation.[36] In February 1634 Laud informed the bishop

> though the canon say the people may receive the communion in the chancel or in the body of the church; yet (the king) likes not that the ordinary (*to*

[33] P. Heylyn, *Antidotum Lincolniense* (1636), epistle dedicatory. Appeals had been made to the royal chapel before (i.e., Laud in GCL Ch. Act 1/4 for the changes in Gloucester Cathedral), but this was the first public recognition for its application to the parish church. Viscount Scudamore's innovations at Dore were based upon the Chapel Royal. See PRO C115/N9/8848–9. *CSPD 1637*, 84.

[34] Nalson, i. 728–9, 771; *CJ*, ii. 35–6; *WWL* iv. 188; *HMC Appendix to the 4th Report*, 89; WSRO Ep. 11/11/3/73; PRO SP 16/361/92 (3).

[35] PRO SP 16/499/42.

[36] LPL MS 943/247, MS 1030/21.

whose discretion this disjuncture is left) should suffer it to be in the body of the church; both because the people usually sit in their seats, and cannot be discerned whether they kneel or not while they receive, and because the minister cannot possibly come with any convenience at them which are placed furthest in their seats to deliver the sacrament to them, unless every other seat should be left void.

This was one of the first indications that Charles was inclining towards uniformity in the matter of receiving in the chancel. Yet it was not now an individual ordinary adopting a particular arrangement for his own parishes, but the Supreme Governor of the Church recommending an arrangement for all subordinate authorities to pursue, a uniformity which might conflict with the Canons of 1604. Since, in January 1634, Laud still personally respected each ordinary's right to place his table during communion according to the canons if he so wished, it is highly unlikely that he steered the king into adopting this novel line of argument or of any blanket order, such as the metropolitical order, which might override the ordinary's authority. Thus between November 1633 and February 1634, Charles I was reneging upon the St Gregory's ruling, which had respected both the ordinary's right and the Canons of 1604.[37]

Thus we can safely say that in the earlier part of 1634, Charles I was disposed to favour the introduction of an order which would attempt to create a uniformity in the position of the table not only outside communion, but during it. But this does not mean that the particular order known as the metropolitical order was already envisaged by the king or that such an order was available in February 1634. The metropolitical visitation of Canterbury diocese (the first to be visited) had already started in November 1633. In February 1634 Brent's personal visitation as vicar-general was one month away (Brent or his commissioners visited each diocese for six weeks only, during the six months of each metropolitical visitation). On 22 February Laud drew up for his vicar-general, pending Brent's visitation of Canterbury, a list of orders which he wished him to implement during the visitation. This list does not contain the celebrated order for the rail, the altarwise position, the reception of communion at the rails. Reference was made to the table but only in

[37] LPL MS 1030/19, MS 943/247. It seems likely that Charles was pressing the practice before this date, since Abbot (uncharacteristically) felt it necessary to introduce it in May 1633, *Documentary Annals*, ii. 226.

its position at the east end where it was generally recognized in law that it ought to stay save during communion.[38]

The decision to introduce the metropolitical order can have been made only very late in February or very early in March 1634 (four months after the start of the metropolitical visitation of Canterbury and Rochester dioceses) and at the initial instigation, not of Laud, but of others, in particular Piers of Bath and Wells. Shortly before 9 March Piers was lobbying for the introduction of the rail and the altarwise position of the table at the east end 'in every church': alterations which he had been introducing since 1633 within his own diocese.[39] But one further development had to take place. The eventual metropolitical order specified that communicants should receive at the rails, something which Piers had never suggested. Laud himself came to believe that the practice was the most decent way of receiving, but he did not believe that communicants should be forced against their consciences to receive at the rail. That he never enforced the practice as archbishop and diocesan, together with the fact that he respected both canonical authority and the ordinary's right to position the table, eliminates him as the person who petitioned for this particular order.[40] Possibly Matthew Wren, Charles's clerk of the Closet and shortly to replace Juxon as dean of the Chapel, asked for it in March 1634. Wren had been a protégé of Andrewes (the first bishop who practised receiving at the rails in his chapel) and during the 1630s he was to be one of only three bishops to enforce it. The king himself would also have liked its introduction, as in the later 1630s he was to approve highly of Wren's strict enforcement of the practice and by 1636 (during the time that Wren was dean of the Chapel) had himself adopted the unprecedented practice of leaving the closet and processing to the rail to receive, the lords following behind. Moreover the document, 'the king's injunctions concerning divine service' (possibly an original draft for the metropolitical order), contains an explicit order for receiving at the rails and requiring that the priests stay behind them at the time of administration.[41]

Thus in March 1634 we may safely conjecture that Charles accepted Piers's suggestion but that he gave his approval also for an order commanding receiving at the rails, for which Laud was not

38 LPL MS 943/247; PRO SP 16/260/90.

30 SRO D/D/Ca 293/3, D/P/Qua. e 4/1/1, D/P/Som 4/1/1; see Ch. 6 n. 88.

40 LPL MS 943/475; see sections ii and iii.

41 *WWL* v. 360; LPL MS 1030/19; PRO SP 16/474/60.

enthusiastic. To force receiving at the rail was to forgo the canonical respect for convenience at the time of communion. It was also, as events proved, an order fraught with unforeseen consequences, and one which in the end went far to discredit the wider altar policy. Laud's reservations about the metropolitical order, his respect for canonical authority, and the fact that the decision to introduce it was taken on the spur of the moment in March 1634 all help to explain why he retained the clause from Abbot's visitation articles, which asked whether the table was placed 'in such convenient sort within the chancel or church as that the minister may best be heard'. This effectively weakened the impact of the order, and could be taken up by opponents of the changes, as on some occasions it was.[42]

It is important to distinguish between the metropolitical order and its mode of enforcement. The metropolitical order itself could only have had the particular sanction of the king and, as suggested above, evolved as late as March 1634, at the instigation of Piers and almost certainly Wren.[43] In 1634, when Laud handed this order to Brent, he gave him also instructions explaining how he thought the metropolitical order should be introduced. Prynne suppressed evidence of this important fact although he probably knew that Laud had given to Brent private instructions as they were referred to in Sir John Lambe's papers which fell into his hands after 1640. The significance of these instructions is such that they alter fundamentally our notion of Laudianism and of Laud's perception of the problem before him. He ordered Brent not to suspend or excommunicate anyone for disobedience to the metropolitical order, nor was he even to compel acquiescence to it; only 'fair persuasions' were to be used. Brent was not to force communicants to come up to the rails against their consciences, only to encourage them. If they refused, and were prepared to receive in the chancel, then the minister was to leave the rails and go down into the chancel to administer the sacraments to them.[44] Such a policy depended for its success on people's habituation to change over time. In establishing a precept Laud clearly hoped that people would come as a matter of course to

[42] PRO SP 16/499/25a; PRO SP 16/327/101; Bodl. Tanner MS 60/160; *WWL* v. 399–452; see sections ii and iii.

[43] PRO SP 16/474/60. The metropolitical order was published in some parishes as a royal order: *The Articles and Charge... against... Dr. Walton* (1641), 2; Richard Dey, *Two Looks Over Lincoln* (1641), 15, 24.

[44] PRO SP 16/485/118.

appreciate its decency. Yet this was hardly a policy of enforcement designed to create uniformity in a short time, for it went far to undermine the peremptory nature of the metropolitical order. It is apparent, then, that our notion of historical Laudianism as tactless, hurried, and as a policy which involved a rigorous distribution of the highest court censures is in need of serious revision.

Laud possibly regarded Brent's introduction of the order as the first process of stirring up affection for change on which the ordinaries could then act if they so wished. In all the extensive documentary material of the 1630s there is no evidence that Laud pressed any of his episcopal colleagues into adopting the order for themselves or others. His reluctance to press the order partly explains why Brent's courts as a rule did not enforce it. An equally important reason was the fact that the metropolitical courts attendant on the visitation of each see were not the most effective means of enforcement: they did not sit long enough and their main function was to take over the business then transacted in the diocesan courts. Thus only in those sees where the ordinary had started to introduce and enforce the rail before Brent's arrival could the metropolitical courts help to enforce it. This was the case in Coventry and Lichfield, London, and Bath and Wells. Brent himself was not keen on the order, confessing in Laud's trial that 'he pressed [it] as sparingly as he might, it being against his own judgement . . . [and] as for himself he never troubled any for it'.[45] Yet as vicar-general he not only published the order in each see but encouraged churchwardens and clergy to inspect churches where it had already been introduced for their model; such as at St Thomas at Cliffe (in the peculiar of South Malling, during the visitation at Lewes).[46] Brent also encouraged those cathedrals and collegiate churches to adopt the rail, if they had yet to introduce it. Clearly it would be useless for the ordinary to appeal to precedent if the most important churches within his jurisdiction had not yet introduced the rail.[47]

The metropolitical visitation of the twenty-one sees of the Southern Province took place over four years. During each of these years Brent issued the formal order for the rail; no general order for the

[45] LJRO B/V/1/55; HTRO ASA 7/31/36^v; SRO D/D/C/299/77^v; W. Prynne, *History of the Trial and Condemnation of Archbishop Laud* (1644), 91.

[46] WSRO Ep./11/11/73.

[47] J. Furley, *Weald of Kent*, 2 vols. (1871), ii. app. 848; PRO SP 16/293/128; LPL MS Reg. Laud 1/ 147^v.

Southern Province as a whole was issued in 1634. During this first year Brent visited Canterbury, Rochester, Lincoln, Salisbury, Exeter, Bristol, Bath and Wells; in 1635 Norwich, Peterborough, Winchester, Chichester, Worcester, Gloucester, Coventry and Lichfield; in 1636 Hereford, St David's, St Asaph, Bangor, Llandaff, and finally in 1637, London. Oxford and Ely were never visited.[48]

Most of the remaining parts of this chapter present an analysis of the introduction of the metropolitical order across the Southern and Northern Provinces. For the sake of clarity a brief summary of ordinary policy in comparison to the metropolitical order is offered here. There are six divisions numbered in relation to the extent to which the diocesan policy differs from the metropolitical order which is taken as the base-line. A different gradation could be drawn up according to the chronology of the changes (their initiation and duration), the degree of censure, or quantitative data, all of which are discussed below.

First, those bishops who enforced the full metropolitical order of the rail, the east-end and altarwise positions, and receiving at the rail: Wren (Norwich and Ely), Towers (Peterborough).

Second, those who pressed the rail, the east-end and altarwise position, but not receiving there: Montagu and Duppa (Chichester), Goodman (Gloucester), Mainwaring (St David's); Davenant (Salisbury), Piers (Bath and Wells), Skinner (Bristol) and Neile (York).

Third, the policy of Juxon and his commissaries in London: the rail, the east-end position, receiving at the rail but not the altarwise position.

Fourth, those who enforced only the rail and the east-end position: Laud (Canterbury), Dee (Peterborough), Thornborough (Worcester), Murray (Llandaff), Roberts (Bangor), Bancroft (Oxford), Wright (Coventry and Lichfield), Warner (Rochester), Curle (Winchester), and Bridgeman (Chester).

Fifth, Williams's idiosyncratic policy in Lincoln: the erection of rails at the east end or in the body of the church.

Finally, the policies of Hall (Exeter), Coke (Bristol and Hereford), Owen (St Asaph), Morton (Durham), and Potter (Carlisle), who might encourage but who took few or no court proceedings to further the order.

48 LPL MS Reg. Laud i/77–185^{v}.

II. THE METROPOLITICAL VISITATION

(i) The first category is the enforcement of the full metropolitical order. The policy of Wren in Norwich, 1636–8, and Ely, 1638–40, is celebrated not only for its unparalleled vigour but for its prying inquisitions. Unlike most other bishops Wren enforced all four stipulations of the metropolitical order and in order to gain compliance resorted to the highest court censures. During the primary visitation of 1636 he ordered his surrogates to enforce minute specifications altering the internal arrangement of churches: all rails were to run from north to south only, to be one yard high; steps were to be erected at the east end for the permanent position of the table, so that congregations could see the minister at the eucharist; all chancels (and not just the east end) were to be cleared of pews and all reading desks were to face east; women were to be churched only at the rail and ministers were to read the second service only at the table.[49] The implementation of Wren's strident policies was partially facilitated by policies initiated by previous ordinaries. As early as the summer of 1631, Archdeacon Byng of Norwich had ordered the churchwardens of his archdeaconry to place their tables on steps at the east end.[50] Later in his primary visitation of October 1633, Bishop Corbet enforced Byng's policy throughout the three other archdeaconries of Norfolk, Sudbury, and Suffolk. Then in 1635, after Brent's visitation, some parishes voluntarily introduced the metropolitical order.[51] Although Wren's orders, issued in the primary visitation of 1636, developed these policies further, his alterations marked a watershed in ordinary policy, in the speed with which they were carried out, their nature, and the degree of censures meted out to offenders. Some parishes which had carried out Brent's orders

[49] Bodl. Tanner MS 68/33, 4, 11v, 33v, 116, 198, 43, 65, 54, 3v–7v, 92, 160, 333–6; Tanner MS 177/7; PRO SP 16/437/91; Bodl. MS Tanner 314/160; BL Egerton MS 1048/24; LPL MS 943/619, MS 943/283; NNRO Sun/4/1 at back; HLRO Jan 8 1641/ Gt. Wratting. For allegations of Wren's arbitrary use of special commissioners and rural deans see *Parentalia*, 106.

[50] NNRO ANW/3/30; NNRO ANW/3/31.

[51] ESFRO FBA 91/E1/1/104,109; NNRO PD 39/74/315, PD 209/478/40, 43, Vis/6/1633, FC 147/E1/1. Dade, Brent's surrogate, went beyond his commission by excommunicating Adams, churchwarden at St Mary Tower, Ipswich, for not removing seats above the table. Subsequently the High Commission prosecuted Adams for attempting to sue Dade in Star Chamber. Although there is no substantive evidence that Laud was behind this prosecution, Prynne held him responsible. (*WWL*, iv. 130–2.)

could not stomach the new medicine of 1636. In fact certain Norwich parishes petitioned the king against Wren, claiming that his policies undermined the decent alterations brought about by Laud's visitor. The king's enigmatic response was to inform Wren not to desist from pressing 'all canonical obedience'.[52]

The destruction of the court *acta* permits a quantitative analysis of the enforcement of the rail in only one of the archdeaconries, Norwich. Within eight of its rural deaneries (some two hundred churches) only one church had not introduced the order by June 1640. As early as 1637 all but three churches within the Lynn deaneries had conformed.[53] Surviving churchwardens' accounts and *comperta* for other rural deaneries suggest that the picture was not very different across the three other archdeaconries.[54] After 1638 Montagu continued the broad outlines of Wren's policies, although he stopped the prosecution and excommunication of those who refused to receive at the rail. At a synod, held in Ipswich in 1639, he informed the clergy of the diocese that he disliked the practice and dissuaded them from pressing it.[55] The large number and searching character of Wren's visitation articles were held against him not only in his impeachment articles but in the Convocation of 1640, where his policy came under attack especially from the lesser clergy.[56] Canon 7 of 1640 in fact marked a triumph for Laud's moderation over Wren's extremism, but by this time the weight of Wren's policies in Norwich and Ely had gone far to discredit the altar policies of the Southern Province as a whole.[57]

The policy of Towers in Peterborough, 1638–40, was not as rigorous as Wren's but, as in Norwich, he pressed the full metropolitical order, and practices such as reading the second service at

[52] Bodl. Tanner MS 70/103–4, MS 68/160; Tanner 89/180.

[53] NNRO ANW/3/35, ANW/3/34, ANW/2/74, ANW/2/75; ANW/30/1/1; ANW/3/33, in particular 1–7, 88, 13.

[54] NNRO PD 58/38(s)59, PD 136/57, PD 191/23/45^{v}, PD 39/74/331, ANF/9/2, Vis/7, Colman MS 651/1641, PD 461/48/1636, PD 111/69/68–68^{v}; PD 26/71(s)218; ESFRO FC 112/E1/1/1637, FB 98/E3/1/22; FB 130/E3/9/1637, FB 22/E1/98; FC 185/E1/2, FB 123/E1+2/1637; FC 99/E1 31/1636, FBA 91/E1/1/113; FC 67/E1/1; PRO SP 16/437/91.

[55] NNRO FCB/5/36.

[56] PRO SP 16/455/47; LPL MS 943/599; *Parentalia*, 76–7; Bodl. Tanner MS 68/219, 240; BL Egerton MS 1048/24/2.

[57] See Ch. 7 section ii; Scudamore, *Notitia Eucharistica* 166, for Wren's activity after the Restoration.

the table.[58] Towers thus completed but also went much further than the policy of his predecessor, Dee, who had commenced court proceedings even before Brent published the order in 1635.[59] Outside the normal period of visitation, the enforcement observed the jurisdictional division of the see: certificates were returned to the consistory at Peterborough for the eastern deaneries (which included Rutland) and to the archidiaconal court at Northampton for the western deaneries, which covered three-quarters of Northamptonshire. Dee introduced the rail in his primary visitation of September 1634 and enforced it not only through his visitation courts but thereafter continually in the consistory.[60] As in Chichester, extensive and detailed *speculae* supplemented the normal inquisitorial machinery of the court. From this, as from other material, it is possible to offer some quantitative conclusions. In the survey of 1637, conducted among 206 churches within the western deaneries, only 29 churches were without rails.[61] By December 1637 their number had fallen to 6. In the eastern deaneries only a handful of churches had to certify after May 1635.[62] By 1640, after two years of Towers's far more vigorous medicine, probably all the parishes under the jurisdiction of the consistory had conformed. The practice of receiving at the rail, however, never won the widespread support or acquiescence of the parishes. In the survey of 1637, parishioners of about 40 out of the 206 churches did not receive there.[63]

[58] NRO X2159/5/1/1/14; HLRO 6 Feb. 1641/97. When Archdeacon Clarke of Derby, surrogate of Northampton, excommunicated the churchwardens of All Saints', Northampton, for not railing in the table, they complained to the court of Arches, where Lambe entered a caveat against them. They appealed to the court of the Delegates, where they procured absolution, although Clarke subsequently threatened the curate of the parish for publishing it. Clarke then persuaded Lambe to take out articles against the petitioners in the High Commission. Appeals by other parishes against Clarke's heavy-handed treatment might be lodged at the Arches or Audience, but with the general inhibition against prohibitions not go very far (HLRO Pet./22 Dec. 1640/Upton; 6 Feb. 1641/97).

[59] LRO DE 2461/39/1634; LRO DE 1784/17/19; NRO Corr. Bk./64/3, 23, 41 ff.–161; Corr. Bk./65/134, 141^{v}, 157, 167–75.

[60] NRO Corr. Bks. 64–70; Arch 58; X2159/5/1; X2159/5/11; X622/6.

[61] NRO X2159/5/11/25–160, X2159/5/11 (western deaneries), X622/6 (eastern deaneries).

[62] NRO X2159/5/1/1–20, X622/6, Corr. Bk./69 (1638–40), Corr. Bk./70 (1639–41), Ep. Visitation 8a.

[63] NRO X2159/5/11/25–160; PRO SP 16/395/79, SP 16/499/44.

(ii) The second category is one of the pressing of the metropolitical order, save for the practice of receiving at the rails. Brent visited Chichester in 1635 at the same time as he visited the exempt deaneries of Pagham, Tarring, and South Malling, and the peculiar of the dean and chapter. However not until 1636 was the rail enforced systematically through the courts.[64] A marked feature of Montagu's policy was his use of the machinery of archdiaconal courts and quarterly visitations to effect the enforcement. As in Essex and Buckingham, the archdeacons carried out detailed surveys to facilitate court activity. After Montagu left for Norwich in 1638, his successor Duppa continued policy along the same lines.[65] Although they enforced the rail rigorously, neither pressed the order for receiving at the rail. In fact Montagu disagreed intensely with Wren's provocative enforcement of the practice in Norwich, and confided to Laud that he thought it 'a new, unnecessary troublesome course, not enjoined by law, not required by canon'.[66] However unlike Laud, he enforced the altarwise position, in which there appears to have been considerable parochial compliance: in a survey conducted among forty-one churches within the archdeaconry of Chichester, only four had not introduced the position by November 1636.[67]

The survival of substantial court material shows that the rail was almost universally present by 1640. Most were erected before 1637, 1636 being the year in which the most intensive activity took place.[68] The process appears to have encountered more opposition in the archdeaconry of Lewes (than that of Chichester), where at least ten parishes were without rails by 1639, although they were subsequently introduced in at least eight of these.[69] The facility with which the rail was introduced is partly explained by the two bishops' refusal to order communicants to receive at the rails. Some ministers pressed the practice without the bishop's knowledge or approbation, and in

64 WSRO Ep. 11/11/3/73, Ep. 111/4/12/210^{v}, Ep. iv/2/15/3^{v}; Ep. 1/17/25/296 ff. See also ESRO 414/9/1/1c/1634.

65 WSRO Ep. 1/17/25, Ep. 1/22/1, Ep. 11/9/18, 23, Ep. 11/15/1 (46–60), 15, Ep. 1/17/27, Ep. 7/26/2.

66 LPL MS 943/619, 943,631; WSRO Ep. 1/17/25/311, 321^{v}, 336^{v}, 338, 361; Ep. 11/9/23/51^{v}, 125^{v}; Ep. 11/15/1/24.

67 WSRO Ep. 1/26/2/15^{v}, 19, 20, 35^{v}; *Sussex Archaeological Collections* (1906), 49.

68 WSRO Ep. 11/9/18, 293–326^{v}; Ep. 11/9/23, 1–134^{v}; Ep. 11/9/24, 1–16^{v}; Ep.1/22/1; Ep. 11/15/15/27–45^{v}; Ep. 1/26/2; Ep. 11/9/23/56–131; Ep. 11/15/1 (1–59); Ep. 11/14/1, Par 106/9/1/53, 48/9/1, 59/9/2/4, MP 245/145, 30/9/1.

69 WSRO Ep. 11/9/24/1–66, Ep. 11/9/23/123–131, Ep. 11/14/1.

consequence brought themselves into disrepute with the lay courts for refusing to administer the communion to parishioners.[70] The rail was also successfully introduced throughout the exempt deaneries of Pagham and Tarring; between April 1635 and October 1636 all parishes within this peculiar had conformed except East Lavant, which did so shortly afterwards.[71] Within the peculiar of the dean and chapter, as early as January 1636 certificates of performance were returned which reveal that by the autumn of 1637 all churches had conformed.[72]

The enforcement of the rail under Goodman in Gloucester was one of the most rigorous of the Southern Province. He republished Brent's orders during the triennial visitation of 1635 and then systematically enforced the rail and altarwise position through the courts from September 1636.[73] By 1640 only a few churches within the city of Gloucester had not introduced the rail, out of a total of 334 churches and chapels within the see.[74] Given the rigorous prosecution in Gloucester diocese, it is rather surprising that Prynne did not list Gloucester among those dioceses where the policy of enforcement was strictest. This was because of the bishop's opposition to the Canons of 1640 and the fact that the Commons rejected petitions critical of Goodman's activity from Gloucester diocese.[75]

In the diocese of Salisbury Brent's order was introduced in 1634 and republished in episcopal visitations during 1635 and 1638. Unlike Hall, his fellow Calvinist in Exeter, whose enthusiasm for the alterations was cool, Davenant enforced them, going in fact further than Laud. He took a very personal interest in implementing the order through both his visitation and the consistory courts, and

[70] J. White, *The First Century of Scandalous Priests* (1643), nos. 25, 43.

[71] WSRO Ep. 1V/2/14, Ep. 1V/2/5/3^{v}.

[72] WSRO Ep. 111/4/12/210–211^{v} (269^{v}, the last being St Olave).

[73] PRO SP 16/354/122, SP 16/381/60; *HMC Various Collections vii Gloucester* (1914), 62; HLRO 1641 Feb. 9/5; GRO P230/CW2/1/1636, P34/CW2/1/1636, P34/CH/1/1636; P154/11/CW2/1 June 1636-May 1637, P154/14/CW2/1/1635, P63/CW2/1/10, P329/CW2/1/248, P154/6/CW2/7 1637; GRO GDR 135 (June 1638), 136 (Oct. 1637), 174 (29 Oct. 1635); GDR 175, 189/1, 190/155–168; 191 (Oct. 1635-Mar. 1637); GDR 195/30–82, 92–176, 207(Jan.–Mar. 1637); GRO P107/CW2/1/17, P320/CW2/1/29, 39. For introduction of the rail in the peculiar of Bibury see GRO P34/CW2/1 Barnsley.

[74] GRO GDR 136, 138, 139, 140, 151, 199, 202, 203, 201/28^{v}–32^{v}; GRO P154/11/CW2/1/1639–40.

[75] Prynne, *CD*, 93; Walker, *Sufferings of the Clergy*, i. 52.

introduced the rail within his personal peculiars.[76] In December 1634 his vicar-general gave a peremptory order to the churchwardens of Edington to rail in their table on a north–south axis at the east end, and to rail in the font. On failure to comply with this order, excommunication was to follow.[77] In December 1637 those parishes without the rail in the archdeaconries of Sarum, Wiltshire, and Berkshire were ordered to return certificates of compliance not only to the archdeacons' visitations but to Davenant's triennial in 1638.[78] The order which the bishop gave to the churchwardens of Aldbourne in May 1637 achieved fame in its own time. Laud, in his speech at the censure of Prynne (and Prynne himself in *Canterburies Doome*), used it as evidence of Davenant's complicity in the alterations. The occasion of the order was that some of the parishioners decided to remove the table from the east end. The matter was brought to Davenant's attention by the king, almost certainly on the representation of the clerk of the Closet, Richard Steward, who was rector of the parish. In his personal communication, Davenant not only proceeded to press but to justify the metropolitical order: 'I . . . require you . . . not to meddle with the bringing down of the . . . table (or) you will answer it at your peril.' As for the position of the table, this was determined only by its convenience, while the power of determining that lay not with the parishioners but with the bishop, for 'the placing of it higher and lower in the chancel, or the church, is by the judgement of the Church a thing indifferent, and to be ordered . . . by the rule of convenience . . . since to judge . . . what is most convenient, belongs not to private persons but to those who have ecclesiastical authority.'[79]

Davenant's policy is distinguishable from Laud's in other ways than a willingness (in this issue) to impose heavy court censures. Unlike the archbishop, he started court proceedings less than a year after Brent's visitation, clearly not giving the parishes much time to become accustomed to the changes. Again Davenant enforced consistently the altarwise (north–south) position through the courts which Laud did not do.[80] His vigorous activity in Salisbury suggests

76 WTRO 1197/21; 189/2/12–13; BERO D/A2/e. 77/81^v; WTRO D3/4 Office 7/56^v.

77 WTRO D1/41/1/2/Citations 42 (unfol. bundle).

78 WTRO D3/4 Office 7/56^v.

79 *WWL* vi. 61; WTRO P 526/2/118; Prynne, *CD*, 100.

80 See nn. 111–26; BERO D/A2/c. 77/153, D/A2/c. 78/69, 255^v; WTRO D3/4 Office 7, 56^v; WTRO D2/4 Office 15, 32, 65^v, 113^v.

that Calvinists were implicated in, and not necessarily hostile to, these alterations, although in his own case there is reason to believe that he would rather they had not been introduced.[81] The largest peculiars within the see were those of the dean and chapter which extended well into Dorset. Under Dean Mason the rail was introduced in 1634 but not enforced until the first and second visitations of Dean Bailey in 1635 and 1638.[82] By July 1638 probably only six out of eighty-five churches within these peculiars lacked the rail.[83] With a determined effort on the part of the ecclesiastical authorities, much of Wiltshire and Berkshire possessed the rail by 1640, for as early as December 1637 the archdeacon of Wiltshire had ordered the churchwardens of Fifield to place their table 'north and south and rail it in as in other churches the same is done'.[84] In at least one of the archdeaconries, Berkshire, where more opposition seems to have been encountered than elsewhere, the courts imposed fines to speed up activity.[85]

Although Prynne marked out Bristol as one of the sees where the policy of enforcement had been the most energetic, probably not until Skinner's visitation in 1637 was the rail enforced. His predecessor, Coke, does not appear to have enforced the changes, although there was some voluntary activity in parishes within the archdeaconry of Dorset, such as at Puddletown, after Brent's visitation of 1634.[86] Like Skinner, Mainwaring of St David's pressed the rail and altar-wise position but possibly only after Brent had visited the Welsh sees in 1636, and during the visitation of his four archdeaconries in 1637. The existence of rails within some of the remotest parts of the archdeaconry of Brecon suggest that the enforcement was systematic.[87]

In Bath and Wells, Piers was the only ordinary of the Southern

[81] Bodl. Tanner MS 67/147.

[82] WTRO D24/3 visitation presentments/1636 July (Bishop's Canon); D24/2 misc.; D5/28 1634/41; D5/28 1635/34, 79; D5/28 1638/41; DTRO PE/SH/CW 108.

[83] WTRO D5/19/40/26ᵛ, 35, 39.

[84] WTRO D3/4 Office 7/56ᵛ.

[85] BERO D/P8/5/1; D/A2/c. 79/339ᵛ. For a small sample of innovating ministers/parishes see BL Add. MS 22084/2–11ᵛ. For the rail within the Windsor peculiar, which fell within much of the diocese see Bodl. MS Top Berks c. 44.

[86] Prynne, *CD*, 93; DTRO CAB CW/29ᵛ, 41; BRO P/St JB/CW/3(b) 1635 P/St P+J/CW/3a/251, 234; P/St W/CW/3b/94, P/St T/CW/71/2, P/St J/CW/1(b) 103, P/All S/CW/1638; P Temple Ch Ca 14(4)1; BRO P/St E/CW/2, P/St W/CW/3b/54, P/St J/CW/1(b) 1624; DTRO PE(PUD) /CW8.

[87] PRO SP 16/298/43; *The Buildings of Powys*, ed. R. Haslam (1983), 333, 340, 362.

Province who introduced and enforced the rail immediately after St Gregory's case.[88] By January 1636 140 churches out of 469 had already introduced the rail and altarwise position.[89] On his own testimony, at this early stage, Piers was prepared to act in a 'persuasive way'. Only later did he resort to the tactless use of court censure, excommunicating churchwardens for not turning their tables altarwise and also preventing clergy from administering the communion in those churches where the alteration had not been introduced, neither of which policies had countenance from Laud as diocesan or metropolitan.[90] As such, Piers, like Wren, earned reproach in 1640 and with him suffered near impeachment in the early days of the Long Parliament. Piers's policies were, however, less extreme than Wren's, for like others in this second category, he did not enforce the practice of receiving at the rails.

Piers informed Lambe that his parishes fell into two groups: 'those whom he spoke to and they no sooner obeyed; and others which refused at first but were soon quickly satisfied and then submitted'.[91] There exists no evidence for the assertion that only a quarter of the churches within the see had rails in 1640.[92] In fact the surviving records suggest the exact opposite, that by 1640 virtually all the churches within the archdeaconries of Bath, Wells, and Taunton had rails, the prosecutions for not having rails ceasing in 1638.[93] The rail was also extensively present within the peculiars of the see, such as those of the dean and chapter, the dean, the chancellor, the precentor, the prebendaries, and of the manor of Ilminster.[94] The exceptional trouble which Piers encountered at Beckington was exacerbated by his determination to make an example of the parish.

[88] Heylyn, *CA* 289; LPL 943/475; SRO D/P/Ilm 4/1/2; D/P cas 4/1/1.

[89] Prynne, *CD* 98–9.

[90] *Articles of Accusation and Impeachment of the House of Commons against William Piers* (1642), 6; *The Correspondence of the Smyth Family 1548–1642*, ed. J. Betly (Bristol Rec. Soc., 25, 1982), 164.

[91] Prynne, *CD* 98–9.

[92] *History*, 69 (Feb. 1984), 135; D. Hirst, *Authority and Conflict* (1986), 168.

[93] SRO D/P/Chlch/4/1/1, Cas/4/1/1, Ax/4/1/1, She/4/1/1, Qua.e/4/1/1, D/P/Lock/4/1/1, Dunn/4/1/1, Stap. g/13/2/1, Wel 4/1/3; Crew 4/1/1; Hal/4/1/1; Blag 4/1/1; Yeo/4/1/1; Crew 4/1/1; Swk/4/1/1; Bur 4/1/1; Kln 4/1/1; Th.co/4/1/1; DD/Wy 1C/306; DD/Sas SE 14/64; SRO D/D/Ca/313/41^v, 138^v; D/D/Ca 277/5^v, 110^v; D/D/Ca/299/57, 77^v; D/D/Ca 309/7, 103, 123, 219, 227, 313, 315; D/D/Ca vols. 297, 314a, 315, 316, 319, 320, 321, 323b, 325, 327, 328, 329, 330, 331, 333; LPL 943/ 563.

[94] SRO D/D/Ca/323d, D/P/Ilm 4/1/2/42, Pilt 4/1/3; D/D/Ca 310 (Cheddar).

Outside influence, identified in 1641 as Laud's, further aggravated the situation.[95] However, Laud's involvement in the affair has not had the close scrutiny it deserves. Piers excommunicated the churchwardens for contempt in refusing to obey his orders and for not offering any sign of compliance. They appealed to the Arches where, contrary to what is thought, Laud absolved them for a month, clearly distancing himself from Piers's provocative action as ordinary. Only after they had appealed a second time, and on this occasion to the court of the Delegates and to the king, did Piers inflict censure.[96]

(iii) The third category consists of the implementation of the metropolitical order, except for the altarwise position. Although Brent's visitation of London occurred in February and March 1637, many parishes within the see had introduced the rail before this date, as Brent had issued the order for the rail as early as May 1636, when he had also distributed the visitation articles and visited St Paul's.[97] However even before this, as early as mid-1635, Juxon's commissary, Aylett, had ordered churchwardens within the jurisdiction of the commissary to rail in their tables at the east end and to press communicants to receive there.[98] In fact London provides the example of a diocese where lesser ordinaries pre-empted the bishop. Archdeacon King of Colchester also appears to have taken early measures to enforce the rail within his archdeaconry; introducing the order in the autumn of 1635 and then enforcing it through the courts after January 1636.[99] The situation may not have been dissimilar in the four other archdeaconries. In March 1634 Archdeacon Paske's registrar drew up an order for the rail in the London church of St Bartholomew by the Exchange, although on this occasion the initiative appears to have come from the parish rather than the court.[100] Not until Juxon's triennial visitation in the summer of 1637, however, did the enforcement of the rail proceed simultaneously and

[95] *WWL* iv. 121. For the parishioners' case see LPL MS 943/ 481, 483; PRO SP 16/499/85.

[96] PRO SP 16/375/84, 16/499/85; PRO Assize 24/20/2/199; LPL MS 943/481, 483, 485, 495, 497; SRO D/D/Ca 277/190^{v}; D/D/Ca 309/324; *Northcote*, 56; *WWL*, iv. 122.

[97] PRO SP 16/327/101; HTRO ASA 7/31/36^{v}.

[98] PRO SP 16/327/101; ERO D/ABA 7/53–186^{v}; D/ABA 8/1–246; D/P 94/5/1/278^{v}; HLRO 1641 Feb. 9/1.

[99] ERO D/ACA 50/166^{v}; D/ACA 51/15^{v}–252^{v}; PRO SP 16/314/130.

[100] GL 4383/1/350.

systematically throughout all the courts. Thereafter parishes were called into one of the five archdeaconry courts or into either of the two commissary courts. During his visitation, Juxon called all parishes, in both diocesan and peculiar jurisdictions, to certify whether or not they had performed the order, although, like his commissary, he did not enquire into the altarwise position.[101] The resulting certificates (and other evidence) suggest the following statistical breakdown. In the archdeaconry of St Alban's (whose 26 churches lay within Hertfordshire and Buckinghamshire) all churches had introduced the rail by December 1637.[102] By the same date all but one of the 46 churches within the archdeaconry of London and all but 10 of the 134 churches within the archdeaconry of Middlesex (covering parts of the county, Essex and Hertfordshire) probably possessed rails.[103] Within the 6 deaneries of the archdeaconry of Colchester, by December 1637 only 23 churches out of 161 had not fulfilled the requirement.[104] In the archdeaconry of Essex, 66 out of 158 churches were without the rail at the end of 1637 but all subsequently introduced them.[105] This breakdown amply confirms the external source in 1640, which implied that by that year all parishes within Essex had introduced the rail.[106] It is not possible to give such a detailed analysis for those parishes within the jurisdiction of the deanery of the Arches, or within that of the commissary of London, which covered many parishes within the City and Middlesex. Yet evidence survives for at least 54 rails within city churches during the 1630s, many of which were introduced during or shortly after Juxon's visitation. The rail was also present in the exempt deaneries of Westminster and St Paul's.[107]

101 ERO D/ALV 2/194ᵛ–327ᵛ; GL 9537/15.

102 HTRO ASA 7/31/36ᵛ; ASA 19/2; PRO SP 16/466/23; GL 9537/15; HLRO Ap. 1640/78; *Articles of Accusation exhibited ... by Parliament against Sir Robert Berkeley* (1641), 5–6.

103 GL 9537/15 (the deaneries of Harlow, Braughing, Dunmow, Hedingham); *The Petition of the Women of Middlesex* (1641); HLRO Pet./May 13 1641 (Kensington); *The Vindication of the Vicar of Isleworth* (1641); WERO B10–11, V22, F3.

104 BL Egerton MS 2651/97, 150; GL 9537/15 (the deaneries of Witham, Lexton, Colchester, Tendring, Samford, Newport); ERO D/ACA 52/137–243ᵛ; D/ACA 53/17–243ᵛ; Essex Sessions Rolls XX/535–6.

105 PRO SP 16/375/83; GLRO DL/C/194; GL 9537/15 (the deaneries of Barnstaple, Dengie, Rochford, Ongar, Chelmsford, Chafford, Barking); ERO 9064/21/23ᵛ; T/P 131; D/AEA 41/75–249ᵛ; D/P 115/5/1/146; D/P50/6/1; D/AEV 7/Sept.–Oct.

106 *The Vindication of a True Protestant ... Daniel Whitby* (1644), 2–3.

107 GLRO DL/C/344/68; GL 9583/1/4/8ᵛ; 5026/1/1638; 5090/2/192; 823/1/

The massive acquiescence in the erection of the rail across the diocese of London was not accompanied by widespread reception of the communion there. This was especially so when Aylett enforced the order before Juxon's triennial. Later, parishioners cited Laud's metropolitical articles against the metropolitical order, as evidence that they need not receive there. In June 1636 Aylett informed Lambe that he had 'caused . . . the people to come up . . . and receive at the rail, although with much opposition, because they see no such thing, they say in the churches of London . . . [and] since the [metropolitical articles] were delivered they have found an article which as they conceive gives them leave to remove the table at the time of celebration'.[108] The number of those opposed to the practice was particularly high within the archdeaconry of Colchester, which possibly explains the rise in presentment of non-communicants after 1636.[109] In 1640 Juxon was able to shield himself from reproach as many of his diocesan duties had fallen on Aylett, Duck, and other surrogates. Yet it is inconceivable that he was unaware of their activities, especially since his visitation courts of 1637 expressly ordered communicants to receive at the rails and that clergy should not administer out of them.[110]

(iv) The fourth category was a policy of enforcing the rail and the east-end position, but not the practice of receiving at the rails or the altarwise position. In Canterbury Laud's primary visitation ran con-

1637; 4835/1/1637–8; 7673/2/1643–4; 1432/4/1636–7; 3556/2/1632–3; 1188/1/139; 2088/1/508; 504/1/11; 4383/1/350–1, 426; 1303/1/94–94^{v}; 1568/589; 942/1/148–155^{v}; 4524/2/61; 9235/2/1633; 6552/1/73; 4423/1/150; 2968/3/355(1629); 4241/1/359; 951/1/92; 6836/151, 166; 4810/2/82; 9583/1/4/8^{v}; 1124/1/122; 3907/1/1634; 4570/2/318; 1176/1/1637; 959/1/193; 6574/1/1638; 11394/1/1637; 2596/2/62, 78; 1013/1/183^{v}; 5714/1/74; 4071/2/137; 2895/2/1629; 524/1/47^{v}; 4825/1/44–5; 5018/1/1637; 645/2/1637?; 2601/1/139^{v}?; 4409/1/148^{v}, 247^{v}; 662/1/94^{v}; 593/2/159 (1640); 1257/1/18 (1631); 1279/3/68^{v}; 4215/1/13,55; 9235/2/1633; *An Answer to a Lawless Pamphlet* (1641); *The Petition of the Parishioners of Christ Church, London* (1643); *The Articles against . . . Dr. Brian Walton* (1641); GL St Bennet, Paul's Wharf/252; GL St Mary Colechurch 66/54^{v}, 56, 74^{v}; Prynne, *CD* , 113; HLRO Pet./30 June 1641; see also GL 9537/15. For St Paul's Pec.: PRO SP 16/499/42; BL Add. MS 12/222/73^{v}; GL 6836/34/1635, *The Petition and Articles against Dr. Fuller* (1641) and note 24 above. For Westminster Pec.: *CJ* ii. 32; WERO E17–E23.

108 PRO SP 16/327/101, SP 16/499/25a.

109 GL MS 4215/1/55; 4051/1; 6574/2 ERO D/ACA 52/e.g. 56. The Colchester courts also excommunicated for not churching at the rail: ERO D/ACA 51/196, 206^{v}.

110 GL 9537/15: Hedingham D./29^{v}–30; Dunmow D./35; Lexton D./22; Dengie D./19; Newport D./41^{v}; GLRO DL/C/343/184.

currently with his metropolitical visitation, but not until his triennial visitation of 1637 was the order to rail in the table enforced systematically through the courts. From December 1637 until early 1641 all those parishes which had not introduced the rail on their own before 1637 were continually cited into court to receive and carry out the order.[111] For the purpose of the enforcement the jurisdictional division between the archidiaconal and episcopal consistories was observed: parishes were cited only into the respective courts of their ordinary. The churchwardens of the consistory parishes received the order first.[112] By 20 December 1638 all had been cited into court, which was the sign for the archdeacon to cite his parishes into court. Much of the *acta* survive, from which it is possible to give a quantitative analysis of the enforcement of the rail in most of the parishes of the consistory and in all the parishes of eight (out of eleven) rural deaneries within the archdeaconry.[113] Before December 1638, 74 out of 194 archdeaconry parishes had introduced the rail.[114] By the beginning of 1641 a further 96 of these had done the same. By the same date at least 31 of the 54 consistory parishes had followed suit,[115] which means that out of 232 parishes (for which some evidence exists) at least 208 had introduced the rail by the beginning of 1641.[116]

Three features emerge most clearly from an analysis of the surviving evidence. First, Laud enforced the rail in the courts systematically only after December 1637, long after most other courts had started prosecutions.[117] From 1634 until December 1637 the rail was introduced gradually and voluntarily in response to Brent's order. Laud clearly hoped that parishes would see the decency of the

[111] CCL Z. 4. 6./125^{v} and following refs.

[112] CCL Z. 4. 6. compared to act books, X. 6. 9., X. 5. 7., X. 6. 6., X. 7. 3., X. 7. 1., X. 6. 11., X. 6. 10., Y. 6. 4.

[113] CCL Z. 4. 6./125^{v}–229^{v}(consistory parishes); X. 6. 11/70; X. 6. 6./243; X. 5. 7./251; Y. 6. 4./388; X. 6. 11/67^{v}. (Sandwich, Westbere, Ospring, Sittingbourne, Bridge, Canterbury, Lympe, Sutton deaneries. The act books for the deaneries of Charing, Dover, Elham appear not to have survived).

[114] Those parishes not cited to receive orders after December 1638, in CCL X. 6. 9, X. 6. 11, Y. 6. 4, X. 6. 11, X. 5. 7, X. 7. 3, X. 6. 10.

[115] Z. 4. 6./125^{v}–229^{v}: (Consistory). Y. 6. 4./379–404; X. 7. 1./22^{v}; X. 6. 9./123–30; X. 6. 11/67^{v}–89^{v}; X. 7. 3./1^{v}–8^{v}; X. 6. 10./191^{v}–202, X. 5. 7./241^{v}–254; X. 6. 6./224–48: (Archdeaconry).

[116] Ibid.; *PCR*, 104, 146, 158, 173, 185, 191, and J. White, *The First Century of Scandalous Priests* (1643), *passim*.

[117] see n. 111.

changes and act accordingly. In order to encourage this the only action which he appears to have undertaken before December 1637 was to encourage the adoption of his own (not the metropolitical) specifications in individual parishes, to remove seats at the east end of a few churches within Canterbury and to cite a handful of consistory parishes into court to certify whether they had carried out the order.[118] In the second place, Laud, unlike Wren and others, enforced neither the altarwise position nor the practice of receiving at the rails. In fact additional diocesan instructions which he gave to Brent (to be distinguished from the private metropolitical instructions) required neither of these alterations within the diocese, thus shielding it from the force of the metropolitical order.[119] Parishes could place their tables altarwise but only of their own volition. It seems likely that only in those parishes where receiving at the rails was generally observed might the courts recommend recalcitrants to obey, for fear of causing disunity, but in all the many cases concerning the rail there is only one example of this.[120] Zealous ministers might present recalcitrant parishes as worthy of censure for not receiving the sacraments or to intimidate them, but the examples of this are minimal, and invariably the courts took no action.[121] Nor did the courts introduce and enforce churching at the rails, as in Norwich and London. In fact in 1638 they prosecuted a minister for pressing this very practice.[122] In the third place, surrogates of Laud and Archdeacon Kingsley never resorted to excommunication or suspension for failure to fulfil the orders of the court within a certain time. Extension of time was continually given, which means that some

[118] PRO SP 16/ 499/71; CCL Z. 3. 16/1; X. 6. 10/91–91^{v}; HLRO MS Braye 8/29.

[119] HLRO MS Braye 8/29; PRO SP 16/499/71; WCO MS Clarke 5/11 (see Prynne's perverted rendering, *CD*, 89, where he corrupts it to read as a general metropolitical order when it was patently a diocesan order for Maidstone (where Laud was rector) and possibly other consistory parishes, issued most likely in preparation for Laud's second ordinary visitation of Canterbury diocese. Tyacke does not clarify this issue, *AC* 203. See Brent's assertion in WCO MS Clarke 5/11 that this order specified that it did not matter whether the table was placed north–south or east–west. Elsewhere Brent could not escape the royal requirement to place tables altarwise (north–south): see the metropolitical order he gave for Chichester: WSRO Ep. 11/11/3/73).

[120] CCL Z. 3. 16/1; Z. 4. 6./250^{v} (although the courts did not enforce receiving at the rails, they did encourage the erection of kneeling boards around them).

[121] BL Add. MS 26, 785/190; *PCR*, 108 and court sessions listed in nn. 113 and 115 above.

[122] *PCR* 197.

churchwardens were cited into court more than thirty times.[123] The only pressure to carry out the order was the mounting cost of citation fees and possibly the occasional fine. It is difficult to know whether the courts inflicted fines in this respect; evidence survives for some parishes but this could refer merely to cumulative citation fees. In 1639, for example, the churchwardens of Headcorn paid over one shilling when they took 'a longer time to rail in the communion table'.[124] Yet the fact that Laud did not force his surrogates to impose the plenary censures of the courts meant that as diocesan he observed those private instructions which he gave to Brent in 1634.[125] It means also that the historiographical understanding of Laudianism is seriously distorted. Neither the propaganda of Prynne nor the activities of individual clergy in Kent (related in White's *Scandalous Priests* or in the petitions received by Dering) is a reliable guide to Laud's policies within the see.[126] As diocesan he never reaped the calumny which others earned and Prynne, in spite of his vicious accusations, found little evidence to use against him. As a result of Laud's cautious, tactful policy, there were disproportionately fewer rails in Canterbury than in other dioceses by 1640.

Within the diocese of Rochester, policy followed similar lines to that in Canterbury. Brent issued the order in 1634 but it was probably only in 1637 during Warner's primary visitation that the rail was enforced.[127] But the rail had been set up in some churches, either in response to the metropolitical recommendations or to the orders issued by Bowle, Warner's predecessor, in his visitation of 1635.[128] The courts did not enforce the altarwise position, which meant that clergy such as Vaughan of Chatham might labour for more than two years to persuade parishes to adopt it.[129] Nor was receiving at the rails enforced, which meant that only through the compulsion of various ministers, such as Vane of Dartford, were communicants

123 CCL Z. 4. 6./127 and n. 115; see also *Dean and Chapter Newes from Canterbury* (1640?), 9, which depicts Archdeacon Kingsley encouraging the introduction of the order in April 1639. The excommunication schedules in CCL V 111/2/2 are not for refusing to introduce the rail but for the usual excommunication inflicted for non-appearance: compare CCL V 111/2/2/202 with CCL Z. 4. 6./198 (Staple).

124 KAO P181/4/1/19 see also CCL U3/99/4/1/1638–9.

125 PRO SP 16/485/118.

126 *PCR*, *passim*; White, *First Century of Scandalous Priests*, *passim*; Prynne, *CD*; BL Harl. 1219/395.

127 PRO SP 16/493/28.

128 KAO P336/5/1; GERO Greenwich ca (no cat. no.).

129 *PCR* 266.

brought to receive there.[130] Presentments might be received on the petition of individual clergy, but as in Canterbury the courts did not prosecute. However, in parishes under his personal jurisdiction, such as St Dionis Backchurch, Warner was prepared to introduce more radical innovations than in his see.[131]

In the visitation of Winchester, during the autumn of 1636, Curle republished Brent's order and thereafter introduced the rail across the archdeaconries of Winchester and Surrey.[132] Many were set up between 1635 and 1636, which suggests that the bishop merely speeded up a process started by Brent in 1635.[133] Although the courts enforced neither receiving at the rails nor the altarwise position, both Mason, chancellor of Winchester, and Hakewill, archdeacon of Surrey, cited some clergy into court for not turning their tables altarwise, including the rector of Lambeth, Daniel Featley, who refused consistently to carry out this requirement, but without prosecution from his next-door neighbour.[134]

Within the diocese of Bangor and Llandaff the courts of Roberts and Murray enforced the rail after 1636, when Brent visited the sees, although neither seems to have introduced the altarwise position or receiving at the rail.[135] Within the diocese of Worcester, no episcopal visitation followed Brent's visitation of 1635 until 1637, but as early as 1636 the consistory was asking for certificates of compliance from the parishes. The archdeacon of Worcester (Thornborough's son) was one of the few archdeacons within the Southern Province whose visitation articles explicitly inquired into the erection of rails.[136] From 1635 the alteration was carried out also within the peculiar of the

[130] *PCR* 118.

[131] PRO SP 16/ 493/28. For further evidence of Warner pressing the innovation outside his diocese: *The Articles and Charge against . . . Dr. Walton* (1641), 2. Evidence suggests that Laud did not call parishes within the archiepiscopal peculiar of Shoreham into court until 1637: *PCR*, 183; KAO P 142/5/1.

[132] HRO V Bk. 32; SPRO/PR4/2/1/St Law/128; PTRO/CHU 3/2A 1/7.

[133] HRO 75 M72/PW7; 41 M64A3/PW1, IM70A/PW1, 49 M67/PR1; SYRO PSH/WOKP/7/8; PSH/SEA/2/69; PSH/MIC/1/1/A/5; PSH/HORS/7/1/13; GLRO P 95/ALL 1/44; IWRO NPT/APR/2B/51–61; SHAL/COM/1; SHOR/APR/2A/1; THOR/APR/2A/1; KTRO KG2 2/3, 2/2/1; 2414/4/1; P52/2/4.

[134] D. Featley, *The Gentle Lash or the Vindication of Dr. Featley* (1644), 10.

[135] CLRO PD/78/1/39; R. Soden, *A Guide to Welsh Parish Churches* (Llandysul, 1984), 68; *RCHM Caernarvonshire*, i (1956), 28, 156; J. R. Guy and E. B. Smith (eds.), *Ancient Gwent Churches* (Risca, 1979), 22, 24, 65.

[136] WARO DR 87/2/114; DR 05/6/22^{v}; DR 446/24; *Articles . . . in the visitation of . . . Edward (Thornborough), Archdeacon of Worcester* (1638), 23.

dean and chapter. As in Canterbury there were still some parishes without the rail in 1640.[137]

In neighbouring Coventry and Lichfield, Wright, traditionally depicted as disaffected with the changes, was one of their most enthusiastic protagonists. Even before Brent visited the see in 1635, he had started enforcing the rail in his consistory.[138] In both 1634 and 1636 the bishop held courts of audience to which he called churchwardens from parishes within the four archdeaconries to receive his personal orders. Later, on the return of certificates, offenders were referred to his counsel or to that of his chancellor.[139] As a result of Wright's early enforcement of the rail, Coventry and Lichfield was one of the few dioceses where the metropolitical courts pressed it.[140] However these courts enforced not the full metropolitical order but Wright's more moderate ones. Although the bishop introduced the rail earlier than Laud in Canterbury, like the archbishop he enforced neither the altarwise position nor receiving at the rail, a policy reflected in that of his four archdeacons. As in Lincoln and elsewhere, certificates of compliance were required at the quarterly archidiaconal visitation, and in 1636 Wright supplemented their activity by calling for certificates in his own triennial visitation.[141]

Of the four archdeacons, Jeffreys of Salop and Clarke of Derby appear as the most zealous for the alterations. In 1637 Jeffreys, together with Latham, the diocesan chancellor, informed against the bishop, believing that Wright was undermining what he considered to be Laud's policy. At Coventry, Wright had given the mayor permission to remove the table at St Michael's out of the rails during the communion because the church was so large. This was particularly contentious because, on a recent visit to the city, the king had ordered that the table should stay in a fixed position at the east end. Laud, however, did not admit of the appeal and dismissed the

[137] WORO b857. 06 BA 2335/16(iv)213^{v}.

[138] C. Cross, *Church and People: 1450–1660* (1976), 178–9; H. R. Trevor-Roper, *Archbishop Laud* (1940), 184, 347; LJRO B/V/1/53, 58 (unfol.); SHRO 1977/4/4; SFRO D13 23/E/1, D3710/1/1, D9/A/PC/1/43.

[139] LJRO B/V/1/57; B/V/1/58/17; B/C/3/16 (May 1638); SFRO D9/A/PC/1/43.

[140] LJRO B/V/1/55; B/V/1/56.

[141] SFRO D9/A/PC/1/43; LJRO B/V/1/58/1, 17, 58; B/V/1/57; B/C/3/15; B/V/1/53; B/C/3/16 (Oct. 1637).

information as 'malice' against the bishop.[142] Clearly Laud thought that the bishop was well within his rights as ordinary to decide the most convenient position of the table during communion, a principle which would ultimately find expression within the Canons of 1640.[143] Within the archdeaconries of Salop and Stafford the courts imposed fines for noncompliance within a given time.[144] By 1636 possibly as few as twelve churches had not introduced the order within the archdeaconry of Derby, while in the archdeaconry of Coventry, which covered half of Warwickshire, most parishes appear to have possessed the rail by 1638.[145] The parishes within the peculiar of the dean and chapter and within the royal peculiar of Wolverhampton received their order not from Wright in 1634 but from Brent in 1635. The altar which Christopher Wren, brother of the bishop, decked out at Wolverhampton achieved notoriety in its own time; Burton lampooned it and in 1640 a handful of townspeople demolished it.[146]

(v) The fifth category covers that of John Williams in Lincoln. The idiosyncratic policy which he pursued in response to the order of 1634 is at once famous and misunderstood. Traditionally it is depicted as a policy at odds with the 'Laudian' metropolitical order.[147] Yet, as the above shows, the policy implicit in the metropolitical order is not necessarily the same as the authentic Laudian policy. The crux of Williams's policy was the railing in of tables in the chancels or the body of the church, and not necessarily at the east end. This

[142] BL Add. MS 4275/326; PRO SP 16/350/52; SP 16/351/18; SP 16/351/38; Prynne *CD* 91; HLRO Pet./6Feb. 1641/97, Pet./Dec. 1640/Upton.

[143] *WWL* v. 607–33.

[144] SFRO D9/A/PC/1/43; SFRO (WSL) M600/134^{v}; SHRO 760/1/77, 2959/4/1, 3848/CW/1, 3793/CW/1, 1379/CW/1.

[145] DBRO D81BA/PW1/1636; D1145 A/PW 1/23, D886A/PW 1/34^{v}; LJRO B/V/1/59; LJRO B/C/3/16 (May 1638); Bodl. Tanner MS 65/209–209^{v}. WARO DR 404/49/14; DR 296/6/79; DR (B) 3/39; DR 50/9/191; CVRO City Annals 920/14.

[146] H. Burton, *For God and the King* (1636), 161; SFRO Q/SR E 1641/11–3; LJRO D20/4/1. For Chester episcopal and archidiaconal activity: Richmond (CBRO WPR, 8, 43, 62, 89, 83); Chester (CCRO CR63/2/203; CRO P13/22/1, P18/3608, P23/3466/9/1, 2, P173/6/1, P39/8/1, P8/13/1, 2, P87/1/1, P1/11, P51/12/1, P20/13/1, P65/8/1, P27/7/1, P63/7/1; LLRO CA/1627–67). One of Bridgeman's domestic chapels (St Anselm, Chester close) survives intact (the only episcopal chapel to survive unaltered from this period), equipped with rail.

[147] E.g. G. W. O. Addleshaw and F. Etchells, *The Architectural Setting of Anglican Worship* (1948), ch. 4.

approach was not significantly different from Laud's approach.[148] Williams, after all, followed the St Gregory's ruling, where incidentally the rails were four-sided. Again like Laud he never enforced the altarwise position nor receiving at the rails. In 1636, when trouble arose in the southern parts of the see over ministers urging their parishioners to receive at the rails, Laud let Williams defuse the problem himself.[149] Nevertheless it is the difference between their policies which is the more striking. Williams, wishing to press home his own interpretation of the issue of conveniency, embarked upon a policy of enforcement far more vigorous than Laud's proceedings in Canterbury. This policy was also more costly to bear because it often countenanced a four-sided rail. During his triennial visitation of 1635 Williams sat in person, the first visitation for years that was conducted by the bishop rather than his chancellor.[150] In August 1635 he gave personal orders for the erection of rails and required churchwardens to return certificates of compliance at their respective archidiaconal visitations in October, and in each quarter thereafter.[151] It was during this triennial visitation of 1635 that Williams erected a rail in the church at Buckden, his country retreat.[152] He also called churchwardens into his own consistory, demanded certificates of performance, and fined those who asked for extra time.[153]

As a result of these orders of 1635, in each of the six archdeaconries, churchwardens were cited into court to certify or to receive further orders.[154] In the small archdeaconry of Stow possibly all seventy-nine parishes had complied with the order by the end of 1636, Flixborough being the last parish to receive further orders for not recertifying as Williams had commanded.[155] *Acta* which survive for the Hertfordshire section of the archdeaconry of Huntingdon reveal that the courts summoned churchwardens for noncompliance several months before Williams issued his own orders in August

[148] Williams, *The Holy Table, Name and Thing*; PRO SP 16/241/18, SP 16/246/42; *HMC Appendix to the 8th Report ii* (Corporation of Leicester), 436ᵛ.

[149] Birch, ii. 277; PRO SP 16/370/6iii; LPL MS 943/261; LPL MS 1030/52.

[150] PRO SP 16/296/27.

[151] LRO 1D41/13/63 (at back).

[152] HNRO 2661/5/1/1635.

[153] LAO St Michael, Lincoln/7/1/24, Vj 28/25, 27ᵛ, 60ᵛ.

[154] LAO viij 3/6, 103, vj 29/137ᵛ; HTRO D/P7 5/1; PRO SP 16/296/27; BKRO MS Archd. papers c. 290, 109ᵛ, 114ᵛ; BDRO P88/5/1/28; LRO ID41/13/64.

[155] LAO viij 3/107; viij 3/6, 103, 116ᵛ, 122ᵛ *et passim.*

1635.[156] The destruction of many rails in the army riots of 1640 in north-west Hertfordshire, in addition to other evidence, suggests that the rail was extensively present here.[157] As ordinary, Holdsworth pursued a policy slightly different to Williams's since he ordered parishes to place their tables at the east end and at times pressed receiving at the rails.[158] When this practice faced opposition in St Ives, Holdsworth informed Lambe that it was his 'weakness . . . to be yielding to tender consciences in cases scrupulary, especially when I meet with ductible spirits and on the contrary, as stout when I see the discipline of the church to be struck at, as it is in this case and by these persons'.[159] In the neighbouring archdeaconry of Bedford, the courts fined churchwardens who asked for further time than the courts permitted for setting up the rail.[160] Although Hacket led the opposition to the altarwise position in the Convocation of 1640, he nevertheless encouraged the clergy of his archdeaconry to take for their model the north–south position at Ampthill.[161] When Williams published *The Holy Table* in June 1637 he supported the episcopal line at a visitation address, for which he had to apologize to the king.[162] After Williams's suspension, some Bedfordshire parishes, as elsewhere in the diocese, took the opportunity to introduce an arrangement more in tune with the metropolitical order.[163] Yet even before 1637 some parishes had followed Brent's rather than Williams's instructions, in the process occasionally exceeding the vicar-general's instructions: in 1636 Jasper Fisher erected a stone altar at Wilden without seeking the permission of either Hacket or Williams. Consequently the bishop visited the church and ceremoniously demolished it.[164] Laud, who believed that Fisher had acted impertinently in not seeking first the advice of his ordinary before carrying out such a controversial action, complained to the

156 HTRO AHH 5/14 (Apr. 9 1635), D3P32 25/1; D/P7 5/1; AHH 5/15 (28 May 1635); PRO SP 16/466/23; SP/16/467/79; SP/16/463/33; SP 16/469/35.

157 PRO SP 16/466/23; 467/79; 463/33; 469/35.

158 HTRO AHH 5/14 (28 May 1635); PRO SP 16/370/6iv, SP 16/444/80a, SP 16/445/22.

159 PRO SP 16/445/22.

160 BDRO P88/5/1/28, P 44/5/2/115.

161 LPL MS 1030/65; for later developments at Ampthill see HLRO Feb. 23/20.

162 LPL MS 943/599; MS 1030/65–7.

163 BDRO P88/5/1/31; HLRO Pet./5 Aug. 1641.

164 LPL MS 1030/51–3; BDRO TW 926.

king about him.[165] Charles's reply reveals that unlike Laud he unreservedly approved of Fisher's action and that he disregarded Williams's rights as ordinary.[166]

The policies pursued within the archdeaconries of Buckingham and Leicester approximated more to Brent's specifications than to Williams's partly because the commissary of Leicester was Sir John Lambe, dean of the Arches, while the archdeacon of Buckingham was Neile's brother. By June 1638 only two out of almost 200 churches within the archdeaconry of Buckingham had not introduced the rail.[167] In Leicester, out of 259 churches all but 8 had set them up by June 1636. By 1640 all these had conformed. In both jurisdictions court activity was earlier and more inquisitive than most sees; the north–south axis, for example, was enforced in both areas. In Leicester the practice of receiving at the rails was pressed, although not to the same extent as in Norwich, since the courts prosecuted ministers for administering outside the rails rather than parishioners for refusing to receive there, both of which were abnegations of Laud's policy.[168]

Throughout the peculiars of the see the rail was widely present. In that of the dean and chapter, receiving at the rail was encouraged, which caused problems at Ketton, where Sir William Armyne, a justice of the peace, refused to receive and proceeded to indict his minister for refusing to give him communion. It was minor incidents such as these which helped to discredit the successful implementation of the rail. Laud did not know how to defuse the problem at

[165] *WWL* v. 342. Williams had informed Laud about the case himself (LPL MS 1030/51) but LPL MS 1030/53 (also Bodl. MS Cherry 2/91) reveals that information had been sent from Lambe and Sibthorpe to Laud concerning the incident, which blackened Williams's name. *WWL* v. 342, however, shows that Laud did not capitalize upon this information when recounting the incident to the king. See also Laud's words to Williams (LPL MS 1030/52) referring to the 'bold and unadvised part in (Fisher) . . . to attempt a business of this nature without the knowledge and approbation of his ordinary'.

[166] *WWL* v. 342: (Charles I) 'This may prove a bold part in the bishop, and the poor priest in no fault.'

[167] PRO SP 16/395/54; SP 16/366/79, 105, 170; SP 16/426/71; BKRO MS Archd. papers c. 290/109^{v}, 114^{v}, MS Archd. papers c. 291/108; PRO SP 16/366/79, 183, 188, 167^{v}, 173^{v}.

[168] LRO 1D41/13/63 (several pages at the back), 1D41/13/61/82^{v}, 100^{v}; 1D41/13/64/9^{v}, 50, 114, 213^{v}, 233^{v}, 287^{v}, 1D41/13/65/76, 191^{v}, 222^{v}, 287, 242^{v}, 296 and vol. 1D41/18/8–12b.

Ketton and delegated its resolution to the Arches.[169] Within the peculiars of Kirton in Lindsey and Louth rails were set up shortly after 1635, which shows that several parishes acted voluntarily on Williams's order, in spite of the fact that consistory had no jurisdiction over them and so could not order certificates of compliance.[170] In 1638 however, all peculiars were called upon to certify whether they had the rail during the second metropolitical visitation of the see, when Laud assumed jurisdiction after the bishop's suspension. Between 1638 and 1639 these courts introduced the rail in recalcitrant parishes, and possibly altered the rail in others. At the end of 1638 perhaps less than forty parishes (in thirteen out of fifteen rural deaneries) in Lincolnshire did not possess the rail.[171] By the 1640s contemporaries found it difficult to discriminate between the policies of Laud and those of Williams. Prynne accused Williams, as he accused Davenant and Morton, of complicity in the alterations of the 1630s.[172] After all, Williams had introduced the rail in what was an early, vigorous campaign when compared to Laud's. Perhaps it was with a measure of self-interest that when Williams drew up the list of innovations for the committee of religion in 1641, he did not include the rail.[173] In his *Two Looks Over Lincoln*, Richard Dey unmasked the ambiguity in Williams's policy in the 1630s and attempted to discredit him when he donned the guise of primitive undefiled episcopacy: 'throughout all the diocese . . . being no small part of the kingdom, there [are] . . . rails and barricadoes . . . [can] any bishop justly be taxed with innovations and be spared, whereas it appears that he exceeded them all'.[174]

(vi) The sixth category comprises those bishops who might encourage, but who took little or no court action to further the order: Hall (Exeter), Coke (Hereford), Owen (St Asaph),[175] Morton

169 PRO SP 16/428/70, SP 16/420/16, SP 16/452/98; HLRO Pet./14 Aug. 1641; ORO MS DD Par Thame b2/299.

170 LAO Louth St James 7/5/88, 109; Kirton in Lindsey 7/1/1638.

171 LAO VII 21/173v; St Michael, Lincoln 7/1/29; LAO Vj, 30/22, 28, 39, 55, 74, 92, 94, 112, 129, 144, 166, 184, 196, 200.

172 Prynne, *CD* 100.

173 Bodl. Eng. misc. MS c. 92/39.

174 R. Dey, *Two Looks Over Lincoln* (1641), pp. ix, viii.

175 The absence of references to the rail in the few surviving parish and court records, and the fact that very few rails survive from before 1640 suggest that Bishop

(Durham),[176] and Potter (Carlisle).[177] In their episcopal visitations they possibly republished the order, as during and after these years several rails were introduced (this is particularly true of Exeter).[178] Hall, like Laud, appears to have ordered the removal of seats at the east end, and looked for a voluntary response to Brent's order. In 1640 he described Cox of Sanford 'as one of the first in my diocese who removed his table voluntarily to an altar position'.[179] Another of these bishops, Coke of Hereford, certainly exploited his rights as ordinary to position the table within the most convenient place at Ledbury.[180] Yet the only instance of the Hereford courts enforcing Brent's order was in Ludlow, arguably the second most important church in the see, as Ludlow was the seat of the Council in Wales and the Marches.[181] However from the general absence of fees expended at court during the 1630s it appears that Coke, like the other four bishops in this category, brought parishes into his con-

Owen did not enforce the rail in St Asaph. This however is not to deny that some parishes adopted the changes during the 1630s: Soden, *Guide to Welsh Parish Churches*, 112; PRO SP 16/371/68; SP 16/383/24; E. Hubbard (ed.), *The Buildings of Clwyd* (1986), *passim*.

[176] Although Prynne and others accused Morton of complicity in the changes (Prynne, *CD* 100; Bodl. Tanner 314/149) and although Morton's work, *Of the Institution of the Sacrament of the Blessed Body and Blood of Christ* (2nd edn. 1635) was republished during the 1630s with glosses (e.g., pp. 36, 462–3, 551) in support of the changes, the lack of references to disbursements and certificates in surviving records suggest that he did not call the parishes into court to receive the order in Durham diocese. Individual clergy however might further the innovations: *The Petition against Dr. Gray, Vicar of Pont Island* (1641).

[177] Much of the court evidence for Carlisle in this period has not survived. In its absence, episcopal and archidiaconal activity can be partially reconstructed from: CBRO PR 116/107, WPR 11, WPR 76. However the survival of many rails in churches in 1700 (see W. Nicholson, *Miscellaneous Accounts of the Diocese of Carlisle, 1703*, ed. R. S. Ferguson (1877)), most of which have now disappeared, suggest that either during the 1630s or the 1670s–1680s the courts enforced it or certainly brought some pressure to bear upon the parish. As there often exists a correlation between the introduction of the rail during the 1630s and its reintroduction in dioceses during the post-Restoration period, given the relatively large number in Carlisle, Potter's inclusion within the sixth category could well be incorrect.

[178] DRO Halberton PW2; Hartland 120/A/PW1; Kilmington PW2/3047; CWRO DDP 126/4/1/177^{v}; *A Second and Most Exact Relation of the Sad and Lamentable Accidents at Widecombe, 21 October 1638* (1638), 18.

[179] DRO 1237A/PW30; PRO SP 16/430/51.

[180] HFRO Box misc. MSS (uncat. containing 1670 visitation returns).

[181] HFRO Box 39/A. Bk. 146/5; *Trans. of the Shropshire Archaeological and Natural History Society*, 2nd Ser., 4 (1892), 129.

sistory neither to receive the order nor to certify of its performance.[182] Archdeacons such as Helyar of Barnstaple, Wilson of Exeter, and Hughes of Hereford might be keen to effect the order, but it is unlikely that they took unilateral actions as ordinaries.[183] The general absence of the rail suggests that most parishes within these five dioceses did not obey the metropolitical order. Yet this disobedience was hardly wilful as the order fell on deaf ears when ordinary activity did not extend to enforcement through the courts and when there was an annual change of churchwardens. Thus the way remained open to independent activity. As a consequence Brent's order was open to individual interpretation, which could lead to the extremes of Ilsington (Exeter), where the vicar, unrestrained from above, had free rein for provocative activities.[184] With little pressure from the courts, the event or extent of alteration depended upon the particular inclination of the vicar or churchwardens. Thus in Hereford diocese as early as 1637 Montgomery had introduced the rail (and receiving there) but it was not until 1639 that Leominster probably received its rail, when Wallop Brabazon, who disliked the vicar, Tombes, introduced it as churchwarden.[185] Of these five dioceses Hereford probably witnessed proportionately more innovations than the others for two reasons. During his primary visitation in 1635, Wren had enforced the altarwise position of the table, an innovation continued by his successor, Field.[186] In the second place, the peculiar of the dean and chapter of Hereford was larger than those of the other capitular authorities. Within this jurisdiction there were possibly more rails than within the entire see, as the Harleian survey of 1640 suggests that under Deans Brown and Richardson, the metro-

[182] HFRO Box 26–7/ AB 95–8; Box 38–9/ AB 144–7; for further evidence see all relevant churchwardens' accounts listed by respective archdeaconries (subdivision 'parish') in the bibliography under CBRO, CWRO, DRO, DURO, HFRO, SFRO, SHRO, WDRO.

[183] *Walker Revised*, ed. A. G. Matthews (1948), 114; J. Brooking Rowe, *Ecclesiastical History of Plymouth* (1876), 16; BL Portland Loan MS 29/173/164.

[184] *The Buller Papers* (private, 1895), 33.

[185] BL Portland Loan MS/29/173/99; *HMC Portland* iii, 76.

[186] *Articles to be enquired... in the visitation of... Matthew (Wren)... Bishop of Hereford* (1635); HFRO Hentland 13/1, Box 27/A. Bk. 97 (Hereford), Box 38/A. Bk. 145 (Ludlow)/Nov. 1635; BL Loan 29/173/99. Contrary to Dr Atherton's argument, Wren was more directly associated with the innovations at Dore than Laud. See PRO C115/N9/8848–9, 8875; I. Atherton, 'Viscount Scudamore's "Laudianism"', *The Historical Journal*, 34/3 (1991), 567–97.

political order had been heavily enforced.[187] In contrast, it was only in 1639 that the rail appeared within Braunton, the tiny peculiar of Peterson, dean of Exeter.[188] In these dioceses, as elsewhere, *sede vacante* records (when jurisdiction lapsed to Canterbury) reveal that Laud did not exploit the opportunity of diocesan vacancies to force the introduction of the metropolitical order, as he might well have done.[189]

Brent never visited the sees of Oxford or Ely metropolitically, although between February and April 1638 he visited Ely *sede vacante*, during which time the metropolitical order was probably published. Laud had intended to visit both sees in 1635–6, but the universities disputed his right of visiting university and diocese simultaneously, and so he delayed the visitation. In both sees proximity to the university could either facilitate or hinder the introduction of the rail in country parishes before 1638: some of the college chapels were redecorated at this time, and not always to the liking of conservative tastes.[190] In the diocese of Oxford, Bancroft probably introduced the rail in his visitations of 1635 and 1638 as several were erected during these years.[191] In Ely Francis White took no measures to introduce the rail, but not before the end of 1636. Before 1637, the erection of the rail in the diocese resulted not from court initiative but from that of the minister of a parish. According to the churchwardens of Girton, their church was 'one of the first... in the county that had rails, and an altar set up, and so an example and precedent to other churches'.[192] In June 1636 the rector, Ling, petitioned Chancellor Eden for permission to carry out this alteration.[193] Only after Wren's primary visitation of 1638 was the rail introduced elsewhere, and churchwardens called to certify in quarterly bills of presentment. By the end of 1639 only a handful of parishes in the southern deaneries

[187] CCO MS 206/20, 21, 24; *WWL* iv. 152.

[188] DRO 1677A/PW1.

[189] LPL Reg. Laud i/175–306ᵛ, ii/1–27ᵛ.

[190] PRO SP 16/386/4; CUL F/5/41; CUL Baker MS 33/193–210, MS 38/455–8, 471–3; *HMC De Lisle and Dudley*, 364; BL Add. MS 15672/1/52; Bodl. Rawl. MS D352.

[191] ORO MS DD Par Oddington e. 3; Par St Martin's a.1/173; Par St Mich.N/gate a.3/1635; Par St Peter in the E. d. I/19; Par Yarnton b. 7/1638; Par Burford c. 36/1636. It appears that his predecessor, Richard Corbet pressed the east-end position in Oxford before 1632, see *The Diary of Thomas Crosfield*, ed. F. S. Boas (1935), 74.

[192] BL Add. MS 15672/29–30.

[193] CUL D/2/48/63ᵛ.

had not obeyed the order, possibly as few as ten.[194] In the deaneries of Ely and Wisbech, 18 churches, noted as without the rail in the episcopal visitation of 1638, had introduced them by mid-1639.[195]

Thus apart from the sees of Exeter, Hereford, St Asaph, Durham, and Carlisle (where court action was minimal) Ely, Oxford, and Canterbury were the last sees in the country to enforce the order for the rail through the courts. However, in virtually all other sees the enforcement of the rail was concentrated during, and subsequent to, 1636. This late but widespread enforcement of the rail did not mean that its introduction was popular.[196] Within a few years it would be removed or destroyed, and as quickly as it had been erected.[197] Nor does it mean that there was widespread acquiescence in the introduction of the wider metropolitical order: the altarwise position and receiving at the rails were almost universally disregarded by the courts and parishes alike.[198]

While there existed parishes which welcomed the rail beyond mere compliance, others went to extremes to oppose it.[199] Reactions to the metropolitical order and to the rail were conditioned by several contingencies. In the first place, as shown above, local acceptance was partly determined by the chronology, rigour, content, and intent of court policy. In the second, the role of the churchwardens was important, although they had little scope for disobedience on this particular issue, due to the extraordinary court activity which it engendered: they were answerable in the courts for its introduction, were responsible for imposing the general parish rate, or soliciting contributions from those who were willing to pay.[200] Thirdly, there were in some parishes individual clergy, impropriators, or parishioners who might wish to outlay the cost themselves, although elsewhere others might try to obstruct the innovation, as an encroachment upon

194 CUL B/2/51/44ᵛ, 40ᵛ; B/2/52/11, 20ᵛ–23, 48–9, 60; B/2/53; BL Add. MS 15672/441.

195 CUL B/2/53/1–68, D/2/51/40ᵛ as compared to B/2/52/1–138ᵛ; see also CARO P17/5/1, P22/5/2–3, P26/5/1, P30/4/1–2, P49/5/1, P76/5/14–9, R51/32/1, P67/5/1, P68/5/1; BL Add. MS 15672/441.

196 G. Bernard, 'The Church of England c. 1529–c. 1642', *History* (1990), 199, surely exaggerates the popularity of the rail.

197 *LJ* iv. 392.

198 See section ii.

199 LPL MS 943/481–497; HLRO /Feb. 6 1641/7; LRO Louth St J/7/5/95; Bodl. Rawl. D. 353/159; NNRO Sun/4/Mar. 1640; ERO D/ACA 52 (1637)/56.

200 For related rating problems see Ch. 2 n. 162.

their parish or chancel.[201] In the fourth place, innovations beyond the metropolitical order but associated with it might occur which could complicate and colour the local response; innovations such as the expensive redecoration of chancels, the levelling of pews, the removal of tombs and impropriatorial seats, and the reorientation of other furniture.[202] As a rule, the more innovations there were the more costly they were, although the rail alone might be sufficiently burdensome to parishes who were already feeling the pressure of other financial exactions. So expensive was the rail to Norfolk and Suffolk that D'Ewes reckoned it was 'to the extreme oppression of the poor inhabitants (whose souls already groaned under the burthens of the Ship-money tax)' and 'amounted unto between thirty and forty thousand pounds, at an indifferent and reasonable estimate and computation'.[203] Finally, there were more overt considerations of principle and conscience, which in many individual cases were as important in creating disaffection. Opposition to the rail or metropolitical order might stem from theological objections, in particular that the innovations represented or encouraged idolatry of the sacraments.[204] Others expressed a more constitutional line: that it deprived the parishioners of the right to position the table and to receive communion in a certain place; that it denied them the facility of hearing or seeing the celebration; and that it prevented the minister from standing at the north side, contrary to statute, the Prayer Book, the canons, or the prescriptive practice of the parish.[205] Any such opposition mirrored awareness of issues of principle at the grassroots level, which reflected a wider constituency than the locality. But perhaps it is in Laud's reservations about the metropolitical order, in

[201] ERO D/ACA 52/165^v, D/ACA 53/49, 64^v, 104^v; GL 4423/1/150; Bodl. Tanner 68/198; see also Ch. 2 n. 156–65; Epilogue, nn. 71, 74.

[202] For a small sample: DTRO PE/LOB P47/CW1/10; PRO SP 16/395/54, 16/259/78, 16/426/71, 16/398/99; *WWL* vi. 459; Clarendon, i. 199–202; HLRO 1641 Feb. 23/20; Bodl. Rawl. 220/2; DPD Corr. Bk. 1635–6/11; SRO D/D/Ca 295/154^v; Collinson, *RP* 188; see also Ch. 2 nn. 156–65; Epilogue, nn. 71, 74. (In the dioceses of Bath and Wells, and Coventry and Lichfield, Piers and Wright rigorously pressed the purchase (sometimes costly) of organs and clocks: SRO D/D/Ca 315/181^v, D/D/Ca 281/139^v, D/D/Sasa Se 14/41^v; and relevant parish refs. for the two dioceses (in bibliography under DBRO, LJRO, SFRO, SHRO, SRO and WARO).

[203] D'Ewes, *Autobiography*, ii. 142; Clarendon, i. 199–202.

[204] ESRO Dunn MS 52/7–14.

[205] E. Kellet, *Tricoenium Christi in Nocte Proditionis Suae* (1641), 81–2; HLRO/Ap. 1640/78; PRO SP 16/445/22(1); Rushworth, i. 197; LPL 943/479, 481–497; *CJ* 275; HLRO Pet./22 Dec. 1640/Upton; Bodl. MS Tanner 89/172; PRO SP 16/314/130, 16/427/30, 16/499/14.

particular over its mode of introduction and enforcement, that we find the most salient evidence for its dubious legality, and the scruples to which it gave rise.

III. THE LAUDIAN ALTAR POLICY

In historiography, the Laudian policy is seen as one of total acquiescence to the full tenor of the metropolitical order. Yet that order cannot be seen as quintessentially 'Laudian' when the archbishop only half-heartedly enforced it. There was a Laudian altar policy but this is not the one identified in historiography. Nor can a 'Laudian' policy be considered as the base-line of activity. That base-line has to be the policy sanctioned by the king and Wren in the metropolitical order, from which all ordinaries differed in degree, in the object and intensity of their enforcement. Ultimately the king himself must take responsibility for the metropolitical order, in whose genesis and enforcement he was heavily involved and implicated.[206] 'Ordinary' activity is distorted if seen through an adversarial framework of Laud versus Williams, or Arminian versus Calvinist. Those designated as 'Puritans' or 'Calvinists' might pursue a line of enforcement, with respect to the metropolitical order, which was similar if not in some respects more rigorous than Laud's. Obedience to the metropolitical order was obedience to the Supreme Governor of the Church rather than to Laud, or to any ecclesiastical faction.[207]

Lord Dacre once described Laud's policy as a preference 'for repression over the slow process of education'.[208] This was far from Laud's own ideas and actions. If we are to speak of the Laudian altar policy as repressive, hurried, impatient then Laud's policy is not 'Laudian'. In Canterbury he started court proceedings later than virtually all other ordinaries of the Southern Province. He believed that to rush the policy was to fail to win the affection of the country for the very 'decency' of the alteration. Even when he enforced the rail systematically through the courts after December 1637 he refrained from using heavy court censures or the force of compulsion. The two practices which he must have realized would take

[206] WTRO 562/2/118; PRO SP 16/351/18; Heylyn, *CA* 288; PRO SP/16/474/60; *Parentalia*, 98; see Ch. 1 section ii.

[207] LPL MS 1030/65–7, 68(b), 97.

[208] Trevor-Roper, *Archbishop Laud*, 435.

longer to effect—the altarwise position and receiving at the rails—he did not enforce through the courts but only encouraged, by pointing out the basis of the one in the Injunctions and by suggesting the decency of the other.[209] At the censure of Prynne, Bastwick, and Burton he spoke with truth of the way in which he had prosecuted the altarwise position: 'and yet here is nothing done either by violence or command, to take off the indifferency of the standing of the holy table either way, but laying it fairly before men, how fit it is there should be order and uniformity: I say still reserving the indifferency of the standing.'[210] In its own way the 'Laudian' altar policy was as distinct as Williams's. Laud's major problem was how to contain pent-up enthusiasm on the episcopal bench and within the parishes for a frontal attack on the Jacobean Church. Among contemporary commentators, Clarendon realized that some of the bishops had acted 'with more passion and less circumspection than they had (for) his example . . . or than he approved'.[211] Many ordinaries, however, clearly did not share Laud's conviction that the force of ecclesiastical censure should not be used to obtain compliance. Among those who resorted to heavy ecclesiastical censure were Piers, Montagu, Goodman, Towers, Wren, and Juxon's commissaries in London. The last three excommunicated for not receiving at the rails. Where they did not excommunicate they resorted to compulsion. Clergy were encouraged not to administer outside the rails and to present offenders who would not come up. This policy was clearly contrary to Laud's instructions and his own views on receiving at the rails.[212] Why then did Laud take no action to prevent the use of force and repression? Clearly it was difficult for Laud to scrutinize the activities of all the ordinaries within their respective jurisdictions. Moreover, with reservations about the metropolitical order, and unsure of its legal implications, he was probably disinclined to get too heavily embroiled in its enforcement. Yet there was a more important reason, for there can be little doubt that the king, as the essential draftsman of the altar policy, and with his liking for receiving at the rails in

[209] See Ch. 4 nn. 111–26. [210] *WWL* vi. 59. [211] Clarendon, i. 128.

[212] NNRO SUN/4/1; Bodl. Tanner MS 68/33ᵛ, 116, 198, 332ᵛ–3; PRO SP 16/437/91; LPL MS 943/283; GL 9537/15/24ᵛ: Hedingham D/29ᵛ–30; Dunmow D./35; Lexton D./22; Dengie D/19; Newport D./41ᵛ; GLRO D2/C/343/184; ERO D/ACA 51/252ᵛ, D/AEA 41/245–252ᵛ, D/ACA 53/17; D/ACA 52/17–18, 104, 208–18, 227, 243–50; *The Vindication of . . . Daniel Whitby*, 3; LRO 1RD41/13/64/50, 114.

particular, was giving free rein to the antics of those advocating hawkish solutions, in particular Wren, his dean of the Chapel.

In January 1637 Laud complained to Charles of the trouble caused in the southern parts of the diocese of Lincoln over ministers urging communicants to receive at the rails. Both Williams and Laud on this occasion turned to the king for advice because the practice was not canonical. That Laud liked the practice cannot be denied, but he asked the king whether he wished him to adopt a more stringent policy. The king's marginalia are revealing. Charles ordered him to try 'your' way for the time being.[213] Clearly the king's ear was open to advice other than Laud's, and to advice which offered a stricter path of enforcement. It is not at all unlikely that towards the second half of 1637 (at a time when he was tightening the screw of conformity generally) Charles ordered the bishops to intensify their enforcement of the metropolitical order.[214] As late as May 1637 Laud's more moderate line may still have had some sanction. During that month Wren temporarily ordered his chancellor not to excommunicate those who refused to receive at the rail, a momentary and belated change in the bishop's policy, which came too late as Corbet had already inflicted heavy censures on Wren's former orders.[215] But clearly Wren could justify a more stringent enforcement by claiming the particular support of the king and the sanction of the order: in 1636 Charles had 'highly approved' of Wren's enforcement of receiving at the rail and when he received a petition against Wren's forceful action he answered it by informing the bishop to continue pressing 'all canonical obedience'.[216]

The issue of receiving at the rail was so controversial that few bishops enforced or pressed it. It was 'a new, unnecessary troublesome course, not enjoined by laws, not required by canon', Montagu informed Laud.[217] That Laud himself never enforced it suggests that he did not seek the order in March 1634. It seems that the archbishop was even prepared to shelter his diocesans from the king's affection for the practice, and their reluctance to press it. In his

213 LPL MS 943/267, 283; LPL MS 1030/52.

214 This helps to explain why Laud should feel the need to make a statement (which the king published, against Laud's wishes, *WWL* vi. 37) at Prynne's prosecution, clarifying his position on the metropolitical changes (*WWL* vi. 59) while nevertheless shielding his limited enforcement of the requirement. See also *CSPD 1637*, 84.

215 Bodl. Tanner MS 68/235.

216 Bodl. Tanner MS 70/103–4; LPL MS 943/283; see also *Parentalia*, 98.

217 LPL MS 943/619.

account of 1638, Laud seemed to condone Wren's activity and to pander to the king's liking for the practice: 'when your Majesty first heard of this business in (Wren's) time you highly approved it therefore I presume you will be pleased to command that the present bishop (Montagu) continue it, and look carefully to it.'[218] That this was mere verbal subterfuge suggests itself from Laud's inaction: he never did order Montagu to force communicants to receive at the rail, and in October 1639 Montagu drew up for the diocese of Norwich orders for the reception of communion in the chancel and not at the rail—orders which Montagu then passed to Laud for his approval.[219] Under cover of the king's belief that his archbishop was pressing receiving at the rail, Laud sanctioned a more moderate policy which allowed a measure of 'convenience' in the reception of the communion. As Laud said at his trial: 'I pressed no one to come up to receive at the rails, no further than the Prayer Book prescribes, which enjoins the people to draw near and to take the Holy Sacrament for their comfort.'[220]

Laud's action in the court of Arches in three appeals emanating from the archdeaconry of Huntingdon fully bears out this statement. In 1639, the rector of Welwyn in Hertfordshire refused to administer the sacrament to certain parishioners as they knelt in the chancel. With no hearing from the archidiaconal court, they appealed to Laud. In his determination Laud ordered the rector to administer the sacrament to those kneeling 'though it be in any part of the chancel, leaving only such to come to the rail and receive as are willing to do . . . the people, being conformable to the laws of the realm . . . canons and rubric of the Church'.[221] In the case of St Ives, in Huntingdonshire, a small number of people, who previously had received at the rails, refused late in 1639. Both minister and recusants appealed to Laud. His answer, delivered by Lambe, again shows his respect for the individual circumstance. As most of the St Ives congregation, about eight hundred in all, had received at the rails for three years, he encouraged the recalcitrant members to return again to the rails, but only through 'fair persuasion' as 'where both unity and uniformity, may be preserved, it is fit the peace of the

[218] LPL MS 943/283. Wren was still prosecuting parishioners for not receiving at the rail in Ely diocese as late as December 1640: HLRO Pet./11 Dec. 1640/Prior.

[219] LPL MS 943/631; NNRO FCB/5/24.

[220] Prynne, *CD* 488.

[221] PRO SP 16/417/16; SJC S. 37(27).

Church be kept'.[222] But it is in the last case, that of Walkern in Hertfordshire, that Laud's latitude most clearly reveals itself. In October 1637, Thomas Humberstone and his wife petitioned their diocesan Williams against their parson Gorsuch, because he refused to administer to them in the chancel and only at the rails. Williams refused to hear Gorsuch's case, with the result that Gorsuch then appealed to Laud. The archbishop's consummate response was to side with Williams against the irritable minister. He suppressed Gorsuch's suit in the Arches, commanded Lambe never to admit his appeal again, and ordered Gorsuch to administer to the parishioners in the chancel; he was to act in the future only in a 'peaceable and Christian-like way'.[223]

As the Walkern incident shows, the problem of whether compulsion should be used to force receiving at the rails was related to the issue of whether clergy should leave the rails to administer in the chancel. In his instructions to Brent in March 1634, Laud had sanctioned this latter policy.[224] Yet by 1637, in Norwich and London, the courts were ordering ministers not to go down into the chancel. That this had the king's explicit backing is not in question as 'the king's injunctions' had ordered priests not to leave the rails, if people refused to come up. It was this refusal to administer the sacrament outside the rails which eventually brought the clergy into contempt of secular justice.[225] In August 1639 Aylett reported to Lambe that at the Chelmsford sessions, indictments were successfully lodged against several Essex ministers for refusing to come out of the rails. In Suffolk, there was also an attempt to indict local clergy, but Lord Chief Bramston refused to admit the suits into the lay courts. Similarly, in neighbouring Hertford, Sir Robert Berkeley quashed indictments presented against the clergy of St Alban's. However, in Essex the Chelmsford jury justified its bold action by saying that they had none other than Laud's sanction for the indictment. Aylett was told that 'the greatest argument they had for it was that my Lord of Canterbury had ordered otherwise and that these (ministers) . . . had insolently disobeyed the archbishop's order'.[226] The rumour that

222 PRO SP 16/442/84, 138; PRO SP 16/444/79–81; PRO SP 16/445/22.

223 PRO SP 16/370/6i–iv. 224 PRO SP 16/427/30.

225 ERO D/ACA 51/252^{v}; *HMC Appendix to the 9th Report*, 498 (28 Feb. 1640); PRO SP 16/474/60; some of the Norwich clergy who refused to administer the sacraments claimed the authorization of the king: MS Tanner 220/3–10.

226 PRO SP 16/427/30; *Northcote*, 55; *Articles against Sir Robert Berkeley*.

Laud himself was opposed not just to the way in which some courts prosecuted the metropolitical order, but to the very order itself, was clearly gaining ground in the localities. In fact as early as May 1639 it was openly reported in Peterborough diocese that 'the Archbishop hath renounced ... having a hand in bringing ... up to the rail to receive the sacrament.' [227]

Apart from Laud's personal reservations about the order, its mode of introduction and enforcement, his dilemma stemmed from the fact that once the ordinaries' rights were asserted, they might carry out policies and countenance actions which he himself found unacceptable. At the same time the metropolitical order was an invitation to individual clerical licence. It is apparent, therefore, that we have confused Laud's more moderate policies with the independent and provocative activities of some ministers (such as those who appear in the scandalous ministers reports) and the policies of some ordinaries, in particular Wren.[228] Historiographical 'Laudianism' is none other than the policy which Wren conducted in Norwich and Ely after 1636; a policy in which he employed full court censure, inquired into hundreds of particulars and ordered many innovations. Corbet, his chancellor, described it neatly as '*censura in summo gradu (suspensa et excommunicatio) prestant potius quam moritio et disputatio*'.[229] In a little-known work, however, Heylyn reprimanded Fuller for failing to discriminate between the policies of Wren and Laud, and for accusing the archbishop of pressing uncanonical practices upon the nation: 'it had been better if he had told us, what those private practices and opinions were which the Archbishop with such a want of moderation did enjoin on others?' Fuller in his reply stood down and confessed, 'this my expression did eye another person related to Bishop Andrewes, whom I forbear to name except by the Animadvertor's reply unto me, I be forced thereto.'[230] The policies which Wren pursued at Norwich and Ely, and which the king had sanctioned in the metropolitical order and forced upon the country, were in fact none other than those which Lancelot Andrewes, his former patron, had practised in his private chapel.

[227] *HMC Appendix to the 9th Report*, 496–7.
[228] For 'scandalous ministers' see *PCR*, *passim*; White, *Scandalous Priests*, *passim*; BL Add. MS 156721, 441, MS 15670/169, MS 22084/2, 4, 8, 9^v, ii^v; *Northcote*, 5; D. Hoyle, 'A Commons Investigation of Arminianism and Popery in Cambridge on the Eve of the Civil War', *Historical Journal*, 29/2 (1986).
[229] Bodl. Tanner MS 68/1. [230] Fuller, *AII* iii. 8.

7
THE CANONS OF 1640

> The general vote of the people will inform you that episcopacy lies at stake ... I dare not (I abhor the thought of it) justify the doings of many bishops least I should not only be patron of wickedness but even of ... novelty. I dare not condemn episcopacy itself as Antichristian and the reverend fathers of the Church as petty popes least I should censure antiquitie ... I commend the success of all to God.
>
> (Thomas Hodges to William Sancroft, 7 Dec. 1640: Bodl. MS Tanner 467/78)

I. THE DISSOLUTION OF THE SHORT PARLIAMENT

In April 1640 it was reported that when the king prayed at the Abbey before opening the new session of Parliament, the 'people cried amen so loud that it made his head-ache'. Their hopes foundered, for a month later, on 5 May 1640, the Short Parliament came to a premature end, without achieving any of the constructive aims for which it had convened. Convocation, which had met at the same time, was due (as was customary) to end on the following day.[1] The clergy had achieved possibly less than Parliament. Charles had commissioned canons from them but within three weeks they had drawn up only a few drafts. They had approved a grant of £20,000 to be paid to the king over six years but they had not worked out any procedure for its collection or assessment.[2] Such a grant might ease the king's financial predicament but it could only worsen the already uneasy relationship that existed between Parliament on the one side and the king and the Church on the other. On 17 April, within a few days of Charles issuing letters patent to the clergy commissioning them to

[1] *HMC Portland iii*, 62; Rushworth, iii. 1144, 1147; PRO SP 16/450/195.

[2] LPL Conv. MS 1/2/2/37; Nalson, i. 362; Heylyn, *CA* 424; *The Records of the Northern Convocation*, ed. G. W. Kitchin (Surtees Soc., 113, 1907), 303.

deliberate upon canons, the House of Commons set up a committee to question the procedure. They claimed that the king had not used the correct channels of communication; that his letters were neither enrolled nor sent out under the signet or the Privy Seal, but rested merely on his own peremptory commands to Convocation.[3] Apart from the issue of impropriety, some Members of Parliament clearly feared that Convocation would make permanent those ecclesiastical changes of the 1630s which they wished to undo. Before and during its session, the Short Parliament had received several petitions from various parts of the country complaining against the innovations and abuses in ecclesiastical government. At the same time several members wished to voice their own grievances against the clergy or the courts.[4] Motivated on the one hand by a desire to put the clock back and on the other by a very conscious fear that their liberties were under attack, the Commons issued a statement that unless Parliament ratified the Canons, they would not recognize them.[5] Thus even before Charles I decided to continue Convocation beyond the Short Parliament (in May 1640), the Commons had disputed his right to call and dissolve Convocation and to commission canons from the clergy without parliamentary approval. This was a novel principle in the constitutional debate, for Elizabethan and Jacobean Parliaments had never sanctioned nor ratified the formulation of canons.[6]

Within Convocation there were mixed reactions to the king's letters of April 15 inviting the clergy to formulate canons.[7] Some of the clergy thought that Parliament would certainly find an increase of clerical power offensive, after eleven years without Convocation, and after a decade of unparliamentary innovations. According to Fuller, some harboured fears also that those who had exceeded the Canons of 1604 by 'ceremonising more than was enjoined' would attempt to

[3] Rushworth, iii. 1144, 1147; LPL MS 577/254; *CJ* (1640), 9.

[4] *The Short Parliament Diary of Sir Thomas Aston*, ed. J. D. Maltby (Camden, 4th ser., 1988), 35; *CJ* (1640), 9. Five days after the dissolution of the Short Parliament, on 10 May, the Council imprisoned John Crew, who had chaired the Commons committee of investigation into the Caroline innovations: Rushworth, iii. 1168, 1196.

[5] Rushworth, iii. 1144, 1147. Relations between the Short Parliament and Convocation were aggravated by the revelation that Dr Beale (Master of St John's, Cambridge) had preached that the king could make laws without Parliament: PRO SP/16/450/94.

[6] PRP SP 16/450/195. As Laud recognized (*WWL* vii. 6): 'the Canons have no other confirmation than the broad seal'. PRO SP 16/474/79 shows that he carefully studied the objections levelled against the Canons of 1604.

[7] PRO SP 16/450/195; LPL MS 577/254.

make their practices canonical and press others to 'do voluntarily what they had pre-practised themselves'.[8] Given these reservations, perhaps a considerable proportion of its members welcomed the end of Convocation.

On 5 May Laud voted at the council table for the dissolution of the Short Parliament, and shortly afterwards sent an order to Convocation to dissolve itself on the following day as was the customary procedure.[9] Yet Laud did not send with this order any writ for dissolution.[10] The reason he gave for this in his trial was simple forgetfulness, which may well have been genuine. Laud, after all, had never presided in Convocation and the last Convocation had sat in 1629.[11] Yet it was a remarkable oversight. Whatever the reason for the omission, within a few hours representatives from Convocation approached the archbishop while at the council table and asked him for a writ.[12] Laud sought from the king a formal writ of dissolution, but received instead what he called an 'unlooked for reply'.[13] Instead of dissolving Convocation Charles had decided to continue it beyond the parliamentary session in order to obtain the subsidies and the canons. Evidently surprised by this decision, Laud pointed out that such a course would be 'excepted against in all likelihood' by many people and he 'desired (him) to advise well upon it'.[14] But the king was fixed in his purpose and had already consulted the Lord Keeper, Finch, about the legal propriety of the act to which Finch had given his assent.[15] Laud received this news as a snub because in an issue directly concerning the privileges of Convocation, the king had not bothered to consult his archbishop.[16]

Charles had clearly decided to continue Convocation regardless of

[8] Fuller, *CH* 406–7. [9] *WWL* iii. 284–5. [10] *WWL* iii. 285.

[11] Ibid. Concerning the Convocation of 1629 and Laud's unfamiliarity with procedures, see PRO SP 16/45/73.

[12] *WWL* iii. 285. [13] Ibid.

[14] Ibid.; HLRO MS Braye 8/30 and also *WWL* iv. 153: 'Nor was this sitting continued by any advice or desire of mine. For I humbly desired a writ to dissolve us; but the best counsel then present assured the king we might legally sit.' Although Laud believed that the continuation of Convocation was a provocative act, he could not object to its continuation in principle; he believed like the other bishops that the calling and dismissal of Convocation rested solely with the royal prerogative. In 1637 he had compiled a volume of texts showing that ecclesiastical synods had formulated canons without parliamentary interference: *WWL* iii. 228; *CSPV 1636–39*, 156; LPL MS 323 (the volume in question).

[15] *WWL* iii. 285. [16] Ibid.

any support which could be brought to reinforce his action. At this time he was possibly unaware of a document discovered by Heylyn, which revealed that the Convocation of 1586 had granted Elizabeth I a benevolence outside parliamentary time, and which Heylyn certainly made known as soon as Parliament was dissolved.[17] In fact it seems not at all unlikely that even before he went to the Lords to dissolve Parliament on 5 May, Charles I had already decided to continue Convocation. His dissolution speech belies what appears to be a thinly veiled sarcasm, the significance of which would not be lost on parliamentarians in the days ahead. He told the House that he would be 'more careful (as I am most concerned) in the preservation of that purity of religion which I thank God is established in the Church of England. And I shall be as careful *out of parliament* as in parliament to do that. My lords I shall not trouble you long with words, it is not my fashion.'[18] Clearly Charles had made up his mind to obtain both the subsidies and the canons. Moreover he wished to challenge the recently espoused claim of the Commons that the Convocation sat and made canons only with parliamentary sanction. Within a few days the king had issued a new commission under the great seal allowing the clergy to continue in session, but this differed from the former commission in one significant respect. Charles added the words '*durante bene placito*': he wished to make it categorically clear to Parliament that it was his prerogative alone to call and dismiss Convocation, when and how he pleased.[19]

According to Fuller, the general expectation within Convocation on 5 May was that they were to meet on the day after the parliamentary dissolution (as was customary) only 'to part and finally dissolve themselves'.[20] Instead they received an order to adjourn until 9

[17] Barnard, *TH* 180–1; Heylyn, *EH* 233; Heylyn, *CA* 429, 440; *WWL* iii. 285.

[18] *The Short Parliament Diary of Sir Thomas Aston*, 145; Bodl. MS Clarendon (SP) 18/1379. This interpretation is confirmed by the fact that in Privy Council on 12 May 1640 (the day on which the new commission was issued) Charles I said that he 'intended *according to his . . . speech* delivered at the dissolution . . . to continue the sitting of the Convocation House for sometime . . . which his Majesty's . . . declaration and resolution the Lords [of the Council] having by his command taken into due consideration, after a serious debate they unanimously approved' (PRO SP 16/453/14; Rushworth, iii. 1172).

[19] LPL Conv. MS 1/1/1/66; PRO SP 16/453/15; LPL MS 577/256; Heylyn, *EH* 229. Was it merely coincidental that these were the same words which Charles had inserted (instead of '*quamdiu bene se gesserint*') into the commissions of the two judges who had ruled against him in the ship-money case? L. Hutchinson, *Memoirs of the Life of Colonel Hutchinson*, ed. J. Sutherland (Oxf., 1973), 48.

[20] Fuller, *CH* 407.

May, which was then extended until 13 May, during which time some clergy within the Lower House apparently motioned that they should finish the canons upon which they had embarked.[21] When the new commission arrived thirty-six clergy (about a quarter of the House) led by four archdeacons, Brownrigg of Coventry, Hacket of Bedford, Holdsworth of Huntingdon, and Westfield of St Alban's, protested against the continuation of Convocation, claiming that such an action was unprecedented and bound to provoke parliamentary wrath, unless new writs of election were issued.[22] Outside there were even more disturbing signs of protest. On 6 May the London apprentices met in St George's Field to hunt 'William the Fox for breach of parliament', while six days later they descended upon Lambeth Palace.[23] Confronted by the strength of the opposition within and outside Convocation, Laud advised Charles to seek the advice of his Council learned in law as to whether the clergy should continue any further.[24] Within a few days, on 15 May, Vane, Secretary of State, appeared in Convocation bearing a legal instrument signed by the Lord Privy Seal, the two Chief Justices, and two other law lords approving the continuation of Convocation. With this document, Vane conveyed a personal message from the king, intimating that if any member should leave the House 'it would incur his greatest displeasure'.[25] Only the day before, Peterson, dean of Exeter, had asked Laud for permission to leave, only to find that the archbishop threatened him 'in a very sharpe and severe manner if (he) did further mention (his) departure'.[26]

According to Fuller the legal instrument pacified the thirty-six protesters, who thereafter accepted the legality of the proceedings.[27] In the following days Charles surrounded Westminster Abbey (where Convocation sat) with several companies of the Middlesex trained bands, under the charge of Endymion Porter. 'To such extremities were the poor clergy brought during these confusions,' declared

[21] Heylyn, *CA* 429; Fuller, *CH* 406; Heylyn, *EH* 229; *HMC Portland iii*, 63.

[22] Heylyn, *EH* 230; Fuller, *CH* 406; Fuller, *AH* iii. 32–5.

[23] *WWL* iii. 284. [24] *WWL* iii. 286.

[25] LPL MS 577/256; LPL MS 1061/4–4v, MS Conv. 1/1/1/67.

[26] Bodl. MS Walker c. 4/224. No copy of any canon could be made nor was there to be any discussion outside the House about the proposals: Ch. Ch. Wake MS 306/389.

[27] Fuller, *CH* 406–7; Heylyn, *EH* 231. On 28 May 1640, however, Archdeacon Byng of Norwich lodged a formal protest against the continuation of proceedings and the formulation of the canons: Ch. Ch. Wake MS 306/391.

Heylyn, 'in danger of the king's displeasure if they rose, and of the people's fury if they sat.'[28] Yet this was far from the sum of Charles's intervention. On 20 May he sent a further letter to Convocation asking them to proceed to the levying of the six subsidies which they had previously approved but requiring them, on the advice of the Council learned in law, to alter the word 'subsidy' in the original grant to 'benevolence', as subsidies could be approved only by Parliament.[29]

The pressing and controversial task of revising the book of subsidies was given to Bishops Hall and Wren, Archdeacons Paske of London and Wilson of Westminster, Heylyn, and Lambe. There appears to have been confusion over whether the resulting book was issued as a separate canonical draft or just as an order of the House. Furthermore Archdeacon Holdsworth said that he never heard it 'read first nor last'.[30] Although a majority of the House voted in favour of the benevolence, no subscriptions were elicited, and some remained stalwartly opposed to the initiative, such as Peterson, dean of Exeter. Bishop Hall, however, did not accept his son-in-law's contention. He believed that Convocation's action was justified by the king's financial necessity, regardless of whether the precedent provided by the benevolence of 1586 validated its present action.[31]

II. THE CANONS OF 1640

The Convocation of 1640 promulgated in all seventeen canons. Three evolved formally within the Upper House (those on popery, the Royal Supremacy, and rites) and thirteen within the Lower House (concerning ecclesiastical jurisdiction, the conversation of the clergy, Socinianism, separatism, the book of visitation articles, and the day of the king's inauguration). Canon 6, which contained the notorious *et cetera* oath, emanated officially from the king.[32]

[28] P. Heylyn, *Observations on the History of the Reign of King Charles* (1650), 181; Heylyn, *CA* 429.

[29] Heylyn, *CA* 429, 440; Fuller, *CH* 407–8; PRO SP 16/450/13.

[30] LPL MS 943/599; Bodl. MS Clarendon (SP) 19/1448–9.

[31] Bodl. MS Walker c. 4/224; J. Jones, *A Life of Joseph Hall* (1826), 252; *WJH* viii. 280. For collection of benevolence see C. Hibbard 'Episcopal warriors in the British wars of religion', in *War and Government in Britain, 1598–1650*, ed. M. Fissel (Manch. 1991), 164–93.

[32] PRO SP 16/455/47 (the original book of canons with subscriptions); *WWL* v.

Throughout the 1630s Laud was morbidly conscious of the popular accusations of popery levelled against himself and his fellow bishops. Yet he had spoken out against the conversions at court and within London more vociferously than any other councillor, and on occasions had begged the king on his knees to expel the main proselytizers.[33] But Laud's opposition to Rome stemmed less from any pronounced personal anti-popery than from his conviction that conversions to Rome would advertise the fact that the Anglican Church was seriously deficient as a true Church. The main theme of Laud's *Conference with Fisher the Jesuit* was to show that the Church of England was a purer expression of catholicity than Rome.[34] At the same time he believed that increasing conversions to Rome would misrepresent (as they did) the changes of the 1630s. The irony of Laud's position was that he believed that there existed a popish plot which would result in his own and the king's assassination. Thus it comes as little surprise that the first measure upon which Laud asked the Lower House to debate was for the formulation of a canon to stem the rise of popery and to restrict the activities of recusants.[35] On the return of the draft from the lower clergy, Laud sent Wren and Skinner to consult with the Lord Chief Justice of the Common Pleas over its legal implications, an unusual condescension on Laud's part to the common law.[36] Yet not every one was pleased with the final canon. Holdsworth thought that it was not as restrictive as existing statute, it being 'too great an honour to the papist to affirm them the freedom of solemn conferences'. Instead he would have preferred that Convocation had petitioned the king to put into execution all existing laws against recusancy, which Charles I was clearly reluctant to do.[37]

607–33; Heylyn, *CA* 430–3; LPL MS 577/269; LPL Conv. 1/2/2/7–32 and 1/1/1/19–34 give lists of all members present within both Houses of the Southern Convocation. For those present within the Northern Convocation see *The Records of the Northern Convocation*, ed. Kitchen, 299–303. See also appendix. As far as the formulation of canons was concerned, the Northern Convocation ratified what the Southern agreed: Bodl. Clarendon MS (SP) 20/1528.

[33] Knowler, ii. 74, 128, 165; Knowler, i. 426; Heylyn, *EH* 260. For Laud's prosecution of recusants within his own diocese see CCL Z/3/14/41.

[34] *WWL* iii. 414–15; *WWL* ii (the Conference). Bodl. MS 888 (partly in Laud's hand) seems to be part of the unfinished Latin edition.

[35] Nalson, i. 362; LPL Conv. MS ix/2/4; Heylyn, *CA* 425.

[36] Nalson, i. 367; *Synodalia*, ii. 619. The draft of the Lower House was drawn up probably by the Prolocutor (Steward), Deans Bargrave of Canterbury and Winniffe of St Paul's, Archdeacons Burgess of Rochester and Cluett of Middlesex: Ch. Ch. Wake MS 306/356.

[37] *WWL* v. 616–20; LPL MS 943/599; PRO SP 16/259/78 suggests that the king

Apart from canon 3, two others originated among the bishops—canon 7, concerning rites and canon 1, explaining the divine right of kings. The bishops compiled a series of six propositions concerning *iure divino* kingship, which they then passed on to the Lower House for approval.[38] The prolocutor of Convocation, Richard Steward (Charles's clerk of the Closet) and Laud's chaplain, Edward Martin (procurator for the clergy of Ely) appear to have played some part in the formulation of the two most controversial heads, the first declaring divine right and the last, justifying the necessity of supply.[39] The propositions declared that the order of kings was sacred and of divine right, founded on Scripture and the laws of nature, and that the protection of the Church and the calling of Convocation rested firmly in royal hands. The fourth and fifth clauses, drawn with particular reference to the Scottish rebellion, proclaimed that it was treason against God and the king to set up any independent co-active power (whether papal or popular) and that to bear arms against the king, even in defence, was to resist the powers ordained of God. The very controversial sixth proposition appears to have caused more opposition in the Lower House than the others. It declared that financial supply was due to kings from their subjects according to the 'law of God, Nature, Nations'.[40] Thus what had previously been an occasionally espoused principle of Elizabeth I and James I to impress their authority had become, under their successor, canonically binding. Some of the clergy, fearful of offending Parliament, thought it better to lodge the royal right to supply not on the law of God or Nature, but on the laws of 'several countries'.[41] Others, including Holdsworth and Brownrigg, felt that the whole canon should be referred to the judges for legal approval before confirmation.[42]

thought that Neile's proceedings against recusants in the Northern Province were too stringent.

[38] *WWL* v. 613–15, 624–6; LPL Conv. MS ix/2/3, Conv. ix/2/9.

[39] Heylyn, *CA* 431–2; Nalson, i. 368.

[40] *WWL* v. 613–15; Heylyn, *CA* 431–2.

[41] Heylyn, *CA* 430–2. The objection to this clause was similar to Abbot's objection to the very similar clause in Sibthorpe's *Apostolike Obedience* (1627), a clause which may have influenced the wording of this canon in 1640; see Rushworth, i. 442 and Bodl. MS Sancroft 18/21–2.

[42] LPL MS 943/599. Among other opponents of this measure were probably Young, dean of Winchester, Ward, archdeacon of Taunton, and Smith, procurator for Bath and Wells: Ch. Ch. Wake MS 306/391. Edward Bagshawe thought this first canon contrary to law, suggesting that it contravened the judges' right to expound the prerogative powers, and invested the Crown with absolute powers. In support of this

The formulation of a canon in 1640 expounding the divine right of kings is not very surprising. Both Charles and Laud visualized *iure divino* episcopacy as a corollary of *iure divino* kingship. Charles for his own part had used the Church to impress upon the country his elevated notion of monarchy, as much as Laud had used the Royal Supremacy to impress upon the Church his conception of episcopacy. During the Convocation Laud may well have presented to the bishops similar propositions concerning divine-right episcopacy.[43] In 1640, together with his *Episcopacy by Divine Right Asserted*, Hall passed to Laud propositions on this very theme for possible inclusion in the work.[44] However, Laud felt that they were better left out and suggested that they might be presented to the bishops during Convocation, although whether as a canon to balance the divine right of kingship remains conjectural.[45]

According to Fuller, shortly after the dissolution of Parliament the Lower House of Convocation contracted into a select committee of twenty-seven with the intention of speeding up proceedings.[46] No member of the House was excluded from being present at the debates of this committee and its decisions were not binding unless first put to the vote of the Lower House, if necessary three times.[47] However, the very existence of the committee meant that discussion of the canons was limited, and that those excluded from openly debating the issues felt that there was insufficient time to study the proposals before the vote of the whole House. Dean Peterson of Exeter said that he desired 'to see the acts before the vote passed the House, at least three times... so that he might maturely advise on them, but he was put off with delays and told they could never obtain that knowledge'.[48] Yet the committee was elected by the Lower House and was not a packed body. Among its members were several clergy out of step with some of the developments of the past decade, such as Archdeacons Brownrigg, Hacket, and Holdsworth, and Fuller, clerk for Bristol, who did not publish the fact of his member-

he appealed to the recent Harrison case and James I's strictures on tyrants: 'those kings are either tyrants or perjurers that govern not according to their law, and that those who persuaded them to do otherwise are vipers and pests both to king and parliament': *Two Arguments in Parliament* (1641), 14.

[43] *WWL* vi. 575–6; iv. 309–11. [44] *WWL* vi. 575–6. [45] Ibid.

[46] Fuller, *CH* 407; Ch. Ch. Wake MS 306/391, 370; Heylyn, *EH* 233; Fuller, *AII* 40.

[47] Heylyn, *CA* 433–4; Fuller, *AII* iii. 40.

[48] Bodl. MS Walker c. 4/224.

ship.[49] Their presence on the board almost certainly served to moderate the more extreme inclinations of other members, especially over rites and ceremonies. The relative weighting of those who advocated consolidation of the changes of the past decade and those who wished their partial dismantling appears to have been almost balanced. When a decision was taken by the board in Holdsworth's absence, he believed that had he been present his representation could have swung opinion in a more moderate direction.[50] Later he contended the matter openly with Richard Steward, which resulted in his temporary removal from the proceedings on the prolocutor's order.[51]

The committee of twenty-seven met in Henry VII's chapel, around the table at which the bishops at other times debated the canons. According to Heylyn, their first function was to draw up a declaration establishing some uniformity in rites and ceremonies, in particular over the contentious issue of the position of the table and the reception of communion, which was then to form the basis for a canonical draft.[52] Each of the members spoke in turn, with Steward and Heylyn speaking first and last, and both almost certainly putting forward the king's views. In fact Heylyn declared his purpose to 'answer all such arguments as had been brought against any of the proposals'.[53] Fuller prepared a canon on rites for the approval of the board but according to Heylyn, this was written 'in such an imperious style . . . it was disliked by all the company but himself' with the result that the others drew up another canonical draft which they then submitted to the bishops, who may have altered it in the Upper House.[54]

Although Heylyn chose to belittle opposition to this particular canon, there may be truth in his statement that it was 'commended generally for its modesty and temper'.[55] In fact it represented a climb-down from the metropolitical order enforced by Wren in Norwich, and in various degrees by all other bishops during the 1630s. As such it vindicated a more moderate, Laudian approach and constituted a triumph for the rights of the ordinary, which Laud had

[49] Ch. Ch. Wake MS 306/391; Heylyn, *CA* 434; Nalson, i. 364; Fuller, *CH* 409; *Synodalia*, ii. 61–2.

[50] Heylyn, *CA* 434; LPL MS 943/599; Fuller, *AII* iii. 40.

[51] Ch. Ch. Wake MS 306/391 (for a possible list of committee members, to which should be added Heath and Lambe 306/370); Nalson, i. 364; *Synodalia*, ii. 61–2.

[52] Heylyn, *CA* 433–4; Ch. Ch. Wake MS 306/391; LPL Conv. MS ix/2/9.

[53] Heylyn, *CA* 433–4. [54] Ibid. [55] Ibid.

first championed in the St Gregory's case of 1633, but which the king had later reneged upon.[56] The bishop or ordinary could now position his table as he wished during communion, which although a salve to Wren, was a greater salve to the inclination of the other bishops. The rail finally achieved canonical recognition, but henceforth the table needed only to be 'decently severed' from the chancel.[57] Thus Wren's north–south rail was not endorsed, and those four- or three-sided rails, which kept alive the notion of 'communion' around the table, remained unaltered.[58] The practice of receiving at the rail, enforced by Wren and two other bishops in the 1630s, did not become canonical, as the canon asked communicants merely to 'draw near' and to receive in the chancel or the body of the church. The ordinary could even dispense with this in individual circumstances and allow reception in the nave or seats.[59] Some members of Convocation, such as Warmestry, clerk for Worcester, and Peterson, dean of Exeter, would object to any of the innovations of the 1630s whether moderate or extreme and they would remain unsatisfied until all were removed.[60] They could hardly agree that the position of the table was a matter of indifference especially since the canon adopted the Injunctions of 1559, and thus ordered the placing of the table altarwise outside communion. Holdsworth particularly objected to the practices of positioning the table altarwise, turning to the east, and bowing towards the table, and protested that instead of declaring what such practices meant, the canon (originally a declaration) recommended their adoption.[61] Although bowing was not to be canonically enforced (those who practised it were not to censure

[56] Ch. 6 sections i–iii; LPL 943/599.

[57] *WWL* v. 624–5. Clarendon noted that this canon was more moderate than what might have been expected, 'countenancing, though not enjoining, what had not been long practised': Clarendon, i. 273.

[58] See Ch. 6 n. 49.

[59] *WWL* v. 625. In spite of this canon, on 7 October 1640 the High Commission interrogated John Bradshaw, vicar of St Paul, Bedford, for leaving the rails and administering to the congregation in the church (possibly the first occasion when the Commission did so). He answered that 'I have not read in any of the new canons any binding injunction that the people should come up to the rails' (PRO SP 16/469/52). This, together with the fact that Laud had encouraged leaving the rails, suggests that by 7 October his influence on the High Commission had been eclipsed by those advocating more repressive expedients to quash dissent.

[60] Bodl. MS Walker c. 4/224; T. Warmestry, *A Convocation Speech... against the new Canons and the Oath* (1641). Warmestry had been one of Laud's metropolitical commissioners in the visitation of Worcester: LPL Reg. Laud 1/141.

[61] LPL MS 943/599.

those who did not, and vice versa) Fuller felt that it had become a qualification for holding office: 'the ceremony was left indifferent as hereafter to sanction but made necessary as here to preferment.'[62]

Apart from canon 6 which Convocation drew up at the express request of the king, the remaining thirteen canons all emanated from within the Lower House. Two of these were personal motions of Heylyn, clerk for Westminster: canon 2 which called for greater observance of the day of the king's accession, 27 March, and canon 9, which ordered the publication of a standard book of visitation articles, which would in effect make redundant the existing metropolitical visitation articles.[63] Canon 2 left Convocation open to the accusation that they had usurped Parliament's privilege to create new holy days and had thus effectively contravened the Henrician statutes limiting the number of such days. At the same time some Members of Parliament would object to the apostheosis of a king whose exalted notions of kingship they had come increasingly to dislike.[64]

According to Holdsworth, Convocation agreed unanimously that there should be a standard book of articles in order to prevent the future appearance of controversial queries.[65] In fact shortly after Heylyn's motion, Brownrigg, Hacket, and others went to Laud and asked him to use his own more moderate metropolitical articles as the basis for the work—the articles which had enabled some in the 1630s to undercut the full weight of the metropolitical order.[66] Laud initially supported their request but then backed Heylyn's proposed book possibly because, in the mean time, canon 7 had appeared, which might relieve some of their scruples, and because (as he asserted later) he 'could not in modesty' press the confirmation of his own metropolitical articles.[67] In the resulting preamble Laud dissociated himself from what he termed 'impertinent, inconvenient or illegal enquiries' in visitation articles such as Wren's, which had caused 'just grievances' during the 1630s.[68] The book of articles received the majority support needed to pass, but for some, Holdsworth included, it still retained some 'offensive enquiries'.[69] Before its

[62] Fuller, *CH* 409; *The Diary of Ralph Josselin*, ed. E. Hockliffe, xv (1908), 8; see Ch. 2 nn. 110–11.

[63] *WWL* v. 615–16, 627; Heylyn, *CA* 425, 436; LPL Conv. ix/2/10, 11.

[64] *WWL* v. 615–16, *Northcote*, 68; Heylyn, *CA* 425.

[65] LPL MS 943/599. After Heylyn compiled the articles they were submitted to Wren, Bancroft, and Hall for examination: LPL 1061/13.

[66] *WWL* iv. 255–6; Heylyn, *CA* 437; Fuller, *AH* iii. 8.

[67] *WWL* iv. 255–6. [68] *WWL* v. 627. [69] LPL MS 943/599.

confirmation, the bishops added a clause enabling Laud to approve any further articles which might be particularly relevant to the needs of their individual sees, but after three years he was to close the articles as a perpetual rule and neither 'at the instance of those who had the right to hold visitation or upon any other occasion' could he make any further alteration to them.[70] These articles were first published for Juxon's second triennial visitation of London in 1640. Appended to them on this occasion were some non-controversial articles, relevant to London and not other sees, which Juxon, in accordance with the above proviso, asked Laud to add.[71] Goodman's sixth visitation fell during the time of his suspension, and although Laud visited the see, he chose to use not the new book of articles but Goodman's more conservative articles for his fifth visitation in 1637.[72]

The new articles did not differ substantially from many visitation articles of the 1630s, but they did emphasize more strongly the institutional and sacramental functions of the episcopacy and the clergy, by incorporating orders from various former codes such as the Advertisements of 1566, the Canons of 1571 and 1597, the Injunctions of 1559, and the rubric of Common Prayer.[73] As such they went some of the way to meet Charles's desire, first mooted in 1629, to restore some of the regulations of the early reformed Church of England.[74] As these visitation articles appeared as canon 9, they were given canonical force, but some already had canonical backing, such as those from the Canons of 1571, which specified that only a minister appointed by the bishop or the bishop in person should excommunicate, that only a bishop could commute penance, and that no work should be done on Sundays or holy days.[75] From the Advertisements of 1566 came the requirement that the minister should carry out preambulations on rogation days, which had entered several previous visitation articles.[76] Among the rubrical orders incorporated were those that the minister should send children to the bishop for confirmation and that only those confirmed and catechized should receive holy communion (rubric of confirmation), that the

[70] Heylyn, *CA* 443; LPL MS 1061/3; PRO SP 16/456/44.

[71] *Articles to be enquired ... in the third triennial visitation of William (Juxon) ... bishop of London* (1640) *appendix*: Heylyn, *CA* 436–7; WCO MS Clarke 5/11.

[72] G. Soden, *Godfrey Goodman* (1953), 314; PRO SP 16/456/44.

[73] *Synodalia*, i. 1–45; *Articles ... (Juxon)*, 2: 4; 3: 3, 6; 5: 3, 4; 7: 5, 6; 9: 1, 3, 4.

[74] PRO SP 16/153/44, 51; 16/158/18; Bodl. Rawl. MS A 127/59, A 127/75.

[75] *Synodalia*, i. 111–45; *Articles ... (Juxon)*, 5: 4; 7: 5, 6; 9: 1, 3, 4.

[76] *Articles ... (Juxon)*, 5: 3; Bodl. MS Rawl. A 127/60^{v}.

minister should read the second service every Sunday or holy day, even if there were no communion (rubric for the communion) and that he should give absolution to all those who confessed their sins (rubric of visitation).[77] There had been much controversy at Oxford during the 1620s and 1630s (most notably between Heylyn and Prideaux) over the issue of whether the Church had power to decide rites and ceremonies, and to give a ruling on controversies of faith. As a result articles of religion 20 and 34 of 1562 affirming this authority entered the book of visitation articles, a controversial move as article 20 in the Latin edition of 1571 had not explicitly vested such authority in the Church.[78] Other visitation articles had their basis in the royal Instructions of 1629 regulating lectures, although the requirement that the lecturer should read service before he preached was omitted.[79] Instead the more moderate stipulation of 1604 that he read the service or administer the sacrament only twice a year was inserted. Absent also was any enquiry into the publication of the book of sports which had entered several visitation articles during the 1630s.[80] Canon 7 concerning rites and ceremonies became an article in its own right, and thus effectively prevented the appearance of more extreme articles over rites in any particular see.

Apart from Heylyn, one other member of the Lower House, Archdeacon Brownrigg of Coventry, is known personally to have sponsored individual canons, which received confirmation in Convocation.[81] According to Heylyn, both his motions passed unanimously because of his wide popularity among the clergy.[82] The first, which appeared as canon 8, ordered all clergy and preachers under pain of suspension, twice a year, to 'positively and plainly preach and instruct the people in their public sermons that the rites and ceremonies in the Church of England were lawful and commendable', and that the people ought not only to conform themselves to these rites and ceremonies but cheerfully submit themselves to the government of the Church as established under Charles I.[83] His other motion called

[77] Heylyn, *CA* 441; *Articles . . . (Juxon)*, 3: 3; 4: 21, 23: PRO SP 16/456/44.

[78] *Synodalia*, i. 34–111; *WWL* v. 87; iv. 30; *Articles . . . (Juxon)*, 2: 4; J. Hutchin, *History and Antiquities of Dorset* (Westminster, 1868), ii. 376.

[79] *Articles . . . (Juxon)*, 4: 7.

[80] *Synodalia*, i. 145–330; R. Cox, *The Literature of the Sabbath Question* (1865), i. 154.

[81] Heylyn, *CA* 428, 437; Heylyn, *EH* 231; Fuller, *AII* iii. 37.

[82] Heylyn, *CA* 428, 437; Heylyn, *EH* 231.

[83] *WWL* v. 626; Heylyn, *CA* 437.

for the same censures against sectaries, 'all Anabaptists, Brownists, Separatists, Familists' as were laid down in canon 3 against papists. This measure, which appeared as canon 5, may be seen as Brownrigg's wish to dissociate himself totally from any taint of sectarianism which anti-Calvinists may have levelled against him during the 1630s.[84]

The divisions over doctrine or rites which existed among the higher echelons of the clergy were relatively insignificant when compared to their unanimous stand against popery and separatism. Yet some members might have felt unease that Convocation had not undertaken more stringent measures against the spread of Arminian doctrine. Davenant asked the bishops to approve the same penalties for printing Arminian books as those inflicted for printing Socinian books, laid down in canon 4, and that all theological works should be printed only in the vernacular to prevent the subtle intrusion of any Arminian or popish tenets.[85] His motion failed, however, because other bishops believed that the proclamation of 1626 and the declaration of 1628 were sufficient safeguards. Yet Davenant's representation provides clear evidence that at least one prominent Calvinist believed that in spite of the king's moratorium Arminian doctrine had increased in recent years.[86] Although Davenant did not regard Charles and Laud as Arminians, he doubtless believed that their refusal to limit the latitude of doctrinal belief in the articles had permitted the intrusion of some Arminian ideas. On the other hand, the bishops moved decidedly against Socinian ideas in canon 4, which possibly received more than the personal confirmation of the king.[87] Throughout the 1630s he had been sensitive to the accusation of Socinianism levelled against himself and the bench, and it may be significant that his clerk of the Closet, Richard Steward, probably formulated much of the canonical draft.[88]

According to Heylyn, the king sent several messages to the clergy to speed up their business, as he wished to disband the soldiers

[84] *WWL* v. 622–3; LPL Conv. ix/2/7. In the original draft, drawn up by Holdsworth and Aglionby (procurator for the Oxford chapter) only 'separatists and familists' were included. Anabaptists and Brownists were added by Convocation, and by Laud personally written into the final version: PRO SP 16/455/47; *Synodalia*, ii. 599. Given Laud's views on Brownism, it would be interesting to conjecture what the views of other members of Convocation were: Ch. 3 nn. 78–9.

[85] NNRO Lee Warner MS 1/2/4.

[86] See Ch. 3 sections ii and iii.

[87] *WWL* v. 620–1.

[88] Heylyn, *CA* 428; Bodl. Tanner 70/103; Nalson, i. 368.

surrounding the Abbey.[89] Consequently several motions were not put before the House, or if put were initially approved but not debated.[90] One such casualty was a canon for a book (or an English 'pontifical' as Heylyn inaptly calls it) which would have contained authorized forms for the coronation (based upon the form of 1626), the consecration of churches (based upon Andrewes's order of 1625), the reconciliation of converts to Islam (based on the order of 1637 drawn up by Hall and Laud together, after several Devon merchants returned from the Middle East and sought reunion), and forms for ordination and confirmation.[91] Another casualty was Laud's motion for a version of the Prayer Book in Latin, for occasional use in the universities.[92] Convocation approved a petition from George Griffiths, clerk for St Asaph, for a new translation of the Welsh Church Bible of 1588, a task which was delegated to the four Welsh bishops, and in particular to Bishop Owen of St Asaph.[93] Other measures failed to achieve canonical status ostensibly for fear that they would be received as innovations, such as reading the entire order for the consecration of the elements, rather than just the consecration prayer, or the practice of mixing water with wine, celebrated by Andrewes and used in the early Church.[94] Certain members asked for a new set form of prayer to be read before and after all sermons, instead of that prescribed in canon 55 of 1604. Ironically this was smothered by Laud 'to prevent the people's jealousy of introducing innovations'.[95] According to Heylyn, the motion won wide approval among the clergy largely because the person to whom they delegated

[89] Heylyn, *CA* 442–4; LPL Conv. ix/2/6.
[90] Heylyn, *CA* 422–4: PRO SP 16/456/44.
[91] Heylyn, *CA* 442–4; PRO SP 16/20/15; *WWL* iv. 247; v. 352.
[92] Heylyn, *CA* 442–4; PRO SP 16/455/54; LPL Conv. 1/1/1/87.
[93] Nalson, i. 370; Fuller, *CH* 408; Heylyn, *CA* 442. According to the official *acta* (*Synodalia*, ii. 623), Griffith petitioned Convocation for a new translation of the Book of Common Prayer into Welsh. Yet according to Fuller and Heylyn (both present) he called for a new translation of the Welsh 'Church' Bible of 1588 and 1620 (*Y Beibl Bach* of 1630 was the popular, five-shilling edition subsidized by two Welsh City merchants, Thomas Middleton and Rowland Heilyn). Fuller's opinion is supported by the fact that he gives samples of printing errors in the former editions of the Bible, to which Convocation's attention was turned. For former editions of both the Welsh Bible and the Book of Common Prayer see Prys Morgan, *A Bible For Wales* (Aberystwyth, 1988); Glanmor Williams, *Recovery, Reorientation and Reformation: Wales c. 1415–1642* (Oxf., 1987), 483.
[94] PRO SP 16/456/44.
[95] Heylyn, *CA* 442–4; PRO SP 16/456/44.

the task of drawing up the prayer was himself reluctant to use set forms.[96]

As at other times, Convocation became an arena not merely for the formulation of canons but for complaints from clergy from across the Southern Province. The Lower House informed the bishops that they and other clergy had suffered at the hands of impropriators and farmers, who had deprived them of their salaries, oblations, and customary fees, and often elected churchwardens merely to vex the minister.[97] The level of these complaints was probably higher in the Convocation of 1640 as a result of the greater activity of the 1630s and the unpopularity of some of the Caroline changes. Yet in these matters, as with more residual socio-economic problems, such were the structural inadequacies of the Church and the strength of the common law that little could be achieved.[98] All that the Upper House could do was send a petition to the Attorney-General demanding immediate redress of grievances.[99]

The feeling of resentment which the clergy as a whole felt towards the lay stranglehold of the Church constituted a prelude for the fierce onslaught which Convocation launched against the apparatus of ecclesiastical jurisdiction. The Lower House received many petitions from different sources, highlighting abuses in ecclesiastical justice, in particular over sentences of excommunication and absolution, commutation of penances, vexatious citations, and the exhorbitant exactions of chancellors.[100] On 22 May it was reported that the whole Convocation 'are as fierce against chancellors and registrars as the Lower House of Parliament was lately against the jurisdiction ecclesiastical'.[101] In order to redress these abuses Convocation passed canons 11–17, all of which evolved in the Lower House but which were either modified or wholly approved of by the bishops.[102]

[96] Heylyn, *CA* 442–4; PRO SP 16/456/44.

[97] Heylyn, *CA* 437–40.

[98] C. Hill, *The Economic Problems of the Church from Archbishop Whitgift to the Long Parliament* (Oxford, 1963); F. M. Heal, 'The Economic Problems of the Clergy', *Church and Society in England: Henry VIII to James I* (1977), ed. F. M. Heal and R. O'Day.

[99] *Synodalia*, ii. 619.

[100] Heylyn, *CA* 438; *Synodalia*, ii. 626 (the petition to Convocation against Coleman, one of the apparitors, and Allen, the deputy public registrar of the archdeaconry of Middlesex, presented by the parishioners of St Clement Dane on 28 May, conveniently put the problem into focus).

[101] SRO D/D/C 1878 bundle 4/unfol. 22 May 1640.

[102] Heylyn, *CA* 438–9; *WWL* v. 628–33; *Synodalia*, ii. 626–7. As early as February

In order to facilitate the task of formulation and, according to Heylyn, to moderate the clerical onslaught, two civilian lawyers, Sir John Lambe, dean of the Arches, and Thomas Heath, judge of the court of Audience, joined the committee of twenty-seven. The notes which Lambe drew up for the board reveal the extent of his personal opposition to many of the proposals.[103] According to Laud, canons 11–17 faced more opposition than the others, opposition which came solely from the civilian elements within the House by which he probably meant Skinner, prolocutor for the chapter of Hereford, and Lambe, Baber, Heath, and Lloyd, prolocutors respectively for the clergy of Lincoln, Gloucester, Peterborough, and Bangor.[104] The civilian opposition to the canons was triggered off by their very radical proposals. Canon 11 reserved to the ordinary all power to grant institutions to benefices, licences to preach and to teach, functions previously disposed of by the chancellors. Henceforth the patents given to chancellors, commissaries, and officials were concurrent only with the episcopate of the bishop who bestowed them.[105] After the appearance of canon 12 no chancellor or official unless in holy orders (which effectively debarred most civilians) could inflict censure on any clergyman in any criminal case, except for non-appearance, and all such cases could be heard only in episcopal audience.[106] Canon 13 declared that all excommunications pronounced other than by the bishop in person or by his delegate were invalid. All penitents henceforth should take absolution upon their knees, which Lambe objected to, on the grounds that it 'may be taken by the better sort of the laity and laid to the clergy as pride'.[107] Canon 14 deprived the chancellors and officials of all power to commute penance unless with the bishop's express permission in writing or in his presence. Failure on the part

1638 Laud had forbidden all common and civil lawyers to interfere in ecclesiastical courts without his permission: PRO SP 16/383/44; Usher, *The Rise and Fall of the High Commission*, 319.

[103] Heylyn, *CA* 438, Richard Steward suggested that the committee of 27 should discuss these issues in closed session in Westminster deanery; *Synodalia*, ii. 627; PRO SP 16/455/57; LPL 1061/116.

[104] *WWL* iii. 287, where Laud uses the word 'canonist' by mistake.

[105] *WWL* v. 628–9. My interpretation of this article is based upon the understanding of the ecclesiastical lawyers in SRO D/D/C 1878 bundle 4/6 June 1640: 'no chancellor shall have his patent but for the bishop's time . . . on the vacancy of every bishop the new bishop may put in a new chancellor.'

[106] *WWL* v. 629. As Edward Bagshawe noted, canons 12 and 13 were contrary to statute 37 HVIII c. 17: *Two Arguments in Parliament* 15–16.

[107] *WWL* v. 629–30; PRO SP 16/455/57 (3g).

of the chancellor to account for any illegal commutations would lead to his peremptory suspension, while the bishop was to ensure that all such commutations were channelled into acceptable and legal uses rather than private purses.[108] The last canons, 15, 16, and 17, attempted to prevent surrogates from mulcting more than their due from unlawful marriages, and regulated cases of concurrent jurisdiction and vexatious citations.[109]

Any evaluation of the significance to which ideas of divine-right episcopacy attained during the 1630s must take into account their alliance in 1640 with the clerical attack on the abuses of ecclesiastical jurisdiction. A lawyer at the Doctor's Commons informed his colleague in the Wells court that the effect of these canons would be 'the getting of ecclesiastical jurisdiction into the bishops' hands'.[110] In yet another way the ordinary power had triumphed over its rivals. So controversial were these last canons that the king and council held a debate in June 1640, at which Laud, representing the bishops and clergy, pitted himself against Sir Henry Martin and possibly Lambe.[111] Martin alleged that the canons tended to the 'visible discouragement' if not the 'plain overthrow of the (civilian) profession'.[112] Laud, supported by the council, retorted that their purpose lay only in the removal of 'execresences and exorbitances'.[113] Three days later the civilian lawyers resorted to their last expedient when the episcopal chancellors and doctors of civil law penned a petition to the king asking him not to approve the canons.[114] But Charles had already made up his mind to support Laud and Con-

108 *WWL* v. 630.

109 *WWL* v. 630–3.

110 SRO D/D/C/1878 bundle 4/unfol. 6 June 1640 ('all ecclesiastical courts will suffer much').

111 Heylyn, *CA* 442–3; SRO D/D/C 188 bundle/4/6 June 1640. Lambe had appeared before the king on several previous occasions over this particular matter: Bodl. Tanner MS 65/82.

112 Heylyn, *CA* 442–4.

113 Heylyn, *CA* 443.

114 PRO SP 16/456/44. It seems that the civil lawyers had difficulty in obtaining a copy: see the petition of Duck, Gwyn, Eden, and Rives to the king, Bodl. Tanner MS 65/82, confirmed by SRO D/D/C/bundle 4/4 July 1640. The king merely referred the petition (and a similar one from the advocates of the Arches) to members of the council (to which Richard Steward and two bishops were called): Bodl. MS Tanner 65/82. Archbishop Neile received notice about what issues to debate in the Northern Convocation from Secretary Windebank only shortly before 9 June 1640, PRO SP 16/456/51. About the same time he received a copy of the canons: SRO D/D/C/1878 bundle 4/30 May 1640.

vocation, and on 30 June he gave his final assent to the whole body of canons.[115] It was singularly ironic that shortly after Laud's fall from power, petitions would flood into Parliament demanding redress of those very abuses which Convocation had undertaken to resolve. The popular attack on ecclesiastical courts (signified by the riot at St Paul's and parliamentary legislation) was preceded by the equally virulent attack sponsored by the clergy and bishops in Convocation.[116]

On 29 May Convocation unanimously subscribed the canons.[117] In the Upper House only one bishop, Goodman of Gloucester, initially refused.[118] According to Fuller, Goodman objected to certain passages in canon 7, which referred to the 'idolatry committed in the Mass for which all popish altars were demolished'.[119] But, according to Laud, his dissent was occasioned rather by the canon for the suppression of popery, which was too stringent for him.[120] The bishop's leanings towards Rome were as yet not popularly known, but both the king and Laud suspected that he was on the verge of lapsing.[121] During Convocation, Goodman had questioned the legality of sitting after Parliament as an attempt to disguise his opposition to the canon, and during the nineteenth session, at his personal request, his opposition was recorded in the official *acta*.[122] Several days before the subscription, and on the day itself, Goodman went to Laud to inform him that he could not assent to the canon and that he would 'be torn with wild horses before he would subscribe that canon'.[123] Apparently he did offer to subscribe *dissentiens*, but this was not sufficient for Laud. With Goodman's open refusal, Laud asked the two Houses to decide upon a suitable censure, with the result that all the Lower House and all the bishops, save for Davenant, Hall, and Wright, called for his suspension *ab officio et a*

[115] Rushworth, iii. 1188, 1209.

[116] Bodl. Tanner MS 65/209v–214; *HMC De Lisle and Dudley vi*, 339; SRO D/D/C/ 1878 bundle 4/2 Oct., 3 Oct.; A. Fletcher, *The Outbreak of the English Civil War* (1981), 110 pp.; *WWL* vi. 585; *WWL* iii. 237.

[117] *WWL* iii. 290–1. Two days before the subscription, on 27 May 1640, Laud read the canons to the king and council: LPL MS 1061/14. Is this not the likeliest occasion for the insertion of the *et cetera*?

[118] *WWL* iii. 288. The five bishops who were absent on the subscription day and who did not sign were Mainwaring, St David's (who probably fearing impeachment stayed away), Juxon, London (Lord Treasurer), Duppa, Chichester (tutor to the royal children), Thornborough, Worcester (over 90, but who signed by proxy of Coke of Hereford), and Williams, Lincoln (suspended): PRO SP 16/455/47.

[119] Fuller, *CH* 408–9. [120] *WWL* iii. 287; iv. 154. [121] *WWL* vi. 539–41.

[122] LPL Conv. 1/1/1/79. [123] *WWL* iii. 287.

beneficio.[124] The three bishops maintained that Goodman should first declare his mind to Convocation and that if he gave satisfaction, he should receive a pardon.[125] It appears that Laud initially threatened Goodman's deprivation, but later backed down, because Davenant thought that some lawyers should first be consulted to determine how far the power of Convocation in such matters extended, and suggested that before the solemn threefold admonition of a bishop, there ought to be a considerable interval between each admonition for deliberation with the defendant.[126] Laud accepted Davenant's advice and allowed him and Hall to speak with Goodman in an attempt to resolve his scruples.[127] As a result the bishop was brought to sign but he failed to satisfy the House on his reason for signing. The whole House then proceeded to suspend him.[128] On hearing of Goodman's refusal Charles was so angered that he imprisoned him in the Westminster Gatehouse.[129] Here, according to Fuller, the bishop got 'by his restraint what he could never have gained by his liberty, namely of one reputed papist, to become for a short time, popular as the only confessor suffering for his subscribing the canons'.[130] Later, on 10 July, the king released him from custody, but only after he had taken the *et cetera* oath with Laud and Juxon, at the Privy Council.[131]

All members of the Lower House subscribed the canons, not necessarily because they agreed with all the particulars, but because it was the custom of Convocation to abide by the majority decision.[132] Only with difficulty did those who were genuinely opposed to individual measures convince their parliamentary accusers of their reluctance to sign. Thomas Warmestry, clerk for Worcester (later, the most vociferous opponent of the canons and the only member who published against them), wrote in 1641 that, if his subscription

124 Fuller, *CH* 409; LPL 1061/17–17^{v}.

125 LPL 1061/17^{v}.

126 M. Fuller, *The Life of John Davenant* (1897), 442; BL Lansd. MS 985/3; PRO SP 16/455/52. Rushworth, iii. 1187: Goodman informed Laud that Montagu of Norwich encouraged him to dissent, 'yet in public to please (Laud) he pressed my deprivation'.

127 *WWL* iii. 290. 128 PRO SP 16/455/51. 129 *WWL* iii. 291.

130 Fuller, *CH* 409. For Goodman's already uneasy relationship with the king see *WWL* vi. 539–41; Birch, ii. 229; Bodl. MS Add. c. 205/8–17; *WWL* vii. 421.

131 *WWL* iii. 236.

132 Fuller, *CH* 409; Heylyn, *EH* 234–5.

implied anything other than abiding by the custom of Convocation, then he did so far 'rescind and condemn it in myself and desire pardon both of God and the Church, resolving by God's grace to be more cautious' in the future.[133] When the Commons threatened to fine all members of the Lower House for formulating the canons, some of those who had protested against the continuation of Convocation in May 1640 claimed immunity.[134] But this found little favour with the Commons, who alleged that the clergy had not subscribed their names at the time of their protest nor drawn up any instrument of protest. Thus their opposition had no legal force whatsoever and was significant only in their own conscience.[135] The accused also faced criticism from nonconformist clergy outside Convocation who accused them, according to Fuller, of 'cowardly compliance' in the changes of the 1630s.[136]

It is easy to exaggerate the strength of protest against the continuation of Convocation when the testimonies of the protesters were issued retrospectively and under parliamentary duress. According to Fuller, the legal instrument which the king sent to the House satisfied most of their scruples and they decided to remain in the session in order to moderate proceedings. At the same time their protest was restrained by the fact that, although it was not customary to hold Convocation outside Parliament, few appear to have thought it illegal.[137] Again there were those who dissented to many particulars, but who did not present a unified oppositionist platform. There was certainly no identifiable 'Calvinist' opposition within the House.[138] Brownrigg was the most prominent Calvinist present. Later he would sit on the committee of religion and was known, like Holdsworth, to disapprove of certain aspects of canon 7 on rites, in particular the altarwise position and the liberty given to those who wished to bow towards the table.[139] Nevertheless in canon 8 he recommended obedience to the rites and ceremonies of the Church, an astute move, which may have won him his bishopric in 1641.

133 Warmestry, *A Convocation speech*, 4.

134 Fuller, *CH* 407.

135 Fuller, *AH* iii. 34–5: the lower clergy were each fined £200 by the House of Commons but the Lords did not agree to it.

136 Fuller, *CH* 458. For subscriptions of the Lower House see PRO SP 16/455/47.

137 Fuller, *CH* 406–7, 409; Heylyn, *EH* 241.

138 Thus I would interpret the Convocations of 1640 in a very different light from Tyacke, *AC* 238–44.

139 *PCR*, 52; LPL MS 943/599.

Again, if certain members dissented in private or openly to particular measures they nevertheless defended the right of the Church to formulate canons. Even Williams, on his return from oblivion, appeared as a 'back-friend' to the canons and was prepared, as events proved, to defend the Church's privileges.[140] In 1641, when Parliament accused the bishops of praemunire for formulating the canons, they defended without equivocation their action in May 1640.[141] Bishop Warner preached the longest defence, but it was Hall of Exeter who preached the noblest. His stand in support of the Convocation of 1640 almost certainly lost him much of the parliamentary support which he had previously held.[142]

Against the accusation that Convocation had acted illegally, Hall justified its action on the basis of the royal letters, the legal instrument, and on the fact that ever since the first synod in Acts 15 ecclesiastical canons were made by the bishops and clergy alone, and not by any popular assembly. If Parliament intended to censure Convocation for illegal practice then they had to censure with them the whole Christian Church, to which the bishop added, 'we shall have too good company in the censure'.[143] As for the ratification and execution of canons this, he said, belonged not to Parliament but only to princes who called the synods in the first place. Neither the Injunctions of 1559 nor the Canons of 1604 had received parliamentary sanction, and if the Canons of 1640 were compared to these codes then they were 'but few and only second to former constitutions'.[144] The canons were to the Church as laws were to the Commonwealth: the Church could no more make canons without the king's approval than Parliament could make laws.

After establishing the principle that Convocation had acted legally, Hall proceeded to praise the contents of the canons, for the 'main drift was to repress and confine the indiscreet and lawless discourse of some either ignorant or parasitical, I am sure offensive

[140] Heylyn, *EH* 241.

[141] *LJ* iv. 273; Rushworth, iii. 1365–6; *CJ* ii. 51–2.

[142] Bodl. Eng. hist. b. 205/23/5; MS b. 205/21; MS b. 205/78, 77^v; G. Lewis, *A Life of Joseph Hall* (1886), 328.

[143] *WJH* viii. 278–80.

[144] *WJH* viii. 278–9. In 1639 Davenant had also welcomed the formulation of canons: 'We want confirmation in these, both old and young' although he wished 'that we could all content ourselves with that doctrine and rites which our predecessors have left unto us. I can see nothing altered or augmented for the better . . . he does an episcopal act, who labours to hold others in that doctrine and discipline, where he found them settled by this church.' Bodl. MS Tanner 67/147.

preachers ... to suppress the growth of Socinianism, Popery and separatism ... to redress some abuses of ... ecclesiastical courts and officers ... in all which I dare say your lordships do heartily concur with them. And even if there were failings in the manner of expression ... the main substance is well meant, and in itself profitable.'[145] It is noteworthy that Hall did not openly praise those canons at which he himself might scruple (such as canon 7) or at which Parliament might take offence such as canons 1 and 2. The bishops may have differed over the content of the canons, yet there existed among them no ostensible disagreement over the right of Convocation to make canons, or the legality of its sitting outside Parliament. As Laud was never openly blamed by any of his episcopal colleagues for the canons, it is singularly ironic that in August 1641, when they were defending the events of May 1640, Charles I chose to isolate himself not only from the canons but from Laud as well.[146] On 4 August 1641 Bishop Warner of Rochester entered in his diary: 'The bishop of Lincoln in the parliament house (about five in the afternoon) tells the bishops of Gloucester and Bangor, which I overheard and (which) Bangor repeated to me presently that the king told him, Canterbury had drawn him to the canons making against his judgment.'[147] Yet as the above account shows, Charles's involvement in the events of April and May 1640 was far from passive. He had decided to continue Convocation to obtain the canons without even consulting Laud. He had procured the legal instrument from the judges and altered the original commission, so that Convocation sat now only at his own pleasure. Moreover the king's statement to Williams reveals that Charles was effectively denying any responsibility for the single act which was to bring down both the canons and Convocation: the ill-fated *et cetera* oath.

[145] *WJH* viii. 278–81.

[146] BL Harl. MS 6424/88^{v}. For the authorship of this diary see C. S. R. Russell, *Bulletin of the Institute of Historical Research*, 411 (Nov. 1968), 229–36.

[147] BL Harl. MS 6424/88^{v}. On the same day Wilde impeached 13 bishops for making the canons and approving the clerical benevolence: Laud, Hall, Wren, Towers, Owen, Piers, Coke, Roberts, Owen, Warner, Curle, Wright, Skinner. By this date Bancroft, Montagu, Davenant, and Thornborough were dead. Mainwaring, Duppa, Williams, and Juxon were not impeached (because they had not signed) nor was Goodman (because of his opposition) or the two surviving bishops of the Northern Province, Morton and Bridgeman (Neile and Potter were dead). This group should not be confused with those later impeached over their right to sit in Parliament. It is ironic but true that the episcopal deaths of 1640–1 parallel those of 1625–6.

III. THE *Et Cetera* Oath

On 18 May 1640 Charles sent a letter to the bishops under his personal signet, requesting that they draw up a canon to include an oath which was taken by all clerics, binding them to the 'doctrine and discipline here established' and that they should not 'give way to any innovations or alterations thereof'.[148] Once this had been drawn up, Charles wished to peruse the oath, and, if necessary, alter it before empowering the clergy to take and administer it. The king justified this intervention in the affairs of Convocation through a clause in the original letters patent, authorizing the formulation of canons. In this clause he reserved a right 'under our sign manual or signet' to ask the clergy to deliberate upon whatever matters he should think fit during the time of Convocation.[149] The oath was in effect Charles's reply to the Scottish covenant, as recognized by the city annalist of Coventry.[150] According to Davenant, all the bishops approved of the oath with 'uniform consent'.[151] Nor did any question the right of Convocation to make such an oath or the ability of the king to interfere in this way. Months later, Laud himself defended the clerical right to make oaths by appealing to Lyndwood, the Canons of 1604, and the Edwardian visitation of the Church.[152] The text of the oath ran as follows:

I, A.B. do swear, that I do approve the doctrine and discipline or government established in the church of England, as containing all things necessary to salvation; and that I will not endeavour by myself or any other, directly or indirectly, to bring in any popish doctrine contrary to that which is so established; nor will I ever give my consent to alter the government of this church, by archbishops, bishops, deans and archdeacons, *et cetera* as it stands now established, and as by right it ought to stand, nor yet ever to subject it to the usurpation and superstitions of the see of Rome. And all these things I do plainly and sincerely acknowledge and swear, according to the plain and common sense and understanding of the same words, without any equivocation or mental evasion, or secret reservation whatsoever. And this I do

148 LPL MS 577/257; LPL MS 1030/103.
149 LPL MS 577/254.
150 CVRO City Annals 920/15.
151 CCO 298/51; GCO MS 291 (1).
152 PRO SP 16/499/65, 16/461/83–5. PRO SP 16/455/134: Laud does not mention the abortive oath of 1606 (see Heylyn, *CA* 444). For other oaths, see those in Canons of 1604: *WWL* iv. 155, Nalson, i. 360.

heartedly, willingly and truly, upon the faith of a Christian. So help me God, in Jesus Christ.[153]

After Convocation agreed on the formulation of the oath, the bishops drew up its basic draft in the Upper House.[154] However, when this appeared in the Lower House, some of the clergy objected that it contained more than what they had originally approved.[155] Holdsworth said that when Laud had first mentioned the oath he advertised it as a measure designed to clear the clergy from the suspicion of popery, 'but when it was drawn in the form of a canon, it came to us with additions', some of which he, Hacket, and Brownrigg criticized.[156] Precisely what these additions were it is difficult to say, but they almost certainly did not include at this point the *et cetera*, which did not enter the oath until the final canonical draft stages. Davenant implied that the words were not present when the oath went through the Upper House the first time, and Heylyn believed the same when it passed through the Lower House.[157] Yet in the manuscript book of canons signed by the whole house on 29 May, the *et cetera* was present.[158] For what his testimony is worth, Heylyn suggested that it entered the oath because the king brought pressure to bear on Convocation to finish its proceedings speedily.[159] This could be a subtle way of implicating the king. As Charles had approved the oath before the subscriptions of 29 May, the possibility exists that he had made the insertion in his characteristic desire to cut out superfluous words. Such a possibility cannot be ruled out as he had expressly reserved for himself the right to alter the oath in any material respect before approving it.[160]

The *et cetera* entered the oath in the printed canons and the oath in the royal commission (and its duplicates) which ordered both archbishops, all bishops, college heads, clergy, masters (save the sons

153 *WWL* v. 623–4; LPL Conv. ix/2/8.

154 Bodl. MS Eng. hist. b. 205/22. The two bishops who drew up the oath were most probably among the four bishops to whom Laud delegated the responsibility of holding consultations (concerning the oath) with the eight representatives elected by the Lower House: Ch. Ch. Wake MS 306/360 (the four were Hall, Curle, Wren, and Skinner).

155 LPL MS 943/599; Heylyn, *CA* 432.

156 LPL MS 943/599.

157 GCC MS 291/6; Bodl. Eng. hist. MS b. 205/21; Heylyn, *CA* 432.

158 PRO SP 16/455/47.

159 Heylyn, *CA*, 444, and his *Observations on the History of the reign of King Charles I*, 189.

160 LPL MS 577/257.

of nobility), bachelors, doctors of divinity, law, physic, actuaries, registrars, proctors, and schoolmasters to take the oath before 2 November.[161] Before long it became apparent that another alteration had occurred in the oath. In the royal commission and its duplicates authorizing the taking and administration of the oath the word 'popish' was mysteriously absent from the clause, 'I will not endeavour . . . to bring in any popish doctrine'.[162] These orders had been drawn up on 5 July in the Lord Keeper's office.[163] The disappearance of the word was serious as it suggested that it was not only popish doctrine which threatened the Church but other, possibly Puritan doctrine as well. But the omission may well have been a scribal error, as Wren believed, when he informed Laud on 16 August 1640 of the disappearance of one 'emphatic' word in 'His Majesty's duplicate'.[164] Although the word 'popish' could be seen in the printed canons, its omission in the duplicates was still serious because those who had to take the oath could justly claim that there was no standard text. Wren considered it important enough not to press the oath any further until he had received instructions.[165] Within a few days and shortly before the king left for York on 20 August, he ordered Laud, at the council table, to inform the bishops in the Southern Province that they should not impose the oath any further on their clergy, except on ordinands and those to be instituted.[166] Yet Charles did not recall the duplicates and the error remained. Moreover it was apparent that the omission continued to agitate the other parties who were still required to take and administer the oath. On 21 September, John Cosin, the master of Peterhouse, complained to Laud that the omission of 'popish' and the intrusion of the *et cetera* were causing considerable unease within the University of Cambridge.[167]

161 Heylyn, *CA* 432.

162 LPL MS 577/258; PRO SP 16/467/129; LPL MS Conv. ix 2/8/6.

163 For an example of the duplicate, see that of Oxford University: Bodl. Univ. Archives MS S.E.P./V2.

164 PRO SP 16/464/13. It is not unlikely that the word 'popish' was dropped in that it seemed to suggest that some popish doctrine was already established (as intimated by *Northcote*, 47, and Bagshawe, *Two Arguments in Parliament*, 17).

165 PRO SP 16/464/13.

166 LPL MS 943/591; LPL MS 577/260. Why this order was not entered into the register of the Privy Council remains a mystery, as the king made the decision when present at the council table. For evidence that Laud acted upon it see PRO SP 16/465/28; LPL MS 577/259.

167 PRO SP 16/467/129.

It is highly unlikely that many took the oath. The dispersal of the 17,500 books of canons across the dioceses of the two provinces constitutes no evidence that the bishops actually administered the oath to the beneficed clergy (and others) before they received Laud's communication of late August.[168] Nor does the existence of petitions from particular areas, as most petitions harboured prospective fears about taking the oath. According to Fuller, some bishops pressed the oath before the end of September, an act which Fuller saw as infringing the royal commission, assuming that the king had given the clergy at least until 29 September to deliberate upon it.[169] But in this he was mistaken, as 29 September was merely the last date by which the book of canons might be bought. As the oath had to be taken before 2 November, in effect it could be administered by the bishops at any time between the receipt of the duplicate of the commission and November.[170] This is an important fact in ascertaining the timing of the administration of the oath as most of the king's duplicates do not appear to have been sent out until August.[171] Of course some bishops may have introduced the oath on the basis of the book itself rather than the duplicate. Fuller is correct in assuming that some had introduced the oath before the end of September, among them Piers of Bath and Wells, Skinner of Bristol, and Davenant of Salisbury.[172] On receiving the king's duplicate and the broad seal, Davenant had taken the oath himself and then administered it to the residentiaries of Salisbury.[173] After the harvest he intended to call the country ministers to take it. As for the ordinands and those seeking institution, the bishop noted that they had 'no more scruple of taking (it) than the beneficed' and he hoped that when the oath was duly weighed, 'few or none in the diocese would refuse to take it'.[174] Davenant may have been a little over-optimistic about the prospects of clerical compliance, and had not Laud's letter arrived (forbearing

[168] PRO SP 16/455/138; LPL MS 577/260.

[169] Fuller, *CH* 410–11; Fuller, *AII* iii. 40–1.

[170] Heylyn, *EH*, 235; PRO SP 16/459/38.

[171] PRO SP 16/464/13. Laud certainly did not press the reading of the oath in Lincoln diocese, where his jurisdiction was metropolitical in 1640 (Williams being under suspension), see S. Clarke, *The Lives of Thirty-Two English Divines* (1677), 199.

[172] Fuller, *CH* 410–11; SRO D/D/C/1878 bundle 4/6 Oct. 1640; *Northcote*, 110 (Piers was possibly the only bishop who enforced the payment of the clerical benevolence); PRO SP 16/465/28; Bodl. MS Walker c. 4/244; *Articles of Accusation and Impeachment . . . against William Piers* (1642), 13, 15.

[173] PRO SP 16/465/28.

[174] PRO SP 16/465/28.

the oath on the beneficed) he would almost certainly have faced considerable opposition.[175] Davenant, like Hall of Exeter, wrote letters to several of his diocesan clergy explaining the oath, 'for . . . as it now stands, in my judgement it cannot trouble any man's conscience, who shall advisedly consider the scope thereof'.[176] According to Fuller, some of the bishops who administered the oath asked their ministers to take it kneeling, which was not required in the taking of the oaths of supremacy and obedience.[177] Even more illegal was the action of the chancellor of London, Arthur Duck, who attempted to make churchwardens take it.[178] Within peculiar jurisdictions the oath was also published, although probably not pressed. Baxter managed to escape taking it within the royal peculiar of Bridgenorth, and only felt threatened when he was reported to the earl of Bridgewater, who was passing through on his way to Ludlow.[179] Most bishops probably did not press the taking of the oath at all (Hall was certainly one of them) as they were aware that the last date for its administration was 2 November, and they were inclined to give their clergy time to think over it.[180] Moreover Laud's letter of late August rescinding the administration of the oath on the beneficed clergy meant that very few clergy, even in those dioceses where proceedings were under way, actually took it.[181]

Although its material inaccuracies went far to discredit the oath, it was eventually brought down by the many petitions which surfaced against it. According to Laud, the oath (and the canons) were at first well received but as soon as the London clergy raised their objections, complaints were voiced all over the country.[182] The petitions of Northamptonshire and Devon were to a large extent based on the London queries, which confirms Laud's opinion.[183] Although the queries were first voiced in July, only on 6 August did a group

[175] LPL MS 943/591; LPL MS 577/260; PRO SP 16/465/28.

[176] PRO SP 16/465/28.

[177] Fuller, *CH* 462; Fuller, *AII* iii. 40.

[178] *HMC Rutland i*, 524.

[179] G. F. Nuttall, *Richard Baxter* (1965), 21. Christopher Love was the first person to be expelled from the Convocation of Oxford University for his failure to subscribe to the Canons: *Records of the County Borough of Cardiff* (1898–1911), v. 470; *The Gospel Atlas* (1855).

[180] *WJH* i, pp. xlvii, l.

[181] PRO SP 16/465/28; LPL MS 943/591.

[182] *WWL* ii. 291; Bodl. Tanner MS 65/42; Rawl. MS D. 353/144; PRO SP 16/461/27; *Northcote*, 50; Heylyn, *EH* 234; Fuller, *AII* 39.

[183] Rushworth, ii. 1207; Bodl. Rawl. MS A 346.

of London clergy formally pen their names to a petition. Among these signatories were Archdeacon Westfield of St Alban's (Laud's appointee) and John Goodwin, vicar of St Stephen, Coleman Street (recently in trouble with Juxon for preaching universal grace).[184] By 8 August the Devon clergy and gentry, headed by the earl of Bath and Sir Francis Seymour, had drawn up their petition, while at Kettering on 26 August twenty-seven clergy of Peterborough diocese composed a similar petition.[185] Some petitions were sent directly to the Privy Council, and then forwarded to the king at York (where he was based between 20 August and 28 October) but not with any great urgency.[186] The council decided to inform him of the Devon petition only on 11 September, and even then they sent it via the Lord Keeper, rather than to him directly.[187] Others were personally handed to the king, such as that of the clergy of Worcester diocese by Clarke, rector of Alcester, which the king received 'without a word', although Bishop Curle of Winchester, who was in attendance at the time, 'frowned extremely'.[188] The signatories to such petitions were generally few in number. In fact many clergy and laity were reluctant to reveal their open defiance. Within given areas there was a varied response to the petition or the request for signatures. A Dorset clergyman wrote that the clerical petition 'stirs very coldly in these parts, though about Sherborne . . . they are more active in it'.[189] Much of this petitioning and the collection of names was performed so discreetly that Archdeacon Fitzherbert first learned of the Dorset petition from Bishop Skinner at Bristol.[190] Often the petitioners looked for oral support in the first place and subscription only later.[191] Yet the speed at which the London queries and other complaints travelled is remarkable. Robert Sanderson informed Laud in September that he had heard of divers papers 'that pass secretly from hand to hand', two of which he had seen with a stranger who passed through his parish of Boothby Pagnell in Lincolnshire.[192]

The objections raised against the oath were various and far more general than those aroused by the omission or the inclusion of words.

184 PRO SP 16/463/54.
185 PRO SP 16/465/8; Bodl. MS Clar. SP 19/1424.
186 LPL MS 577/260.
187 Bodl. MS Clar. SP 19/1424 (nor according to Windebank did the Council 'think fit to be sudden in answering it').
188 S. Clarke, *The Lives of Sundry Eminent Persons* (1683), i, 7–8.
189 PRO SP 16/467/63. 190 Ibid. 191 Ibid.
192 PRO SP 16/467/56; LPL MS 577/259.

One was the basic question of whether it was lawful to administer or take the oath, because Convocation had sat outside Parliament and because Parliament had not approved it. Edward Bagshawe asserted that only an act of Parliament or common law could impose a new oath, and Henrician statutes had specifically deprived the clergy of this right. According to Fuller, 'the exception of exceptions against the canons was because they were generally condemned as illegally passed to the prejudice of the fundamental liberty of the subject.'[193] One of the Devon petitions called the oath 'a project to suppress all parliaments for ever' because the clergy could not draw up canons, much less create or impose an oath, unless Parliament confirmed them.[194] For the London ministers, the clergy in convocation had contravened both the Petition of Right and the Henrician statutes by making ecclesiastical laws against the state.[195] Again there existed the question of what the oath understood by the 'doctrine and discipline established within the Church' and whether that doctrine and discipline contained 'all things within necessary to salvation'.[196] For the petitioners of York such a clause was offensive to God because 'it seemed to make His Word insufficient to salvation'.[197] Many objections rose through the understanding that to bind the swearer against future alterations was in effect to make him swear against the Royal Supremacy, or the power of the king, and an invitation to commit perjury.[198] Again there existed considerable doubt over the meaning of the phrase 'as it now stands established and by right it ought to stand', which implied that discipline existed by *iure divino* alone, and not *iure humano* or *ecclesiastico*.[199] For some of the Devon petitioners the oath would precipitate the decline of a preaching ministry and of the universities, as the laity would seek education elsewhere.[200] Given its general ambiguity many clergymen felt that they simply could not take the oath 'according to the plain and common sense

[193] Fuller, *CH* 410–11; *Northcote*, 8–9, 45–51, 65–9, 72–5; Bodl. Rawl. D.831/103; Bagshawe, *Two Arguments in Parliament*, 16.

[194] Rushworth, iii. 1207; *Northcote*, 47.

[195] Bodl. MS Tanner 65/42 (1).

[196] Bodl. MS Tanner 65/42 (2, 3).

[197] PRO SP 16/466/42.

[198] Bodl. Tanner 65/42 (4); Rushworth, iii. 1207; *Northcote*, 47: some thought that the oath appeared to deny that the king was Supreme Governor of the Church unless this was comprehended in the *et cetera*, 'an unworthy place for the king'.

[199] Bodl. MS Tanner 65/42 (7, 5).

[200] Bodl. MS Rawl. A 346; Rushworth, iii. 1209.

and understanding of the same words, without any equivocation or mental evasion, or secret reservation whatsoever'.[201] And yet to refuse would be to face the prospect of a severe penalty of suspension or deprivation. It was, as Thomas Warmestry said, 'a strange kind of sinning to make a benefice the price of perjury'.[202]

Davenant, Hall, and Warner were among those bishops who answered the various objections raised against the oath or who explained it in order to relieve clerical scruples.[203] For Davenant the London queries were so weak that 'there was not one of them where full satisfaction may not be given to any men who were not unwilling to be satisfied'.[204] But, like Hall, he regretted that the oath was not better worded so that 'the weakest eyes might at first view have discovered that we place not the same necessity to salvation in matters of order and discipline', as in doctrine.[205] Against the objection that the oath could not be legally binding, Davenant appealed to the fact that all Christians had to submit themselves to perform particular acts at various times by which they were not previously bound by any human positive law, and the taking of lawful oaths constituted such an act.[206] As for the oath's legality, like Warner, he based this on the authority of the great seal and the ruling of the council learned, whose authority was greater than that of any individual judge.[207] As the clergy had already taken the oath of obedience to the bishops, which bound them to obey both the doctrine and discipline, they could hardly refuse to swear to an oath which required the same.[208] As for the 'doctrine established' this was, according to Davenant,

201 Bodl. MS Tanner 65/42 (6); Rushworth, iii. 1207.

202 Warmestry, *A Convocation Speech*, 4.

203 CCO MS 298/50–3; GCC MS 291; Bodl. Eng. hist. MS b. 205/21; PRO SP 16/464/30; *WWL* iii. 125; *WWL* iv. 156: in 1641 Laud wrote an extensive answer to the speech of Nathaniel Fiennes against the Canons of 1640 (14 December 1640, Rushworth, iii. 105). At one time this was in Sancroft's hands (LPL MS 577/289) but it was subsequently lost. Some of Laud's preparatory notes are among: PRO SP 16/458/114–15, 16/461/85, 16/455/134–6. Some clergy also wrote apologies (Bodl. Rawl. C. 262), while Holdsworth and Brownrigg were among those who interviewed clergy with scruples. Davenant suggested that they were 'the fittest to give satisfaction touching the queries and scruples made about it': CCO 298/50.

204 PRO SP 16/465/28; CCO MS 298/50: 'in my judgment it cannot trouble any man's conscience who shall advisedly consider the very scope thereof and fairly interpret the words' (Davenant, 1640).

205 CCO MS 298/50; Bodl. Eng. hist. MS b. 205.

206 CCO MS 298/52.

207 GCC MS 291 (1); Bodl. Eng. hist. MS b. 205/21.

208 GCC MS 291 (1).

only the thirty-nine articles ratified by the king's declaration of 1628 whereas 'discipline established' meant the canons.[209] A relevant objection here was that some canons had fallen into disuse and others had been superseded by the recent canons and consequently it was impossible to know which to obey and which not. But Davenant met this objection by pointing out that they were asked to swear not to a particular discipline (or doctrine) but to the discipline (and doctrine) established in general. Moreover the oath bound no man to a further approbation of any canon than that approved by the authority of those who first established them.[210]

Some of the petitioners understood the phrase 'in the doctrine and discipline of the Church of England all things are contained which are necessary to salvation' in the sense of 'all things which are contained in the doctrine and the discipline of the Church are necessary to salvation'.[211] Thus the petitioners objected to a false premiss of their own making. They then proceeded to base several other erroneous arguments upon this, such as that the oath condemned all Reformed Churches abroad.[212] As Davenant pointed out, the petitioners had in effect accused the Church of England of holding a Tridentine position on doctrine and discipline.[213] Yet unlike Rome it would not argue that all its doctrinal conclusions were necessary for salvation, even if it regarded them to be true. Even less would it maintain that all matters pertaining to discipline were necessary for salvation.[214]

The phrase 'nor will I ever give my consent' to alter the government of the Church was also open to misconstruction. Some held that to swear not to consent to alterations was against the Royal Supremacy and against the king's power to carry out alterations.[215] Both Davenant and Warner pointed out that the oath could bind the swearer against consenting to alter only those things which were inalterable, for neither the king nor the bishops would abridge themselves for the future of the power to alter things alterable or bind the clergy against their own authority.[216] As such the Church could alter 'matters indifferent', such as rites, ceremonies, and those officers

209 Ibid. 210 Ibid. 211 GCC MS 291 (3).
212 Ibid. 213 Ibid.; CCO MS 298/50. 214 GCC MS 291 (2, 3).
215 GCC MS 291' (4).
216 Ibid.; Bodl. Eng. hist. MS b. 205/21.

within the Church whose position was held only *iure humano* or *ecclesiastico*, (like deans and archdeacons).[217] But the order of bishops, on the other hand, was inalterable as it stood *iure divino*.[218] Although the bishops might disagree over the extent to which episcopacy was of divine right, they would all defend its *iure divino* origin. There may have been differences among them over certain doctrinal issues, but on the doctrine of authority they exhibited near unanimity. The oath had in effect caused the bishops to close ranks, to defend their rights and their action in Convocation, and their ability to make laws for the Church without parliamentary sanction. In fact Davenant did not regret the oath at all. He regarded it as 'the best assurance we could (give) of our sincerity and constancy to those who either out of ignorance or malice have persuaded themselves and go about to persuade others that the bishops and many of our clergy were about changing of our established religion and bringing in of Popery'.[219]

But these episcopal apologetics written to meet clerical scruples and objections to the petitions could not stem the tide of opposition to the oath. Bishop Warner believed that unless an official interpretation of the oath was forthcoming 'it would empty the Church of more preachers than all the ceremonies ever did'.[220] Sanderson thought that the king should publicly explain the ambiguous statements through an official circular which could be read out at the administration of the oath, 'otherwise the peace of the Church is apparently in danger to be disquieted . . . though there be little by this occasion,' he informed Laud, 'than by anything that has happened in our memory'.[221] Sanderson perceived correctly that the *et cetera* oath polarized opinion to a far greater extent than the various innovations of the 1630s. The oath was offensive not only to the 'preciser sort' of clergy 'whose dislike is the less to be regarded because they like nothing not of their own way' but those in 'every way conformable'.[222] Even such a stalwart advocate of the Caroline ecclesiastical policies in the 1630s as Martin Blake, vicar of Barnstaple, felt that he could not take the oath because of his mental reservations and that there were hundreds like him.[223] Sir Francis Fane assured the earl of Rutland

217 GCC MS 291 (5). 218 Ibid.
219 CCO MS 298/50; GCC MS 291 (1).
220 Bodl. Eng. hist. MS b. 205/22.
221 PRO SP 16/467/56; LPL MS 570/259.
222 PRO SP 16/467/56.
223 Bodl. Tanner MS 65/197.

that thousands would leave their livings rather than take the oath.[224]

The real casualty of the oath was of course Laud himself. As early as July it was reported that the effect of the Devon petition was 'to grow mens' mouths extremely against the archbishop'.[225] In face of the alienation of moderate clergy, the representation of the likes of Cosin and Sanderson, and the mounting tide of petitions, Laud moved to extricate himself completely from its shackles. Before the end of September 1640, and less than a month later Laud warned the bishops not to administer it to the beneficed clergy, and before its formal renunciation by the king, the oath was dropped completely within his own diocese of Canterbury.[226] This resignation was in stark contrast to the aggressive policy being advocated by some other members of the Privy Council. As late as 18 September, Windebank, Secretary of State, wrote to the king (then at York) informing him that the Privy Council advised him to imprison those who petitioned against the canons. This was met with the enigmatic and desperate response of a king whose kingdom was fast falling through his hands: 'I could wish [that] you would show as much stoutness there as you council me [to] here.'[227] Twelve days later, however, on 30 September, either on the promptings of others or on his own initiative, Charles issued an official order to Neile and Laud commanding them to delay the administration of the oath until after the next Convocation, due to meet in November.[228] Laud did not receive this letter until 3 October, by which time he had already taken action in his own diocese.[229] Once in his hands he then dispatched letters to the bishops asking them not to administer the oath until after the parliamentary session, as the king had requested.[230]

Nevertheless when the oath disappeared, agitation against it continued not least because of fears that it would be introduced in the November Convocation. As such it served to fan the flames of

224 *HMC Rutland i*, 522.

225 Rushworth, iii. 1209; Heylyn, *CA*.

226 G. Swincock, *The Life and Death of Thomas Wilson* (1672), 14; LPL MS 577/260, 259; PRO SP 16/465/28.

227 Bodl. MS Clar. SP 19/1425. Windebank's words were that the lordships 'most humbly beseech your Majesty to show resentment of this insolency . . . and to cause the presenters of such a petition . . . to be committed close prisoners'. The role of the Privy Council in the promotion of Carolinism clearly needs further and careful analysis, as intimated elsewhere in this work (see eg. Ch. 5 nn. 26, 60; Ch. 6 n. 32).

228 LPL MS 943/591, MS 577/260.

229 LPL MS 943/591; Swincock, *Life and Death of Thomas Wilson*, 14.

230 LPL MS 943/591.

mounting opposition to alterations in Church and government. The petitions continued but the focus of attention had now shifted towards the elections to Parliament and Convocation. The last days of October witnessed the most heated contests as clergy attempted to wrest the right of electing Convocation clerks from the bishops. Hall recorded that there was 'great working secretly for the designation and election of the clerks ... where now the clergy were stirred up to contest with and oppose their diocesans, for the choice of such men as were most inclined to the favour of an alteration'.[231] In the diocese of Exeter only with the greatest difficulty did Hall hold on to his own nominees who were contested by clergy, incited by 'some busy interlopers of the neighbouring country'.[232] In the diocese of Hereford, clergy within the archdeaconry of Ludlow met to vote, only to find that Bishop Coke's supporters had already decided the result. According to Stanley Gower, 'in all business that concerns ... the clergy the bishop's party are alone, and exempt us from the vote.'[233] Many clergy had received no notice of the elections, and most of those who had, had received no legal writ. In the diocese of Bath and Wells, Piers found his election of Lute of Chard contested notably by the minister of Doulting, who went to Wells and proposed 'in a violent manner' the name of Alleine, the minister of Ditchet, and demanded to know 'who had given the name of Mr. Lute to be convocation clerk'.[234]

Other clergy looked less to Convocation than to Parliament itself for relief against the oath. Blake of Barnstaple took comfort in his belief that the king wished Parliament to remedy ecclesiastical grievances.[235] This is precisely what Charles did to save face, an abnegation of the principle which he had consistently espoused throughout his reign, that Parliament should not discuss the 'cause' of the

231 *WJH* i, p. xlvii; *Bishop Hall's Hard Measure*, 32. Both houses of Convocation met again on 4 November: *WWL* iii. 238. Neile died a few days before: Heylyn, *CA* 446.

232 *WJH* i, p. xlvii, where Hall also states that it was usual for bishops to recommend names to their clergy as clerks for Convocation, the clerical election being a formality.

233 *HMC Portland iii*, 69, 67.

234 *HMC Portland iii*, 67; SRO D/D/C/1878 bundle 4/unfol. 2 Nov. 1640; 2 Oct. 1640.

235 Bodl. Tanner MS 65/199, 209. Sir Simon D'Ewes informed the earl of Worcester in October 1640 that the withdrawal of the *et cetera* oath and the ship money were the prerequisites to communication between the king and the new Parliament. Ship money went first: 'last Monday morning, December the seventh, we utterlie damned the ship-money': D'Ewes, *Autobiography*, i. 243, 252.

Church. In the meanwhile petition after petition flooded into the Long Parliament from all parts of the country, and 'those liked the best that fly the highest'.[236] In the Lower House of Convocation which convened in November, Warmestry suggested that the clergy should withdraw the canons, but a majority of the members were not willing to condemn themselves until formally accused.[237] In the Upper House, Laud and the bishops considered abrogating the canons but decided that to do so was tantamount to recognizing parliamentary interference in their affairs.[238] Charles in the meanwhile retreated to the sidelines, and surreptitiously dissociated himself from the oath, the canons, and the ecclesiastical policies of the 1630s, which he had espoused. On 29 November, the day before the Commons debate on the canons, Laud wrote to his friend Selden, promising that if the debate did not proceed he would ask the king for a licence to abrogate them. However Laud's conciliatory gesture failed: the debate proceeded and the archbishop was left to face his accusers. Once again the king was about to distinguish between a churchman and a church cause.[239]

236 Bodl. Tanner MS 65/209^{v}–214.
237 Heylyn, *CA* 446.
238 Heylyn, *CA* 446; *WWL* vi. 589; Bodl. MS Selden supra 108/137.
239 Bodl. MS Selden supra 108/137; *WWL* vi. 338.

EPILOGUE

> Heresy, bribery and oppression, and a world of other notorious crimes, will be ready to walk impudently at noon-day, when the good and godly are without hope, and the evil and wicked without fear of a Parliament. For kings are but men.
>
> (D' Ewes, *Autobiography*, ii. 133)

It is now time to take a broader look at the canvas and to examine the contribution of this work to the historiography of the early seventeenth century, and in particular to the controversy surrounding the religious origins of the British Civil War and the English Revolution. Four questions appear pertinent: the extent to which Carolinism was innovatory within the context of previous Anglican history; the rationale for Charles I's subversion of the Jacobean polity; the extent of popular reception for Carolinism; and finally, the role it played (and that of religion generally) in the collapse of Charles I's regime in 1640 and in the outbreak of hostilities two years later.

I. CAROLINISM IN THE ANGLICAN CONTEXT

While disagreeing fundamentally with the revisionist thesis that Charles I was an Arminian revolutionary, that Arminian doctrine was substituted for Calvinist doctrine, and that the major ecclesiastical developments of the reign were an expression of this doctrinal shift, this work reinforces the particular revisionist platform which asserts that the king undermined a Jacobean consensus, in the process radicalizing Puritans and making dissidents of those who were not particularly critical of the Anglican Church. These developments, in their own turn, prepared the broad outlines of post-Restoration Anglicanism, from which nonconformity was doctrinally and ecclesiologically alienated.[1] In reaction to this 'revisionist' interpretation,

[1] Tyacke, *AC* 8 *et passim*. In his *The Struggle for the Constitution: England in the Seventeenth Century* (1963), 48, G. E. Aylmer broached a revisionist notion of Charles I well before the advent of fully-fledged revisionism.

some historians have asserted that Charles I merely continued the policies of his predecessors.[2] For two main reasons their argument does not convince. In the first place, they emphasize the monarchical origins of the Church to the exclusion of its parliamentary and populist basis. Anglicanism was distinctive for contemporaries because it was established by 'the Prince *and* Parliament'. In the second place, they play down the relative difference between the policies of Charles I and those of his predecessors. Whereas it may be feasible to see James I as promoting 'comprehensive, eirenic, politique policies in order to hold together a religiously divided society and church', it is difficult to see his son in the same light.[3] Lucy Hutchinson voiced what appeared in 1640 to be a generally held verdict on Charles: 'as in the primitive times it is observed that the best emperors were... stirr'd up by Sathan to be the bitterest persecutors of the Church, so this king was a worse encroacher upon the civil and spiritual liberties of his people by farr than his father.'[4]

Historians who depict Charles I as breaking the Anglican mould would question the suitability of 'Anglicanism' as a term to describe the confession and practice of the early reformed Church of England. They would suggest that the delineation of an identifiable Anglicanism throughout history is anachronistic and misleading, since the historiographical term has more exclusive connotations in present-day usage than for the sixteenth or early seventeenth centuries. Yet, although 'Anglicanism' as a word was unknown, 'Anglianisme' had appeared in print by 1616. Thomas Harrab's definition placed 'Anglianisme' firmly within the context of European Protestantism and bestowed upon it a meaning somewhat different from that which it later acquired. Thus what is in question is not the validity of Anglicanism as a term for the confession of the early reformed Church, but its definition. When redefined in the light of modern scholarship, early Anglicanism appears even more attuned than before to the vision of its sixteenth-century architects: an Anglicanism relativized by the historical developments which it absorbed and with which it interreacted, but retaining basic constituents over time

[2] G. Bernard, 'The Church of England c.1529–c.1642', *History*, (1990), 183–206, 192, 201; P. White, 'The Rise of Arminianism Reconsidered', *Past and Present*, 101 (1983), 34–54.

[3] Bernard, 'The Church of England', 192; T. Harrab, *Tessaradelphus or the Four Brothers* (1616), 'to the reader'.

[4] Lucy Hutchinson, *Memoirs of the Life of Colonel Hutchinson*, ed. J. Sutherland (Oxford, 1973), 46.

and revealing more than previously its characteristic genius as an accommodation.[5]

It was this accommodation that Charles I destroyed. Although the king died a martyr for the Church of England, he died for a very different Church from that which had existed during the 1630s. By 1640–1 the Church had been brought to the brink of dissolution, with calls for the removal of its bishops 'root and branch', the abolition of its liturgy, and the destruction of its jurisdiction.[6] This work has attempted to throw light on the reasons for this crisis by showing how, after 1625, Carolinism altered the early reformed Church of England. What are the broad characteristics of Elizabethan and Jacobean Anglicanism alongside which any conclusions stemming from this analysis of Caroline policy presented in the previous pages must be placed?

1. The Jacobean Church, like its Elizabethan predecessor was a national Church, whose Supreme Governor was the monarch and whose constitutional arrangements had been established through the co-operation of Crown and Parliament between 1530 and 1560. Although the scope and content of the royal prerogative in ecclesiastical affairs had always been a contentious issue, Charles I destroyed a working relationship by promoting highly controversial ecclesiastical measures without parliamentary support and by threatening parliamentary privileges. Although the royal supremacy was not openly questioned, the way in which the Church had become enmeshed in the promotion of arbitrary government was. It was the Caroline Church which had assumed the key role in the royal programme to assert prerogative rights over 'popular' and 'Puritan' tendencies, aiming (so the king believed) at the overthrow of his authority.[7]

[5] Harrab, *Tessaradelphus*, 'to the reader'; see Ch. 1 nn. 1–6. The major works which have contributed to this redefinition are: Collinson, *RP*; Parker *ES*; Tyacke *AC*; N. R. N. Tyacke, 'Puritanism, Arminianism and Counter-Revolution,' in C. S. R. Russell (ed.), *Origins of the English Civil War* (1973), 119–43; K. Fincham and P. Lake, 'The Ecclesiastical Policy of James I', *Journal of British Studies*, 24 (1985), 169–201; K. Fincham, *Prelate as Pastor: the Episcopate of James I* (Oxf., 1990); P. Lake, *Moderate Puritans and the Elizabethan Church* (Cambridge, 1982); Lake, *AP*; J. S. Morrill, 'The Religious Context of the English Civil War', *TRHS*, 5th ser., 34 (1984), 155–78. For the contribution of literary historians to the redefinition of Puritanism see Ch. 1 n. 10.

[6] J. S. Morrill, 'The Church in England, 1642–9', in his (ed.) *Reactions to the English Civil War* (1982); A. Fletcher, *The Outbreak of the English Civil War* (1981), 91 *et passim*; W. Abbott, 'The Issue of Episcopacy in the Long Parliament: The Reasons for its Abolition' (Oxford D.Phil. thesis, 1981).

[7] See section iv; C. Cross, *Church and People, 1450–1660* (1976); id., 'Churchmen and the Royal Supremacy', in F. Heal and R. O'Day (eds.), *Church and Society in England: Henry VIII to James I* (1977).

2. The Reformation Church possessed a jurisdictional capacity emanating from the Crown, which exerted some consistorial discipline over religious, moral, and social irregularities. Abbot's application and extension of social justice through the High Commission and the Star Chamber foreshadowed Laud's policy. However the Caroline Church differed from its predecessors in that it witnessed an unparalleled number of prosecutions in diocesan consistories, in particular over canonical disobedience. Whereas James I had incorporated religious nonconformity within the structures of the established Church, it was not tolerated under his successor. Thus, as a result of Carolinism, discipline effectively joined preaching and the administration of the sacraments as the third mark of the Anglican Church.[8]

3. The structure of the early reformed Church was Erastian and proprietorial, as its patronage and financial resources were effectively in the hands of the laity or the Crown. By supporting the Laudian programme to reduce lay influence within the Church and in particular to restore its impropriated lands, tithes, and advowsons, Charles I did nothing to allay fears that the secularization of church property (the economic investment which helped to bind the laity to the preservation of the Church) would be reversed. Apart from the direct resumption of royal and ecclesiastical rights in support of the institutional Church, Carolinism also reversed the Jacobean laicization of the Church by restricting lay religious expression and activities, and by advancing an aggressive professionalism and corporate identity among the clergy.[9] Thus the Root and Branch Petition of 1640 complained of 'the encouragement of ministers to despise the temporal magistracy, the nobles and gentry of the land ... knowing that they, being the bishops' creatures, shall be supported'. As Johann Sommerville has suggested, the petition's failure to name the king as one of the 'temporal magistrates' implies that its drafters were convinced that the king was opposed to their interests.[10]

4. The officially sanctioned ceremonies and rites of early

[8] See all chapters. Cross, *Church and People*; Fincham and Lake, 'The Ecclesiastical Policy of James I', 169–201; Bodl. MS J. Walker c. 9/31–57ᵛ.

[9] See Ch. 1, Ch. 2 section iii, Ch. 4; C. Hill, *The Economic Problems of the Church from Archbishop Whitgift to the Long Parliament* (Oxford, 1956), id., *Society and Puritanism in Pre-Revolutionary England* (1964); F. M. Heal, 'The Economic Problems of the Clergy', in Heal and O'Day, *Church and Society in England*, 99–119.

[10] J. P. Sommerville, *Politics and Ideology in England 1603–1640* (1986), 221.

Anglicanism were few. Although some of these were given more canonical force in the Canons of 1604, they remained largely unimposed for most of James I's reign. Moreover, whereas in 1616 the ceremonies of Anglicanism were 'daily decreasing', the period after 1625 witnessed the introduction of several uncanonical rites and orders, as well as the first serious attempt to enforce the Canons of 1604.[11] Thus Carolinism widened considerably the bounds of conformity, and disaffection to the Church grew appreciably. This stands in sharp contrast to the period after 1640, when these accretions were largely swept away and the Prayer Book surfaced once again as a unifying feature of restored, primitive Elizabethan and Jacobean Anglicanism.[12]

5. Early seventeenth-century Anglicanism had a strongly evangelical complexion. Rather than being alienated from the Church, evangelical Puritans were integral to its mainstream. Although some might scruple at the retention and enforcement of certain rites, many conformed. Laity and clergy alike increased the limited evangelistic capacity of the Church through the establishment of lectureships, prophesyings, repetitions, fasts, and exercises. Charles I's determination to assert the discipline of the institutional Church over its voluntary forms, and to elevate the liturgy over popular preaching emasculated many of these initiatives and created the impression that he did not favour the gospel. In fact he loathed evangelical Puritanism, its perceived individualistic and nonconformist tendencies, and sought to marginalize it from the Church.[13] Consequently, during his reign, the name of 'Puritan' became 'the very inquisition of England'.[14] Thus the advent of Carolinism increased nonconformity, reopened the question of Presbyterianism, and drove many Puritans to seek asylum in the Low Countries, Scotland, or

[11] See esp. Ch. 1 section ii, Ch. 2 section ii, Chs. 6 and 7; Harrab, *Tessaradelphus*, 'to the reader'; Collinson, *RP*, chs. 2–3, 6; K. Fincham, *Prelate as Pastor*, 253–76 *et passim*.

[12] Morrill, 'The Church in England 1642–9', in his (ed.) *Reactions to the English Civil War* (1982). The growth of disaffection to the Caroline Church within the provinces can be traced in the many localist works listed in the bibliography, and in the petitions of 1640–1 (for the context see Fletcher, *Outbreak of the English Civil War*, (111, *et passim*).

[13] See esp. Ch. 1 section i, Ch. 4; Collinson, *GP*, esp, 467–99; Collinson, *RP*, chs. 2–3, 6; Fincham, *Prelate as Pastor*, 253–276 *et passim*; Bodl. MS J. Walker c. 9/31–57^{v}.

[14] Hacket, *SR* ii. 39.

America.[15] In opposition to this thesis, some historians have denied the 'Puritan' complexion of the Jacobean Church, and have suggested that Charles I merely upheld Anglican moderation against Puritan radicalism.[16] This ignores the fact that the king and his bishops were prepared to go out of their way to taunt the Jacobean Church with the name of Puritan, and that within the Jacobean context their own anti-Puritan views were in the minority (even if they were to become the established and advocated position under Charles I). This is sufficiently revealed by Thomas Triplett, who, fearing a Puritan backlash in May 1640, reminded Archbishop Laud of a time when, apart from himself, 'my ever honoured dead lord [Howson?]', and two or three others in the whole university [Oxford] 'there was scarce any durst show themselves for the Church [so great was] the power of prevailing Puritans'.[17]

6. The numerical and social weight of many evangelical Puritans within the later Elizabethan and Jacobean Church, together with the interest of many justices in the preservation of the status quo, contributed to the creation of consensual views on sabbatarian and moral issues among many of the Jacobean élites.[18] After 1630 this sabbatarian consensus was eroded when Charles I promoted Sunday pastimes and anti-sabbatarian ideas. Whereas James I had shelved his declaration of sports because of the degree of opposition it encountered, Charles I not only reintroduced it but pressed ministers

[15] For the emigration issue see N. C. P. Tyack's thesis: 'Migration from East Anglia to New England before 1660' (London Univ. Ph.D. thesis), and the work in progress of Dr Susan Hardman. Bernard, 'The Church of England', 199, suggests that migration to New England was either economic in motivation or constituted the migration of 'religious extremists whose views few high Calvinists would have tolerated, and who left not because of any new "crisis" in England in the 1620s and 1630s but because of the much deeper dilemma of living among the "prophane".' However Sir Simon D'Ewes (a moderate Calvinist, a first-hand witness of the emigration from East Anglia, and who himself had considered emigrating), had no doubt that the major reason for the exodus was the reactionary ecclesiastical policies of Charles I: D'Ewes, *Autobiography*, i. 112–13, 117–99, 145. Likewise Pym; Bodl. Tanner 61/215: that those who emigrated, left not 'by reason of scarcity of bread' but the 'bread of life'. Avihu Zakai, 'The Gospel of Reform: The Origins of the Great Puritan Migration', *Journal of Ecclesiastical History*, 37/4 (Oct. 1986), 584–603, puts the migration of the 1630s into a wider context, but his evidence does not explain away (as he claims, p. 601) the religio-political origins of the migration of those years.

[16] See note 2 above.

[17] PRO SP 16/447/27. For popular Puritanism in the countryside see Collinson, *RP* chs. 3, 5–6; and M. Spufford, *Contrasting Communities: English Villages in the Sixteenth and Seventeenth Centuries* (Camb., 1974), 262–3.

[18] See Ch. 5; Parker, *ES passim*.

to read it. The moral and political consequences of Caroline anti-sabbatarianism should not be underestimated, for according to many contemporaries who looked back over the 1630s it was the abuse of the Lord's day which 'was a principle procurer of God's anger, since poured out on this land, in a long and bloody civil war'.[19]

7. In 1616 Harrab thought 'Anglianisme' a useful term, because the English Church did not acknowledge any particular theologian as its founder. Calvin was respected but not markedly more than many of the second generation of indigenous, Anglican reformed theologians. Certainly Anglican doctrine, as represented in its main codes, in Puritan soteriology and within the schools, was more Reformed than Lutheran.[20] However, the 'unofficial' doctrine held by many of its clergy and members may have reflected a broader and less orthodox doctrinal complexion; within some parishes it may have taken on more Erasmian overtones.[21] By restricting rigid predestinarian opinions, attacking conventional sabbatarianism, stigmatizing Puritanism, and cold-shouldering the continental Reformed congregations, Charles I made it clear that he did not subscribe to the reformed doctrinal 'consensus' which had existed within the Jacobean polity among the clerical and lay élites. Instead he attempted to carve out a different kind of peace, characterized less by an anti-Calvinist purge than by the absence of doctrinal discussion and the propagation of his sacramental kingship.[22]

8. Since the Church did not recognize papal supremacy, its survival was closely tied to that of European Protestantism as well as the

[19] Fuller, *CH* iii. 425; see Ch. 5.

[20] See Ch. 3; Harrab, *Tessaradelphus*; B. Hall, 'The Early Rise and Gradual Decline of Lutheranism in England 1520–1660', in D. Baker (ed.), *Reform and Reformation in England and the Continent c. 1500–1700* (Oxford 1979); R. T. Kendall, *Calvin and English Calvinism to 1649* (Oxf., 1979); P. Lake, 'Calvinism and the English Church, 1570–1635', *Past and Present*, 114 (1987); id., *Moderate Puritans*; id., 'Protestants, Puritans and Laudians', 618 ff.

[21] By 'Erasmian' I mean that the moral injunctions of Christianity were emphasized to the exclusion of its evangelistic message; that the message conveyed was that Christianity was a philosophy of life rather than a way of salvation. To describe such beliefs as 'Erasmian' is preferable to 'rustic Pelagianism' since this has too many 'Arminian' connotations, although 'Pelagian', like 'Arminian', was in use as a term of abuse whereas 'Erasmian' was not. As for Erasmus's influence upon the English scene see among others: A. Fox and J. Guy (eds.), *Reassessing the Henrician Age: Humanism, Politics and Reform 1500–1550* (Oxf., 1986), chs. 1–3. As a matter of interest, Erasmus's *Paraphrases* were often to be found in Anglican churches (NRO X2159/5/11); BL Harl. MS 6272/38.

[22] See especially Chs. 1 and 3, and all others as well.

survival of the Protestant succession.[23] At a time when the frontiers of European Protestantism were being pushed back, the recatholicization of Anglicanism under Charles I (the introduction of new ceremonies, the elevation of the institution of the Church, the assertion of episcopal power and clerical autonomy), conversions to popery, and the perceived toleration of recusancy served to create the impression that the king and the bishops were conspiring either to return the country to Rome or to set up an English popery.[24]

9. Whereas James I had been content to establish just the basic minimum of conformity between the Church of England and the Churches of Scotland and Ireland, Charles I attempted to bring them into a closer canonical and liturgical unity. It was the attempt to impose a prayer book on Scotland which triggered off the Scottish Rebellion, and which attuned the country to the reality of Civil War four years before the outbreak of formal hostilities.[25]

Taking into account these issues, there can be little question that Charles I fundamentally altered the nature of Elizabethan and Jacobean Anglicanism, with fateful consequences for himself and the country. As such, whether he saw himself as an innovator is irrelevant. Although the king's policies did not have a uniform impact upon the country, their effects transcended ecclesiastical boundaries and created deep scruples of conscience, which led contemporaries to question the demands of authority. This meant that the opposition to Carolinism in 1640 would be national rather than merely localist. Moreover the attempt in the early days of the Long Parliament to resurrect the Jacobean religious compromise failed precisely because Charles I had so effectively discredited the notion of Anglican moderation.[26] Carolinism also hindered all future attempts during the following twenty years to find a suitable ecclesiastical system to

[23] Harrab, *Tessaradelphus*; T. Cogswell, *The Blessed Revolution: English Politics and the Coming of War, 1621–1624* (Camb., 1989).

[24] C. Hibbard, *Charles I and the Popish Plot* (Chapel Hill, NC, 1983); Morrill, 'The Religious Context of the English Civil War', 171–2.

[25] C. S. R. Russell, 'The British Problem and the English Civil War', *History*, 72 (1987); id., *The Causes of the English Civil War* (Oxf., 1990), chs. 2, 5; id. *The Fall of the British Monarchies 1637–1642* (Oxford, 1991); see also Ch. 1 section iii.

[26] Morrill, 'The Religious Context of the English Civil War', 165–75; id., 'The Attack on the Church of England in the Long Parliament, 1640–1642', in D. Beales and G. Best (eds.), *History, Society and the Churches* (Camb., 1985); id., 'The Church in England, 1642–49', in his (ed.), *Reactions to the English Civil War 1642–1649* (1982).

replace what had been destroyed. But, in the long term, after the eirenic interlude of the Cromwellian Church, Charles I posthumously triumphed over his foes, through the official expulsion of nonconformists after 1660 and the recognition of his martyrdom. This helped to mould a more exclusive established Church than that which had existed before 1625, and went some way to realizing what the king had only half-achieved.[27]

II. THE REASONS FOR THE CAROLINE REACTION

Some revisionists have located the reasons for Charles I's hostility to the Jacobean polity in his supposed conversion to Arminianism. This, it is held, made him anathematize its doctrinal opposite, Calvinism, the assumed doctrine of the Anglican confession. Furthermore, to underline his dissociation from Calvinists within the Church hierarchy, the king, it is claimed, associated their Calvinism with Puritanism, by subscribing to the notion that a specific 'doctrinal Puritanism' existed, i.e., Calvinism. As Laud and his disciples were seen as 'Arminians' who had poisoned the king's mind against Calvinism, the archbishop surfaced in revisionist historiography as the greatest calamity to befall the Church of England and the person who, more than any other, was responsible for the collapse of the Stuart regime.[28]

Given the degree of the king's hostility to individual religious expression and his obsession with his sacramental credentials, it is not easy to see what role doctrinal 'Arminianism' might have played in destroying the character of early Anglicanism. Moreover this work has questioned the current definition of Arminianism and has suggested that the misplaced attention given to it has diverted our attention from other features more or equally worthy of consideration.[29] The revisionist writing which challenged the conventional interpretation of the English Civil War generated reasons for the collapse of the Stuart regime other than Arminianism, but these writings nevertheless accepted Dr Tyacke's thesis uncritically, in some areas overstated its argument, and in several cases used it as an

[27] C. Cross, 'The Church in England 1646–1660', in G. E. Aylmer (ed.), *The Interregnum: The Quest for Settlement 1646–1660* (1975), 99–121.

[28] N. Tyacke, 'Puritanism, Arminianism and Counter-Revolution', 119–43; id., *AC*, *passim*; n. 97.

[29] See chs. 1–3 in particular, but all others as well.

apology for things which could not easily be explained. This is not to deny Tyacke's formidable achievement in generating discussion, altering our perspectives, and in delineating the growth of anti-Calvinism, nor is it to deny that the Laudians were sometimes accused of Arminianism.[30]

There are three main axioms in the current revisionist understanding of Arminianism: that Charles I was an Arminian revolutionary, who gave his full backing to a clerical Arminian fifth column within the Church;[31] that Arminian doctrine was substituted for Calvinist doctrine, as the king destroyed the previous Calvinist consensus;[32] and that the major ecclesiastical developments of the 1630s (the sacramental changes, the anti-sabbatarianism, the campaign to restore clerical over lay rights) were an expression of this doctrinal shift, as Arminianism found expression in a programme of Arminianization.[33] Each of these points has been addressed at length in this work.

1. The king disliked doctrinal dispute intensely and attempted to attain throughout his reign a doctrinal vacuum, by supporting neither an Arminian nor a Calvinist interpretation of the articles, regardless of the impact this would have on the prevalent reformed doctrine of the Church. Those who received patronage from him did so in the first place because they met his criteria for office, which had no particular doctrinal conditions attached to it. Certainly the king's dislike of nonconformity made him susceptible to the advice of those who were not (on their own reckoning) 'doctrinal Puritans'. Yet this did not mean that these clergy were doctrinally Arminian; in some respects (and to varying degrees) they were anti-Calvinist; but what effectively united them was a dislike of the Jacobean Church's toleration of nonconformity and the (perceived) elevation of its preaching over its sacramental life, both of which they might identify as the handmaids of reformed doctrine. Whereas their efforts to impress the discipline of the Church were unequivocally supported by the king, the

30 As a sample, C. S. R. Russell, *Parliaments and English Politics, 1621–1629* (Oxford, 1979), 29–32; A. G. R. Smith, *The Emergence of a National State: The Commonwealth of England, 1529–1660* (1984), 282–3; A. J. Fletcher, *A County Community in Peace and War: Sussex 1600–1660* (1975); B. Coward, *The Stuart Age* (1980), 148–9; see also the list in Bernard, 'The Church of England', 183–4.

31 Tyacke, 'Puritanism, Arminianism and Counter-Revolution', 119–43; Tyacke, *AC* 8, *et passim*, 246–7.

32 Tyacke, *AC* 246–7, 8, *et passim*.

33 Ibid., 162, ch. 8; 'Puritanism, Arminianism and Counter-Revolution,' 133.

demands of royal policy circumscribed their anti-Calvinism. In fact, due in part to the Woodstock meeting of 1631, which clarified the king's attitudes towards predestinarian controversy further than the proclamation of 1626 and the declaration of 1628, the 1630s witnessed a distinct diminution in anti-Calvinist tactics.[34]

2. These considerations help to explain why the reformed doctrine of the English Church survived 1640. There never was any question of Arminianism replacing Calvinism: as Peter Lake has written of the anti-Calvinists, 'the positive thrust of their own position was not towards the propagation of an alternative Arminian orthodoxy'.[35] The question was how far could the reformed doctrine of the Church be watered down so that it no longer presented the (perceived) threat to the liturgy and discipline of the Church, without undermining the essential Protestantism of the Anglican Church or the credal predestinarianism of its leaders. There took place after 1625 not a proscription of Calvinism (the doctrine of election was inviolate, as long as it was not antinomian) but an attempt to excise its rigid predestinarian offshoots, above all the doctrine of reprobation and its antinomian tendencies. The opinion that Calvinism was proscribed after 1625 also rests on an over-optimistic expectation of (and misreading of the purpose of) central edicts.[36] Moreover recent work on sermons, catechisms, and censorship during the early modern period points to the survival of Calvinism within Anglicanism during the 1630s. The charged anti-reformed atmosphere of the Caroline Church certainly created a climate which could promote the growth of Arminian ideas, as well as other heterodoxies. But in any case, the articulation of English Arminianism belonged to the future, not to the early seventeenth century.[37]

3. In the light of these considerations, the notion of an Arminianization of the Church during the 1630s looks decidedly questionable. Dr Tyacke saw in such developments as the increased sacramentalism, anti-sabbatarianism, and the reinvestment of the clerical and institutional authority of the Church the peculiar marks of

[34] See Ch. 3 section iii. [35] Lake, *AP* 228–9. [36] See Ch. 3 section i–iii.

[37] I. Green, '"For Children in Yeeres and Children in Understanding": The Emergence of the English Catechism under Elizabeth and the Early Stuarts', *Journal of Ecclesiastical History*, 37 (1986), 411–12; Lake, 'Calvinism and the English Church'; S. Lambert, 'Richard Montagu, Arminianism and Censorship', *Past and Present*, 124 (Aug. 1989); P. White's forthcoming work on predestinarianism and hermeneutics. See *Short Title Catalogue* for the many new editions of Calvinist works which appeared during the 1630s.

ascendant English Arminianism. Conditioning this perception was his adoption of a simple Weberian polarity of predestination versus grace, which made little concession to the doctrinal nuances which existed in the early seventeenth century, and which overlooked the fact that those whom he designated as Calvinists could be found often supporting measures which Weberian logic dictated that they should not. Moreover neither the patronage connexions of the period nor the index of ecclesiastical preferment correspond to a Calvinist-versus-Arminian hypothesis. Whether they liked it or not, Calvinists were effectively trapped between their allegiance to the Crown and the personal demands of the monarch. Their complicity in the changes of the 1630s revealed their obedience to the Royal Supremacy rather than their eclipse by any particular ecclesiastical faction.[38]

If the Arminian thesis as an explanation of the ecclesiological shift of the reign is redundant (which is not to deny its importance in the reconstitution of early Anglican history), then how are we to explain the changes of the 1630s? This work has suggested that they stemmed from the confluence of two distinct (if sometimes converging) developments: one more long term, the recatholicization of the Church, emanating in part from its patristic and historic reinvestment, which forced reformed doctrine to relate itself to a wider context and asserted the liturgy and discipline of the Church over the primacy of the pulpit; and the other short term (and of more immediate consequence): the determination of Charles I to impress his sacramental notions of kingship upon the country, to carve out a greater Anglo-Catholic identity and to undermine evangelical Puritanism and its perceived handmaid, nonconformist persuasion. In order to highlight the distinct identities of these two interrelated developments, this work has denoted them 'Laudianism' and 'Carolinism'. However Carolinism is a more suitable umbrella term as it was the lowest common denominator of all that was innovatory in the reign. It also suggests that the role of the king has been seriously underestimated and that more coherence existed behind the royal policy than is traditionally allowed.[39]

As an explanation for the king's reaction against the reformed Church of England, the role of doctrine was negligible (and in stark

[38] Tyacke, *AC* 10, *et passim*; Sommerville, *Politics and Ideology*, 43, 208, 223; P. Lake, 'Serving God and the Times: The Calvinist Conformity of Robert Sanderson', *Journal of British Studies*, 27/2 (Apr. 1988), 81–117.

[39] See Chs. 1–2.

opposition to its importance in the popular defence of traditional Anglicanism). Charles I was not attracted by doctrinal debate and he did not easily articulate his theological beliefs; if we can describe his opinions in doctrinal terms at all, then they approximated to an anti-scholastic and anti-fideistic humanism. He was more concerned with the reformation of manners than any reformation of belief, more with matters of morality than personal salvation. Consequently where there was little room for revelation, superstition crept in; and 'if a man by eschewing superstition grow to be profane, what hath he gotten?', asked the king.[40]

Although the king never committed to paper what he understood by 'profanity', it seems most likely that it meant the associated evils against which much of the wider Caroline policy was directed: 'popularity' and 'Puritanism'. As early as 1626 Charles appears to have been convinced of a Puritan conspiracy against his throne, orchestrated by elements within the Commons, judiciary, and the populace at large. Although (as Professor Russell has shown) there was no such identifiable Puritan opposition to Charles I in the 1620s, this was far from the king's perception.[41] Some clergy exploited the king's paranoia and might implicate Calvinism, in varying degrees, with this 'Puritan' conspiracy, but there is no evidence that he subscribed to this particular interpretation. Whatever his understanding of the 'opposition', Charles's defence against it was to retreat into the shelter of divine-right monarchy, which thereafter he elevated as a buffer against Jacobean disaffection and as a device to forge conflicting passions into Caroline allegiance.[42]

The assertion of prerogative rule in Church and Commonwealth after 1629, the promotion of conformity, and the propagation of

[40] See Ch. 1 section i; the king penned this question in his copy of Bacon's *Advancement of Learning*, cited in R. Smuts, *Court Culture and the Origins of a Royalist Tradition in Early Stuart England* (Philadelphia, 1987), 242.

[41] K. Sharpe, 'The Personal Rule of Charles I', in H. Tomlinson (ed.), *Before the English Civil War* (1983), 58–63, id., *Criticism and Compliment: The Politics of Literature in the England of Charles I* (Camb., 1987); R. Smuts, *Court Culture*, 258–62; R. Cust, *The Forced Loan and English Politics 1626–1628* (Oxford, 1987), 328–9, 332, 336; C. S. R. Russell, *Parliaments and English Politics*, 26–8; R. Cust and A. Hughes (eds.), *Conflict in Early Stuart England: Studies in Religion and Politics, 1603–1642* (1989), 84–6.

[42] PRO SP 16/175/69, SP/16/177/8, SP/16/176/46; Thomas Jackson, *A Treatise of Divine Essence and Attributes* (1628) epistle dedicatory; L. J. Reeve, *Charles I and the Road to Personal Rule* (1989), ch. 6, 172–80, 295–300; Cust, *Forced Loan*, 13–90, 324–32; *Conflict in Early Stuart England*, ed. Cust and Hughes, 18–21, 84–6.

his sacramental kingship constituted the response of a monarch convinced that repression would succeed where discourse could not. Whereas Parliament might spurn his prerogative, the established Church could not easily escape his advances. Under the Royal Supremacy there existed no effective insurance against the misuse of the ecclesiastical prerogative. At the same time reformed Calvinists advocated *iure divino* kingship as much as their Laudian associates, and thus effectively disabled themselves from adopting a more critical stance.[43] Moreover the Anglican Church provided Charles with a subsidiary apparatus of local control to shire administration, and one more attuned to the propagation of his prerogative and sacramental rights. During the 1630s canonical obedience, or conformity to initiatives such as the Instructions of 1629 and reading the book of sports became as much a test of loyalty to the Crown as it did to the Church. The eyes of the king peered down from the walls of the High Commission Court, while the repainting of the royal arms often accompanied the internal reorientation of the church.[44] As Lucy Hutchinson diagnosed, the interests of state religion had infiltrated the sanctuary of true religion. Through the reorientation of the parish church according to the perspective and liturgy of the Chapel Royal, Charles had effectively translated the doctrine of the divine right of kings into a seductive and aesthetic spectacle. But unlike the masque, the Caroline liturgy was not symbolic allegory, which offered little scope for political realism or public audience, but a powerful advertisement of the king's sacramental notions of personal authority, which reached into every parish of the land. Purgative and paternalistic at the same time, the cult of Carolinism served to atone for the mistakes of the Jacobean past and to open the nation to the beneficent light of the Caroline countenance.[45]

The political implications for Charles I's rule of Laudianism during the 1630s have been addressed by Lord Dacre. However, in contradiction to his argument, Laudianism itself had little political momentum. If it attained political importance it was because the king harnessed its energies to his own requirements, rather than because he came to recognize the force of its political argument. Charles I's

[43] Sommerville, *Politics and Ideology*, 206–7, 223.
[44] *The Confession of John Bastwick* (1641); PRO SP 16/362/9; PRO SP 16/366/79.
[45] L. Hutchinson, cited in L. Marcus, *The Politics of Mirth: Johnson, Herrick, Milton, Marvell and the Defense of Old Holiday Pastimes* (Chicago, 1986), 6; see especially Ch. 1 section ii, Ch. 6.

attempt to subvert the Church for his own purposes was necessarily more controversial than Laud's attempt to utilize the state in support of the Church, although such was the loyalty to the concept of the Royal Supremacy it was necessarily the latter rather than the former development which became the focus of attack in 1640. Without the backing of Charles I Laudianism would have remained as it was under Andrewes: a movement enriching the sacramental life of the Church, while advancing a healthy, if socially disturbing, criticism of the Erastian Reformation, combined with an unfortunate reluctance to preach from the pulpit, if not from the table.[46]

Perhaps only in 1640 did Laudianism and Carolinism come together as fully compatible and equal partners. Only then did *iure divino* episcopacy sit down with *iure divino* kingship as equal partners. With the passing of the Canons of 1640 Laud could at last prosecute change with the force of canonical authority. Yet the Canons of 1640 were far from being the logical expression of an overriding metropolitical power or an English 'papal tyranny'. Any such pretensions were undercut by the new-found power of the ordinary in ecclesiastical jurisdiction. The Canons of 1640 were less a victory for Laud over fissiparous forces than a vindication of his belief in the divine right of the episcopacy. Nor did the canons give retrospective canonical confirmation to the Caroline innovations of the 1630s without discrimination. While they reinforced many of the reactionary developments of the past years, they nevertheless moderated others. Significantly they failed to condone some policies which had been pursued unilaterally by individual ordinaries. From these Laud had isolated himself during the 1630s through disengagement, sponsoring a more persuasive means of extracting compliance, or by undercutting the letter of the royal demands. Those who had ordered otherwise, he protested in his trial, had done so 'without [his] knowledge or against [his] direction', and he had 'sharply chid some for this very particular'.[47]

In fact, when it came to the realization of controversial non-canonical measures, Laud was seriously out of step with the pace and some of the objectives of Caroline policy. Policy had passed him by. Yet as this work reveals, Laud was more politically pragmatic than

[46] H. R. Trevor-Roper, 'Laudianism and Political Power' in his *Catholics, Anglicans and Puritans* (1987), 41, 40–119.

[47] See esp. Ch. 7 section ii, Ch. 6 section iii; *WWL*, vi. 126.

Charles I, confirming the archbishop's opinion that the king neither knew 'how to be, or be made great'.[48] It was Laud who advised him against two of the most impolitic decisions of the reign: the publication of Mainwaring's treatise and the continuation of Convocation beyond the Short Parliament. In fact all the attributes which historians have traditionally awarded Laud: intransigence, intolerance, authoritarianism, paranoia, duplicity, suit the king better. According to Lucy Hutchinson, Charles I 'was a prince that had nothing of faith or truth, justice or generosity in him: he was the most obstinate person in his self-will that ever was, and was so bent upon being an absolute uncontrollable Sovereigne that he was resolv'd either to be such a king or none'.[49] If Charles I is a historical enigma it is because Laud has carried his mask for too long. As diocesan and metropolitan the archbishop tempered and undercut the letter of the king's orders introducing and pressing the three most controversial ecclesiastical initiatives of the 1630s: the altar policy, the restraint of lecturers, and the book of sports. As for other non-canonical measures Laud advertised them as decent or creative of order, but issues not to be forced, expressing the hope that the clergy would become habituated to them in time. This was an attitude and policy which served to restrain the drive to Caroline conformity and one which allowed a measure of tolerance for individual conscience under the law.[50] But Laud failed, as Clarendon noted, to make his intentions appear as 'candid' as they were.[51] While he might allow others to shoulder the responsibility for introducing and pressing controversial policies, his high notion of kingship, together with the insecurity of his own position, minimized any outward expression of dissent to policies pursued by others under royal patronage. His respect for ordinary authority certainly served to prevent him from making a more positive stand against those who pursued policies less accommodating than his own. The recognition of an authentic Laudian policy was hindered also by the fact that in the Caroline reaction to the Jacobean establishment differences over policy might

[48] See all chapters; *WWL* iii. 443; Cust, *Forced Loan*, 325.

[49] Hutchinson, *Memoirs of the Life of Colonel Hutchinson*, 47. While my work confirms the depiction of the king's character and policies in John Reeve's study, *Charles I and the Road to Personal Rule*, (see ch. 6 and pp. 172–9 in particular) it conflicts with his analysis of Laudianism and Arminianism.

[50] See esp. Ch. 2 section ii; Ch. 1 section iii; Chs. 4–6.

[51] Clarendon, i. 125.

appear as matters less of substance than of circumstance. Laud's personal defects—his temperamental character, his lack of social and courtly graces, his convinced self-righteousness—all served to make him an isolated figure whose true intentions were easily open to misconstruction. Moreover the acerbity of his drive to impress the canonical discipline and monopolies of the institutional Church, in particular against the laity in High Commission and Star Chamber, meant that many would feel little volition to find any redeeming features in one who had pitted clerical pretensions against their vested interests: 'the angry wasp', who, according to Sir Harbottle Grimstone, 'had stung . . . the tail of everything'.[52]

Thus in 1640 the archbishop surfaced as the obvious scapegoat for Carolinism. To blame Laud avoided implicating the king directly, while allowing him room for manœuvre to alter his policies. Thus Laud was added to the long list of those who had trusted Charles and had later found themselves abandoned. Isolated from the king, he became the focus for all objectivized venom against the regime, a necessary counterpoise to Charles I in the royal bid to recover the initiative and a shadow of credibility in the political impasse of 1640–1. The archbishop's refusal to reveal all of his warrants and orders, 'lest anything might prejudice the king his master's honour', served to cover some of the king's traces.[53] Yet in the aftermath of the Personal Rule contemporaries became increasingly aware that culpability for the subversion of the Jacobean polity fell more widely, randomly, and higher than they had previously thought. As early as January 1641 certain peers were impressed by Laud's 'patient and moderate carriage', while four earls personally informed him that the 'Lords were not so sharp against [him] as they were at first; and that they were resolved only to sequester [him] from the king's counsels and to put [him] from [his] archbishopric'.[54] In 1641 Laud did not follow Strafford to the block and by May of that year, according to Coke, Secretary of State, the case against him was 'asleep'.[55]

[52] Cited in J. S. Morrill, 'The Religious Context of the English Civil War', *TRHS*, vol. 34, 164; PRO SP 16/499/78.

[53] Bodl. Tanner 61/243 (3); Reeve, *Charles I and the Road to Personal Rule*, 175; Fletcher, *A County Community*, 6.

[54] *WWL* iii. 395; Reeve, *Charles I and the Road to Personal Rule*, 175; Sommerville, *Politics and Ideology*, 207. Laud informed Heylyn that the worst he expected was to be sequestered and confined to his diocese (like Abbot in 1627), Heylyn, *CA* 464.

[55] *HMC Cowper ii*, 284.

Deprived of bail, Laud survived the outbreak of hostilities and languished in the Tower for four years. Then in 1644, to satiate the appetite above all of the Presbyterian Scots and as an expendable pawn in the royal negotiations leading to Uxbridge, he was put on trial, attainted of High Treason, and executed.[56]

III. THE RECEPTION OF CAROLINISM

It is axiomatic to the general revisionist argument that the ecclesiastical policies of Charles I's reign were unpopular, as they are seen as having overturned a previously existing consensus.[57] Other historians who see Charles I as merely affirming and continuing the traditions of Anglican moderation necessarily adopt the opposite line, that the changes were welcome. Consequently these latter historians are forced into seeking explanations for the collapse of the regime and the opposition to the ecclesiastical policies in short-term considerations, which are mostly extraneous, such as the Scottish rebellion, in spite of the fact that oppositionist voices in 1640 based their platform not merely on developments after 1637, but the whole gamut of ecclesiastical policies since 1625.[58]

By the end of 1640 Charles I's governorship of the Church had received an almost unanimous vote of no confidence. The canons appeared to be an attempt to make permanent policies which many had hoped were only temporary aberrations. Even after their abrogation, the Commons distrusted the king's intentions. D'Ewes noted the general scepticism of the House when Charles promised to restore the Church to the status quo, not as it had existed under

[56] Bodl. Tanner 61/240; *WWL* iv. 413–25; D. Nicholas, *Mr. Secretary Nicholas 1593–1669: His Life and Letters* (1955), 204; H. R. Trevor-Roper, *Archbishop Laud*, 427, 430–3; C. Carlton, *Archbishop William Laud* (1987), 223; PRO SP 16/499/1. Herne, Laud's solicitor, advised him to drop the accusation of 'traitors' against Parliament in his scaffold speech, the day before his execution, so that it would not hazard the royal negotiations with Parliament: Bodl. Tanner 61/240. The king believed that Laud's death would further the royal cause: J. O. Halliwell, *Letters of the Kings of England* (1846), ii. 361. The only lords who voted for Laud's condemnation were Kent, Pembroke, Salisbury, Bolingbroke, North, and Grey of Wark: Heylyn, *CA* 527–8. See also W. G. Palmer, 'Invitation to a Beheading: Factions in Parliament, the Scots and the Execution of Archbishop William Laud in 1645', *Historical Magazine of the Protestant Episcopal Church*, 52/1 (1983), 17–27.

[57] See n. 1 above.

[58] Bernard, 'The Church of England', 205; *LJ* iv. 392.

James, but under Elizabeth. The attempt to revamp the Jacobean ecclesiastical compromise collapsed in 1641–2 as Pym and others realized that Carolinism had compromised the position of the more moderate bishops and that the subversion of the Church had been a failure not just of a Laudian personnel but of an entire ecclesiastical system. Consequently this induced calls not merely for remedial measures but for the reconstruction of the entire Elizabethan Settlement.[59]

Perhaps the most noticeable feature about the parliamentary attack on Carolinism in 1640 was that although the Lords thought the innovations unpopular and supported their withdrawal, the House of Commons adopted a far more trenchant stand against the innovations than the Upper House after November 1640. The removal of Laud in 1641 was only one objective envisaged by the Commons in the piecemeal dismantling of the apparatus of the Caroline experiment assembled since 1625. As early as December 1640 the Lower House had voted against the canons but not until June 1641 did the Lords join them in their condemnation.[60] Again only later did the peers finally endorse the Commons bill (drawn up long before) to remove the rail and to destroy all 'popish' innovations introduced during the previous fifteen years.[61] As 1641 progressed, the Commons became increasingly exasperated at the Lords' inactivity. In March 1641 the peers had appointed a Committee of Religion to examine the innovations, on which ten of the Caroline bishops (including Wren) sat to investigate the innovations which they had helped to authorize. However, even before its first meeting the Commons had drawn up

[59] W. Abbott, 'The Issue of Episcopacy', chs. 1–4 (this important thesis has not had the attention it deserves since it runs against the grain of prevailing Tyackean historiography); D'Ewes, *Autobiography*, i. 262. As Stanley Gower informed Harley: 'No, the fault is not personal but official, and to (have) redress the government must be set upon a new base': *HMC Portland iii*, 79. Bernard's contention ('The Church of England', 199) that the petitioners of 1640–1 were supporting the Church of England *with* its Caroline accretions runs contrary to the substantial evidence showing the opposite. The petitioners harkened back to a Church with fewer ceremonies and more relaxed discipline, see: Morrill, 'The Religious Context of the English Civil War', *TRHS*, 5th series, xxxiv (1984), 165, 175–7; id., 'The Church in England, 1642–1649', in his (ed.), *Reactions to the English Civil War 1642–1649* (1982), 89–114; id., 'The Attack on the Church of England in the Long Parliament, 1640–1642', in D. Beales and G. Best (eds.), *History, Society and the Churches* (Camb., 1985); Fletcher, *A County Community*, 91–124.

[60] *CJ* ii. 51–2; *LJ* iv. 272–3; Bodl. MS Clarendon (SP) MS 19/1460, 1470.

[61] *CJ* ii. 246, 278–9, 283, 287; *LJ* iv. 392–5; Fletcher, *Outbreak of the Civil War*, 115–17, *et passim*.

bills removing the bishops from the Lords and debarring clergy from all secular offices.[62] By September 1641, however, the Lords had effectively lost the initiative to the Commons: the bishops' temporal and judicial power caved in with the passing of bills to abolish the Star Chamber and the High Commission, and to incapacitate the ecclesiastical courts. Fear of religious radicalism within and outside the Commons, as well as the king's personal identification with the innovations, doubtless inhibited the conservative majority in the Lords from adopting the positive opposition staged by many in the Commons.[63]

Another means of gauging the reception of Carolinism is the way in which freedom of expression surfaced in the early 1640s. The relaxation of censorship between November 1640 and October 1641 brought into the open a whole plethora of religious sentiments which had crystallized during years of suppression and censorship. According to one observer, 'there is such giddiness in the profession of religion, that every one almost is led by his own opinions; and most men in matters of judgment are divided one against another.'[64] Separatism increased dramatically, as congregations felt the relaxation from consistorial oversight. People flocked to hear preachers, while ordinary 'mechanicks' expounded the Word in freedom. Others petitioned for a massive reallocation of ecclesiastical resources to prepare for the inauguration of another more far-reaching reformation.[65] Responding to these developments, Parliament ordered all cathedral authorities to provide sermons in the close and permitted the establishment of lectures in all parishes, and at any time of the day.[66]

As John Morrill has shown, the fear of religious radicalism among many conservatives played into the king's hands, and eventually provided him with the support that he had previously lacked. With the withdrawal of the religious moderates after the outbreak of

[62] See Abbott, 'The Issue of Episcopacy', chs. 3–4; *LJ* iv. 174, 256–7; Fletcher, *Outbreak of the Civil War*, 99 *et passim*.

[63] Fletcher, *Outbreak of the Civil War*, 115 *et passim*; Bodl. Tanner MS 65/272; Morrill, 'The Religious Context of the English Civil War', *TRHS*, 5th ser. xxxiv (1984), 167 ff. These fears were played upon by the king, e.g. *LJ* iv 100.

[64] Fletcher, *Outbreak of the Civil War*, 91; Bodl. Tanner MS 65/236.

[65] Bodl. Tanner MS 65/209–14; CCO MS 206/24; Seaver, *PL* 266; *The Anatomy of the Separatists, alias Brownists, the factious brethren in these times* (1642); J. T. Cliffe, *Puritans in Conflict: The Puritan Gentry During and After the Civil Wars* (1988), 3; Morrill, 'The Religious Context', 167–8, 173.

[66] *CJ* ii. 283, 287; J. Walker, *The Sufferings of the Clergy* (1714), I. 18.

hostilities, there was little to prevent those who remained from staging a frontal assault on the vestiges of the Caroline apparatus. Of the major initiatives (and perhaps out of deference to its royal title) the book of sports alone survived the outbreak of hostilities in the summer of 1642, even if sabbath-day observance was pressed after 1640. Yet it awaited an ignominious end, being consigned, under parliamentary order, to the flames at Cheapside in May 1643, and at the hands of the common hangman.[67] Within the following three years, as Presbyterian Scotland impinged more assertively upon events south of the border, episcopacy was formally abolished and the Prayer Book, which had been the mainstay of Anglican worship since 1559, replaced by the Directory of Worship. After these and other remedial and preventive measures, the parish system, with its lay impropriations and tithes, was all that remained of the Church which Charles I had inherited.[68] Thus what had been in part an attempt to sever the Church from the lay reformation, produced, in its backlash, a triumph for Erastianism and property.

Among Carolinism's gravest offences had been the threat it presented to the prescriptive rights and attitudes of the provincial élites. They responded in kind. According to Bartholomew Parsons, 'too many gentlemen of our times are most prodigal upon law suits and most pernicious towards God's worship.' Clarendon believed that, between them, Wren and Piers had alienated most of the gentry of East Anglia and Somerset. Here and elsewhere the provincial élites had often been socially downgraded by provocative clergy determined to assert their new-found professional confidence.[69] They had been humiliated by being prosecuted in the ecclesiastical courts over petty and not so petty moral offences;[70] suits over proprietorial and rating disputes and the restoration of chancels;[71] the redrafting of city and

[67] *CJ* ii. 287; Walker, *Sufferings of the Clergy*, i. 25; Bodl. Tanner MS 65/83; Cliffe, *Puritans in Conflict*, 3; Morrill, 'The Religious Context', 167 ff.

[68] Morrill, 'The Church in England 1642–1649', in his (ed.) *Reactions to the English Civil War* (1982), 93–5; W. A. Shaw, *The History of the English Church during the Civil War and under the Commonwealth*, 2 vols. (1900); C. Cross, 'The Church in England 1646–1660', in *The Interregnum: The Quest For a Settlement*, ed. G. E. Aylmer (1972), 99–121.

[69] B. Parsons, *A Sermon Preached at the Funeral of Sir Francis Pile* (1636), 33; Clarendon, i. 272; PRO SP 16/499/78; Foster, 'Church Policies of the 1630s', *Conflict in Early Stuart England*, ed. Cust and Hughes, 209.

[70] Clarendon, iv. 489; i. 125, 372; see Ch. 2. section iii.

[71] See Ch. 2 section iii; NRO Corr. 64/81^{v}; LAO Vi/27/5, Vii/19/134, 165, Vii/20/224; GDR 175/7 Sept. 1635; HLRO 1641 Feb. 23/20; LRO R D1D41/13/64/288; Foster, 'Church Policies of the 1630s', 216.

cathedral charters to the advantage of the close;[72] and the weight of ecclesiastical innovations.[73] Their pews had been cut down to size[74] and they had been forced to adopt unseemly liturgical gestures.[75] As watch-dogs of the local peace they did not need to be doctrinally Puritan in order to recognize that the relaxation of sabbatarian inhibitions among the lower echelons threatened social cohesion within their communities and hindered the continued application of a reformation of manners.[76] For many within the parishes the Caroline innovations had been expensive and had served further to alienate the laity from the clergy, who were often exempt from payment, while increasing rating disputes at a time when royal taxation demands were mounting. 'Superstition is costly,' wrote John Tombes, 'this evil . . . ['wil-worship'] tends to the detriment of men's goods, the pillaging of men's purses, for no benefit to the owners, much hindrance to the poor, labouring ministers and commonwealth on which it should be bestowed.'[77]

From the vantage-point of the 1640s it is perhaps easy to write off the Caroline religious experiment as doomed to failure from the start. Yet there can be little doubt that, had it not been for a groundswell of support and considerable compliance in the localities, the innovations of the 1630s could not have been introduced, even less enforced.[78] In retrospect the young John Evelyn saw 1637 as the time when the Church of England was 'in her greatest splendour, all things decent, and becoming the peace, and the Persons that governed'.[79] Yet throughout the 1630s outward compliance might cover inward disaffection. If (as Underdown has implied) Carolinism, like later

[72] PRO SP 16/499/78; WORO 13945/712.17147; Foster, 'Church Policies of the 1630s', 208; A. Fletcher, 'Factionalism in Town and Countryside: The Significance of Puritanism and Arminianism', *Studies in Church History*, 16 (1979).

[73] See esp. Ch. 6 section iii; Foster, 'Church Policies of the 1630s', 216.

[74] LRO R 1D41/14/50, 18/9/3a; Foster, 'Church Policies of the 1630s', 216.

[75] LRO R 1D41/14/35, 86.

[76] K. Wrightson, *English Society 1580–1680* (1982); id., 'Alehouses, Order and Reformation in Rural England 1590–1660', *Popular Culture and Class Conflict 1590–1914*, ed. E. and S. Yeo (Brighton, 1981).

[77] See Ch. 2 n.; Ch. 6 n.; Foster, 'Church Policies of the 1630s', 215–16; Sommerville, *Politics and Ideology*, 220; Tombes, *Fermentum Pharisaeorum, or, The Leaven of Pharisaicall Wil-Worship* (1643), 11; see also CCO MS 206/22.

[78] Bodl. MS Clar. SP 20/1503; PRO SP 16/470/83, 16/163/45, 16/161/43, 54, 16/260/68; Heylyn, *EH*, 234; *A Relation of a Short Survey of 26 Counties*, ed. L. G. Wickham Legg (1904), 92; *Associated Architectural Society Reports and papers* (1875), ed. E. Venables, xiii (1875), pp. i, 59; *An Answer to a Lawless Pamphlet* (1641); *A Magazine of Scandall or a Heape of Wickednesse* (1642); CCO MS 206/20; *HMC Portland*, iii, 76.

[79] *The Diary of John Evelyn*, ed. E. S de Beer (1959), 12.

popular royalism, appealed to a residual festive culture within the country, nevertheless communities often protected themselves against administrative or religious innovations from outside. In this respect, Carolinism might be as much a threat as a buttress to the 'cherished ideas of parochial harmony' or the paternalistic household, for it could undermine patriarchal notions and level social distinctions within the parish church.[80] If Carolinism had convinced supporters within the parishes they were likely to be found less among the provincial élites than among the 'plain country people' who in 1640 'wondered' at the actions of Parliament.[81] While different constellations of social, political, and cultural forces might help to determine allegiance in 1640–2, they were somewhat put to confusion in the 1630s by the very subjective response to what one individual, D'Ewes, characterized as the 'highest step of wickedness and prevarication against God and his honour'.[82]

The petitions of 1640–1 which flooded into Parliament suggest that Carolinism split many parishes down the middle. Other evidence, however, such as the 'scandalous ministers' reports, give neither a good indication of the level of alteration nor the unpopularity of innovating clergy in the 1630s. Those 'scandalous' clergy who were eventually deprived were singled out, often randomly, in response to pressure for purges from the centre rather than selected on the weight of local evidence or because of the singularity of their complicity in the Caroline changes.[83] Informers were sometimes sent down into the parishes to act as 'neighbours' to prepare information against 'persecuting and innovatory' ministers.[84] As Archdeacon Marler noted, the Commons's circular, inviting people to present allegations against their ministers, went far beyond the intention of moderate members like Hyde. It was an invitation to some 'very sour

[80] Underdown, *Revel, Riot and Rebellion: Popular Politics and Culture in England, 1603–1660* (Oxford, 1985), 40–1.

[81] Bodl. MS Clar. SP 20/1503.

[82] D'Ewes, *Autobiography*, 114.

[83] I. Green, 'The Persecution of "Scandalous" Ministers and "Malignant" Parish Clergy during the English Civil War', *English Historical Review*, 94 (1979); Morrill, 'The Church in England 1642–1649', in his *Reactions to the English Civil War* (1982), 100–3; Bodl. MS Clar. SP 19/1498, 20/1506; *Walker Revised*, ed. A. G. Matthews (Oxford, 1948); *A Magazine of Scandall*; Bodl. MS Clar. SP 20/1506.

[84] Bodl. MS Clar. SP 19/1498.

people' to discredit not just selected individuals but to 'overthrow ... the hierarchy of the Church'.[85]

It is difficult to gauge the nature of the popular reception and acceptance of Caroline innovations from the evidence of their withdrawal or destruction (in the case of the rail the distinction is important for whereas the rail was to be withdrawn, altars were to be levelled).[86] Within many parishes the excision of Carolinism was effected unilaterally, sometimes earlier, sometimes later than the parliamentary bills ordering the removal of innovations. Very often the response was conditioned by the pressure of local parties, riots, and rumours. What, however, is not in doubt was that during the 1640s the country witnessed the greatest wave of iconoclasm since the mid-sixteenth century.[87]

The widespread enforcement of the rail during the 1630s did not mean that the altar policy of the 1630s was a 'success': the two most controversial parts of the metropolitical order, the altarwise (north–south position) and receiving at the rail, were introduced by few church courts and adopted by only a relatively small percentage of parishes. Nor did it mean that the introduction of the rail was popular. The acceptance and reception of the rail, as of ship-money, is to be gauged less by its enforcement than by its longevity, and by its potential for creating community division. Considering the eventual fate of the rail there is little reason to doubt that one Exeter citizen in 1640 spoke for many across the country: the rails 'cost blood in setting them up and ... they would cost somewhat a do before they could be pulled down'.[88] As such, it may not be

[85] Bodl. MS Clar. SP 20/1506.

[86] *LJ* iv. 392; *CJ* ii. 279; Walker, *Sufferings of the Clergy*, i. 25.

[87] Morrill, 'The Church in England, 1642–1649', in his *Reactions to the English Civil War* (1982), 109–10; *The Diary of John Rous*, ed. M. A. E. Green (Camden, 50, 1856), 99; *LJ* iv. 106, 133, 272; PRO SP 16/499/65ᵛ; HLRO Pet. 10 June 1641/1000; Pet. 1641 15 June 105; PRO SP 16/461/24, 25, 463/27, 33, 90; 466/23; 467/79; 469/35; *Mercurius Rusticus* (1685) 119–214; *The Autobiography of Sir John Bramston*, 75, 95; HLRO 10 Dec. 1640; P. Lake, 'Anti-popery: The Anatomy of a Prejudice', in Cust and Hughes (eds.), *Conflict in Early Stuart England*, 94; J. Phillips, *The Reformation of Images: The Destruction of Art in England, 1535–1660* (Los Angeles, 1973). To suggest as Bernard does ('The Church of England', 199) that the iconoclasm of 1640–1 was 'the work of minorities and of soldiers' overlooks the fact that its general timing was orchestrated by Parliament: *CJ* ii. 279, 289.

[88] See Ch. 6 n. 203; DRO Exeter City Muniments Bk. 63 Quarter Sessions Minutes 1630–42.

coincidental that the three areas which proved to be the strongest bastions of later royalist support were precisely those parts of the country where the courts did not enforce the rail: the far West (diocese of Exeter), the far North (the dioceses of Carlisle and Durham), and a considerable tract of the Welsh Border, on both sides (the dioceses of Hereford and St Asaph).[89]

At the same time the patent acceleration of policy towards 1640 intensified oppositionist tendencies. Whereas many could tolerate the rail, they could not stomach the introduction and impact of altars and postures. When the demands of royal taxation were greatest, the costs of the Caroline innovations weighed heavily.[90] Regulations governing the use of the pulpit were seemly, but when they shaded into a frontal attack on the gospel, Antichrist stalked the land. With the start of the Scottish rebellion in 1637, the country was already being attuned to the realization of a more trenchant resistance to the demands of authority.[91] Yet it was the Canons of 1640 and not, as has been recently suggested, the Scottish policy of Charles I which offers 'the best explanation of criticisms of royal religious policies in 1640–2', for it was the canons which brought to a head all the controversial ingredients of Carolinism in the 1630s: the extension of the royal prerogative and ecclesiastical power over the parish, common law, and civil law; and the retrospective confirmation of much of the controversial Caroline programme.[92] Moreover, it was the occasion of the canons and the *et cetera* oath in May 1640 which more than any other factor explains why the simmering discontent of the Short Parliament in April boiled over in the strident opposition of the Long Parliament six months later.[93]

[89] See Ch. 6 section ii. In his recent article, Bernard, 'The Church of England', 201, has cited three of my seminar papers as support for his views. They did not describe the policies of the 1630s as 'modest, largely uncontroversial' or assert 'that no one was punished for offences against any single policy alone'. The central thesis of these papers was the contrast between the extreme policy of Wren (and what has passed for Laudianism) and the more moderate policies of Laud as ordinary.

[90] *A Complaint to the House of Commons* (1642); Clarendon, i. 199–202; Sommerville, *Politics and Ideology*, 220; DRO Exeter City Muniments, Bk. 63, Quarter Sessions Minutes 1630–42; see Ch. 6 n. 203, Ch. 2 n. 164.

[91] *The Letters of Lady Brilliana Harley*, ed. T. T. Lewis (Camden Soc 58, 1854), 41.

[92] As Bernard, 'The Church of England', 204, has suggested.

[93] See Ch. 7.

IV. THE ROLE OF RELIGION IN THE COLLAPSE OF THE PERSONAL RULE

Did religion play the same role in the collapse of the Caroline regime as in the later outbreak of hostilities? John Morrill (supported by the work of Anthony Fletcher) contends that only deeply-held religious convictions were powerful enough to cause the split of 1642 and provide the momentum for war. Thus the British Civil War could be seen as Europe's last war of religion (his major premiss).[94] But was religion the same determinant of the divisions before 1641, during the regime, and after its collapse, as it was in the split of 1641–2? He has asserted that the causes of Charles I's problems in 1640 emanated far more from the religious sphere than other spheres, and that during the 1630s the 'religious perception' far exceeded the 'localist or legal-constitutionalist perception' of misgovernment or tyranny (his minor premiss).[95] Can such a distinction be maintained? Those historians who have attacked Morrill's *minor* premiss have avoided this rather crucial issue. Instead they have focused their attention on events between 1637 and 1640, in particular the Scottish rebellion, as the major precipitants of the collapse of the regime.[96] This underrates both the collective mentality of the 1630s and the significance of Morrill's thesis. For what is really in question here is the viability of the revisionist interpretation of 'religion' and 'ideology' in the early seventeenth century.

It is axiomatic to revisionist historiography that in spite of all the factional, functional, personal, and local issues (which it depicts as 'political' problems of the Stuart monarchy), it was religion which caused the collapse of Charles I's regime in 1640. For most revisionists, influenced by Nicholas Tyacke's work, that means Arminianism, and Laud in particular. These two assumptions have fundamentally influenced revisionist historiography, and prevented it from broaching a more contextualized notion of early seventeenth-century religion, because in the traditions of modern thought what is doctrinal and ecclesiastical is assumed to be opposed to what is

[94] Morrill, 'Religious Context', 178 *et passim*; Fletcher, *The Outbreak of the English Civil War*.
[95] Morrill, 'Religious Context', 164 *et passim*.
[96] Bernard, 'The Church of England', 183.

secular or political.[97] But avoiding the particular question of the importance and definition of Arminianism and Laudianism, both of which are dealt with above (and which are not in the last resort absolutely necessary to the revisionist case), the question remains to be asked: is the revisionist depiction of two spheres, one religious, the other political, intellectually tenable? If it is not, and if *political religion* or *religious politics* are concepts more compatible when studying the Caroline Church, then the origins of the British Civil War look somewhat different from those delineated in current historiography.[98]

Revisionism lost its bearings, it could be argued, as soon as it played down ideology and principle, and concentrated instead upon (neo-Namierite) factors of material self-interest and administrative paralysis.[99] Against this tendency some historians, in particular Richard Cust, Derek Hirst, Clive Holmes, Ann Hughes, and Johann Sommerville, have reasserted the importance of ideological considerations in early seventeenth-century history, and in particular, in the opposition to the policies of Charles I.[100] They have shown that the ideological implications of the Caroline policies were scrutinized and thoroughly discussed at the provincial and national level.[101] Differences over what was in 'the self-interest' betrayed issues extending beyond material considerations and broaching matters of principle.[102]

[97] As exemplified by 'if there is one person to whose actions and policies the fall of the Stuart monarchy can be attributed' in R. Ashton, *The English Civil War: Conservatism and Revolution, 1603–1649* (1978), 110, and by 'the greatest calamity ever visited upon the English Church' in Collinson, *RP* 90.

[98] See Chs. 2 and 3 in particular.

[99] A general survey of revisionist literature is given in R. Cust and A. Hughes, 'After Revisionism', in Cust and Hughes (eds.), *Conflict in Early Stuart England.* While the editors are critical of revisionism, for the most part this is less true of their contributors; Sommerville, *Politics and Ideology*, intro.

[100] D. Hirst, *Authority and Conflict: England 1603–1658* (1986), id., 'Local Affairs in Seventeenth Century England', *Historical Journal*, 32 (1989), 437–448; id., 'Revisionism Revised: Two Perspectives in Early Stuart Parliamentary History: The Place of Principle', *Past and Present*, 92 (1981); Cust and Hughes (eds.), *Conflict in Early Stuart England: Studies in Religion and Politics 1603–1642*; Cust, *Forced Loan*; C. Holmes, 'The County Community in Stuart Historiography', *Journal of British Studies*, 19 (1980); A. Hughes, *Politics, Society and Civil War in Warwickshire, 1620–1660* (Camb., 1987); Sommerville, *Politics and Ideology*. Reeve, *Charles I and the Road to Personal Rule*; and Underdown, *Revel, Riot and Rebellion, England*, may also be added to this list.

[101] For a critique of the 'county-community' school of revisionists see, in particular, Holmes, 'The County Community in Stuart Historiography'.

[102] Sommerville, *Politics and Ideology*, 232–4; Cust, *The Forced Loan*, 3 *et passim*; Reeve, *Charles I and the Road to Personal Rule*, 4–5, 294–5.

But the revisionist problem is not just theoretical, it is also empirical. Those who questioned governmental policies did not readily disclose their views on paper, while the surviving documentary evidence of the period is mostly of an administrative rather than personal nature, and more likely to highlight functional rather than ideological concerns.[103] If the ideological factor has been underestimated in historiography, a recognition of the constitutional implications of Carolinism can only help to reinstate it.

Perhaps the most grievous offence of Carolinism was that it violated the conscience, as it forced people to decide between the demands of the Crown and the authority of God. Throughout the 1630s moral and constitutional awareness increased, as minds were conditioned to question the intent and demands of authority. The opposition to Charles I's ecclesiastical policies could not fail to have principled origins when the conscience was informed about what was a state of normality and what was not.[104] Moreover, in that it distorted the distinction between popery and orthodoxy, Carolinism convinced many that the king was turning the tide against the Reformation and attempting to reintroduce an English popery. Their fears were not without justification, for although Charles I was not attempting to reintroduce popery he was certainly attempting to mould the Anglican Church into a Catholic identity to rival the national Churches of Spain and France. The backdrop of the conflagration of the Thirty Years War, the growth of recusancy, and the perceived enticement of 'cheap-grace' all seemingly gave credence to the hypothesis that Charles I and his bishops were covert papists.[105]

In 1640 this perception of popery was intimately associated with the perception of the subversion of the state. As the Church was an established element within the constitution and since popery was seen as a natural ally of absolutist rule, the advent of the Caroline Counter-Reformation was perceived as the most insidious expression

[103] Cust and Hughes 'After Revisionism', in their *Conflict in Early Stuart England* (1989), 12–15; Sommerville, *Politics and Ideology*, 232–4.

[104] For a review of recent works which reinstate the significance of ideology at all levels of early seventeenth-century society see Derek Hirst, 'Local Affairs in Seventeenth Century England', 440–1, 439, 437–48.

[105] Hibbard, *Charles I and the Popish Plot*; GCC MS 291 (4); Heylyn, *EH* 260; D'Ewes, *Autobiography*, 113–14; Even those who did not think the bishops were papists nevertheless accused them of it: 'we charge the prelaticall clergy with popery to make them odious though we know they are guilty of no such thing', John Selden, *Table Talk of John Selden*, ed. Sir Frederick Pollock (1927), 99.

of a mounting Caroline absolutism in the state.[106] Axiomatic to this view was the opinion that Parliament was necessary to the constitutional well-being of the state. D'Ewes was convinced that the subversion of the Church in the 1630s had occurred precisely because of the lack of parliamentary accountability and advice. In its absence, the statute law governing the Church had been undermined or ignored. The crux of the Commons attack on the ecclesiastical developments of the 1630s was that some things had been enjoined and other things prohibited 'without warrant of law'. Even the least significant of the Caroline innovations, such as the collection of money for St Paul's or the attempt to restrict the gentry's chaplains, could be seen as contrary to the Petition of Right and Magna Carta. The opposition to the bishops in 1640 was couched in the most explicit constitutional terms. 'Wiser than the laws, [they] have found out a better form of government,' declared Waller in April 1640, 'the king must be a more absolute monarch than any of his predecessors and to them he must own it.'[107] Of the articles of impeachment levelled against Laud in 1641 few concerned the ostensible ecclesiastical innovations with which he has been inextricably identified in history. The majority dealt with his alleged attempt to subvert parliamentary and individual liberty, through arbitrary government, unparliamentary taxation, elevating the king's authority over statute, undermining the Royal Supremacy, usurping patronage, and advancing the Crown towards what Pym called 'absolute and unlimited power'.[108] Thus complaints against Charles I's government were not limited, as Morrill contends, to the misuse of agreed powers, but highlighted his attempt to usurp 'the constitution' through evolving new prerogative powers and by breaking the law. It is not surprising therefore to find that before attempting to remove the Caroline excrescences, the Commons looked to protect their own privileges. As there is 'nothing more easy than to impose a religion on a people

[106] J. Sommerville, 'Ideology, Property and the Constitution', in Cust and Hughes (eds.), *Conflict in Early Stuart England*, 65; Sommerville, *Politics and Ideology*, 211–24. I do not deny that some may have seen the subversion of the Church in essentially religious terms, e.g. Nehemiah Wallington: P. Seaver, *Wallington's World: A Puritan Artisan in Seventeenth Century London* (Stanford, CA, 1985), 158.

[107] D'Ewes, *Autobiography*, i. 133; *CJ* i. 279; Bodl. MS Add. c. 132/80/20; see Ch. 2 n. 180; Ch. 4 n. 211.

[108] *WWL* iii. 275–462; iv. 1–400; Bodl. Tanner MS 61/215–224^{v}, 220^{v}.

deprived of their liberties,' declared Waller, 'so there is nothing more hard than to do the same upon freemen.'[109]

Although some contemporaries may have distinguished (as Morrill has done) between a localist, religious, and legal-constitutional perception of tyranny before 1640, such a perception could only become blurred after the passing of the canons in May of that year.[110] Both the Commons and Lords eventually condemned the canons as contrary 'to the rights of parliament, the property of the subject and fundamental law'. 'The exception of exceptions against the canons', wrote Fuller, was that 'they were generally condemned as illegally passed to the prejudice of the fundamental liberty of the subject'.[111] Apart from the fact that Convocation formulated its canons after the dissolution of Parliament and that they passed without its approval, individual canons seriously encroached upon parliamentary and legal rights: canons 11–17, extricating the Church from the civil law; canon 6, enacting the *et cetera* oath, and canon 1, which constituted the clearest exposition of the principle of the divine right of kingship propagated under Charles I and which justified the royal right to supply in near absolutist terms.[112]

Thus the purgative medicine applied to the Church in 1640, which removed the canons and the accretions of the previous fifteen years, was designed not just to stem the growth of an ecclesiastical tyranny but constituted part of the wider parliamentary platform to restore the 'nation in general to their fundamental and vital liberties, the property of their goods and the freedom of their persons'.[113] It was not only the Puritan godly who perceived the destruction of Caroline idolatry during the 1640s as 'the casting down of imaginations and every high thing that exalteth itself against the knowledge of God'.[114] For a majority of the political nation the breaking of the ecclesiastical yoke was the essential prelude to the restoration of the constitutional status quo and the first stage in the daunting task of convincing

[109] Bodl. MS Add. c. 132/80/21^v; Morrill, 'The Religious Context of the English Civil War', 160.

[110] Morrill, 'The Religious Context of the English Civil War', 162.

[111] *LJ* iv. 273; Fuller, *CH* 410; Heylyn, *CA* 442–3.

[112] See Ch. 7 section ii.; Edward Bagshawe highlighted in particular canons 1, 6, 12, and 13 as contemptuous of the law, broaching new prerogatives, and tending towards absolutism: *Two Arguments in Parliament* (1641), 14–16.

[113] Bodl. MS Add. c. 132/80/22.

[114] 2 Corinthians 10: 5.

Charles I that divine rights entailed divine obligations. With Carolinism rather than Arminianism on the centre stage, and with Charles I, not Laud, assuming the leading role in his ecclesiastical perspective theatre, another window opens on to a post-revisionist world. 'Religion was not the thing at first contested for, but God brought it to that issue at last.'[115]

[115] Cromwell, cited C. Hill, *God's Englishman: Oliver Cromwell and the English Revolution* (1970), 204.

APPENDIX

(i) The Upper House of Convocation April–May 1640 and November–February 1640/1

The Southern Province

Canterbury	William Laud
London	William Juxon
Winchester	Walter Curle
Salisbury	John Davenant
Rochester	John Warner
Chichester	Brian Duppa
Norwich	Richard Montagu[1]
Lincoln	suspended[2]
Worcester	John Thornborough[3]
Oxford	John Bancroft
Coventry and Lichfield	Robert Wright
Gloucester	Godfrey Goodman
Llandaff	Morgan Owen
St David's	Roger Mainwaring[4]
St Asaph	John Owen
Bangor	William Roberts
Bristol	Robert Skinner
Bath and Wells	William Piers
Exeter	Joseph Hall
Ely	Matthew Wren
Hereford	George Coke
Peterborough	John Towers

The Northern Province

York	Richard Neile[5]
Chester	John Bridgeman[6]
Carlisle	Barnaby Potter[7]
Durham	Thomas Morton[8]
Sodor and Man	Richard Parr

[1] Present in April but absent from the November Convocation (appeared in proxy by Bancroft of Oxford).

[2] John Williams was not called to either Convocation, as under suspension.

[3] Over 90; absent from both; appeared in proxy by Juxon of London and Coke of Hereford.

[4] Absent in the April–May Convocation but present in November.
[5] Died a few days before the November Convocation met.
[6] Absent; appeared in proxy by Hodson, Procurator for the chapter of York.
[7] Absent; appeared in proxy by Dawes, Procurator for the chapter of Carlisle.
[8] Absent; appeared in proxy by Nailer, Procurator in the chapter of Durham.

(ii) The Lower House of Convocation

Names in brackets represent the procurators for the chapter or clergy who appeared in the November–February Convocation (if different to the April procurators).

The Southern Province

Canterbury

Dean of Canterbury	Isaac Bargrave
Archdeacon of Canterbury	William Kingsley[a]
Procurator for the chapter	William Bray
Procurator for the clergy	John Oliver
	John Swinnock

London

Dean of St Paul's	Thomas Winniffe
Archdeacon of London	Thomas Paske[b]
Archdeacon of Middlesex	Richard Cluett
Archdeacon of St Alban's	Thomas Westfield
Archdeacon of Essex	Edward Layfield
Archdeacon of Colchester	Henry King
Procurator for the chapter	John Montfort
Procurator for the clergy	Samuel Baker (John Downham)
	Thomas Wykes (Anthony Smith)

Winchester

Dean of Winchester	John Young
Archdeacon of Winchester	Edward Burby
Archdeacon of Surrey	George Hakewill[1]
Procurator for the chapter	James Halsey
Procurator for the clergy	Thomas Turner
	Benjamin Laney

Salisbury

Dean of Sarum	Richard Bailey
Archdeacon of Salisbury	Thomas Marler
Archdeacon of Berkshire	John Ryves[c]
Archdeacon of Wiltshire	Thomas Leche

Procurator for the chapter	William Chillingworth
Procurator for the clergy	Thomas Chaffin (Gilbert Wimberley)
	John Littleton (Hugh Halkwell)

Rochester

Dean of Rochester	Henry King
Archdeacon of Rochester	Elizeus Burgess
Procurator for the chapter	John Larkin (Edmund Jackson)
Procurator for the clergy	Henry Hammond (Henry Valentine)
	Richard Chase (Thomas Backner)

Chichester

Dean of Chichester	Richard Steward (Prolocutor)
Archdeacon of Chichester	James Marsh
Archdeacon of Lewes	William Hutchinson
Procurator for the chapter	James Larkin (Joseph Henshaw)
Procurator for the clergy	Granada Chester
	Stephen Gosse (Edward Burton)

Norwich

Dean of Norwich	John Hassel[d]
Archdeacon of Norwich	Andrew Byng
Archdeacon of Norfolk	Robert White
Archdeacon of Sudbury	Theophilus Kent
Archdeacon of Suffolk	Robert Bostock
Procurator for the chapter	Foulke Robartes (Edward Young)
Procurator for the clergy	Edward Franklin (Edmund Porter)
	Lawrence Britton (Simon Sumpter)

Lincoln

Dean of Lincoln	Anthony Topham
Archdeacon of Lincoln	Morgan Wynne
Archdeacon of Stow	Nicholas Walker
Archdeacon of Leicester	William Warr
Archdeacon of Bedford	John Hacket
Archdeacon of Buckingham	Robert Newell
Archdeacon of Huntington	Richard Holdsworth
Procurator for the chapter	Robert Meres (Hamlet Marshall)
Procurator for the clergy	Sir John Lambe (Thomas Sanderson[e])
	Thomas Hurst[e]

Worcester

Dean of Worcester	Christopher Potter
Archdeacon of Worcester	Edward Thornborough

Procurator for the chapter	William Smith
Procurator for the clergy	Giles Thornborough (George Wall)
	Thomas Warmestry

Oxford

Dean of Christ Church	Samuel Fell
Archdeacon of Oxford	Barton Holiday
Procurator for the chapter	George Aglionby (Thomas Walker)
Procurator for the clergy	Thomas Walker
	Edward Fulham

Coventry and Lichfield

Dean of Lichfield	Griffith Higgs
Archdeacon of Stafford	Martin Tylney[2]
Archdeacon of Salop	William Jeffreys
Archdeacon of Coventry	Ralph Brownrigg
Archdeacon of Derby	Samuel Clarke
Procurator for the chapter	William Higgins
Procurator for the clergy	John Arneway (Arthur Richards)
	James Fleetwood (Richard Vines)

Gloucester

Dean of Gloucester	Accepted Frewen[3]
Archdeacon of Gloucester	Hugh Robinson
Procurator for the chapter	Gilbert Sheldon (George Palmer)
Procurator for the clergy	Francis Baber
	Thomas Temple

Llandaff

Archdeacon of Llandaff	Thomas Pritchard[4]
Procurator for the chapter	Francis Mansell (John Clegg[f])
Procurator for the clergy	Hugh Lloyd (Michael Hughes)
	Francis Davies[f]

St David's

Precentor of St David's	Griffith Higgs
Archdeacon of St David's	Robert Rudd[5]
Archdeacon of Carmarthen	William Beeley
Archdeacon of Brecon	Isaac Singleton[6]
Archdeacon of Cardigan	Thomas Brand
Procurator for the chapter	William Heywood
Procurator for the clergy	Evan Owen
	William Edwards

Bangor

Dean of Bangor	Griffith Williams
Archdeacon of Bangor	William Mostyn
Archdeacon of Merioneth	Robert White[g]
Archdeacon of Anglesey	in commendam to Bishop
Procurator for the chapter	John Griffith (Robert Morgan)
Procurator for the clergy	David Lloyd
	Robert Morgan (William Beale)

St Asaph

Dean of St Asaph	Andrew Maurice
Archdeacon of St Asaph	in commendam to Bishop
Procurator for the chapter	Lewis Hughes
Procurator for the clergy	George Griffiths[h]
	Edward Powell (John Price[h])

Bristol

Dean of Bristol	Matthew Nicholas
Archdeacon of Dorset	Richard Fitzherbert
Procurator for the chapter	John Weekes
Procurator for the clergy	Thomas Fuller
	Gilbert Ironside

Bath and Wells

Dean of Wells	George Warburton[7]
Archdeacon of Wells	Gerard Wood
Archdeacon of Bath	William Piers
Archdeacon of Taunton	Samuel Ward
Procurator for the chapter	Sebastian Smith
Procurator for the clergy	Edward Kellet (John Fabian)[i]
	Henry Anchetill (William Lute)[j]

Exeter

Dean of Exeter	William Peterson
Archdeacon of Cornwall	Robert Hall
Archdeacon of Exeter	Aaron Wilson[k]
Archdeacon of Barnstaple	William Helyar
Archdeacon of Totnes	Edward Cotton
Procurator for the chapter	William Cotton[l]
Procurator for the clergy	Robert Dove (George Hall)
	William Cotton (John Pyne)

Ely

Dean of Ely	William Fuller
Archdeacon of Ely	Daniel Wigmore[m]
Procurator for the chapter	Daniel Wigmore (Radulpum Brownrigg)
Procurator for the clergy	Edward Martin
	Thomas Wilson

Hereford

Dean of Hereford	Jonathan Brown
Archdeacon of Hereford	John Hughes
Archdeacon of Ludlow	Morgan Godwyn
Procurator for the chapter	William Skinner
Procurator for the clergy	William Sherburn
	Peter Mewes

Peterborough

Dean of Peterborough	Thomas Jackson[n]
Archdeacon of Northampton	John Quarles
Procurator for the chapter	John Pocklington (John Quarles)
Procurator for the clergy	Thomas Heath
	William Beale (Edward Reynolds)

Westminster

Dean of Westminster	(Williams—under suspension[o])
Archdeacon of Westminster	Thomas Wilson
Procurator for the chapter	Peter Heylyn

Wolverhampton

Dean of Windsor and Wolverhampton	Christopher Wren
Procurator for the chapter	Robert Dove

Those absent for the April–May Convocation but present for the November–February Convocation

[1] Appeared in proxy by Winniffe, Dean of St Paul's.

[2] Appeared in proxy by Brownrigg, Archdeacon of Coventry and Lambe, Procurator for the clergy of Lincoln.

[3] Appeared in proxy by Jackson, Dean of Peterborough and Bailey, Dean of Sarum.

[4] Appeared in proxy by Lloyd, Procurator for the clergy of Llandaff.

[5] Appeared in proxy by Owen, Procurator for the clergy of St David's.

[6] Appeared in proxy by King, Archdeacon of Colchester, Turner, Procurator for the clergy of Winchester, Wykes, Procurator for the clergy of London.

[7] Appeared in proxy by Baker, Procurator for the clergy of London.

Those absent for the November–February Convocation but present for the April–May Convocation

[a] Appeared in proxy by Bray, Procurator for the chapter of Canterbury.

[b] Appeared in proxy by Bray, Procurator for the chapter of Canterbury.

[c] Appeared in proxy by Wimberley, Procurator for the clergy of Salisbury.

[d] Appeared in proxy by Young, Procurator for the chapter of Norwich.

[e] Both were contested as Procurators for the clergy of Lincoln by Anthony Tuckney and Herbert Palmer. The Prolocutor controversially ruled in favour of the sitting incumbents, which caused a heated debate over the extent of his powers in the November Convocation.

[f] Both ultimately appeared in proxy by Hughes, Procurator for the clergy of Llandaff.

[g] Appeared in proxy by Morgan, Procurator for the chapter of Bangor.
[h] In the November Convocation Robert Morgan and Edward Powell appeared instead.
[i] Appeared in proxy by Montfort, Procurator for the chapter of London.
[j] See Ch. 7. n. 234.
[k] Appeared in proxy by Cotton, Archdeacon of Totnes, and Hall, Procurator for the clergy of Exeter.
[l] Joined as Procurator for the chapter by William Hutchinson and Lawrence Burwell.
[m] Appeared in proxy by Burgess, Archdeacon of Rochester.
[n] Jackson, Dean of Peterborough, died in the interval between the sessions.
[o] The sub-dean of Westminster (Robert Newell) was called instead to both Convocations.

The Northern Province (April–May 1640)

Those marked * were absent and appeared in proxy; attendance at the Northern Convocation being more of a formality than a necessity.

York

Dean of York	John Scot*
Archdeacon of York	Henry Wickham
Archdeacon of Nottingham	William Robinson*
Archdeacon of East Riding	John Cosin*
Archdeacon of Cleveland	John Neile
Procurator for the chapter	Phineas Hodson
Procurator for the clergy of York	George Riddell
	Henry Aiscough
Procurator for the clergy of Nottingham	Edward Mottershed
	Francis Wittington
Procurator for the clergy of East Riding	Edward Mottershed
	Robert Perrot
Procurator for the clergy of Cleveland	William Berman
	Richard Brandsby
	Thomas Squire
	Richard Eskrigge
Procurator for the chapter of Ripon	John Favor*
Procurator for the chapter of Southwell	Thomas Benson
Procurator for the clergy of Southwell Pec.	John Neile
	George Barlowe
Procurator for the dean and chapter Pec. *et al.*	William Easdall

Durham

Dean of Durham	Walter Balcanquall*
Archdeacon of Durham	Gabriel Clarke
Archdeacon of Northumberland	Everard Gower*

Procurator for the chapter	Joseph Nailer
Procurator for the clergy of Durham	Ferdinand Merecroft
	William James
Procurator for the clergy of Northumberland	Yeldard Alvey
	Thomas Triplett

Chester

Dean of Chester	Thomas Mallory*
Archdeacon of Chester	George Snell*
Archdeacon of Richmond	Thomas Dod*
Procurator for the chapter	William Bispham
Procurator for the clergy of Chester	Thomas Byrom
	John Ley
Procurator for the clergy of Richmond	John Ley
	Thomas Byrom

Carlisle

Dean of Carlisle	Thomas Comber*
Archdeacon of Carlisle	Issac Singleton*
Procurator for the chapter	Lancelot Dawes
Procurator for the clergy	Lancelot Dawes
	William Richardson

Sodor and Man

Archdeacon of Man	Samuel Rutler*
Procurator for the clergy	Samuel Hynderson

Sources

PRO SP 16/455/47—subscriptions to the Book of Canons (Southern Province); LPL Conv. 1/2/2/7–32; LPL Conv. 1/1/1/19–34 (Southern Province) Ch. Ch. Wake MS 306/315–326; *The Records of the Northern Convocation*, ed. G. W. Kitchin (Surtees Soc., 113, 1907), 299–303.

BIBLIOGRAPHY

For published works, place of publication is London unless otherwise indicated. Works included in the Abbreviations section are not listed here.

PRIMARY SOURCES

Manuscripts

The following are the major sources consulted for this work. This is far from a complete list of the surviving, relevant records. Sources are listed under record repositories, which are ordered alphabetically. I have attempted to catalogue them according to type and respective jurisdictions. Due to restrictions of space, the description of the collections is necessarily curtailed. Further details of particular collections can be found in my thesis. The maps contained in the *Phillimore Atlas and Index of Parish Registers* were an invaluable aid in establishing ecclesiastical boundaries. The archdeaconry of Salop in Hereford diocese is termed the archdeaconry of Ludlow to distinguish it from the archdeaconry of Salop in Coventry and Lichfield. Please see abbreviations for this section, p. xvii.

BEDFORDSHIRE RO (BDRO)

Ay of Bedford

Parish

P. 10/5/1; 12/5/1; 13/5/1; 44/5/2; 53/8/1; 60/12/1; 88/5/1; 118/5/1.
J. 1224–30
TW. 835; 936

BERKSHIRE RO (BERO)

Ay of Berkshire

Parish

D/P 8/5/1; 23/5/1; 24/5/1; 35/5/1; 62/5/1; 78/5/1; 97/5/3; 114/5/2; 116/5/1

Court

MS Archd. papers c. 73–80, 1633–45, *acta*, office and instance

BODLEIAN LIBRARY, OXFORD (Bodl.)

MSS Tanner 65–74, 82, 88, 114–15, 125, 129, 137, 141–8; 220, 240, 276, 281, 290, 314
MSS Rawlinson A 127, 289, 346, 409, 441; B 372–3, 488; C 106, 262, 421, 573, 579, 674, 687; D 158, 320, 353, 376, 392, 399, 814, 831, 857, 924, 1104; 1331; 1347; 1480–1; E 21
MSS Add. a. 55; c. 132
MSS Ashmole 1131; 1144
MS Bankes 62
MS Bodl. 888
MS Carte 103
MS Cherry 2
MSS Clarendon (SP) 18–20
MSS Eng. Hist. b. 205; d. 222
MSS Eng. letters b. 1; c. 130
MSS Eng. misc. f. 49; c. 92
MSS Eng. theol. e. 57; f. 20
MS Film dep. 953
MS Gough Eccles Top 3 (SC 17,679)
MS Jones misc. papers 17
MS Lister 11
MSS Sancroft 18, 78
MS Selden supra 108
MSS Smith 23, 40
MS Top Berks c. 44
MS Top Cheshire c. 6/5
MS Top Eccles e. 9
MS Twyne 7
MS Univ. Archives S. E. P. V2
MS Walker c. 1–9

BORTHWICK INSTITUTE, YORK (BI)

Archdiocese of York

Court

Chan. A. B. 22–28, 1629–40, *acta*, chancery and audience
Cons. A. B. 71–4, 1633–9, *acta*, consistory
Sub Bk. 2, 1632–40, subs (also Neile 1628–32)

Visitation

V. CB, *acta* 1629–30, Chester
V. CB 1, 2a, 2b, 1633, York, Chester
V. papers Manchester, 1630s
V. CB pres., 1636
V. CB exhibit bk., 1640

APec. of York

ca: Millington

Ay of York

Parish

ca: York: Hy Trin Goodrangate; St J. Ousebridge; St Mart. Coney St; St Mart. cum Gregory; St Mich. le Belfrey; St Mich. Spurriergate

Ay of Cleveland

Court

C. V. /CB 1 + 2, *acta*, 1632, 1634

DCh. of York

Court

D/C AB 11, *acta*, 1624–34

Visitation

D/C V/CB 1 1630s DCh. Nottingham Pec.

High Commission of York

Court

HC /AB 18–19, *acta* 1631–4; 1638–41

BRISTOL RO (BRO)

Con. of Bristol

Administrative

Ep. A/5/3 (institutions) 1630s.
Ep. A/10/1/1–2 (subs.) 1630s.
Ep. A/30/1 St Paul's coll.
Ep. E/13/2, lease bk.

Court

Ep. J/1/20–5, 1630–40 *acta*, instance and office with some *detecta*

Visitation

Ep. V/2/1; V/3, 1626–42, visitation papers and pres.

Parish

P/St. All S./CW/3; Xch./CW/16; JB/CW/3: a, b; P + J/CW/3a; T./CW/63–72; W./CW/3b; T. Ch./CW/Ca 13, 14; E./CW/2, 3c; J./CW/1(b)

DCh. of Bristol

Misc.

DC A/9/1/5, 6, accounts
F/1/1, Wright's vindication
City of Bristol MSS
21 c3 Common Council proceedings, 1621–39
Smythe MSS: Ashton Court MSS 36,214

BRITISH LIBRARY (BL)

Egerton MSS 238; 784; 1048; 2651
Sloane MSS 34; 827; 2728; 3945; 4177
Lansdowne MSS 213; 966; 985–6; 991
Harleian MSS 159; 832; 984; 1219; 4274; 4931; 6424; 7000–1; 7032; 7517; 11,055
Stowe MS 743
Portland Loan MSS 29/119, 172–3, 202, 206
Add. MSS 4221; 4274–6; 4460; 5155; 5783; 11,043; 11,051; 11,055; 12,222; 14,919; 15,645; 15,672; 18,773; 19,398; 20,065; 22,084; 23,146; 26,785; 29,586; 29,975; 34,141; 34,217; 36,937; 37,343; 39,527; 42,504; 45,388; 45,498; 46,885

BUCKINGHAMSHIRE RO (BKRO)

Ay of Buckingham

Court

MS Archd. papers c. 276–79, 1635–40, *acta*, instance

Visitation

MS Archd. papers c. 267, 1630s, *speculae*, visitation
c. 289–91, 1633–7, *detecta*, and pres.
c. 308, 1633–5, office memorials

Parish

PR 52/5/1; 138/5/1; 140/5/1; 234/5/1; 235/5/1

Pec. of Leighton Buzzard

Court

MS Archd. papers c. 309, 1631–3 instance, causes and fees

Pec. of Aylesbury

Court

MS Archd. papers c. 302, 1632–41, *acta*, office, instance

APec. of Monks Risborough and Newington

Court

MS Archd. papers c. 200, 1626–40, *acta*, (office)

Ay of St Albans

Parish

PR 7/5/1

CAMBRIDGE UNIVERSITY LIBRARY (CUL)

Pec. of Tredington

Court

Add. 2377, 1576–1686, *acta*

DCh. of Peterborough

MSS Peterborough c/30; c/20 misc. papers, 1630s
ZA 3836, *acta*, 1630s

Con. of Ely

Visitation

B/2/32, 40a, 47a, 49–51, *libri cleri*, 1625–38

Court

D/2/40–51, assignation bk., instance and office, 1626–39
B/2/41–53, assignation bk., office, 1631–9
F/5/34, 39, 41 precedent books, 1636–8
G/2/1, Wren's papers
H/2/1/B/30, 1630s, reg. corr.
Baumgartner MS, 8/200–2 1614, visitation
Baker MSS 33; 42/35 sequestrations, East Anglia

CAMBRIDGESHIRE RO

Ay of Ely

Parish

P17/5/1; P22/5/2–3; P26/5/1; P30/4/1–2; P49/5/1; P76/5/14–9 R51/32/1

Pec. of Bp. of Ely

Parish

P67/5/1; P68/5/1

CANTERBURY CATHEDRAL LIBRARY (CCL)

(for metropolitical jurisdiction see also LPL)

Con. of Canterbury

Administrative

Z. 3. 14, registry, 1628–40
J/J/55–65, court, 1628–40
V111/2/2, excommunication schedules, 1630s

Court

Z. 2. 1; Z. 2. 2; Z. 1. 19; X. 3. 1, *acta*, instance, 1634–41
Z. 4. 6; Z. 4. 7, *comperta* and *detecta*, office and visitation, 1636–43

Visitation

V/V/44–51, 1630s, *libri cleri*
X. 6. 2, 1637, *liber cleri*

Parish

U3 99/4/1; 30/8/1; (uncat.) Boughton under Blean ca

Ay of Canterbury

Court

Z. 3. 16–17; X. 3. 1; Y. 6. 11, *acta*, instance, 1634–9.
X. 7. 4; X. 5. 7.; X. 7. 2.; X. 6. 10; X. 7. 3.; X. 6. 6.; X. 6. 8.; Y. 6. 4.; X. 7. 1; X. 6. 9; X. 6. 11 pt. 1; X. 6. 11 pt. 11; X. 6. 2., *acta*, office and visitation *comperta* and *detecta*, 1615–32, 1632–40

Parish

U3 5/5/1; 2/5/1; 39/5/1; 137/5/1; 48/28/1; 34/5/1

CHESHIRE RO (CRO)

Ay of Chester

Parish

P13/22/1; P18/3608; P23/3466/9/1, 2; P173/6/1; P39/8/1; P8/13/1, 2; P87/1/1; P1/11; P51/12/1; P20/13/1; P65/8/1; P27/7/1; P63/7/1

CHRIST CHURCH, OXFORD (Ch. Ch.)

Convocation

MS Wake 306, convocation papers

CITY OF CHESTER RO (CCRO)

Ay of Chester

Parish

CR63/2/203

CLWYD RO (CLRO)

Ay of Bangor

Parish

PD 78/1

CORNWALL RO (CWRO)

Ay of Cornwall

Parish

DDP 36/8/1; 126/4/1; 144/5/3/1–23; 162/5/1; 214/5/1; 322/3/1

Pec. of Bp. of Exeter

Parish

DDP: 19/5/2–32; 170/5/1

Borough MSS

E/Bor/Bod/246; Lis/28

CORPUS CHRISTI COLLEGE, OXFORD (CCO)

MSS 206; 288; 308; 316

COVENTRY RO (CVRO)

City of Coventry MSS

CAR AC A79/69, 90, 134–6, 156–8, 169, 186, admin. 1630s
City Annals 920
LM 166, corp. accounts misc. 33

CUMBRIA RO (CBRO)

Con. of Carlisle

Administrative

DRC 1/33 ep. reg., 1629–41 (at Carlisle)

Court

DRC 3/3 misc. court papers (at Carlisle)

Ay of Carlisle

Parish

PR 116/107 (at Carlisle)
WPR 11; 76 (at Kendal)

Ay of Richmond

Parish

WPR 8; 43; 62; 89; 83 (at Kendal)

DEPT. OF PALAEOGRAPHY AND DIPLOMATIC, DURHAM UNIVERSITY (DPD)

Con. of Durham

Administrative

Reg. 1/4, ep. reg., 1617–72

Court

111/12–3, 1629–37 *acta*, office and instance
Mickleton and Spearman MSS 2–91
Cosin Letter Bk. IA

DERBYSHIRE RO (DERO)

Ay of Derby

Parish

D: 11145 A/PW1; 803 M/Z9; 638 A/PW1; 886 A/PW1; 81 BA/PW1; 1632 A/PW1
M 154
MS 184/09

DEVON RO (DRO)

Con. of Exeter

Court

CH: 803–8, 13, *acta*, instance, 1629–41
CH: 866, 180, 11035, depositions, 1634–59

Administrative

CH: 6, cause papers, 1630–9
CH: 22–5, 43, 50 ep. reg., 1627–41
CH: 57, patent bk., 1630s

CH: 90–2, 141, 146, 166, 176–8, 724–5, 853–4, 884, 1075, mostly cause papers, 1610–40
45 Moger PR BC4, misc. ecc. papers, 1630s

Visitation

CH: 217–18, *libri cleri*, 1628, 1638

Pec. of Bp. of Exeter

Visitation

CH: 905a, 1637–40 pres.

Parish

Chudleigh/PW1

Ay of Barnstaple

Parish

482A/ PW46; 1201A/PW1; 3047A/PW2; 2021A/PW1; 2914A/PW1

Ay of Totnes

Parish

269A/PW8; 2660A/PW1

Ay of Exeter

Parish

1146A/PW1; 3030A/PW1; R4/1/Z/PX5; 3147A/PW5; DD70963–7; 3004A/PW3,4; 1718A/PW5; 51/1/5/PW; 1639A/PW1; 1302A/PW1

Pec. of Dn. of Exeter

Parish

1677A/PW16

Pec. of DCh. of Exeter

Parish

2932A/PW1

Pec. of VCh. of Exeter

Parish

Woodbury/PW1

Other MSS

Exeter City MS 63, Quarter Sessions Minutes, 1630–42

DORSET RO (DTRO)

Ay of Dorset

Parish

PE CAB/CW1; CHM/CW1; DO(HT)/173/CW1, 2; IWC/RE1; LAL/207/CW1;
PUD/CW8; SSN/36/CW1; SYM/CW1
3/CD7–9

Pec. of Corfe Castle

Court

uncat. *acta*, 1630s

Pec. of Wimborne Minster

Parish

PE WM/CW1/41(20, 42) pres., 1630s

Visitation

PE WM/CP2/8–18

Pec. of Dn. of Salisbury

Parish

PE BER/CW6, 7; CMR/RC; LOB/CW1; SH/CW/100–109; SH/VE/1

Pec. of Gillingham

Parish

PE, MOT/CW1

RPec. of Lyme Regis

7/M1

Borough MSS

B 2/8/1–4, Dorchester court bk., 1629–37

DR WILLIAMS'S LIBRARY, LONDON (DWL)

Baxter MSS, Correspondence 1–6

DURHAM CATHEDRAL LIBRARY (DCL)

Con. of Durham

Court

Corr. Bks., 1635–8, *acta*
Hunter MSS, 67/145, Neile MS

DURHAM RO (DURO)

Con. of Durham

Parish

Ep. Ch. le St/1; Da. SC/35; Ga. SM/4/1; Mer. 34/1; Ryt. 4/1; WG 1/1; LN/1

DYFED RO (DFRO)

Ay of St David's

Parish

HPR 68/33

EAST SUFFOLK RO (ESFRO)

Ay of Sudbury

Parish

FB: 77/E2/3; 130/E3; 23/E1/1 + 2; 198/E1/1 + 2; 198/C1/1; 153/E1/1;
E: BA121/E1/1

Ay of Suffolk

Court

FAA: 3/5, 1640 allegations; 4/2, 1621–1732, misc. coll.

Parish

FB: 51/E1/1; 51/E2/1; 98/E3/1; 22/E1/1; 19/E4/2
FBA: 91/E1/1
FC: 112/E1/1; 68/E1/1; 25/E1/1; 83/E1/1; 171/E1/1; 119/E1/1; 149/

E2/1; 147/E1/1; 131/E1/1; 62/E1/3; 84/E2/1; 99/E1/1; 101/E2/22; 185/E1/2; 80/E4/1–7; 89/A2/1 + 2
FD: 51/E2/1

EAST SUSSEX RO (ESRO)

Ay of Lewes

Parish

P 235/9/1; 237/9/1; 289/12/1; 293/12/1; 308/12/1; 309/9/1; 361/12/1; 414/9/1/1c; 462/12/1; 465/10/3/1; 481/9/2,9

APec. of South Malling

Parish

P 415/9/1a

Other MSS

Rye 1/1; 47/133, papers conc. High Commission and Star Chamber
QR, E 57/60–5, 1642 depositions
Frewen MSS: FRE 4223
Dunn MSS: DUNN 52, 57

ESSEX RO (ERO)

Con. of London

Court and Visitation

D/ALV, 1–2, visitation pres. and *detecta*, 1625, 1629, 1634–6

Comm. in Essex and Herts

Court

D/ABA, 3–9, *acta* office, 1625–41
D/ABC, 5–7, causes, 1631–42
D/ABD, 1–8, deposition and cognate docs., 1618–42

Visitation

D/ABV, 1, 1633–9, visitation

Parish

D/P 16/5/5; 94/5/1

Ay of Colchester

Court

D/ACA, 46–54, 1634–41, *acta*
D/ACC, 14–16, 1627–40, *acta*
D/ACD, 5–7, 1626–41, deposition and cognate docs.

Visitation

D/ACV, 5, 1633, pres.

Parish

T/P 131
D/P 192/5/2

Ay of Essex

Court

D/AEA, 36–42, *acta*, 1626–40
D/AEC, 10–12, 1629–37, causes
D/AED, 8, 1626–42, deposition and cognate docs.

Visitation

D/AEV, 6–7, 1638, pres., *liber cleri*

Parish

D/P, 248/5/1; 356/5/1

Ay of Middlesex

Parish

D/P, 11/4/1

Pec. of Havering and Hornchurch

Parish

D/P, 115/5/1

Pec. of Roxwell and Writtle

Parish

D/P, 50/5/1

Pec. of the Liberty of the Sokens

Visitation

D/APs, VI/E6, 1630–7, Soken visitation pres.
Barrington Hall MS D/DBa, OI/1, 1632, St Paul's coll.
Quarter Sessions MSS Q/SR, XX, 1640, Essex Session Roll

GLOUCESTER CATHEDRAL LIBRARY (GCL)

DCh. of Gloucester

MS Act Bk. 1, *acta*, 1617–60
D936A1/1 + 2 accounts, 1609–64

GLOUCESTERSHIRE RO (GRO)

Con. of Gloucester

Administrative

27A, reg., 1612–56
142A A, reg., 1612–56

Court and Visitation

GDR: 135–40, 151, 174–5, 181, 186–7, 190–1, 195, 198–9, 201–3, 1619–41, *detecta*
GDR: 166, 185, 189, 1628, 1634, 1635 (metrop.), ep. visitation book
GDR: 167, 169–173, 179, 1628–32, *acta*, office
GDR: 168, 204–5, 1628–49, depositions
GDR: 177–8, 182–4, 188, 192–3, 196–7, 200, 1631–1639, *acta*, instance
GDR: 180, 1633, *liber cleri*

Ay of Gloucester

Parish

P: 63, CW2/1; 107 CW2/1; 127 CW2/1; 154/11 CW2/1; 154/14 CW2/1; 154/14/6 CW2/7; 197 CW2/1; 216 CW2/1; 217 CW2/1; 230 CW2/1; 276 MI/1; 320 CW2/1; 368 MI/1/2

Pec. of Bibury

Parish

P 34 CW2/1

Pec. of Withington

Parish

P 34 CH/1

Ay of Wiltshire

Parish

P 186, CW2/1

City of Gloucester

GBR B3/1 + 2; F4/5; G3/50–60, misc. city records
H2/2/199, court bk., 1630s
D 1280, mayorial accounts, 1625–78

GONVILLE AND CAIUS COLLEGE, CAMBRIDGE (GCC)

MS 291, eccles. and theol. tracts

GREATER LONDON RO (GLRO)

Ay of Middlesex

Parish

DRO 2/B2/1; 21/B1/1A

Comm. of London

Parish

DRO A/H2
P 79/JN.1/B7/59

APec. of Croydon

Parish

DRO 8/BI/1
P 95/MRY/1/413

Con. of London

DL/C/ 25–30, 1628–1641, *acta*, instance
87–90, 1633–44, assignation books
194, 1621–39, personal answers
231–5, 1627–40, deposition bk.

317–22, 26–7, 1627–33, *acta*, office
342–4, 1623–44, vicar gen. books
623–4, 1627–Jan. 1629, *acta*, office (related to DL/C/317–27)
630, Nov. 1632–Feb. 1635, deposition bk. (related to DL/C/231–35)

Ay of Surrey

Parish

P 95/TRI/1/1; 78/N10/44; 95/ALL 1/44
92/SAV/512–590 St Saviour. visitation pres.

GREENWICH RO (GERO)

Ay of Rochester

no cat. no., St Alfege, Greenwich ca

GUILDHALL LIBRARY (GL)

Con. of London

Administrative

9531/13–15, ep. reg., 1577–1660
9539a/1 + 2, subs.
9535/2, ordination reg., 1578–1628

Visitation

9537/15, 1637, Juxon's second visitation

Comm. of London

Court

9064/20–1, 1635–41, *acta*, office

Visitation

9583/1

Parish

1279/3; 7673/2; 3556/2; 1303/1; 942/1; 4524/2; 6552/1; 4423/1; 2968/3; 951/1; 4810/2; 3907/1; 4570/2; 959/1; 1,1394/1; 2596/2; 4071/2; 524/1; 1257/1; 977/1; 2593/1; 1016/1; 1046/1; 4457/2; 5026/1; 1013/1; 559/1; 4409/1

Ay of London

Court

9057/1, 1632–8, depositions
9052/7–8, 1630s, wills

Parish

5092/2; 823/1; 4835/1; 1432/4; 2088/1; 504/1; 4383/1; 9235/2; 4241/1; 577/1; 1635/6; 1124/1; 1176/1; 66/1; 1002/13; 5714/1; 2895/2; 4825/1; 645/2; 662/1; 593/2,4; 1455/1; 590/1; 3891/1; 1179/1; 2601/1; 818/1; 3989/1

Dy of the Arches

Parish

4051/1; 1188/1; 4215/1; 6574/1; 5018/1; 7882/1

Pec. of DCh. of St Paul's

Parish

6836/1

Chamber of London MSS

25,474, 1–6, accounts of national collection for rebuilding of St Paul's, 1633–40

HAMPSHIRE RO (HRO)

Con. of Winchester

Administrative

A/1/1/30–1, ep. reg., 1628–47
C/10/B:
112, 1631, depositions
113–15, 117–19, 121–5, 1631–2, 1634–43, *acta*, instance
116, 1633, personal answers
120, 1636–8, *acta*, office
C/1/A/1a,b, 17th cent. misc. papers

Visitation

B/1/A/3/32–3 1636, 1641–2, *detecta*

Ay of Winchester

Parish

63M70/PW 1; 113M82/P22; 1M70A/PW1; 49M67/PR1; 28M79A/PW1; 90M71/PW1; 72M72/PW1; 24M82/PW1; 44M81M/PW6, 7

Pec. of the Incumbent

Parish

41M64A/PW1

HEREFORD CATHEDRAL LIBRARY (HCL)

DCh. of Hereford

MS 1555–65, visitation returns, 1634–7

HEREFORDSHIRE RO (HFRO)

Con. of Hereford

Administrative

AL19/17–18, 1617–67, ep. reg.

Ay of Hereford

Court

Box 26–7, vols. 95–8, 1630–9, *acta*, office

Parish

H13/1

Ay of Ludlow

Court

Box 38–9, vols. 144–7, 1631–40, *acta*, office

HERTFORDSHIRE RO (HTRO)

Ay of Huntingdon

Parish

D/P: 7/5/1; 71/5/2; 12/5/1; 12/8/1; 18/5/1; 114/18/1; 105/8/1; 95/5/1; 46B/5/1; 110/5/1

Court

5/14–16, 1634–40, *acta*, office

Ay of St Alban's

Parish

D/P: 26/10/1; 93/5/1; 95/2

Court

ASA 7/30–2, 1633–40, *acta*, office

Ay of Middlesex

Parish

D/P: 13/5/1

Comm. of London

Parish

D/P: 43, 3751/1; 21 5/2; 21 29/1

HOUSE OF LORDS RO (HLRO)

MS Braye 8, account of Laud's trial
MS Main Papers/Petitions 1640–1

HUNTINGDONSHIRE RO (HNRO)

Pec. of the Bp. of Lincoln

Parish

2661/5/1

Ay of Huntingdon

Parish

2688/5/1–4; 2280/28; 2735/5/1

ISLE OF WIGHT RO (IWRO)

Ay of Winchester

Parish

NPT/APR/2B/51–61; SHAL/COM/1; SHOR/APR/2A/1; THOR/APR/2A/1

KENT AO (KAO)

Con. of Rochester

Administrative

DRC R/8–9, ep. reg., 1540–1666

Court

PRC 44, misc. papers, 1620–40

Ay of Rochester

Court

DRB PA 33 *detecta*, 1634–5
JD 2, interrogations, 1631–6

Visitation

DRA Vb5, *liber cleri*, 1587–1620

Parish

P 29/5/1; 188/5; 52/5/1; 85/8/1; 85/5/1; 336/5/1

APec. of Shoreham

Parish

P 142/5/1

Ay of Canterbury

Parish

P 26/5/1; 75/5/1A; 100/5/1; 181/4/1; 289/5/1; 321/5/1; 364/5/14; 253/5/1

Con. of Canterbury

Parish

P 78/5/1; 233/5/1

Con. of Oxford

Court

PRL 44/2, misc. papers, 1630s

RPec. of Stratford upon Avon

Visitation

U269
Q24, *detecta*, 1622–4
Q27, Thornborough dispute
Darrell MSS, Darrell papers U386, Q1
Dering MSS, Dering papers U320, A1–4; C2; L1–6; Q1–5
Filmer MSS, Filmer papers U120, C1–10

KINGSTON (Surrey) RO (KTRO)

Ay of Surrey

Parish

KG2: 2/3; 2/2/1; 2414/4/1
P52/2/4

LICHFIELD JOINT RO (LJRO)

Con. of Coventry and Lichfield

Administrative

B/A/1/16, ep. reg., 1619–32
4A/17–23, subs., 1614–40

Court

B/C/3/14–7, 1629–42, *acta*, office
B/C/4, 1635, met. visitation
B/C/5, 1630–40, cause papers

Visitation

B/V/1/57, 62, 1636–9, *liber cleri*
B/V/1/47, 1625, *acta, comperta*
B/V/1/48–56, 1626, 1629–35, +pres.
B/V/1/58–61, 1636, *acta, comperta*
B/V/1/63–6, 1639, *acta, comperta*
B/V/3, 1630s, misc. articles of visitation
B/V/4, 1626, citations
B/V/2/14, 1630s, excommunications

Pec. of the Dn. of Lichfield

Parish

D20/4/1

DCh. of Lichfield

Visitation

D + Ch VI, 1629, visitation

RPec. of Wolverhampton

Court

Pec. Wolv/Ch., 1636/7, chapter papers

LINCOLNSHIRE AO (LAO)

Con. of Lincoln

Administrative

Reg. XXX/1 + 2, ep. reg., 1621–63
Add H Reg. 3, reg., 1608–54, 'the Red Book'
Sub 1, subs., 1613–41
Corr. B/3, Williams corr.
L/1, corr. relating to ay of Leicester
M/2 misc. corr., 1601–43

Court

Cj, 23–32, 1626–42 *acta*, office and instance
Responsa IX–XII, 1611–41, responses in suits
Fac 1/5, 1630s, misc. papers

Visitation

LC, V, *liber cleri*, 1634 (ay of Stow and Lincoln)
Ch, C/L 1, call bk. 1638 (2nd met. visitation)
Ch, P 12/27–8, presentments (Bedford ay), 1631
Vj, 27–30, *detecta* and *comperta*, 1631, 1635–6, 1638 (Lincoln ay)
Vj, 31, *detecta* and *comperta*, 1640 (Stow ay)

Ay of Lincoln

Visitation

Ch, C/L/1, 1638–40, call bk.
Vij, 19–21, 1629, 1637–8, visitation bk.

Parish

P: 7/1 Algarwick; 10/1 Mk Deeping; 7/1 + 7/6 Horbling; 7/1 Lincoln St Michael
L1, 5/12 Lincoln St Martin

Ay of Stow

Visitation

Viij, 2–3, 1631–5, visitation bk.

Parish

P: 7/1 Scotherne

Pec. of Sub-Dn. of Lincoln

Parish

P: 7/1 Kirton in Lindsey

Pec. of the Prebendary of Louth

Parish

P: 7/5 Louth St James

DCh. of Lincoln

D + Ch, Fabric, Bj/7, rolls

LIVERPOOL RO (LLRO)

Ay of Chester

Parish

CA/1627–67

LAMBETH PALACE LIBRARY (LPL)

Wharton MSS: 577, 585, 595
Tennison MSS: 663, 669, 680, 731, 847
Gibson MSS: 942–3
Miscellaneous MSS: 1030, 1061, 1113, 2872, 2686
Lambeth MSS: 323

Metropolitical MSS: Province of Canterbury

Archiepiscopal reg.

Abbot II–III, 1619–33
Laud I–II, 1633–42
VB, 2/1, 1633–1639

Convocation

Conv.

1/1/1, *acta*, Lower House of Convocation, 1640
1/2/2, *acta*, Upper House of Convocation, 1640
1X/2/1–12 drafts for Canons 1640

Dy of the Arches

Arches

F7, 1635–63, muniment bk.
B3, 1639–40, sentences
A1, 1635–40, *acta*

APec. of Croydon and Shoreham

VP II/3a/1, 1637–42, *liber cleri*

Sede Vacante

VX IA/2E, subs.: Hereford and Norwich, 1630–40
VX IIA/1/1A, papers relating to suspension of Williams July 1637–Aug. 1638

Vicar General

In this case relating to metropolitical jurisdiction within the diocese of Canterbury not the Province of Canterbury
VG/4 12–22, 1629–30, 1634–7, *comperta* and *detecta*

LEICESTERSHIRE RO (LRO)

Ay of Leicester

Administrative

1D41/34/1, 1626–42, subs.
1D41/40/3/1–8, 1638/9, procurations and levies

Court

1D41/11/63–72, 1628–40, mostly instance
1D41/4/ii: Boxes i–iv 1622–8, cause papers; Boxes vi–xxiii, 1629–40, cause papers; Boxes xxv–xxvii, 1639–42; Box v, 1628–38 (loose papers from files); Box xxiv, 1638–40 (loose papers from files)
1D41/8/1–2, 1607–50, excommunications and caveats

Visitation

1D41/13: 57–66, 1625–41, *acta*, office, corr. (including some assignations)
1D41/18: 6–12, 1630–9, *speculae* (certain deaneries only)
1D41/21: file 1635, 1638–9, 1640–1, pres.
1D41/17: 1–11, 1638–9, monitions, citations, calls
1D41/14/1: 1–158, 1638, 2nd met. visitation misc. papers

Con. of Peterborough

Parish

DE: 2461/39; 1784/17

NATIONAL LIBRARY OF WALES (NLW)

Con. of St David's

Administrative

SD/BR/3, ep. reg., 1636–1705

Ch. of St David's

Administrative

SD/Ch/B/3, 4, *acta*, chapter

Con. of St Asaph

Administrative

SA/MB/15, ep. reg., 1629–70

Court

SA/CB/5–8, 1631–6, *acta*, instance
SA/Misc., 547, 568–74, 1775, misc. papers, 1630s

Con. of Bangor

Administrative

B/BR/2, ep. reg., 1542–1637
B/DL, lease bk., 1630s

Ch. of Bangor

B/QA/1/22, misc. papers

Derwydd MSS: 674, 683, 787
Kinmel MSS: coll. 1637 for St Paul's

NORTHAMPTONSHIRE RO (NRO)

Con. of Peterborough

Administrative

PDR X959/4, 1623–43, ordination bk.
PDR X957/6–7, 1616–48, ep. reg.

Court

Corr. Bk. 64–70, 1634–41, *acta*, office

Visitation

Ep. Visit 7–8b, 1633, 1635, 1640–1, *liber cleri*
X622/6, 1640, *speculae* X650/1 + 2, 1634, abstract of met. visitation

Parish

P 199/77/1–33

Ay of Northampton

Parish

P 74/31/3

Court and Visitation

Arch 32, 59, 1618–33, 1637, *liber cleri*
Arch 55, 61, 1631–34, 1639, *acta*, office
Arch 58, 1636, *detecta*
X622, *speculae*, 1631 (western deaneries)
X2159/5/11, *speculae*, 1637 (western deaneries)
X2159/5/1, *acta*, office 1637 on above

NORTH YORKSHIRE RO (NYRO)

Ay of Richmond

Parish

Thornton Watlass ca; Bedale ca

Ay of Cleveland

Parish

Thirsk ca

APec. of Ripon

Parish

Little Ouseburn ca; Kirby Malzeard ca

NORWICH AND NORFOLK RO (NNRO)

Lee Warner MSS 1/2/4

Con. of Norwich

Administrative

Reg., 15/21, 1603–29, ep. reg.
Reg., 16/22, 1603–29, ep. reg.
Reg., 16/23, 1629–38, ep. reg.
Reg., 18/24, 1638–56, ep. reg.
Sub/1, 1637, subs.
FCB/5, 1630s, misc. registry docs.

Court

Acts 61, 63, 66–7, 1631–7, *acta*, instance
Con 13, 1633–7, transmitted cases
Con 15, 1636, personal answers

Con 16, 1637–41, misc. court files
Sun 4, 1637–40, excommunications, citations
Dep 42–3, 1635, 1638, depositions

Visitation

Vis. 5–7, 1629, 1633, 1636, misc.

Ay of Norfolk

Court

ANF 9/2–3, 1640–1, *acta*, instance

Parish

PD: 197/64; 144/44; 219/58; 50/35; 136/57; 111/69; 382/29
PHI: 610, 611

Ay of Norwich

Administrative

ANW 21/1, misc. reg., 1630s

Court and Visitation

ANW 1/20, 26–7, 29, 1629–31, 1634, *libri cleri*
ANW 2/26, 70, 73–6, 1630–1641, *acta*, office
ANW 71–2, 1634–7, *comperta*
ANW 3/30–6, 1630–41, *comperta*
ANW 6/8, 1637–41, pres.
ANW 30/1/1–4, 1638, *comperta*
ANW 30/1/1–4, 17/2, 1638, consignation bk.

Parish

PD 124/30; 39/74; 90/69; 26/71(S); 58/38(S); 461/48; 59/54; 209/478; 437/14; 276/30
R 154D
Colman MS 651

NOTTINGHAMSHIRE RO (NTRO)

Ay of Nottingham

Court and Visitation

A42, 44–5, 47, *acta*, 1633–41

Parish

PR: 22 765; 2794; 1517; 547

OXFORDSHIRE RO (ORO)

Con. of Oxford

Administrative

Oxf. dio. papers: c. 264, 1604–63, ep. reg.; c. 265, 1579–1638, ep. reg.; e. 13, 1630s, subs.

Court

c. 26–7, 1629–39 deposition bk.; c. 1–2, 1629–31, *acta*, office and instance

Visitation

e. 1, 1630–41, *liber cleri*

Ay of Oxford

Court

Archd. papers: c. 11–3, 1632–40, *acta*, office and instance

Visitation

e. 1, 12, 1630–2, 1635, 1641, *liber cleri*

Parish

DD Par:, Burford c. 36 ca; Langford c. 2 ca; Oddington e. 3 ca; Pyrton c. 1 ca; Spelsbury d. 5 ca; Witney c. 9; Woodstock c. 12; Yarnton b. 7 ca; Oxford, St Peter le Bailey b. 3 ca; Oxford, St Peter in the East a. 2 + d. 1 ca; Oxford, St Aldates b. 17–18 ca; Oxford, St Martin a. 1 ca; Oxford, St Michael Northgate a. 3 ca; Oxford, St Mary the Virgin c. 2 ca; Oxford, St Mary Magdalene a. 9–19, b. 32–7 ca

Pec. of the DCh. of Lincoln

Banbury, Cropredy, Hornton, King's Sutton

Court

Oxf. dio. papers c. 16, 17, 155, 1626–36, *acta*, office and instance

Dorchester

Court

Archd. papers c. 158, 1629–1638, *acta*, office and instance

Thame

Court

Oxf. dio. papers c. 18, 1636–40, *acta*, office

Parish

DD Par, Thame b. 2 ca

Pec. of Bibury

Court

Archd. papers misc. c. 1–2, 1635, 1638–9, *acta*, office

PUBLIC RO (PRO)

SP: 14/State Papers Domestic: James I, 105, 137–8, 142, 165–7, 485
SP: 16/State Papers Domestic: Charles I, 2, 20, 27–9, 32, 36, 51, 54, 61, 83, 103, 108, 114, 117, 123–4, 134, 136–7, 142, 144, 148–151, 153–4, 157–8, 160, 162, 175–6, 178, 183, 186, 192–3, 201, 205, 218, 220, 226, 229, 232, 239–40, 242–8, 250, 252, 254–60, 266, 267, 269, 274, 281, 284, 286, 295–6, 308, 312, 327, 345, 347, 351, 354, 366, 368–370, 372, 375–6, 383, 386, 395, 398, 414, 424, 426, 430, 432–3, 436–7, 441, 444–5, 447, 450, 453, 455, 457, 459–461, 463–9, 474–5, 483, 485–6, 489, 491, 493, 497–9, 520, 525, 529, 531, 533–7, 540, 577, 595
SP: 38/State Papers Domestic: Docquets, 14–15
SP: 39/27–8, State Papers Domestic: Warrants
SO: 1/2, 1630s, Irish Letter Book: Signet Office
SO: 3/10–12, 1630s, Docquet Book: Signet Office
C: 115, N2–17, Chancery: Duchess of Norfolk Deeds: Scudamore; M12–M28, Papers
C: 58, 40–3, 1635–40, Chancery: Dispensation Rolls
DEL: 3/2, 1630s, Delegates: examination; 4/15, 1630s, Delegates: *acta*; 5/8, 1630s, Delegates: sentences
8/70, 1630s, Delegates: miscellanea
LC: 3/1, 1641, Lord Chamberlain: reg.; (4/14–17, Lord Chamberlain: recognizance rolls)

5/38, 1622–30, Lord Chamberlain, wardrobe, copies of warrants
5/50–1, 1603–35, Lord Chamberlain, wardrobe, copies of warrants, dormant
5/179–80, 1603–40, Lord Chamberlain, household regulations, Cha. I
9/98–103, 1623–40, Lord Chamberlain, accounts, Gt. Wardrobe

5/134, 1635–7, list of ordinary chaplains, Lenten
5/132, 1627–40, preachers, etc.
PC: 2/43, 1635, Privy Council: reg.
MPF: 286, 1635, Woolston map

Sta. Cha.

9, 1625–40, Star Chamber, 1 bundle Cha. I

Assize

24, 20/2/19, assize refs. to Beckington dispute
24, 20/2/55, order concerning ales and revels, 1632

PORTSMOUTH RO (PTRO)

Ay of Winchester

Parish

CHU: 3/2A/1

ST JOHN'S COLLEGE, CAMBRIDGE (SJC)

MS S/29(17), directions of 1622
MS 37(27), petition of Welwyn (Ay of Huntington)
MS 41, Ad. Westfield sermons
I/4, Buckeridge's defence of royal power
I/18, tract concerning episcopacy
I/25, 'Sabbatum Redivivum'

SHEFFIELD RO (SERO)

Ay of York

Parish

PR: 54/86

SHROPSHIRE RO (SHRO)

Ay of Ludlow

Parish

2280/6/1a; 219/CW/1

Ay of Salop

Parish

790/1; 1877/4/3, 4; 4462/1/1–12; 3848/1; 2959/4/1; 3793/1; 2310/1

RPec. of St Mary Shrewsbury

Parish

1379/1; 1041/2

RPec. of Bridgenorth

Court

uncat., *acta*, 1620–40

Parish

4030/1 + 2; 3662/1

SIDNEY SUSSEX COLLEGE, CAMBRIDGE (SSC)

MSS, 44–5, papers of Samuel Ward

SOMERSET RO (SRO)

Con. of Bath and Wells

Administrative

D/D/B: Reg. 20, ep. reg., 1632–70

Court and Visitation

D/D/Ca: 258, 260–1, 277, 281–3, 286–7, 289, 294, 297, 299–302, 304, 308–9, 313, 315–7, 319–20, 324–8, 330–1, 333, 1627–1641 office; 288, 310, 314a, 321, 1633, 1636–9, *comperta*
D/D/Cd: 74, 76, 78–9, 1633–7, depositions; 80–2, 90, 1635–7, excommunications
D/D/O1: 27, 29, 31–2, 1630s, rough journals
D/D/Vc: c. 22, 1630s, clerical list; c. 38, 1640, consignation book; c. 86, 1634, consignation book
D/D/(o): C/1878, 1630s, misc. court papers and correspondence bundles 1–4 in boxes L2/B5/7 + L2/B4/1 (not yet catalogued)

Pec. of the DCh of Wells

Court

D/D/Pg: 3, 1630s, subs.

Parish

D/D: Sas SE/14

Pec. of Prebendaries

Parish

D/D: Wy 37/1

Pec. of Prec.

Parish

D/P: Pilt, 4/1/3

Pec. of Chan.

Parish

D/P: K. ep., 4/1/1, 2

Ay of Bath

Parish

D/P: Swk, 4/1/1

Ay of Taunton

Parish

T/PH: BM 27
D/P: Bic 4/1/2–20; Chlch 4/1/1; Wel 4/1/3; Crew 4/1/1; Durs 4/1/1; Gst 4/1/1; Hin.g4/1/1; Kg.St.m 4/1/1; Long 4/1/1–3; Kln 4/1/1; M. St M 4/1/1; Mon 4/1/1; Qua.e 4/1/1; Rode 4/1/1; Stap. g 13/2/1; Hal 4/1/1

Ay of Wells

Parish

D/P: Bur 4/1/1; Cad. 4/1/1; Cas 4/1/1; Chi. dom 4/1/1; Blag. 4/1/1; Ch. mu 4/1/1; Yeo 4/1/1; Gla.j 4/1/22–9; Lock 4/1/1; She 4/1/1; Som 4/1/1; Th. co 4/1/2; Tin 4/1/2; Ban 4/1/2, 3; Chl 4/1/1

Pec. of Ilminster

D/P: Ilm 4/1/1–3

Ay of Salisbury

Parish

D/D, Wy, 37/1

Phelips MSS

D/D, PH, 216–20, Phelips coll., 1630s

SOUTHAMPTON RO (SPRO)

Ay of Winchester

Parish

PR4, 2/1

City of Southampton MSS

SC 5/3/15–8, mayorial acc., 1630s

STAFFORDSHIRE RO (SFRO)

Ay of Stafford

Parish

D: 689/P6/1/1; 3539/2/1; 1386/2/1/1; 9/A/PC/1; 113/A/PC/1; 705/PC/1/1; 730/4/1; 1538/4/1; 3710/1/1; 3451/2/2; 1323/E/1

RPec. of Wolverhampton

Court

D: 260/M/PV/1, misc. papers

Pec. of Dn. of Lichfield

Parish

D: 932/5

Quarter Sessions MS

Q/SR: E, 1641, depos

STAFFORDSHIRE RO (William Salt Library) (SFRO (WSL))

RPec. of Wolverhampton

Parish

HI: TP. 952, temp. deposit

Ay of Stafford

Parish

SR: 231, 14/2/46
M: 600

Pec. of Pby of Eccleshall

Parish

Salt MS, 236/27

SURREY RO (SYRO)

Ay of Surrey

PSH: MIC/1/1/A; HORS/7/1; WOK P/7/1; SEA/2/1; COM/6/1; EL/6/1; CL. E/7/1; CHOB/7/1/3; COB/6/17–9; SEN/2/3; STR DAB/1/1; NE/1/1/1; MCH/1/2

Borough MSS

BR/OC/61 1630s, Guildford acc

THE QUEEN'S COLLEGE, OXFORD (QCO)

MS: 390, Crosfield diary, 1626–40

UNIVERSITY COLLEGE, SWANSEA (UCS)

Ay of Carmarthen

Parish

D2, 3
I1

WARWICKSHIRE RO (WARO)

Ay of Worcester

Parish

DR: 212/30; 446/24; 87/2
DRO: 5/6

Ay of Coventry

Parish

DR: 404/48–9; 223/38; 11/8; 158/19; 296/6; 50/9; 581/45–6, 64
DRB: 3/39; 64/63; 27/5
DRN: 4/18
CR: 2134/20

WESTMINSTER RO (WERO)

RPec. of Westminster

Parish

E17–E23

Ay of Middlesex

Parish

B10, B11
V22
F3

WEST DEVON RECORD OFFICE (WDRO)

Ay of Totnes

Parish

731/34; 600/58; 694/52; 542/46

Borough MSS

W48, Plymouth 'The White Book'
W370–1, 1630s, clerical dispute

WEST SUFFOLK RO (WSFRO)

Ay of Sudbury

Parish

FL: 501/5/1; 509/5/1

Court

909/6, 1636, *acta*, office
E: 14/1/13, faculties
E: 11/1–7, faculties
E: 5/1, induction bk.

APec. of Bocking

Court

FB. 81, C6/1, 1637–41, *acta*, office (Hadleigh)

WEST SUSSEX RO (WSRO)

Con. of Chichester

Administrative

Ep. 1: 1/9, 1628 (for 1629–34 see Bodl. Ashmole 1144)
Ep. 1: 3/1, 1625–41, subs.
Ep. 1: 7/3, 1637–9, episcopal mandates for induction

Ay of Chichester

Court and Visitation

Ep. 1:
10/38–45, 1628–42, *acta*, instance
11/15–6, 1631–41, deposition book
12/2, 1631–7, citation book
13/1, 2, 1631, 1640, excommunication papers
15/3/30–9, 1631–40, misc. court papers
17/22–7, 1626–41, *detecta* and *comperta*
18/37, 1631–35, *liber cleri*
19/10, 1634–5, reg. of orders
20/11–7, 1628, 1631, 1634–5, 1639, 1641, visitation papers
22/1, 1628, 1636, 1640, pres.
26/2, 1636, *speculae*
43/3, 1638–42, *acta*, office

Parish

48/9/1; 197/9/1; 176/9/5; 183/9/1

Ay of Lewes

Parish

59/9/2; 30/9/1; 100/9/1; 516/9/1–6

Court and Visitation

Ep. 11:
1/1, 1630s, subs.
4/17–21, 1628–37, *acta*, instance
5/14–17, 1632–41, depositions
6/1–2, 1619–41, citations
9/18–24, 1628–41, *detecta*
10/3, 1626–41, *liber cleri*
11/2, 3, 1628–40, reg. of orders
14/1, 1641, pres.
15/1, 1637–9, reg. of pres.
29/1, 1600–40, formulary

Pec. of the Dn. of Chichester

Court and Visitation

Ep. 111
4/11–3, 1622–43 *acta*, instance, *detecta*, and *liber cleri*
5/2–3, 1623–40, depositions
7/1–9, 1630s, pres.

DCh. of Chichester

Capitular

Cap
1/2/5, 1636, met. orders
1/3/1a, 1618–41, *acta*
1/4/1, 1630s, minutes
1/6/5–8, 1630s, election papers

Exempt Dy of Pagham and Tarring

Court and Visitation

Ep. 1V
2/13–16, 1629–42 instance *acta*, *detecta*, *liber cleri*
3/2, Mar. 1626–Mar. 1641, depositions

Parish

106/9/1

APec. of South Malling

Court and Visitation

Ep. V
3/4, 1627–32, *acta*, office
8/1, 1625–40, *liber cleri*

Parish

416/9/1

Quarter Sessions

Sessions Rolls 42/50; 46/5

WEST YORKSHIRE ARCHIVE SERVICE (WYAS)

Ay of York

Parish

40: Spofforth (at Leeds)
Misc: 8/125/1 (at Calderdale)

WILTSHIRE RO (WTRO)

Con. of Salisbury

Administrative

D1: 2/21, ep. reg., 1620–41
D1: 2/21, subs., 1620–40
D1: 2/21, convocation mandates 1639–40

Court and Visitation

D1: 39/1 49–54 *acta*, instance 1622–1623, 1627–1631, 1634–1638, 1640–2
D1: 39/2, 11–2 *acta*, office 1622–1635; citations, 1631–1640 (unfol.); excommunications 1628–1640 (unfol.); libels, 1633 (unfol.)
D1: 42/42–57, depositions, 1627–41

Pec. of Bp. of Salisbury

Parish

P: 9036/1; 189/2; 1197/21

Ay of Salisbury

Court

D2: 4/14–15, *acta*, office, 1624–30, 1636–41; citations, 1626–40; uncat. excommunications, 1607–30

Parish

P: 730/97/1; 1899/65
Phelips MS 12362

Ay of Wiltshire

Court

D3: 4/6–7, 1622–41, *acta*, office

Visitation

D3: 15, 1602–42, visitation

Parish

P: 1819/13; 1532/10; 1271/18; 526/2

Subdn. of Salisbury

Court

D4: 5/citations, 1612–38; libels, 1610–39

Visitation

D4: 10, presentments, 1612–39; presentments, 1633–40

Dn. of Salisbury

Administrative

D5: 6/ preaching licenses, 1634;
D5: 19/ subs., 1630–40

Court and Visitation

D5: 19/29–41, *acta*, mixed, 1623–45;
D5: 21/ citation bundles, 1629–41; excommunications, 1632–3; libels files, 1626–41;
D5: 22/11–4, deposition, 1629–41

Visitation

D5: 28/visitation mandates, 1625–40; churchwarden pres., 1627–41

Pby of Bishopstone

D6:

Visitation pres.; 1627–37

Pby of Chute and Chisenbury

D8:

Court

citations, 1626–36
misc. papers, 1630–40

Visitation

pres. Chute, 1625–32
Winterborne Dauntsey, 1626–36; returns, 1626–40

Pby of Dunford

D9: 2

Court

acta, office, 1635–9

Visitation

mandates, 1632–41; uncat. pres. and returns

Pby of Highworth

D10:

Court

acta, mixed, 1624–36
excommunications, 1624–33

Visitation

mandates 1624–6; pres. 1624–36

Parish

P: 1565/35

Pby of Hurstbourne and Burbage

D11:

Court
acta, mixed, 1630–5

Visitation
returns and pres., 1637–40

Pby of Netheravon
D12: 3

Court and Visitation
acta, pres., citations, 1626–39

Pby of Wilsford and Woodford

Court and Visitation
D13: *acta* and citations

Pby of Lyme and Halstock

Court and Visitation
D16: *acta*, pres., citations, 1632–8

Pby of Netherbury in Ecclesia

Court and Visitation
D17: pres., *acta*, 1632–40

Pby of Uffculme

Court and Visitation
D20: corr., 1639–56; *acta*, pres., 1623–40

Pec. of the Lord Warden of Savernake Forest

Court and Visitation
D21: *acta* 1623–32; *acta*, pres., 1636–40

Pec. of Trowbridge

Court and Visitation
D22: *acta*, pres., 1622–34

Pec. of the Dn. and Canons of Windsor

Court and Visitation

D23: pres., misc. papers, 1620–41

Pec. of DCh. of Salisbury

Court

D24: libels, 1620–38; citations, 1630–4

Visitation

D24: 2, mandates 1620–38; 3–4, 16, pres., 1627–38; misc. papers and accounts, 1630s

Pec. of Prec.

Court

D25: 6, *acta*, 1620–36

Visitation

D25: 12, pres., 1614–40

Pec. of Treas.

Court

D26: *acta*, 1630s

Visitation

D26: pres., 1630–40

Parish

P: 2083/1

Ay of Dorset

Court

D28: loose papers (Bp. of Bristol's sub-registry for Dorset) 17th cent.

WINCHESTER CATHEDRAL LIBRARY (WCL)

DCh. of Winchester

MS, XXII diary of Dn. Young
MS, *Acta* 1622–45

WORCESTER COLLEGE, OXFORD (WCO)

MS Clarke 5/11, account of Laud's trial (unfol.)

WORCESTERSHIRE RO (WORO)

Con. of Worcester

Administrative

2648/716.093, ep. reg., 1625–46

Court

795.02/2302/3, misc. court papers
3945/712.17147, dispute between city, Potter and Thornborough

Pec. of DCh. of Worcester

Parish

b.857.06.BA, 2335/16 (iv)

Published Works (Select)

The number of printed works included in this list is necessarily small. For further works readers are referred to: *A Short-Title Catalogue of Books Printed In England, Scotland and Ireland and of English Books printed Abroad 1475–1640*, comp. A. W. Pollard and G. R. Redgrave (2nd edn. 1986, W. A. Jackson, F. S. Ferguson, and K. F. Pantzer); and *Short-Title Catalogue of Books Printed 1641–1700 in England, Scotland, Ireland, Wales and British America and of English Books printed in other Countries 1641–1700*, ed. D. Wing, 2 vols. (New York, 1972).

ABBOT, G., *A Treatise of the Perpetual Visibility and Succession of the True Church in all Ages* (1624).
ABBOTT, W. C., *The Writings and Speeches of Oliver Cromwell*, 4 vols. (1937–47).
Acts of the Privy Council (1637–45).
ANDREWES, L., *The Works of Lancelot Andrewes*, ed. J. Bliss, 11 vols. (Oxf., 1841–54).
Antidotum Culmerianum (1644).
Articles agreed upon . . . reprinted by His Majesty's Commandment (1628).
BALCANQUALL, W., *The Honour of Christian Churches* (1633).
BARGRAVE, I., *A Sermon Preached Before King Charles* (1637).
BARNARD, J., *Theologo Historicus, or The True Life of Peter Heylyn* (1683).
BAYNE, R. (ed.), *Of the Laws of Ecclesiastical Polity: The Fifth Book of Richard Hooker* (1902).

BEDFORD, T., *A Treatise of Sacraments* (1638).
BERINGTON, J. (ed.), *The Memoires of Gregorio Panzani* (Birmingham, 1793).
(BERKELEY, Sir ROBERT), *Articles of Accusation exhibited by Parliament against Sir Robert Berkeley* (1641).
BETLEY, J. (ed.), *The Correspondence of the Smyth Family 1548–1642* (Bristol Record Society, 25, 1982).
BIRCH, T. (ed.), *The Court and Times of Charles I*, 2 vols. (1848).
BOAS, F. S. (ed.), *The Diary of Thomas Crosfield* (1935).
BROWNRIGG, R., *Sixty-Five Sermons* (1674).
BURTON, H., *Babel, No Bethel* (1629).
—— *A Divine Tragedy Lately Enacted* (1636).
—— *For God and the King* (1636).
B(ULTEEL) J., *A Relation of the Troubles of the Three Foreign Churches in Kent . . . caused by the Injunctions of William Laud in 1634* (1645).
CARDWELL, E. (ed.), *Documentary Annals*, 2 vols. (Oxf., 1844).
CLARKE, S., *The Lives of Sundry Eminent Persons*, 2 vols. (1683).
—— *The Lives of Thirty-Two English Divines* (1677).
COLLIER, J., *An Ecclesiastical History of Great Britain* (1708).
COLLINS, W. E. (ed.), *Archbishop Laud Commemoration* (1895).
COOPER, J. P. (ed.), *The Wentworth Papers*, Camden, 4th ser., 12 (1973).
COSIN, J., *A Collection of Private Devotions* (1627).
CULMER, R., *A Parish Looking Glasse for Persecutors of Ministers* (1657).
DEY, R., *Two Looks Over Lincoln* (1641).
DONNE, J., *The Works of John Donne*, ed. 1f. Alford, 6 vols. (1839).
DOW, C., *Innovations unjustly charged unto the present Church and State* (1637).
—— *A Discourse of the Sabbath Day* (1636).
EVELYN, J., *The Diary of John Evelyn*, ed. E. S. de Beer (Oxf., 1955).
FEATLEY, D., *The Gentle Lash or the Vindication of Dr. Featley* (1644).
FELL, J., *The Life of Dr. Henry Hammond* (1661).
FRERE, W. H. (ed.), *Visitation Articles and Injunctions* (Alcuin Club Collections, 16, 1910).
GARDINER, S. R. (ed.), *Cases in the Courts of Star Chamber and the High Commission* (Camden, NS, 39, 1886).
GIBSON, E., *Synodus Anglicus* (1702).
GOODWIN, J., *Redemption Redeemed* (1651).
GREY, T., *The Petition against Dr. Gray, vicar of Ponteland* (1641).
HALE, W. H. (ed.), *Precedents in Causes of Office* (1841).
HALL, J., *The Works of Joseph Hall*, ed. P. Wynter, 10 vols. (Oxf., 1863).
HAMILTON, A. H. A. (ed.), *Sir John Northcote's Notebook* (1877).
HARRAB, T., *Tessaradelphus or The Four Brothers* (1616).
HAUSTED, P., *Ten Sermons* (1636).
HEYLYN, P., *A Brief and Moderate Answer* (1636).
—— *The History of the Sabbath Day* (1636).

—— *A Coale from the Altar* (1637).
—— *Antidotum Lincolniense* (1637).
—— *Observations on the History of the Reign of King Charles* (1650).
(HEYWOOD, W.), *An Answer to a Lawless Pamphlet* (1641).
(*HMC*) *Historical Manuscript Commission Reports*
—— *Appendix to the 4th Report*
—— *Appendix to the 8th Report ii*
—— *Appendix to the 9th Report*
—— *Buccleuch (Whitehall) i, iii*
—— *Cowper ii, iii*
—— *De Lisle and Dudley, vi*
—— *Portland ii, iii*
—— *Rutland i*
—— *Skrine*
—— *Various Collections vii*
—— *Addenda: New Series: House of Lords xi*
HOLMES, C. (ed.), *The Suffolk Committee for Scandalous Ministers 1644–6* (Suffok Record Soc., 13, 1970).
HUMPHERY-SMITH, C. (ed.), *The Phillimore Atlas and Index of Parish Registers* (1984).
JACKSON, T., *A Treatise of Divine Essence and Attributes* (1628).
KELLET, E., *Tricoenium Christi, in Nocte Proditionis Svae* (1641).
KITCHIN, G. W. (ed.), *The Records of the Northern Convocation* (Surtees Soc. 113, 1907).
KNOWLER, W. (ed.), *The Letters and Dispatches of Thomas, Earl of Strafford*, 2 vols. (Dublin, 1740).
LAKE, A., *Sermons with some religious and divine meditations by Arthur Lake, Bishop of Bath and Wells* (1629).
LARKIN, J. F. (ed.), *Stuart Royal Proclamations*, ii (Oxf., 1984).
LAWRENCE, T., *The Duty of the Laity and the Privileges of the Priest* (Oxf., 1635).
—— *A Sermon preached before the King's Majesty at Whitehall* (1637).
LEGG, J. W. (ed.), *English Orders for Consecrating Churches in the Seventeenth Century* (Henry Bradshaw Soc., 12, 1911).
LONGSTAFFE, J. (ed.), *The Memoirs of Ambrose Barnes* (Surtees Soc., 1, 1866).
LOOMIE, A. J. (ed.), *Ceremonies of Charles I: The Notebooks of Sir John Finet, Master of Ceremonies, 1628–1641* (New York, 1987).
MACDONOUGH, T. M. (ed.), *Brief Memoirs of Nicholas Ferrar* (1837).
MAINWARING, R., *Religion and Allegiance* (1627).
MALTBY, J. (ed.), *The Short Parliament Diary of Sir Thomas Aston* (Camden, 4th ser., 1988).
MATTHEWS, A. G. (ed.), *Walker Revised* (Oxf., 1948).
MAYO, R., *The Life and Death of Edmund Staunton* (1673).

MEDD, P. G. (ed.), *The Greek Devotions of Lancelot Andrewes* (1892).
—— *Appello Caesarem, a just appeal from two unjust informers* (1625).
MONTAGU, R., *A Gagg for the new Gospel? No: a new Gagg for an old goose* (1624).
MORE, R., *The True Relation of Enoch ap Evans* (1641).
MORTON, T., *Of the Institution of the Sacrament* (1635).
—— *A Sermon Preached Before The King* (1639).
(PARKER, H.), *A Discourse Concerning Puritans* (1641).
PARSON, D. (ed.), *The Diary of Henry Slingsby* (1836).
—— *The Petition of the Parishioner of Christ Church, London* (1643).
(PIERS, W.), *Articles of Accusation and Impeachment of the House of Commons against William Piers* (1642).
PORTER, R., *The Life of Mr. John Hieron* (1691).
POTTER, C., *Dr. Potter's Vindication of Himself... 1629* (1651).
PRESTON, J., *Life Eternal or a Treatise of the Knowledge of the Divine Essence and Attributes* (1629).
—— *The Life... of... Dr. Preston writ... by Thomas Ball in 1628*, ed. E. W. Harcourt (1885).
PRYNNE, W., *The Perpetuitie of a Regenerate Man's Estate* (1627).
—— *A brief survay and censure of Mr. Cozens his couzening devotions* (1628).
—— *Anti-Arminianisme or the Church of England's Old Antithesis to New Arminianisme* (1630).
—— *Lame Giles his Haultings* (1631).
—— *Historio-Mastix* (1633).
—— *A Looking Glasse for All Lordly Prelates* (1636).
—— *News from Ipswich* (1636).
—— *A Breviate of the Life of William Laud* (1644).
QUARTERMAYNE, R., *Quartermayne's Conquest over Canterburies Court* (1642).
—— *Reliquiae Sacrae Carolinae* (1650).
RIMBAULT, E. F. (ed.), *The Old Cheque Book of the Chapel Royal* (Camden, NS 3, 1872).
ROBARTES, F., *God's Holy House and Service, according to the primitive and most Christian form Thereof* (1639).
ROBERTS, P., *Y Cwtta Cyfarwydd*, ed. D. R. Thomas (1883).
SANDERSON, R., *The Works of Robert Sanderson*, ed. W. Jacobson, 6 vols. (Oxf., 1954).
SHELFORD, R., *Five Pious and Learned Discourses* (1635).
SIBTHORPE, R., *Apostolike Obedience* (1627).
SKINNER, R., *His Speech at the Visitation at Dorchester, September 18 1637* (1744).
SMART, P., *The Vanitie and Downfall of Superstitious Popish Ceremonies* (Edinburgh, 1628).

SMITH, D. N. A. *Characters of the Seventeenth Century* (1918).
STEWARD, R., *Three Sermons Preached by ... Dr. Richard Stuart* (1658).
STOW, J., *Annales*, ed. Edmund Howes (1615).
STUDLEY, P., *The Looking Glasse of Schisme* (1635).
SWINCOCK, G., *The Life of Thomas Wilson* (1672).
TOMBES, J., *Fermentum Pharisaeorum, or, the Leaven of Pharisaicall Wil-Worship* (1643).
(TWISS, W.), *Tuissii Vita et Victoria*, ed. G. Kendall (1657).
UDALL, E., *Communion Comeliness* (1641).
UNDERHILL, E. B. (ed.), *Records of a Church of Christ meeting at Broadmead, Bristol, 1640–1687* (Hanscrd Knollys Society, 1847).
—— *The Vindication of the vicar of Isleworth in ... Middlesex* (1641).
VERNON, G., *The Life of Heylyn* (1682).
WALKER, J., *The Sufferings of the Clergy* (1714).
WALTON, B., *The Articles against ... Dr. Brian Walton* (1641).
WALTON, IZAAK, *The Life of Herbert* (1670; 1907 edn.).
—— *The Life of Sanderson* (1678; 1907 edn.).
WARMESTRY, T., *A Convocation Speech ... against the new Canons and the Oath* (1641).
WHARTON, H., *The History of the Troubles and Trial of William Laud* (1695).
WHITBY, D., *The Vindication of a True Protestant* (1644).
WHITE, F., *A Treatise of the Sabbath Day* (1635).
WHITE, J., *The First Century of Scandalous Priests* (1643).
WICKHAM-LEGG, L. G. (ed.), *A Relation of a Short-Survey of Twenty-six counties* (1904).
WILLIAMS, B. (ed.), *The Subscription Book of Bishops Towson and Davenant* (Devizes, 1977).
WILLIAMS, J., *The Holy Table, Name and Thing* (1637).
WILTON HALL, H. R. (ed.), *Records of the old archdeaconry of St. Alban's* (1908).
WOLFE, D. M. (ed.), *The Complete Prose Works of John Milton* (Yale, 1953).
WORTH, R. N. (ed.), *The Buller Papers* (Plymouth, 1895).

SECONDARY SOURCES

Published Works (Select)

ADDLESHAW, G. W. O., and ETCHELLS, F., *The Architectural Setting of Anglican Worship* (1948).
ALLEN, J. W., *English Political Thought 1603–1644* (1938).
ASHTON, R., *The City and the Court* (Cambridge, 1979).

—— *The English Civil War: Conservatism and Revolution 1603–1649* (1978).

ASTON, T. (ed.), *Crisis in Europe 1560–1660* (1965).

ATHERTON, I., 'Viscount Scudamore's "Laudianism": The Religious Practices of the First Viscount Scudamore', *The Historical Journal*, 34/3 (1991).

ATKINS, J. M., 'Calvinist Bishops, Church Unity and the Rise of Arminianism', *Albion*, 18/3 (1986).

AYLMER, G. E., 'Attempts at Administrative Reform, 1625–40', *EHR*, 72 (1957).

—— *The King's Servants: The Civil Service of Charles I* (1961).

—— (ed.), *The Interregnum: The Quest for Settlement 1646–1660* (1972).

—— 'Collective Mentalities in mid Seventeenth Century England: 1. The Puritan Outlook', *TRHS*, 36 (1986).

—— *Rebellion or Revolution? England from Civil War to Restoration* (Oxf., 1986).

BABBAGE, R., *Puritanism and Richard Bancroft* (1962).

BAKER, E., *Plato and Aristotle* (1906).

BARNES, T. G., 'County Politics and a Puritan Cause Célèbre: Somerset Church Ales, 1633', *TRHS*, 5th ser., 9 (1959).

—— *Somerset 1625–1640: A County Government during the 'Personal Rule'* (1961).

BATTEN, J. M., *John Dury: Advocate of Christian Reunion* (Chicago, 1941).

BENNETT, G. V., 'Archbishop Laud', in G. Rowell (ed.), *To The Church of England* (1988).

BENNETT, H. S., *English Books and Readers 1603–1640* (Cambridge, 1970).

BOLTON, F. R., *The Caroline Tradition of the Church of Ireland* (1958).

BOULTON, J., *Neighbourhood and Society: A London Suburb in the Seventeenth Century* (Camb., 1987).

BOURNE, E. C. E., *The Anglicanism of William Laud* (1947).

BRIGHT, F. E., *Liturgies Eastern and Western* (1986).

BRINKWORTH, E. R. C., 'The Laudian Church in Buckinghamshire', *University of Birmingham Historical Journal*, 5 (1955–6).

BROOKS-DAVIES, D., *The Mecurian Monarch* (Manchester, 1984).

BUTLER, M., *Theatre and Crisis, 1632–42* (Camb., 1984).

—— 'Early Stuart Court Culture: Compliment or Criticism?', *The Historical Journal*, 32 (1989).

CALDER, I. M. (ed.), *Activities of the Puritan Faction of the Church of England 1625–1633* (1957).

CARLTON, C., *Archbishop William Laud* (1987).

CHANTER, J. F., *The Life of Martin Blake* (1910).

CLARK, P., *English Provincial Society from the Reformation to the Revolution: Religion, Politics and Society in Kent 1500–1640* (1977).

—— SMITH, A. G. R., and TYACKE, N. R. N., *The English Commonwealth 1547–1640: Essays Presented to Joel Hurstfield* (Leicester, 1979).

COGSWELL, T., *The Blessed Revolution: English Politics and the Coming of War, 1621–1624* (Camb., 1989).

COPE, E., 'The Short Parliament of 1640 and Convocation', *Journal of Ecclesiastical History*, 25 (1974).

COWARD, B., *The Stuart Age* (1980).

COX, R., *The Literature of the Sabbath Question*, 2 vols. (1865).

CRAGG, G., *Freedom and Authority* (Philadelphia, 1975).

CRANFIELD, N., and FINCHAM, K., 'John Howson's Answers', *Camden Miscellany*, Camden, 4th ser., 29 (1987).

CRESSY, D., *Coming Over: Migration and Communication between England and New England in the Seventeenth Century* (Camb., 1987).

CROSS, C., *Church and People: 1450–1660* (1976).

CUMING, G. J., 'Eastern Liturgies and Divines', *Studies in Church History*, 13 (1976).

CURTIS, M. H., 'Hampton Court Conference and its Aftermath', *History*, 46 (1961).

CUST, R., *The Forced Loan and English Politics 1626–1628* (Oxford, 1987).

—— and HUGHES, A. (eds.), *Conflict in Early Stuart England: Studies in Religion and Politics, 1603–1642* (1989).

—— and LAKE, P. G., 'Sir Richard Grosvenor and the Rhetoric of Magistracy', *BIHR*, 54 (1981).

DAVIES, G., 'Arminian versus Puritan in England, c.1620–1640', *Huntington Library Bulletin*, 5 (1634).

DAVIES, H., *Worship and Theology in England*, 5 vols. (Princeton, NJ, 1975–).

DONALD, P., *An Uncounselled King: Charles I and the Scottish Troubles 1637–1641* (Cambridge, 1991).

DONALDSON, G., *The Making of the Scottish Prayer Book of 1637* (Edinburgh, 1954).

ECCLESHALL, R., *Order and Reason in Politics* (1978).

ELTON, G. R., 'A High Road to Civil War?', in C. H. Carter (ed.), *From the Renaissance to the Counter-reformation: Essays in Honour of Garrett Mattingly* (New York, 1965).

EVANS, J. T., *Seventeenth Century Norwich: Politics, Religion and Government 1620–1690* (Oxf., 1979).

EVERITT, A., *The Community of Kent and the Great Rebellion, 1640–1660* (Leicester, 1966).

FIELDING, J., 'Opposition to the Personal Rule of Charles I: the diary of Robert Woodford, 1637–1647', *Historical Journal*, 31 (1988).

FINCHAM, K., 'Prelacy and Politics: Archbishop Abbot's Defence of Protestant Orthodoxy', *Historical Research*, 61 (1988).

—— *Prelate as Pastor: The Episcopate of James I* (Oxf., 1990).

—— and Lake, P. G., 'The Ecclesiastical Policy of James I', *Journal of British Studies*, 24 (1985).
Finlayson, M., *Puritanism and the English Revolution: The Religious Factor in English Politics before and after the Interregnum* (Toronto, 1983).
Fisch, H., *Jerusalem and Albion: The Hebraic Factor in Seventeenth Century Literature* (New York, 1964).
Fletcher, A. J., *A County Community in Peace and War: Sussex 1600–1660* (1975).
—— *The Outbreak of the English Civil War* (1981).
—— 'New Light on Religion and the English Civil War', *Journal of Ecclesiastical History*, 38/1 (1987).
—— and Stevenson, J., *Order and Disorder in Early Modern England* (Cambridge, 1985).
Fuller, M., *The Life, Letters and Writings of John Davenant* (1897).
George, C. H., and George, K., *The Protestant Mind of the English Reformation 1570–1640* (Princeton, NJ, 1961).
Gordon, M. D., 'The Collection of Ship Money in the Reign of Charles I', *TRHS*, 4 (1910).
Gorman, G. E., 'A Laudian Attempt to 'tune the pulpit': Peter Heylyn and his Sermon against the Feoffees for the Purchase of Impropriations', *Journal of Religious History*, 8/9 (1975).
Govett, L. A., *The King's Book of Sports* (1890).
Green, I., 'The Persecution of "Scandalous" and "Malignant" Parish Clergy during the English Civil War', *EHR*, 94 (1979).
—— 'Career Prospects and Clerical Conformity in the Early Stuart Church, *Past and Present*, 90 (1981).
—— '"For Children in Yeeres and Children in Understanding": the Emergence of the English Catechism under Elizabeth and the Early Stuarts', *Journal of Ecclesiastical History*, 37 (1986).
Haigh, C. A. (ed.), *The Reign of Elizabeth I* (1985).
Hall, B., 'Calvin against the Calvinists', *Proceedings of the Huguenot Society*, 20 (1962).
—— 'Puritanism: The Problem of Definition', *Studies in Church History*, 2 (1965).
—— 'The Early Rise and Gradual Decline of Lutheranism in England 1520–1660', in O. Baher (ed.), *Reform and Reformation in England and the Continent c.1500–1700* (Oxf., 1979).
Haller, W., *The Rise of Puritanism* (New York, 1938).
Harris, J., Orgel, S., and Strong, R. (eds.), *The King's Arcadia: Inigo Jones and the Stuart Court* (1973).
Harrison, A. W., *The Beginnings of Arminianism* (1926).
—— *Arminianism* (1937).
Heal, F. M., and O'Day, R. (eds.), *Church and Society in England: Henry VIII to James I* (1977).

—— *Princes and Paupers in the English Church* (Leicester, 1981).
HEXTER, J. H., 'Power Struggle, Parliament and Liberty in Early Modern England', *JMH*, 50 (1978).
HIBBARD, C., *Charles I and the Popish Plot* (Chapel Hill, NC, 1983).
HILL, C., *The Economic Problems of the Church from Archbishop Whitgift to the Long Parliament* (Oxf., 1956).
—— *Society and Puritanism in Pre-revolutionary England* (1964).
—— *The Intellectual Origins of the English Revolution* (Oxf., 1965).
—— 'Parliament and People in Seventeenth Century England', *Past and Present*, 92 (1981).
—— *Collected Essays* (1985–).
HILL, J. W. F., *Tudor and Stuart Lincoln* (Camb., 1956).
HIRST, D., 'Revisionism Revised: Two Perspectives in Early Stuart Parliamentary History: The Place of Principle', *Past and Present*, 92 (1981).
—— *Authority and Conflict: England 1603–1658* (1986).
—— 'Local Affairs in Seventeenth Century England', *Historical Journal*, 32 (1989).
HOLMES, C., *Seventeenth Century Lincolnshire* (Lincoln, 1980).
—— 'The County Community in Stuart Historiography', *Journal of British Studies*, 19 (1980).
HÖPFL, H., *The Christian Polity of John Calvin* (Camb., 1982).
HOYLE, D., 'A Commons Investigation of Arminianism and Popery in Cambridge on the Eve of the Civil War', *Historical Journal*, 29/2 (1986).
—— *Politics, Society and Civil War in Warwickshire 1620–1660* (Camb., 1987).
HUGHES, A., 'Thomas Dugard and His Circle in the 1630s: A "Parliamentary-Puritan" Connexion?', *Historical Journal*, 29 (1986).
HUNT, W., *The Puritan Moment: The Coming of Revolution to an English County* (Cambridge, Mass., 1983).
HUTTON, S., 'Thomas Jackson, Oxford Platonist and William Twiss, Aristotelian', *Journal of the History of Ideas*, 39 (1978).
INGRAM, M., *Church Courts, Sex and Marriage in England 1570–1640* (Cambridge, 1987).
JAMES, M., *Family, Lineage and Civil Society: A Study of Society, Politics and Mentality in the Durham Region 1500–1640* (1974).
JONES, J., *The Life of Bishop Hall* (1826).
KEARNEY, H. F., *Strafford in Ireland 1633–41* (Manch., 1959).
KENDALL, R. T., *Calvin and English Calvinism to 1649* (Oxf., 1979).
KENYON, J. P., *The Stuart Constitution* (1986).
KIRBY, E. W., 'The Lay Feoffees: A Study in Militant Protestantism', *Journal of Modern History*, 14 (1942).
LAKE, P., 'The Significance of the Elizabethan Identification of the Pope as Antichrist', *Journal of Ecclesiastical History*, 31 (1980).
—— 'The Collection of Ship Money in Cheshire during the 1630s: A Case

Study in the Relation between Central and Local Government', *Northern History* (1981).
—— *Moderate Puritans and the Elizabethan Church* (Camb., 1982).
—— 'Puritan Identities', *Journal of Ecclesiastical History*, 35/1 (1984).
—— 'Calvinism and the English Church, 1570–1635', *Past and Present*, 114 (1987).
—— 'The Impact of Early Modern Protestantism', *Journal of British Studies*, 28 (1989).
—— 'Protestants, Puritans and Laudians', *Journal of Ecclesiastical History*, 42/4 (1991).
—— and DOWLING, M. (eds.), *Protestantism and the National Church in the Sixteenth Century* (1987).
LAMBERT, S., 'Richard Montagu, Arminianism and Censorship', *Past and Present*, 124 (Aug. 1989).
LAMONT, W., *Godly Rule: Politics and Religion 1603–1660* (1969).
—— 'The Rise of Arminianism Reconsidered', *Past and Present*, 107 (1988).
LE NEVE, J., *Fasti Ecclesiae Anglicanae*, ed. T. D. Hardy, 3 vols. (Oxford, 1854).
LEONARD, H. H., 'Distraint of Knighthood: The Last Phase 1625–41' *History*, 63 (1978).
LEVACK, B., *The Civil Lawyers in England 1603–41: A Political Study* (Oxf., 1973).
LEWALKSKI, B., *Protestant Poetics and the Seventeenth Century Lyric* (1979).
LEWIS, G., *A Life of Joseph Hall* (1886).
LINDLEY, D. (ed.), *The Court Masque* (Manchester, 1984).
LOCKYER, R., *Buckingham: The Life and Political Career of George Villiers, First Duke of Buckingham, 1592–1628* (1981).
LIU, TAI, *Puritan London: A Study of Religion and Society in the City Parishes* (1986).
MAGRATH, A., 'Reformation to Enlightenment', in P. Avis (ed.), *The Science of Theology* (1986).
MARCHANT, R. A., *The Puritans and the Church Courts in the Diocese of York, 1560–1642* (1960).
—— *The Church under the Law: Justice, Administration and Discipline in the Diocese of York, 1560–1640* (Cambridge, 1969).
—— 'The Restoration of Nottinghamshire Churches 1635–1640', *Thoroton Society Transactions*, 5 (1961).
MARCUS, L. S., *The Politics of Mirth: Johnson, Herrick, Milton, Marvell and the Defense of Old Holiday Pastimes* (Chicago, 1986).
MATTHEWS, A. G., *The Congregational Churches of Staffordshire* (1925).
MCADOO, H. R., *The Spirit of Anglicanism: A Survey of Anglican Theological Method in the Seventeenth Century* (1965).
MCCLUNG EVANS, W., *Henry Lawes: Musician and Friend of Poets* (New York, 1941).

McGEE, J. S., 'William Laud and the Outward Face of Religion', in R. L. De Molen (ed.), *Leaders of the Reformation* (1987).
MILLAR, O., *The Age of Charles I* (1972).
—— *Vandyke in England* (1982).
MILTON, A., review of Tyacke, *Anti-Calvinists*, in *Journal of Ecclesiastical History*, 39/4 (1988), 613–16.
MILWARD, P., *Religious Controversies of the Jacobean Age: A Survey of Printed Sources* (1978).
MORE, E., 'John Goodwin and the Origins of the New Arminianism', *Journal of British Studies*, 22 (1982).
MORGAN, I., *Prince Charles' Puritan Chaplain* (1957).
MORGAN, P., *A Bible For Wales* (Aberystwyth, 1988).
MORRILL, J. S., *Cheshire 1630–1660* (Oxf., 1964).
—— *The Revolt of the Provinces* (1976).
—— (ed.), *Reactions to the English Civil War 1642–1649* (1982).
—— 'The Religious Context of the English Civil War', *TRHS*, 5th ser., 34 (1984).
—— 'The Attack on the Church of England in the Long Parliament, 1640–1642', in D. Beales and G. Best (eds.), *History, Society and the Churches* (Cambridge, 1985).
O'DAY, R., *The English Clergy: The Emergence and Consolidation of a Profession 1558–1642* (Leicester, 1979).
—— *The Debate on the English Reformation* (1986).
—— and HEAL, F. (eds.), *Continuity and Change: Personnel and Administration of the Church of England 1500–1642* (Leicester, 1976).
O'DONOVAN, O., *On the Thirty-Nine Articles: A Conversation with Tudor Christianity* (1986).
ORGEL, S., *The Illusion of Power* (Berkeley, CA, 1975).
OWEN, D. M., *The Records of the Established Church of England* (British Rec. Association, vol. i, 1970).
PALME, P., *The Triumph of Peace* (Stockholm, 1956).
PARKER, G. (ed.), *The Thirty Years War* (1984).
PARKER, T. M., 'Arminianism and Laudianism in Seventeenth Century England', in C. Dugmore and C. Duggan (eds.), *Studies in Church History* (1964).
PARRY, G., *The Golden Age Restored: The Culture of the Stuart Court 1603–1642* (Manchester, 1985).
PENNINGTON, D. H., and THOMAS, K. V. (eds.), *Puritans and Revolutionaries: Essays Presented to Christopher Hill* (Oxf., 1978).
PETTEGREE, A., *Foreign Protestant Communities in Sixteenth Century London* (Oxf., 1986).
PEVSNER, N., *et al.* (eds.), *The Buildings of England and Wales* (1956–).
PHILLIPS, H., 'The Last Years of the Court of the Star Chamber 1630–41', *TRHS*, 4th ser., 21 (1939).

PLATT, J. E., 'Eirenical Anglicans at the Synod of Dort', in D. Baker (ed.), *Reform and the Reformation: England and the Continent, c.1500–1750* (Oxf., 1979).

PORTER, H. C., *Reform and Reaction in Tudor Cambridge* (Camb., 1958).

QUASTEN, J., *Patrology*, 4 vols. (Utrecht, 1986).

QUINTRELL, B. W., 'The Royal Hunt and the Puritans 1604–5', *Journal of Ecclesiastical History*, 31 (1980).

RANGER, T., 'Strafford in Ireland: A Revaluation', in T. Aston (ed.), *Crisis in Europe 1560–1600* (1975).

REARDON, B. M. G., *Religious Thought in the Reformation* (1981).

RICHARDS, J., '"His nowe majestie" and the English Monarchy: the Kingship of Charles I before 1641', *Past and Present*, 113 (1986).

RICHARDS, T., *A History of the Puritan Movement in Wales 1629–1652* (1920).

—— *Cymru a'r Uchel Gomisiwn, 1633–1640* (Liverpool, 1930).

RICHARDSON, R. C., *Puritanism in North-West England: A Regional Study of the Diocese of Chester to 1642* (Manchester, 1972).

—— *The Debate on the English Revolution* (1977).

RUSSELL, C. S. R., 'Arguments for Religious Unity in England 1530–1650', *Journal of Ecclesiastical History*, 18/2 (1967).

—— (ed.), *The Origins of the English Civil War* (1973).

—— *Parliaments and English Politics 1621–1629* (Oxford, 1979).

—— 'The British Problem and the English Civil War', *History*, 72/236 (Oct. 1987).

—— *The Causes of the English Civil War* (Oxford, 1990).

—— *The Fall of the British Monarchies 1637–1642* (Oxford, 1991).

SALT, S. P., 'The Origins of Sir Edward Dering's Attack on the Ecclesiastical Hierarchy c.1625–1640', *Historical Journal*, 30 (1987).

SASEK, L., *The Literary Temper of English Puritanism* (Baton Rouge, LA, 1961).

SCHWARZ, M., 'Lay Anglicanism and the Crisis of the Church in the Early Seventeenth Century', *Albion*, 14 (1982).

SCUDAMORE, W., *Notitia Eucharistica* (1876).

SEAVER, P., *Wallington's World: A Puritan Artisan in Seventeenth Century London* (Stanford, CA, 1985).

SHARPE, K., 'Archbishop Laud and the University of Oxford', in H. Lloyd-Jones, V. Pearl, and B. Worden (eds.), *History and Imagination: Essays presented to Lord Dacre* (1981).

—— 'Archbishop Laud', *History Today*, 33 (1983).

—— *Criticism and Compliment: The Politics of Literature in the England of Charles I* (Camb., 1987).

—— 'Honour and Retrenchment: The Court and Household of Charles I', in D. Starkey (ed.), *The English Court from the Wars of the Roses to the Civil War* (1987).

SHAW, W. A., *The History of the English Church during the Civil War and under the Commonwealth*, 2 vols. (1900).

SHRIVER, F., 'Hampton Court Revisited: James I and the Puritans', *Journal of Ecclesiastical History*, 33 (1982).

SLACK, P. A., 'Religious Protest and Urban Authority: The Case of Henry Sherfield, Iconoclast 1633', in *Schism, Heresy and Religious Protest: Studies in Church History*, ix. ed. D. Baker (Cambridge, 1972).

SMITH, A. G. R., *The Emergence of a Nation State: The Commonwealth of England, 1529–1660* (1984).

SMITH, D. M., *A Guide to the Bishops' Registers of England and Wales* (1981).

SMITH, H., *The Ecclesiastical History of Essex* (Colchester, n.d.).

SMUTS, R., *Court Culture and the Origins of a Royalist Tradition in Early Stuart England* (Philadelphia, 1987).

SOMMERVILLE, J. P., 'The Royal Supremacy and Episcopacy "*jure divino*" 1603–1640', *Journal of Ecclesiastical History*, 34/4 (1983).

—— *Politics and Ideology in England 1603–1640* (1986).

SPRINGER, K. L., 'Archbishop Laud's campaign against Puritans at the Hague', *Church History*, 44 (1975).

SPUFFORD, M., *Contrasting Communities: English Villagers in the Sixteenth and Seventeenth centuries* (Camb., 1974).

STEVENSON, D., *The Scottish Revolution 1637–1644* (Newton Abbot, 1973).

STIEG, M., *Laud's Laboratory: The Diocese of Bath and Wells in the Early Seventeenth Century* (Lewisburg, Pa, 1982).

STONE, L., *Social Change and Revolution in England, 1540–1640* (1965).

—— *The Causes of the English Revolution, 1529–1642* (1972).

STRONG, R., *Charles I on Horseback* (1970).

TAIT, J., 'The Declaration of Sports for Lancashire', *English Historical Review*, 32 (1917).

THOMAS, K., *Religion and the Decline of Magic* (1971).

TIGHE, W., 'William Laud and the Reunion of the Churches', *Historical Journal*, 30/3 (1987).

TODD, M., *Christian Humanism and the Puritan Social Order* (1987).

TOMLINSON, H. (ed.), *Before the English Civil War* (1983).

TREVOR-ROPER, H. R., *Archbishop Laud* (1940).

—— 'The Church of England and the Greek Church', *Studies in Church History*, 14 (1978).

—— *Catholics, Anglicans and Puritans* (1987).

TRIMBLE, W., 'The Embassy Chapel Question 1625–1660', *Journal of Modern History*, 28 (1946).

TURNER, E. R., *The Privy Council of England in the Seventeenth and Eighteenth Centuries, 1603–1784*, 2 vols. (Baltimore, 1927–8).

TYACKE, N. R. N., 'Puritanism, Arminianism and Counter-Revolution', in C. S. R. Russell (ed.), *The Origins of the English Civil War* (1973).

—— 'Arminianism and English Culture', in A. C. Duke and C. A. Tamse (eds.), *Britain and the Netherlands*, 7 (The Hague, 1981).
—— 'The Ambiguities of Early Modern English Protestantism', *The Historical Journal*, 34/3 (1991).
TYLER, P., 'The Significance of the Ecclesiastical Commission at York', *Northern History*, 2 (1967).
UNDERDOWN, D., *Revel, Riot and Rebellion: Popular Politics and Culture in England, 1603–1660* (Oxford, 1985).
—— *Somerset in the Civil War and Interregnum* (Newton Abbot, 1973).
USHER, R. G., *The Reconstruction of the English Church*, 2 vols. (New York, 1910).
—— *The Rise and Fall of the High Commission* (1910).
VEEVERS, E., *Images of Love and Religion: Queen Henrietta Maria and Court Entertainments* (Cambridge, 1989).
VEITH, G., *Reformation Spirituality: The Religion of George Herbert* (1985).
WALLACE, D. D., *Puritans and Predestination: Grace in English Protestant Theology* (Chapel Hill, NC, 1982).
—— 'The Anglican Appeal to Lutheran Sources: Melancthon's Reputation in Seventeenth Century England', *Historical Magazine of the Protestant Episcopal Church*, 52/4 (Dec. 1983).
WALZER, M., *The Revolution of the Saints* (Cambridge, Mass., 1965).
WEDGWOOD, C. V., *Strafford 1593–1641* (1935).
WELSBY, P. A., *Archbishop Abbot: The Unwanted Archbishop* (1962).
WHITE, P., 'The Rise of Arminianism Reconsidered', *Past and Present*, 101 (1983).
—— 'A Rejoinder', *Past and Present*, 115 (1987).
WILLIAMS, F. B., 'The Laudian Imprimatur', *Library*, 5th ser., 29 (1966).
WILLIAMS, G., *Recovery, Reorientation and Reformation. Wales c.1415–1642* (Oxford, 1987).
WRIGHTSON, K., 'Alehouses, Order and Reformation in Rural England 1590–1660', in E. and S. Yeo (eds.), (Brighton, 1981).
—— *English Society 1580–1680* (1982).

Unpublished Theses

I consulted the following dissertations when conducting the research for my thesis. I should like to thank their authors for making their works available for me to read.

ABBOTT, W., 'The Issue of Episcopacy in the Long Parliament, 1640–1648: The Reasons for its Abolition' (Oxford D.Phil. thesis, 1981).
ALLEN, E. J. I., 'The State of the Church in the Diocese of Peterborough 1601–1642' (Oxford B.Litt. thesis, 1972).

BOORMAN, D. W., 'The Dioceses of Norwich and Ely under Wren' (Oxford B.Litt. thesis 1959).
BRINKWORTH, E. R. C., 'A Study of the Visitation Books of the Archdeaconry of Buckingham 1633–7', (Oxford B.Litt. thesis 1948).
FOSTER, A. W., 'A Biography of Archbishop Richard Neile 1562–1642' (Oxford D.Phil. thesis, 1978).
HEWLETT, A. W., 'The University of Oxford and the Church of England in the time of William Laud' (Oxford B.Litt. thesis, 1934).
HAJZKY, H., 'The Church in Lincolnshire, c. 1595–1640' (Cambridge Ph.D. thesis, 1980).
MACAULAY, J. S., 'Richard Montagu, Caroline Bishop 1575–1641' (Cambridge Ph.D. thesis 1965).
MCELROY, L., 'Laud and his Struggle for Influence from 1628 to 1640' (Oxford D.Phil. thesis 1943).
OLANDER, P. M., 'Censorship of the Press during the Personal Rule of Charles I' (Oxford B.Litt. thesis, 1976).
PARKER, L., 'The English Sabbath 1558–1640' (Cambridge Ph.D. thesis 1984).
PEAKE, T., 'Somerset Clergy and the Church Courts' (Bristol M.Litt. thesis, 1978).
SLATTER, M. D., 'A Biographical Study of Sir John Lambe (c. 1566–1646)' (Oxford B.Litt. thesis, 1952).
TYACK, N. C. P., 'Migration from East Anglia to New England before 1660' (London Ph.D thesis, 1951).
TYACKE, N. R. N., 'Arminianism in England: Religion and Politics 1604–40' (Oxford D.Phil. thesis, 1968).

INDEX

The following abbreviations are used:

ABp.	Archbishop	Dn.	Dean
Ad.	Archdeacon	DPec.	Decanal/capitular Peculiar
APec.	Archiepiscopal Peculiar	Dy.	Deanery
Ay.	Archdeanery	EPec.	Episcopal Peculiar
Bp.	Bishop	Pec.	Peculiar
Comm.	Commissary	RPec.	Royal Peculiar
Dio.	Diocese		

I should like to thank Mr Charles Patrick for helping me to compile this index.